FIFTH EDITION

Introduction to Teaching

Becoming a Professional

DON KAUCHAK
University of Utah

PAUL EGGEN
University of North Florida

PEARSON

Boston Columbus Indianapolis New York San Francisco Upper Saddle River
Amsterdam Cape Town Dubai London Madrid Milan Munich Paris Montreal Toronto
Delhi Mexico City São Paulo Sydney Hong Kong Seoul Singapore Taipei Tokyo

Vice President and Editorial Director: Jeffery W. Johnson
Executive Editor: Ann Castel Davis
Editorial Assistant: Krista Slavicek
Executive Development Editor: Hope Madden
Vice President, Director of Marketing: Margaret Waples
Marketing Manager: Darcy Betts-Prybella
Senior Managing Editor: Pamela D. Bennett
Senior Project Manager: Sheryl Glicker Langner
Senior Operations Supervisor: Matthew Ottenweller
Senior Art Director: Diane C. Lorenzo
Cover Designer: Candace Rowley
Cover Image: Shutterstock
Media Producer: Autumn Benson
Media Project Manager: Rebecca Norsic
Composition: S4Carlisle Publishing Services
Printer/Binder: Courier/Kendallville
Cover Printer: Lehigh-Phoenix Color
Text Font: ITC Garamond Std Book, 10/12

Library of Congress Cataloging-in-Publication Data

Kauchak, Donald P.
Introduction to teaching: becoming a professional / Don Kauchak, University of Utah, Paul Eggen, University of North Florida.—Fifth edition.
pages cm
Includes bibliographical references and index.
ISBN 978-0-13-283563-3—ISBN 0-13-283563-0
1. Teachers. 2. Teaching—Vocational guidance. 3. Education—United States. I. Eggen, Paul D., II. Title.
LB1775.K37 2014
371.1—dc23

2012032663

10 9 8 7 6 5 4 3 2 1

ISBN 13: 978-0-13-283563-3
ISBN 10: 0-13-283563-0

PREFACE

Welcome to the fifth edition of the most applied introduction to education book in the field!

For the Student

We've made major changes to the fifth edition of *Introduction to Teaching: Becoming a Professional.* This edition is more interactive, engaging, and personal. We know that our students learn better when we relate new ideas to their own lives and experiences. We've tried to describe important changes in education in terms of their implications for you as a prospective teacher. We think that this book will be both interesting and useful for you because it's about you and your decision to become a teacher.

Our emphasis on understanding the realities of today's students, classrooms, and schools helps you answer two fundamental questions:

- Do I want to become a teacher?
- What kind of teacher do I want to become?

The first question is important, and our goal isn't to convince you to become a teacher. Instead, it's to help you decide if teaching is for you. Teaching isn't for everyone, and some of our most rewarding experiences in working with students like you have been in helping them answer this important, personal question. Some have said, "No," and walked away from our courses with a better understanding of education and themselves. For many others, this book was a major step toward a rewarding career working with young people. We're glad that both groups of students found this book helpful and informative.

The second question, "What kind of teacher do I want to become?" is also a crucial one. If you decide to become a teacher, you'll be faced with myriad decisions about yourself, the way you interact with students, and how you'll teach when you have your own classroom. The interactive features in this edition, such as *This I Believe, Teaching and You, Issues You'll Face in Teaching,* and *Diversity and You,* invite you to begin wrestling with these decisions in a personal way.

We believe our own experiences in schools will help you make good decisions. We have both taught in public schools, and since we moved to higher education, we have spent literally hundreds of hours working with teachers in classrooms ranging from kindergarten through grade 12. We continue to work in schools and talk with teachers on a regular basis. We're also married to teachers, and several of our children are teachers. Hopefully, our experiences in schools, which we share throughout the book, will help you make the right decisions about teaching as a career.

In our continuing efforts to create the most applied and meaningful book in the field, we've also added new content and features to this edition.

New to This Edition

Did you know this book is also available as an enhanced Pearson eText? The affordable, interactive version of this text includes 3–5 videos per chapter that exemplify, model, or expand upon chapter concepts. To learn more about the enhanced Pearson eText, go to www.pearsonhighered.com/etext.

Making good decisions about becoming a teacher requires the most current information about the constantly changing education profession. So we've added new features and a new chapter, as well as information across the book on many new topics.

New Topics!

Common Core State Standards Initiative
Cyberbullying
Differentiating instruction
Dropouts and new compulsory attendance laws
The gender gap in teaching
Merit/performance pay
Money and your first job
New collective bargaining restrictions
Professional organizations and reform
Race to the Top
Reform in teacher education
Response to intervention
Sexting
Social justice in the curriculum
Value-added models of teacher evaluation
Technology and 21st-century skills

Text Themes

The fifth edition highlights the following major themes: *reform, diversity,* and *professionalism*. These themes are integrated into every chapter to provide a comprehensive guide to teaching in today's classrooms. Within these themes we strive to provide real-world applications to life as a teacher.

Reform

Reform is everywhere in education, reshaping every aspect of teachers' lives. Schools, as never before, are being seen as integral to not only the well-being of our country but also the futures of our students. Students can't succeed in our fast-paced, technologically driven society without a quality education. And increasingly, a quality education is being equated with effective teachers, the focus of many reforms. The fifth edition explores reforms aimed at improving teachers and teaching with a complete chapter on reform (Chapter 12) and with sections on reform throughout other chapters.

NEW! Chapter 12: Educational Reform and You

This chapter explains how reform will transform schools and classrooms. Standards, accountability, high-stakes testing, value-added models of teacher evaluation, restrictions on tenure, and moves toward merit pay are reshaping the profession.

Chapter Topics

We also integrated coverage of reform into other chapters:

- Reform in Teacher Education (Chapter 1)
- The Federal Government's Role in Pursuing Equality (Chapter 4)
- Emerging Issues in School Governance and Finance (Chapter 7)
- Standards and Accountability (Chapter 9)
- Teacher Evaluation (Chapters 12 and 13)

Special Features

NEW! *Issues You'll Face in Teaching* presents the pros and cons of different educational reforms and asks you to make a personal decision about the value of these reforms to the profession.

ISSUES YOU'LL FACE IN TEACHING

A National Curriculum?

The leaders who drafted our country's constitution placed curriculum decisions directly in the hands of the states by passing the Tenth Amendment, and the principle of state control of curricula has been in place since that time.

Today, this principle is being questioned by many who advocate national standards, and by extension, a national curriculum (D. Hoff, 2009b; Porter, 2011). And the politics of this controversy have become blurred. Historically, political liberals have advocated a strong federal role in education, whereas conservatives have supported states' rights and have advocated a smaller federal presence. However, the NCLB legislation was a massive federal intervention and was promoted and passed by the conservative Bush administration. Though it still left control of the curriculum in states' hands, NCLB exerted a powerful federal influence on how different states implement and test for these standards. For some, a national curriculum with mandated federal testing is a logical next step.

THE QUESTION

Is the idea of national standards leading to a national curriculum a good idea? Arguments for and against a national curriculum include the following:

PRO

- The rigor of standards varies significantly from state to state; some states have much lower standards and levels of achievement than others. A national curriculum would create uniform standards for all and help raise achievement for low SES and cultural minority students in all states (C. Finn & Petrilli, 2009).
- Students in countries such as Germany and Japan, which have national standards and national exams, achieve higher than American students (National Center for Education Statistics, 2011e).
- A national curriculum would provide stability and coherence. The population in the United States is highly mobile: Twenty percent of Americans relocate every year, some urban schools have a 50% turnover rate during the school year, and by the end of third grade, 1 of 6 children has attended three or more schools (Hartman, 2006). Teachers working with new students from different districts or states often can't tell what they have or haven't already studied.

CON

- It will create a massive and unwieldy federal bureaucracy, which will also weaken local control and accountability.
- A national curriculum won't be responsive to regional differences and will ignore the needs of diverse students in different parts of the country.
- The national standards being proposed are no more rigorous than existing ones and won't provide the rigor that is frequently lacking in current state standards (Porter, 2011).

YOU TAKE A STAND

Now it's your turn to take a position on the issue. Should our country have national standards and a national curriculum, or should curriculum decisions be left in the hands of the states?

Go to *Issues You'll Face in Teaching* in the MyEducationLab™ Book Resources that accompany this text to log your thoughts and receive feedback from your authors.

Diversity

As in the first four editions, in this text we continue to highlight the importance of diversity and adapting teaching to meet the needs of students from diverse backgrounds. Culture, language, gender, and exceptionalities are just some of the dimensions of diversity that require both teacher understanding and the ability to adapt classroom practices to maximize student learning. You'll explore today's diverse classrooms and their implications for classroom teaching through multiple chapters and features:

Chapter 2: Changes in American Society: Their Influences on Today's Students

This chapter describes ways that changes in the American family and our students affect the classroom, and it addresses the influence of socioeconomic factors on students.

Chapter 3: Student Diversity: Culture, Language, Gender, and Exceptionalities

This chapter guides you through the impact of cultural and language diversity, as well as gender differences and exceptionalities, and provides information on meeting the needs of all students in every classroom.

Special Features

NEW! Exploring Diversity is a new section in every chapter that considers how diversity affects classrooms in the context of each chapter's focus.

NEW! Diversity and You features in every chapter explore how diversity will influence your life and success as a teacher. Diversity comes in many forms—culture, language, gender, socioeconomic status, and exceptionalities are just a few. This feature describes different dimensions of diversity and then presents a case-based problem to analyze.

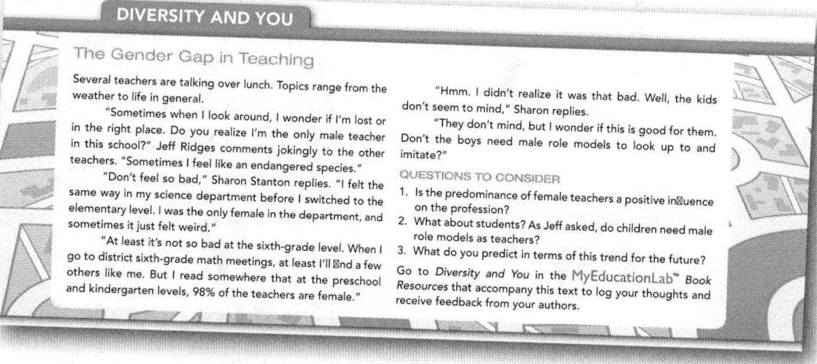

DIVERSITY AND YOU

The Gender Gap in Teaching

Several teachers are talking over lunch. Topics range from the weather to life in general.

"Sometimes when I look around, I wonder if I'm lost or in the right place. Do you realize I'm the only male teacher in this school?" Jeff Ridges comments jokingly to the other teachers. "Sometimes I feel like an endangered species."

"Don't feel so bad," Sharon Stanton replies. "I felt the same way in my science department before I switched to the elementary level. I was the only female in the department, and sometimes it just felt weird."

"At least it's not so bad at the sixth-grade level. When I go to district sixth-grade math meetings, at least I'll find a few others like me. But I read somewhere that at the preschool and kindergarten levels, 98% of the teachers are female."

"Hmm. I didn't realize it was that bad. Well, the kids don't seem to mind," Sharon replies.

"They don't mind, but I wonder if this is good for them. Don't the boys need male role models to look up to and imitate?"

QUESTIONS TO CONSIDER

1. Is the predominance of female teachers a positive influence on the profession?
2. What about students? As Jeff asked, do children need male role models as teachers?
3. What do you predict in terms of this trend for the future?

Go to *Diversity and You* in the MyEducationLab™ *Book Resources* that accompany this text to log your thoughts and receive feedback from your authors.

NEW! Urban Education chapter sections introduce you to the challenges and rewards of teaching in urban settings and discuss how effective teachers adapt their teaching to meet the needs of students in urban classrooms.

Professionalism

Teaching is at a crossroads; it will either continue to develop as a profession or become an occupation in which teachers follow the directives of others. We believe professionalism has the potential both to make teaching more attractive to bright young people and also to improve the quality of teaching in every classroom. But professionalism requires teachers who understand the issues facing education and who are willing to act courageously on their knowledge and convictions. The fifth edition provides readers opportunities to construct personal, professional identities through interactive activities focused on decision making.

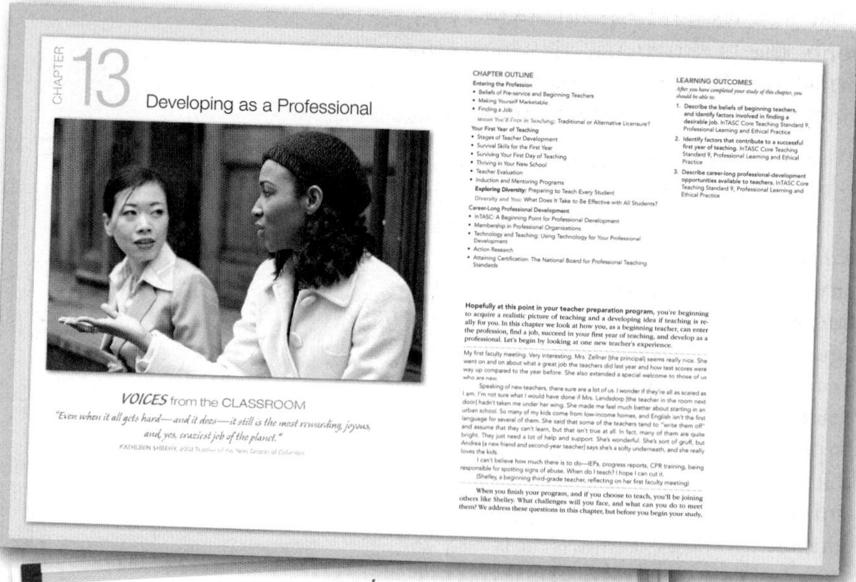

CHAPTER 13 Developing as a Professional

VOICES from the CLASSROOM

"Even when it all gets hard—and it does—it still is the most rewarding, joyous, and, yes, craziest job of the planet."

Chapter 13: Developing as a Professional

This chapter provides valuable information about strategies for finding a desirable teaching position, describes factors that contribute to a successful first year in teaching, and provides guidance toward career-long professional development.

Special Features

This I Believe features begin each chapter, inviting you to assess your own beliefs about important issues in teaching and learning.

NEW! Revisiting My Beliefs features in every chapter ask you to revisit your responses to the chapter-opening *This I Believe* inventory and to reflect on the new information you've learned over the course of the chapter.

NEW! Teaching and You. This book is not only about the field of education but also about prospective teachers—how they enter, adapt to, and change the world of teaching. *Teaching and You* asks questions you will need to be prepared to answer when you begin teaching, and invites you personally to consider basic ideas in education and evaluate their applicability and value as a prospective teacher. This feature is interspersed throughout each chapter to encourage you to evaluate new educational ideas and how they'll change your life as a teacher.

This I Believe

CURRICULUM DECISIONS AND MY CLASSROOM

For each item, circle the number that best represents your belief. Use the following scale as a guide:

4 = I strongly believe the statement is true.
3 = I believe the statement is true.
2 = I believe the statement is false.
1 = I strongly believe the statement is false.

1. Because it is important to remain objective about what students should learn, I should be careful to avoid letting my attitudes and values influence decisions about what I teach.
   1 2 3 4
2. Decisions I make about what *not to teach* are sometimes as important as the decisions about what to teach.
   1 2 3 4
3. School activities, such as clubs and sports, can provide positive outlets for students and are an essential part of schooling.
   1 2 3 4
4. Because standards and accountability are so important in today's schools, the most important decisions about what I will teach are now out of my hands.
   1 2 3 4
5. Sex education should be taught in the home, and it should not be a topic that is addressed in schools.
   1 2 3 4

Application

Content, pedagogy, philosophies—these essential concepts stay with all of us longer, help us make career decisions, and help us mold our own teaching if we can envision them in action. That's why we strive to bring these ideas and materials to life throughout each chapter with cases and applications and with videos on your Pearson eText and the MyEducationLab™ that accompanies this text.

Teaching and You

How would you like to make $125,000 a year working as a teacher? What if you had to work longer hours? What if your salary also depended on your students' standardized test scores and you could be terminated if your performance did not satisfy your principal?

Case-Based Approach

In *Preparing Teachers for a Changing World,* Linda Darling-Hammond and her colleagues (2005) point out that grounding teacher education in real classrooms—among real teachers and students and among actual examples of students' and teachers' work—is an important, and perhaps even an essential, part of training teachers for the complexities of teaching in today's classrooms. We capture realistic images of classroom life through case studies inserted throughout the book. We use cases to illustrate ideas and show how they affect the lives of real teachers and their students. This case-based approach maximizes your understanding of the book's content by providing concrete frames of reference in every chapter. Each chapter begins with a case that

"Let's see what we remember about adding fractions," she says, displaying the pizzas as shown here.

She then removes three pieces from the first and two pieces from the second so they appear as shown here.

She continues, "What fraction of one whole pizza did we eat?"

After giving her students several seconds to think about their answers, she asks, "How many pieces of the first pizza did we eat? . . . Jacob?"

"Three."

"And how about this pizza? How many pieces did we eat? . . . Emma?"

"Two."

She then writes 3/8 + 2/8 on the board and, pointing to these numbers, asks, "Why did I write 3/8 here and 2/8 there? . . . Aiden?"

"You have eight pieces in each pizza, and you ate three of them in that one," Aiden responds, pointing to the one on the left.

"Good," Shirley smiles. "And what about the second one? How many pieces of that pizza did we eat? . . . Sophia?"

"Two."

"So what fraction of a total pizza did we eat altogether? . . . Mason?"

"Five eighths of a pizza?" Mason responds after thinking for a few seconds.

"Good, Mason. . . . And why is it 5/8 . . . Claire?"

". . ."

"How many pieces altogether in each pizza?"

"Eight," Claire answers.

"Good, and how many did we eat, altogether?"

"Five."

"Yes," she smiles at Claire, "so we ate 5/8 of one pizza."

Shirley then writes these problems on the board: 3/7 + 4/7 = ?, 2/5 + 1/5 = ?, and 4/8 + 2/8 = ? and reviews them as she did with her pizzas.

"Now remember," she emphasizes, "in each of these problems, the two fractions have the same denominator. . . . Be sure to keep that in mind as we continue our study of fractions.

provides the framework for the content that follows, and we integrate other, shorter vignettes throughout every chapter to help you experience vicariously the real world of teaching. We designed these realistic classroom snapshots to help you understand how educational ideas are connected to classrooms and schools.

NEW! Windows on the Profession feature. How are professionals in the field responding to the changes occurring in education? This feature provides access to professionals who know. Video clips linked directly from your enhanced Pearson eText and available on the MyEducationLab™ that accompanies this text show real classrooms, as well as interviews with first-year and experienced teachers, principals, and superintendents, so you can see and hear what professionals think about current changes to education and how they are affecting their professional lives.

Voices from the Classroom features begin and end every chapter and invite you to go to MyEducationLab™ to witness exemplary teachers in their classrooms as they describe their personal reasons for why they chose teaching as a career, and what teaching means to them.

Technology and Teaching sections, which appear throughout the text, provide a comprehensive and up-to-date introduction to technology and how it is changing the teaching profession. Because we've interspersed this topic throughout the text, you'll learn about technology as an integrated piece of the instructional and learning process rather than a separate entity.

MyEducationLab™

MyEducationLab™ is an online homework, tutorial, and assessment resource designed to improve results by helping you quickly master concepts and by providing your instructor with a robust set of tools for easily gauging and addressing the performance of individuals and classrooms.

MyEducationLab™ engages you with high-quality multimedia learning experiences to help you build critical teaching skills and prepare you for real-world practice. In practice exercises, you'll receive immediate feedback so you'll see mistakes right away, learn whether any concepts are holding you back and precisely which concepts they are, and you'll then master those concepts through targeted practice.

Visit www.myeducationlab.com to explore your online learning resources.

For Instructors

For educators, MyEducationLab™ provides highly visual data and performance analysis to help quickly identify gaps in student learning and make a clear connection between coursework, concept mastery, and national teaching standards. And because MyEducationLab™ comes from Pearson, it's developed by an experienced partner committed to providing content, resources, and expertise for the best digital learning experiences.

In the MyEducationLab™ for this course, educators will find the following features and resources:

Advanced Data and Performance Reporting Aligned to National Standards

Advanced data and performance reporting helps educators quickly identify gaps in student learning and gauge and address individual and classroom performance. Educators easily see the connection between coursework, concept mastery, and national teaching standards with highly visual views of performance reports. Data and assessments align directly to national teaching standards and support reporting for state and accreditation requirements.

Study Plan Specific to Your Text

MyEducationLab™ gives students the opportunity to test themselves on key concepts and skills, track their own progress through the course, and access personalized *Study Plan* activities.

The customized *Study Plan* is generated based on students' pretest results. Incorrect questions from the pretest indicate specific textbook learning outcomes the student is struggling with. The customized *Study Plan* suggests specific enriching activities for particular learning outcomes, helping students focus. Personalized *Study Plan* activities may include eBook reading assignments and *Review, Practice, and Enrichment* activities.

After students complete the enrichment activities, they take a posttest to see the concepts they've mastered or areas where they still may need extra help.

MyEducationLab™ then reports the *Study Plan* results to the instructor. Based on these reports, the instructor can adapt course material to suit the needs of individual students or the entire class.

Assignments and Activities

Designed to enhance students' understanding of concepts covered in class, these assignable exercises show concepts in action (through videos, cases, and/or student and teacher artifacts). They help students deepen content knowledge and synthesize and apply concepts and strategies they have read about in the book. (Correct answers for these assignments are available to the instructor only.)

Building Teaching Skills and Dispositions

Building Teaching Skills and Dispositions are unique learning units that help students practice and strengthen skills essential to effective teaching. After examining the steps involved in a core teaching process, students receive an opportunity to practice applying this skill via videos, student and teacher artifacts, and/or case studies of authentic classrooms. Providing multiple opportunities to practice a single teaching concept, each activity encourages a deeper understanding and application of concepts, as well as the use of critical thinking skills. After practice, students take a quiz that is reported to the instructor gradebook and performance reporting.

Teacher Talk

The *Teacher Talk* feature emphasizes the power of teaching through videos of master teachers, each speaker telling their own compelling stories of why they teach. Each of these featured teachers has been awarded the Council of Chief State School Officers Teachers of the Year award, the oldest and most prestigious award for teachers.

IRIS Center Resources

The IRIS Center at Vanderbilt University (http://iris.peabody.vanderbilt.edu), funded by the U.S. Department of Education's Office of Special Education Programs (OSEP), develops training-enhancement materials for pre-service and practicing teachers. The IRIS Center works with experts from across the country to create challenge-based interactive modules, case study units, and podcasts that provide research-validated information about working with students in inclusive settings. In your MyEducationLab course, we have integrated this content where appropriate.

Simulations in Classroom Management

One of the most difficult challenges facing teachers today is how to balance classroom instruction with classroom management. These interactive cases focus on the classroom management issues teachers most frequently encounter on a daily basis. Each simulation presents a challenge scenario at the beginning and then offers a series of choices to solve each challenge. Along the way students receive mentor feedback on their choices and have the opportunity to make better choices if necessary. After completing each simulation, students will have a clear understanding of how to address these common classroom management issues and will be better equipped to handle them in the classroom.

Book Resources

Issues You'll Face in Teaching

Students learn about current reforms within this text feature and then go to MyEducationLab™ to explore different perspectives on the issue and determine their personal stance on these important changes in education. Students receive structured hints to help them analyze both sides of an issue and decide how the issue will affect their professional lives. Students receive immediate feedback once they submit their response.

Diversity and You

In this feature, students examine and consider diversity issues and their implications for today's classrooms. Students apply these issues to their own teaching through activities on MyEducationLab™, where they receive hints and feedback.

Course Resources

The *Course Resources* section of MyEducationLab™ is designed to help students put together an effective lesson plan, prepare for and begin a career, navigate the first year of teaching, and understand key educational standards, policies, and laws. It includes the following:

- The Lesson Plan Builder is an effective and easy-to-use tool that students can use to create, update, and share quality lesson plans. The software also makes it easy to integrate state content standards into any lesson plan.
- The Certification and Licensure section is designed to help students pass licensure exams by giving them access to state test requirements, overviews of what tests cover, and sample test items.

  The *Certification and Licensure* section includes the following:
- State Certification Test Requirements: Here, students can click on a state and be taken to a list of state certification tests.
- Students can click on the Licensure Exams they need to take to find:
  - Basic information about each test
  - Descriptions of what is covered on each test
  - Sample test questions with explanations of correct answers
- National Evaluation Series™ by Pearson: Here, students can see the tests in the NES, learn what is covered on each exam, and access sample test items with descriptions and rationales of correct answers. Students can also purchase interactive online tutorials developed by Pearson Evaluation Systems and the Pearson Teacher Education and Development group.
- ETS Online Praxis™ Tutorials: Here students can purchase interactive online tutorials developed by ETS and by the Pearson Teacher Education and Development group. Tutorials are available for the Praxis I exams and for select Praxis II exams.
  - The Licensure and Standards section provides access to current state and national standards.

- The Preparing a Portfolio section provides guidelines for creating a high-quality teaching portfolio.
- Beginning Your Career offers tips, advice, and other valuable information on:
  - *Resume Writing and Interviewing*: Includes expert advice on how to write impressive resumes and prepare for job interviews.
  - *Your First Year of Teaching*: Provides practical tips to set up a first classroom, manage student behavior, and more easily organize for instruction and assessment.
  - *Law and Public Policies:* Details specific directives and requirements needed to understand under the No Child Left Behind Act and the Individuals with Disabilities Education Improvement Act of 2004.
- The Multimedia Index aggregates resources in MyEducationLab™ by asset type (for example, video or artifact) for easy location and retrieval.

Visit www.myeducationlab.com for a demonstration of this exciting new online teaching resource.

Support Materials for Instructors

The following resources are available for instructors to download on www.pearsonhighered.com/educators. Instructors enter the author or title of this book, select this particular edition of the book, and then click on the "Resources" tab to log in and download textbook supplements.

Instructor's Resource Manual and Test Bank (0-13-300686-7)

The *Instructor's Resource Manual and Test Bank* includes suggestions for learning activities, additional *Experiencing Firsthand* exercises, supplementary lectures, case study analyses, discussion topics, group activities, and a robust collection of test items. Some items (lower-level questions) simply ask students to identify or explain concepts and principles they have learned. But many others (higher-level questions) ask students to apply those same concepts and principles to specific classroom situations—that is, to actual student behaviors and teaching strategies.

PowerPoint Slides (0-13-300689-1)

The PowerPoint slides include key concept summarizations, diagrams, and other graphic aids to enhance learning. They are designed to help students understand, organize, and remember core concepts and theories.

MyEducationLab Correlation Guide (0-13-301848-2)

This guide connects chapter sections with appropriate assignable exercises on MyEducationLab™.

TestGen *(0-13-300691-3)*

TestGen is a powerful test generator that instructors install on a computer and use in conjunction with the *TestGen* test bank file for the text. Assessments, including equations, graphs, and scientific notation, may be created for both print or testing online.

TestGen is available exclusively from Pearson Education publishers. Instructors install *TestGen* on a personal computer (Windows or Macintosh) and create tests for classroom testing and for other specialized delivery options, such as over a local area network or on the web. A test bank, which is also called a Test Item File (TIF), typically contains a large set of test items, organized by chapter and ready for use in creating a test, based on the associated textbook material.

The tests can be downloaded in the following formats:

TestGen Testbank file—PC
TestGen Testbank file—MAC
TestGen Testbank—Blackboard 9 TIF
TestGen Testbank—Blackboard CE/Vista (WebCT) TIF
Angel Test Bank (zip)
D2L Test Bank (zip)
Moodle Test Bank
Sakai Test Bank (zip)

Acknowledgments

Writing a book such as this is the result of the collective efforts of many people that we would like to both thank and acknowledge. First, special thanks to our editor, Ann Davis, who helped us understand national trends and turn our ideas into a book that addresses these trends and speaks to pre-service and beginning teachers. Hope Madden, our developmental editor, brought energy and direction to the project and helped steer the book through both design and production. Luanne Dreyer Elliott, our copy editor, made it the cleanest and clearest of our five editions of this text. Sheryl Langner, our production editor, conscientiously steered the final project to completion, ensuring the highest level of text quality. Darcy Betts, our link to instructors, helped us craft our thoughts into a text that will hopefully help teachers develop to their fullest potential. We are deeply grateful for all their efforts.

In addition we would like to acknowledge the reviewers who helped us understand what students and instructors need and want: Sharon Teets, Carson-Newmam College; Deron Boyles, Georgia State University; LueLinda Egbert, College of Southern Idaho; Mara Jane Cawein, University of Central Arkansas; and Brian Yusko, Cleveland State University.

Finally, we would much appreciate any feedback you can give us about the text and the supplements that accompany it. Please feel free to contact either of us at any time. Our email addresses are: don.kauchak@gmail.com and peggen@unf.edu. We will respond to you as quickly as possible.

About the Authors

DON KAUCHAK Don has taught and worked in schools and in higher education in nine different states across the country and at every level, including preschool and kindergarten. He is married to a teacher and his son is also a teacher. He has published in a number of scholarly journals, including the *Journal of Educational Research, Journal of Experimental Education, Journal of Research in Science Teaching, Teaching and Teacher Education, Phi Delta Kappan,* and *Educational Leadership.* In addition to this text, he has co-authored or co-edited six other books on education. He has also been a principal investigator on federal and state research grants examining teacher development and evaluation practices. He currently volunteer-tutors in a local elementary school. Besides helping him keep in touch with classrooms, teachers and students, it's also a lot of fun, and provides him with valuable insights into how hard it is to be a good teacher.

PAUL EGGEN Paul has worked in higher education for nearly 40 years, and during that time he has spent literally hundreds of hours in public and private school classrooms working directly with teachers and students at all levels ranging from kindergarten through 12th grade. He is a consultant for public schools and colleges in his university service area and has provided support to teachers in 12 different states. Paul has also worked with teachers and in classrooms in 23 different countries in Africa, South Asia, the Middle East, Central America, South America, and Europe. He has published numerous articles in national journals, is the co-author or co-editor of six other books, and presents regularly at national and international conferences.

Public school education is central to Paul's life. His wife is a middle school teacher in a public school, his daughter is also a public school teacher, and his daughter and son are graduates of public schools and state universities.

BRIEF CONTENTS

CONTENTS

PART I TEACHERS AND STUDENTS 2

3 Student Diversity: Culture, Language, Gender, and Exceptionalities 70

PART II FOUNDATIONS 106

4 Education in the United States: Its Historical Roots 106

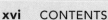

7 Governance and Finance: Regulating and Funding Schools 212

8 School Law: Ethical and Legal Influences on Teaching 242

SPECIAL FEATURES

Introduction to Teaching

The students look at the list, and after several seconds David continues, "Now, what have we been studying?"

"Inertia," Taneka responds after hesitating briefly.

"Exactly," David says, smiling. "So let's review for a minute. What is inertia? . . . Go ahead, Dana."

"The tendency . . . of something moving to keep on moving . . . straight."

"Or something not moving to remain still," Jamal adds.

"Excellent," David responds with a nod. "Now, let's answer the questions on the board using the idea of *inertia.*"

With David's guidance, students conclude that if cars suddenly stop, their bodies tend to keep moving because of inertia, and seatbelts stop them, so they don't get hurt. They also decide that inertia separates water from clothes in the washer because the water goes straight out through the holes in the drum, but the clothes are kept in it. Finally, they determine that as the dog shakes one way, and then stops, the water keeps moving, and the same thing happens when it shakes the other way. So the dog uses the principle of inertia to shake the water from itself.

"Neat," Rebecca says. "Where'd you get that stuff, Mr. Ling?"

"I just thought up the questions," David replies. "The more I study, the more examples I find. . . . That's what we're here for. We study science so we can learn how the world around us works."

Revisiting My Beliefs

Our survey (Table 1.1), found that "the opportunity for a lifetime of self-growth" (Item 6) and "interest in a subject matter field" (Item 5) were major reasons for considering teaching, ranking 3 and 4 of 6. Learning more about ourselves and the world and seeing students get excited about the topics we teach are two personal and intellectual rewards of teaching. Not surprisingly, these intellectual rewards also help keep veteran teachers in the field. One researcher studying exemplary veteran teachers concluded, "Without exception, intellectual stimulation is a burning need of the teachers I interviewed" (Williams, 2003, p. 72).

Occupational status is another intrinsic reward. In spite of perceptions to the contrary, teachers enjoy high regard and high status. If you have doubts about the status of teachers, consider how parents feel as they approach their first parent–teacher conference: They want nothing more than to hear that you really care about their child, that everything is okay in school, and that their child is growing academically and socially. Into no other profession's hands is so much care of young people placed.

This positive view of teachers is corroborated by national polls. For example, one poll indicated that nearly 70% of the public view teachers as honest and ethical, second only to nurses in the helping professions, and above doctors, the clergy, and judges (Jones & Saad, 2010). A second poll found that nearly 3 of 4 people said they had confidence and trust in teachers, and 2 of 3 said they would be in favor of their own children becoming teachers (Bushaw & Lopez, 2011). People believe in teachers, and this fact is reassuring to all of us as we work in classrooms on a day-to-day basis.

Extrinsic Rewards

Extrinsic rewards also attract people to teaching. For example, job security and summer vacations ranked fifth and sixth, respectively, in our survey. The job security in teaching is greater than in most other occupations. For instance, people in the business world are terminated or let go much more frequently than are teachers. And the existing teaching force is aging, so demographic trends suggest that job security is likely to remain high.

Schools are also positive places to work in; you're surrounded by others like yourself—colleagues who are optimistic about young people and want to make the world a better place. And then there are the long vacation breaks that allow you to recharge your batteries and explore new places and ideas. According to an old joke, a student asked to identify three reasons for going into teaching responded, "June, July, and August." In addition, if you decide to teach, you'll have vacations at times when they're the most attractive—the Friday after Thanksgiving, the winter holiday season, and spring break, for example.

Besides job security and desirable vacations, teachers' work schedules are also attractive. For instance, their schedules are similar to those of students, so their own children don't go home to empty houses after school. For many, family is central to their lives; teaching provides opportunities to spend valuable time with their partners and children.

Revisiting My Beliefs

In addition to intrinsic rewards, teaching also has extrinsic benefits (Items 1 and 2 of the *This I Believe* survey). Teaching has greater job security than many other careers, and favorable schedules enable teachers to stay positive about themselves and their jobs and to spend time with the people they care about.

Challenges in Teaching

A number of challenges also exist in teaching, the first of which is simply finding a job.

Teaching and You

How hard is teaching? Can anyone become a good teacher? What will be your major challenges when you teach?

Finding a Job

Finding a job is the first challenge you'll face. With the downturn in our country's economy, and states cutting many services, the job market in the second decade of the 21st century has been tight. The long-term prospects for jobs are quite positive, however (Hussar & Bailey, 2011). For example, more than a third of the nation's teachers are projected to retire in the near future, which should open up over a million new teaching positions (S. Dillon, 2009).

Several factors influence the availability of positions, and student demographics make up one of the most important. The P–12 student population has increased steadily in recent years, and public school enrollments are projected to increase 6% between 2007 and 2019 (Hussar & Bailey, 2011). The number of public school elementary teachers is also projected to increase 9%, with slightly slower rates of increase for secondary teachers. Opportunities will also be greater in rural and urban schools than in the suburbs, and they're also greater in districts with higher numbers of low-income students and students who are members of cultural minorities (Kaiser, 2011).

Once you've secured a position and begin teaching, your working conditions will be the primary challenge you'll face. Let's examine them.

Working Conditions

Despite the positive work environments described earlier, your actual working conditions will present challenges when you begin teaching. Let's look at one new teacher's experience.

All I do is work. I work every night; I work all weekend. Perri [her high school-aged daughter] and I went on a short day trip last weekend, and I worked all the way there and all the way back while she drove. I know I'm in my first year of teaching, but this is just about too much.

The kids have been off the wall, and the EOC is coming up [EOC refers to the "end of course" exam], and part of my year-end evaluation will be based on how well they do on the test. If next year doesn't get easier, I'm not sure I can do this. (Suzanne Schellenberg, Personal Communication, February 29, 2012)

Think about this as you anticipate your first job. If you're teaching in an elementary school, you will be responsible for 20 to 30 children all day, every day. Or, if you work in a middle or secondary school, you'll have five different classes of similar numbers of students. You will be responsible for their safety, and you'll be expected to promote their learning and help them grow socially and personally. You'll experience frustration, and, after a tough day many teachers have said something like, "Why am I doing this? The kids don't seem to care, and I'm not making any progress with them."

You will have a limited amount of time during the day to plan, which means that you will almost certainly need to work on school-related tasks during your evenings and weekends. For example, Judy, Paul's wife and recipient of the note connection between feeling effective and feeling satisfied, but can't be absolutely sure.) More than 9 of 10 experienced teachers described themselves as "very competent." As teachers gain experience, they also become more confident in their ability to work with students and help them learn (Feistritzer, 2011). These highly satisfied teachers also believe that they are capable of promoting learning in their students regardless of students' ability, backgrounds, and home life (MetLife, 2009).

Despite their general positive perspectives on the profession, teachers also identified problems. Incompetent or unmotivated colleagues are one of the biggest. Teachers believe that too many of their peers aren't getting the job done and believe they should be removed, regardless of seniority (Feistritzer, 2011). Teachers also identify low salaries as a second major problem. (We discuss teacher salaries later in this section.)

This generally positive perspective on the profession has shifted recently with the publication of the latest Metlife Survey of the American Teacher (Metlife, 2012). This latest survey found a sharp drop in teacher job satisfaction since the previous one (Metlife, 2009), with a large increase in the number of teachers who are considering other occupations. Why this sharp decrease in teacher satisfaction with their jobs? Pollsters point to a deterioration in public support for education, ranging from less money for school services to decreased job security for teachers. As cash-strapped state governments cut back on a range of educational services including support staff, art, music and after-school programs, as well as health and social services, teachers' jobs and job security also suffered. Whether these shifts in teacher attitudes are primarily the result of cyclical economic conditions or more long-term changes in our country's support for teachers and the profession is not clear.

But what about first-year teachers? You might be one of these in the near future. What do new teachers think about teaching and their place in the profession?

First-Year Teachers Weigh In

New teachers are also satisfied with their jobs, the vast majority (over 90%) are confident in their abilities, and most (over 80%) believe their students are lucky to have them as teachers (Rochkind et al., 2008). They're also optimistic; almost 3 of 4 believe that good teachers can promote learning in all students, including those with uninvolved parents and from poor families. We hope they retain that optimism, and they will if they continue to produce good teaching results in the classroom. There is no substitute for seeing children learn and develop as a result of your efforts.

The vast majority (over 80%) of new teachers believe that teaching is what they should be doing, and there is no other job they'd rather have. And, more than 6 of 10 say they believe they'll still be in a classroom 10 years from now. Despite the stereotype that teachers go through "hell and high water" in their first years of teaching, first-year teachers seem to be both confident and happy in their new profession.

Job satisfaction is closely linked to **teacher efficacy**, teachers' beliefs in their ability to promote learning and make a difference in students' lives, regardless of background or home conditions. It's almost certain that seeing their students learning is the primary reason a large majority of teachers describe themselves as satisfied with their decision to teach. Few experiences are more rewarding than seeing students grow and develop over time because of our efforts. Most teachers have gone home at night saying, "Today was a good one. I could actually feel them learning. Maybe, just maybe, I'm making a difference in their lives." It's a wonderful, intoxicating, almost euphoric feeling. The opposite is also true; teachers who fail to experience that success and confidence soon burn out (Yarrow, 2009).

Classrooms are complex learn
occur simultaneously.

Unfortunately many teachers (too many) don't feel appreciated, supported by their principal, or optimistic about their ability to influence student learning. Experts call these teachers disheartened; another name might be discouraged. Again, every teacher has experienced that sinking feeling when lessons don't go right, when management is a constant struggle, and students seem to be resisting our best efforts. Fortunately for most of us, we can go home, lick our wounds, and come back the next day with new ideas and renewed optimism. When that doesn't happen, it's time to get out of teaching.

In *Teaching and You* at the beginning of this section, we asked if you believe that you will be teaching in 5 or 10 years. If you're similar to the teachers in these surveys, many of you will be. Admittedly, some teachers change their minds, for a variety of reasons. However, if you decide to teach, surveys suggest that you will be very satisfied with your career choice, and believing you're making a difference in students' lives will be a primary reason for remaining.

This information has important implications for all of us who work with students. Mastering the knowledge and skills needed to promote student learning and seeing that we're making a difference in our students' lives will ultimately determine how satisfied we are with our decision to teach.

How Much Is a Teacher Worth?

Teaching and You

How would you like to make $125,000 a year working as a teacher? What if you had to work longer hours? What if your salary also depended on your students' standardized test scores and you could be terminated if your performance did not satisfy your principal?

An expanding body of research is now examining the economic impact of teachers, and the results are striking; large-scale studies—studies examining millions of students—indicate that good teachers have effects on their students that last a lifetime (Chetty, Friedman, & Rockoff, 2011). Let's take a look.

The Economic Impact of Teachers

The economic impact of teachers begins in kindergarten. For example, one study found that students who were fortunate to have a good kindergarten teacher (one whose students were learning at the 75th percentile) versus a poor one (one whose students were learning at the 25th percentile) resulted in students who were more likely to attend college and adults who were more likely to own a home, earn more over a lifetime, and have sizable retirement savings (Chetty et al., 2011).

And the economic impact continues as students move through school. Having a good teacher in fourth grade, for example, results in increased adult incomes, an increased likelihood of going to college, and a decreased likelihood of teenage pregnancy. The cumulative economic effects of good teaching are dramatic; if the profession could replace as few as the bottom 5% of teachers (again identified by their students' test scores) and replace them with teachers of no more than average ability, an increased cumulative earnings of $52,000 for each student, or $1.4 million for a class, would result (Kristoff, 2012). This is indeed a stunning result, and many argue that teachers aren't being paid enough. Let's take a closer look at teacher salaries.

Teacher Salaries

Teacher salaries are the subject of considerable debate. They are low compared to other professions, such as medicine, law, architecture, and engineering, and they are a primary reason teachers leave the profession. The general public agrees; more than half of Americans believe teachers are paid too little, and two thirds of teachers agree (Metlife, 2012). However, politically conservative critics contend that when benefits such as medical insurance and pensions are factored in, teacher salaries are competitive with, or even higher than, similar occupations (Biggs & Richwine, 2011). Teachers who have to moonlight to make ends meet obviously disagree (Parham & Gordon, 2011).

Salaries for all teachers are improving, however. The average teacher salary in the United States for the 2009–2010 school year was $55,350, ranging from a high of $71,470 in New York to a low of $35,136 in South Dakota. The average beginning salary nationwide was about $35,000.

Your beginning salary will depend on a number of factors, including the location of the school district and the cost of living in your area. Local property taxes are a major funding source for schools, so your salary will depend on property values in your district. Also, urban districts typically have higher salaries than their rural counterparts because of a higher cost of living.

Other economic factors also influence the attractiveness of teaching. For example, in many states annual salary increases are often automatic, and, as you saw earlier in the chapter, vacation periods are ideal. Medical, dental, and retirement benefits are usually provided. In addition, you will be paid a supplement for extra duties, such as being a club sponsor, coaching, chairing academic departments (e.g., chairing the English department in a middle school), and mentoring beginning teachers. In schools with year-round schedules, teachers work 11 months of the year versus 9 or 10 and are paid accordingly.

Table 1.2 lists the average and beginning teacher salaries for each state in the 2009–2010 school year. Take a look at your state and any others that you might be considering. Would you consider these salaries to be a reward or a challenge if you entered the teaching profession?

Is money an incentive? One study asked what would happen if teacher salaries began at $65,000 and went as high as $150,000. Researchers found that the percentage of high-performing graduates who said they would choose teaching would jump from fewer than 15% to nearly 70% (Sawchuk, 2012b). The answer to our question apparently is yes.

Now, let's consider the first question we asked in *Teaching and You* in this section: "How would you like to make $125,000 a year working as a teacher?" This wasn't merely hypothetical; an innovative charter school in New York offered teachers exactly that amount ($125,000), and 600 teachers nationwide applied (Equity Project, 2012)! An intensive screening process followed in which the principal interviewed 100 teachers in person and observed 35 in their classrooms. Out of this pool, 8 were chosen. This exceptional experiment was grounded in the premise that effective teachers are the key to a successful school, and an expanding body of research is consistently confirming this premise (Chetty et al., 2011).

Now, think about the other questions we asked in *Teaching and You*: "What if you had to work longer hours?" and "What if your salary also depended on your students' standardized test scores and you could be terminated if your performance did not satisfy your principal?" These questions are now being considered by policy makers. For example, educational leaders are suggesting that the much higher salaries we describe here should be tied to longer hours, both during the regular school year and summers, as well as to larger class sizes, reduced retirement benefits, and virtually nonexistent job security, that is the principal could terminate you without recourse if he or she felt you were not doing an adequate job (Gootman, 2009).

Perhaps now your answer to the offer of a $125,000 salary has changed—or maybe not. Your dilemma is one that a number of teachers are facing nationwide as reforms attempt to link higher teacher salaries to more rigorous forms of teacher evaluation, including student test scores (Honawar & Olson, 2008). As you begin thinking about your first job, the conditions of employment, including your salary structure, and what you'll need to do to receive pay increases will become increasingly important.

Our goal in writing this section has been to provide you with realistic information about the rewards and challenges of teaching, to help you begin making a decision about whether you want to teach. In the next section, we turn to a discussion of professionalism, one of the major themes of this text.

TABLE 1.2 Average and Beginning Teacher Salaries for United States in 2009–2010

State	Average Salary ($) (Rank)	Beginning Salary ($) (Rank)
Alabama	47,156 (34)	36,144 (16)
Alaska	59,729 (9)	42,687 (4)
Arizona	46,952 (36)	31,888 (36)
Arkansas	49,051 (30)	30,525 (45)
California	70,458 (2)	41,181 (6)
Colorado	49,505 (28)	31,285 (42)
Connecticut	64,350 (7)	40,079 (8)
Delaware	57,080 (14)	36,633 (15)
District of Columbia	64,548 (6)	NA
Florida	46,912 (37)	34,605 (22)
Georgia	54,274 (18)	33,424 (25)
Hawaii	58,168 (11)	43,157 (2)
Idaho	46,283 (40)	31,581 (40)
Illinois	62,077 (8)	35,464 (18)
Indiana	49,986 (27)	32,761 (28)
Iowa	50,547 (24)	32,001 (34)
Kansas	46,957 (35)	31,763 (37)
Kentucky	48,354 (33)	34,631 (21)
Louisiana	50,349 (25)	38,523 (10)
Maine	46,106 (42)	30,732 (44)
Maryland	65,333 (4)	42,297 (5)
Massachusetts	68,000 (3)	38,570 (9)
Michigan	57,958 (13)	35,164 (19)
Minnesota	53,069 (20)	32,315 (33)
Mississippi	45,644 (46)	30,090 (46)
Missouri	45,317 (47)	29,309 (47)
Montana	45,759 (45)	24,685 (50)
Nebraska	46,080 (43)	27,030 (48)
Nevada	51,524 (22)	34,193 (23)
New Hampshire	51,365 (23)	32,549 (30)
New Jersey	64,809 (5)	44,872 (1)
New Mexico	46,401 (38)	36,003 (17)
New York	71,470 (1)	41,079 (7)
North Carolina	48,648 (31)	31,892 (35)
North Dakota	42,964 (50)	25,793 (49)
Ohio	55,931 (15)	31,656 (38)
Oklahoma	44,143 (48)	31,611 (39)
Oregon	55,224 (17)	31,556 (41)
Pennsylvania	58,124 (12)	38,229 (13)
Rhode Island	59,636 (10)	38,466 (11)
South Carolina	48,417 (32)	38,466 (11)
South Dakota	35,136 (51)	34,016 (24)
Tennessee	46,290 (39)	32,525 (31)
Texas	46,157 (41)	32,868 (27)
Utah	43,068 (49)	32,393 (32)
Vermont	49,053 (29)	33,100 (26)
Virginia	49,999 (26)	36,634 (14)
Washington	53,653 (19)	35,018 (20)
West Virginia	45,959 (44)	30,815 (43)
Wisconsin	52,644 (21)	32,643 (29)
Wyoming	55,694 (16)	43,010 (3)
U.S. AVERAGE	**55,350**	**34,558**

NA = not available.

Sources: National Education Association. (2009). *State affiliates.* Retrieved from http://www.nea.org/home/49809.htm
National Education Association. (2010). *Rankings and estimates: Rankings of the states 2009 and estimates of school statistics 2010.* Retrieved from http://www.nea.org/assets/docs/010rankings.pdf

Data used by permission of National Education Association.

Check Your Understanding

1.1 Identify the four most commonly cited reasons people give for entering teaching.
1.2 What are the major rewards in teaching?
1.3 What are the major challenges in teaching?
1.4 How do experienced and beginning teachers feel about the rewards and challenges of teaching? What are the implications of these findings for you as a beginning teacher?

For feedback, go to the appendix, *Check Your Understanding,* located in the back of this text.

The Teaching Profession

Are teachers professionals? This question is becoming increasingly important, because current reform efforts in our country are resulting in many professional decisions being made *for*, rather than *by,* teachers (Wilson & Tamir, 2008). In the opinion of prominent educational leaders, these efforts are misguided.

> "What are the right incentives to have in place for teachers?" The very question itself is jarring. It implies that teachers don't want to perform well and that they need incentives, which in today's parlance translates into rewards (money) and reprimands (fear of loss of benefits or position). Let me present a very different picture: Teachers should be regarded as and behave like professionals. (Gardner, 2011, paras. 1–2)

Making teaching a profession comparable to medicine or law, advocates contend, would benefit both teachers and their students; it would mean better-prepared teachers, higher standards for performance and ethics, and greater trust in teachers by parents. As authors, we support this position. We believe in the potential of **professionalism** to transform teaching in many positive ways, which is why we've made it the subtitle of your text and a major theme for its content. Let's examine the issue further.

What Does Being a Professional Mean?

Established professions such as medicine and law have the following characteristics:

- A specialized body of knowledge
- Autonomy
- Emphasis on decision making and reflection
- Ethical standards for conduct (Hurst & Reding, 2009; Wilson & Tamir, 2008)

Teaching and You

What do you look for when you visit a doctor or dentist? How important are their confidence, competence, or expertise?

Let's look at these characteristics of professionalism.

A Specialized Body of Knowledge

Professionals understand and use a specialized body of knowledge in serving their clients (see Figure 1.3). A physician, for example, recognizes and understands symptoms of diseases and prescribes medications, surgical procedures, or other forms of therapy to eliminate both the symptoms and their causes. People seek the advice and help of physicians because of their specialized knowledge.

Do teachers possess specialized knowledge? Researchers believe the answer is yes and suggest this knowledge exists in four forms (Darling-Hammond, 2008):

- *Knowledge of content:* The more teachers know about a content area, such as algebra, American history, or chemistry, for example, the more effective they will be in teaching it (Krauss et al., 2008). Acquiring a deep understanding of the content you'll teach will be one of the biggest challenges you'll face as a beginning teacher.

- *Pedagogical content knowledge:* Understanding a content area is essential for teaching, but, in itself, is not sufficient. Being able to make the content understandable to others requires an additional form of professional knowledge (Murray, 2008). The ability to illustrate abstract ideas, such as equivalent fractions in math or the concept *nationalism* in history, in ways that are understandable to students reflects **pedagogical content knowledge**.
- *General pedagogical knowledge:* General principles of teaching and learning, such as the ability to maintain an orderly and learning-focused classroom and guide student learning using skilled questioning, constitute a third form of professional knowledge called **general pedagogical knowledge** (Darling-Hammond, 2008).
- *Knowledge of learners and learning:* Understanding the different ways students learn and develop is another form of professional knowledge. Young children, for example, aren't merely miniature versions of those who are older; they think and learn differently (Berk, 2012). Your ability to understand your students and adjust your lessons accordingly will determine, to a large extent, your teaching effectiveness.

FIGURE 1.3 Professionalism Requires a Specialized Body of Knowledge

To see these different kinds of professional knowledge used in classrooms at different levels, click on the video *Types of Professional Knowledge* (6:52).

To these four we add *knowledge of the profession*, which includes understanding the social, historical, philosophical, and legal aspects of teaching. These different forms of knowledge will help you make professional decisions in your school and classroom (Krull, Oras, & Sisask, 2007).

The inclination to continue learning is also essential for professionals. Just as physicians must continually upgrade their knowledge of therapies, medications, and surgical procedures, you will need to stay abreast of research in your field. For instance, intuition suggests that we should encourage students who aren't successful to work harder, but research indicates that this can be counterproductive. Students in general believe they are already working hard, so they're bewildered by the suggestion, and older students often believe that an admonition to work hard suggests low ability in the student. If you're aware of this research, you will encourage students to change the *way* they study instead of the *amount* they study, and doing so can have a significant influence on their motivation to learn (Schunk, Pintrich, & Meece, 2008). The more professional knowledge you possess, the better able you will be to adapt your instruction to best meet each student's needs. Our primary goal in writing this text is to help you develop these different forms of professional knowledge.

Extended Training for Licensure. Extended training for licensure is required to develop these different types of professional knowledge. As with physicians, lawyers, and engineers, teachers must earn a license that allows them to practice their profession. The license certifies that you're competent, and as with other professions, you will be required to periodically renew your license to confirm that you are staying current in your field. Teachers need at least a bachelor's degree before licensure, and in many states they must complete the degree in a content area, such as math or English, before they begin their teacher preparation experiences. Licensure also requires clinical experiences, such as internships, which are designed to ensure that you can apply your professional knowledge in the real world of schools.

FIGURE 1.4 Professionalism Requires Autonomy

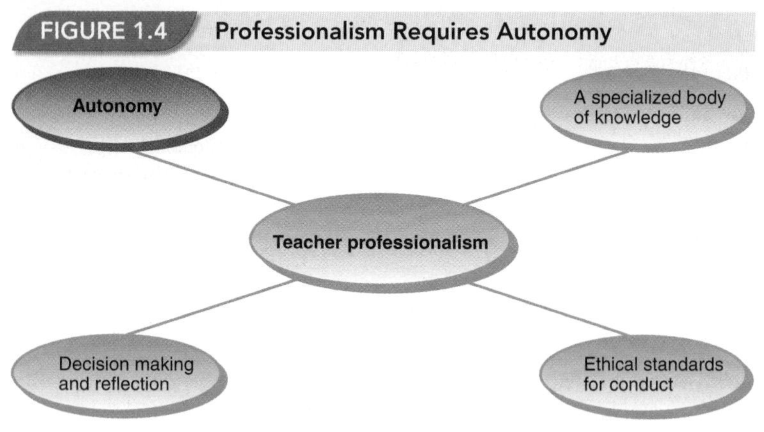

Autonomy

With knowledge comes **autonomy**, the capacity to control one's own professional life. Professionals have the authority to make decisions based on their specialized knowledge (see Figure 1.4). When a person sees a physician because of stomach problems, for example, no set of standards mandates specific treatments or medications; doctors have the authority to treat patients as they see fit. Some suggest that teaching isn't a profession because states and districts, instead of teachers, prescribe what teachers teach (the **curriculum**) as well as how student understanding is measured (**assessment**) (Imig & Imig, 2008).

Indeed, states and districts prescribe **standards**, statements specifying what students should know or be able to do after completing an area of study, and districts often require students to meet these standards before moving from one grade to another or graduating from high school. However, in spite of these mandates, you will have a great deal of autonomy when you begin teaching. You will have control over the specific content you teach, how you teach it, and—even though yearly standardized assessments are often mandated—how you will decide how to assess your students' learning. Although some argue that teachers lack the autonomy to be called true professionals, we disagree: You will, in fact, have considerable autonomy to determine what goes on in your classroom.

Emphasis on Decision Making and Reflection

As you saw earlier in the chapter, classrooms are complex, and teachers make many decisions in ill-defined situations. For example, when Sylvia accused Joey of calling her a fat jerk, Ken had to decide whether to ignore the incident or to intervene. And if he decided to intervene, what should this intervention be? Should he take Joey out of the classroom and talk to him? Make him apologize or write a note to Sylvia? Call his parents? And, what if Sylvia wasn't telling the truth, or misunderstood what Joey said? David Ling, in his lesson on inertia, had to decide how to begin his lesson, what examples to use, what students to call on and in what order, how long to give them to answer, what kind of follow-up question to ask if they didn't respond, and a host of other decisions. Both Ken and David faced ill-defined situations, yet decisions had to be made. This is why professional knowledge is so essential: Without it, wise decision making is virtually impossible.

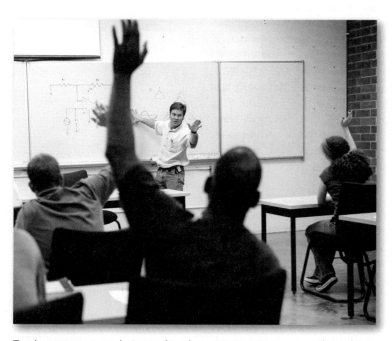

Teacher autonomy to design and implement instruction comes with teacher professionalism.

But how will you know if you've made wise decisions? Unfortunately, you will receive little formal feedback about the effectiveness of your work. Typically, teachers are observed by administrators a few times a year at most, and they receive only vague, sketchy, and often uncertain feedback from students and parents; they get virtually no feedback from their colleagues, unless the school has a peer coaching or mentoring program. To develop as a professional, you will need to be able to assess your own decisions.

The ability to conduct this self-assessment requires that teachers develop a disposition for continually and critically examining their work; this is the essence of a simple, yet powerful idea called **reflection**, the act of thinking about and analyzing your actions (Howard & Aleman, 2008). Reflective teachers are thoughtful and critical about their teaching. They plan lessons carefully and take the time to analyze them afterward.

FIGURE 1.5 Professionalism Requires Decision Making and Reflection

Autonomy

A specialized body of knowledge

Teacher professionalism

Decision making and reflection

Ethical standards for conduct

Reflection is essential because it improves our teaching and helps us develop as professionals. As we analyze our work, we gradually develop a coherent philosophy of education that helps us integrate theory and research into our classrooms and continually refine our practice (Oner & Adadan, 2011) (see Figure 1.5).

Professional Ethics

Teaching is—and has historically been—described as a moral enterprise in which teachers are continually asked to make ethical decisions (Goodlad, Soder, & Sirotnik, 1990; Murrell, Diez, Feiman-Nemser, & Schussler, 2011). Fortunately, teachers have ethical standards to guide their actions. To understand what this means, consider the following problems:

An ardent advocate of gun control, you believe that access to guns should be strictly regulated, and you have said so in class. Eric, one of your students, brings a newspaper editorial to school that makes a compelling argument against gun control. Because of your beliefs, you don't allow him to share the editorial with the class.

Greg is a difficult student in one of your classes. He is disruptive and periodically shouts insults at other students and sometimes even at you. You've tried everything you know to control his behavior, but you've been unsuccessful. Finally, in exasperation one day, you walk up to him while he is talking, clap your hands together, and say angrily, "Greg, I've had it with you! You can't keep your mouth closed for more than 1 minute, and you're an embarrassment to yourself and the other students in this class. I don't want to hear another sound out of you the rest of the period." Surprisingly, it works; Greg sits quietly for the remainder of the period. Now, finding that anger seems to be the only way to keep Greg from being disruptive, you sometimes use it to manage his behavior.

Professional ethics guide teachers in their interactions with students, parents and caregivers, and colleagues.

Have you behaved "ethically" in these examples? How do you know? **Ethics** are sets of moral standards for acceptable professional behavior, and all professions have codes of ethics intended to guide professionals as they make decisions about how to act (see Figure 1.6). In its code of ethics, the National Education Association (NEA), the largest professional organization in education, addresses the issue of how teachers should interact with their students (see Figure 1.7).

FIGURE 1.6 Professionalism Requires Ethical Standards for Conduct

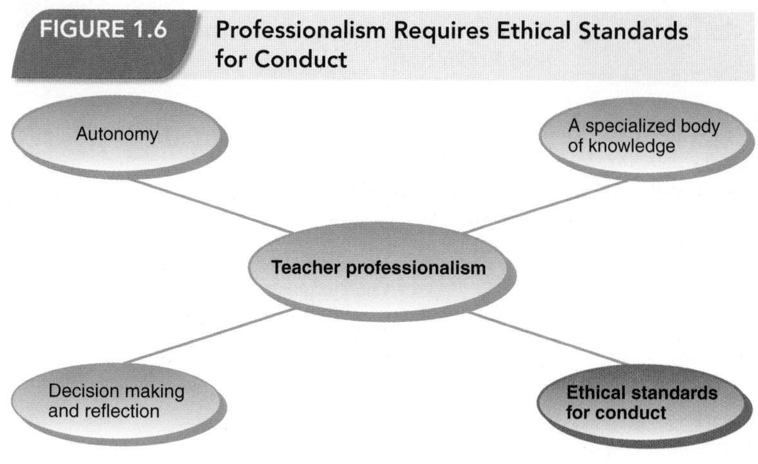

Let's evaluate your actions based on the information in the NEA Code of Ethics. Item 2 of Principle I, Commitment to the Student, states that a teacher "shall not unreasonably deny the student access to varying points of view." In the first example, you didn't let Eric share the editorial with other students, so you have denied them access to a view that differs from your own. Whether your denial was "unreasonable" is open to interpretation, as is the case with ethical standards in any profession.

In the second example, you were desperately searching for a way to manage Greg's behavior, and by chance you found that anger (and possibly intimidation) was the only thing that seemed to work. However, Item 5 of Principle I says a teacher "shall not intentionally expose the student to embarrassment or disparagement." This case is clear: In your desperation and frustration, you intentionally used anger and disparagement as a strategy with Greg, so you are in violation of the ethical code.

Other examples of ethical lapses sometimes seen in teaching include retaliating against students for alleged slights or offenses by grading unfairly or making unfair placement decisions, accepting fees for tutoring one's own students, and cheating on state tests by giving students more than the prescribed time or by giving them clues and/or answers. Ethical standards are so important to professionals that they are often written into employment contracts; they are also valuable because they can provide a basis for your own professional decision making.

Are Teachers Professionals?

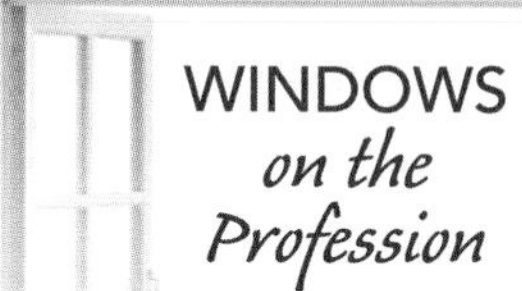

To hear two principals' views on what it means to be a professional, click on the video *Teachers as Professionals: Two Principals' Views* (4:38).

Not everyone believes that teachers are professionals. Critics' arguments most commonly include lack of rigorous training and lack of autonomy (Imig & Imig, 2008; Labaree, 2008). Let's examine these arguments.

Lack of Rigorous Training

The academic rigor of teachers' professional training has historically been criticized (Sedlak, 2008). Entrance into teaching isn't as competitive as entrance into professions such as medicine or law, and many critics suggest that content knowledge is all teachers need to teach successfully. This position is not supported by research (Darling-Hammond, 2008). The complexities of teaching requiring split-second decision making, and the responsibility of guiding the lives of young people suggests that teaching is a demanding profession requiring a great deal of specialized knowledge. Training in any profession can always be more rigorous, but suggesting that teaching doesn't require deep, extensive, and varied knowledge reflects a lack of understanding of the profession.

Lack of Autonomy

In the previous section, we argued that teachers have a great deal of autonomy. We maintain this position, but we acknowledge that teachers have less autonomy than other professionals. For example, unlike physicians and lawyers, teachers are supervised and evaluated by their principals, and states and districts mandate a portion of the curriculum. Teachers have little to say about the standards for licensure, and some teachers even have to sign in at the beginning of the day and sign out at the end. The extent to which these requirements detract from the definition of teaching as a true profession continues to be debated.

FIGURE 1.7 National Education Association Code of Ethics

Preamble

The educator, believing in the worth and dignity of each human being, recognizes the supreme importance of the pursuit of truth, devotion to excellence, and the nurture of democratic principle. Essential to these goals is the protection of freedom to learn and to teach and the guarantee of equal educational opportunity for all. The educator accepts the responsibility to adhere to the highest ethical standards.

The educator recognizes the magnitude of the responsibility inherent in the teaching process. The desire for the respect and confidence of one's colleagues, of students, of parents, and the members of the community provides the incentive to attain and maintain the highest possible degree of ethical conduct. The Code of Ethics of the Education Profession indicates the aspiration of all educators and provides standards by which to judge conduct.

The remedies specified by the NEA and/or its affiliates for the violation of any provision of this Code shall be exclusive and no such provision shall be enforceable in any form other than one specifically designated by the NEA or its affiliates.

Principle I—Commitment to the Student

The educator strives to help each student realize his or her potential as a worthy and effective member of society. The educator therefore works to stimulate the spirit of inquiry, the acquisition of knowledge and understanding, and the thoughtful formulation of worthy goals.

In fulfillment of the obligation to the student, the educator—

1. Shall not unreasonably restrain the student from independent action in the pursuit of learning.
2. Shall not unreasonably deny the student access to varying points of view.
3. Shall not deliberately suppress or distort subject matter relevant to the student's progress.
4. Shall make reasonable effort to protect the student from conditions harmful to learning or to health and safety.
5. Shall not intentionally expose the student to embarrassment or disparagement.
6. Shall not on the basis of race, color, creed, sex, national origin, marital status, political or religious beliefs, family, social or cultural background, or sexual orientation unfairly:
   a. Exclude any student from participation in any program;
   b. Deny benefits to any student;
   c. Grant any advantage to any student.
7. Shall not use professional relationships with students for private advantage.
8. Shall not disclose information about students obtained in the course of professional service, unless disclosure serves a compelling professional purpose or is required by law.

Principle II—Commitment to the Profession

The education profession is vested by the public with a trust and responsibility requiring the highest ideals of professional service.

In the belief that the quality of the services of the education profession directly influences the nation and its citizens, the educator shall exert every effort to raise professional standards, to promote a climate that encourages the exercise of professional judgment, to achieve conditions which attract persons worthy of the trust to careers in education, and to assist in preventing the practice of the profession by unqualified persons.

In fulfillment of the obligation to the profession, the educator—

1. Shall not in an application for a professional position deliberately make a false statement or fail to disclose a material fact related to competency and qualifications.
2. Shall not misrepresent his/her professional qualifications.
3. Shall not assist entry into the profession of a person known to be unqualified in respect to character, education, or other relevant attribute.
4. Shall not knowingly make a false statement concerning the qualifications of a candidate for a professional position.
5. Shall not assist a noneducator in the unauthorized practice of teaching.
6. Shall not disclose information about colleagues obtained in the course of professional service unless disclosure serves a compelling professional purpose or is required by law.
7. Shall not knowingly make a false or malicious statement about a colleague.
8. Shall not accept any gratuity, gift, or favor that might impair or appear to influence professional decisions or actions.

Source: National Education Association. (2008). Code of Ethics of the Education Profession, NEA Representative Assembly. Reprinted by permission.

Are Teachers Professionals? Revisiting the Question

The issue of teaching as a profession is controversial and won't be resolved anytime soon. Without question, the training required for professions such as medicine and law is more rigorous than the training required for teaching, although rigor in teacher education is increasing (Imig & Imig, 2008). Prospective teachers are expected to know and do more, and their professional knowledge is now assessed with tests that measure their understanding of the content they teach, as well as their understanding of how to help students learn. We discuss these tests later in the chapter.

With respect to autonomy, a battle is currently being fought on both sides of the issue (Whitcomb, Borko, & Liston, 2007). Some would curtail teachers' autonomy by mandating what and how to teach and how to assess student learning. Others argue that this technical view of teaching isn't feasible, because teaching requires too many split-second decisions to be reduced to mandates, and good teachers need to be sensitive to different student's needs (Gardner, 2011).

It is clear that teachers share many characteristics of established professions: They possess a specialized body of knowledge; they make an enormous number of decisions as they work; and they have a significant amount of autonomy. Effective teachers also take time to reflect on their actions and are careful to follow the ethical standards established by educational leaders. Are teachers professionals? This remains an unanswered question. However, you can behave like a true professional by becoming as knowledgeable as possible, exercising your autonomy in the classroom wisely, and behaving ethically in all your dealings with students. This is as much as individuals do in any profession.

TECHNOLOGY and TEACHING: The Influence of Technology on the Profession

To say that technology is an integral part of our lives is an understatement. It has changed both the way we live and the way we learn and teach in many different ways. For instance, cell phones, Facebook, and Twitter have revolutionized the way we communicate. Internet search engines, such as Google, Dogpile, and Yahoo, have radically altered the way we find information, and have made print encyclopedias and dictionaries anachronisms. We don't find locations on a map anymore; we go to www.mapquest.com. And our vehicles are equipped with GPS systems that send us straight to our desired destination. Technological literacy has become a basic skill, virtually equal in importance to reading, writing, and math.

Our students report spending over 7½ hours with media each day (Rideout, Foehr, & Roberts, 2010). Ninety-seven percent of teachers report that they have computers available in their classrooms, and almost 70% use them to augment their instruction (N. Thomas & Lewis, 2010). Both teacher and student use of technology has increased dramatically in the last 20 years.

Technology is increasingly being seen by many as the key to economic survival in a global economy (Manzo, 2009b). Countries such as China and India have invested heavily in educational technology in attempts to make their countries more competitive economically. Experts are asking, "Are U.S. students' tech skills keeping up with their international peers?"

Although other technologies have advanced as well, the most dramatic growth has occurred in the area of computer technology. Currently, virtually all schools have access to the Internet, and 4 of 10 classrooms have wireless network capability (National Center for Education Statistics, 2010c). The ratio of students to computers has fallen dramatically, and experts now estimate the number at 3 to 1. The vast majority of homes with school-age children have a computer, and most have access to the Internet (Rainie, 2010).

Initially, computer literacy, or preparing students for life in the age of computers, was the focus of most computer use in the schools. Over time, instructional uses of computers have expanded to include:

- Computer-assisted instruction, including simulations, multimedia instruction, drill and practice, and tutorials
- Information tools for students, including spreadsheets, data bases, and other capabilities for information retrieval, processing, and multimedia learning
- Computer-managed instruction, including student record keeping, diagnostic and prescriptive testing and test scoring and analysis, and design of instructional materials, including text and graphics (Roblyer & Doering, 2013)

Technology has become an essential component of education in our country. However, implementing technology in our schools isn't as simple as it appears on the surface, and it has also raised a number of issues that influence learning and teaching in today's education. To address these issues, we include 12 *Technology and Teaching* sections in 10 different chapters of your text. For example, in Chapter 2 we focus on cyberbullying, an issue that has received a great deal of publicity in recent years. In Chapter 3 we examine technology access issues for different student groups, and in Chapter 9 we discuss Internet censorship issues in schools. Our goal in each of these sections is to provide you with current information about technology use in our schools, issues involved in this use, and how it will affect your life as a teacher. We hope you find these sections a valuable addition to your understanding of the profession.

Check Your Understanding

2.1 What are the essential characteristics of professionalism?

2.2 What are the primary arguments that teaching is a profession?

2.3 What are the major arguments that teaching is not a profession?

2.4 How do the arguments for and against teacher professionalism balance each other?

For feedback, go to the appendix, *Check Your Understanding*, located in the back of this text.

Diversity: The Changing Face of American Classrooms

When you walk into your first classroom, you will likely be struck by one fact: Our students have become remarkably diverse. Nationwide, for example, more than 4 of 10 students in P–12 classrooms are students of color. In our 25 largest cities, these students make up more than half the student population (National Center for Education Statistics, 2011f), and in 2011, the majority (51%) of students in the California public schools were Hispanic (California Department of Education, 2011). By the year 2020, the P–12 population is projected to increase by nearly 10%, and most of this increase will occur in Hispanic (25%), Asian and Pacific Islander (36%), and American Indian and Alaska Native (17%) student populations. Percentages of white students will actually decrease during this same time span. Combined with this cultural and ethnic diversity, you will likely teach students who speak a native language other than English.

Your students' **socioeconomic status**—the combination of their parents' income, level of education, and jobs—will also differ, and these differences will strongly affect their learning (Macionis, 2011). Some parents can afford trips to other states and even countries, for example, whereas others are barely able to provide a place to live and enough to eat. Some students will have trips to zoos, museums, and other places that provide the school-related experiences that prepare them for learning, but others' experiences will be limited. These differences result in dramatic differences in their school success (Maxwell, 2012b).

In a single grade you will also have learners who are mature for their age and others who are slower in developing. Some will be poised and self-confident; others, shy and hesitant. You will certainly have a mix of boys and girls, and you're likely to have students with learning problems who will require extra help.

Each of these forms of diversity can affect students' success in your classroom, and how you respond to these differences will influence how much your students learn, how they feel about school, and your own enjoyment of teaching. In addition, federal mandates require states to report student progress in terms of specific ethnic and cultural groups.

Unfortunately, many beginning teachers feel ill-prepared to teach this diversity. One new teacher commented, "I was completely unprepared for dealing with the poverty issues and social issues that occur in my school" (MetLife, 2009, p.4). Because learner diversity is so important to your future teaching success, we have made diversity the second theme (together with professionalism) of this text. Consistent with this theme, we devote all of Chapters 2 and 3 to the topic, and we include special sections called *Exploring Diversity* and *Diversity and You* in every chapter.

EXPLORING DIVERSITY: Teaching in Rural, Suburban, and Urban Schools

Teaching and You

Where would you like to teach after you graduate? Will you be most happy/comfortable in a school similar to the one you attended as a student? With what kinds of students will you be most effective?

Exploring Diversity in each chapter examines a diversity-related issue, and in this chapter we consider teaching in rural, suburban, and urban contexts. Understanding different learning and teaching contexts will be important for you when you begin teaching because these environments present different opportunities and challenges (Gardner, 2008). We begin with rural schools.

Teaching in Rural Schools

In 1900, 60% of the population in our country lived in rural areas; today that figure is 16% (U.S. Bureau of Census, 2010b). Approximately 1 in 5 students attends a rural school, and enrollments in these schools grew 22% between 1999 and 2009 (Strange, Johnson, Showalter & Klein, 2012). In 15 states, students in rural areas make up a majority of the public school population. South Dakota has the highest percentage of rural students (79%), and Massachusetts the lowest (7%). As we'd expect, rural schools are much smaller than their urban and suburban counterparts; in 2007, in fact, 327 one-teacher, one-room schools remained in rural areas of our country (Brimley, Verstegen, & Garfield, 2012). Because they're small, student–teacher ratios are low, with the smallest rural schools averaging 11 students per class compared to 17 for their counterparts in larger districts (U.S. Government Accounting Office, 2006).

Students in rural districts tend to be less culturally diverse than those in urban and suburban districts, although this is rapidly changing and varies from state to state. For example, cultural minorities make up more than 80% of the student population in New Mexico, compared to less than 5% in Rhode Island (Strange et al., 2012). Immigrants from Latin America and Asia are finding their way into rural America, seeking jobs in construction, meatpacking, and other food-processing industries (Macionis, 2011). Twenty-six percent of rural students are members of minority groups, and the Hispanic population grew over 150%

between 1999 and 2009. Many of these students don't speak English as their native language (Strange et al., 2012).

Poverty is also an issue in rural districts, particularly in the South and Southwest. For example, more than 40% of students in rural districts qualify for free or reduced-price lunch programs, and many rural students come to school with inadequate health care (Mattingly & Stransky, 2010; National Center for Education Statistics, 2010d).

Teaching in rural schools has both advantages and disadvantages. Because the districts are small, they have a strong sense of community, with schools often serving as the social center for the community. Because of small class sizes, communication with parents is often easier. And rural districts' small size can make innovation and change easier to accomplish than in larger districts. However, rural districts often aren't able to offer all of the services found in larger school districts.

Teaching in Suburban Schools

The last half of the 20th century resulted in unprecedented growth in the suburbs of our major cities. By the turn of the 21st century, many people had moved to suburbs from both rural and urban areas, and now the majority of our population lives there (Macionis, 2011). This exodus brought with it a growing tax base, which resulted in more money for suburban schools (Macionis & Parrillo, 2010; Spring, 2011). Increased revenue translates into smaller class sizes and greater access to resources such as science labs and technology.

Suburban schools are also more culturally diverse than their rural counterparts, but much of the diversity comes from well-educated professionals working in high-tech industries (Macionis, 2011). They are less diverse than urban schools, however, and average household incomes tend to be higher than in rural or urban areas.

Most of the highest-achieving school districts in our country are found in suburban areas, and many suburban families select neighborhoods based on the reputation of the schools in that area (Brimley et al., 2012; Spring, 2011). Because teaching in suburban schools is considered to be highly desirable, competition for jobs in them is stiff, and, as a beginning teacher, getting a job in one will be a challenge.

Teaching in Urban Schools

With respect to jobs, urban schools are "where the action is." Consider the following statistics (Council of Great City Schools, 2011):

- Our nation's 100 largest school districts represent less than 1% of all districts but are responsible for educating 16% of our students. For example, the New York City Public Schools and the Los Angeles Unified School District, the two largest in the nation, each have enrollments greater than the total enrollments of 27 states.
- The 100 largest districts employ more than a sixth of the nation's teachers.

Urban schools provide job openings and opportunities for personal and professional growth.

Eighty percent of students in urban schools are members of cultural minorities, and this number exceeds 95% in some (Macionis & Parrillo, 2010). More than 65% of all urban students are

Some of the more prominent of these reform efforts include:

- *Standards:* Statements describing what students should know and be able to do at the end of a period of study. All states have specified standards in most content areas.
- *Test-based accountability:* The process of using standardized tests to determine whether students have mastered essential knowledge and skills and basing promotion and graduation on test performance.
- *Choice:* Attempts to provide parents with alternatives to regular public schools by creating alternative charter schools and providing parents with financial vouchers that allow them to send their children to schools of their choosing.

We discuss these reforms and the implications they will have for your life as a new teacher in detail in later chapters. Reforms that focus on changes in teacher preparation, however, will have an immediate impact on you, and we examine them in the next section.

Changes in Teacher Preparation

Increased emphasis on professionalism, combined with concerns that too many underqualified teachers enter the field, have resulted in a number of reforms in teacher education, most enacted at the state level (Hightower, 2012). These reforms include:

- Raising standards for admission into teacher training programs
- Requiring teachers to take more rigorous courses
- Expanding teacher preparation programs from 4 to 5 years
- Requiring experienced teachers to take more rigorous professional-development courses
- Requiring higher standards for licensure, including teacher competency tests (McDiarmid & Clevenger-Bright, 2008; Rhee & Oakley, 2008)

You have already experienced, or are now experiencing, some of the outcomes of these reform efforts. For example, you are taking the required courses, and you can decide if you believe they are appropriately rigorous.

With respect to teacher preparation, teacher testing is one of the most significant reform efforts implemented, and it will affect you and every other teacher candidate in our country. Let's look at it in more detail.

Comprehensive Teacher Testing

Almost all (47) states in our country now test prospective teacher candidates before they're licensed (Hightower, 2012). A few states have created their own state tests, but the vast majority uses the Praxis Series™, published by Educational Testing Service. The Praxis Series (*praxis* means "putting theory into practice") exists at three levels (Educational Testing Service, 2012):

- *Praxis I: Pre-professional Skills Test.* These academic skills tests are designed to measure basic skills in reading, writing, and math that all teachers need. The items you see in *Teaching and You* on the following pages are similar to those you'll encounter in these pre-professional skills tests and also similar to those you might encounter in state-specific basic skills tests.
- *Praxis II: Subject Assessments.* The subject assessments are intended to measure teachers' knowledge of the subjects they will teach. In addition to 70 content-specific tests, Praxis II includes the Principles of Learning and Teaching (PLT) tests, which measure professional knowledge. The four

PLT tests are designed for teachers seeking licensure in Early Childhood or in grades K–6, 5–9, and 7–12. Each of the grade-level tests has two parts: The first consists of 24 multiple-choice questions similar to items in the test bank that accompanies this text, and the second part presents case histories with three short-answer questions to read and analyze. The topics these tests cover are outlined in the Praxis Correlation Matrix at the beginning of this text (Educational Testing Service, 2012).

- *Praxis III: Classroom Performance Assessments.* These tests use classroom observations and work samples to assess beginning teachers' ability to plan, instruct, manage, and understand professional responsibilities. In addition, Praxis III assesses a teacher's sensitivity to learners' developmental and cultural differences. You are most likely to encounter Praxis I before being admitted to a teacher licensure program, Praxis II during and after its completion, and Praxis III during your first years of teaching.

Comprehensive teacher testing is part of a broader reform effort, and as with most reforms, it's controversial. This leads us to the idea of issues that you'll face when you begin your teaching career.

Teaching and You

How would you answer the following questions?

1. Which of the following fractions is the smallest?

   a. $\frac{12}{11}$ b. $\frac{99}{100}$ c. $\frac{3}{4}$ d. $\frac{15}{16}$ e. $\frac{201}{200}$

2. Read the following sentence, and decide if it is grammatically correct. If not, how should it be changed to make it correct?

   A teacher should never assume that the students they teach understand something if they explain it correctly.

   a. The sentence is grammatically correct.

   b. The sentence is NOT grammatically correct and should be changed in this way:

   ____

   ____

Issues You'll Face in Teaching

Because reform is one of the themes for this book, we ask you to examine a variety of current reform efforts with a feature in each chapter titled *Issues You'll Face in Teaching*. We introduce the feature in this section and illustrate how you can use it to increase your understanding of educational reforms and how they'll influence you as a teacher.

The feature incorporates the following elements:

- A discussion of a reform issue such as zero tolerance policies (Chapter 2), grade retention (Chapter 6), money and your first job (Chapter 7), or teacher tenure (Chapter 12)
- Positions taken by both proponents and critics of the reform effort
- An opportunity for you to take a position with respect to the issue

Because teacher testing is an important and controversial reform issue that will affect your life directly in the near future, we use it to illustrate our *Issues You'll Face in Teaching* in this chapter. If you haven't already encountered teacher tests as an entrance requirement for admission into a teacher education program, you likely will as you move through your program and apply for licensure in your state.

Check Your Understanding

4.1 How is the current reform movement in education changing the teaching profession?

4.2 Describe the major changes in teacher preparation that have resulted from the reform movement in education.

4.3 What is the Praxis Series, and how does *praxis* relate to the reform movement?

4.4 What are the major arguments for and against testing teachers?

For feedback, go to the appendix, *Check Your Understanding*, located in the back of this text.

ISSUES YOU'LL FACE IN TEACHING

Testing Teachers

Currently, most states require some form of testing for prospective teachers, but the exact form that this testing takes varies from state to state (Hightower, 2012). Most states (39) require tests of basic skills either before admission to a teacher education program or after, and others test professional knowledge after program completion. In addition, most states (43) require tests of your knowledge of the subjects you'll be teaching, especially if you're a middle or high school teacher. Virtually all of these tests exist in a paper-and-pencil format, and new teachers will also be evaluated on their classroom performance during their first year.

Testing teachers is not new; for example, teachers were tested all the way back in the 1840s using oral exams that focused primarily on candidates' moral qualifications (Wilson & Youngs, 2005). The current emphasis on testing teachers is part of a larger accountability movement in education in which students, teachers, and even principals are being tested, and the results are being used to evaluate the effectiveness of educational efforts.

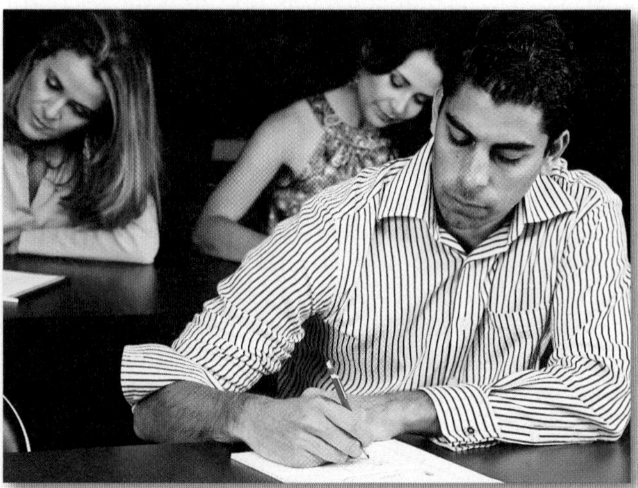

Prospective teachers are being asked to demonstrate their professional knowledge on state and national tests.

THE QUESTION

Is teacher testing an effective way to improve the teaching profession, or does it create barriers to talented people entering the profession? Arguments exist on both sides of the issue.

PRO

- Standardized tests are valid and necessary because they keep unqualified teachers out of classrooms.
- These tests are fair, and they minimize or even eliminate evaluator bias; a test doesn't know if the test taker is male or female, or if he or she is a member of a cultural minority. Further, research indicates that teachers' verbal ability is strongly correlated with student learning (Good & Brophy, 2008).
- The tests are economical and cost-effective, and the public at large supports teacher testing, with nearly 80% of the general public believing that teachers should have to pass a national test in the subjects they teach (Bushaw & Gallup, 2008).

CON

- Critics of teacher testing argue that the tests aren't valid because they fail to differentiate between good and bad prospective teachers. Performance on a test does not guarantee performance in the classroom, which further detracts from their validity (Sawchuk, 2012a). It's difficult, if not impossible, for a paper-and-pencil test to measure something as complex as teacher competency.
- Cutoff scores established by different states are arbitrary, based more on the demand for new teachers than on any objective measure of minimal teacher competency. Too often, the pass rates, which stand at 96% nationally, fail to distinguish between qualified and unqualified teacher candidates (Sawchuk, 2012a).
- The tests penalize cultural minorities and nonnative speakers because they rely on verbal and test-taking skills that may or may not influence teaching effectiveness (Bennett, McWhorter, & Kuykendall, 2006; Zumwalt & Craig, 2008).

YOU TAKE A STAND

Now it's your turn to take a position on the issue. Are teacher tests an effective way to ensure teacher quality, or are there better ways to guarantee teacher competency?

Go to *Issues You'll Face in Teaching* in the MyEducationLab™ *Book Resources* that accompany this text to log your thoughts and receive feedback from your authors.

VOICES from the CLASSROOM

"I teach because of the awesome pay, the perks, and the low-stress work environment that comes with being a teacher. Okay, I'm just kidding on that one. That's not why I teach. I teach because somewhere deep inside me, I'd like to think that sometimes, just sometimes, we make a difference."

MICHAEL SMART, 2008 Teacher of the Year, Minnesota

CHAPTER 1 Summary

1. Describe major rewards and challenges in teaching.
   - Rewards in teaching include both intrinsic and extrinsic benefits. Intrinsic rewards include both helping young people grow emotionally, socially, and academically and opportunities for a lifetime of intellectual growth. Examples of extrinsic rewards are desirable vacation times, convenient work schedules, and occupational status.
   - The first challenge in teaching is finding a job. Other challenges in teaching include the complexities of classrooms as well as the multiple roles that teachers perform. Classrooms are multidimensional, and the events that occur in classrooms are simultaneous, immediate, unpredictable, and public. Teachers' roles include creating productive learning environments, serving as ambassadors to the public, and working with other professionals as collaborative colleagues.
   - Teachers, both experienced and new, are positive about the profession and confident in their competence as professionals. A vast majority (80%) said they planned to be teaching in 5 years, and most (90%) believed they did a good job of teaching students. However, teachers at all levels identified incompetent or unmotivated teachers as a major professional problem.
2. Describe the essential characteristics of professionalism, and explain how they relate to teaching.
   - Characteristics of professionalism include a specialized body of knowledge, autonomy, the ability to make decisions in ill-defined situations and reflect on one's own performance, and ethical standards that guide professional conduct.
   - Some argue that teachers aren't professionals, suggesting their training isn't rigorous and they lack autonomy. Others contend that teaching is a developing profession that is still evolving.
   - The future status of teaching as a profession will be largely determined by current reform efforts.
3. Identify different dimensions of diversity, and explain how diversity affects the lives of teachers.
   - The following dimensions of diversity influence student learning: culture and ethnicity; socioeconomic status; cognitive, physical, and emotional maturity; gender; and learner exceptionalities.
   - Understanding different learning and teaching environments is important for beginning teachers because these environments present different opportunities and challenges.
   - Rural districts tend to be smaller and more homogeneous in terms of diversity. Suburban districts are intermediate in size and funded better than other districts, but competition for teaching jobs is greater there. Urban districts present unique challenges and opportunities, are more culturally diverse, and also offer the most teaching opportunities for first-year teachers.
4. Explain how the current reform movement in education is changing the teaching profession.
   - Prospective teachers will encounter reforms calling for higher standards, more rigorous training,

and increased teacher testing. In addition to increased use of licensure exams, beginning teachers will be asked to demonstrate their competence in the classroom.

- Testing teachers has been proposed as a major way to improve education in the United States. Advocates claim that teacher tests are a valid and reliable way to ensure teacher quality, and that these tests are practical and economical. The public supports the testing of teachers.
- Critics counter that these tests are neither valid nor reliable, that they fail to capture the complexities of successful performance in the classroom, and that they punish minority candidates and those whose first language is not English, because they are language based.
- The Praxis Series is the most widely used teacher test; four versions test teachers at the pre-K and elementary, middle, and high school levels. The Praxis tests are designed to assess teachers' basic skills, subject matter mastery, and classroom performance. The Principles of Learning and Teaching (PLT) tests assess teacher knowledge.

Important Concepts

assessment
autonomy
curriculum
ethics
extrinsic rewards
general pedagogical knowledge
intrinsic rewards
pedagogical content knowledge
productive learning environment
professionalism
reflection
reforms
socioeconomic status (SES)
standards
teacher efficacy

Portfolio Activity

Teacher Licensure and Testing in Your State

InTASC Core Teaching Standard 9: Professional Learning and Ethical Practice

The goal of this activity is to familiarize you with the current teacher licensing requirements in your state. Locate the website for your state's office of education. Within the website, find the teacher licensing requirements in your state and the role of teacher testing in the process.

a. What are the major requirements to become licensed in your state?

b. What tests are required for teachers? When will you have to take these tests?

c. What are the specific contents of these tests? What are the cutoff scores for each test?

d. What aids are available to prepare for these tests?

Based on this information, what can you do right now to begin preparing yourself for these tests?

Portfolio Activities similar to this one and related to chapter content can be found at MyEducationLab™.

Do I Want to Be a Teacher?

Go to the topic *The Teaching Profession* in the MyEducationLab (www.myeducationlab.com) for *Introduction to Teaching*, where you can:

- Find learning outcomes for *The Teaching Profession,* along with the national standards that connect to these outcomes.
- Complete *Assignments and Activities* that can help you more deeply understand the chapter content.
- Apply and practice your understanding of the core teaching skills identified in the chapter with the *Building Teaching Skills and Dispositions* learning units.
- Access video clips of CCSSO National Teachers of the Year award winners responding to the question, "Why Do I Teach?" in the *Teacher Talk* section.
- Check your comprehension on the content covered in the chapter with the *Study Plan.* Here you will be able to take a chapter quiz, receive feedback on your answers, and then access *Review, Practice, and Enrichment* activities to enhance your understanding of chapter content.
- Check the *Book Resources* to find opportunities to share thoughts and gather feedback on the *Diversity and You* and *Issues You'll Face in Teaching* features found in this chapter.

MyEducationLab™

CHAPTER 2

Changes in American Society: Their Influences on Today's Students

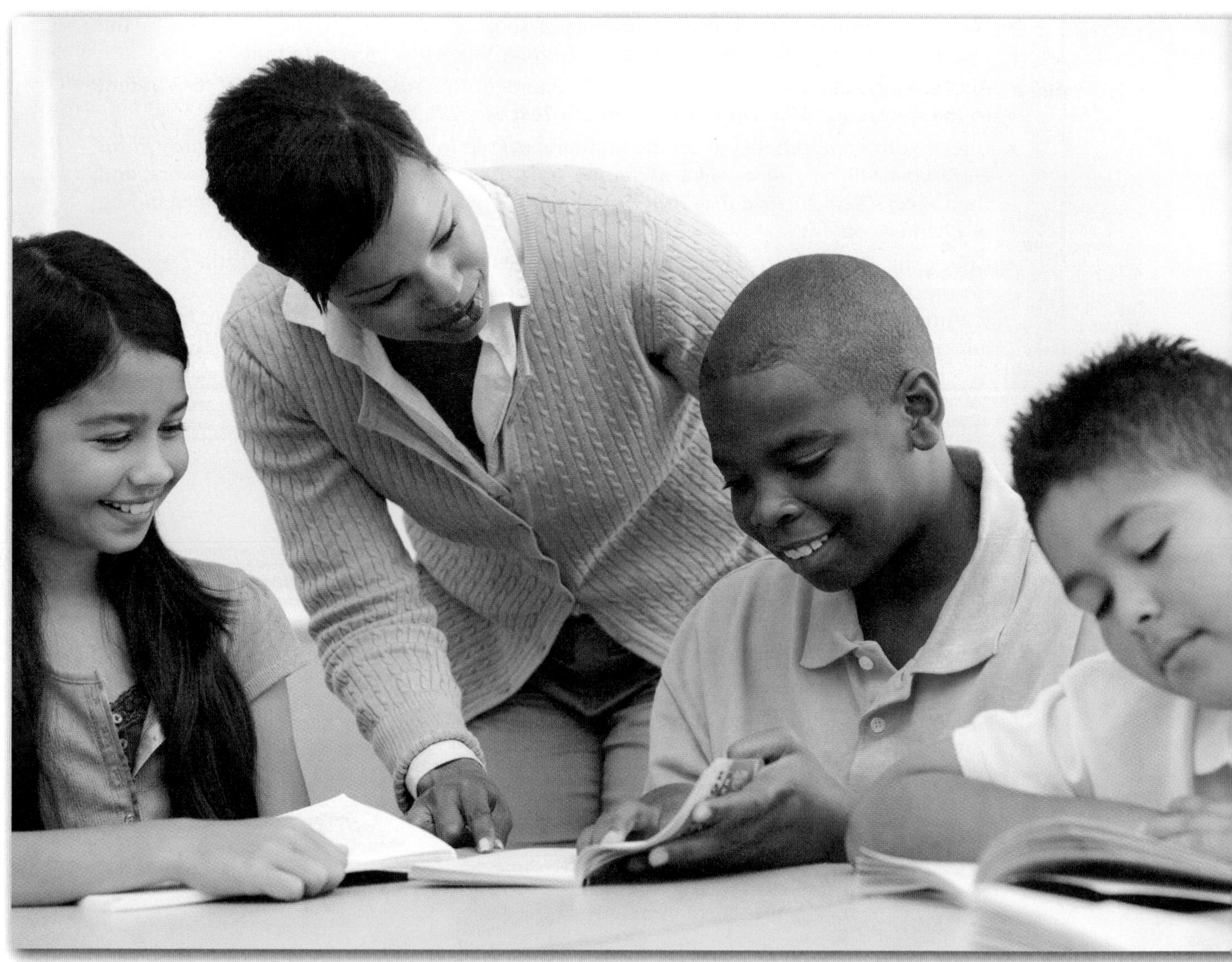

VOICES from the CLASSROOM

"We live in a society that is founded on the ideal of equal opportunity for all, yet this principle is not a reality for far too many students. . . ."

KELLY KOVACIC, 2010 Teacher of the Year, California

CHAPTER OUTLINE

LEARNING OUTCOMES

After you've completed your study of this chapter, you should be able to:

1. **Describe changes that have occurred in the American family over the last 50 years.** InTASC Core Teaching Standard 2, Learning Differences
2. **Describe societal changes and the implications of these changes for education.** InTASC Core Teaching Standard 2, Learning Differences
3. **Define socioeconomic status, and explain how different socioeconomic patterns influence school success.** InTASC Core Teaching Standard 1, Learner Development

Teaching today is more challenging than at any point in our nation's history, in large part because our society is changing. As you read the following case study, think about the children in it, how societal issues are influencing them, and how these issues will affect your life as a teacher.

It is the end of August, and Carla Torres, a second-year teacher, is excited about the new school year. Relocating to the Midwest because of her husband's job, she has been assigned a first-grade classroom in a large city. Looking forward to her new position, she has spent much of the summer planning for the year.

Two weeks into the school year, Carla shuffles into the faculty lounge on her lunch break.

"You look tired. Been getting enough sleep?" her hall mate, 20-year veteran Rae Anne Johnson, asks.

"No, I'm not tired," Carla responds, collapsing in a chair. "Just discouraged."

"Anything you want to talk about?" Rae Anne asks.

"It's my kids," Carla replies. "I had such high hopes. . . . I had my room all set up with learning centers and neat stuff. I knew what I was going to teach, and I was really looking forward to it. But these kids . . . I don't know. I'm really struggling, and now I'm beginning to wonder if it's me."

Rae Anne shrugs. "Maybe, but you're so conscientious. . . . I doubt it's you. What's got you so down?"

"Well, I can't quite figure it out. Some of the kids are really squirrelly, and it's almost impossible to get them to sit down at all. Others literally fall asleep in the middle of lessons. Four are still sucking their thumbs—in first grade for heaven's sake. Frankly, a lot of them just don't seem ready for first-grade work. I hand out a worksheet, and they look at it like I wrote it in Greek or something."

"You might be right. . . . I know it's tough. I have some of the same problems. One of my kids was upset yesterday, so I sat her down after our lunch break, and she told

This I Believe

SOCIETAL CHANGES AND OUR STUDENTS

For each of the following statements, circle your choice using the following options:

4 = I strongly believe the statement is true.
3 = I believe the statement is true.
2 = I believe the statement is false.
1 = I strongly believe the statement is false.

1. Most of the mothers and fathers of the children I'll be teaching will both work outside the home.
   1 2 3 4
2. Parents of today's students don't want schools to teach sex education, preferring to provide it themselves.
   1 2 3 4
3. In recent years, student use of drugs and alcohol has declined.
   1 2 3 4
4. If I see what I suspect is an instance of child abuse, I'm required by law to report it to the proper authorities.
   1 2 3 4
5. Parents' educational background strongly influences their children's success in school.
   1 2 3 4

me that her parents had had a big fight the night before. And then there's Johnny. . . . He's always so droopy, so I asked him if he'd had breakfast this morning. He said he never eats it, so I called his home and told his mother about the school's free breakfast program. I had to call three times to get her—I didn't want to just leave a message on the machine. She was apologetic about sending him to school without it, but she works weird hours, and she's a single mom, so I know it's tough for her, too. It's hard for a lot of kids."

"I guess you're right, but they didn't prepare me for this. I was so eager and, I guess, idealistic about making a difference. Now, I'm not so sure."

When you begin teaching, you will likely face some of the same problems Carla and Rae Ann experienced. Today's students are indeed different from those in years past. Fewer come from homes where their father is the sole breadwinner and their mother is the primary caregiver, and more come to school hungry, tired, or emotionally drained because of conditions in their homes and communities. Students are more sexually active, and alcohol and drug use is a persistent problem for many students. Many come to school with "baggage" that students didn't have in the past, and these problems are often linked to societal issues.

How do these issues affect our students, and how will they affect your life as a teacher? We address these questions in this chapter, but before you begin your study, please respond to the items shown in *This I Believe: Societal Changes and Our Students.*

Changes in American Families

As teachers, we want to provide a quality education for all our students, and for many, we can. Many come from stable, supportive families, and they come to our classrooms with experiences that prepare them to succeed in school. Unfortunately, for other students, this isn't the case.

MyEducationLab™

Visit the MyEducationLab for *Introduction to Teaching* to enhance your understanding of chapter concepts with a personalized *Study Plan.* You'll also have the opportunity to hone your teaching skills through video and case-based *Assignments and Activities* and *Building Teaching Skills and Disposition* lessons.

Different Family Patterns

Joey looks puzzled when he is asked how many brothers and sisters he has—a seemingly simple question, he's uncertain about the answer. He furrows his brow, pushes back in his chair, and begins counting on his fingers. "Four?" "Five?" "Wait, six." "That's a hard question." "My dad was married to three different ladies, and he had lots of kids."

Joey's story, although extreme, graphically illustrates the ways the American family has changed. The "traditional" family—a husband who is the primary breadwinner, a mother who doesn't work outside the home, and two school-age children—made up only slightly more than 1 of 20 households in the United States in 2000.

Other changes have occurred:

- Families headed by married couples made up slightly more than two thirds of all households, compared to close to 80% in 1980.
- Seven of 10 women with children are in the workforce.
- The divorce rate quadrupled from 1978 to 2000.
- Nearly 1 of 4 children live only with their mothers, 5% live only with their fathers, and 4% live with neither.
- The incidence of poverty among single-parent families was nearly 10 times higher than in families headed by married couples. (Federal Interagency Forum on Child and Family Statistics, 2010; U.S. Bureau of Census, 2007a)

Poverty, divorce, both parents working outside the home, and families headed by a single father or mother all pose challenges for both parents and their children. Because of busy schedules, parents and children spend less time together than they did in previous generations, and even when they have time, many parents are uncertain about how to help their children with schoolwork. The combination of less time and less support results in children coming to school less prepared to learn.

What does this information suggest for you when you begin teaching? First, remember that family patterns have changed. For instance, when students are told, "Take this home and have your mother sign it," they may not be living with their mothers. One California teacher commented, "I stopped using the word 'parents' with my kids because so many of them don't have them. Amanda's mom died in October. She lives with her 30-year-old brother. (A thousand blessings on him.) Seven kids live with their 'Grams,' six with their dads. A few rotate between parents. So 'parents' is out as a descriptor" (Karrer, 2011, p. 23). When you talk with students, communicate that different family configurations exist and are acceptable, and attempt to be flexible with meeting times for parent–teacher conferences. These actions communicate that you care about your students, that you're committed to their education, and that you're aware of the pressures that today's parents are experiencing.

Revisiting My Beliefs

This section addresses the first item in *This I Believe:* "Most of the mothers and fathers of the children I'll be teaching will both work outside the home." This statement is true. Today, 7 of 10 mothers work outside the home, which raises questions about both child care and "latchkey" children.

Affordable, quality child care is an important issue for today's working parents.

Child Care

Quality child care is an important issue for the more than 6 of 10 working mothers with a child under 6 (U.S. Department of Health and Human Services, 2009). When both parents work outside the home, or if a working parent is single, young children spend a great deal of time in child care, and questions about its impact on children's development have been asked for years. Critics contend that young children need the presence of a mother in the home, and that child care isn't an adequate substitute. Supporters counter that children readily adapt to different care patterns and learn valuable lessons from interacting with other children.

Researchers examining this issue focus on the quality of the child care instead of the larger issue of working parents. Their research indicates that high-quality child care is positively correlated with children's long-term cognitive and emotional development, higher earnings later in life, and greater marital stability. It also reduces delinquency, teenage pregnancy, drug use, and dropout rates (Berk, 2012; F. Campbell et al., 2012). The term *high-quality* is important: Poor-quality child care can have the exact opposite effect.

Although quality child care is important for all children, it is essential for the children of poverty. Unfortunately, children from low-income families are the least likely to have access to early childhood education programs such as nursery school and prekindergarten. And the rate of participation for poor families has decreased in recent years. The reasons are uncertain, but money is a definite factor. Our country is losing an important opportunity to invest in its children; research shows that quality child-care programs can have lasting effects on participants, and these benefits last long into adulthood (F. Campbell et al., 2012).

Latchkey Children

Ana Rosa opens the door to her apartment, goes inside, and quickly relocks it, remembering what her mother has said about strangers. She drops her school pack on the sofa, deciding to do her homework later. The house is quiet, too quiet. She goes in the living room, turns on the TV, and surfs through the menu of talk shows, cartoons, and soap operas. Then, she heads to the kitchen and checks out snacks. A soft drink and chips look good. She returns to the living room and settles in with the TV. Her mom will be home from work in 3 hours.

Latchkey children—children who return to empty houses after school and who are left alone until parents arrive from work—are another problem many parents face: 15 million children return to an empty house or apartment after school (Ash, 2009). This raises issues ranging from concerns about children's safety to questions about supervision, excessive time spent watching television, and lack of help with homework. You can address the last issue by ensuring that your students understand exactly what is expected of them on their homework assignments and can do the work before sending them home. If your students understand what is expected of them, they're more likely to do it. Some schools respond with after-hours offerings, but a more common solution is for schools to cooperate with community agencies, such as YMCAs or youth clubs, to offer after-school programs. In addition to providing safe, supervised environments, these programs teach children how to respond to home emergencies, use the phone to seek help, make healthful snacks, and spend time wisely.

Check Your Understanding

1.1. Describe changes that have occurred in the American family over the last 50 years.

1.2. What implications do the changes in American families have for child care in this country?

1.3. Who are latchkey children? What problems do they encounter in their homes?

For feedback, go to the appendix, *Check Your Understanding*, located in the back of this text.

Changes in Our Students

Just as families have changed over time, our students have also changed, and these changes will present special challenges to you when you begin teaching. Consider these statistics from a survey of high school students (Centers for Disease Control and Prevention, 2010):

- Seventy-two percent had experimented with alcohol, 10% drove after drinking, and nearly 3 of 10 rode in a car when a driver had been drinking.
- Nearly 40% had used marijuana; 12% had sniffed glue, and 23% reported being offered an illegal drug on school property.
- Nearly 1 of 5 reported carrying a weapon during the preceding month, and 32% reported being in a fight during the past year.
- 6% attempted suicide within the last 12 months, and 14% had seriously contemplated it.

Our students are engaging in risky and often dangerous activities. In this section and in Figure 2.1, we examine these and other risk factors that pose problems for students' safety and healthy development.

Sexuality

In the past, we tacitly thought that teenagers were either asexual or restrained. We knew they were going through puberty, but we assumed that they weren't sexually active—or chose not to think about it.

The facts suggest otherwise. In recent surveys, nearly half of teens reported being sexually active by the end of high school, but only 61% reported using a condom. In addition, nearly 1 of 10 said they had sex before age 13, and another 1 of 10 said they had four or more sex partners before they completed 10th grade (Centers for Disease Control and Prevention, 2008, 2010). And the average age for first intercourse has dropped steadily over the years and is now 17 (Guttmacher Institute, 2011a). This level of sexual activity poses a number of risks, including teenage pregnancy and sexually transmitted diseases.

Teaching and You

How much do you know about the sexual habits of the students you'll teach? What percentage is sexually active, and when do they typically begin their first sexual contact? How many have had more than one sexual partner? How do your answers to these questions compare to your own experiences?

FIGURE 2.1 Changes in Our Students

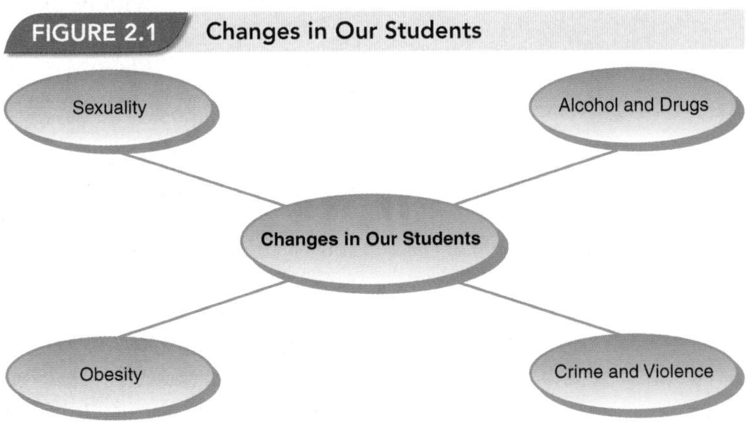

Teenage Pregnancy

Although the annual teenage birthrate declined steadily from a high of 89 births per 1,000 students in 1960 to 42 per 1,000 in 2008, the United States still has the highest rates of teenage pregnancy and births in the industrialized world (National Campaign to Prevent Teen

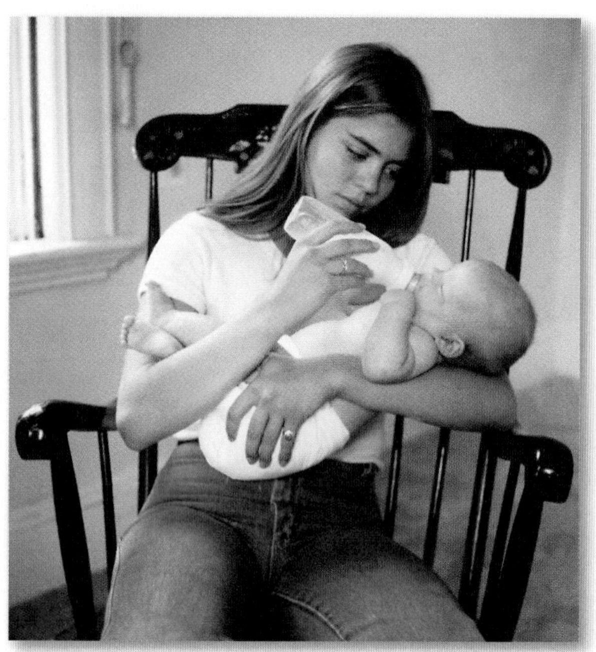

Teen pregnancies force children to mature too rapidly, diverting attention from their own personal development.

and Unplanned Pregnancy, 2010; Orr, 2009). Experts attribute the decline to both decreased sexual activity and increased use of contraceptives. Eighty percent of teens who become pregnant aren't married, and nearly 6 of 10 teenage mothers keep their babies (Guttmacher Institute, 2011a). These pregnancies present a major problem for both the mothers and the children.

Becoming a teenage parent forces students to mature too quickly, diverting energy from their own development to the care of a baby. And more than half of the households headed by teen mothers live in poverty (Macionis, 2011). Juggling child rearing with work and school, teenage mothers are more likely to drop out, develop poor work skills, and have limited employment opportunities. Their babies also fare poorly: Because of inadequate prenatal care, they are often born prematurely or with health problems.

Efforts to deal with the problem of teenage pregnancy focus on programs that encourage mothers to complete their education through home instruction, or programs in which mothers bring their babies to school and attend child-care and regular classes. Despite these efforts, the majority of teen mothers drop out of school.

Sexually Transmitted Diseases

Many teens have sex without protecting themselves from sexually transmitted diseases (STDs) such as herpes, human papillomavirus, chlamydia, genital warts, syphilis, and gonorrhea. One survey found that 1 of 4 sexually active teenage girls, or more than 3 million, were infected with at least one form of STD (Altman, 2008). AIDS (acquired immune deficiency syndrome), which can be transmitted through sexual activity, has made the problem more urgent and deadly. Although it was first believed that the AIDS virus was transmitted primarily through sexual contact between male homosexuals or through intravenous drug use, we now know HIV is also spread through heterosexual sex.

As you read earlier, almost half of teenagers report being sexually active, and some have several partners. Nevertheless, only about 60% of teenagers reported using condoms, the only reliable defense—other than abstinence—against sexually transmitted diseases (National Campaign to Prevent Teen and Unplanned Pregnancy, 2010).

Revisiting My Beliefs

This section addresses the second question in *This I Believe*, "Parents of today's students don't want schools to teach sex education, preferring to provide it themselves." This statement is not true: Polls suggest that most parents want schools to provide sex education for their children.

Sex Education

In response to teenagers' increasing sexual activity, many school districts have implemented sex education, but because sex education is controversial, the form and content of instruction vary widely. Polls suggest that the vast majority of parents (around 90%) favor sex education (Constantine, Jerman, & Huang, 2007; Eisenberg, Bernat, Bearinger, & Resnick, 2008), and courts have consistently upheld districts' rights to offer sex education courses (Schimmel, Stellman, & Fischer, 2011). Parents who object are free to take their children out of the programs.

Teaching and You

Did you know about any students in your school who were lesbian, gay, or bisexual? Were any of these students your friends? How were these students treated by others? What obstacles did they face as they were growing up? Did any of these obstacles affect you personally?

Sexual Orientation and Identity

Experts estimate that between 3% and 10% of U.S. students differ in their sexual orientation, but accurate figures are hard to obtain because of the social stigma involved (Berk, 2012). The labels *lesbian, gay, bisexual*, and *straight* refer to a person's sexual orientation; *transgender* refers to sexual identity. Lesbian, gay, bisexual, and transgender (LGBT) students are often rejected by both peers and society, leading to feelings of alienation and depression, drug use, and suicide rates considerably higher than in the heterosexual population (Berk, 2012; Macionis, 2011).

Discussions about sexual orientation and identity are controversial, with some believing that they're genetic and others attributing them to learning and choice (Gollnick & Chinn, 2013). Those arguing that the causes are genetic ask why someone would voluntarily choose an orientation or identity that would result in discrimination and rejection, and their position has considerable research support. For example, if one identical twin is homosexual, the other twin is much more likely also to be homosexual than is the case with fraternal, or nongenetically linked, twins (Berk, 2012).

LGBT students often go through a three-phase sequence in their attempts to understand who they are sexually. The first is feeling different, a slowly developing awareness that they aren't like other children. One gay student described his experience:

> As long as I can remember, I always felt a little different when it came to having crushes on other people. When I was in elementary school I never had crushes on girls, and when I look back on that time now, I was probably most attracted to my male friends. I participated in some of the typical "boy" activities, like trading baseball cards and playing video games, but I was never very interested in rough sports. (McDevitt & Ormrod, 2010, p. 567)

In the second phase, which typically occurs during adolescence, students are frequently confused. In this phase, LGBT students attempt to understand their developing sexuality, looking for both social support and role models. The same gay male described his feelings during this phase:

> To my dismay, middle school and the onset of puberty only brought more attention to my lack of interest in girls. The first time I thought about being gay was when I was in the 6th grade, so I was probably 11 or 12 years old at the time. But in my mind, being gay was not an option and I began to expend an incredible amount of energy repressing my developing homosexual urges. (McDevitt & Ormrod, 2010, p. 567)

Finally, in the third phase, the majority of gay and lesbian teenagers reach a point where they accept their homosexuality and share it with those who are close to them. Unfortunately, rather than experiencing understanding, LGBT students are often subjected to harassment.

In *Teaching and You* we asked about your own experiences with students who were gay or lesbian. Often these students are ostracized and even bullied; rarely are they accepted like other students. You can make a huge difference in the way these students are treated by the implicit and explicit messages you send about these students. Make a special effort to ensure that your classroom is a safe haven for all students.

Sexual Harassment

> "Hey, babe. Lookin' good in that sweater!"
>
> "Hey, sugar. Want to make me happy tonight?"

Comments like these, heard in many classrooms and hallways in our nation's schools, constitute **sexual harassment**, unwanted and/or unwelcome sexually oriented behavior that interferes with a student's life. Sexual harassment is a problem affecting both males and females and can also interfere with a student's learning and development. In a recent survey, nearly half of 7th- to 12th-grade students reported being sexually harassed during the last school year; for girls the figure was higher (56%) (Hill & Kearl, 2011). Sexual comments, gestures, and looks, as well as touching and grabbing, were most commonly cited. And 87% of

FIGURE 2.2 Sexual Harassment in U.S. Schools

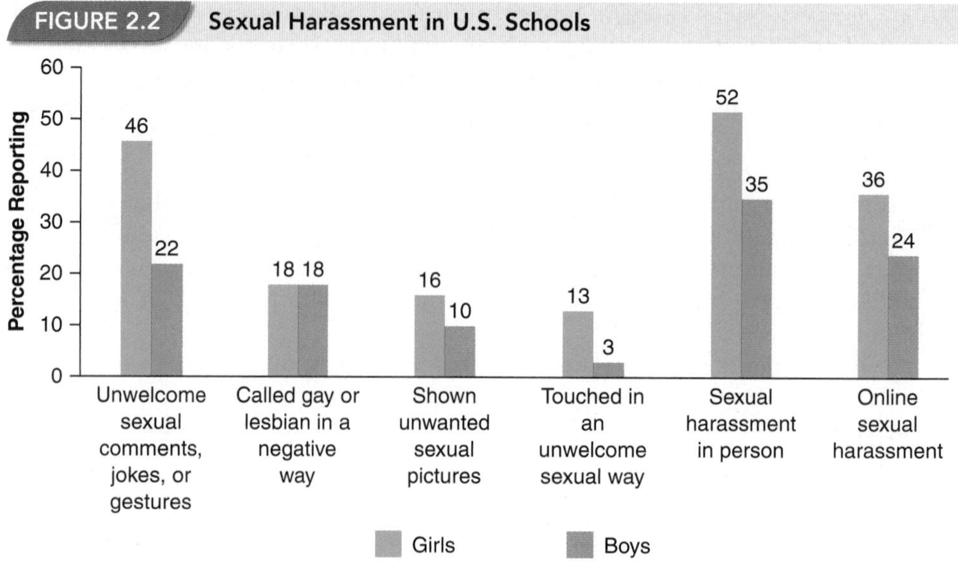

Source: Based on Hill and Kearl (2011).

students who were sexually harassed reported negative personal consequences, such as poor sleep, stomachaches, or absenteeism. The percentages of boys and girls who were subjected to various forms of sexual harassment are outlined in Figure 2.2. Equally disturbing is a college survey indicating that two thirds of college students experienced sexual harassment, including nearly one third of first-year students (American Association of University Women, 2006).

The problem of sexual harassment is especially acute for students who are LGBT. One national survey found that 90% of homosexual students frequently hear expressions such as, "That's so gay" or "You're so gay"; 75% frequently encountered terms such as "faggot" or "dyke"; and more than 60% reported other forms of verbal harassment (Kosciw & Diaz, 2006). One teenage boy commented, "To call someone gay or fag is like the lowest thing you can call someone. Because that's like saying that you're nothing" (Warner, 2009, p. 2). And the abuse often goes beyond verbal; many homosexual students reported physical harassment, and 6 of 10 reported not feeling safe at school (Maxwell, 2008). Harassment such as this contributes to higher rates of depression, drug abuse, and suicide for LGBT students. Unfortunately, many teachers and school counselors feel unprepared to deal with these issues (M. Wood, 2005).

Schools and teachers need to do a better job of making classrooms and hallways safe for every student. A Supreme Court ruling that holds school districts legally responsible in cases where sexual harassment is reported but not corrected is likely to make both teachers and administrators more sensitive to this issue (Schimmel, Stellman, et al., 2011).

All students—boys and girls, straight and LGBT—have a right to harassment-free schools, and you play an essential role in ensuring that this happens. Talk with your students about the problem, and emphasize that no form of harassment, sexual or otherwise, will be tolerated.

Use of Alcohol and Other Drugs

> **Teaching and You**
>
> What was the alcohol and drug picture like in the schools you attended? Were these available and common to students or limited to a small group of students? Did any of your friends use alcohol or drugs? Did you?

Consider the following statistics from 2009 (Centers for Disease Control and Prevention [CDC], 2010):

- More than 4 of 10 high school students used alcohol, and nearly 25% reported binge drinking.
- Two of 5 high school students have experimented with marijuana.

- Twenty percent of high school students have taken a prescription drug, such as Oxycontin, Ritalin, or Xanax, without a doctor's prescription.
- Nearly 1 of 5 high school students report current use of cigarettes.

The problems of drug use are well known and occur on multiple levels. You will likely have students in your classes who come from families where alcohol and drug abuse are persistent problems. Teenagers who abuse alcohol and drugs place themselves at risk for many problems including damage to their health, car accidents, and even suicide. Alcohol and drug users have a myriad of school-related problems including alienation from school and their classmates, poor attendance, decreased learning, and an increased likelihood of dropping out. And they are less likely to develop healthy mechanisms for coping with life's problems (Berk, 2012). Although student use of alcohol and other drugs has declined in recent years, substance abuse still poses a serious problem for our teenagers.

What leads teenagers to alcohol and other drug use? Experts identify several potential causes, including the stresses of growing up, unstable families, as well as peer pressure (Berk, 2012). Some also blame the mixed messages teens receive from the media and our culture at large. The tobacco industry spends billions on advertising, and these billions influence behavior; students who are exposed to smoking in advertising and movies are more likely to smoke than peers who aren't (Molnar, Boniger, Wilkinson, & Fogarty, 2009; Molnar, Boniger, Wilkinson, Fogarty, & Geary, 2010). Although educators and parents talk about the dangers of these substances, the media—and particularly teenage pop culture—often glorify using alcohol, tobacco, and other drugs, implying that it's acceptable and often the best way to deal with problems such as stress, loneliness, or depression.

What can teachers and schools do about the problem of substance abuse? Nationally, the federal government made teenage substance abuse a priority by including the Safe and Drug Free School and Communities Act as an integral part of the No Child Left Behind Act of 2001. Unfortunately, the primary focus of these actions is enforcement rather than prevention. Other programs attempt to teach students facts about drugs and help them learn to make wise personal decisions and develop strategies for understanding and avoiding peer pressure. Probably best known is the Drug Abuse Resistance Education (DARE) program, which uses local police officers to deliver anti-crime, anti-gang, and anti-drug messages. Research on these programs is mixed, and delivering the "Just Say No" message without further intervention efforts is rarely effective (Viadero, 2005).

This is where you come in. One study of effective drug prevention programs found that teachers were central to program effectiveness (Beets et al., 2009). Teacher interactions with students about drugs and emphasis on a healthy lifestyle were identified as crucial to successful efforts to prevent drug abuse. You can do a lot to help prevent drug abuse by talking about the problem and helping your students understand the benefits of dealing with their problems in a positive and proactive manner.

Revisiting My Beliefs

This section addresses the third item in *This I Believe* at the beginning of the chapter, "In recent years student use of drugs and alcohol has declined." This statement is true, but research suggests that large numbers of students are still abusing different forms of drugs and that this abuse interferes with healthy development.

Obesity

A health-care worker at the Obesity Center of Children's Hospital, Los Angeles, encountered the following:

> One of my patients, 16-year-old Max, who weighed close to 300 pounds, told me that he drank a six-pack of sweetened soda every day. I was appalled: he was consuming more than a thousand empty calories every day just in soda. And I was puzzled, too. Max was on his high school's junior varsity football team, which meant he arrived at school early in the morning and left

Teaching and You

Did you ever struggle with your weight as you were growing up? (Most of us did—we thought we were either too skinny or too fat.) Did the school you attended do anything to help with or exacerbate the problem?

late in the afternoon, after practice. How, I asked, did he manage to drink six cans of soda in the remaining hours of the day?

> The answer floored me: Max explained that he bought five cans of sugared soda from school vending machines every day, one each before his first class, his second class, and lunch. Before football practice he downed a fourth can, and he topped it off with a fifth can of soda when practice was over. That left one for home. I asked why he didn't drink water. He told me the water that came out of the fountains was brown and smelly and the vending machines didn't sell it. The rest of his diet was equally bad. In the mid-morning he bought a candy bar at the student store, at lunch he had high-calorie, high-fat burrito and fries or cheese nachos, and after football practice there were boxes of doughnuts . . . there was literally nothing in his daily environment that was both nutritious and appealing. (F. Kaufman, 2005, p. 243)

Obesity is a major health issue in our country, and this is equally true for our young people. Nationally, 1 of 6 students—more than 9 million—is overweight, triple the proportion in 1980 (Ogden & Carroll, 2010). This figure is even higher for children living in poverty and cultural minorities such as African Americans, Hispanic Americans, and Native Americans who often don't have access to affordable healthy foods (L. Tanner, 2009). In addition to immediate health risks such as high blood pressure and joint problems, overweight youth also face rejection from their peers and the risk of developing into heavy adults with additional health problems, such as heart disease and Type II diabetes (Vedantam, 2010).

The causes of this epidemic are multifaceted and range from lack of exercise to just plain unhealthy diets. School-age children spend more than 44 hours a week in front of either a television or a computer screen and less than 2 hours a day in outdoor play (McDonough, 2009). In addition, children 8 to 12 years old watch an average of 21 food ads a day—more than 7,600 a year—on television (Hellmech, 2007). And advertisers spend more than $10 billion a year marketing food and beverages to children, mostly for non-nutritious products; more than a third of the food ads push candy and snacks, and none promote fresh fruits and vegetables.

Schools themselves are often part of the problem. Districts, strapped for cash, sign lucrative contracts with corporations to place soft-drink machines in school hallways (Molnar et al., 2010). (A typical can of nondiet soda has 10 teaspoons of sugar and 150 calories; students drinking three or four cans a day can gain 6 pounds in a month.) In addition, school lunches often contribute to the problem; one study of middle school students found school lunches often loaded with cheap, high-energy, low-nutrition foods (Eagle et al., 2010; Shah, 2011f).

State legislatures have responded with both stricter nutritional guidelines for school lunches and bans on soft-drink sales during school hours (Winterfeld, 2008). In addition, beverage companies such as Coca-Cola and PepsiCo, under pressure from a number of advocacy groups, agreed to limit sales of sugar-laden soft drinks in schools (Samuels, 2006). Under the agreement, the companies would sell only water, unsweetened juice, and low-fat milk to elementary and middle schools, and only diet sodas to high schools. The federal government has also issued new guidelines for school lunches, requiring more vegetables and fruits and limiting foods high in calories as well as fats and sodium (Shah, 2012). These efforts may be paying off: one report found that after a 25-year increase, the percentage of U.S. children who are overweight or obese has leveled off (Parker-Pope, 2008). This is a start, but lack of exercise and unhealthy diets still need to be addressed.

You can help deal with the problem. Information is a start; one study found that many students have a limited understanding of healthy eating (Powers, Bindler, Goetz, & Daratha, 2010). Talk about the foods you eat, and help your students understand how their diets affect their health. And your own modeling can be a powerful tool in helping students understand how exercise and a good diet can contribute to their own good health.

School Violence and Crime

Anthony, one of the main characters in the documentary *Waiting for Superman* (Guggenheim, 2011), grew up in a world of crime and violence. He never knew his mother, and his father, who was involved with drugs, died when he was in second grade. The trauma of losing his only parent contributed to his being held back a year in second grade. His grandmother, who raised him, cautions him every morning before he leaves for school, "Be careful."

Unfortunately, crime and violence sometimes enter school doors. The problem of school violence came to national attention in 1999 with the tragedy at Columbine High School in Littleton, Colorado, in which 2 students went on a rampage, gunning down 13 students before killing themselves. It was then amplified in 2005 when a high school student in Red Lake, Minnesota, killed seven people, including a teacher and a security guard, and wounded seven others.

Teaching and You

Were the schools you attended safe places to learn? If so, what did your teachers do to make them safe and secure? If not, what could the teachers have done to make them safer?

Consider these statistics:

- During the 2007–2008 school year, there were 1,701 homicides and 1,231 suicides of school-age children; of these, 38 were school-associated violent deaths, including 24 homicides and 14 suicides.
- In 2007–2008, 85% of public schools recorded one or more incidents of crime.
- Students aged 12 to 18 were victims of 1.9 million nonfatal crimes, including 1.2 million thefts and 740,000 violent crimes.
- In the same time period, 8% of high school students reported being threatened or injured with a weapon; male students were twice as likely to be threatened or injured as females.
- Most of the schools you'll work in have written plans for bomb threats (94%) and for shootings (84%) (National Center for Education Statistics, 2011a, 2011c).

Despite these statistics, three trends are clear: First, the incidence of violence in schools is declining; second, students are safer in schools than on the streets where they live. Third, school violence is more common in some school contexts than in others; incidents of violence are highest at the middle school level and decline as students get older (National Center for Education Statistics, 2011a, 2011c). Also, violence is more common in urban than in suburban or rural schools, and concerns about violence are greatest in high-poverty areas. School violence is often associated with gangs, and more than 1 of 5 secondary students reported that street gangs were present at their school (National Center for Education Statistics, 2011c).

Bullying is common in schools, and teachers play a major role in protecting their students from this problem.

What can teachers and schools do to increase school safety? The answer is, a lot! A study of Chicago schools found that school safety depends more on the schools and their teachers than the poverty and crime surrounding them (Sparks, 2011b). Some schools were safe havens for students, while others in similar neighborhoods were centers for violence. While safe neighborhoods count, students' academic success and relationships with adults were even more important. This is where you come in. You need to make sure that your students are learning and experiencing academic success and that they believe that you care about them and want them to succeed. This can be a challenge, but it is both important and possible. A principal from one of the safe schools in Chicago noted, "If a child doesn't have someone to talk to, they will carry [their problems] into the classroom" (Sparks, 2011c, p. 13). When students enter her school, they are greeted by name by both teachers and school staff. A parent commented, "When a kid feels loved, they know that, and they know that when they come to school they are safe" (Sparks, 2011c, p. 13). You can make a big difference in your students' lives by showing you care and helping them succeed, both academically and personally.

Bullying

How would you react to the following incidents?

You are monitoring students on the playground when you overhear one student say to another, "No, way. Absolutely not! I already told you that you can't play with us." The student leaves and is isolated, playing alone for the remaining time with tears in her eyes. This is not the first time this individual has kept someone from joining her group of playmates.

You have assigned the students in your class to work in groups of four on their projects. While the students are getting in their groups, you see one student push another with enough force that he falls to the ground. The push was clearly intentional and was not provoked. The child that fell yells, "Stop pushing me around! You always do this, just leave me alone." (Adapted from Bauman & Del Rio, 2006)

Bullying, a more subtle form of school violence that involves a systematic or repetitious abuse of power between students, is receiving increased attention as educators better understand its damaging effects on students and possible links to suicides and school shootings (Berger, 2007). As of 2011, 21 states had passed antibullying laws (Zubrzycki, 2011b).

All of us remember teasing and taunting in the halls and on school playgrounds, and many parents and teachers considered this to be a normal rite of passage. But research now links bullying to a number of antisocial and aggressive behaviors that can have negative consequences for both bullies and victims (Raskauskas & Stoltz, 2007). Research suggests that bullying is a major factor in many school shooting incidents such as the Columbine tragedy; both bullies and victims are more likely to carry a weapon, bring it to school, and become involved in serious fights (Fast, 2008).

People who bully take advantage of imbalances in power, such as greater size or strength, higher status, or the support of a peer group. Typical victims include students who are obese, gay, or have disabilities (Berk, 2012). The bullying itself can be a face-to-face attack, threats, teasing about perceived sexual orientation, or refusing to let someone participate or play. It can also include behind-the-back behaviors, such as spreading malicious rumors, writing harmful graffiti, or encouraging others to exclude a child. Though physical bullying declines with age, more subtle forms persist, such as excluding others from a peer group, "No, way. Absolutely not! I already told you that you can't play with us" (Berger, 2007).

Bullying is more common than many adults realize. In one survey of high school students, half admitted they had bullied someone in the past year, and nearly the same percentage reported being the victim of bullying (Josephson Institute Center for Youth Ethics, 2010). Another study found that nearly 75% of 8- to 11-year-olds and more than 85% of 12- to 15-year-olds reported bullying in their schools (W. Roberts, 2006). As with other forms of violence, bullying is most prevalent at the middle school level and declines at high school levels (National Center for Education Statistics, 2011c). Experts think the incidence of bullying is actually higher than reported because it usually occurs in areas where students interact informally, such as playgrounds, hallways, cafeterias, and school buses, and where they have little adult supervision (Berk, 2012).

Bullying is most commonly learned, with modeling and reinforcement by parents and peers playing major roles (Berk, 2012). For example, bullies tend to come from homes where parents are authoritarian, hostile, and rejecting. The parents may have poor problem-solving skills and use fighting as a solution to conflicts; their children then imitate these behaviors. Bullies are often emotionally underdeveloped, and they're unable to understand or empathize with others' perspectives or regulate their own behavior.

Teachers often fail to take steps to address the problem because they perceive bullying incidents as part of the normal rough-and-tumble give-and-take that amounts to a rite of passage for young people. Here's what one student wrote about his own experiences with bullying.

> A student pushed a 10-year-old boy off a school bus causing him to land face down on the ground, "just to be funny." The bus driver drove away after asking only half-heartedly if the boy was "okay." Imagine this same boy shoved into the corner of the school building while three students held him down, twisting and pinching his skin. . . . The principal dismissed the actions as "just boy's horseplay." The boy felt scared, hurt, and alone. I was that boy. (Gourley, 2009, p. 26)

Students are often hesitant to report bullying because they fear reprisals or don't want to appear weak or unable to solve their own social problems (R. Newman, 2008). Unfortunately, beginning teachers are less likely than veterans to respond to incidents of bullying (Bauman & Del Rio, 2006).

Bullying is an important issue that affects not only specific students but also school climate and the way students feel about your own classroom. You need to be proactive in communicating that bullying won't be tolerated (Sherer & Nickerson, 2010). When bullying does occur, you should intervene immediately and apply appropriate consequences for the perpetrators. Perhaps more importantly, you can use the incident as a teachable moment because bullying is often tolerated and even encouraged by peers (Engel & Sandstrom, 2010; Graham, 2010). Discuss the idea of right and wrong, the way we should treat others, tolerance for differences, and abuse of power. Teachers working together can make a difference, not only in their classrooms but also in their schools.

TECHNOLOGY and TEACHING: Cyberbullying

The growing presence of the Internet in students' lives has resulted in **cyberbullying**, a new form of bullying that occurs when students use electronic media to harass or intimidate other students. Cyberbullying received national attention after the suicides of Megan Meier, an eighth grader who was bullied on MySpace, and Rutgers University freshman Tyler Clementi, who committed suicide after his roommate streamed video of his encounter with a male student. Since then, both school officials and parents have become alarmed about this growing problem (Shah, 2011a).

Cyberbullying tends to follow the same patterns as traditional forms of bullying; students who are bullies and victims on the playground play similar roles in cyberspace (Raskauskas & Stoltz, 2007). The anonymity of the Internet distinguishes cyberbullying from other types, and this anonymity can make bullies even more insensitive to the hurtful nature of the bullying incidents.

Cyberbullying is hard to measure, but an informal poll revealed that almost half of the middle schoolers polled had experienced some form of cyberbullying (Hoffman, 2010). Given the popularity of Internet use among teenagers (most teenagers use it every day), cyberbullying is likely to remain a persistent problem (Davis, 2011).

Attempts to prevent bullying often focus on helping students understand the consequences of their negative behaviors and teaching alternative prosocial behaviors. Because of your close contact with students, you will be instrumental in helping your students understand how their actions influence others. One of the unfortunate outcomes of bullying is suicide, which we discuss in the next section.

School-wide safety programs are designed to make schools safe places to learn.

School-Wide Safety Programs

School-wide safety programs are designed to make schools safe havens for teaching and learning through comprehensive antiviolence and antibullying programs (Graham, 2010). Recently, New Jersey passed a new antibullying law that requires each school to appoint a safety team to review all bullying complaints and requires principals to begin a review within one school day of any reported bullying incidents (Hu, 2011). The aim of this new law, called the Anti-Bullying Bill of Rights, is to make schools accountable for the safety of their students. When school safety programs work, school leaders establish policies that clearly communicate that violence and bullying will not be tolerated, and parents, administrators, and teachers then monitor playgrounds, lunchrooms, and hallways, areas where these incidents are most common. When an incident occurs, it's quickly identified and defused, and consequences are administered to perpetrators.

In other attempts to increase school safety, many schools are adopting comprehensive security measures, such as having visitors sign in, closing campuses during lunch, and controlling access to school buildings. Schools are also adding prevention policies that include use of hallway police, student photo ID badges, transparent book bags, handheld metal detectors, and Breathalyzers to check for alcohol consumption. In many districts, visitors are screened through an electronic system that matches drivers' licenses to a database of convicted sex offenders (Maxwell, 2006). Students are warned to avoid jokes about violence and are given hotline numbers to anonymously report any indications that a classmate could turn violent. Schools are also creating peer buddy systems and adult mentorship programs and are teaching conflict-resolution skills as alternatives to violence (D. Johnson & Johnson, 2013).

The enormous publicity generated by school shooting incidents has led many schools around the country to experiment with new approaches to making schools safe. One of the most controversial involves the issue of **zero-tolerance policies**, which call for students to receive automatic suspensions or expulsions as punishment for certain offenses, primarily those involving weapons, threats, or drugs. Such policies have become increasingly popular across the nation. We examine controversies surrounding zero-tolerance policies in our *Issues You Will Face in Teaching* feature that follows this section.

Suicide

Think about this statistic: Suicide is the third-leading cause of teen death, surpassed only by car accidents and homicide (U.S. Bureau of Census, 2010a)! About a half million young people attempt suicide each year, and between 2,000 and 5,000 succeed; accurate figures are hard to obtain because of the social stigma attached to suicide (Fisher, 2006; J. Moore, 2007). The suicide rate among adolescents has quadrupled in the last 50 years. Girls are twice as likely as boys to attempt suicide, but boys are 4 times more likely to succeed. Boys tend to employ more lethal means, such as shooting themselves, whereas girls choose more survivable methods, such as overdosing on drugs.

Causes of teen suicide vary, but most are related to the stresses of adolescence; they include family conflicts, parental unemployment and divorce, drug use, failed peer relationships, and peer harassment, especially for LGBT youngsters (Berk, 2012). In addition, students who are socially isolated as well as those who display antisocial behaviors such as fighting, bullying, increased risk taking, and drug use are more likely to attempt suicide.

Indicators of potential suicide include:

- An abrupt decline in the quality of schoolwork
- Withdrawal from friends or classroom and school activities
- Neglect of personal appearance or radical changes in personality
- Changes in eating or sleeping habits
- Depression, as evidenced by persistent boredom or lack of interest in school activities
- Student comments about suicide as a solution to problems (Berk, 2012)

If you observe any of these indicators in a student, contact a school counselor or psychologist immediately; early intervention is essential.

Child Abuse

You're a middle school teacher in a rural district, and you meet with your homeroom students every day. You use homeroom to take care of daily routines and get to know your students as individuals. Janine has always been a bright, happy student who gets along well with her classmates. Lately, she seems withdrawn, and her personal appearance is disheveled. When you look at her, she seems hesitant to make eye contact. You ask her to come in after school to talk. She says she has to go right home to help care for her younger brothers and sisters, so you suggest her lunch break instead. She reluctantly agrees.

When she comes in, she appears nervous, fidgeting with her hands and refusing to look at you. You ask her how she feels, and she replies, "Fine." You mention that she seems to be different lately, preoccupied. She only shrugs. You ask if there is anything bothering her, and she shakes her head no. You reaffirm your availability if she ever wants to talk, and she smiles briefly. As she gathers her book to get up and leave, her sweater slides off her shoulder, revealing bruises.

"Janine, what happened to your arm?"

"Oh, I fell the other day."

"But how did you hurt the inside of your arm?"

Janine's pained and embarrassed expression suggests that a fall wasn't the cause.

"Did someone try to hurt you, Janine? You can tell me."

"Only if you promise not to tell," she blurts out.

Without thinking, you agree. She proceeds to tearfully tell you about an angry father who has been out of work for months and who becomes violent when he drinks. As she leaves, she makes you promise that you won't tell anyone.

What would you do in this situation?

Teachers play a major role in reporting and preventing child abuse.

Child abuse is another serious problem today's young people face. In 2009, child protective services agencies across the country received 3.3 million reports of child abuse, and further investigation found more than 700,000 children had been victims of abuse or mistreatment (U.S. Department of Health and Human Services, 2010). Because abuse and neglect are often hidden, reliable figures are difficult to obtain. More than 78% of abuse victims suffered from neglect, about one fifth experienced physical abuse, and about 10% were sexually abused. When sexual abuse occurs, it most commonly involves a family member or friend. Although child abuse can occur at any

ISSUES YOU'LL FACE IN TEACHING

Zero Tolerance

The era of zero tolerance began in 1994, when Congress passed the Gun-Free Schools Act, requiring states receiving federal funds to expel for 1 year any student who brought a firearm to school. The Safe and Drug Free Schools and Communities Act broadened the focus from firearms to all weapons and also included expelling students for possessing drugs or drug paraphernalia. This act became part of the No Child Left Behind Act of 2001 and continues to have a powerful effect on teachers and their classrooms.

This issue will affect you because you have the most direct contact with students and you will be expected to report incidents of noncompliance.

THE QUESTION

The need for safe schools is obvious, and the premise of zero-tolerance policies—that students who endanger or disrupt the learning environment for the majority of the school population should be removed—is intuitively sensible. But are zero-tolerance policies the best way to make our schools and classrooms safe? Leaders disagree, and the following are arguments on both sides of the issue:

PRO

- Our schools need to be safe havens where parents can send their children, and zero-tolerance policies have resulted in safe, less-violent schools. In recent years, incidents of crime and violence have decreased in schools, largely because of zero-tolerance policies.
- Students can't learn if they don't feel physically and emotionally safe. Safety is a basic human need, and students need to feel both emotionally and physically safe so they can devote their full energies and attention to learning.
- Parents and other taxpayers rank school safety and the problems of drug use as critical problems facing U.S. schools (Bushaw & Lopez, 2011). In addition, both teachers (70%) and parents (68%) believe zero-tolerance policies to be effective deterrents to crime and violence in schools (Public Agenda, 2004).

CON

- Largely because of zero-tolerance policies, the suspension rate of students has increased dramatically. In 2011, almost 1 in 14 students were suspended, with the vast majority for noncriminal offenses (LaMarche, 2011).
- When expulsions occur, fewer than 6 of 10 students are sent to an alternative placement; the rest are sent home to fend for themselves, making the likelihood of truancy and crime even greater. One study found that students suspended only once during a year were nearly 3 times as likely to end up in the juvenile justice system in the subsequent year (Schwarz, 2011).
- The implementation of the policies is inconsistent and some say biased. Nationally, 15% of black students were suspended in 2006–2007, compared with 8% of Native Americans, 7% of Hispanic and 5% of white students (Shah, 2011e).
- The policies fail to discriminate between major and minor disruptions, so schools sometimes punish students for minor transgressions. For example, a food fight in a Chicago middle school resulted in the suspension and arrest of 25 students (Wald & Thurau, 2010).

YOU TAKE A STAND

Now it's your turn to take a position on the issue. Do zero-tolerance programs make schools safer and better places to learn, or do the related negative side effects outweigh the benefits?

Go to *Issues You'll Face in Teaching* in the MyEducationLab™ *Book Resources* that accompany this text to log your thoughts and receive feedback from your authors.

level of society, it tends to be associated with poverty and is often linked to parental substance abuse.

You will be in a unique position to identify child abuse because you'll work with children every day. Possible symptoms of abuse include:

- Neglected appearance
- Sudden changes in either academic or social behavior
- Disruptive or overly compliant behavior
- Repeated injuries such as bruises, welts, or burns

Teachers in all 50 states are legally bound to report suspected child abuse, and you and your school are protected from lawsuits if a report is made honestly and includes behavioral data, such as observations of the symptoms just listed (Schimmel, Stellman, et al., 2011).

Revisiting My Beliefs

This section addresses the fourth item in *This I Believe*, "If I see what I suspect is an instance of child abuse, I'm required by law to report it to the proper authorities." This statement is true. Every state and the District of Columbia require that teachers report instances of child abuse either to school authorities or to the police. The intent of the laws is to encourage teachers to report these problems and to protect them if they do.

Check Your Understanding

2.1. What changes have occurred in student sexuality over time? What are the implications of these changes for education?
2.2. Explain the trends in student use of alcohol and other drugs over the last several years, and describe the implications of these changes for education.
2.3. How has the rate of student obesity changed over the years? How are schools responding to this problem?
2.4. How have crime and violence changed in U.S. schools? What are the implications for education?

For feedback, go to the appendix, *Check Your Understanding*, located in the back of this text.

The Influence of Socioeconomic Factors on Students

As you begin this section, think about the amount of time your students will spend in your classroom compared to the rest of their day. It's actually quite limited; experts estimate that school-age children spend five times as many hours in their homes and neighborhoods as they do in school (Berliner, 2005). During this out-of-school time, students learn a great deal about the world, and they develop attitudes and values that shape the ways they'll act and learn in your classroom.

The family is the primary influence on students in their out-of-school time, and interest in the influence that families have on learning peaked in 1966 when the famous and controversial Coleman Report suggested that family background was the primary factor influencing student achievement (Coleman et al., 1966; Viadero, 2006). More recently one expert noted, "We have moved from a society in the 1950s and 1960s in which race was more consequential than family income, to one today in which family income appears more determinative of educational success than race." (Tavernise, 2012a, p. A3). A recent study confirmed that conclusion; not only has the achievement gap between rich and poor children grown in the last three decades, it is nearly twice as large as the black–white achievement gap (Maxwell, 2012c).

Family income is a major factor in determining **socioeconomic status (SES)**, the combination of family income, parents' occupations, and level of parental education. Researchers describe socioeconomic status using four classes—upper, middle, working, and lower—with finer distinctions within each (Macionis, 2011). Table 2.1 outlines characteristics of these different socioeconomic classes. Before you continue, look at Table 2.1, see where you are, and think about how your family background influenced your attitudes and values related to school. We'll share ours later in this section.

The **upper class**, composed of highly educated, highly paid professionals (people who usually have a bachelor's degree or higher and make more than $170,000 per year), is at the top of the SES pyramid. Though only a small part of the total population (about 5%), the upper class controls a disproportionate amount of the wealth (some estimate that the top 1% controls nearly half of the wealth in this country, and the top 5% control almost 60%). The gap between the upper and other classes is growing (Chinni, 2011; Macionis, 2011), and this growing disparity was the primary factor in the "Occupy Wall Street" protests in the fall of 2011—when thousands of people in cities all across the nation attempted to force our nation's leaders to address this issue.

The **middle class** is composed of managers, administrators, and white-collar workers. As a teacher, you'll be in this class; you will hold a bachelor's or higher degree, join a professional organization, and, as you saw in Chapter 1, earn around $50,000 per year (National Education Association, 2010a). Middle-class incomes

TABLE 2.1 Characteristics of Different Socioeconomic Classes

	Upper Class	Middle Class	Working Class	Lower Class
Income	$170,000+	$80,000–170,000 (1/2) $40,000–80,000 (1/2)	$25,000–$40,000	Below $25,000
Occupation	Corporate or professional (e.g., doctor, lawyer).	White collar, skilled blue collar.	Blue collar.	Minimum-wage unskilled labor.
Education	Attended college and professional schools and expect children to do the same.	High school, college, or professional schools. Strive to help their children do the same or higher.	High school; may or may not encourage college.	High school or less; cost a major factor in education.
Housing	Own home in prestigious neighborhood.	Usually own home.	About half own a home.	Rent.

Sources: Information from Macionis (2011) and U.S. Bureau of Census (2007b).

typically range between $40,000 and $170,000, and about 4 of 10 families in the U.S are middle class (Macionis, 2011).

Working-class families, also called *lower middle class,* earn between $25,000 and $40,000 per year and compose about a third of the population. Most have a high school education and hold steady blue-collar jobs involving manual labor, such as construction or factory work. About half of this group owns a home. College is a reality for only about a third of working-class children.

Families in the **lower class** typically make less than $25,000 per year, have a high school education or less, and work in low-paying, entry-level jobs. About 1 of 5 families in our country falls into this category, and the percentage is increasing. Only half of lower-class family members complete high school, and only 1 of 4 reaches college. People in the lowest-earning segment of this category often depend on public assistance to supplement their incomes and are often the third or fourth generation to live in poverty.

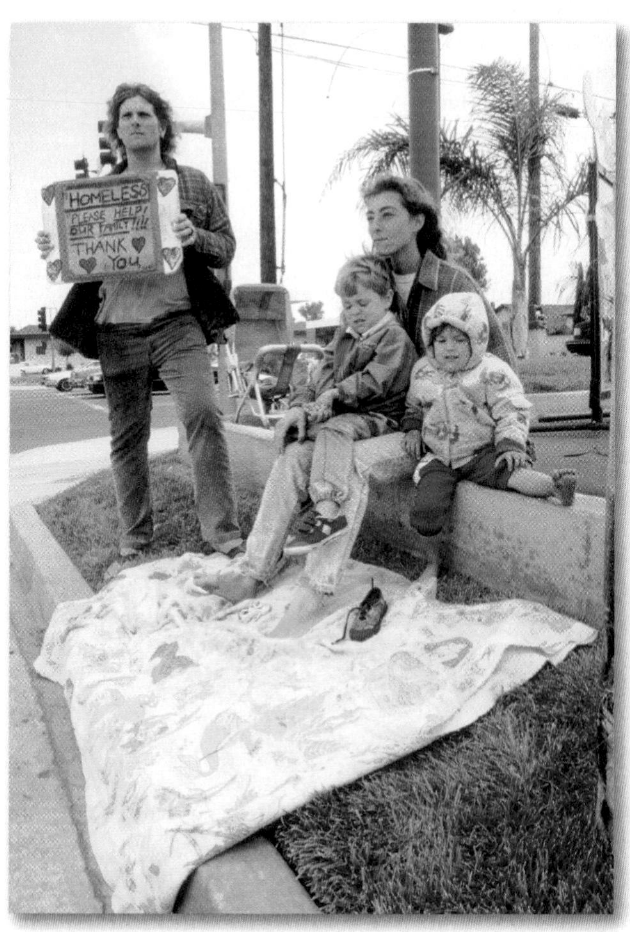

Poverty can exert a powerful negative influence on school success.

The term **underclass** is often used to describe people with low incomes who continually struggle with economic problems. Escaping from the underclass is very difficult, and poverty poses special challenges to these families and their children, a topic we examine in the next section.

Poverty

When Kirsten gets a spare moment (and there aren't many of these), she loves to draw fantasy creatures on her computer (When it works. When it doesn't, she uses paper and pencil). She likes to draw mermaids, fairies, and monsters—escapes from reality. But Kirsten's life is not a fairy tale. She hurries home from school with her brother, fixes them both a snack, and does her homework. Then she straightens up the small apartment, cleans up the room she shares with her brother, does the dishes left over from breakfast and dinner last night, and cooks dinner. Quite an accomplishment for a fifth grader! Her greatest fear is that the money will run out and she and her mother and brother won't have enough to eat and will get sick. Who would take care of the family then?

Kirsten has to work like this because her mother, who has severe diabetes, works 10 hours a day on two jobs—one as a waitress, the other cleaning other people's houses. When her mother returns home from work, she collapses on the sofa exhausted. When Kirsten comes home from school, this is how she usually finds her. Life is not easy.

Poverty exerts a toll on both families and children. To assist families, the federal government establishes **poverty thresholds**, household income levels that represent the lowest earnings required to meet basic living needs. In 2011, the poverty level for a family of four was $22,350 (U.S. Department of Health and Human Services, 2011). These levels are determined primarily by food costs and largely ignore other factors such as the cost of housing, transportation, and energy.

Several disturbing patterns exist in our country with respect to poverty. As we've moved into the second decade of the 21st century, the number of children living in poverty rose by 33% between 2000 and 2009, with young, teenage and single-parent families overrepresented (U.S. Bureau of Census, 2010a). And, the percentage of U.S. families below the poverty level is consistently higher than in other industrialized countries (Rebell & Wolff, 2012). Nearly 1 of 5 U.S. students live in poverty, in New York City that figure is 30%, and almost half of the U.S. poor are young people under the age of 25 (Macionis, 2011; Rebell & Wolff, 2012). The fact that one third of the children living in poverty have at least one parent working full time is disconcerting; the low-paying jobs available to poorly educated parents can't keep up with the continually rising cost of living (Federal Interagency Forum on Child and Family Statistics, 2010).

Many of our students, like education students nationwide, come from the suburbs and think that they won't encounter poverty in their classrooms. This isn't true; we used to think of poverty as something we'd only find in large urban or remote rural areas, but that has changed in recent years. Nationwide 55% of the poor population in metropolitan areas now lives in the suburbs; in Cleveland between 2000 and 2010 the suburban poverty rate increased by 53%, fueled by unemployment and real estate problems (Tavernise, 2011). This suggests that no matter where you teach, you'll end up dealing with the negative effects of poverty in your classroom.

Poverty is not distributed equally among children from different racial or ethnic groups (see Figure 2.3). The actual number of white children living in poverty is greater than for any other group, but their percentage is the lowest among all ethnic groups. For example, 12% of white children live in poverty, whereas 33% of Hispanic children, 34% of Native American, and 36% of black children experience the same plight (Wight, Chau, & Aratani, 2011).

The federal government addresses the problems of poverty through the National School Lunch Program. In 2008, children from a family of four with income below $27,650 a year were eligible for free breakfasts and lunches; families earning below $39,220 qualified for 30-cent breakfasts and 40-cent lunches (S. Dillon, 2008a). Although virtually all schools participate in the program, most families that qualify for free or reduced meals don't participate, being either too proud or unaware that the programs are available (Brimley, Verstegen, & Garfield, 2012). This problem is not new, as the following quote indicates, and it has important implications for all teachers:

> What this means is that at least one-fifth of all children who come through the schoolhouse door in America today are likely to be experiencing poverty-associated problems such as substandard housing, an inadequate diet, threadbare or hand-me-down clothes, lack of health insurance, chronic dental or health problems, deprivation and violence in their communities, little or no funds for school supplies, and whose overburdened parents subsist on welfare or work long hours at miserably paid jobs. These facts pose enormous problems for America's schools. (Biddle, 2001, p. 5)

FIGURE 2.3 **Child Poverty Rates by Race/Ethnicity**

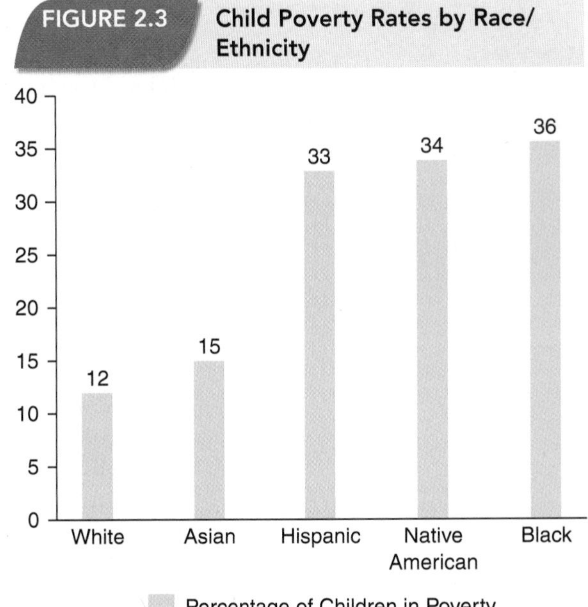

Source: Based on U.S. Bureau of Census. (2011). *Income, poverty, and health insurance coverage in the United States: 2010.* Report P66N.238 Table B-2, pp. 68–73. Retrieved from http://www.census.gov/prod/2011pubs/p60-239.pdf

Teachers report that almost 65% of their students periodically come to school hungry (Shah, 2011c), and they respond in a variety of ways, such as keeping boxes of crackers, granola bars, and other snacks in their desks. They also help students sign up for free or reduced-priced meals at school.

Poverty can have a devastating effect on students. For instance, one study found that children of poverty are five times more likely to drop out of school than are their more affluent peers (Chapman, Laird, Ifill, & KewalRamani, 2011). To address the effects of poverty on students, a number of districts across the country have implemented integration-by-income programs, including Louisville, Kentucky; Omaha, Nebraska; and San Francisco (Bazelon, 2008; Kahlenberg, 2012). These programs integrate students from different SES levels in a variety of ways, including magnet schools, vouchers, and even busing. All are based on the belief that high concentrations of students from impoverished backgrounds limit a school's ability to meet students' learning needs (Zehr, 2010c). Research indicates that these programs are effective. For instance, in North Carolina, more than 60% of integrated-by-income students passed state-mandated end-of-course exams compared to less than 50% in comparable surrounding areas (Kahlenberg, 2006).

Homelessness

Homelessness is a direct result of poverty. An accurate count of homeless students is difficult, but experts estimate that 1.5 million children are homeless sometime during any given year, and families with children account for 40% of the homeless population (Dill, 2010). Homeless children often come from unstable families, suffer from inadequate diets, and lack medical care; a large percentage of homeless children fail to attend school regularly because of either family or logistical problems such as not being able to get to their old school after having to relocate to a homeless shelter (P. Miller, 2011). A major provision of the 2001 No Child Left Behind Act requires that districts provide homeless students with transportation to their original schools, but cash-strapped districts are finding it difficult to comply with this law. Homeless children suffer from a number of learning challenges and are much more likely to repeat a grade and drop out of school than other children (M. Anderson, 2011).

Schools respond to the problem of homelessness in several ways, becoming sanctuaries or havens for children whose lives have been turned upside down (Dill, 2010). Recognizing that students' home situations are difficult, they attempt to make school admission, attendance, and course requirements flexible; they provide outreach services such as counselors, after-school programs, and financial aid for transportation; and school officials coordinate with other community agencies to ensure that basic needs, such as food and shelter, are met.

Several urban schools across the country target homeless children as their primary clients (M. Anderson, 2011; Zehr, 2010a). They send school buses around their cities to pick up the children, and they maintain rooms in which students can shower, wash clothes, and get clean underwear and changes of clothes. Volunteer pediatricians staff on-site clinics and provide free medical care and immunizations. One school even handed out alarm clocks (old-fashioned windups because many of the children don't have access to electricity) to help them get to school on time (Sandham, 2000). Teacher dedication and effort make these schools work. One teacher commented, "There's something about watching the buses roll out of here, with all the kids' faces pressed against the windows. I get this feeling it's what I should be doing" (Sandham, 2000, p. 29).

The problem of homelessness has been exacerbated by the recent economic downturn that hit the U.S. economy, and many families that were just getting by now face being evicted from their homes (Winerip, 2011d). Families that used to own homes or were renting now find shelter in one-room motel rooms—if they have any shelter at all, forced there by an inability to pay the up-front costs of renting, such as security and utility deposits (Eckholm, 2009). Often as many as six members of a family share one room, which serves as living room, kitchen, and bedroom. Homework is a challenge when the TV is on and there is no quiet place to work.

Homelessness is obviously very difficult for students, but you can help. For instance, being a willing ear is a start. You might be the only person students will confide in, because they fear the scorn of peers and will do everything they can to mask this personal problem (Winerip, 2011a). Second, make a special effort to maintain high expectations for all your students, regardless of their dress or appearance. Research suggests that factors such as dress and grooming can influence teachers' instructional decisions (Ready & Wright, 2011). Third, talk with experienced teachers about community resources available for these students and their families, and pass this information on to parents. Most importantly, care and flexibility are essential. Demonstrating that you genuinely care about students and their learning is important for all children; for those who are homeless, it's critical.

Socioeconomic Status and School Success

Socioeconomic status consistently predicts a number of indicators of school success, including achievement test scores, grades, and truancy, dropout, and suspension rates (Lareau, 2011). But what is the link between SES and school success? A researcher went to the house of a struggling fifth grader named Socorro to find out why she struggled. While interviewing Socorro's mother, here is what he found.

> Nick [Socorro's uncle] passed through the apartment apparently returning to work after taking a brief break. The phone rang. Socorro's 5-year-old stepbrother curled up in his mother's lap and began talking into her ear. The television was on. There is a television in every room; one is Socorro's. The apartment is spotlessly clean. Life is busy, very busy. Once off the phone, the mother exclaims, proudly, "I let her do whatever she wants . . . she does whatever she wants." Working two jobs, one in housekeeping at a nearby hospital and another, an evening job as a parking lot attendant to obtain money . . . leaves her no option: She is not home often. . . . "I want to support my kids," the mother says, and this requires that she is "never home for them." She works very hard.
>
> Socorro's problem in school, her mother asserts, is that "her mind wanders." Her teachers tell another tale: Socorro cannot read and is struggling. Her mother seems unconcerned that Socorro frequently misses school. As her teacher said, "She is out of school more than she is in it." Attending school irregularly, Socorro is slipping further and further behind her classmates. Concerned, teachers made arrangements to place Socorro for part of the day with the special education teacher. They didn't know what else to do, having failed to gain the mother's help in getting Socorro to school regularly. (Bullough, 2001, p. 33)

Socioeconomic status influences school success in a number of ways but has its most powerful influence at the lower income levels. Frequently, low-SES children come to school ill-prepared to learn: low-SES elementary students are more than twice as likely as their higher SES peers to fall below basic levels of reading, and they are only one third as likely to achieve at a proficient level. As you saw earlier, children of poverty are 5 times more likely to drop out than their more fortunate peers (Chapman et al., 2011). And only about 1 of 4 high school graduates from lower SES classes goes to college and earns a degree, compared to nearly 8 of 10 graduates from the highest SES classes (Macionis, 2011).

But what accounts for these dramatic differences in achievement? Experts identify the following factors:

- Fulfillment of basic needs
- Family stability
- School-related experiences
- Interaction patterns in the home
- Parental attitudes and values

Most families in our country take for granted basic needs, such as food, shelter, and medical care. Many low-SES families lack adequate medical care, however, and an increasing number of children come to school without proper nourishment. In 2010, more than 37 million people in the United States reported going hungry, and 14 million of these were children (Feeding America, 2010). One in eight Americans now rely on outside help to feed their families, and one third of these report having to choose between food and other basic needs such as rent, utilities, or medical care. Poor nutrition affects attention and memory and can even lead to lower scores on intelligence tests (Berk, 2012).

In high-poverty schools, the school nurse often serves as a substitute for the family doctor because families in poverty don't have medical insurance and can't afford to seek medical help. One school nurse reported,

> Mondays we are hit hard. It's not like in the suburbs, where families call the pediatrician. When our kids get sick on the weekends, they go to the emergency room, or they wait. Monday morning, they are lined up, and they have to see the nurse. (F. Smith, 2005, p. 49)

It is hard to learn when you're sick or hurting.

Children of poverty also relocate frequently; in some low-income schools, mobility rates are above 100%, which means you could have a complete turnover in students during an academic year if you taught in a school such as this (Gruman, Harachi, Abbott, Catalano, & Fleming, 2008). Nearly a third of the poorest students attend three schools by third grade, compared to only 1 of 10 for middle-class students. These frequent moves are stressful for students and will be a challenge for you as you attempt to develop caring relationships with them.

Family stability also influences learning and school success. In many low-SES families, daily struggles and economic problems result in parental frustration and anger, which can lead to marital conflicts and unstable home environments. Children often come to school lacking the sense of safety and security that would equip them to tackle school-related challenges. Children from families with high amounts of internal conflict have higher rates of behavioral and mental health problems (Sturge-Apple, Davies, & Cummings, 2010).

School-related experiences in the home influence students' learning as well (Aikens & Barbarin, 2008). High-SES parents are more likely than their low-SES counterparts to provide their children with educational activities outside school, such as visits to museums, concerts, and libraries; to have materials at home that support learning (e.g., newspapers and computers with Internet access); and to arrange for formal out-of-school learning experiences, such as music or dance lessons, participation in tennis and soccer camps, and computer classes. Parents at the upper end of the income spectrum spend five times as much per child on education-related enrichment activities as lower-income parents, and children from wealthy families spend 1,300 more hours before the age of 6 visiting museums and other enriching environments than those from poor families (Tavernise, 2012). These activities provide an experiential foundation that helps students succeed in school activities. Low-SES students are also less likely to participate in extracurricular activities provided by schools, often because of parents' work demands or transportation problems, or because their parents don't know these opportunities exist.

Interaction patterns in the home also influence learning. High-SES parents tend to talk with their children more than do lower SES caregivers, and this verbal give-and-take provides students with practice in developing their language skills (Lareau, 2011). These discussions also prepare children for the kind of verbal interaction found in the schools. Sometimes called "the curriculum of the home," these rich interaction patterns, together with the enrichment experiences described in the previous paragraph, provide a solid foundation for reading and vocabulary development.

Experts estimate that by the age of 3, children of professional parents have heard 30 million words; children with working-class parents, 20 million; but children with parents on welfare, only 10 million (Chance, 1997). High-SES parents are also more likely to treat their children as conversational partners, explain ideas and the causes of events, encourage independent thinking, and emphasize individual responsibility (Berk, 2012). Low-SES parents, by contrast, are more likely to "tell" rather than explain, their language is less elaborate, their directions are less clear, and they are less likely to encourage problem solving.

Finally, parental attitudes and values shape the way students think about schools and learning (Lareau, 2011). Reading materials are more common in high-SES homes, and children learn that reading is an important part of people's lives. Parents who enjoy books, newspapers, and magazines communicate that the information they contain is valuable and that reading is a useful activity for its own sake. When children see their parents read, they imitate the behavior, which influences their learning at school (G. Tompkins, 2013).

Parents also communicate their attitudes about education through the expectations they hold for their children and through their involvement in their children's activities (Benner & Mistry, 2007). High-SES parents are more likely to encourage their children to graduate from high school and attend college. They also support their children's education by attending curricular and extracurricular activities. One mother commented, "When she sees me at her games, when she sees me going to open house, when I attend her Interscholastic League contests, she knows I am interested in her activities. Plus, we have more to talk about" (Young & Scribner, 1997, p. 12).

Revisiting My Beliefs

This section addresses the fifth question in *This I Believe*, "Parents' educational background strongly influences their children's success in school." This statement is true; parents' level of education influences learning in a number of ways including attitudes and values, as well as the kinds of experiences children have as they grow up.

SES: Some Cautions and Implications for Teachers

It's important to remember that the information in this section describes group differences; individuals within groups will vary widely. For example, many low-SES parents read and talk to their children, encourage their involvement in extracurricular activities, and attend school events. Both of your authors come from low-SES families, and we were given many enriching experiences associated with high-SES parents. Conversely, belonging to a high-SES family does not guarantee that a child will have enriching experiences and caring, involved parents. When you work with your students, consciously avoid stereotypes; remember that your students are individuals, and treat them as such (Ready & Wright, 2011). Keep your expectations appropriately high for all students.

One popular staff development program that targets the children of poverty has been criticized for stereotyping these children. Based on Ruby Payne's *A Framework for Understanding Poverty* (2005), these workshops help teachers understand how the values and beliefs of low-SES children are different from those of middle-class students and adversely affect school success. Critics contend that the book oversimplifies issues related to poverty and encourages teachers to treat these children as having collective deficits rather than as individuals with potential (Gorski, 2008). Despite these criticisms, the book has sold more than 800,000 copies, and the author has been called the "dominant voice on class and poverty" in education (Gorski, 2008, p. 130).

A second, related, caution: We know that certain home conditions make it more difficult for students to succeed in school, but we also know that schools and teachers can do much to overcome these problems (Lowery, 2012). As you'll see later in the chapter, schools that are safe, nurturing, and demanding, and teachers who hold high expectations for their students' success and teach effectively can make a significant difference in all students' lives.

Check Your Understanding

3.1. Define *socioeconomic status.*
3.2. Explain how different socioeconomic patterns influence school success.
3.3. How does the government define *poverty*? How does poverty influence learning?
3.4. How does homelessness influence learning?

For feedback, go to the appendix, *Check Your Understanding,* located in the back of this text.

Students at Risk

Laurie Ramirez looks over the papers she has been grading and shakes her head. "Fourth grade, and some of these kids don't know what zero means or how place value affects a number. Some can't add or subtract, and most don't understand multiplication. How am I supposed to teach problem solving when they don't understand basic math facts?"

"Reading isn't much better," she thinks. "I have a few who read at a fourth-grade level, but others are still sounding out words like *dog* and *cat.* How can I teach them comprehension skills when they are struggling with ideas this basic?"

Struggling students can be found in any school. Many reasons exist, but many students are exposed to a combination of conditions that decrease their chances for success. **Students at risk** are in danger of failing to complete their education with the skills necessary to function effectively in modern society. The term *at risk* is derived from medicine, which uses the term "risk factors," such as high cholesterol and obesity, to describe dangers to our health. *At risk* became widely used after 1983, when the National Commission on Excellence in Education proclaimed the United States a "nation at risk," emphasizing the growing link between education and economic well-being in today's technological society (National Commission on Excellence in Education, 1983). The report recognized that success in life depended on success in school, and many of our students weren't making it.

Since 1983, researchers have focused considerable attention on problems involving students at risk. Table 2.2 outlines the academic, social, and emotional problems these students encounter. You will almost certainly have these students in your classes.

TABLE 2.2 Characteristics of Students at Risk

Background Factors	Educational Problems
Low SES/Poverty	High dropout rates
Transient/Homeless	Low grades
Divorced Families	Retention in grade
Inner City	Low achievement
Minority	Low participation in extracurricular activities
Nonnative English Speaker	Low motivation
Environments with Alcohol and Drug Abuse	Poor attendance
High Neighborhood Criminal Activity Rates	Misbehavior in classes
	Low self-esteem
	Low standardized test scores
	Lack of interest in school
	High suspension rates

The Dropout Problem

Because it has an enormous impact on subsequent employment and income, dropping out of school is one of the most pernicious outcomes of being at risk. Dropouts not only decrease their own chances of personal success, they also are more likely to have problems with transiency, crime, and drug abuse (Macionis, 2011). High school dropouts often end up in dead-end minimal wage jobs earning $7.25 an hour. In a year, that comes to $14,500; try living on that, much less raising a family on it. The average high school dropout earns almost 50% less than a high school graduate; over a lifetime, a high school dropout earns $400,000 less than someone with a high school diploma (Swanson, 2011). In addition, dropping out of high school closes the door to college and well-paying jobs that require advanced training and expertise with technology. In the past, factory and farm jobs offered viable alternatives for dropouts; today with outsourcing to other countries and consolidation of smaller farms, these jobs no longer exist.

Getting a handle on the dropout problem was difficult in the past because states couldn't agree on how to accurately count the number of high school dropouts, but now a uniform system of counting compares the number of students who enter high school versus those who leave 4 years later with a high school diploma. In 2008 that figure was 72%, but huge differences exist across the country and between different groups of students (EPE Research Center, 2011a). For example in 2008, New Jersey had a graduation rate of 87% compared to Nevada's 44%. Dropout rates also vary dramatically by ethnicity; while overall, 72% of students graduate from high school, Hispanic (58%), black (57%), and Native American (54%) students had much lower graduation rates (see Figure 2.4) (Swanson, 2011). In addition, males (68%) have lower graduation rates than females (75%). Think about this: Nearly one third of the students who enter ninth grade won't graduate in 4 years, and the dropout rate increases to almost one half for cultural minorities!

FIGURE 2.4 Graduation Rates by Ethnicity and Gender

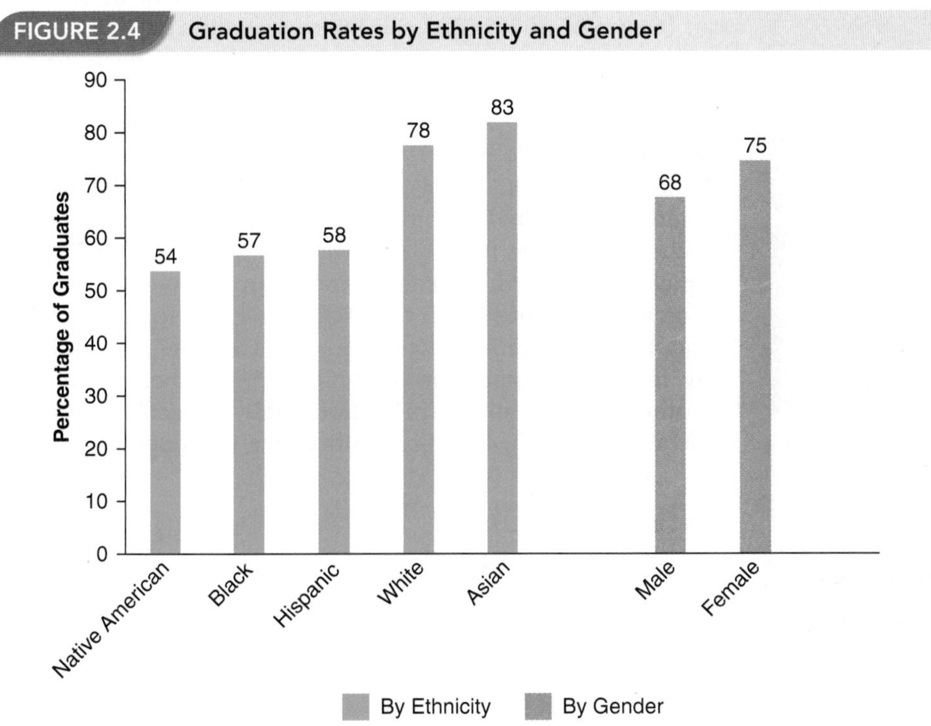

Source: Based on National Center for Education Statistics. (2012). *Trends in high school dropout and completion rates in the United States: 1972–2009* (Compendium Report). Retrieved from http://nces.ed.gov/pubs2012/2012006.pdf

Dropout rates are strongly affected by poverty; as you saw earlier, students from low-income families are 5 times more likely to drop out than those from high-income families (Chapman et al., 2011). Other factors contributing to high dropout rates include unstable families, high rates of student mobility, as well as higher graduation standards and high school exit exams (Barton, 2006). Typically, large urban districts have lower graduation rates, but graduation rates in urban districts vary greatly; Chicago had a graduation rate of 70% in 2008 compared to Detroit's 33% (EPE Research Center, 2011b). Even within a district, dropout rates can vary dramatically, with some schools with abysmally low graduation rates identified as "dropout factories" (Sparks, 2010). This wide variability both between and within districts suggests that schools and the teachers in them can have a powerful influence on retaining students in school.

Recently, the dropout problem received national attention in President Obama's 2012 State of the Union address. In it he urged every state to require that all students stay in school until they graduate or turn 18 (Maxwell, 2012c). When he made that speech, 18 states had legal dropout ages of 16. Unemployment statistics bolster the case for changing the legal dropout age; in January 2012, the national unemployment rate was 8.3%; for those with less than a high school diploma, it was 13.1% (Editorial, 2012). Nationally, the most successful dropout-prevention programs provide students with multiple pathways to graduation, including career and technical programs, as well as flexible options to complete high school degrees (Gewertz, 2012a).

What can you do to address this problem? Some people think that dropping out is a high school problem, but it isn't. A number of educationally related problems contribute to dropping out, including low achievement and grades, retention in grade, poor attendance, behavior problems, and poor self-esteem. These problems often develop in the early elementary grades (Alonso, Anderson, Su, & Theoharis, 2009; Bryk, Sebring, Allensworth, Luppescu, & Easton, 2010). Student motivation is also a major factor in dropping out. Nearly 70% of dropouts in one study said they weren't motivated or inspired to work hard, almost half said their classes weren't interesting, and 2 of 3 identified a lack of challenge as a major factor in dropping out (Gewertz, 2006). You can make a significant difference in your classroom through the way you teach and relate to your students.

Meaningful relationships with students make urban schools and classrooms more inviting places to learn.

Potential dropouts need better teachers, and a move is now under way to ensure that the best teachers are available to them (Sawchuk, 2010a). In the past, low-performing, high-poverty schools had problems attracting and retaining the best teachers. Now the federal government is funding an initiative to pay high-performing teachers who can produce achievement gains in their students up to $10,000 to move to, and teach in, schools with large numbers of students at risk. The additional pay, increased support from administers, and help from teams of other teachers make this a potentially attractive option for teachers who want to make a difference in students' lives.

URBAN EDUCATION: Students at Risk and Urban Schools

Urban schools can be tough places to teach and learn, both for teachers and their students. Consider one teacher's experience.

> I'm teaching in a barrio in California. I had 32 kids in my class last year. I love them to tears. They're 5th graders. That means they're 10 years old, mostly. Six of them

> were 11 because they were retained. Five more were in special education, and two more should have been. . . . Here's the kicker. Fifty percent of my students have set foot in a jail or prison to visit a family member. (Karrer, 2011, p. 23)

Students at risk face special challenges in urban schools, which tend to be large and located in high-poverty areas. As you saw earlier in the chapter, poverty often has an adverse effect on student achievement, and urban environments have higher rates of poverty than areas outside central cities (Macionis & Parrillo, 2010). Poverty, crime, unsafe neighborhoods and drugs all create environments that place students at risk. They are less well funded than their suburban counterparts, and because they are large, they can become impersonal. Urban high schools can be tough, confusing places where students can easily get lost (C. Payne, 2008).

The diversity found in urban neighborhoods, the distances students often must travel over public transportation, and the fact that urban teachers typically don't live in the same neighborhoods make it difficult for teachers to connect with students and empathize with their lives outside school. Extracurricular activities, which can serve as a way to meet and get to know students, are often inaccessible, compounding the problem of establishing supportive interpersonal relationships with students. One study found that only 20% of urban African American males and less than 30% of African American females believed that their teachers supported them and cared about their success (Noguera, 2003). It is difficult for teachers to influence their students' development without mutual trust and caring.

Lower incomes and the lower residential property values that go with them also mean less money for schools. Less money often means that class sizes are larger and schools have fewer resources, such as computers and science lab equipment (Brimley et al., 2012).

Finally, because working in urban areas is viewed as challenging and with fewer rewards, veteran teachers often choose jobs in the suburbs instead of in urban settings (Sawchuk, 2010a). As a result, urban students, who most need experienced professionals, are unlikely to get them. This can present opportunities for you: If you consider working in an urban environment, the likelihood of getting a job is high. In addition, as you saw in the previous section, schools are increasingly offering incentive pay for teachers willing to work in urban schools, and working with urban students can be rewarding as you help them develop, both personally and intellectually.

The challenge for urban educators is to create contexts in which students can interact meaningfully with both teachers and other students. One proposed solution is to create smaller schools, or schools within a school, that allow for the creation of more personal learning communities. Students in smaller schools "behave better, are more likely to be involved in extracurricular activities, . . . fight less, feel safe, and feel more attached to their schools" (Ilg & Massucci, 2003, p. 69).

Although teachers alone can't create smaller schools, you can make a special effort to create learning communities within your classrooms that nurture both the social and the cognitive development of your students. Let's see what an urban seventh grader has to say about one of her teachers.

> She's probably the strictest teacher I've ever had because she doesn't let you slide by if you've made a mistake. . . . If you've made a mistake she's going to let you know it. And if you're getting bad marks, she's going to let you know it. She's one of my strictest teachers and that's what makes me think she cares about us the most. (Alder, 2002, pp. 251–252)

Effective urban teachers combine high expectations for academic success with clear messages about the need for student effort and responsibility.

Additional research suggests that the human factor is essential: Students considering dropping out need to believe that they belong in school and that someone cares about them as people and about their success (Barton, 2006). This is where your work is crucial, because you and your colleagues are the only people in the school who interact with students every day. Make it a point to

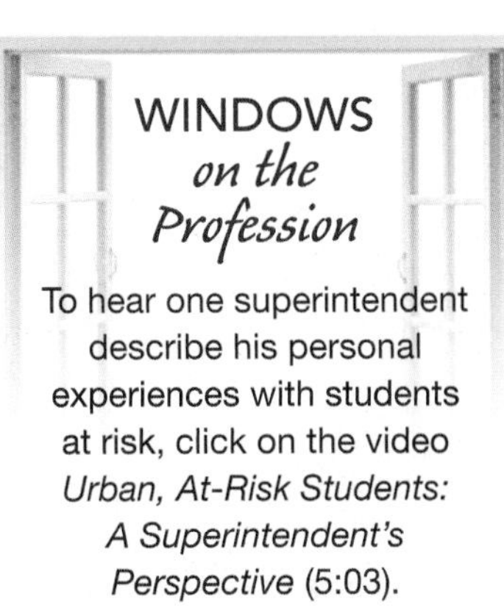

To hear one superintendent describe his personal experiences with students at risk, click on the video *Urban, At-Risk Students: A Superintendent's Perspective* (5:03).

learn about your students and their families, and share information about your own life. You are not trying to be their "buddy"; rather, you're an adult who cares about them and wants to see them succeed.

It Takes a Village: The Community-Based Approach to Working with Children at Risk

Though schools can have a powerful influence on the success of students at risk, they can't do it all without outside help. Effective schools involve parents and other members of the community in redesigning schools to better meet the needs of these learners.

Full-service schools serve as family resource centers that provide a range of social and health services. Recognizing that many of the risk factors students encounter occur outside school walls, and that supporting families also strengthens children, full-service schools attempt to create a safety net of services for students and their families. Services provided by these schools are listed in Table 2.3.

The School Development Program, created by Yale psychiatrist James Comer, is one example of a full-service model (Emmons & Comer, 2009); it integrates schools and the community by bringing principals, teachers, and parents together in school planning and management teams. School services, such as counseling and support for students with learning or behavioral problems, are coordinated through teams of psychologists, counselors, and special educators. This coordination is important because services for students are often fragmented. Comprehensive school programs address this problem by coordinating services and focusing on each child's physical, social, emotional, and academic growth in integrated efforts. They offer free dental care, free immunizations and physicals at the beginning of the school year, and family visits to a health clinic where the fees are on a sliding scale based on family income (Zehr, 2011a).

From its start in New Haven, Connecticut, the School Development Program has spread to more than 500 schools across the country. Evaluations indicate that the program is effective; researchers report increases in achievement and student self-concepts and declines in absences, suspensions, and management problems in schools where the program is fully implemented (Emmons & Comer, 2009). Research on other comprehensive school programs shows similar positive effects (Zehr, 2011a).

Your role in a full-service school will change from one of instructor to partner with the community. If you work in one of these schools, you'll be asked to serve on community councils that attempt to link schools with their surrounding communities, and you'll also be asked to be proactive in making contacts with parents and other caregivers. Your workload will be greater, but the rewards that come from seeing your students succeed because of your outreach efforts will be substantial.

TABLE 2.3 Services Provided by Full-Service Schools

Child care
Medical and dental screening
Immunizations
Nutrition/weight management
Employment and housing assistance
Legal and immigration advice
Individual counseling/mental health services
Substance abuse treatment
Recreation, sports, and culture
Parent education
After-school teacher assistance with homework

EXPLORING DIVERSITY: Promoting Student Resilience

Despite the obstacles they encounter, many students succeed against the odds and graduate from school with the skills necessary to succeed in life. **Resilient students** are students at risk who have been able to rise above adverse conditions to succeed in school and in other aspects of life.

Resilient children have well-developed "self-systems," including high self-esteem and confidence that they are in control of their destinies. They set personal goals, possess good interpersonal skills, and have positive expectations for success. They are motivated to learn and are satisfied with school (Reis, Colbert, & Hébert, 2005).

How do these adaptive skills develop? First, resilient children have relationships with caring adults who hold high moral and academic expectations for them (Poplin et al., 2011). Second, they come from schools that are both demanding and supportive; in many instances, schools serve as homes away from home. Let's look more closely at how you can foster resilience in your students.

Effective Schools for Students at Risk

Effective schools for students at risk focus on personal responsibility, cooperation, and mutual respect between teachers and students. Effective schools emphasize:

- A safe, orderly school climate in which students understand the meaning behind and the purpose of school and classroom rules
- Academic objectives focusing on mastery of content
- Cooperation, a sense of community, and prosocial values
- Student responsibility and self-regulation with decreased emphasis on external controls
- Strong parental involvement
- Caring and demanding teachers who hold high expectations for all students (Bryk et al., 2010; Poplin et al., 2011)

The combination of these factors creates a web of support that allows resilient students to grow and develop.

Effective Teachers for Students at Risk

Well-run and academically focused schools are important, but they aren't enough; students also need good teachers. Effective teachers in these schools are simultaneously caring and demanding and hold high moral and academic expectations for their students. In essence, they refuse to let students fail. One high school teacher reported:

> A graduate whom I had not seen for many years stopped by after school when he saw me working late. His eyes were thick with tears as he spoke: "You never gave up on me. You never ignored me. You always encouraged me to get my work in and pass all of my classes, even when I wasn't nice to you. Thank you." (Barnoski, 2005, p. 37)

This kind of teacher commitment is essential because the needs and personal sensitivities of students at risk make them vulnerable to failure, personal slights, hints of favoritism, and doubts about the relevance of school.

Teachers who are ineffective with students at risk are more authoritarian and less accessible. They distance themselves from students and place primary responsibility for learning on them. They view being emotionally supportive as "babying students" or "holding students' hands." Lecture is a common teaching strategy, and motivation is the students' responsibility. One urban high school student observed, "Some teachers are here to work and some are just here to get paid. . . . The bad teachers at Fremont just sit their behind down all day and expect us to work without them helping us to work" (Alonso et al., 2009, p. 103). Students perceive these teachers as adversaries, to be avoided if possible, tolerated if not.

In addition to being caring and demanding, what do effective teachers of students at risk need to do? They also have to be effective instructors.

Effective Instruction and Support

Teachers of students at risk don't have to teach in fundamentally different ways; instead, they need to systematically apply the strategies that are effective with all students (Eggen & Kauchak, 2013). They provide enough instructional support to ensure success while teaching students active learning strategies that allow them to take control of their own learning. Effective instruction for students at risk includes:

- High classroom structure with predictable routines
- Clear learning objectives
- High levels of interaction between the teacher and students
- Frequent and thorough assessment
- Informative feedback to promote student success
- Emphasis on student responsibility (Brophy, 2010; Lemov, 2010)

Let's see how one teacher does this.

When students enter Dena Hine's second-grade classroom after recess, they see a review assignment on the chalkboard. As Dena takes roll, students get out their books and start on the assignment. Five minutes later, Dena begins with a brief review of the previous day's lesson. Because the students answer her questions quickly and correctly, she believes that her class knows the content and is ready to move on.

As she introduces two-column subtraction, she comments that this is an important skill that everyone will be able to learn. Then she presents the following problem and discusses how two-column subtraction will help them solve it:

Teresa was saving her money to buy a toy for her little sister. The toy cost $.99, and she has already saved $.67. How much more money did she need to buy the toy?

Next, she gives each student bundles of 10 craft sticks bound together with rubber bands. She guides students through the subtraction steps by having them take apart the bundles to illustrate the process, asking many questions as she proceeds. She also uses questioning to help them link the craft sticks to the numbers she writes on the board. Then she has students solve problems on their own mini-chalkboards and hold them up to allow her to check their solutions. Whenever mistakes occur, she stops, explains the errors, and helps students correct them.

When most of the class is correctly solving the problems, Dena starts the students on additional practice problems, which they check in pairs. As they work, she helps those still having difficulty, moving around the room to respond to pairs who disagreed with each other or who have questions.

Effective teachers actively involve their students in learning activities, and they provide instruction that is challenging, motivating, and connected to students' lives.

A final word about a major problem often associated with students at risk, which you saw in Table 2.2: low self-esteem. This problem is real, and we've seen it at all grade levels as we've worked in classrooms around the country. Students sit passively, pretending that they're not there and hoping that the teacher won't call on them, because they don't think they know the answer. They have a history of failure, and a low sense of self-worth is the result.

The solution? Teach them something, and make sure that they know that hard work and effort contributed to their learning. The best way to address low self-esteem in students at risk is to design your instruction so that everyone in

DIVERSITY AND YOU

Teaching Students Who Are at Risk

Wendy Kaughman sighs as she enters the teachers' lounge at Lincoln Middle School, located in a large urban center in the Northeast.

"What's wrong, Rookie?" Joe Patterson, one of the other social studies teachers, asks. "Are the kids winning?"

"Sometimes it feels like it," Wendy replies with a grin, "but I didn't think that teaching was going to be a game with winners and losers. If I could just get them to settle down and cooperate, I might be able to teach them something."

"Don't forget what I told you at the beginning of the year," Joe responds. "Don't smile 'til Christmas. You've still got 2 months to go, and I'll bet you've already smiled. You have to teach them that you mean business. Once they learn that, you can teach them something."

"Don't listen to Joe," Emma Harris interjects with a smile. "He's been teaching in this school too long and forgets what it's like to be human. It's okay to smile at the kids—just not too long or too often. Just kidding. I've only been teaching 5 years, but I found that these kids respond to the human touch. They like to know that you care, and you can't do that when you have them sitting quietly in rows while you lecture to them. They need opportunities to work in groups, to learn to work with others, and to express their own thoughts and ideas. Don't be afraid to be human—they like that."

"Wait a minute," Joe responds. "You can't argue with success. I've been here for 17 years, and my referrals to the principal's office are virtually nonexistent. I lay it on the line the first day of class and refuse to take crap from anyone. They have to know that you mean business. Once you convince them of that, it's all downhill. They'll sit quietly; some will listen and even take notes, and most learn something. Not a lot, but what can you expect? This is a tough school in a rough neighborhood. Survival is important for them, and it should be for you. Toughen up, Wendy, and maybe you'll be around in 17 years."

QUESTIONS TO CONSIDER

1. Classroom management is a perennial concern for beginning teachers. Which approach to classroom management—Joe's or Emma's—makes the most sense?
2. What about instruction? Which advice—Joe's or Emma's—makes the most sense?

Go to *Diversity and You* in the MyEducationLab™ *Book Resources* that accompany this text to log your thoughts and receive feedback from your authors.

the class learns something and knows it afterward. When students are successful, their confidence improves, and their self-esteem grows. This isn't an easy task, but many classroom teachers do this on a daily basis (Lemov, 2010; Poplin et al., 2011).

We have one more suggestion; at the beginning of the year, look every student in the eye and say, "I guarantee that each and every one of you can learn if you work hard and try. I promise to work hard to make that happen, but I need your cooperation. If we work hard together, each of you, and I mean everyone, can succeed and learn in my classroom." Then the challenge is to make this happen in your own classroom. It can be done.

WINDOWS *on the Profession*

To see a teacher using effective teaching skills in an urban middle school classroom, click on the video *Essential Teaching Skills in an Urban Classroom* (14:01).

Check Your Understanding

4.1. What are the characteristics of students at risk?
4.2. What unique challenges do urban schools present to students at risk?
4.3. What can schools and teachers do to help students at risk achieve success?

For feedback, go to the appendix, *Check Your Understanding*, located in the back of this text.

VOICES from the CLASSROOM

"I teach because I know I'm investing in the future of our world . . . and the compounding rewards are endless."

PAMELA LYNCH WILLIAMS, 2011 Teacher of the Year, Georgia

CHAPTER 2

Summary

1. Describe changes that have occurred in the American family over the last 50 years.
   - The traditional family, which historically has been described as a father who is the breadwinner and a mother who works in the home and cares for two children, has become rare in this country.
   - The majority of mothers now work outside the home, raising concerns about child care. Quality child care can provide an environment where children learn both cognitive and interpersonal skills; these skills then provide a foundation when students enter school. In addition, the benefits of quality early child care extend into adulthood.
2. Describe societal changes and the implications of these changes for education.
   - Students are becoming sexually active at an earlier age, placing themselves at risk for pregnancy and sexually transmitted disease. Schools attempt to deal with these problems through sex education programs. Other aspects of student sexuality include homosexuality and sexual harassment. Teachers play an essential role in communicating that sexual harassment won't be tolerated in schools or classrooms.
   - The use of alcohol and other drugs, violence, suicide, and child abuse all present challenges to youth as well as the teachers who work with them. Although the use of alcohol and drugs is declining, significant numbers of students experiment with and use these at an early age.
   - Obesity has become another health issue threatening students. Although it's increasingly common in all students, its negative effects are seen more often in low-SES and cultural minority youths.
   - Crime and violence are on the decline in schools as well as society as a whole but still pose a problem to educators. Bullying is a major school safety issue because of its potential not only to damage individuals but also to lead to more serious forms of violence. In response to these issues, schools have implemented school-wide safety programs.
   - A major response to crime and violence in the schools has been the implementation of zero-tolerance policies that expel students from school for any infraction involving drugs or weapons. Although adopted by a number of school districts, zero-tolerance policies have problems, ranging from increased student dropout rates to punishing students for minor offenses, and differential treatment of minority students.
3. Define socioeconomic status, and explain how different socioeconomic patterns influence school success.
   - Socioeconomic status (SES) describes the combined effects of income, occupation, and educational level on people's attitudes, values, and behaviors. SES can also have powerful influences on how children respond to schools.
   - Poverty presents a number of challenges, ranging from lack of basic needs to unstable home environment. Recently, the rate of childhood poverty has increased, creating challenges for both teachers and students.
   - SES influences educational success in several ways, including whether students' basic needs, such as nutrition and medical care, are met. It also influences the language skills and school-related experiences students bring to the classroom. Finally, SES shapes parents' and students' attitudes and values about the importance of education and school.
   - Homelessness affects large numbers of children, influencing their ability to succeed in school. High percentages of homeless children don't attend school regularly, and when they do, they suffer from inadequate diets and substandard medical care as well as unstable families.
   - Students at risk face a number of challenges to school success, ranging from poverty to transience and unstable families. These conditions result in educational problems that create barriers to school success.
   - Urban schools present many challenges to students at risk. Urban schools are often in high-poverty areas and have less experienced teachers. They are also less well funded than their suburban counterparts and tend to be larger and more impersonal.
   - Community-based approaches to working with students at risk actively involve parents and the community in designing and implementing comprehensive educational programs. Community-based programs attempt to integrate the services available to students by linking various support agencies.
   - Effective schools for students at risk create a safe, orderly learning environment that emphasizes

academic goals. Studies of successful or resilient children suggest that caring home and school environments with supportive, understanding adults can help these students withstand societal challenges. Effective teachers for students at risk combine supportive interpersonal contacts with instructional structure and support.

Important Concepts

bullying
cyberbullying
full-service schools
latchkey children
lower class
middle class
poverty thresholds
resilient students
sexual harassment
socioeconomic status (SES)
students at risk
underclass
upper class
working class
zero-tolerance policies

Portfolio Activity

School Safety and Security

InTASC Principle 9: Professional Learning and Ethical Practice

This activity is designed to familiarize you with school safety and security procedures in the schools in your area. Locate the websites of several local school districts. Browse the sites for information on student conduct policies and procedures, and read how each district handles discipline and safety issues. How are the procedures similar and different? How would they affect your life as a teacher?

Portfolio Activities similar to this one and related to chapter content can be found at MyEducationLab™.

Changes in American Society: Their Influences on Today's Students

Go to the topic *School and Society* in the MyEducationLab (www.myeducationlab.com) for *Introduction to Teaching*, where you can:

- Find learning outcomes for *School and Society,* along with the national standards that connect to these outcomes.
- Complete *Assignments and Activities* that can help you more deeply understand the chapter content.
- Apply and practice your understanding of the core teaching skills identified in the chapter with the *Building Teaching Skills and Dispositions* learning units.
- Examine challenging situations and cases presented in the IRIS Center Resources.
- Access video clips of CCSSO National Teachers of the Year award winners responding to the question, "Why Do I Teach?" in the *Teacher Talk* section.
- Check your comprehension on the content covered in the chapter with the *Study Plan.* Here you will be able to take a chapter quiz, receive feedback on your answers, and then access *Review, Practice, and Enrichment* activities to enhance your understanding of chapter content.
- Check the *Book Resources* to find opportunities to share thoughts and gather feedback on the *Diversity and You* and *Issues You'll Face in Teaching* features found in this chapter.

MyEducationLab™

This I Believe

STUDENT DIVERSITY AND ME

For each of the following statements, circle your choice using the following options:

4 = I strongly believe the statement is true.
3 = I believe the statement is true.
2 = I believe the statement is false.
1 = I strongly believe the statement is false.

1. Culturally sensitive teachers treat all students the same way.
   1 2 3 4
2. Students who aren't native English speakers learn English most effectively by hearing the teacher use correct English.
   1 2 3 4
3. Boys generally get better grades in school than girls.
   1 2 3 4
4. It is important for me to adapt my instruction to the individual learning styles of my students.
   1 2 3 4
5. Experts in special education advocate the creation of special classrooms to meet the needs of students with exceptionalities.
   1 2 3 4

FIGURE 3.1 The Four Dimensions of Student Diversity

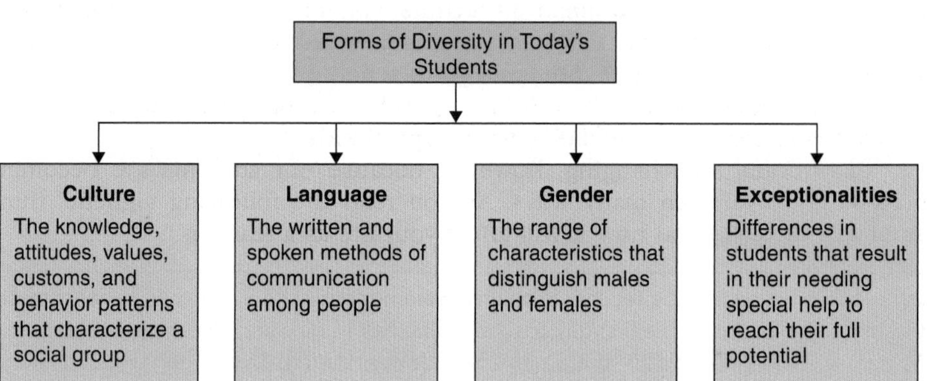

MyEducationLab™

Visit the MyEducationLab for *Introduction to Teaching* to enhance your understanding of chapter concepts with a personalized *Study Plan.* You'll also have the opportunity to hone your teaching skills through video and case-based *Assignments and Activities* and *Building Teaching Skills and Disposition* lessons.

Cultural Diversity

The clothes you wear, the kind of music you like, and even the food you eat, along with other dimensions such as language and religion, are all part of your **culture**, the knowledge, attitudes, values, customs, and behavior patterns that characterize a social group (Banks, 2008). Culture is a powerful force on our lives and will also influence your students' learning as well as your success as a teacher. **Cultural diversity** refers to the different cultures you'll encounter in classrooms and how these differences influence learning.

To see how culture influences us, let's look at eating as a simple example. Do you sit down for dinner at 6:00 in the evening, or do you often wait until 8:00 p.m. or later? Does your family sit down together, or do you "eat on the run"? Do you eat with a knife and fork or perhaps with chopsticks, or even your hands? And if you use a knife and fork, do you cut a piece of meat and then transfer the fork back to your right hand or leave it in your left hand? These patterns are all influenced by culture, and it, of course, influences what we eat as well, as evidenced by the many ethnic restaurants around our country.

Ethnicity, a person's ancestry and the way people identify themselves with the nation from which they or their ancestors came, is an important part of culture. Members of an ethnic group share an identity defined by their history, language (although sometimes not spoken), customs, and traditions. Experts estimate that nearly 300 distinct ethnic groups currently reside in the United States (Gollnick & Chinn, 2013).

Immigration and other demographic shifts have resulted in dramatic changes in our country's school population. Most immigrants during the early 1900s came from Europe, but more recently they have come from Latin America (53%), and Asia (28%), with only 13% having Europe as their point of origin (U.S. Bureau of Census, 2009). U.S. census estimates indicate that members of cultural minorities now make up more than a third of our nation's population (Santa Cruz, 2010), and the 2000 census found, for the first time, that the Hispanic surnames Garcia and Rodriguez are among the 10 most common in our country (S. Roberts, 2007).

This trend is reflected in our classrooms, where more than 4 of 10 students in the P–12 population are members of cultural minorities (Tavernise, 2011). Children of color now make up the majority of school-age youth in 10 states. In Arizona, for example, only 42% of school-age youth are white, compared to 83% of the over-65 population. Experts worry that this generational divide may mean less support from taxpayers who no longer identify with the school population. Further, over 90% of the student population in Detroit, New York, the District of Columbia, Chicago, Houston, and Los Angeles are members of cultural minorities.

For the first time in our history, less than half of 3-year-olds in our country are white (Frey, 2011). This means that white students will no longer be a majority as these children move through our classrooms, and it helps us understand why the backgrounds of Carla's students are so diverse (see Figure 3.2).

FIGURE 3.2 Percentages of Public School Students by Race/Ethnicity

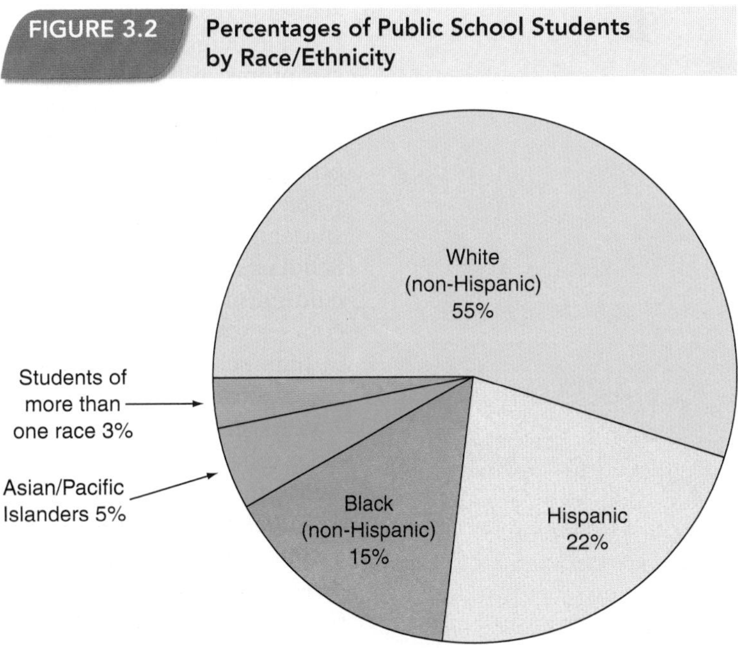

Source: National Center for Education Statistics. (2011). *The condition of education 2011.* Washington, DC: Author.

By the year 2050, the U.S. population will see many more changes (see Figure 3.3). Experts predict considerable increases in the percentages of all groups of people except white, non-Hispanic. During this time, the percentage that is white will decrease from 65% to just half of the total population (U.S. Bureau of Census, 2010b). By 2050, no single group will be a majority among adults.

Cultural Attitudes and Values

Our students come to school with a history of learning influenced by the cultures of their homes and neighborhoods. Some of these attitudes and values complement school learning; others do not (Gollnick & Chinn, 2013).

Language is one example. Students are sometimes hesitant to drop the use of nonstandard English dialects in favor of "school English" because doing so might alienate their peers

FIGURE 3.3 Projected Changes in U.S. Population, 2010 to 2050

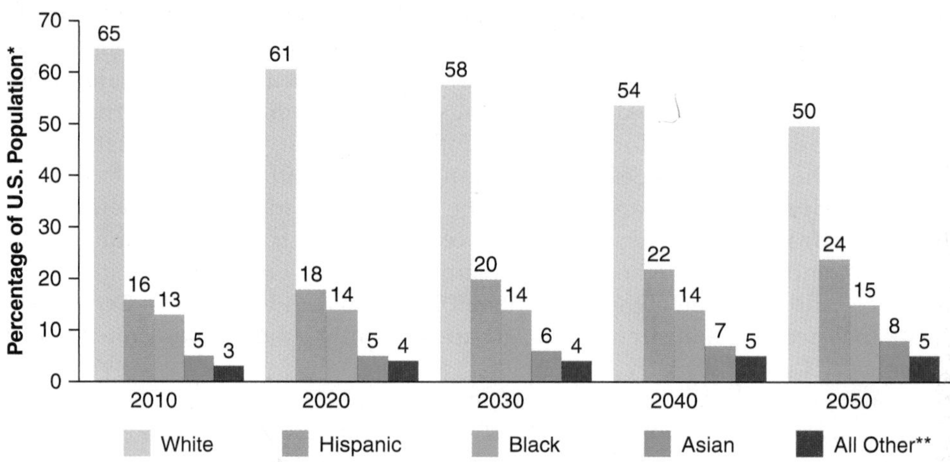

Source: U.S. Bureau of Census (2010b).

(Ogbu, 1999). The same problem occurs in classrooms where students are asked to learn English and to quit using the languages of their homes. Programs encouraging students to drop their native languages can distance them from their parents, who often can't speak English (Shankar, 2011).

Even school success can be an issue. Members of minorities sometimes interpret succeeding in school as rejecting their native culture; to become a good student is to become "white"—to embrace and uphold only white cultural values. Members of minorities who study and succeed academically risk losing the friendship of their peers. John Ogbu, an anthropologist who studied the achievement of minority students, found that in many schools students form what he called "resistance cultures," in which peer values either don't support school learning or actually oppose it (Ogbu & Simons, 1998). Low grades, classroom management and motivation problems, truancy, and high dropout rates are symptoms of this conflict.

In other cases, students' attitudes and values can complement learning. For instance, researchers studying the amazing academic success of Vietnamese and other Asian American students found that hard work, perseverance, and pride were heavily emphasized in the home (Kristoff, 2006). In 2005, Asian American students scored highest (an average 1091) on the math and verbal parts of the Scholastic Aptitude Test (SAT), outscoring white students by 23 points and other cultural minorities by an average of 168 points. Willingness to take challenging courses was a factor. For example, 4 of 10 Asian American students took calculus in high school, compared to fewer than 3 of 10 in the general population. One Vietnamese student who became the valedictorian at her high school after only 7 years in the United States commented, "Anybody can be smart, can do great on standardized tests. But unless you work hard, you're not going to do well" (Kristoff, 2006, p. 13).

Research on Indian students' success in U.S. national spelling bees found a similar emphasis on hard work and study (Bracey, 2005). Children of Indian descent consistently place high in these academic contests, winning much more often than other ethnic groups. Experts joke about an Indian "spelling gene," but emphasize instead the hard work and determination instilled by cultural attitudes and values.

Cultural Interaction Patterns

Our students learn to interact with others at home, but cultural conflict can occur when they enter our classrooms. Let's look at an example:

Cynthia Cole, a second-grade teacher in an elementary school in the Southwest, is reading a story. "What do you think is going to happen next? . . .Tony?" Cynthia asks in response to his eagerly waving hand.

"I think the boy is going to meet his friend."

"How do you think the boy feels about meeting his friend?" she continues.

After Tony responds, Cynthia calls on Sharon Nighthawk, one of the Native Americans in her class, even though Sharon has not raised her hand. When Sharon doesn't answer, Cynthia prompts her by rephrasing the question, but Sharon continues to look at her in silence.

Slightly exasperated, Cynthia wonders if Sharon understands her questions, or if she is asking the right kind of questions, because Sharon seems to be enjoying the story and also understands it. Why won't she answer?

Thinking about the lesson after school, Cynthia realizes that this has happened before, and that, in fact, her Native American students rarely answer questions in class. She can't get them to talk.

How might we explain this problem? Some experts suggest that Native American children aren't used to the fast-paced, question-and-answer patterns found in most American classrooms. When involved in discussions, such as the one in Cynthia's class, they are uncomfortable and reluctant to participate (Banks, 2008). Similar issues can exist with students who are members of other cultures.

So, how should you respond? We address this question when we discuss *culturally responsive teaching* later in this section.

Educational Responses to Cultural Diversity

Historically, social commentators have used different metaphors to describe the relationships among the diverse cultures in our country; a "melting pot" was one of the first. Those who saw the United States as a melting pot emphasized **assimilation**, a process of socializing people so that they adopt dominant social norms and patterns of behavior. Assimilation attempted to make members of minority cultural groups "similar" to those belonging to the dominant cultural group in our country—typically, white people of northern European descent.

The melting pot metaphor was especially popular in the early 1900s, when large numbers of immigrants from southern and eastern Europe came to the United States. Society assigned schools the task of teaching immigrants how "Americans" were supposed to think, talk, and act. Immigrants, eager to become "American" and share in this country's economic wealth, generally accepted assimilation efforts.

About the middle of the 20th century, a shift in thinking occurred. People realized that assimilation had never totally worked, as indicated by neighborhoods and groups that continued to speak their home languages, celebrate their unique cultural holidays, and maintain their cultural habits, such as eating ethnic foods from their home countries. In other words, a true "melting pot" never existed. The contributions of different cultural and ethnic groups were increasingly recognized, and leaders began to realize that some educational practices aimed at assimilation were actually counterproductive. For example, in an effort to encourage English language acquisition, schools in the Southwest didn't allow students to speak Spanish, even on playgrounds. Schools became hostile places where students had to choose between family, friends, and school. The policy probably did as much to alienate Hispanic youth as it did to encourage English language development (Spring, 2010).

Multicultural Education

To address these problems, educators began developing new approaches to addressing cultural diversity. **Multicultural education** describes a variety of strategies schools use to accommodate cultural differences in teaching and learning. Instead of trying to create a melting pot, these approaches align with new metaphors that describe the United States as a "mosaic" or a "tossed salad," in which society recognizes and values each culture's unique contributions.

Multicultural education is controversial. Critics contend that it's divisive because it emphasizes differences between cultural groups instead of what we have in common (Lacey, 2011; Zirkel, 2008b). Textbooks have been scrutinized, and a major controversy even erupted over singing the national anthem in Spanish (D. Goldstein, 2006). Critics argued that the national anthem is a symbol of unity for our country and its Constitution. Criticism became so widespread that bills were submitted in Congress mandating English as the exclusive language for the anthem, even though it has historically been translated and sung in a number of languages, including French, Polish, and Italian.

Proponents of multicultural education assert that building on students' cultures is nothing more than sound teaching. By recognizing, valuing, and utilizing students' cultures and languages in their instruction, teachers help them link the topics they study to what they already know, a process consistent with effective teaching and learning (Eggen & Kauchak, 2013). Proponents also assert that the United States has always been a nation of immigrants and that diversity has long been recognized. They point out, for example, that our society embraces holidays, such as St. Patrick's Day, Cinco de Mayo, Hanukkah, and the Chinese New Year, as well as the music and foods of many cultures. Multicultural education continues this tradition by recognizing and building on students' cultural heritages.

Multicultural education will evolve as educators discover what works and what doesn't. Culturally responsive teaching is one approach to working with students from diverse backgrounds that appears to have promise.

EXPLORING DIVERSITY: Culturally Responsive Teaching

Shannon Wilson, a fifth-grade teacher in a large urban elementary school, walks around her classroom, helping students as they work on a social studies project. A number of hands are raised, and she feels relieved that she has Maria Arguelas, her special education resource teacher, to help her. Shannon has 27 students, 7 of whom speak a first language other than English. Five are Hispanic, and fortunately, Maria can help them with language-related problems. Shannon often spends extra time with Kwan and Abdul, the other two non-English speakers.

Culturally responsive teaching builds on students' cultural backgrounds, accepts and values differences, and accommodates different cultural learning styles.

Shannon's class is preparing for Parents' Day, an afternoon when parents and other caregivers join the class in celebrating the students' ancestral countries. The students present information about the countries' history, geography, and cultures in their projects. The class has already prepared a large world map with pins marking the students' countries of origin. Although several of the pins are clustered in Mexico and Central and South America, the map shows that students also come from many other parts of the world. Each student is encouraged to invite a family member to come and share a part of the family's native culture. The parents can bring food, music, and native dress from their different homelands.

Culturally responsive teaching is instruction that acknowledges and capitalizes on cultural diversity (Gay, 2005; Leonard, 2008). It attempts to do this in three ways:

- Accepting and valuing cultural differences
- Accommodating different patterns of cultural interaction
- Building on students' cultural backgrounds

Accepting and Valuing Cultural Differences. Communicating that you recognize and value student diversity is an important first step, and it's particularly important because members of cultural minorities sometimes feel alienated from school. As a simple example, Shannon had her students identify their ethnic homelands on the map; this showed an interest in each student and helped him or her feel accepted and valued.

Genuine caring is essential in making students feel welcome in classrooms. You can communicate caring in several ways:

- Devote time to students—for example, be available before and after school to help with schoolwork and to discuss students' personal concerns.
- Demonstrate interest in students' lives—for example, ask about Jewish, Muslim, Latin American, and African American holidays and festivals.
- Involve all students in learning activities—for example, call on all students as equally as possible.

Each of these suggestions communicates that you welcome and value all students.

Accommodating Cultural Interaction Patterns. Being sensitive to possible differences between interaction patterns of home and school and adapting your instruction to best meet your students' needs is a second important step. For example, you saw earlier that the communication patterns of Native Americans might clash with typical classroom practices. Recognizing that some of your students may not be comfortable in question-and-answer activities that require one specific answer, you can use more open-ended questions, such as "What do you notice?" and "How do these items compare?" that allow a variety of acceptable responses. Questions such as these involve students and encourage them to respond, while simultaneously removing the pressure to give "the" right answer. Effective teachers also use different cooperative-learning activities to complement their question-and-answer sessions and involve all students.

As another example, when a teacher realized that her routines might clash with her students' cultures, she made a simple adaptation.

> I traditionally end every day with the students lining up and receiving a hug before they leave. My Vietnamese kids were always the stiff huggers until October. Through my understanding of their cultures, I now give all students the choice of a hug, handshake, or high five. This simple act may make children feel more comfortable interacting with me. (McAllister & Irvine, 2002, p. 440)

Accommodating different interaction patterns can help students from diverse backgrounds adapt to the existing culture of schools, without losing their native identities, a process called "accommodation without assimilation" (Ogbu, 2003). Accommodation without assimilation helps students function comfortably in both cultures, including using different language patterns in school than in the home or their neighborhoods. Your challenge is to help students understand the "culture of schooling"—the norms, procedures, and expectations necessary for success in school—while honoring and valuing their home cultures.

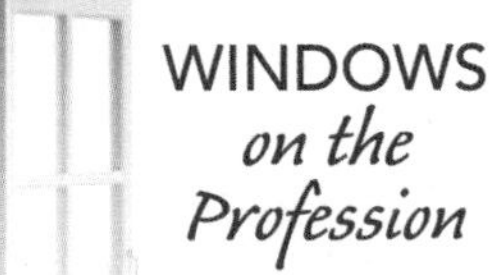

To see an example of culturally responsive teaching in an elementary classroom, click on the video *Culturally Responsive Teaching* (4:16).

Building on Students' Backgrounds. Learning about students' cultures and using this information to promote personal pride and motivation is a third step, as we saw in Shannon's class. Let's look at another example:

Jack Seltzer, a high school biology teacher on the Navajo Nation Reservation, uses his students' background experiences to illustrate hard-to-understand science concepts. He uses Churro sheep, a local breed that Navajos use for food and wool, to illustrate genetic principles. When they study plants, he focuses on local varieties of squash and corn that have been grown by students' ancestors for centuries. He uses geologic formations in nearby Monument Valley to illustrate igneous, sedimentary, and metamorphic rocks. (D. Baker, 2006)

Both students and their parents benefit from building on students' cultural backgrounds. Student achievement increases, and parents become more positive about school, both of which enhance student motivation (Leonard, 2008). Shannon recognized this when she invited parents and other caregivers to share their cultural heritages with her class, and Jack capitalized on this idea by providing examples the students could personally understand and identify with.

URBAN EDUCATION: Cultural Diversity in Urban Schools

The term *cultural minority* is often used to refer to various non-white cultural groups. Based on sheer numbers, this term may soon be obsolete and is already a misnomer in many parts of the country, especially in urban areas. For example, Hispanics, African Americans, and Asians—when combined—now make up the majority of the population in almost half of the 100 largest U.S. cities (Macionis, 2011). In addition, as you saw earlier in the chapter, more than 90% of the students in Detroit, New York, the District of Columbia, Chicago, Houston, and Los Angeles are children of color (Tavernise, 2011).

DIVERSITY AND YOU

Cultural Discontinuities

You've been invited to a community awards ceremony at a local church of Pacific Island immigrants to honor students from your school. (This invitation and the events that followed actually happened to one educator.) You gladly accept, arrive a few minutes early, and are ushered to a seat of honor on the stage. After an uncomfortable (to you) wait of over an hour, the ceremony begins, and the students proudly file to the stage to receive their awards. Each is acknowledged, given an award, and applauded. After this part of the ceremony, you have another eye-opening experience.

The children all go back and sit down in the audience again, and the meeting continues with several more items on the agenda. The kids are fine for a while, but get bored and start to fidget. Fidgeting and whispering turn into poking, prodding, and open chatting. You become a little anxious at the disruption, but none of the other adults appear to even notice, so you ignore it, too. Soon, several of the children are up and out of their seats, strolling about the back and sides of the auditorium. All adult faces continue looking serenely up at the speaker on the stage. Then the kids start playing tag, running circles around the seating area, and yelling gleefully. No adult response—you are amazed, and struggle to resist the urge to quiet the children. Then some of the kids get up onto the stage, run around the speaker, flick the lights on and off, and open and close the curtain! Still nothing from the Islander parents who seem either unaware or unconcerned about the children's behavior! You are caught in the middle of a conflict of cultures—yours and the Pacific Islanders'. You don't know what to do (Based on Winitzky, 1994).

QUESTIONS TO CONSIDER

1. This section discussed two potentially conflicting ideas: accepting and valuing cultural differences and accommodation without assimilation. How do these ideas relate to this dilemma?
2. So, what would you do in this situation, both short-term and long-term?

Go to *Diversity and You* in the MyEducationLab™ *Book Resources* that accompany this text to log your thoughts and receive feedback from your authors.

The growth of minority student populations in urban areas is the result of immigration coupled with higher birth rates. For example, between 1990 and 2000, Hispanic populations increased 43% and Asian populations surged 40% in urban areas (Lichter & Johnson, 2006). Urban centers are often called "gateway cities" for recently arriving immigrants, and this diversity is reflected in urban schools. Across the United States, minority students currently attend schools with populations that are almost half minority; in one high school in New York City, researchers found that African American and Hispanic students made up 97% of the student population, and only 0.5% were white (Goldsmith, 2011; Kozol, 2005). Many of these students don't speak English as their first language, which will pose a challenge for you if you teach in an urban school. Teachers skilled in helping students simultaneously learn English and the content of their classes are sorely needed.

Revisiting My Beliefs

This section addresses the first item in *This I Believe*, "Culturally sensitive teachers treat all students the same way." This statement isn't true and is, in fact, the opposite of culturally responsive teaching. To be most effective, you'll need to adapt your instruction to your students' cultural backgrounds.

TECHNOLOGY and TEACHING: Technology Access Issues

"Technology is everywhere," has become almost a cliché, but this isn't true for all students. Many don't have access to technology, and if they don't, they obviously can't use it to learn.

Surveys of educational technology use across the country found that by 2008 virtually all public schools had Internet access and nearly 4 of 10 had wireless network capability (National Center for Education Statistics, 2010c). Between 1998 and 2008, the ratio of students per Internet-connected computer dropped from 12 to slightly more than 3. So, if your school is typical, and you have a class of 30 students, your classroom should have about 10 Internet-connected computers available. This statistic is misleading, however, because many schools cluster computers in labs where they are accessible only once or twice a week. Teachers still need to do instructional juggling to provide computer access to all students when they need it. In a national survey 91% of teachers said they had access to computers in their classrooms, but only 1 in 5 said they had the right level of technology in their classrooms; cost was identified as a major obstacle (PBS LearningMedia, 2012). When we asked teachers about barriers to effective use of technology, they identified insufficient number of computers as a major problem. Research suggests that the number and quality of computers influence teachers' use of technology (Roblyer & Doering, 2013). When obstacles are too great, teachers tend not to use it, which deprives their students of valuable learning opportunities.

In the past, research revealed disparities in tech access between urban and suburban schools and between schools serving high percentages of students in poverty and those serving more-affluent families (National Center for Education Statistics, 2007). More recent research shows that these differences in tech availability have largely vanished, but there are significant disparities in how technology is actually used in schools. For instance, schools with high concentrations of low-income students are more likely to use computers for practice on basic skills versus for writing essays or developing student-initiated multimedia projects (Gray, Thomas, & Lewis, 2010). These differences become important when students seek entrance to college or jobs in high-skill industries. Home–school communication was also an issue; teachers in high-poverty schools were much less likely to use the Internet to communicate with either parents or students about school-related problems or issues and were less likely to use regular posts to keep parents informed about class progress. These differences create a two-tiered system in which computers are used in very different ways by high- and low-poverty schools.

There is also considerable variation in access to technology among different ethnic groups and particularly among families with differing levels of income and parental education. For example:

- Seventy-six percent of white households have access to the Internet, compared to 70% for African American and 60% of Hispanic households.
- Ninety eight percent of high-income families own computers, and 94% of these families have access to the Internet, whereas 65% of low-income families own computers, and 60% have access to the Internet (Rainie, 2010).
- Ninety four percent of students whose parents have a college degree reported access to the Internet at home versus 39% for households where parents failed to complete high school.

When students are expected to complete assignments at home that require computers and information from the Internet, access can be a serious problem. Long term, access to computers can also influence the career options available to students: Students are less likely to pursue high-tech careers in areas such as science and engineering if they have inadequate technology backgrounds or haven't been introduced to ways that technology can be used in these areas. Preparing all students to compete in such an environment can be a challenge.

But access to technology, alone, might not be the "Great Equalizer" that narrows the achievement gap between poor and wealthy students and minorities and nonminorities. Several studies, both in this country and elsewhere, show that access to computers is only the first step in increasing student learning (Stross, 2010). Left on their own, students tend to use computers to play games and interact with each other instead of accessing the wealth of information available on the Internet or developing their skills with technology. Encouragement and close supervision from adults are essential to increase student learning through access to computers (Stross, 2010).

There is a lesson in this for classroom teachers—just throwing technology at students doesn't guarantee learning. As educators we're tempted to view technology as a "magic bullet" that can solve all of our educational problems, but this is far from true. Classroom teachers need to plan carefully when they use technology, structure lessons strategically, monitor students while they are using it, and evaluate both students and the technology afterward to ensure that using it translates into learning for students.

Check Your Understanding

1.1. Explain how cultural diversity influences learning.
1.2. Describe three ways in which effective teachers respond to cultural diversity in their classrooms.
1.3. Describe the relationship between urban schools and cultural diversity.

For feedback, go to the appendix, *Check Your Understanding*, located in the back of this text.

Language Diversity

Teaching and You

Have you ever tried to learn a language different from the one spoken in your home? Was it easier to learn to speak the language, understand it when spoken, or read it? How proficient were you after 2 or 3 years? How successful would you have been if all the instruction in your other classes were in that language?

Think about the questions we asked in "Teaching and You," and also imagine trying to help students make sense of a topic you're teaching if they can't understand the words you're saying. And what if you can't understand what they're trying to say to you? This is the challenge many teachers in today's schools face.

Language is one of the most important parts of any culture, and language influences learning more than any other single factor. Let's see how one school responds.

Ellie Barton, a language arts teacher at Northeast Middle School, is the school's English language learner (ELL) Coordinator. (You'll also encounter the term English learner [EL], as both are used in education.) She teaches ELL classes and is also in charge of the school's testing and placement program.

Her job is challenging, as her students vary considerably in their knowledge of English. For instance, one group of Somali-Bantu children just arrived from a refugee camp in Kenya. They cannot read or write, because there is no written language for Mai-Mai, their native tongue. Language isn't their only challenge; many had never been in a building with more than one floor, and others found urinals and other aspects of indoor plumbing a mystery. At the other end of the continuum is a young girl from India who can read and write in four languages: Hindi, the national language of India; Urdu, the language of her Persian ancestors; Telegu, a regional language in India; and Arabic.

To sort out this language diversity, the district uses a placement test that categorizes students into three levels: newcomer classrooms for students who have little or no expertise with English; self-contained ELL classrooms, where a primary emphasis is on learning to read and write English; and sheltered English, where students receive structured help in learning academic subjects such as science and social studies. However, the placement process is not foolproof, since English skills are sometimes nonexistent, and some parents don't know the exact ages of their children. Ellie's principal deals with this information void in creative ways; he recently asked a dentist friend to look at a student's teeth to estimate the child's age. (Based on Romboy & Kinkead, 2005)

As you saw earlier in the chapter, immigration has brought increasing numbers of students with limited backgrounds in English to our country's classrooms. The number of **English learners (ELs)**, students whose first language is not English and who need help in learning to speak, read, and write in English, increased by more than 60% between 1995 and 2009, totaling more than 5 million students, or more than 10% of the student population (National Clearinghouse for English Language Acquisition, 2011). Currently, over 22% of our students are either foreign-born or have at least one foreign-born parent. Experts predict that by 2030 two of five students will be enrolled in programs designed to teach English (Shah, 2012). Currently, 440 languages are spoken in the United States, with Spanish (73%), Chinese (4%) and Vietnamese (3%), the most common (Migration Policy Institute, 2010).

Language Diversity: The Government's Response

Public interest in educating students who are ELs increased with the passage of the No Child Left Behind (NCLB) Act of 2001, which required states to document the educational progress of each specific group of students, including ELs. The federal government, through legislation and court rulings, initially attempted to address the needs of EL students through bilingual approaches, strategies intended to maintain the first language while students learned English. In 1968, Congress passed the Bilingual Education Act, which provided federal funds for educating nonnative English speakers. In the controversial 1974 *Lau v. Nichols* case, the Supreme Court ruled unanimously that the San Francisco School District unlawfully discriminated against minority students by failing to address non-English-speaking children's language problems (Schimmel, Stellman, & Fischer, 2011). But in 1998 more than 60% of the voters in California passed Proposition 227 to replace bilingual education programs with a fast-track to English; EL students were provided with a special pullout English immersion program for 1 year and then shifted into mainstream English-only classrooms (McCloskey, Pellegrin, Thompson, & Hakuta, 2008). And 29 different states have passed legislation making English the official language in that state (see Figure 3.4). The effectiveness of these actions is still being debated, as you'll see in the *Issues You'll Face in Teaching* feature in this chapter.

FIGURE 3.4 States with Official Language Legislation

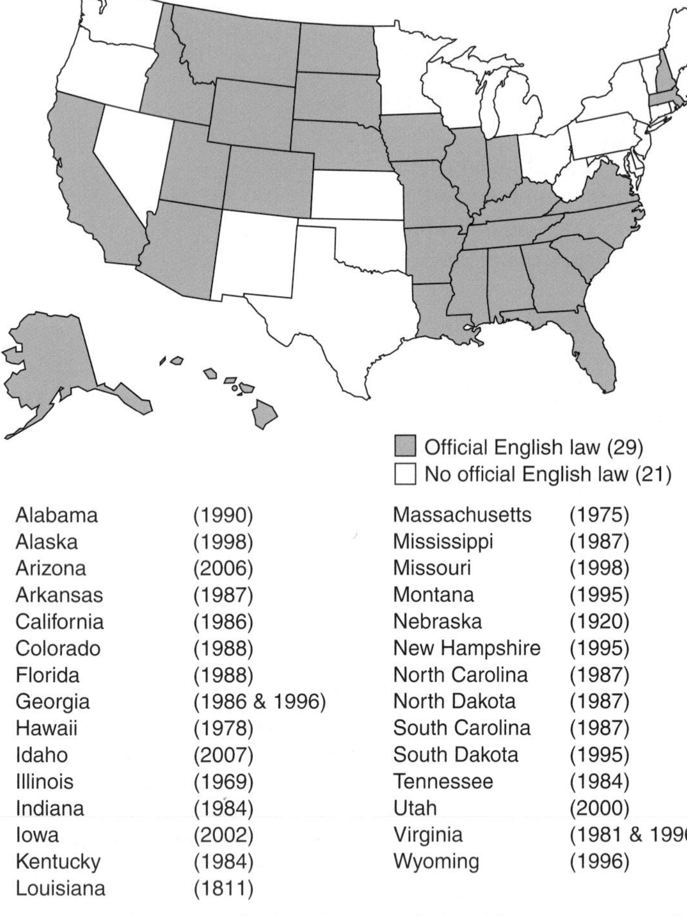

Alabama	(1990)	Massachusetts	(1975)
Alaska	(1998)	Mississippi	(1987)
Arizona	(2006)	Missouri	(1998)
Arkansas	(1987)	Montana	(1995)
California	(1986)	Nebraska	(1920)
Colorado	(1988)	New Hampshire	(1995)
Florida	(1988)	North Carolina	(1987)
Georgia	(1986 & 1996)	North Dakota	(1987)
Hawaii	(1978)	South Carolina	(1987)
Idaho	(2007)	South Dakota	(1995)
Illinois	(1969)	Tennessee	(1984)
Indiana	(1984)	Utah	(2000)
Iowa	(2002)	Virginia	(1981 & 1996)
Kentucky	(1984)	Wyoming	(1996)
Louisiana	(1811)		

Source: U.S. English. (2011). *Official English: Why is official English necessary?* Retrieved from http://www.usenglish.org/view/10

Bowing to public pressure, the federal government has more recently changed course, advocating that schools should teach English, with little attempt to preserve minority languages. With this shift in thinking, the previous federal Office of Bilingual Education now has become the Office of English Language Acquisition (OELA). In 2006, during a debate on immigration reform, the U.S. Senate voted to designate English as the national language (Hulse, 2006). Now the federal government's major goal is to teach English to students who are ELs as quickly as possible.

Language Diversity: Schools' Responses

Despite the federal position on EL instruction, schools across the country, when faced with the reality of educating EL students, have responded to the challenge of language diversity in very different ways (see Figure 3.5). Although all of the programs are designed ultimately to teach English, they differ in how fast English is introduced and to what extent the first language is encouraged and maintained.

Bilingual maintenance language programs place the greatest emphasis on using and sustaining the first language while teaching English. In these programs, students initially receive most or all of their instruction in their first language, which is usually Spanish, and a corresponding small percentage in English (Tong, Lara-Alecio, Irby, Mathes, & Kwok, 2008). The emphasis on English then increases in each subsequent grade. The future of maintenance programs is uncertain, given the English Acquisition component of NCLB, which discourages such programs.

Educational responses to language diversity differ in the degree to which they build on and attempt to maintain students' first language.

At the opposite end of the continuum, **immersion** and **English as a second language (ESL) programs** emphasize rapid transition to English, with no efforts to maintain students' native language. ESL programs, the most common educational response to linguistic diversity, vary across the country, with some focusing on general education classroom-based ESL, others on pullout ESL instruction, and still others on sheltered or structured English instruction (Viadero, 2009b). Halfway between the two ends of the continuum, **transition programs** maintain the first language until students acquire sufficient English to succeed in English-only classrooms; the primary goal is to help students reach English proficiency.

Logistics are often a factor when schools consider which type of program to use. For example, transition programs can be effective when classes are composed of large numbers of EL

FIGURE 3.5 Different EL Instruction Programs

Bilingual Maintenance	Transition Programs	English as a Second Language	Immersion
Teach English while still maintaining students' native language.	Use students' first language initially, and then introduce English gradually.	Provide instruction in English, but attempt to adapt instruction to learner needs.	Place students in English-only classes with minimal adjustments to the curriculum or instruction.

students who speak the same language, such as Spanish-speaking students in Los Angeles, because a teacher who speaks the students' native language can be hired. This isn't possible when several first languages exist. This happened at Northeast Middle School and is a primary reason why Ellie Barton teaches in an ELL program that places minimal emphasis on students' first language.

ISSUES YOU'LL FACE IN TEACHING

Bilingual Education

Bilingual education is controversial and reflects our country's changing views about immigration and assimilation. Through the Bilingual Education Act of 1968 and guidelines drafted as a result of *Lau v. Nichols* in 1974, the federal government signaled its commitment to providing services for nonnative English speakers. But in 2002, Congress failed to renew the Bilingual Education Act, instead packaging funds for English language learners into NCLB, which requires students to attain "English fluency" in 3 years and requires schools to teach students in English after that time period (Viadero, 2009b). In addition, state-level proposals, similar to Proposition 227 in California, passed in 26 other states and sharply curtailed the use of bilingual programs across the country, replacing them with English-only immersion programs (R. Garcia, 2006).

The essence of bilingual programs is an attempt to maintain and build on students' native languages while they learn English. Proponents claim that maintaining and building on students' native language not only make sense from a learning perspective but also produce adults who can navigate in other languages. Critics contend that bilingual programs are divisive and slow down the rate of English acquisition.

THE QUESTION

Are bilingual programs designed to maintain students' native languages an effective way to teach English, or are other approaches, such as English immersion, more effective? Here are the arguments on both sides of the issue.

PRO

- Bilingual programs make sense educationally because they build on and reinforce students' first language (Hakuta, 2011; Tong et al., 2008).
- Immersion programs place unrealistic demands on students who are faced with the dual task of learning English and a content area at the same time (Gollnick & Chinn, 2013).
- Because bilingual programs produce students who can speak two languages, they make sense economically. People who can speak more than one language will become increasingly valuable in today's global economy.
- Research shows that knowledge and skills acquired in a native language are "transferable" to the second language, providing students with a better understanding of the role of language in communication and how language works (Gugliemi, 2008).

CON

- Critics of bilingual education contend that it is divisive, encouraging groups of nonnative English speakers to remain separate from mainstream American culture.
- Bilingual programs are ineffective, slowing the process of acquiring English for ELL students.
- Bilingual programs are inefficient, requiring expenditures for the training of bilingual teachers and materials that could be better spent on quality monolingual programs (U.S. English, 2011).

YOU TAKE A STAND

So what is the best way to help EL students learn English? Do bilingual maintenance programs provide a more effective and humane way to learn English, or is it better to immerse students in an English-rich environment to speed up the process?

Go to *Issues You'll Face in Teaching* in the MyEducationLab™ *Book Resources* that accompany this text to log your thoughts and receive feedback from your authors.

Language Diversity in Your Classroom

As you work with EL students, it's easy to fall into the trap of tacitly assuming that they're all similar in terms of their backgrounds in their native languages. This isn't true (Zehr, 2009). As with students in general, some come from homes where books, newspapers, and the Internet are a regular part of their lives, but others come from families whose members can barely read and write in their native language. When these students enter your classroom, they bring considerable diversity in terms of their grasp of the mechanics and power of language.

Also, the ability to converse in English doesn't mean students can learn effectively in English (Hakuta, 2011). Students who are ELs usually pick up enough English to communicate with peers and teachers after 3 or 4 years, but it can take up to 8 years to learn enough English to function effectively in academic content areas.

The likelihood is high that you'll have students in your classroom whose first language is not English. Your ability to make informed professional decisions will be essential to help them learn. In working with students from diverse cultural and language backgrounds, your professional knowledge will be tested, perhaps more than in any other area of your work. If you have ever tried to learn another language, you can understand how difficult the process is. Vocabulary and grammar are constant challenges and often interfere with understanding. Try to remember your own struggles as you work with students attempting to master English.

Teaching EL Students

Research offers a number of suggestions for working with students from varying language backgrounds (Echevarria & Graves, 2011; Peregoy & Boyle, 2009):

- Create a warm and supportive classroom environment by taking a personal interest in all students and involving everyone in learning activities. Get to know students, and strive to personalize the content you're teaching.
- Mix whole-class instruction with group work and cooperative learning to allow students to interact informally and practice their developing language skills with the topics they study.
- Use question-and-answer sessions to involve all students in classroom activities and concrete examples to provide reference points for new ideas and vocabulary. Continually check for understanding through questions, assignments, and quizzes. Misunderstandings are a normal part of teaching and are even more common with students who are members of cultural minorities. Use these checks to adjust instruction.
- Avoid situations that draw attention to students' lack of English skills, such as making students read aloud in front of the whole class.

These strategies represent good instructional practice for all students; for ELL students, they're essential.

How will language diversity affect you as a teacher? First, although bilingual programs have been reduced, the need for teachers with EL expertise will only increase. Experts estimate that in the near future, U.S. schools will need almost 60,000 additional teachers with ESL certification to meet the demands of these students, and 11 states have incentive policies to encourage teachers to pursue studies in this area (Honawar, 2009). In addition, the U.S. Department of Labor has targeted bilingual teachers as a critical need area, especially in urban and rural districts (Bureau of Labor Statistics, 2011). Teacher candidates who speak two languages, especially Spanish, are in high demand across the country.

Revisiting My Beliefs

This section addresses the second question in *This I Believe*, "Students who aren't native English speakers learn English most effectively by hearing the teacher use correct English." This statement isn't true: The only truly effective way for students to learn English is to practice it in language-related activities.

Check Your Understanding

2.1. What has been the government's response to language diversity in our nation's schools?

2.2. Bilingual education and other approaches that primarily focus on teaching English differ radically in both philosophies and practices. What are the primary differences in these two major approaches schools use in working with English language learners?

2.3. What are the major ways that teachers can adapt their instruction to meet the needs of students with varying language backgrounds?

For feedback, go to the appendix, *Check Your Understanding*, located in the back of this text.

Gender

What Geri Peterson sees on her first day of teaching Advanced Placement calculus is both surprising and disturbing: Of the 26 students watching her, only 4 are girls, and they sit quietly in class, responding only when she asks them direct questions. One reason that Geri has gone into teaching is to share her interest in math with other females, but this situation gives her little chance to do so.

Teaching and You

Think about this class. What is the ratio of males to females? Is it similar to other classes you're taking? How would the ratio be different if it were an engineering or computer science class?

Lori Anderson, the school counselor at an urban middle school, looks up from the desk where she is working on her annual report to the faculty. From her course work at the university and her internship, she knows that boys traditionally outnumber girls with respect to behavioral problems, but the numbers she sees are disturbing. In every category—referrals by teachers, absenteeism, tardies, and fights—boys outnumber girls by more than 2 to 1. In addition, the number of boys referred to her for special education testing far exceeds referrals for girls.

Gender and Society

Why did you choose your current major? Did your gender play a role in the decision? If you are like students in other areas, there's a chance it did. For example, 85% of teachers are female, but instructors of computer science courses at the university level report just the opposite; the vast majority of their students are male (Feistritzer, 2011).

The fact that males and females are different is so obvious that we often don't think about it, but research has uncovered some important gender-related differences. For example, females generally are more extroverted, anxious, and trusting; they're less assertive and have slightly lower self-esteem than males of the same age and background; and their verbal and motor skills tend to develop faster than boys' (Berk, 2012). In addition, the play habits of boys and girls differ, with boys typically preferring more "rough and tumble" play. These gender differences will also influence learning and teaching in your classroom.

Why do these differences exist? As with most other individual differences, research suggests the influence of both genetics and environment (Berk, 2012). Genetics largely determines physical differences such as size and growth rate and may also influence temperament, aggressiveness, and early verbal and exploratory behaviors. And some researchers now believe that boys' and girls' brains are wired differently for learning. For example, components of the brain that focus on words and fine-motor skills are developmentally a year ahead in girls, which gives them an advantage in reading, small-motor tasks, such as using pencils and scissors, and printing and cursive writing. Emotional centers in the brain are also more advanced for girls, making them calmer and more able to sit still for the long periods that classrooms often require (Eliot, 2010). Some wonder if schools, as they currently exist, may be more compatible with girls' genetic makeup (Gurian & Stevens, 2007).

Our environment also influences gender differences. From the day we're born, boys and girls are treated differently (Berk, 2012). Girls are given pink blankets, are called cute and pretty, and are handled delicately. Boys are dressed in blue, are regarded as handsome, and are seen as tougher, better coordinated, and hardier. Fathers are rougher with their sons and involve them in more physical stimulation and play; they tend to be gentler with their daughters and offer more gender-stereotyped toys, such as dolls and stuffed animals. Not surprisingly, boys and girls grow up looking and acting differently.

Gender and Classrooms

Differences between boys and girls should generally be celebrated, but **gender bias** becomes a problem when forces in schools and the larger society limit the growth and academic potential of either boys or girls, as happened in Geri Peterson's AP calculus class. In high school, girls score lower than boys on the math sections of the SAT and the ACT, two tests that are essential for college admission, and women score lower on all sections of the Graduate Record Exam, the Medical College Admissions Test, and admissions tests for law, dental, and optometry schools (Alperstein, 2005; Halpern, Benbow, Geary, Gur, Hyde, & Gemsbacher, 2007; O'Shea, Heilbronner, & Reis, 2010). These tests are important because they serve as gatekeepers to high-paying professions.

But as you saw in Lori Anderson's school, boys have their own problems (Berk, 2012; Wallace, Goodkind, Wallace, & Bachman, 2008). They're retained or held back in grade more often, they're more than twice as likely to be placed in **special education** classes, and they far outnumber girls in remedial English and math classes. Boys receive both lower grades and the majority of failing grades, and they are more likely to drop out of school. They are also cited for disciplinary infractions much more often than girls.

So, we have an uneven picture of male and female strengths and weaknesses, but historically, concerns about girls received the most attention. For instance, in *How Schools Shortchange Girls*, the American Association of University Women (AAUW, 1992) argued that differential treatment of boys and girls by both teachers and society seriously hampered the educational progress, self-esteem, and career choices of girls. In the 1998 *Gender Gaps: Where Schools Still Fail Our Children*, the AAUW reiterated many of its earlier claims.

These assertions are controversial and have been countered by others. For example, popular books such as *The Problem with Boys' Education* (Martino, Kehler & Weaver-Hightower, 2009) and *Guyland: The Perilous World Where Boys Become Men* (Kimmel, 2008) assert that males are being shortchanged by our educational system. Yet it's the myth of the fragile girl that continues to receive the lion's share of attention, these authors argue.

Boys' educational problems extend into college. Women are more likely to attend college, earn a degree (57% to 43%), get higher grades, and earn a master's degree (59% to 41%). And women earn the majority of research PhDs awarded to U.S. citizens (Sommers, 2008).

As with gender differences in general, a combination of genetics and the environment probably explains the relative strengths and weaknesses of boys and girls in school. Because little can be done about genetics, more attention has been given to the environment, particularly the part gender-role identity differences play in shaping student behaviors. **Gender-role identity** describes societal differences in expectations and beliefs about appropriate roles and behaviors of the two sexes. Society treats boys and girls differently and expects them to develop different gender-role identities. These identity differences aren't a problem unless they perpetuate stereotypes or negatively influence behavior, learning, or expectations for school success. A **stereotype** is a rigid, simplistic caricature of a particular group of people. For example, "Women aren't good at math" and "Men don't make good nurses or teachers" are both inaccurate and damaging stereotypes because they limit career choices.

Revisiting My Beliefs

This section addresses the third item in *This I Believe*, "Boys generally get better grades in school than girls." This statement is not true, and in fact, the opposite is the case: Girls generally do better than boys on a number of academic measures, with grades being one of the most obvious.

Gender and Career Choices

Look around your classroom for this course; if it's a typical education course, the vast majority of the students are women. The same would be true for classes in nursing, but you would find the opposite in math, science, engineering, and computer-related fields (Cavanagh, 2008).

Where do stereotypes of "appropriate" careers for boys and girls originate? Some are perpetuated by society, but ironically, parents—and particularly mothers—also play a major role. For example, when mothers believe that math is a male domain—a negative gender-stereotyped view—their daughters take fewer math classes, get lower grades in them, and are less likely to view math positively (Cavanagh, 2008).

Nontraditional role models can help prevent students from forming gender-stereotypic views about appropriate careers.

Gender-stereotypic views can also negatively influence career decisions (Hill, Corbett, & Rose, 2010). For example, only 20% of the bachelor's degrees in engineering and physical and computer sciences go to women. At the high school level, only 19% of students taking the College Board Advanced Placement test in Computer Science in 2009 were women, only slightly higher than the percentage of undergraduate female majors (19%) (Hafner, 2012; National Center for Women and Information Technology, 2010). While slightly more than 50% of all doctorates are earned by women, the percentage in science-related fields remains low—33% in physics and earth science, 27% in math and computer science, and 22% in engineering (Jaschik, 2010). Many of the gender-stereotypic views of math, science, and computer science careers begin in middle and high school, where too many females avoid taking challenging advanced math and science courses; this problem is especially acute for minority females (Riegle-Crumb & King, 2010).

Similar gender-related problems exist for men. Go to any elementary school, and you'll see that the faculty is overwhelmingly female. This is especially true at the kindergarten and preschool levels, where 97% of the teachers are female (MenTeach, 2010). And although more men are choosing nursing as a career, they remain a distinct minority (just 7% of registered nurses) (Vigeland, 2012).

Single-Sex Classrooms and Schools

What would you say to a class of fifth graders who weren't working hard enough? Here is how one urban teacher responded, "You—let me see you trying! Come on, faster!" Another, right across the hall, said this, "This is so sloppy, honey. Remember what I spoke to you about? About being the bright shining star that

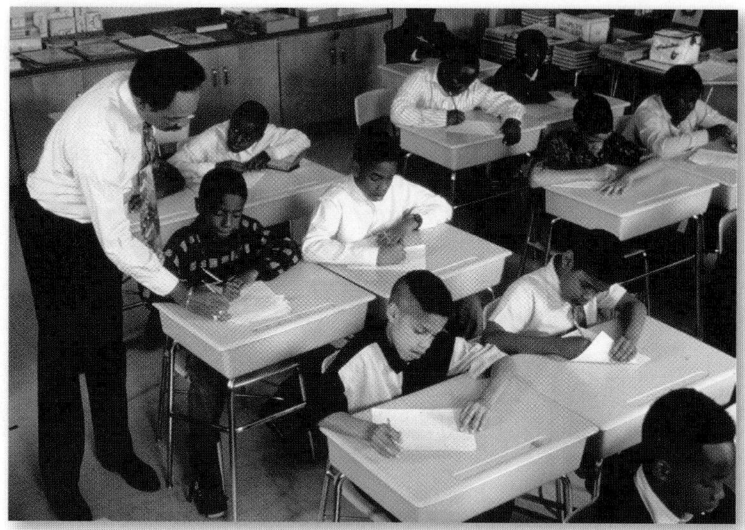

Single-sex classrooms attempt to build on students' strengths and remove the distractions from the other sex.

you are?" (Medina, 2009b, p. A24). Can you guess which teacher was talking to an all-girls class and which was addressing a room full of boys?

The creation of **single-sex classes and schools**, where boys and girls are segregated for part or all of the day, is one response to gender-related learning problems. One argument for single-sex classrooms is that they minimize distractions from the other sex that interfere with learning. One director of a single-sex school notes, "The boys don't feel like they need to put on a big show for the girls, and the girls feel like they can strive academically without having to dumb down their ability" (Standen, 2007, p. 47). Separating boys and girls also allows teachers to adjust their teaching to the specific needs and interests of each.

The number of single-sex classrooms in the United States has increased dramatically, from less than a dozen in 2000 to 510 in 2011. In addition, there are now 95 completely single-sex schools in the United States (Medina, 2009b; Zubrzycki, 2012).

Why this interest in single-sex classrooms and schools? Advocates claim that both girls and boys benefit from single-sex schools (Sullivan, Joshi, & Leonard, 2010). Girls in these schools are more likely to assume leadership roles, take more math and science courses, and have higher self-esteem. Advocates of all-male schools claim that they promote male character development and are especially effective with boys from low-income and minority families (Patterson, 2012).

However, a more recent study on single-sex schooling disputes these claims and even calls for a ban on the practice (Halpern et al., 2011). These critics assert that academic achievement is no higher in single-sex classrooms, gender stereotypes are reinforced, boys become more aggressive, and girls' assertiveness is reduced.

Research raises other issues. Because boys and girls are isolated from one another, single-sex schools and classes might not prepare students for the "real world," where males and females must work together (Standen, 2007). One critic observed, "a boy who has never been beaten by a girl on an algebra test could have some major problems having a female supervisor" (Medina, 2009b, p. A24). Some critics also question the legality of single-sex schools and classrooms based on Title IX, the federal law that prohibits discrimination on the basis of sex, but recent federal directives suggest that these are legal if participation is voluntary and comparable educational opportunities are available to both sexes (Schimmel, Stellman, et al., 2011). More research is needed to determine the long-term effects of this experiment and whether these changes are effective for helping students learn and develop. At this point, the research is inconclusive (Zubrzycki, 2012).

Interestingly, single-sex classrooms, or at least segregation of the sexes, were common in colonial schools in the United States. On the other hand, England, with a long history of private, single-sex schools, is currently moving away from them and toward coeducational classrooms (Younger & Warrington, 2006).

Gender and Classrooms: Implications for Teachers

What can you do to promote gender equality in your classroom? The following suggestions offer guidance:

- Communicate openly with students about gender issues and concerns. Simply telling your students that teachers often treat boys and girls differently and that you're going to work to treat them equally is a positive first step.

- Encourage equal participation in all classes. One demanding but extremely effective technique is to call on everyone in your classes individually and by name, regardless of whether their hands are raised (Kauchak & Eggen, 2012).
- Make an effort to present examples of men and women in nonstereotypical roles, such as women who are engineers and men who are first-grade teachers.
- Encourage girls to pursue science-related careers and boys to consider careers in nontraditional male fields, such as nursing and teaching.
- Talk to parents—and particularly mothers—and remind them to be careful about how they talk to their daughters about careers in math-related fields. Let's see how one high school math teacher addresses this problem.

Effective teachers are sensitive to gender differences in the classroom and make a conscious effort to involve all students.

> When I meet my parents at open house, one of the things that I emphasize is the importance of avoiding negative comments about math, such as, "Well, I was never very good at math either." It almost gives the girls in my class an excuse for not doing well. Then, I re-emphasize it during parent–teacher conferences. My dad used to say to me, "None of this 'Math isn't for girls' stuff in this house," when I was growing up, and it made a huge difference. I never considered the possibility that math wasn't a field for me because I was a girl. (Nicole Shantz, Personal Communication, November 26, 2012)

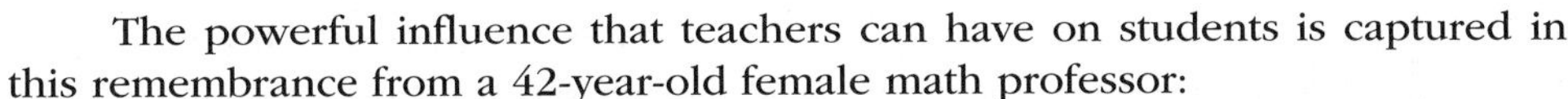

The powerful influence that teachers can have on students is captured in this remembrance from a 42-year-old female math professor:

> It was the first time I had algebra, and I loved it. And then, all of a sudden, I excelled in it. And the teacher said, "Oh no, you should be in the honors course," or something like that. So, there's somebody who definitely influenced me because I don't think I ever even noticed. I mean, I didn't care one way or the other about mathematics. It was just something you had to do. I remember she used to run up and down the aisle. She was real excited. . . . She said, "Oh, you gotta go in this other class. You gotta." And she kind of pushed a little bit, and I was willing to be pushed. (Zeldin & Pajares, 2000, p. 232)

The student ended up majoring in math and ultimately became a math professor. When teachers believe in their students, students start believing in themselves. No one is suggesting that boys and girls are, or should be, the same. Nevertheless, you should strive to provide the same academic opportunities and encouragement for all your students.

Check Your Understanding

3.1. Explain how society influences gender differences in our students.

3.2. How should teachers respond to gender differences?

For feedback, go to the appendix, *Check Your Understanding*, located in the back of this text.

Learners with Exceptionalities

In our country more than 6.5 million students are diagnosed as having **exceptionalities**, learning or emotional needs that result in their requiring special help to succeed and reach their full potential. Most get help in general education classrooms, which means you will, without question, work with these students when you begin your teaching career (Samuels, 2010). How will exceptionalities influence your teaching? Let's look at one teacher's experience.

Celina Curtis, a beginning first-grade teacher in a large elementary school, has survived her hectic first weeks. She is beginning to feel comfortable, but at the same time, some things are bothering her.

"It's kind of frustrating," she admits to Clarisse, a veteran who has become her friend and confidante. "I think I'm teaching, but some of the kids just don't seem to get it.

"For instance, there's Rodney. You've seen him on the playground. He's cute, but his engine is stuck on fast. I can barely get him to sit in his seat, much less work. The smallest distraction sets him off. He can usually do the work if I can get him to stick to it, but it's tough. I've talked to his mother, and he's the same way at home.

"Then there's Amelia; she's so sweet, but she simply doesn't get it. I've tried everything under the sun with her. I explain it, and the next time, it's as if it's all brand new. I feel sorry for her, because I know she gets frustrated when she can't keep up with the other kids. When I work with her one-on-one, it seems to help, but I don't have enough time to spend with her. She's falling farther and farther behind."

"Maybe it's not your fault. You're supposed to do your best, but you're going to burn yourself out if you keep this up," Clarisse cautions. "Check with one of the special ed teachers. Maybe these students need some extra help."

When you begin your teaching career, you will have experiences similar to Celina's. You will have students like Rodney and Amelia, both of whom may have an exceptionality, which means they need special help to succeed in school. And you may also have students who are **gifted and talented**, learners with abilities at the upper end of the continuum who require support beyond general education classroom instruction to reach their full potential.

That's why we're introducing you to the study of students with exceptionalities at this early point in your teacher preparation program. In today's schools almost 1 of 10 students has some type of exceptionality that requires extra help (Hardman et al., 2011). And the trend is to place more and more of these students in general educational settings instead of segregated facilities. In 2009, for example, 95% of **students with exceptionalities** were educated in general education schools (National Center for Education Statistics, 2011d).

The terms *children with exceptionalities, students with special needs*, and *individuals with* **disabilities** have all been used to describe students needing additional help to reach their full potential, and you may encounter any of them when you begin teaching. Notice that in these terms, *children, students*, and *individuals* come first. This "people-first" mind-set emphasizes that, foremost, these individuals are people like all of us, and they deserve to be treated with the same care and respect.

Because it plays an important role in understanding and helping students with exceptionalities, we begin by examining the concept of *intelligence*.

Intelligence

We all know people we think are "sharp," because they're knowledgeable, perceptive, or learn new ideas quickly and easily. These are intuitive notions of **intelligence**, which experts define as the ability to acquire and use knowledge, solve problems and reason in the abstract, and adapt to new situations in our environments (Garlick, 2010; Gläscher et al., 2010).

The ability to benefit from experience is a simple way to think about intelligence. For instance, if we could hypothetically give two people exactly the same set of experiences, the more intelligent of the two will derive more benefit from them. Intelligence is important for all of us involved in teaching, because it relates to important aspects of learning, such as success in school and behavior problems. For example, high intelligence correlates with academic achievement, whereas low intelligence correlates with higher incidence of school problems and delinquent behavior (Laird, Pettit, Dodge, & Bates, 2005).

Experts suggest that you're likely to have students with intelligence test (IQ) scores ranging from 60 or 70 to 130 or 140 in an average, heterogeneously grouped classroom (Hardman et al., 2011). This range is so great that students at the lower end would be classified as intellectually handicapped, whereas students at the upper end might be considered gifted and/or talented. You're likely to encounter the full spectrum of ability levels when you begin teaching.

Changes in Views of Intelligence: Multiple Intelligences

Historically, researchers believed that intelligence was a single trait and that all people could be classified along a single continuum of "general" intelligence (Salvia, Ysseldyke, & Bolt, 2010). Thinking has changed, however, and many researchers now believe that intelligence is composed of several distinct dimensions that may occur alone or in various combinations in different individuals. In other words, we can be "smart" in many ways instead of just one.

Howard Gardner, a psychologist who did groundbreaking work in this area, is one of the best-known proponents of this idea (Gardner, 1983; Gardner & Moran, 2006). He proposed a theory of **multiple intelligences**, which suggests that overall intelligence is composed of eight relatively independent dimensions (see Table 3.1).

Gardner's theory makes sense intuitively and is popular with teachers (Cuban, 2004a). We all know people who don't seem particularly "sharp" analytically but who excel in getting along with others, for example. This ability serves them well, and in some instances, they're more successful in life than their "brighter" counterparts. Others are extraordinary athletes or accomplished musicians. Gardner describes these people as high in interpersonal, bodily-kinesthetic, and musical intelligence, respectively.

On the other hand, Gardner's work has a number of vocal critics. For instance, some caution that the theory and its applications have not been validated by research and have no support from research in cognitive neuroscience (Waterhouse, 2006). Others disagree with the assertion that abilities in specific domains, such as music, qualify as separate forms of intelligence (McMahon, Rose, & Parks, 2004). Some even argue that it isn't truly a theory (Chen, 2004).

Also, despite the theory's popularity with teachers, most classrooms focus heavily on the linguistic and logical-mathematical dimensions of Gardner's theory and virtually ignore the others (Seider, 2009). To develop the other dimensions,

TABLE 3.1 Gardner's Dimensions of Intelligence

Dimension	Description	Individuals Who Might Be High in This Dimension
Linguistic intelligence	Sensitivity to the meaning and order of words and the varied uses of language	Poet, journalist
Logical-mathematical intelligence	The ability to handle long chains of reasoning and to recognize patterns and order in the world	Scientist, mathematician
Musical intelligence	Sensitivity to pitch, melody, and tone	Composer, violinist
Spatial intelligence	The ability to perceive the visual world accurately and to re-create, transform, or modify aspects of the world on the basis of one's perceptions	Sculptor, navigator
Bodily-kinesthetic intelligence	A fine-tuned ability to use the body and to handle objects	Dancer, athlete
Interpersonal intelligence	An understanding of interpersonal relations and the ability to make distinctions among others	Therapist, salesperson
Intrapersonal intelligence	Access to one's own "feeling life"	Self-aware individual
Naturalist intelligence	The ability to recognize similarities and differences in the physical world	Biologist, anthropologist

Source: Based on H. Gardner and Hatch (1989) and Chekles (1997).

students need to explore and practice them. For example, if well-organized and carefully supervised, cooperative learning activities can help students develop interpersonal intelligence, participation in sports or dance can improve bodily-kinesthetic abilities, and playing in a band or singing in choral groups can improve musical intelligence.

Emotional Intelligence

Have you ever had a person make a rude remark to you and thought, "I'd love to tell him [or her] where to go!"? But you don't. In restraining yourself, you might be demonstrating **emotional intelligence**, the ability to manage our emotions so we can cope with our world and accomplish goals. It's another important form of intelligence and includes factors such as:

- Controlling impulses to behave in socially unacceptable ways (controlling the impulse to tell the other person where to go)
- Managing negative emotions (able to forget about the rude remark after initially feeling angry about it)
- Behaving in socially acceptable ways (deciding to talk calmly to the person about the remark, or simply leaving)

Students who can manage their emotions are happier, better adjusted, and better able to make and keep friends than those who can't. In addition, they're also better students, because they're able to focus their emotions on the learning task (Berk, 2013).

As we would expect, children differ considerably in their ability to control and regulate their emotions. Older children are better at it than their younger counterparts, and language plays a role, providing a tool they can use to examine and monitor their emotions (e.g., "I know I feel badly about how I did on the test, but I'll try to study harder for the next one."). Boys have a harder time than girls controlling negative emotions, and consequently boys tend to act out more (Berk, 2012).

You can help your students develop emotional self-regulation by openly talking about emotions and discussing strategies for dealing with them. In the process, you can remind students that feeling a variety of emotions is completely normal, but some ways of responding to them are better than others. For example, feeling hurt and angry is normal, but responding calmly is much better than lashing out.

Using literature in your teaching also offers opportunities to develop emotional intelligence. As you read and discuss stories, you can ask questions about characters' motives, feelings, and actions. Our goal is for students to become aware of their own emotions, how they influence our behavior, and ultimately how to control them, so they don't control us. If we can help our students understand and control their emotions, they will have acquired an ability that will serve them well throughout their lives.

Learning Styles

To understand something, do you need to "see" it? Or hear it described? Or touch it? People often describe themselves as visual, verbal, or tactile learners. These descriptions reflect your unique **learning style**, or your preferred way of learning, studying, or thinking about the world.

Learning styles also influence classroom teaching, as Chris Burnette discovers.

Teaching and You

How do you like to learn? When do you learn best? Do you prefer to study in the morning or later in the day? Do you like to study alone or with other people? Do you prefer to read about a topic or hear someone lecture about it? How will your learning preferences differ from the students you'll teach?

One thing Chris remembers from his methods classes is the need for variety. He has been primarily using large-group discussions in his middle school social studies classes, and most of the students seem to respond okay. But others seem uninterested, and their attention often drifts.

Today, Chris decides to try a small-group activity involving problem solving. The class has been studying the growth of American cities, and he wants the students to think about solutions to some of the problems of big cities. As he watches the groups interact, he's surprised at what he sees: Some of the students who are most withdrawn in whole-class discussions are leaders in the groups.

"Great!" he thinks. But at the same time, he notes that some of his more active students are sitting back and not getting involved.

Each of us approaches learning differently, but which of these differences are important? One approach to learning styles distinguishes between deep and surface approaches to processing information (C. Evans, Kirby, & Fabrigar, 2003). For instance, when you study a new idea, do you ask yourself how it relates to other ideas, what examples of the idea exist, and how it might apply in a different context? If so, you're using a deep-processing approach. On the other hand, if you simply memorize the definition, you're using a surface approach. As you might expect, deep-processing approaches result in higher achievement if subsequent tests focus on understanding and application, but surface approaches can succeed if tests emphasize learning and memorizing facts.

Other perspectives on learning styles contrast analytic and holistic, and visual versus verbal approaches to learning. Analytic learners tend to break learning tasks into their component parts, whereas holistic learners attack problems more globally (Norenzayan, Choi, & Peng, 2007). Visual learners prefer to see ideas, whereas verbal learners prefer hearing them (Mayer & Massa, 2003). In general, an analytic approach is more beneficial for learning and develops as students mature. You can encourage this learning style with the kinds of questions you ask and the kinds of assignments, tests, and quizzes you give. You can also present information in both visual and verbal forms to capitalize on differences in this area.

Like multiple intelligences, these preferences or "styles" make intuitive sense. We've all heard people say, "I'm a morning person" or "Don't try to talk to me until I've had my cup of coffee." Many people describe themselves as visual, verbal, or tactile. And, as with multiple intelligences, the idea of learning styles is very popular with teachers.

The idea is highly controversial, however. Learning style advocates claim the match results in increased achievement and improved attitudes (Lovelace, 2005); critics counter by questioning the validity of the tests used to measure learning styles (Pashler, McDaniel, Rohrer, & Bjork, 2008). They also cite research indicating that attempts to match learning environments to learning preferences have resulted in no increases in achievement and, in some cases, even decreases.

Most credible experts in the field question the wisdom of teachers' allocating energy and resources to accommodate learning styles.

> Like other reviewers who pay close attention to the research literature, I do not see much validity in the claims made by those who urge teachers to assess their students with learning style inventories and follow with differentiated curriculum and instruction. First, the research bases encouraging these urgings are thin to nonexistent. Second, a single teacher working with 20 or more students does not have time to plan and implement much individualized instruction. (Brophy, 2010, p. 283)

Others speak more strongly. "I think learning styles represents one of the more wasteful and misleading pervasive myths of the last 20 years" (Clark, 2010, p. 10).

While little evidence supports attempts to match instruction to students' learning style, the concept of *learning style* does have implications for us as teachers. First, it reminds us that we should vary our instruction, because no instructional strategy works for all students, or even the same students all the time (Brophy, 2010). Second, we should help our students understand how they

Revisiting My Beliefs

This discussion addresses the fourth item in *This I Believe*, "It is important for me to adapt my instruction to the individual learning styles of my students." This statement is not supported by credible research. Varying instruction is important, but little evidence supports the contention that achievement is increased by attempting to match instruction to each child's individual learning style. This would create enormous logistical problems and would also fail to teach students to broaden and develop their different learning abilities.

learn most effectively, something that they aren't initially good at (Berk, 2012). Third, our students differ in ability, motivation, background experiences, needs, and insecurities. The concept of learning style can sensitize us to these differences, help us treat our students as individuals, and do everything we can to help each one learn as much as possible.

Next we discuss special education and our country's efforts to best serve students with exceptionalities.

Special Education and the Law

Historically, students with exceptionalities were separated from their peers and placed in segregated classrooms or schools. Unfortunately, instruction in these settings was often inferior, achievement was no better than in general education classrooms, and students didn't learn the social and life skills they needed to function effectively in the outside world (Heward, 2013).

To address these issues, the U.S. Congress passed Public Law 94–142, the Individuals with Disabilities Education Act (IDEA), in 1975. The guarantee of a free and appropriate public education for all students with exceptionalities was central to this act. IDEA, combined with later amendments, provides the following guidelines for working with students having exceptionalities:

- Guarantees an appropriate education for all students with exceptionalities
- Identifies the needs of students with exceptionalities through assessment that doesn't discriminate against any students
- Involves parents in decisions about each child's educational program
- Creates an environment that doesn't restrict learning opportunities for students with exceptionalities
- Develops an individualized education program (IEP) of study for each student

Since 1975, Congress has amended IDEA three times to ensure that all children with disabilities are protected and provided with a free appropriate public education (Sack-Min, 2007). For example, one amendment extended the provisions of IDEA to children aged 3 through 5 and held states accountable for locating young children who need special education services. A second helps ensure protection against discrimination in testing, requires districts to keep confidential records of each child, and shares them with parents on request. The third amendment requires schools to establish methods to reduce the number of students from culturally and linguistically diverse backgrounds who are inappropriately placed in special education, likely a response to the fact that students who are culturally and linguistically diverse are overrepresented in special education classes. This amendment also provides for procedures that allow districts to remove students from the classroom who "inflict serious bodily injury" on others.

The Move Toward Inclusion

As educators realized that segregated classes and services weren't meeting the needs of students with exceptionalities, they searched for alternatives. **Mainstreaming**, the practice of placing students with exceptionalities in general education classrooms, often for selected activities only, was their first effort. Mainstreaming began the move away from segregated services, but it had problems. Students with exceptionalities were often placed in general education classrooms without adequate support and services, and the results were unsatisfactory, however, as one student's experience documents:

When I got to sixth grade, they put me in regular ed. classes. The work was way too hard, and the teachers did not try to help me. They went way too fast, and I got confused. I got scared and angry. I needed the help, but none of the teachers seemed to care. They didn't pay attention to me. No one ever noticed that I couldn't keep up with the work they were giving me. They were too busy teaching. (Schrimpf, 2006, p. 87)

To remedy problems identified with mainstreaming, educators developed an alternative approach to educating students with exceptionalities, now commonly called **inclusion**, a comprehensive approach to educating students with exceptionalities that incorporates a total, systematic, and coordinated web of services (Heward, 2013). Inclusion has three components:

- Include students with special needs in a general education school campus.
- Place students with special needs in age- and grade-appropriate classrooms.
- Provide special education support within the general education classroom.

Inclusion is broader than mainstreaming, and it means that as a general education classroom teacher you will have students with exceptionalities in your classroom, with the support of special educators to assist you with these students.

Individualized Education Program

To ensure that inclusion works and that learners with exceptionalities don't get lost in general education classrooms, a team of educators prepares an **individualized education program (IEP)** for every student who has an exceptionality. As a general education classroom teacher, you will be part of this team, which will also include a special education specialist, resource professionals, and parents. An IEP includes:

- An assessment of the student's current level of performance
- Long- and short-term objectives
- Strategies to ensure that the student is making academic progress
- Schedules for implementing the plan
- Criteria for evaluating the plan's success

Teachers and other professionals work with parents to design an IEP that meets each student's individual learning needs.

The IEP provides sufficient detail to guide general education classroom teachers and special education personnel as they implement the plan. Signatures from each participant indicate that all were consulted and agree on the recommended course of action.

IEP conferences are a source of comfort for parents who have seen their child struggle again and again in school. One mother wrote this note to her child's teacher:

> Thank you so much for attending the IEP. Because of your advocacy, concern, and belief in Sam, the IEP was a nice experience for us. To be surrounded by people who see that all is good and possible in Sam was just wonderful. Thanks. (Kostelnik, Onaga, Rohde, & Whiren, 2002, p. 114)

An **individualized family service plan (IFSP)** provides the same type of planned care as an IEP but targets developmentally delayed preschool children. A product of PL 99-457, an IFSP provides for early intervention and care for children from birth to age 2. It differs from an IEP in two important ways

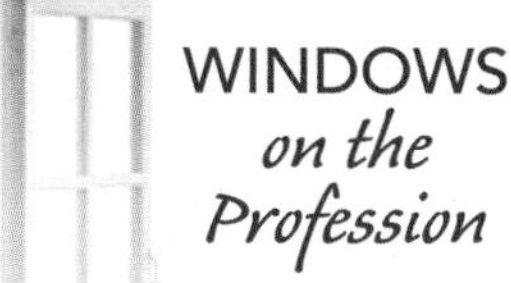

To see how an IEP helps guide instructional planning for one student, click on the video *Reviewing an IEP* (3:43).

(Heward, 2013). First, it targets the child's family and provides supplemental services to the family as well as the child. Second, it includes interventions and services from a variety of health and human services agencies in addition to education; these could include physical therapy as well as family training and counseling.

Categories of Exceptionalities

More than 6 million students in the United States are enrolled in special education programs, two thirds of them for relatively minor problems (Heward, 2013). Approximately 1 of 10 students in a typical school receives some form of special education services; most of these occur in a general education classroom for a significant portion of the school day.

Federal legislation has created categories to identify students eligible for special education services, but the use of categories is controversial. Advocates argue that categories provide a common language for professionals and encourage specialized instruction that meets each student's specific needs (Heward, 2013). Opponents claim that categories are arbitrary, that many differences exist within each, and that categorizing students encourages educators to treat them as labels instead of people. Despite the controversy, these categories are widely used, so they should be part of your professional knowledge base.

IDEA lists 13 different categories of disabilities, outlined in Figure 3.6. More than three fourths of the students with exceptionalities fall into four categories:

- learning disabilities
- communication disorders (speech or language impairment)
- intellectual disabilities
- behavior disorders/emotional disturbance

FIGURE 3.6 **Percentage of Students Ages 6 to 21 Receiving Special Education Services Under the Federal Government's Disability Categories**

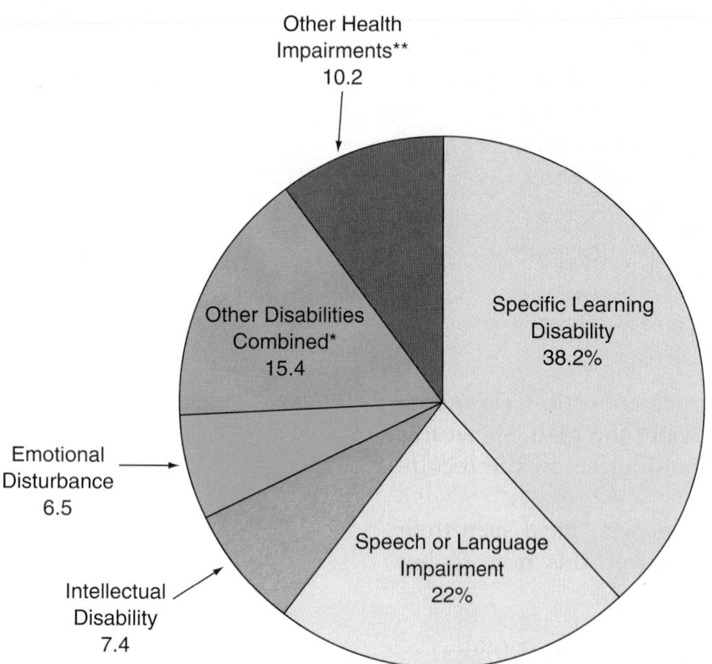

*Autism 5.2
Multiple disabilities 2.0
Developmental Delay 5.5
Hearing Impairment 1.2
Orthopedic Impairment 1.1
Visual Impairment 0.4

**Asthma, attention-deficit disorder, diabetes, epilepsy, a heart condition, hemophilia, lead poisoning, leukemia, hepatitis, rheumatic fever, sickle cell anemia

Source: National Center for Education Statistics (2011g).

Learning disabilities, the most frequently occurring, involve difficulties in acquiring and using listening, speaking, reading, writing, reasoning, or mathematical abilities. **Communication disorders** interfere with students' abilities to receive and understand information from others and to express their own ideas or questions. **Intellectual disabilities**, which used to be called *mental retardation,* include limitations in intellectual functioning, as indicated by difficulties in learning, and problems with adaptive skills, such as communication, self-care, and social interaction. This category relates to our earlier discussion of intelligence. Children with intellectual disabilities fall toward the lower end of the intelligence continuum.

Behavior disorders involve the display of serious and persistent age-inappropriate behaviors that result in social conflict, personal unhappiness, and school failure. This category relates to our earlier discussion of emotional intelligence. Learners with behavior disorders also tend to be lower than their peers in emotional intelligence. The term *behavior disorder* is often used interchangeably with *emotional disturbance, emotional disability,* or *emotional handicap*, and you may encounter any of these in your work. Researchers prefer the term *behavior disorder* because it focuses on overt behaviors that can be targeted and changed (Turnbull, Turnbull, & Wehmeyer, 2013).

Students in each of these categories require extra assistance to help them succeed in the general education classroom.

Revisiting My Beliefs

This section addresses the fifth item in *This I Believe*, "Experts in special education advocate the creation of special classrooms to meet the needs of students with exceptionalities." This statement isn't true; special educators recommend that students with exceptionalities should be educated in general education classrooms, whenever possible. This movement toward inclusion reflects research that suggests that these students learn more and develop more effective social skills when they have opportunities to interact with other students in general education classrooms.

Students Who Are Gifted and Talented

As a classroom teacher, you'll likely also work with learners who are gifted and talented, students at the upper end of the ability continuum. What is it like to be gifted or talented in a general education classroom? Here are the thoughts of one 9-year-old:

> Oh what a bore to sit and listen,
> To stuff we already know.
> Do everything we've done and done again,
> But we still must sit and listen.
> Over and over read one more page
> Oh bore, oh bore, oh bore.
> Sometimes I feel if we do one more page
> My head will explode with boredness rage
> I wish I could get up right there and march right out the door.
>
> (Delisle, 1984, p. 72)

Although we don't typically think of gifted and talented students as having exceptionalities, they often have learning needs not met by the general education curriculum, and they need special services to reach their full potential. The National Center for Education Statistics (2011c) reports that over 3 million students are gifted and talented, slightly more than 6% of the total student population. At one time, the term *gifted* was used to identify these students, but the category has been enlarged to include both students who do well on intelligence tests and those who demonstrate above-average talents in a variety of areas such as math, creative writing, and music (Hardman, et al., 2011).

Meeting the needs of students who are gifted and talented requires both early identification and instructional modifications. Conventional procedures often miss students who are gifted and talented because they rely heavily on standardized test scores and teacher nominations; as a result, females, students with low socioeconomic status, and students from cultural minorities are typically underrepresented in these programs (Gootman & Gebelof, 2008; J. Lewis, DeCamp-Fritson, Ramage, McFarland, & Archwamety, 2007). To address this problem, experts recommend more flexible and less culturally dependent methods, such as creativity measures, tests of spatial ability, and peer and parent nominations in addition to test score or teacher recommendations.

As a general education classroom teacher, you will probably be responsible for adapting instruction for students who are gifted and talented, because special programs for these students have declined in recent years. Different ways of helping these students are typically based either on **acceleration**, which keeps the curriculum the same but allows students to move through it more quickly, or on **enrichment**, which provides richer and varied content through strategies that supplement usual grade-level work. Table 3.2 lists different acceleration and enrichment options. Failure to address the needs of these students can result in gifted underachievers, with social and emotional problems linked to boredom and lack of motivation.

TABLE 3.2 Acceleration and Enrichment Options for Students Who Are Gifted and Talented

Enrichment Options	Acceleration Options
1. Independent study and independent projects	1. Early admission to kindergarten and first grade
2. Learning centers	2. Grade skipping
3. Field trips	3. Subject skipping
4. Saturday and summer programs	4. Credit by exam
5. Simulations and games	5. College courses in high school (Advanced Placement Courses)
6. Small-group inquiry and investigations	6. Correspondence courses
7. Academic competitions	7. Early admission to college

Adapting to Students' Abilities and Exceptionalities: Your Role as a Teacher

Teaching and You

Do you have an exceptionality? Did you know any students with exceptionalities when you were in school? Do you have any of these students in your close circle of friends? How were students with exceptionalities treated by other students in the schools you attended?

Because of inclusion, you—the general education teacher—now are central to helping students with exceptionalities learn and develop to their full potential. You will have three important roles in this process:

- Identify students you suspect have exceptionalities.
- Collaborate with other professionals.
- Modify instruction to meet students' needs.

This process begins with identification, an important first step in understanding and diagnosing learning problems. Following identification, classroom teachers collaborate with special educators and other support personnel to design and implement the IEP. Finally, and perhaps most importantly, classroom teachers adapt instruction to meet the learning needs of students with exceptionalities. The process begins with identification.

Identifying Students with Exceptionalities

Because you work directly with students every day, you are in the best position to identify students who may have exceptionalities. For example, Celina's ongoing observations of Rodney—in the case study at the beginning of this section—led her to conclude that "his engine is stuck on fast" and he might need special help. No one else in the school was in a better position to raise the question of whether or not Rodney needed additional support. The same was true for her experiences with Amelia.

In the past, a **discrepancy model** was used to identify students with exceptionalities. This model looked for differences between:

1. Performance in the classroom and scores on standardized tests
2. Scores on intelligence and achievement tests
3. Intelligence test scores and classroom achievement
4. Subtests on either intelligence or achievement tests

Performance in one area, such as an intelligence test, should predict performance in others; when the two were inconsistent, a learning problem was suspected.

Many experts became dissatisfied with the discrepancy model, arguing that it identified a disability only after a problem surfaced, sometimes after several years of failure and frustration (Lose, 2008). Instead, they argued, educators need early screening measures, so they can prevent failure before it occurs. Critics also contended that the discrepancy model didn't provide specific information about the nature of the learning problem or what should be done to correct it.

The **response to intervention (RTI) model of identification** addresses both of these problems. RTI typically begins at the start of the school year with pretesting designed to identify potential learning problems as early as possible (Samuels, 2011). If a potential learning problem is identified, the classroom teacher adapts instruction in an attempt to meet the student's needs. Common interventions include working with individual students while the majority of the class does seat work, one-on-one tutoring outside of regular school hours, and small-group work. RTI also emphasizes developing study strategies, such as highlighting important vocabulary, using a dictionary, reading assignments aloud, and finding a quiet place to study free of distractions. If the interventions are unsuccessful, a learning exceptionality is likely. You will note what works and what doesn't and document how the student responds to the intervention. This is the source of the label "response to intervention."

Collaboration

Collaboration with other professionals is your second important role in the inclusion process. Initially, inclusion provided for additional services to help students with exceptionalities function in general education school settings (Turnbull et al., 2013), but the concept of collaboration gradually replaced this additive approach. Collaboration involves communication with parents and other professionals, such as special education specialists, school psychologists, and guidance counselors, to create the best possible learning environment for students with exceptionalities. You will work closely with special education teachers to ensure that learning experiences are integrated into the general education classroom curriculum. For example, rather than pulling a student with special needs out of the classroom for supplementary instruction in math, a special education teacher will coordinate instruction with you and will then work with the student in your classroom on tasks linked to the standard math curriculum, as the following example illustrates:

Sharon Snow notices that Joey Sanchez is having difficulties with three-digit addition problems. After checking the IEP she has helped design in collaboration with the special education team, she finds that mastering math problems such as these is one of Joey's goals. She meets with Ken Thomas, the resource teacher, after school, and examines some recent work samples from Joey's math homework and quizzes. They discover he is having trouble with problems that involve place value and carrying values over to the next column, such as the following:

$$\begin{array}{r} 345 \\ +296 \\ \hline \end{array}$$

During the next week, when Sharon's class is working on similar problems, Ken stops by Joey's desk to help him. At first, they work in the back of the room, and Ken reviews place values for him. When Ken thinks Joey understands how place value affects the addition problems, he sends him back to his seat to work on the next few problems. Both Sharon and Ken monitor Joey's progress carefully so he won't get discouraged. When the number of problems seems to overwhelm Joey, Ken breaks them down into smaller blocks of five, providing feedback and encouragement after each block. Slowly, Joey starts to catch on and gain confidence. Collaboration is working.

Collaboration enabled the classroom teacher and the special educator to coordinate their efforts to help Joey succeed.

Unquestionably, having learners with exceptionalities in your classroom will make your teaching more demanding, but helping a student with a disability adapt and even thrive can be one of the most rewarding experiences you'll have as a teacher. One teacher shared this story about her efforts to help a student struggling with a communication disorder.

> At the end of the year, his dad took me aside and said, "We don't know what we would have done without this program. We were getting desperate. He's a different child today from what he was in August. We are so happy. He is just a different little boy" That felt pretty good. (Kostelnik et al., 2002, p. 129)

In *Teaching and You,* we asked if you knew any students with exceptionalities in the schools you attended. Most of us did, either directly or indirectly, and some of us had family members who struggled in school. It isn't easy being different or struggling to understand topics that seem effortless for other students. When you work with these students in your own classroom, try to remember your own struggles in encountering challenging topics, and help them in every way you can.

Modifying Instruction to Meet Students' Needs

Modifying your instruction to meet the needs of students with exceptionalities is your third important role. But the modifications you will use will not differ drastically from your general instruction practices (Vaughn & Bos, 2012). "In general, the classroom management and instruction approaches that are effective with special students tend to be the same ones that are effective with other students" (Good & Brophy, 2008, p. 223). In other words, you don't teach students with exceptionalities in ways that differ fundamentally from the way you teach all students; you simply do it that much better.

You can use these instructional modifications to help learners with exceptionalities succeed in your classroom (Turnbull et al., 2013):

- Teach in small steps, and provide detailed feedback on homework.
- Involve students with exceptionalities by calling on them as often as other students in your classes.
- Carefully model solutions to problems and other assignments.
- Provide outlines, hierarchies, charts, and other forms of organization for the content you're teaching.
- Increase the amount of time available for tests and quizzes.
- Use available technology.
- Teach learning strategies.

In inclusive classrooms, teachers play a major role in identifying students needing extra help, collaborating with other professionals, and adapting instruction to meet students' needs.

The last item on the list is particularly important. Students with learning difficulties often approach tasks passively or use the same strategy for all objectives (Vaughn & Bos, 2012). These students can learn to use strategies, and strategy training is one of the most promising approaches to working with students having exceptionalities, but the strategies need to be taught explicitly (M. Coyne, Carnine, & Kame'enui, 2011). For example, a student with a learning disability in reading was taught the following strategy. In attempting to understand the content of a chapter, he first looked at the chapter outline to see how the chapter was organized. Then, he used the outline as a guide as he skimmed the chapter. He then read the chapter to himself aloud, stopping every few paragraphs to summarize what he had just read. If he was unable to summarize the information, he reread the section.

Success is essential for struggling learners, and you'll need to provide additional support to help students overcome a history of failure and frustration and to convince them that they can succeed if they're willing to make the effort. For instance, while the majority of the class is completing a seat-work assignment, you might work with an individual student or a small group; this is how Sharon and Ken helped Joey with his math skills. Positive reinforcement and support are crucial. One teacher reported,

Anytime Brian did what I asked him to do, I made sure to help him recognize that he had been successful. I would make a little face, put my thumbs up, or say, "Good job." I wanted him to get the message "You're doing okay," or "You're on the right track." Sometimes, I just wanted him to know that I saw him and noticed what he was doing—not because he had accomplished anything in particular, but just because it was fun to have him around. (Kostelnik et al., 2002, p. 127)

Peer tutoring has also been used effectively, providing benefits to both the tutor and the person receiving the tutoring. It not only helps with content learning, but also provides an opportunity for students to interact with and learn about students with exceptionalities.

Home-based tutoring programs that involve parents are especially effective (Vaughn & Bos, 2012). Parents often want to help with their children's schooling but aren't quite sure how. Some simple directions and encouragement from you are often all that parents need.

TECHNOLOGY and TEACHING: Employing Technology to Support Learners with Disabilities

Julio is partially deaf, barely able to use a hearing aid to understand speech. Kerry Tanner, his seventh-grade science teacher, works closely with the special education instructor assigned to her classroom to help Julio. Seated near the front of the room to facilitate lipreading, Julio takes notes on a laptop computer during teacher presentations. Other students take turns sharing their notes with him so he can compare and fill in gaps. He especially likes to communicate with other students on the Internet, because this levels the communication playing field. When he views video clips on his computer, he uses a special device with earphones to increase the volume.

Jaleena is partially sighted, with a visual acuity of less than 20/80, even with corrective lenses. Despite this disability, she is doing well in her fourth-grade class. Terrence Banks, Jaleena's teacher, has placed her in the front of the room so that she can better see the chalkboard and overhead projector and has assigned students to work with her on her projects. Using a magnifying device, she can read most written material, but the computer is giving her special problems: The small letters and punctuation on websites and other information make it difficult for her to use the computer as an information source. Terrence works with the special education consultant in his district to get a monitor that magnifies the display. He knows it's a success when he sees Jaleena quietly working alone at her computer on the report due next Friday.

Assistive technology, a set of adaptive tools that support students with disabilities in learning activities and daily life tasks, can be a powerful tool for students with exceptionalities. These assistive tools are required by federal law under the Individuals with Disabilities Education Act (IDEA) and include motorized chairs, remote control devices that turn machines on and off with the nod of the head or other muscle action, and machines that amplify sights and sounds (Heward, 2013; Roblyer & Doering, 2013).

Probably the most widespread use of assistive technology is in the area of computer adaptations.

Adaptations to Computer Input Devices

To use computers, students must be able to input their words and ideas; however, this can be difficult when visual or other physical disabilities impede standard keyboarding. Enhancing the keyboard, such as making it larger and easier to see, arranging the letters alphabetically to make them easier to find, or using pictures for nonreaders are adaptations that accommodate these disabilities (Schultz, 2012). AlphaSmart, one widely used program, helps developing writers by providing spell-check and word-prediction scaffolding. When a student hesitates to finish a word, the computer, based on the first few letters, then either completes the word or offers a menu of suggestions, freeing students to concentrate on ideas and text organization.

Additional adaptations bypass the keyboard altogether. For example, speech/voice-recognition software translates speech into text on the computer screen (Roblyer & Doering, 2013). These systems can be invaluable for students with physical disabilities that affect hand and finger movement. Other adaptations use switches activated by an eye or body movement, such as a head nod, to interact with the computer (Schultz, 2012). Touch screens also allow students to go directly to the monitor to make responses.

Research also indicates that students with learning disabilities encounter difficulties translating ideas into written words (Hallahan, Kauffman, & Pullen, 2012). Speech-recognition technology eases this cognitive bottleneck by bypassing the keyboard, helping to produce initial drafts that are longer, with fewer errors.

Adaptations to Output Devices

Adaptations to computer output devices also assist learners with exceptionalities (Roblyer & Doering, 2013). For example, the size of the display can be increased with a special large-screen monitor, such as the one Jaleena used, or with a magnification device. For students who are blind, speech synthesizers read words and translate them into sounds. In addition, special printers can convert text into Braille and Braille into text.

Diversity in Your Classroom

These technologies are important because they prevent disabilities from becoming obstacles to learning. Their importance to students with exceptionalities is likely to increase, as technology becomes a more integral part of classroom instruction.

Students will be naturally curious when you introduce any of these new technologies into your classroom. Use this as an opportunity to discuss the whole topic of exceptionalities: emphasize that everyone is different, with unique strengths and abilities, and that knowing these allows us to make the most out of what each of us possesses.

Check Your Understanding

4.1. Define the concept of *intelligence,* and explain how the idea of multiple intelligences changes this definition.
4.2. Explain the legal foundation of special education.
4.3. What are the major categories of exceptionalities found in classrooms?
4.4. What roles do classroom teachers play in helping students with exceptionalities succeed in their classrooms?

For feedback on these exercises, go to the appendix, *Check Your Understanding,* located in the back of this text.

VOICES from the CLASSROOM

"I found the reason why there's a special in special education: those children are such special gifts to our world, and where people saw a disability, I saw a possibility. And I knew that it would be my job to help them reach their possibilities."

DANIELLE DOVACH, 2011 Teacher of the Year, New Jersey

CHAPTER 3 Summary

1. Explain how cultural diversity influences learning and how effective teachers respond to this diversity.
   - As students from diverse cultural backgrounds enter our classrooms, they bring with them unique attitudes and values. Sometimes these cultural attitudes and values complement school learning; at other times, they don't.
   - Diversity also results in differences in the cultural interaction patterns students bring to our classrooms. Often the interaction patterns of the classroom conflict with those of the home. Teachers who recognize this problem can adapt their instruction to meet the needs of students and also teach them how to adapt to the interaction patterns of the classroom.
   - Educational responses to cultural diversity have changed over time. Initially, the emphasis was on assimilation, or socializing students to adopt the dominant social norms and patterns of behavior. Multicultural education, and especially culturally responsive teaching, recognizes, accommodates, and builds on student cultural differences.
   - Urban areas are often called "gateway cities," because many of the immigrants to the United States first settle there. Consequently, the number of cultural minorities attending urban schools is large. In addition, many of these recent immigrants don't speak English as their first language.
2. Describe the major approaches to helping EL students learn.
   - Language diversity is increasing in U.S. classrooms. During the 1960s and 1970s, the federal response to this diversity was to encourage bilingual programs. Currently, the federal emphasis is on the rapid acquisition of English with little or no emphasis on preserving students' home languages.
   - Educational responses to language diversity range from recognizing and building on the home language to teaching English as quickly as possible. Currently, despite research that suggests advantages for maintaining the first language, political sentiment favors teaching English as quickly as possible.
   - Teachers who have EL students in the classroom can do several important things to help them learn. In addition to creating a warm and inviting classroom, they can provide multiple opportunities for students to practice their developing language skills with their peers. Teachers also should use a variety of concrete examples and graphics to illustrate abstract ideas and concepts.
3. Explain how gender differences influence school success and how effective teachers respond to these differences.
   - Males and females are different, and these differences reflect genetic influences as well as differences in the way society treats boys and girls. Parents also exert powerful influences on gender differences.
   - Evidence suggests that both boys and girls encounter problems in today's schools. For girls, these problems focus more on achievement and career choices, especially in math, science, and computer science, whereas for boys, the problems are more behavioral and connected to learning problems. Suspected causes of these problems range from societal and parental expectations to differential treatment in classrooms. Teachers play a major role in ensuring that gender differences don't become gender inequalities.

4. Explain how schools have changed the ways they help students with exceptionalities.
   - The legal foundation for special education was established in 1975 with the passage of the Individuals with Disabilities Education Act. IDEA, combined with later amendments, mandates a free appropriate public education, protection from discrimination in testing, parental involvement, a learning environment that doesn't restrict learners, and an individualized program of study for learners with exceptionalities.
   - Students with exceptionalities require extra help to reach their full potential. The majority of students with exceptionalities fall into four major categories: learning disabilities, communication disorders, intellectual disabilities, and behavior disorders. A substantial number of students with exceptionalities are also gifted and talented.
   - General education classroom teachers collaborate with other professionals to provide individualized educational services to students with exceptionalities. This collaboration begins with helping to identify students with exceptionalities, continues with collaboration during the creation of IEPs, and extends into the classroom, where teachers adapt their instruction to meet the learning needs of these students. Throughout this process, the teacher maintains continual communication with parents, school administrators, and other school professionals.
   - Effective teachers use the same basic instructional strategies that work with all students, but they also provide additional support for students with exceptionalities. The emphasis is on helping students with exceptionalities succeed on their academic tasks. Effective teachers use modeling, provide peer and one-on-one tutoring, break large tasks into smaller ones, provide visual aids, use assistive technology, and teach students how to use learning strategies.

Important Concepts

acceleration
assimilation
assistive technology
behavior disorders
bilingual maintenance language programs
collaboration
communication disorders
cultural diversity
culturally responsive teaching
culture
disabilities
discrepancy model of identification
emotional intelligence
English as a second language (ESL) programs
English learners (ELs)
enrichment
ethnicity
exceptionalities
gender bias
gender-role identity
gifted and talented
immersion programs
inclusion
individualized education program (IEP)
individualized family service plan (IFSP)
intellectual disabilities
intelligence
learning disabilities
learning style
mainstreaming
multicultural education
multiple intelligences
response to intervention (RTI) model of identification
single-sex classes and schools
special education
stereotype
students with exceptionalities
transition programs

Portfolio Activity

Exploring Cultural Diversity

InTASC Core Teaching Standards 2: Learning Differences

The purpose of this activity is to introduce you to the cultural diversity in an area where you might teach. Contact the State Office of Education in a state where you're thinking of teaching (addresses and websites can be found on the

Internet). Or contact a district in which you might teach (school district websites can be found on the Internet, or telephone numbers can be found in the White Pages of the telephone directory, in the Business Section under "Schools"). Ask for demographic information on cultural minorities and ELL students. Summarize the information briefly, identifying major cultural groups and possible implications for your teaching.

Portfolio Activities similar to this one and related to chapter content can be found at MyEducationLab™.

Student Diversity: Culture, Language, Gender, and Exceptionalities

Go to the topic *Student Diversity* in the MyEducationLab (www.myeducationlab.com) for *Introduction to Teaching*, where you can:

- Find learning outcomes for *Student Diversity,* along with the national standards that connect to these outcomes.
- Complete *Assignments and Activities* that can help you more deeply understand the chapter content.
- Apply and practice your understanding of the core teaching skills identified in the chapter with the *Building Teaching Skills and Dispositions* learning units.
- Examine challenging situations and cases presented in the IRIS Center Resources.
- Access video clips of CCSSO National Teachers of the Year award winners responding to the question, "Why Do I Teach?" in the *Teacher Talk* section.
- Check your comprehension on the content covered in the chapter with the *Study Plan.* Here you will be able to take a chapter quiz, receive feedback on your answers, and then access *Review, Practice, and Enrichment* activities to enhance your understanding of chapter content.
- Check the *Book Resources* to find opportunities to share thoughts and gather feedback on the *Diversity and You* and *Issues You'll Face in Teaching* features found in this chapter.

MyEducationLab™

CHAPTER 4

Education in the United States: Its Historical Roots

VOICES from the CLASSROOM

"Every day students come to me who are trying to keep their head above the water, who are trying to float in this world. They come to us from abusive situations, they come to us from poverty, they come to us from group homes and from homelessness. They come to us for breakfast, for lunch, for their health care, for love, for support, and yes, for education."

BARBARA WALTON-FARAI, 2009 Teacher of the Year, Rhode Island

CHAPTER OUTLINE

The Colonial Period (1607–1775)
- Differences in Colonies
- Teaching in Colonial Schools
- European Influences on American Education
- The Legacy of the Colonial Period

The Early National Period (1775–1820)
- The Constitution Shapes Education
- How the Early National Period Shaped Education Today

The Common School Movement:
The Rise of State Support for Public Education (1820–1865)
- Making Education Available to All
- Teaching in the Common School Era
- The Legacy of the Common School Movement

The Evolution of the American High School
- Historical Roots of the Comprehensive High School
- Redefining the High School
  Urban Education: The Challenge of Teaching in Large Urban High Schools
- Junior High and Middle Schools
- Technology and Teaching: A Brief History of Technology in the Classroom

Searching for Equality: The Education of Cultural Minorities
- Education of Native Americans
- Education of African Americans: Up from Slavery to . . .
- Education of Hispanic Americans
- Education of Asian Americans
- The Search for Equality: Where Are We Now?

The Modern Era: Schools as Instruments for National Purpose and Social Change
- The Cold War: Enlisting America's Schools
- The War on Poverty and the Great Society
- Schools and the Battle for Economic Survival
- The Federal Government's Role in Pursuing Equality
  Exploring Diversity: A Look Back at Teaching Through the Lens of Gender
  Diversity and You: The Gender Gap in Teaching
  Issues You'll Face in Teaching: Is Compulsory Attendance the Solution to Absenteeism and Dropouts?

LEARNING OUTCOMES

After you have completed your study of this chapter, you should be able to:

1. Explain how the diversity of the original colonies shaped our educational system, and describe the role of religion in colonial schools. InTASC Core Teaching Standard 9, Professional Learning and Ethical Practice
2. Explain how the early national period influenced education in this country. InTASC Core Teaching Standard 9, Professional Learning and Ethical Practice
3. Explain how the common school movement influenced education in our country today. InTASC Core Teaching Standard 9, Professional Learning and Ethical Practice
4. Describe the historical roots of contemporary secondary schools. InTASC Core Teaching Standard 9, Professional Learning and Ethical Practice
5. Identify similarities and differences in minority groups' struggles for educational equality. InTASC Core Teaching Standard 9, Professional Learning and Ethical Practice
6. Explain how schools became instruments for national purpose during the modern era. InTASC Core Teaching Standard 9, Professional Learning and Ethical Practice

Education in our country is unique. The way we organize schools, the content we teach, and our teaching methods differ from those in other countries. The reasons for these differences lie in the historical roots of our education system. As you read the following case study, think about the ways that history will affect the schools in which you'll teach.

"I've about had it," Dave Carlisle, a first-year teacher at Westmont Middle School, says as he drops into a chair in the teachers' lounge.

"Having a bad day?" Monica Henderson, one of Dave's colleagues, asks.

"Bad day. You could say that," Dave replies. "We had lunch money missing again today. And I'm pretty sure there was cheating on the test I gave last week. They think cheating is fine if they can get away with it. It's almost like these kids have no ideas about right and wrong. I sometimes think they could use some religion."

"We already tried that," Monica replies, looking up from the papers she is grading.

"When?" Dave asks.

"Back in our country's history, and often since then."

"Oh, no. Not more of that history stuff. . . . What's that class you're taking?"

"Actually, it's interesting. I understand much better why our schools are the way they are, and why some of the issues politicians fight about still exist. It's really good," Monica replies with a smile.

"Yeah, I know, 'Those that don't know history are destined to repeat it,'" Dave says, rolling his eyes, "but how will it help me with my cheating and stealing problems?"

MyEducationLab™

Visit the MyEducationLab for *Introduction to Teaching* to enhance your understanding of chapter concepts with a personalized *Study Plan*. You'll also have the opportunity to hone your teaching skills through video and case-based *Assignments and Activities* and *Building Teaching Skills and Disposition* lessons.

Studying our country's educational history won't give Dave a direct answer to his questions, but it can help you understand why the schools and classrooms in which you'll teach are the way they are. Our goal in writing this chapter is to help you see how our nation's history helped shape today's schools. But, before you begin your study, please respond to the items in *This I Believe*.

Think again about Dave's lament: "We had lunch money missing again today. And I'm pretty sure there was cheating on the test I gave last week. . . ." His comment relates to the issue of moral and character education in our classrooms. Educators generally agree that schools should promote students' moral development, but they don't agree on how to accomplish it. Some want to link it to religious values taught in homes and churches, but others argue that basing moral education on religion is neither desirable nor possible, given the religious diversity in the United States (Gollnick & Chinn, 2013). Parents who believe

This I Believe

HISTORY OF EDUCATION AND ME

For each item, circle the number that best represents your thinking. Use the following scale as a guide:

4 = I strongly believe the statement is true.
3 = I believe the statement is true.
2 = I believe the statement is false.
1 = I strongly believe the statement is false.

1. The Constitution of our country requires that religion and public schooling be kept separate from each other.

   1 2 3 4

2. A free public education for students like me has always been a cornerstone of education in the United States.

   1 2 3 4

3. The American high school has historically attempted to meet the needs of all students.

   1 2 3 4

4. When slavery ended in our country, cultural and ethnic minorities were welcomed into our public schools.

   1 2 3 4

5. In recent times, the federal government has used our nation's schools as instruments to achieve national goals.

   1 2 3 4

schools should teach values and morals often send their children to private, church-supported schools, and supporters argue that these schools have as much right to federal education money as do our country's public schools. Opponents counter that federal support of parochial schools violates the Constitution.

Religion and schools are closely linked in many states. Some public schools, for example, want to allow prayer in classrooms, hold religious assemblies, and give students Bibles (LaMorte, 2012; Schimmel, Stellman, & Fischer, 2011). They argue that this emphasis promotes positive values, but critics, as with support for religious schools, contend that these practices violate our country's Constitution.

These and other controversies in today's schools have their roots in the colonial period in our nation's history. This is where we begin.

Teaching and You

Most of us have an idea of how we want to teach when we enter our first classroom. But what would you do if you didn't have access to computers or the Internet, or even electricity? Or chalkboards or white boards? Or even textbooks? What was it like to be a teacher in colonial times? How did the challenges colonial teachers faced compare to those today?

The Colonial Period (1607–1775)

The roots of American education began with the Jamestown colony, the first permanent English settlement in North America. Religion was an integral part of the colony from its beginning. King James of England, after whom the colony was named, wanted to establish a foothold for Protestantism in the New World, for both spiritual and political reasons. The English believed it was their duty to spread the gospel and convert Native Americans to Protestant Christianity, and King James also recognized the importance of countering the colonizing efforts of the Spanish, who were zealously converting native people in their colonies to Roman Catholicism (Glasson, 2007). Colonial schools were formed in response to this need, and they laid the foundation for many of the controversies that exist today (see Figure 4.1).

As you would expect, the schools reflected the settlers' values and beliefs, and as a result, schooling in colonial America had the same class and gender distinctions common in Europe at the time. Formal education was reserved for wealthy white males, and ignored females, people of color, and those less wealthy. Differences in the colonies existed, however, and we examine them next.

Religion was a major reason early settlers came to America and was a major force in shaping colonial schools.

FIGURE 4.1 The Colonial Period

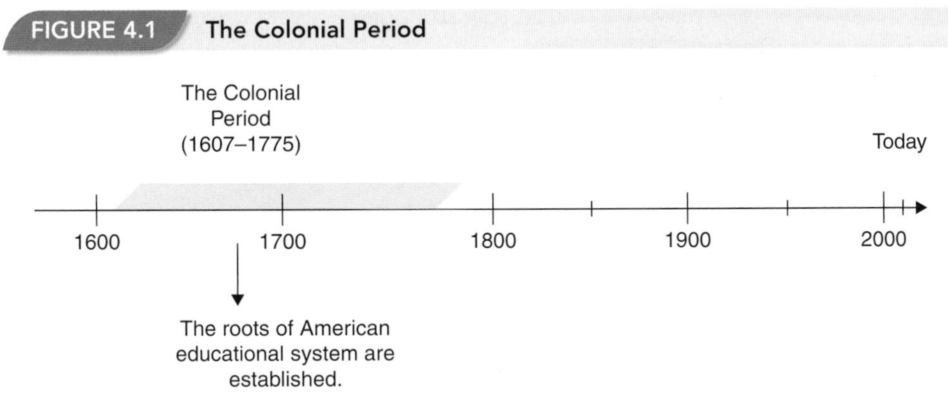

FIGURE 4.2 Regional Differences in Colonies

Southern Colonies
Middle Colonies
New England Colonies
New Hampshire
Massachusetts
New York
Rhode Island
Connecticut
Pennsylvania
New Jersey
Maryland
Delaware
Virginia
North Carolina
South Carolina
Georgia

Differences in Colonies

After Jamestown was settled, many people from Europe came to the New World, and although most spoke English, others came from a number of countries and settled in each of the 13 colonies. They were similar in some ways, such as being linked to Europe and desiring better lives, but geography, economics, and their reasons for coming resulted in regional differences (see Figure 4.2).

The Southern Colonies

If you'd lived in Georgia in 1700, your life not only would have differed dramatically from your life today, but it also would have differed from life in New York or Massachusetts in 1700. Life in the Southern colonies—Maryland, Virginia, the Carolinas, and Georgia—was linked to the land and revolved around agriculture, often on large plantations where African slaves and indentured servants worked land owned by wealthy landlords. Poor white settlers worked small farms on the margins, barely scratching out an existence.

You wouldn't have attended a public school, because they didn't exist at the time. If your parents weren't wealthy, you probably wouldn't have gone to school at all. Life for most people in the colonial South was hard, and formal education was a luxury reserved for those with money (Pulliam & Van Patten, 2013). Private tutors often lived on plantations, or parents pooled their resources to hire a tutor to teach the children of several families. Private schools sponsored by the Church of England—the religion of the original Jamestown settlement—and boarding schools for the wealthy sprang up in larger Southern cities, such as Charleston and Williamsburg. The English tradition of education for the wealthy few made an easy leap over the Atlantic to the Southern colonies.

The Middle Colonies

The middle colonies—New York, Rhode Island, New Jersey, Delaware, and Pennsylvania—were more diverse than the Southern colonies. For example, substantial pockets of Dutch in New York, Swedes in Delaware, and Germans in Pennsylvania brought their native cultures to the New World. As a result, middle colonists belonged to a number of religious groups, such as Dutch Reformist, Quaker, Lutheran, Baptist, Roman Catholic, and Jewish (Pulliam & Van Patten, 2013). Because religious freedom was an important reason for coming to America, and because religion played a central role in people's lives, it was difficult to create schools that satisfied everyone.

In response to this diversity, families in the middle colonies created parochial schools, schools that included the study of religion in addition to the three R's. Students learned in their native languages, and local religious beliefs, such as the study of the Lutheran religion in German schools, were an integral part of the curriculum.

The New England Colonies

We've all heard maxims such as, "Idle minds are the Devil's workshop" and, "Spare the rod and spoil the child," as well as the three R's—"readin', 'riting, and 'rithmetic." Let's see where they came from.

The New England colonies—Massachusetts, Connecticut, and New Hampshire—differed from the other colonies in two important ways. First, they were culturally and religiously homogeneous, which made consensus about school goals easier to achieve. Second, industry and commerce encouraged the clustering of people into towns, which allowed the formation of common schools.

For example, in Massachusetts where the Puritans, followers of John Calvin, settled, religion played a huge role in people's lives. The Puritans came to America because of conflicts with the Church of England, which they believed had grown too liberal and tolerant of "immoral practices." Puritans believed that humans were inherently evil, having fallen when Adam and Eve committed original sin. They advocated a "purity" of worship and doctrine, hence the name "Puritan," and education was viewed as the vehicle for helping people follow God's commandments and resist the devil's temptations (Spring, 2011). By learning to read and write, people gained access to God's word through the Bible. Education was important because it made people more righteous, industrious, resourceful, and thrifty.

Teaching in Colonial Schools

You saw earlier that schooling in the southern colonies was largely accomplished by private tutors, and in the middle colonies, different religious groups formed their own parochial schools. The schooling in the New England colonies was heavily based on religion and has had the most influence on many controversies in today's schools.

The Puritans' views shaped the schools they created. They saw children as savage and primitive, requiring education (and religion) to become civilized and God-fearing. Puritans viewed play as idleness and considered children's talk to be prattle. They commonly used corporal punishment, such as beating students with switches or forcing them to kneel on hard pebbles, as punishment for unacceptable behavior. Puritans believed in the adage, "Spare the rod and spoil the child."

Religion also influenced both what was taught (the curriculum) and how it was taught (instruction), and this helps answer the questions we asked in *Teaching and You* in this section. If you'd taught in one of these schools, you would have focused on the four R's—reading, writing, arithmetic, and religion—and you would have emphasized memorization and recitation. Your students would have been expected to sit quietly for long periods of time, and you wouldn't have allowed students to ask questions or express their opinions. You would have had no formal professional preparation, such as the class you're now taking, and you would have had virtually no textbooks or other curriculum materials to support your efforts.

These negative features of colonial classrooms were not limited to New England; most classrooms in colonial times were unpleasant places in which to work and learn. If you had taught in any of these classrooms, you would have been underpaid and underappreciated, and your students usually didn't want to be there, both because of the unpleasant experience and a curriculum irrelevant to their future lives. If you were a woman, the likelihood of being a teacher was almost nonexistent, because almost all teachers were men, either preparing or waiting for a position in the ministry.

Paradoxically, a landmark piece of legislation, the Massachusetts Act of 1647, also known as the **Old Deluder Satan Act,** arose from this grim educational landscape. The law was designed to produce citizens who understood the Bible and could thwart Satan's trickery, and it required every town of 50 or more households to hire a teacher of reading and writing. This act is enormously significant historically, because it gave birth to the idea that public education could contribute to the greater good of our country. It provided the legal foundation for public support of education, which is a cornerstone of schooling in our country.

European Influences on American Education

Schools in the colonies focused on religion and emphasized memorization and recitation, but change was occurring in Europe and gradually making its way across the Atlantic. Prominent European philosophers were changing the way people thought about schools, teachers, and children. Although their ideas came from different places, all involved a more humane, child-centered, and practical view of education. These philosophers are important because they planted the seeds of educational change that would fundamentally alter the education of students in the United States. Some of the more prominent include:

John Amos Comenius (1592–1670; Czech philosopher), who questioned the effectiveness of memorization and recitation, and instead emphasized the importance of basing teaching on children's interests and needs

John Locke (1632–1704; English philosopher), who emphasized the importance of firsthand experiences in helping children learn about the world

Jean-Jacques Rousseau (1712–1778; Swiss philosopher), who viewed children as innately good and argued that teachers should provide children with opportunities for exploration and experimentation

Johann Pestalozzi (1746–1827; Swiss philosopher), who criticized authoritarian educational practices that stifled students' playfulness and natural curiosity and recommended that teachers use concrete experiences to help children learn

The Legacy of the Colonial Period

The colonial period shaped today's education in three important ways. First, it was the source of inequality in American schools: With few exceptions, poor whites, females, and minorities such as Native Americans and African Americans were excluded from schools (Spring, 2010). William Berkeley, the aristocratic governor of Virginia, supported this exclusion, and in 1671 railed against both free public education and access to books:

> "I thank God, there are no free schools nor printing, and I hope we shall not have them these hundred years, for learning has brought disobedience, and heresy, and sects into the world, and printing has divulged them, and libels against the best government. God keep us from them both." (Pulliam & Van Patten, 2007, p. 88)

European ideas of class structure and privilege didn't die easily in the New World. Given attitudes such as these, it's easy to see why equality of educational opportunity wasn't a legal reality until the mid-20th century, and some critics argue that today's schools are still racist and sexist (Spring, 2010).

Second, although education was a privilege reserved for wealthy males, with the passage of the Old Deluder Satan Act, the colonial period also laid the foundation for public support of education and local control of schools, two principles shaping education in our country today.

Third, and perhaps most significantly, the relationship between religion and schooling, so dominant in the colonial period, helps us understand why religion continues to be an important and contentious issue in education today.

Check Your Understanding

1.1. How did the diversity of the original colonies shape the educational system in the United States?

1.2. What role did religion play in colonial schools?

1.3. How did this emphasis on religion influence schools today?

1.4. Why was the Old Deluder Satan Act of Massachusetts important for the development of our American educational system?

For feedback, go to the appendix, *Check Your Understanding,* located in the back of this text.

The Early National Period (1775–1820)

Teresa Sanchez has moved with her family from a large urban center in the Northeast to a sprawling city in the South. Although the teenager encounters changes in climate and lifestyle, she finds her new high school surprisingly similar to her old school. The buildings and physical layout are similar, with long hallways lined with lockers and interspersed with classrooms. Even the central office seems the same, and the guidance counselor who works with her assures her that she won't lose credits because of the move.

But there are differences. Teresa rides a district school bus instead of using public transportation. The students, although friendly, talk differently, and their interests differ from those of her friends back home. And the textbooks she receives, although covering the same basic material, do so in different ways.

Her mother, an elementary teacher, also notices both similarities and differences. She is hired almost immediately but is told that her teaching certificate is only temporary and that she'll have to take additional course work for it to become permanent. The textbooks she is given are different from the ones she had previously used, but the principal's emphasis on testing at the end of the year isn't. Some things never change.

As you travel across our country, the United States appears homogeneous. A McDonald's in California looks much like one in Ohio, for example, and television programs, movies, and music across the country are similar. But there are many regional and state differences (Gollnick & Chinn, 2013).

The same paradox occurs if you look at schools across the country. Although schools across the country appear similar, if you look closely, you will see important regional and state differences. For example, students in Texas study Texas state history and take specially constructed tests to determine grade advancement and even graduation, and students in other states study their own history and take their own state-specific graduation tests (M. Miller et al., 2009). Education to assist English learners (ELs) exists in all states, but the form of this assistance varies considerably (Echevarria & Graves, 2011). Why do these differences exist? Answers can be found in the early national period of our country (see Figure 4.3).

Before 1775, the United States was a loose collection of separate colonies that looked mostly to Europe for trade and ideas. During the 45 years from 1775 to 1820, however, the separate colonies became the United States of America, and this country shaped its future through the Constitution and the Bill of Rights, as you see in the next section.

The Constitution Shapes Education

The U.S. Constitution, written in 1787 and adopted in 1789, played a major role in shaping the educational system you'll teach in today. It has had 27 amendments,

FIGURE 4.3 The Early National Period

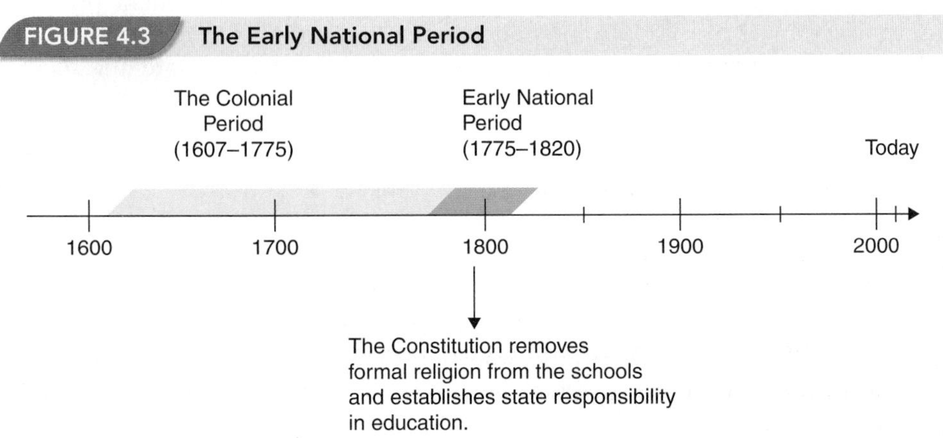

Teaching and You

You've taken your first teaching job in a public elementary, middle, or high school, and a discussion of religion comes up in one of your classes. Is it okay for you to be involved with your students in this discussion?

the first 10 of which are known as our Bill of Rights. As you saw in the previous section, the original colonies were very religiously diverse, and because of this diversity, our country's founders concluded that no religion should be placed above others. This led to the "establishment clause" of the First Amendment, which prohibited the government from passing legislation to establish any one official religion over another. This created the principle widely known as *separation of church and state*.

Considering the importance of religion in the colonies, it's easy to see how the principle of separation of church and state led to controversies about religion that continue today. Questions such as the following occur frequently:

- Should prayer be allowed in schools?
- Should federal money be used to provide instruction in religious schools?
- What role should religion play in character education?

This discussion also addresses the question we asked in *Teaching and You* in this section. It is perfectly okay for you to discuss religious topics with your students if they relate to your content or if students ask a question or bring the topic up. But it wouldn't be okay for you to advocate one religion over another; doing so would violate the principle of separation of church and state.

Severing the federal government's ties between religion and education also raised another question: Who should be responsible for organizing and managing education in our new country? Establishing a national education system was one suggestion. Proponents argued that a national system would best meet the country's growing agricultural, industrial, and commercial needs. Opponents cited the monolithic and unresponsive systems in Europe. Opponents also argued that the beginnings of viable local and state systems, such as those in Massachusetts, already existed, so why create another level of bureaucracy and control when it wasn't needed?

The Constitution's framers sidestepped the issue with the Tenth Amendment, which said that areas not explicitly assigned to the federal government would be the responsibility of each state. This amendment was important for two reasons: First, it implicitly removed the federal government from a central role in running and operating schools, and second, it passed this responsibility on to the individual states. This helps us understand why standards, accountability, and the high-stakes tests, so common in today's education, currently originate at the state level.

To support states' efforts, Congress passed the Land Ordinance of 1785 (Brimley, Verstegen, & Garfield, 2012). At that time, Congress didn't have the power to directly tax American citizens, so the Land Ordinance was designed to raise money by selling land in the territories west of the original colonies acquired from Britain at the end of the Revolutionary War. The ordinance divided land into townships consisting of 36 one-square-mile sections, with the income from one section reserved for support of public education. Although not directly involved in governing or operating schools, the federal government provided monetary support for schools and education, a tradition that persists to this day. With respect to education, the lines of responsibility between state and federal governments were already being blurred.

How the Early National Period Shaped Education Today

Three important events occurred during the early national period. First, the principle of separation of church and state was established, and second, legislators removed control of education from the federal government and gave it to the states. Third, in passing the Land Ordinance of 1785, the federal government established a role for itself in public education.

We continue to feel the influence of these actions in today's schools. For example, courts have repeatedly upheld the principle of separation of church and state, and decisions about school and classroom policy are made by individual states and local school districts instead of by the federal government. However, the federal government does play an important role in education: Public schools receive federal funding and must adhere to federal laws, and the federal government continues to use our schools to achieve national goals. For example, when Russia launched the Sputnik satellite in 1957 and appeared to be winning the space race, a torrent of federal funds was released with the goal of improving instruction in math and science in our country. More recently, based on the belief that significant segments of our country's students were underachieving, the No Child Left Behind (NCLB) Act of 2001 was passed, which required all states to develop a comprehensive accountability plan to ensure that all students acquire basic skills, with primary emphasis on reading and math.

Revisiting My Beliefs

This section addresses the first item in *This I Believe* at the beginning of the chapter, "The Constitution of our country requires that religion and public schooling be kept separate from each other." This statement is essentially true: The framers of our Constitution wanted to avoid problems associated with governments—federal, state, or local—establishing any one official religion. It's difficult to keep the two completely apart, however, as you'll see at different points in the text.

Check Your Understanding

2.1. Explain how the early national period influenced education in this country.

2.2. What is the Tenth Amendment to the Constitution? Why is it important for education today?

2.3. What was the historical significance of the Land Ordinance of 1785?

For feedback, go to the appendix, *Check Your Understanding*, located in the back of this text.

The Common School Movement: The Rise of State Support for Public Education (1820–1865)

Most of you reading this text will become teachers of elementary, middle, or high school students, and you'll work in public schools. Think about these schools for a moment. The students you'll teach won't be charged for their schooling and will be required by law to be there; all states require students to attend school until they're 16. Your salary and the salaries of other teachers and administrators, the building itself, materials and supplies, buses that take students to and from school, and even some of your students' lunches will be publicly supported, meaning a portion of federal, state, and local taxes will pay for them.

The common school movement made education accessible to the common person.

Typically, your school will be organized into grade levels. At the elementary level, 5-year-olds will be in kindergarten, 6-year-olds will be in the first grade, and so on; at the middle and high school levels, classes will focus on different content areas, such as ninth-grade English, chemistry, or geometry. You will have a designated grade level or content area to teach.

Getting a job will require you to be licensed. You'll have to complete a specified set of university courses, which is one reason you're in this class, and you'll complete clinical experiences in schools, including an internship. You'll probably also have to take a standardized test—the content of which will vary from state to state—to assess your competency.

FIGURE 4.4 The Common School Movement

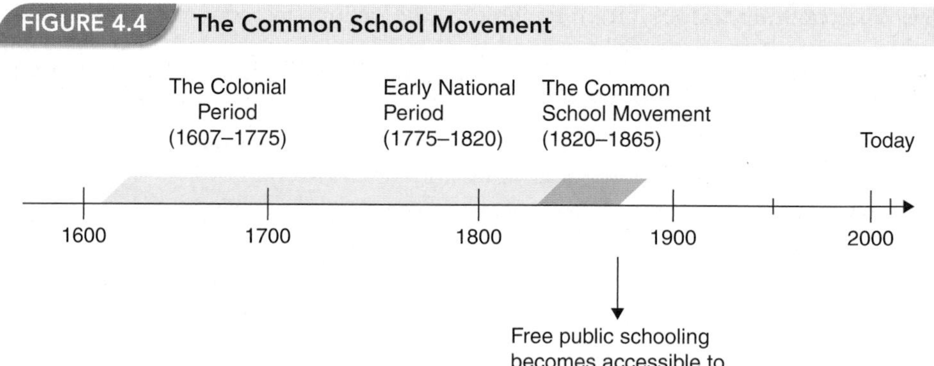

Teaching and You

Did your parents pay to send you to school? Were your classmates the same age as you? Did your friends attend school regularly and graduate on time? Did your parents talk about education as an option, or as a necessity? Your responses to these questions are probably related to important changes that occurred during the common school era.

The origins of all these structures and policies occurred during the common school period, from 1820 to 1865.

American education between the years 1775 and 1820 (the early national period) was still largely reserved for the wealthy. The common school movement changed that (see Figure 4.4).

Historians describe the period from 1820 to 1865 as the "Age of the Common Man." Two important factors contributed to this trend. First, Andrew Jackson, the popular and down-to-earth hero of the War of 1812, was elected president. Second, westward expansion provided opportunities for the poor and landless to start over by pulling up stakes and heading west. The land area of the United States nearly doubled between 1830 and 1865, and the population increased from 13 to 32 million, 4 million of whom were new immigrants (Urban & Wagoner, 2009).

This unprecedented growth presented both opportunities and challenges. Industrialization created jobs and contributed to the growth of cities such as New York and Boston, but it also resulted in pollution, crime, and urban slums. Many immigrants didn't speak English and weren't accustomed to the American way of life. And most citizens were functionally illiterate. The country needed an informed citizenry that could participate in politics and contribute to the nation's economy, so America turned to its schools for help (Tyack, 2003).

Making Education Available to All

What was it like to teach and learn during the common school period? If you taught at the beginning of the 19th century, you would have encountered an American educational system that was a patchwork of private and quasi-public schools. "Public" schools often charged partial tuition, discouraging all but the wealthiest from attending. States didn't coordinate their efforts, and the quality of education was uneven at best (Pulliam & Van Patten, 2013).

Around 1820, changes began to occur that marked the beginning of the **common school movement**, a historic attempt to make education available to all children in the United States. Important events that occurred during this period include:

- States and local governments directly taxed citizens to support public schools. Educators attempted to increase the attendance of underrepresented groups such as the urban poor and freed slaves.
- States created state education departments and appointed state superintendents of instruction.
- Educators organized schools by grade level and standardized the curriculum.
- States improved teacher preparation.

The Contributions of Horace Mann

Horace Mann, a lawyer turned educator, was a key figure in the common school movement (Urban & Wagoner, 2009). Secretary of the Massachusetts State Board of Education from 1837 to 1848, he was an outspoken advocate for public education, believing that it was the key to developing our country and improving the quality of life for all people.

Under Mann's influence, Massachusetts became the leader of education in the United States. It doubled state appropriations for education, built 50 new secondary schools, increased teacher salaries by 50%, and passed the nation's first compulsory school attendance law in 1852. (By 1900, 32 other states had passed similar laws.) Mann's most important legacy, however, was the idea that public education, in the form of tax-supported elementary schools (common schools), should be a right of all citizens.

Expansion of the Common School Movement

The common school movement prospered despite obstacles, such as business interests that feared a loss of cheap child labor, citizens who objected to increased taxes and having to pay to educate other people's children, and competition from private and parochial schools. The reasons for this unprecedented growth include:

- Parents began viewing education as a way of improving their children's lives.
- National and local leaders saw education as the vehicle for assimilating immigrants and improving national productivity.
- Industry and commerce were growing and required an increasingly educated populace.

By 1865, 50% of American children were enrolled in public schools and 28 of 35 states had established state boards of education. During the common school movement, tax-supported public elementary schools were firmly established as a cornerstone of our country's educational system. (New Jersey, the last state to do so, eliminated the requirement that parents pay for their children's elementary education in 1871.)

Although free public elementary school slowly became available to all, the same didn't occur in secondary education until much later. For example, in 1906, 150,000 students entered first grade in Tennessee, 10,000 remained by the eighth grade, and only 575 graduated from high school (Tyack, 2003). (We examine the evolution of the American high school in the next section of the chapter.) By the 1930s, however, the majority of American children attended high school, a stark contrast with England, where less than 10% of 17-year-olds were enrolled in school. Economists believe this greater access to schooling played a major role in our country's economic growth during that period (Goldin & Katz, 2008).

Teaching in the Common School Era

Although the common school movement dramatically increased access to education, as a teacher you would have encountered a number of obstacles and challenges. During the early to mid-1800s, here's what your life would have been like.

Your workload would have been very heavy, and you would have taught only fundamentals, such as reading and math. The building you taught in would have been poorly constructed, and it's unlikely that you would have had textbooks, writing boards, or other materials. Buildings were not kept up, lighting was not adequate, and quite often one poorly trained teacher was in charge not only of one school but also of an entire district. You probably would have had no more than an elementary school education yourself (Pulliam & Van Patten, 2013).

Teaching was especially tough if you taught in a rural school; students didn't want to be in school, so they often misbehaved. Your resources would have been virtually nonexistent. One rural school had two teachers for 108 students (D. Manning, 1990). Imagine teaching 54 students at a time, and having to teach all grade levels; at this point in our schools' history, grade levels were nonexistent (Cuban, 2012)! Another teacher reported building a rock walk to the outhouses with her students so they could use them without tracking mud and dirt into the classroom. This teacher was one of the lucky ones; in other schools no outhouses were available, so everyone used the bushes near the school.

If you had worked in one of these schools, you would have been expected to sweep floors and take care of other janitorial responsibilities such as chopping wood and hauling water. Because your own education would have been limited, you would have struggled to stay a day ahead of your students.

Improving Education

But this was soon to change; then, as now, teachers were seen as keys to improving schools. The creation of **normal schools**, 2-year institutions developed to prepare prospective elementary teachers, was the first significant attempt to improve education during the common school era (Selak, 2008). As we mentioned earlier, before normal schools, the typical teacher was a man, either preparing or waiting for a position in the ministry. Because teachers had no training in education, they used primitive methods, such as memorization and recitation, and they maintained order with stern disciplinary measures, including corporal punishment. Normal schools, in contrast, targeted women as potential teachers and attempted to provide both content background and pedagogical training beyond the high school level.

Many of today's state colleges and universities began as normal schools, such as Eastern Michigan University (formerly Michigan State Normal School), Illinois State University (formerly Illinois State Normal University), Sam Houston State University (formerly Sam Houston Normal Institute), and perhaps most famous, UCLA, the University of California at Los Angeles (formerly Los Angeles Normal School). The functions of normal schools are now performed by undergraduate and graduate schools of education in a college or university such as the one you're now attending.

The second significant change was an improvement in school quality, which occurred when larger elementary schools began separating students into grade levels. This eliminated congested conditions and the overlapping curricula often found in one-room schools. When enrollments were small, one-room schools were the norm, and different-aged students learned together. (Can you imagine trying to teach 6- and 7-year-olds in the same room as 13- and 14-year-olds?) Dividing schools into grade levels resulted in more age-appropriate instruction and allowed content to be taught in greater depth for older students. Finally, as paper and printing presses became more common, more textbooks became available, and educational materials improved.

The Legacy of the Common School Movement

In our *Teaching and You* feature at the beginning of this section, we asked if your parents paid for your education, and if you and your classmates were the same age. We also asked if your friends attended regularly and graduated on time from high school. Your answers to these questions reflect important developments during the common school movement. It was a turning point in American education because the idea of universal access to a tax-supported education was planted and took root (Tyack, 2003). The number of children who attended elementary schools increased steadily during this time, and public support for education grew. State governance and control of education were institutionalized with the creation of state departments of education, and teacher training and quality improved with the development of normal schools.

Organizing elementary schools into grade levels similar to what we have today was another important contribution of the common school era. This makes sense; grouping students together by age makes it easier for teachers to design instruction to meet students' developmental needs.

Despite these advances, the common school movement left two issues that remain today. One involves the inequitable funding of education from state to state and district to district, both of which affect quality. In his book *Savage Inequalities* (1991), Jonathan Kozol, a prominent educational commentator, addresses this issue:

> Americans abhor the notion of a social order in which economic privilege and political power are determined by hereditary class. Officially, we have a more enlightened goal in sight: namely, a society in which a family's wealth has no relation to the probability of future educational attainment and the wealth and station it affords. By this standard, education offered to poor children should be at least as good as that which is provided to the children of the upper-middle class. (1991, p. 207)

This often doesn't occur, however; wide differences in funding exist among states and even districts within states. For example, in Kansas, the wealthiest districts spend almost triple the amount per pupil spent in poorer districts in the state ($16,969 versus $5,655) (Brimley et al., 2012). That extra money means better facilities and resources and the ability of wealthy districts to pay their teachers more and keep them longer.

Teacher quality is the second contentious issue that remains from the common school movement, and educational leaders continue to debate the question of what constitutes a well-qualified teacher. Two contradictory movements in education today illustrate this debate. Alternative licensure, which allows people to become teachers more easily and quickly, is the first. The effort to increase teacher professionalism by making entry into teaching more intellectually rigorous is the second, and it is a theme of this text (Cochran-Smith, Feiman-Nemser, McIntyre, & Demers, 2008). How the issue will be resolved in the future is unclear.

Table 4.1 outlines the important events in our country's early history, their influence on education, and the issues that remain today.

Revisiting My Beliefs

This section addresses the second item in *This I Believe*, "A free public education for students like me has always been a cornerstone of education in the United States." This statement isn't true: Originally, access to education was reserved for the wealthy, and only slowly did this access spread to students from all walks of life.

TABLE 4.1 **A Summary of Historical Periods in American Education (1607–1865)**

Period	Significant Features	Issues That Remain Today
Colonial period, 1607–1775	• Education reserved for wealthy white males • Seeds planted for public support of education • Religion at the core of education	• Whether prayer should be allowed in schools and in what circumstances • Tax support for religious schools • The relationship between religion and character education
Early national period 1775–1820	• The principle of separation of church and state established • Control of education given to the states, rather than to the federal government • Education viewed as crucial for furthering the national interest	• The role of the federal government in education • National testing of students • A national curriculum
Common school movement, 1820–1865	• Access to tax-supported education for all established • Grade levels introduced in elementary schools • Normal schools created to prepare teachers	• Inequities in funding among states and school districts • Teacher quality and alternative routes to teacher certification

Check Your Understanding

3.1. Explain how the common school movement influenced education in our country today.

3.2. How was the common school movement linked to the growing number of immigrants coming to the United States?

3.3. Who was Horace Mann, and what was his contribution to education in the United States?

For feedback, go to the appendix, *Check Your Understanding*, located in the back of this text.

The Evolution of the American High School

Teaching and You

What was your high school experience like? How big was your high school? How big was your graduating class? Did your school have a vocational or technical track? Did you have many friends in other tracks?

Kareem and Antonio walk to high school together, have lockers that are side by side, and even have the same homeroom period. But that's where their contact ends. Kareem is in a college preparation track, along with about a third of the other students in his school. As he goes from class to class, he sees many of the same students. Antonio is in a vocational track, and many of his classes are designed to explore different career options. A technology class focuses on business applications of computers and introduces him to jobs in the computer field. A metalworking class includes welding and even allows him to work on his family's car as a class project. Once Kareem and Antonio leave homeroom, they often don't see each other until soccer practice at the end of the day.

Think about your own experience in high school. Many of you probably took honors classes in English, chemistry, or math, whereas some of your classmates were in "standard" classes, designed for students of average ability. You may also have enrolled in some vocational courses, such as word processing or woodworking, designed to give you skills you could use immediately after graduating from high school. You may have even taken driver's training or nutrition and cooking or other "life management" courses. These options existed because you attended a unique American invention, the **comprehensive high school**, a secondary school that attempts to meet the needs of all students by housing them together and providing a variety of curricular options geared toward different ability levels and interests. How did this uniquely American invention evolve?

Today's modern comprehensive high school can be traced back to academies, such as Franklin's Academy of Philadelphia, and English classical schools, such as the English High School in Boston.

Today, a high school education is seen as essential for success in life, but this wasn't always the case: Before the turn of the 20th century, fewer than 10% of students progressed beyond elementary school (U.S. Department of Education, 1995). In contrast, currently 96% of teenagers attend high school (National Center for Education Statistics, 2010a). A high school education has evolved from a luxury to a right, and now to a necessity.

Historical Roots of the Comprehensive High School

The high school you attended is the result of a long evolutionary history. A time line illustrating this development appears in Figure 4.5 and is discussed in this section.

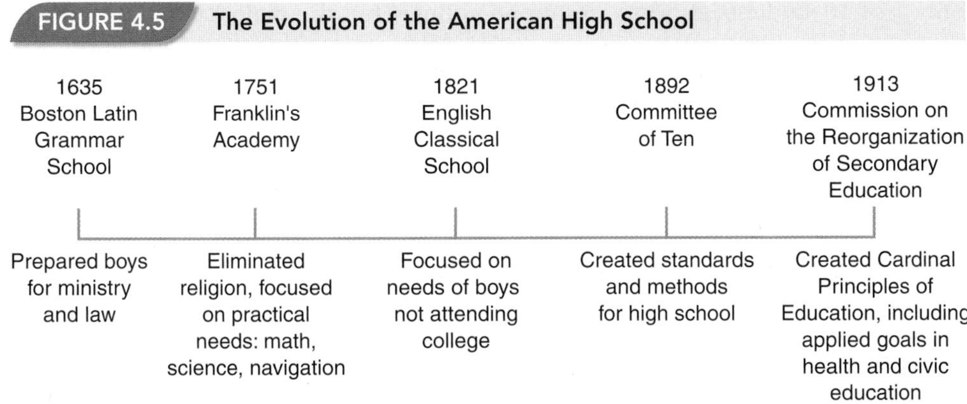
FIGURE 4.5 The Evolution of the American High School
1635 Boston Latin Grammar School
1751 Franklin's Academy
1821 English Classical School
1892 Committee of Ten
1913 Commission on the Reorganization of Secondary Education
Prepared boys for ministry and law
Eliminated religion, focused on practical needs: math, science, navigation
Focused on needs of boys not attending college
Created standards and methods for high school
Created Cardinal Principles of Education, including applied goals in health and civic education

To understand the evolution of today's high schools, we need to go all the way back to 1635, when *The Boston Latin Grammar School* was established. It was the first American high school, but it served only the colonial elite and had a strong European flavor. As the name suggests, it was a **Latin grammar school**, a college-preparatory school designed to help boys prepare for the ministry or a career in law. If you were female, you didn't attend, because you could be neither a minister nor a lawyer. The narrow curriculum—Latin and Greek were the core components—and high cost made Latin grammar schools unattainable and irrelevant for most Americans.

In reaction to this narrow academic orientation, Benjamin Franklin opened the Academy of Philadelphia in 1751. Free of religious orientation and uniquely American, an **academy** was a secondary school that focused on the practical needs of colonial America. Math, navigation, astronomy, bookkeeping, logic, and rhetoric were all taught, and both boys and girls attended. Students selected courses from this menu, which created the precedent for electives and alternative programs at the secondary level that exist today.

Merchants and craftsmen, who had questioned the emphasis on Latin and Greek in the Latin grammar schools, enthusiastically supported this curriculum. By 1860, a quarter of a million students were enrolled in 6,000 tuition-charging academies, and they were the most common type of high school until about 1890 (Reese, 2005).

The academies made three important contributions to American education. First, they shifted emphasis to a practical curriculum, an idea still prominent today, and second, they removed religion from the curriculum. Third, they were partially supported by public funds, which established a trend that flourished during the common school movement. These characteristics—practical, secular, and public—are themes that remain in today's schools.

In addition to the academies, another uniquely American educational institution appeared: In 1821, Boston established the first **English classical school**, a free secondary school designed to meet the needs of boys not planning to attend college. It offered studies in English, math, history, science, geography, bookkeeping, and surveying, and to reflect its practical emphasis, the name was changed to the English High School in 1824.

Schools modeled after the English High School spread slowly because of competition from the academies and public opposition to tax-supported schools. Unconvinced of the practical or economic benefits of a high school education, taxpayers disagreed with the idea that secondary schools should be free, natural extensions of elementary education. The schools were also unable to decide whether their mission was practical or college preparatory, so they responded by offering both types of classes. This uncertainty also affected students: In 1900,

Revisiting My Beliefs

This section addresses the third item in *This I Believe*, "The American high school has historically attempted to meet the needs of all students." This statement isn't true; a high school education was initially a luxury reserved for the wealthy elite. And problems remain today. Even though all students have access to a high school education, many—as high as a third by some estimates—fail to graduate on time, and this figure is higher for cultural minorities (S. Dillon, 2008c).

only 1 of 10 students expected to attend college, but the majority took a college-preparatory curriculum. As you see in the next section, this confusion about the American high school's mission continued into the 20th century and persists even today.

Redefining the High School

The American high school in the late 1800s was an institution in search of an identity. Educational leaders recognized the problem, so in 1892, the National Education Association (NEA) appointed a group called *The Committee of Ten* to examine the high school curriculum and make recommendations about standards, programs, and methods. The committee concluded that students who planned to go no further than high school needed content and teaching methods that were the same as those who were college bound—an idea that continues to be debated today.

Three factors shaped the committee's conclusions (Spring, 2011). First, it was composed of only college professors and administrators—no high school teachers or parents were included—so the bias toward a college-preparatory curriculum isn't surprising. Second, the committee believed in *faculty psychology*, the view that exercising the powers of the mind promoted intelligence. Proponents of this view held that everyone should practice mental discipline to achieve a "stronger" mind. A third factor influencing the committee was the large number of non-English-speaking immigrants and a growing lower class that threatened to create divisions in American society. The committee felt that a different curriculum for college- and non-college-bound students might create a class-based system of education and damage national unity.

Educators recognized, however, that the college-preparatory curriculum wasn't providing prospective workers with the skills needed for increasingly complex jobs. To resolve this dilemma, NEA appointed a second committee, the Commission on the Reorganization of Secondary Education. Its 1918 report, *The Cardinal Principles of Secondary Education*, broadened the high school curriculum to include basic skills such as reading and math, together with vocational education, personal health, worthy home membership, civic education, effective use of leisure time, and ethical character (Urban & Wagoner, 2009). To accommodate these more applied goals, the commission proposed the idea of comprehensive high schools with different tracks for different students; the hope was that the diverse student body, separated into different tracks, would be integrated by sports and other extracurricular activities (Spring, 2010).

Efforts to solve the problems of intellectual and cultural diversity persist today. Although different tracks are designed to provide a customized education for all students, they create two negative side effects (Oakes, 2008). First, the curriculum in the non-college-bound tracks often offers little intellectual challenge; teachers tend to have low expectations for students, and they often use primitive and ineffective teaching methods, such as extensive lecture and seat work (Good & Brophy, 2008). Second, the move to make high schools comprehensive often made them very large, particularly in urban areas.

URBAN EDUCATION: The Challenge of Teaching in Large Urban High Schools

More than 70% of American high schools have enrollments of 1,000 or more, and some urban districts have high schools with more than 5,000 students (U.S. Department of Education, 2009b). Their size creates problems. Classrooms are crowded, and teachers have trouble getting to know their students. Students get lost in the shuffle and are treated as numbers rather than as people.

If you teach in a large urban school, how can you respond to these problems? One way is to create a learning community in which you and your students work together to create a supportive environment in your classroom (Milner & Tenore, 2010; Poplin et al., 2011). Effective teachers in large urban high schools make a special effort to get to know students as people by quickly learning their names, discussing their hopes and fears, and spending out-of-class time with them. They model courtesy and respect for all students and expect similar courtesy in return. And they create clear standards for behavior that require students to treat each other the same way. This creates a sense of community in their classrooms that can reduce the impersonal feel of large high schools. This is very challenging, but it's an ideal worth striving for.

Effective urban teachers create warm, caring learning communities in their classrooms.

Junior High and Middle Schools

While groups such as the Committee of Ten and the Commission on the Reorganization of Secondary Education wrestled with curricular issues, other educators questioned the effectiveness of the then-prevalent organizational pattern of 8 years of elementary and 4 years of high school. Critics argued that too much emphasis was being placed on basic skills like reading and language arts in the upper elementary grades, time that should be spent learning content in depth. Developmental psychologists also noted that early adolescence is a time of intellectual, emotional, and physical transition, and students undergoing these transitions require a different kind of school. In response to these arguments, educators created **junior high schools** to provide a unique academic curriculum for early adolescents. The first junior high, for grades 7, 8, and 9, opened in Columbus, Ohio, in 1909. The concept spread quickly, and by 1926, junior highs had been set up in 800 school systems (Kliebard, 2002).

The 6–3–3 organizational pattern (6 years of elementary school, 3 of junior high, and 3 of high school) was more a change in form than substance, however. Most "junior" highs were exactly that—imitations of high schools with emphasis on academic disciplines and little attention to adolescent development.

In spite of these problems, junior highs remained popular until the 1970s, when continued criticism caused fundamental change. The creation of **middle schools**, targeted at grades 6 to 8 and designed to meet the unique social, emotional, and intellectual needs of early adolescents, was a response to these criticisms (Kellough & Carjuzaa, 2009).

Middle schools attempted to create stronger teacher–student relationships by creating teams. For example, a science, English, math, and social studies teacher would form a team and would all have the same group of students for the school year; this organization allowed teachers to share information about learner progress and make the topics they were teaching more meaningful to students. For instance, if you were a science teacher working on the acceleration of falling bodies, you might integrate the topic with the math teacher on the team, who would demonstrate how the acceleration could be represented graphically. And the social studies teacher, whose students are studying the Civil War, might work with the English teacher, who would have her students read *The Red Badge of Courage,* a novel that focuses on a young soldier's reactions to a Civil War battle. This integration promotes both intellectual and emotional development. In addition, educational psychologists encouraged teachers to move away from lecture-dominated instruction, so prominent in high schools, and focus more on interactive instruction guided by teacher questioning.

This middle school philosophy has grown in popularity, and the number of junior highs has decreased in recent years.

American Secondary Schools: Future Directions

In our *Teaching and You* feature at the beginning of this section we asked you to describe your own high school experiences. Those experiences were influenced by historical trends that shaped the high schools we have today.

The history of American secondary schools also helps us understand important questions facing today's educators. For example, are the tracking systems common in high schools meeting students' needs? Are middle schools rigorous enough academically? Begun as college-preparatory institutions, high schools became comprehensive in an effort to meet the needs of a diverse student body. To help adolescents make the transition from elementary to high school, junior highs were created; when those schools failed to fulfill that mission, educators created middle schools. The academic pendulum has now swung back, however, and some leaders are calling for a redesign of middle schools to make them more academic and rigorous (Schwerdt & West, 2011). Have American secondary schools been too trendy, quickly zigzagging in response to changes in society, or have they been too conservative, hanging on to outmoded academics that are no longer relevant? We examine these questions later in the chapter when we discuss the modern era in American education.

TECHNOLOGY and TEACHING: A Brief History of Technology in the Classroom

The year is 1770, and Anthony and his 17 elementary classmates are involved in a math lesson with Mr. Willis, who has been assigned to teach in the school while he waits for his appointment to a congregation as a minister.

Mr. Willis asks Anthony to recite his "4s" times table orally, while the other students listen quietly. After Anthony is finished, Mr. Willis has James repeat the process with the "5s" times table. He continues through the rest of the times tables, calling on a different student for each table.

As you begin reading this section, you may be asking yourself, "How does this relate to technology?" The answer is, "A great deal."

Although there is no precise definition for the term *technology,* most experts agree that it includes the development and use of tools, machines, and methods of organization designed to perform a specific function. A history of technology can be traced back to prehistoric times with the domestication of fire, an essential tool for improving nutrition, or the invention of the wheel, certainly one of the most important technological advances in history. With respect to education, two of technology's most common functions were communication and presenting information.

Advocates have historically suggested that technology would "revolutionize" education, and some of the advances that we take completely for granted, and typically don't even consider to be technology, did indeed revolutionize education. Easy access to paper and efficient writing pens are two examples. For instance, paper was scarce and expensive during colonial days, which made books even scarcer, so parchment was used originally. The parchment was laid on a flat wooden board, and a transparent piece of cow's horn was fastened onto the parchment to protect it from daily use. These "hornbooks" were used for children's first lessons, such as learning the alphabet or numbers. Constructing hornbooks was time-consuming and expensive, so written materials weren't widely used in colonial classrooms.

This helps us understand how technology relates to the vignette with Mr. Willis and his class. The recitation method, which you saw illustrated, was admittedly inefficient and crude, but was used, in large part, because tools we take for granted today, such as paper and books, were scarce and copy machines were still far in the future. Abe Lincoln reportedly learned math by writing with charcoal on the back of a shovel, and the recitation method was a popular assessment tool because paper wasn't available on which to print tests (Pulliam & Van Patten, 2013).

The use of pens that made writing efficient is another example. Quill pens, made from bird feathers that required students to repeatedly dip the quills in inkwells, were used until about 1830. As you might expect, using them was slow, tedious, and messy, so teachers avoided having their students do much writing. The fountain pen, a pen that held an internal reservoir of ink, was a major technological advance, as was the ballpoint pen, which wasn't widely available until nearly the middle of the 20th century (Pulliam & Van Patten, 2013). Gradually, as books, writing paper, and pens and pencils came into widespread use, education in the 19th and early 20th century advanced dramatically.

Similarly, the use of other technologies in education also rapidly increased. A brief time line of some of the tools that were historically used include:

- (1930s) *Projectors and filmstrips*: This instructional technology, commonly used through the 1980s, and still used in some areas today, allowed teachers to show still photographs in classes, sometimes with accompanying narrative. The instructor turned on a film projector that showed the first frame (image) of the filmstrip. The instructor might then turn on a record or cassette tape containing the audio material for the filmstrip. At the appropriate point, a tone signaled the teacher to turn a knob, advancing the presentation to the next frame.
- (1940s) *Overhead projector*: You might be familiar with overhead projectors, as they were often used to present information to classes until recent years, when they were replaced by smart boards and other more-flexible tech tools. They require information to be placed on transparent plastic for projection, a primary disadvantage.
- (1950s) *Programmed and Computer-Based Instruction*: Originally developed as teaching machines in the 1920s, programmed instruction got a big boost from the famous psychologist B. F. Skinner. Programmed instruction focused on forming behavioral objectives, breaking instructional content into small units, and rewarding correct responses immediately and frequently. Today's computer-based drill-and-practice software, common in basic skills areas at the elementary level, is largely grounded in Skinner's original ideas.
- (1950s–1970s) *Educational television,* the *video cassette recorder* (VCR), and *video home system* (VHS) *tapes*: VCRs and VHS tapes are still familiar to most of us but are rapidly being replaced by DVRs and DVDs. These were used to bring the outside world into the classroom.
- (1967) *Hand-held calculators*: Introduced by Texas Instruments, these large and initially bulky tools paved the way for the sophisticated calculators used in today's classrooms.

The 2000s marked the use of streaming video in classrooms; the use of handheld devices, such as smartphones and clickers; the replacement of overhead projectors with document cameras and chalkboards with whiteboards; the widespread use of the Internet as a source of information; and the increasing popularity of distance learning. Common to all these technological innovations was the claim that they would revolutionize education and perhaps even replace the teacher (Cuban, 1986, 2001). But history has proven these claims to be inaccurate. Although different forms of technology have found their way into classrooms, the teacher is still the center of classroom instruction, and technology's effectiveness depends heavily on the teacher using it.

In the 21st century, we've seen a shift in the use of technology both in and outside of classrooms. Historically, technology was used primarily as a tool for presenting information. Today it is more commonly used to access information via the Internet and communicate with others. For example, a survey conducted in 2010 found that teens who text send and receive an average of 50 texts per day, and even adults who text send and receive 10 per day. In fact, teens now prefer texting to talking on their phones (Kerr, 2012). Further evidence of this technology fervor could be seen in the state of Idaho, where state legislators mandated that students complete two one-semester on-line courses before graduating from high school (Cavanagh 2011e).

Critics argue, however, that technology is not having the impact on teaching and learning that many thought it would, and the reason is that it failed to act as a "magic bullet," curing all of education's problems (Cuban, 1986, 2001; Roblyer & Doering, 2013). For example, a considerable amount of research suggests that students in distance learning and virtual school environments often learn less than their counterparts in brick-and-mortar schools (Collins, 2011; Gabriel & Richtel, 2011; Glass & Welner, 2011). In addition, research suggests that sometimes technology improves learning, while other times it doesn't (Roblyer & Doering, 2013). Simply throwing technology at students without careful planning and execution doesn't work.

Without question, technology is having a profound effect on the way we live. However, the history of technology in classrooms tells us that it is a tool, but only a tool, that you can use to support your instruction. You, the teacher, are still the key to student learning, and you always will be. You will never be replaced by a teaching machine, website, video, or any other form of technology, now or in the future.

Check Your Understanding

4.1. Describe the historical roots of contemporary secondary schools.
4.2. How have the goals of high school education changed over time?
4.3. How are junior highs and middle schools different from each other?

For feedback, go to the appendix, *Check Your Understanding,* located in the back of this text.

Searching for Equality: The Education of Cultural Minorities

To this point, the history of American education has been generally positive. Despite lurches and false starts, the quality of education improved, and it became accessible to more people. The story isn't so positive if you were a member of a cultural minority, however. For example, as a group, students who are cultural minorities:

- Score lower on achievement tests at all grade levels
- Are more likely to drop out of school and fail to graduate with a high school diploma
- Are less likely to attend and graduate from college (Macionis, 2011; Macionis & Parrillo, 2010)

History helps us understand the reasons for these patterns. In this section, we outline the experiences of four minority groups: Native Americans, African Americans, Hispanic Americans, and Asian Americans. We begin with Native Americans.

Education of Native Americans

> The first thing to do was to clean them [Native Americans] thoroughly and to dress them in their new [military] attire. . . . [Then] everything except swallowing, walking, and sleeping had to be taught; the care of person, clothing, furniture, the usages of the table, the carriage of the body, civility, all those things which white children usually learn from their childhood by mere imitation, had to be painfully inculcated and strenuously insisted on. In addition to this, they were to be taught the rudiments of an English school course and the practical use of tools. (U.S. Bureau of Indian Affairs, 1974, p. 1749)

The history of Native American education is a story of largely unsuccessful attempts to assimilate different tribes into the American mainstream (W. Fleming, 2006). **Assimilation** is the process of socializing people to adopt the dominant society's social norms and patterns of behavior. Historically, schools have sought to bring minorities, and particularly Native Americans, into the mainstream of American life by teaching basic skills and instilling white, middle-class values. In doing this they asked Native Americans to reject important aspects of their own histories and cultures. The quote that introduces this section illustrates this policy.

As with American education in general, the education of Native Americans began with a religious orientation. During the 1700s and 1800s, mission schools run primarily by the Catholic Church designed classrooms that focused on basic skills, agriculture, vocational education, and religion. Although instruction was in the native language, mission schools attempted to assimilate Native Americans by helping them bridge the gap between tribal, communal life and one in which individuals owned land, had jobs, and followed the dominant culture (Spring, 2010).

Attempts at assimilation were formalized by the federal government, which was involved in the education of Native Americans from the beginning of our country (see Figure 4.6). From 1771 to 1870, it signed nearly 400 treaties with Native American tribes designed to provide federal assistance for agriculture, medical care, and education. From 1890 to 1930, the federal government established boarding schools run by the Bureau of Indian Affairs. The best way to "Americanize" the children, educators thought, was to remove them from tribal settings and provide them with a strict program of cultural transformation. Consequently, children were forced to live at the schools, English was spoken and taught, and native languages and customs were forbidden.

These boarding schools were a complete failure. For example, in 1901 only 300 of 5,000 eligible Navajo children attended these schools, and many who did initially attend later ran away and returned to the reservation (Button & Provenzo, 1989). Those who graduated quickly returned to reservations.

Despite the failure of boarding schools, federal control of Native American education continued through the 1960s (Lomawaima & McCarty, 2006). Tribal schools, which added Native American culture to the curriculum, opened in 1965, but teachers were poorly paid, instructional materials were limited, and schools depended on the federal government for finances, all problems difficult to overcome.

FIGURE 4.6 Time Line of Native American Education

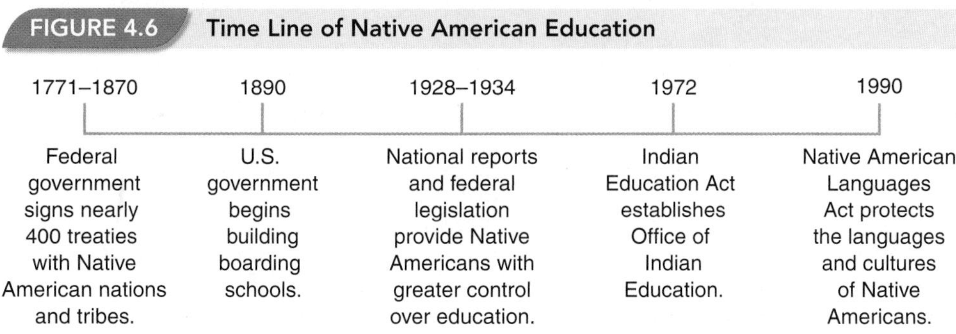

1771–1870
Federal government signs nearly 400 treaties with Native American nations and tribes.
1890
U.S. government begins building boarding schools.
1928–1934
National reports and federal legislation provide Native Americans with greater control over education.
1972
Indian Education Act establishes Office of Indian Education.
1990
Native American Languages Act protects the languages and cultures of Native Americans.

Source: N. Dillon (2007) and W. Fleming (2006).

Legislation during the 1970s gave Native Americans greater control over their schools, and more recently, the federal government shifted responsibility for Native American education from tribal schools to public schools. Currently, there are approximately 4.4 million American Indian and Alaska Natives in the United States; most are clustered in western states, with Alaska (27%), Oklahoma (19%), Montana (11%), and New Mexico (11%) having the highest percentages of Native American students (Zehr, 2008). Of these, only 540,000 live on reservations or trust lands, with nearly 60% living in metropolitan areas (W. Fleming, 2006). Despite this shift and increased involvement by tribal governments, problems with Native American education persist, including high rates of poverty and unemployment, underachievement, high dropout rates, and low rates of college attendance (Spring, 2010).

There is an ongoing debate among Native American educators about the benefits of reservation schools versus nearby public schools (K. Johnson, 2008). Although acknowledging that public schools may offer better academic programs in areas such as advanced science and math, Native American educators fear their students are losing an important part of their cultural heritage, including their native languages (W. Fleming, 2006).

Education of African Americans: Up from Slavery to . . .

The first African Americans arrived in America shortly after the founding of Jamestown in 1607. Brought as slaves, they had few educational opportunities before the Civil War, and many states had laws forbidding the education of slaves (Spring, 2010). Even in "free states" the education of African Americans was limited. For example, in 1850 about 4,000 black students in slave states and 23,000 in free states attended schools—less than 2% of the African American population. The result was a literacy rate of less than 10% (Reese, 2005).

The Civil War (1861–1865) ended legal slavery in the United States, but the policy of **separate but equal**, which formalized the segregation of African Americans in education, transportation, housing, and other aspects of public life,

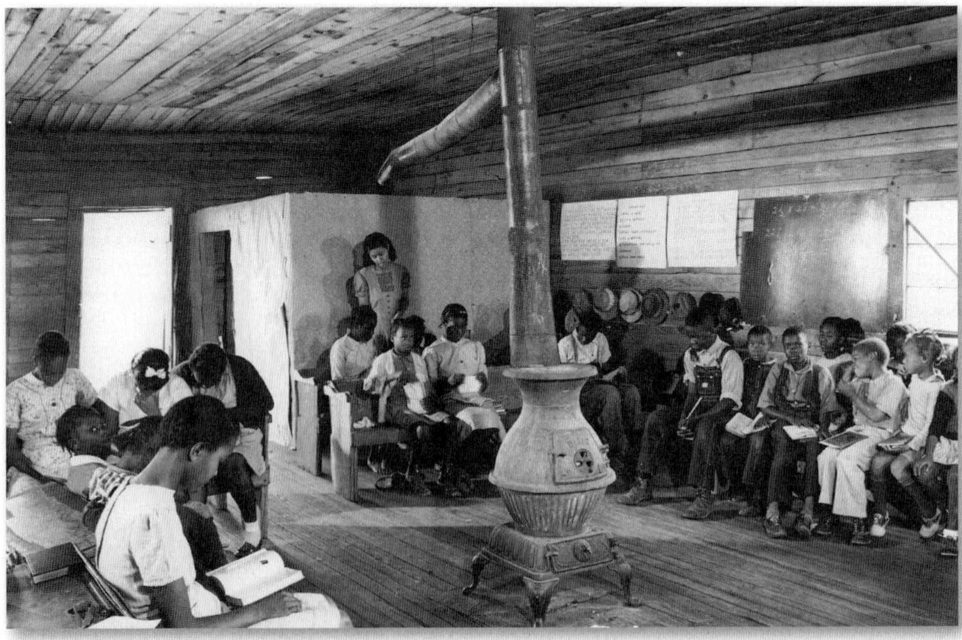

Early efforts at educating African Americans were often substandard because of inadequate funding and resources.

replaced it (Urban & Wagoner, 2009). This policy justified segregation by claiming that African Americans were receiving different but equal treatment under the law. In education, the policy was implemented by creating separate schools with different curricula, teaching methods, teachers, and resources. Some historians believe that these efforts were well intentioned but misguided, whereas others argue that they were inherently racist (Spring, 2011). The policy remained in place until it was overturned by the Supreme Court in 1954 in the famous watershed case, *Brown v. Board of Education of Topeka* (1954).

Unfortunately, the *separate but equal* policy resulted in schools that could more accurately be described as *separate* and *unequal* (E. Gordon, 2007). Funding for African American schools was consistently lower than for white schools, and the schools were consistently substandard. In 1913, for example, South Carolina spent $1.09 per African American student but $9.65 per white student. By 1929, the disparity had grown to $5.20 compared to $52.89 per white student (Urban & Wagoner, 2009). In the early 1900s, white teachers in Alabama were paid 5 times more than African American teachers. In Georgia in the late 1920s, 99% of the money budgeted for teaching equipment went to white schools, even though African Americans made up more than a third of the state's student population (E. Gordon, 2007). *Separate but equal* wasn't working, and the reason was that "equal" wasn't equal.

Proposed Solutions to the Problem

The education of African Americans was clearly inferior to that of whites, but a solution to the problem remained elusive. Finally, two leaders, with sharply different perspectives, emerged.

Booker T. Washington (1856–1915) was born a slave and taught himself to read. Educated at Hampton Institute, a vocational school for African Americans, he established the Tuskegee Institute in 1881. Short of resources, he had his students build the school themselves, and this hands-on approach to learning illustrates his strategy for bettering the education and lives of African Americans in the South. He believed that hard work, practical training, and economic cooperation with whites were the keys to success. His philosophy became popular, and he was often invited to address white audiences on the topic of African American education. Washington also encouraged his students to become teachers; he believed that attempting to enter other professions or politics was premature and would lead to conflict with the white power structure in the South.

Although Washington was accepted by many African Americans and was popular with whites, his policy of accommodating segregation angered other African American leaders. W. E. B. Dubois (1868–1963) was an important opponent whose resistance to Washington's stance was predictable, given the differences in their backgrounds. Dubois was born in Massachusetts and educated in integrated schools. He attended colleges and universities in the United States and Europe and was the first African American to receive a PhD in the United States (Pulliam & Van Patten, 2013).

Dubois was committed to changing the status of African Americans and advocated a determined stand against segregation and racism. He focused his energies on the top students, believing that they would provide leadership and create opportunities for the rest of the African American population. He also believed that this group could take its place among the business, professional, and intellectual leaders of the white population. Dubois believed that Washington's separatist approach implied inferiority and, although expedient in the short term, would impede the educational progress of African Americans in the long run. He advocated social activism and was a leader in establishing the National Association for the Advancement of Colored People (NAACP). This organization played a major role in the Civil Rights Movement in the 20th century.

The Courts Examine "Separate but Equal"

Before the Civil War, African Americans lived apart from the white majority because of slavery and legal restrictions. African Americans were excluded from schools and often forbidden to learn to read or write. Segregation continued after the Civil War because of the *separate but equal* policy. A federal challenge to the policy came in Louisiana in 1896 in a court case involving segregated railroads. In *Plessy v. Ferguson,* the Supreme Court ruled that separate but equal railroad facilities didn't violate the Constitution (Spring, 2011). This decision was also applied to education, and separate but equal remained for almost 50 years.

Education of Hispanic Americans

Hispanic is a label that refers to a diverse group of people who speak Spanish or are of Latin American or Caribbean heritage: Mexican Americans in the Southwest, Puerto Rican Americans in the Northeast, and Cuban Americans in Florida are all included in this group. Currently, the Hispanic population in our country consists of 64% Mexican Americans, 13% Central and South Americans, 9% Puerto Ricans, 3% Dominican, 3% Cuban and 8% from other Spanish-speaking countries (U.S. Bureau of Census, 2008). The term *Hispanic* is more popular in the Northeast, with groups in the Southwest preferring *Latino* (*Latina*, female). The term *Chicano* (*Chicana*, female) refers to Hispanics of Mexican American heritage.

Hispanics are both the largest and the fastest-growing minority group in the United States. Between 1987 and 2007, the Hispanic public school population almost doubled, and experts predict that by 2021 one in four students will be Hispanic (Gándara, 2010). In several states, such as California and Texas, nearly half the school population is now Hispanic.

Hispanic education in America began with Catholic mission schools in the Southwest, but it shifted to public schools after the Mexican–American War in 1848. Assimilation was the initial policy; classes were taught in English, Spanish was forbidden, and students' Hispanic heritage was either ignored or disparaged (Spring, 2010). As with African Americans, schools were often segregated with limited resources allocated unevenly.

Apathy, resistance to school, and dropping out, problems similar to those with Native Americans, were pervasive. These educational problems persist today: In 2008, for example, 64% of the Hispanic school-age population graduated, compared to 81% of white students and 91% of Asian and Pacific Islanders (National Center for Education Statistics, 2010c). Also, only about 1 of 8 25- to 29-year-old Hispanics had a bachelor's degree in 2009, compared to more than 1 of 3 for Whites and nearly 1 of 5 for African Americans (National Center for Education Statistics, 2010e).

Language differences have been the source of many problems in the education of Hispanics. Language symbolizes differences between Hispanics and the dominant culture, and language differences often interfere with student learning. Some experts argue that Hispanic students have historically scored lower on both intelligence and achievement tests largely because of language barriers (Echevarria & Graves, 2011; Solórzano, 2008).

Education of Asian Americans

Like Hispanics, Asian Americans are a diverse group of people with varied histories (Gollnick & Chinn, 2013). The first Asian Americans were Chinese who came to the United States to work in the California gold mines and on the first transcontinental railroad. Japanese immigrants came to California and Hawaii in the late 1800s as farm workers. More recently, Korean and Southeast Asian immigrants came to the United States seeking a better life and an escape from the Korean and Vietnam Wars.

Asian immigrants initially were welcomed because they relieved an acute labor shortage in the West. However, in the late 19th and early 20th centuries, racism and competition for jobs resulted in changes in immigration laws that prevented further Chinese and Japanese immigration (Spring, 2011). A dark page in Asian American history came during World War II, when more than 100,000 Japanese American citizens were forced out of their homes near the Pacific coast and into internment camps in barren areas of the West.

Like other minority groups, Asian Americans experienced discrimination. For example, in 1906, San Francisco established segregated schools for Asian Americans. Instruction was in English, which resulted in problems similar to those that Native Americans and Hispanics encountered. In *Lau v. Nichols* (1974), a federal court ruled that the San Francisco school system had violated the rights of Chinese American students and students who found their educational experience "wholly incomprehensible" should be taught in their first language if that language was not English.

As a group, Asian Americans have generally fared better in American schools than members of other minorities (Gollnick & Chinn, 2013). For example, Asian Americans typically score higher on achievement tests and have higher rates of college attendance and completion than that of both other cultural minority groups and the white population (National Center for Education Statistics, 2010c, 2010e). This success has led some educators to label this group "the model minority," a stereotypic term that can be misleading: Many Asian American students have problems in school, and language and poverty remain obstacles (Gollnick & Chinn, 2013). In addition, considerable differences exist between the educational experiences of different Asian American groups (Pang, Han, & Pang, 2011). Chinese and Korean students, for example, enroll in colleges at much higher rates than Cambodians and Hmong. Focusing on group memberships can result in inappropriate expectations for and unjust treatment of individual members of those groups. In short, you need to remember that your students are individuals and treat them that way.

The Search for Equality: Where Are We Now?

The United States has always had ambivalent attitudes toward ethnic and cultural diversity. While accepting and even valuing this diversity in the form of music, food, and holidays, such as the Chinese New Year or Cinco de Mayo, our country values assimilation and uniformity. Some argue for cultural homogeneity and emphasize the need for common values and language, whereas others counter that cultural diversity contributes unique ideas and perspectives that make our country vibrant and rich (Spring, 2011). As our country continues to attract immigrants from different countries and cultures, the debate is likely to continue.

Because of this ambivalence, the federal government's role in the education of cultural minorities remains poorly defined. In the past, federal courts played a major role in desegregation. During the 1960s, the commendable goal of integration, which sought to provide opportunities for cultural minorities and white majority students to attend school together and learn about each other, often became synonymous with the highly unpopular policy of forced busing (Pulliam & Van Patten, 2013). Parents who wanted their children to attend neighborhood schools resisted busing, public support for integration waned, and a resegregation of cultural minorities in urban schools has resulted (Orfield, Frankenberg, & Siegel-Hawley, 2010). Because of the public's attitudes, the federal government has become reluctant to impose busing and other legal mechanisms to achieve integration.

As with the federal courts, the legislative branch also remains uncertain. Once an advocate for cultural diversity, the Senate voted 63 to 34 in 2006 to designate English as the national language (Hulse, 2006). We examine this changing federal role in education in the next section.

Revisiting My Beliefs

This section addresses the fourth item in *This I Believe*, "When slavery ended in our country, cultural and ethnic minorities were welcomed into our public schools." This statement isn't true: Even today, many cultural minorities fail to benefit from educational opportunities in our country.

Check Your Understanding

5.1. What are the similarities and differences in different minority groups' struggles for educational equality?
5.2. How does the concept of assimilation relate to Native American boarding schools?
5.3. How does "separate but equal" relate to African Americans' educational experience in the United States?
5.4. How did the process of assimilation relate to Hispanic Americans and their native languages?

For feedback, go to the appendix, *Check Your Understanding*, located in the back of this text.

The Modern Era: Schools as Instruments for National Purpose and Social Change

The modern era in education began after World War II and continues to the present (see Figure 4.7). It is characterized by an increased national emphasis on education, which people now view as the key to both individual success and the progress of the nation. Given this perspective, it isn't surprising to see the federal government more actively involved in education than in the past. This increased involvement occurred in four major areas:

- Education and the Cold War
- The War on Poverty
- The enlistment of schools in a worldwide economic battle
- The government's role in equity issues

The Cold War: Enlisting America's Schools

After World War II, the United States became involved in the Cold War, with ever more powerful weapons being stockpiled on both sides. It was called the "Cold War" because no shots were fired. But the struggle for world leadership between our country and the Communist bloc—primarily the USSR—significantly impacted education in our country.

The Russian launching of the satellite Sputnik in 1957 was a key event of this period. Believing the United States was losing the technology war, our government authorized a fivefold increase in the funding of the National Science Foundation, which had been created in 1950 to support research and improve science education. Congress also passed the National Defense Education Act (NDEA) in 1958, which was designed to enhance "the security of the nation"

FIGURE 4.7 The Modern Era

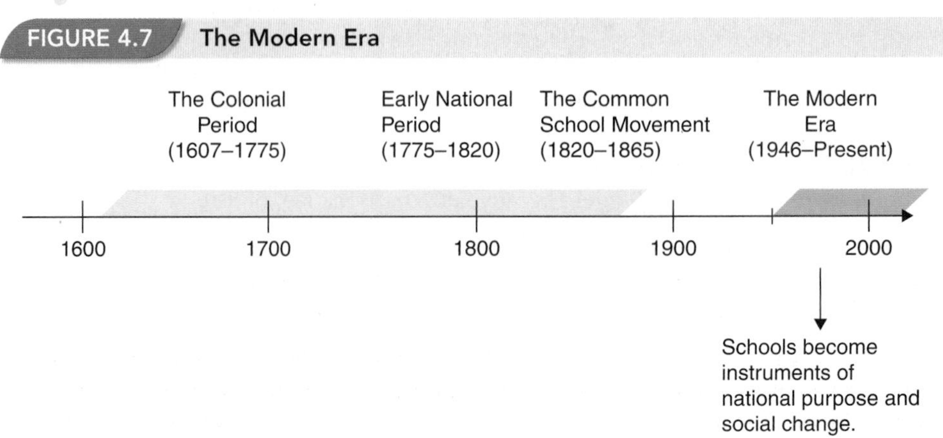

by improving instruction in math, science, and foreign languages. The NDEA provided funds for teacher training, new equipment, and the establishment of centers for research and dissemination of new teaching methods. During this period, Admiral Hyman Rickover, the father of the American nuclear navy, called education the first line of defense against our enemies (Pulliam & Van Patten, 2013).

The War on Poverty and the Great Society

During the 1960s, leaders began to realize that despite the economic boom following World War II, many Americans were living in poverty. The United States was becoming a nation of "haves" and "have-nots," and the problem was exacerbated by an economy that required ever-increasing skills from its workers.

For the unfortunate, a cycle of poverty began with inadequate education, which decreased employment opportunities, led to a poorer quality of life, and resulted in lowered achievement for the next generation (Macionis, 2011). To break this cycle and create a "Great Society," in which all could participate and benefit, President Lyndon Johnson stated in his 1964 State of the Union address that "this administration today, here and now, declares unconditional war on poverty in America."

Teaching and You

Did you attend preschool? Kindergarten? Did most of the students in your neighborhood do the same? Were these public or private schools?

The **War on Poverty**, a general term for federal programs designed to eradicate poverty during the 1960s, emphasized education as its major thrust. During this period, the federal government's involvement in education increased significantly. Initiatives included:

- *Increased federal funding for K–12 education,* which grew from $900 million and about 4.4% of the total spent on education in 1964 (before Johnson's initiatives) to $3 billion and 8.8% of the total educational budget by 1968.
- *The development of the Job Corps.* Modeled after the Civilian Conservation Corps of the 1930s, the Job Corps created rural and urban vocational training centers to help young people learn marketable skills while working in government projects.
- *The creation of the Department of Education in 1979.* The department was originally part of the Department of Health, Education, and Welfare, but education was considered so important that it was elevated to its own cabinet-level position during President Carter's administration.
- *Support for learners with exceptionalities,* such as students who struggled in a particular area like reading or math. In 1975, Congress passed Public Law 94-142, the Individuals with Disabilities Education Act (IDEA), which required a free and appropriate public education for all students, including those with exceptionalities. In 1976–1977, the nation educated about 3.3 million children with exceptionalities; today, the schools serve more than 6 million, an increase of nearly 100% (Heward, 2009).
- *The creation of national compensatory education programs.*

Let's look at these compensatory programs in more detail.

Compensatory Education Programs

Compensatory education programs are government attempts to create equal educational opportunities for disadvantaged youth. These programs provide supplementary instruction and attempt to prevent learning problems before they occur. The two best known are Title I and Head Start.

Title I: Improving the Academic Achievement of the Disadvantaged. Title I is a federal compensatory education program that funds supplemental education services for low-income students in elementary and secondary schools. Title I provided

were equal at your school. They probably weren't; Title IX is attempting to fix that, but societal pressures in favor of male sports often run counter to that change.

Title IX has become controversial at the college level. Critics argue that to achieve an equal number of male and female athletes, schools have had to eliminate many of the "minor" men's sports, such as wrestling, swimming, gymnastics, and tennis. Supporters of Title IX argue that the extraordinary cost of college football skews the issue, and that a modest cut in football expenditures would allow for a greater investment in women's sports with no cuts to other men's sports. Colleges and universities typically have used Internet surveys to poll female students about their interest in participating in sports programs, but a recent change in federal policy now requires schools to provide additional forms of data, such as actual participation rates (Associated Press, 2010).

Evaluating Federal Equality Efforts

So, how has federal intervention affected the struggle for equality in education? With respect to integration, progress is uncertain. For example, in the South in 1988, nearly 44% of African American students attended integrated schools, up from virtually none in 1954. By 1996, however, the figure had shrunk to slightly more than a third (Hendrie, 1999). In the North, segregated housing patterns led to de facto segregated schools. This problem has been exacerbated in urban areas by "white flight" to the suburbs. Consider these statistics:

> In Chicago, by the academic year 2000–2001, 87 percent of public school enrollment was black or Hispanic; less than 10 percent of children in the schools were white. In Washington, D.C., 94 percent of children were black or Hispanic; less than 5 percent were white. In St. Louis, 82 percent of the student population was black or Hispanic by this point, in Philadelphia and Cleveland 78 percent, in Los Angeles 84 percent, in Detroit 95 percent, in Baltimore 88 percent. In New York City, nearly three quarters of the students were black or Hispanic in 2001. (Kozol, 2005, p. 8)

Currently, more than three fourths of Hispanic students attend schools populated predominantly by members of cultural minorities, and nearly 4 of 10 attend schools that are 90% to 100% minority (Orfield, 2009).

Various strategies have been proposed to achieve greater racial diversity, such as school boundary realignments, and the mandatory busing we discussed earlier. In the 1970s, **magnet schools**, public schools that provide innovative or specialized programs and accept enrollment from students in all parts of a district, were developed to integrate white and minority students.

Magnet schools capitalize on school choice, avoiding the problems associated with mandatory busing to achieve racial integration (Orfield & Siegel-Hawley, 2008). These schools organize their curricula around high-interest or high-need areas such as math, science, and computer science, or around high-quality general programs designed to prepare students for college. They're most common in large cities, and they attract large proportions of cultural minorities and low-income students who are looking for alternatives to existing schools (Orfield & Siegel-Hawley, 2008). The federal government supports the growth of magnet schools by targeting annual grants of $100 million of federal funds to school districts (Chandler, 2012).

In spite of strong governmental support, magnet schools haven't always met their original goals. For instance, they tend to attract the highest-achieving minority students, robbing students from other schools of role models. And when they attract bright members of cultural minorities, they sometimes can't attract high-performing white students into the same schools. Although magnet schools are more racially diverse than charter schools, social class differences between wealthier and poorer students and cultural differences within magnet schools can thwart true integration and the development of cohesive learning communities (Orfield & Siegel-Hawley, 2008).

Civil rights and women's equity efforts also continue to be highly controversial. Some minority leaders and women's groups assert that progress for cultural minorities and women has been too slow, and the government should do more. On the other hand, conservative leaders contend that civil rights efforts have gone too far: They charge that women and minorities are receiving preferential treatment, which amounts to reverse discrimination. These debates are likely to continue in the future as critics on various sides become increasingly vocal and polar in their positions.

Diversity in Your Classroom

Although you may feel limited in what you can do about these issues at the national or state levels, there is much you can do in your own classroom. You play a major role in creating a classroom climate that welcomes and encourages all students (Hallinan, 2008). You establish the rules and procedures, and you set a moral tone when you introduce your students to them. You also act as a role model in the way you treat students. You also have frequent opportunities to teach about fairness and equity in your everyday interactions with students, including who you call on in class and who receives extra help and encouragement. You can make your classrooms a microcosm of the kind of world you'd like your students to grow up in.

Check Your Understanding

6.1. How did schools become instruments for national purpose during the modern era?
6.2. How were federal efforts during the Cold War similar to and different from its efforts to achieve racial equality in education?
6.3. What are magnet schools, and how do they relate to attempts to achieve equality in our schools?
6.4. What is Title IX, and how is it related to the concept of equality?

For feedback, go to the appendix, *Check Your Understanding*, located in the back of this text.

EXPLORING DIVERSITY: A Look Back at Teaching Through the Lens of Gender

Currently more than 3 of 4 teachers in our country are female, and the proportion of teachers who are women continues to increase. But it wasn't always this way (Ingersoll, 2010). In fact, in colonial times, most teachers were male, and women were considered ill-suited to the demands of teaching. Women were thought of as inferior, both physically and intellectually, and not up to the rigors of disciplining unruly students with the "rod." The story of women in teaching is an interesting one that mirrors changes in our society, and these changes continue today as more and more women are attracted to teaching. To understand these changes, let's return to colonial times.

During colonial times, men dominated teaching, and women were viewed as second-class citizens, with few property rights and little say in government. (Women weren't allowed to vote until 1920, when the 14th Amendment to the Constitution was passed.) **Dame schools,** in which women taught small groups of children in their homes, were the exception to this rule, but few of them existed, and they depended on donations of money or food from parents of schoolchildren (Pulliam & Van Patten, 2013; Urban & Wagoner, 2009).

This pattern of male domination in the teaching force continued until the Civil War, when three events occurred, both in and outside of schools. First, large numbers of men were killed during the Civil War, which created a labor shortage. Second, the industrial revolution took hold in America after the Civil war, resulting in higher wages for men in factories. And third, access to public schooling

FIGURE 4.8 **Women and Teaching: A Historical Look**

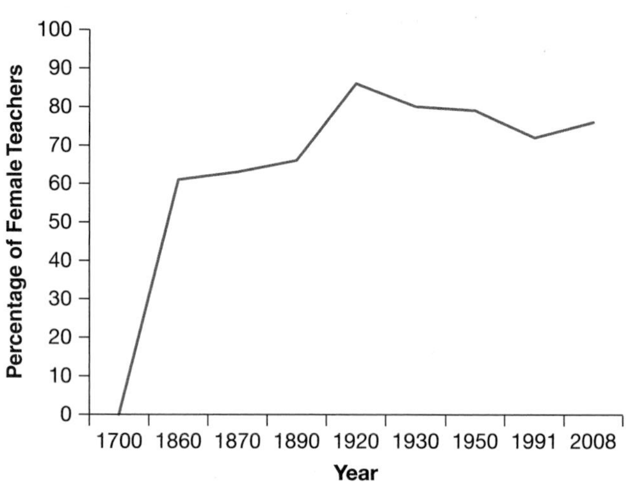

Source: Holmes and Weiss (1995); Tyack and Hansot (1986); and Urban and Wagoner (2009).

increased dramatically, resulting in large numbers of students who needed teachers—especially women who would work for lower wages.

The shift in the gender composition of the teaching force was dramatic (see Figure 4.8). By the late 1800s, two thirds of teachers in our country were women, and the figure rose to 90% in urban areas, largely because men left teaching for better-paying factory jobs. The proportion of female teachers in rural areas at the same time was much lower (1 of 3 teachers was female), because men in rural areas didn't have access to higher-paying factory jobs, and women were needed on the farm to help with the work. By 1920, the number of female teachers in the United States increased to 86%, and remained at about 70% through the rest of the 20th century.

Despite increasing numbers, female teachers faced a number of obstacles, including lower pay, resistance to hiring during tough economic times, and restrictions on their private lives (Urban & Wagoner, 2009). In terms of salary, female teachers were typically paid less than their male counterparts. In Boston in the late 1890s, female high school teachers were paid $756 per year, with $48-yearly increments for experience; male teachers earned $1,380 with $144-annual increments. The top salary for females in Boston was $1,300; for males it was $2,880. Female teachers endured these inequities because viable alternatives in the workplace didn't exist.

In addition to low pay, female teachers also had to endure restrictions on their private lives. For example, during the 1920s, many urban districts prohibited hiring married female teachers; the logic was that if teachers were married, their husbands should support them, and they shouldn't take jobs from men who really needed them. In addition, it was common practice to require female teachers to take a leave of absence when they became pregnant. It was not until 1978 that Congress passed the Pregnancy Discrimination Act that forbids such discriminatory practices (LaMorte, 2012). Finally, it was common for districts to prescribe female teachers' personal appearance, placing explicit restrictions on clothing, make-up, and fingernail polish (Urban & Wagoner, 2009).

DIVERSITY AND YOU

The Gender Gap in Teaching

Several teachers are talking over lunch. Topics range from the weather to life in general.

"Sometimes when I look around, I wonder if I'm lost or in the right place. Do you realize I'm the only male teacher in this school?" Jeff Ridges comments jokingly to the other teachers. "Sometimes I feel like an endangered species."

"Don't feel so bad," Sharon Stanton replies. "I felt the same way in my science department before I switched to the elementary level. I was the only female in the department, and sometimes it just felt weird."

"At least it's not so bad at the sixth-grade level. When I go to district sixth-grade math meetings, at least I'll find a few others like me. But I read somewhere that at the preschool and kindergarten levels, 98% of the teachers are female."

"Hmm. I didn't realize it was that bad. Well, the kids don't seem to mind," Sharon replies.

"They don't mind, but I wonder if this is good for them. Don't the boys need male role models to look up to and imitate?"

QUESTIONS TO CONSIDER

1. Is the predominance of female teachers a positive influence on the profession?
2. What about students? As Jeff asked, do children need male role models as teachers?
3. What do you predict in terms of this trend for the future?

Go to *Diversity and You* in the MyEducationLab™ *Book Resources* that accompany this text to log your thoughts and receive feedback from your authors.

Despite these restrictions, women flocked into teaching because historically it provided one of the few occupations accessible to them. Factory jobs were a male province (except during World War II, when men went to war and women were needed on the assembly line), and alternatives in industry were often limited to clerical or secretarial work. Although this is no longer the case, and women are finding their way in record numbers into areas like medicine, law, and industry, societal forces still draw women into teaching and men away from the profession (Lenz, 2011). Currently, 76% of teachers are female, and experts predict this figure will increase to 80% in the near future (Ingersoll, 2010). In a profession once dominated by males, females have taken control, at least in terms of numbers.

ISSUES YOU'LL FACE IN TEACHING

Is Compulsory Attendance the Solution to Absenteeism and Dropouts?

Dropping out of school has become a social issue as well as an educational problem. When students drop out of school, they not only decrease their own personal chances for success, they also increase the probability of being unemployed as well as increased likelihood of drug abuse and crime (Macionis, 2011). Compulsory attendance laws in every state currently require students to attend school until a predetermined age, which varies from state to state, from 16 to 18. But are compulsory education laws working, and are they the best strategy to address our country's dropout problem?

If you had asked citizens during colonial times the same questions, they would have looked at you with a puzzled stare. Not only were children not required to attend school, it was a privilege reserved for a select few—the wealthy. Slowly over time, the importance of school attendance for later success in life became apparent, and Massachusetts passed the first compulsory attendance law in 1852. Pallid by current standards, it required 12 weeks of school attendance, at least 6 of which had to be continuous (Urban & Wagoner, 2009). Despite public resistance (Why does my son or daughter need to go to school to learn how to farm or be a wife?) and lax enforcement, public school attendance increased significantly over time. In 1860, less than half of 5- to 19-year-olds attended school regularly; by 1920, the figure had increased to almost 80% (Urban & Wagoner, 2009). Currently 69% of students graduate on time, down from 77% in 1970, and the figure is much lower for cultural minorities (Swanson, 2010).

School attendance is important for several reasons, the most important being learning. Learning suffers when students aren't in class, and absenteeism also creates logistical problems for teachers when students miss important lessons. Unfortunately, in large urban districts like Chicago, the average high school attendance rate is 86%, which means students miss 1 of 7 school days, and this absentee rate increases for cultural minorities, children in poverty, and students with exceptionalities (Cullotto, 2011). Some high-poverty Chicago high schools have attendance rates of only 54%, and two thirds of these students miss more than a month or more of school during the year (Cullotto, 2011).

THE QUESTION

So what is the best way to address this pressing problem? Some call for stricter enforcement of existing compulsory attendance laws, while others contend that poor attendance is a symptom rather than a cause. Here are the arguments on both sides of stricter compulsory attendance laws.

PRO

- There is a strong link between attendance and school success as well as dropping out of school and problems in later life. Compulsory attendance laws address these connections.
- Compulsory attendance laws currently exist in all 50 states. They need to be enforced better; nonenforcement of these laws sends the wrong message to truants.
- New technologies allow schools to track truancy and address the problem more efficiently (Roblyer & Doering, 2013).

CON

- Compulsory attendance laws don't work. The students who normally attend school aren't affected by them, and the students who need them the most, disregard them.
- Nonattendance and truancy are symptoms of larger problems, and are not the problem itself. Poverty is a major factor affecting school attendance, and many students miss school because of family or health problems (Macionis, 2011). In addition, students fail to attend school and drop out because school is meaningless to them and fails to connect to their lives.
- Instead of more attention to coercing students to attend, personalized alternative programs are needed that motivate students and address their problems. These have proven successful in a number of high-poverty and urban settings (Ready & Lee, 2008).

YOU TAKE A STAND

Are compulsory education laws the best answer to the attendance and dropout issues, or is there a better way to address the problem?

Go to *Issues You'll Face in Teaching* in the MyEducationLab™ *Book Resources* that accompany this text to log your thoughts and receive feedback from your authors.

VOICES from the CLASSROOM

"I like to think that I stretch the children's minds, and I move out poverty, I remove hate, discrimination, and I put in their places love, music, beautiful music that can transform the world."

PHIL WILSON, 2011 Teacher of the Year, Alabama

CHAPTER 4 Summary

1. Explain how the diversity of the original colonies shaped our educational system, and describe the role of religion in colonial schools.
   - Major geographic, economic, and cultural differences existed in the original 13 colonies. These differences spilled over into religious differences, which strongly influenced the decision to separate church and state.
   - Early colonial educational practices were largely negative and repressive. Over time, European philosophies that were more humane and child centered made their way across the Atlantic.
   - The colonial period resulted in three historical legacies. First, early schools were elitist, catering to wealthy white males. Second, the foundation of public support for education was established by the Old Deluder Satan Act. Finally, the tangled relationship between religion and education began.
2. Explain how the early national period influenced education in this country.
   - During the early national period, the framers of the Constitution used the First Amendment to separate religion from government control or influence.
   - The Tenth Amendment placed the primary responsibility for funding and governing education in the hands of state and local governments.
   - During this period, the federal government separated church and government, relegated educational responsibility to the states, and established the idea that schools were essential for improving the quality of life and helping the nation grow.
3. Explain how the common school movement influenced education in our country today.
   - During the years leading up to the Civil War, states laid the foundations for universal access to tax-supported schools. States established state departments of education to govern schools and built normal schools to improve the professional training for teachers.
   - The common school movement was a turning point in American education because it planted the idea of access to a tax-supported education for all. Though this ideal was not achieved in practice until later, establishing the principle was important.

4. Describe the historical roots of contemporary secondary schools.
   - The history of the comprehensive American high school began with the Boston Latin School, the first secondary school in the colonies. This college-preparatory institution focused on the classics. Benjamin Franklin's Academy of Philadelphia introduced the idea of a practical curriculum. The English High School targeted non-college-bound students and was supported by public funds.
   - The comprehensive American high school evolved as a compromise out of a tug-of-war between committee reports that advocated either academic or applied orientations. The goal of the comprehensive high school is to meet the needs of all students—general education, vocational, and college preparatory—under one roof.
   - Current middle schools began as more traditional junior highs created in the early 1900s. Junior high schools were more academically oriented and were often "mini" versions of high schools. Middle schools were created to meet the unique developmental needs of young adolescents.
5. Identify similarities and differences in minority groups' struggles for educational equality.
   - The education of cultural minorities in the United States aimed at assimilation. Although attempts were made to create schools that were separate but equal, they succeeded in the goal to separate but failed dismally to create equal quality of education. Native American education efforts attempted to assimilate students through boarding schools.
   - The education of African Americans in the United States had a long history of separate but unequal treatment that was finally challenged in the Supreme Court in 1954.
   - Education for Hispanic Americans had a similar, uneven history, with both segregation and unequal funding. Language was a central issue in the education of Hispanic students, and bilingual education, designed to preserve students' first language, has been a central controversy in the education of Hispanics.
   - Asian Americans experienced educational problems similar to those of other cultural minorities. In attempts to assimilate them quickly, schools often ignored Asian Americans' native languages and cultures. Asian American groups and students are widely diverse, both in terms of cultural backgrounds as well as facility with the English language.
   - The federal government's proper role in pursuing equity in education is continually being debated. The debate includes advocates of local control and questions about whether equity efforts should come from states or the federal government.
6. Explain how schools became instruments for national purpose during the modern era.
   - During the modern era, the federal government took a more active role in education, using it as an instrument of national purpose. During the Cold War with the Soviet Union, the federal government spent large amounts of money improving math, science, and foreign language education.
   - During the War on Poverty and the Great Society, the federal government also used courts and federal spending to battle poverty and inequities in schools.
   - The federal government also enlisted schools in its economic struggles with other countries. *A Nation at Risk* called for improved education to maintain U.S. "preeminence in commerce, industry, science, and technological innovation." No Child Left Behind, the latest attempt at federal reform, aimed to reform education through testing and accountability.
   - Currently, consensus is lacking about the federal government's proper role in achieving education equity. Although most believe that reform is needed, whether the focal point of change should be federal or local is still undecided.

Important Concepts

assimilation
common school movement
compensatory education programs
comprehensive high school
dame schools
de jure segregation
de facto segregation
English classical school
Head Start
junior high schools
Latin grammar school
magnet schools
middle schools
normal schools
Old Deluder Satan Act
separate but equal
Title I
War on Poverty

Portfolio Activity

Investigating Title I Programs and Students

InTASC Core Teaching Standard 2: Learning Differences

The goal of this activity is to familiarize you with the Title I programs in your area. Locate the websites for your state's office of education or for several local school districts. (Phone numbers for local school districts can be found under "Schools" in the commercial White Pages at the back of a phone book. The offices you call will provide website addresses.) Browse the sites for information on Title I programs, and answer the following questions:

a. Which districts or schools offer the largest number of these programs?
b. What kinds of students (i.e., students from which cultural minority groups) are found in these programs?
c. What is the curriculum in these programs?
d. What is instruction like in these programs?

Based on this information, what are some ways that you can prepare yourself to teach in schools that have high percentages of Title I students?

Portfolio Activities similar to this one and related to chapter content can be found at MyEducationLab™.

Education in the United States: Its Historical Roots

Go to the topic *History and Philosophy of Education* in the MyEducationLab (www.myeducationlab.com) for *Introduction to Teaching*, where you can:

- Find learning outcomes for *History and Philosophy of Education,* along with the national standards that connect to these outcomes.
- Complete *Assignments and Activities* that can help you more deeply understand the chapter content.
- Apply and practice your understanding of the core teaching skills identified in the chapter with the *Building Teaching Skills and Dispositions* learning units.
- Access video clips of CCSSO National Teachers of the Year award winners responding to the question, "Why Do I Teach?" in the *Teacher Talk* section.
- Check your comprehension on the content covered in the chapter with the *Study Plan.* Here you will be able to take a chapter quiz, receive feedback on your answers, and then access *Review, Practice, and Enrichment* activities to enhance your understanding of chapter content.
- Check the *Book Resources* to find opportunities to share thoughts and gather feedback on the *Diversity and You* and *Issues You'll Face in Teaching* features found in this chapter.

MyEducationLab™

CHAPTER 5

Educational Philosophy and Your Teaching

VOICES from the CLASSROOM

"I became a teacher because I believe that teaching is one of the few careers that you can wake up each morning and you can change the world. I know that might sound a little exaggerated, but I truly believe it. I believe that teachers have the power to send children down paths that they had no idea they were interested in going down."

JOSEPH MASIELLO, 2011 Teacher of the Year, Delaware

CHAPTER OUTLINE

Philosophy and Philosophy of Education

- Philosophy and Teacher Professionalism
- The Relationship Between Philosophy and Theory

Branches of Philosophy

- Epistemology
- Metaphysics
- Axiology
- Logic

Philosophies of Education

- Perennialism
- Essentialism
- Progressivism
- Social Reconstructionism
- Technology and Teaching: Educational Technology and Philosophy
- Philosophies of Education and Cultural Minorities

  Exploring Diversity: Philosophy and Cultural Minorities

  Diversity and You: Philosophy and the Classroom

  Issues You'll Face in Teaching: The Essential Knowledge Debate

Developing Your Philosophy of Education

- The Role of Beliefs in a Philosophy of Education
- Examining Your Beliefs
- Forming a Philosophy

  Urban Education: Philosophy of Education in Urban Environments

LEARNING OUTCOMES

After you've completed your study of this chapter, you should be able to:

1. **Define philosophy, and explain the difference between philosophy and theory.** InTASC Core Teaching Standard 9, Professional Learning and Ethical Practice.
2. **Describe the branches of philosophy, and identify examples that illustrate each.** InTASC Core Teaching Standard 9, Professional Learning and Ethical Practice.
3. **Describe the major educational philosophies, and identify examples that illustrate each.** InTASC Core Teaching Standard 9, Professional Learning and Ethical Practice.
4. **Explain why a personal philosophy of education is important, and describe the steps involved in forming one.** InTASC Core Teaching Standard 9, Professional Learning and Ethical Practice.

How do you plan to teach when you have your first classroom? What content or topics will you focus on? What teaching strategies will you use to help your students learn? How will you relate to your students? Educational philosophy can help answer these questions. Most beginning teachers have an educational philosophy that guides them in the classroom, but often this philosophy is implicit rather than explicit, meaning that it's there but you're often not aware of its existence or how it will influence your actions as a teacher. Our goal in this chapter is to help you think about your own personal philosophy of education and how it will affect your professional life.

Philosophy often seems rather remote and disconnected from our everyday lives, but it is not. We all have philosophical views about many aspects of daily living and may even use the phrase, "My philosophy on this is . . ." as we describe some belief. And we all have a "philosophy of life," which might be as simple as "Live life to the fullest," "Live for the moment, because we never know about tomorrow," or "Hard work is the key to success." **Philosophy** is a set of principles we choose to live by, even though we often don't consciously think about them.

As with individuals, teachers have philosophies that guide their practice. As you read the following case study, think about the philosophical differences that guide the thinking of these two middle school teachers.

"What's happening?" Brad Norman, a middle school English teacher, asks Allie Skinner, a colleague who teaches science, as he walks into the teachers' lounge after school.

"Working on this quiz," Allie mumbles, glancing up at him.

"You sure do test the heck out of your kids, don't you? Every time I come in here, you're either writing a quiz or scoring one."

"Well, this is what I believe. . . . I've given all this a lot of thought, and this is the best I've been able to come up with so far. . . . Everything I read in journals talks about how important background knowledge is for new learning. Everything we learn depends on what we already know. . . . And there's real, practical stuff out there that kids need. They have to be good readers, they need to be able to write and do math, and they need to understand this stuff, the science I'm teaching. I'm not doing my job if I don't get them to learn as much as possible. And practice, thorough assessment, and detailed feedback are some of the best ways we have of getting them to learn. That's reality."

"I like the idea of kids knowing stuff, too, but school involves more than that. Where in your scheme do kids learn to solve problems and make choices and wise decisions? Everything I read says that kids need lots of experience in making decisions and solving problems. The only way they're going to get good at making decisions is to be put in situations where they're forced to make decisions. . . . That's how the world works, and I would be doing the kids, their parents, and ultimately our whole society a disservice if I didn't try to prepare them for life outside school.

"And," Brad continues, "exactly what is reality? You said, 'There's real, practical stuff out there that kids need.' I think being put in situations where they have to practice making decisions is 'real, practical, stuff.' Reality is, in fact, what you perceive it to be, and there's no objective source out there to decide which view is the 'right one.'"

"Aw, c'mon," Allie counters. "Sure, perception is important, but look at that oak tree outside the window. You can perceive it to be anything you want, but it's still an oak tree. And, it doesn't matter what anybody thinks: Two plus two is four—not three, not five, not anything else."

The bell rings, cutting off their conversation. They laugh, agree to disagree, and promise to continue the discussion later.

MyEducationLab™

Visit the MyEducationLab for *Introduction to Teaching* to enhance your understanding of chapter concepts with a personalized *Study Plan.* You'll also have the opportunity to hone your teaching skills through video and case-based *Assignments and Activities* and *Building Teaching Skills and Disposition* lessons.

This I Believe

EDUCATIONAL PHILOSOPHY AND ME

For each item, circle the number that best represents your belief. Use the following scale as a guide:

4 = I strongly believe the statement is true.

3 = I believe the statement is true.

2 = I believe the statement is false.

1 = I strongly believe the statement is false.

1. The purpose of educational philosophy is to help me and other prospective teachers understand how past experts have thought about teaching.

   1 2 3 4

2. Children should learn morals in the home. Teaching morals in school is not part of my job.

   1 2 3 4

3. As a teacher, my primary goal should be to help students master essential content rather than to help them develop emotionally and socially.

   1 2 3 4

4. Our nation's schools should focus on teaching students to think and solve problems in the real world.

   1 2 3 4

5. I should encourage my students to think about their personal role in making the world a better place.

   1 2 3 4

We address the issues raised in Allie and Brad's conversation as the chapter unfolds, but before we begin, please respond to the items in the *This I Believe: Educational Philosophy and Me* feature on the preceding page. We know you're only beginning your teacher preparation program, but now is the time to start thinking about your own philosophy of education. We address each of the feature's statements in this chapter.

Philosophy and Philosophy of Education

Think about the questions we asked in *Teaching and You*. The answers are "philosophical." If you believe, for example, that your math, science, history, and other content courses are most important in helping you learn to teach, you are making a philosophical decision. We believe that these courses are indeed important, but so is educational philosophy. Here's why. Studying educational philosophy helps you become more aware of your beliefs about teaching and learning and helps you make decisions about the kind of teacher you want to become. Teachers' beliefs strongly influence they way they approach their work with students and the way they teach (Woolfolk Hoy, Davis, & Pape, 2006). That's why we've written this chapter—to help you examine your beliefs and translate them into actions in the classroom.

Teaching and You

What courses are most important for you in your teacher preparation program? How important is educational philosophy as part of this program?

At its most basic level, **philosophy** is a search for wisdom (Ozmon, 2012), but in a formal sense, it's a study of theories of knowledge, truth, existence, and morality—matters of right and wrong. We see evidence of philosophy in Allie and Brad's discussions in our opening case. Allie, for example, said, "I've given all this a lot of thought, and this is the best I've been able to come up with so far." Just as your responses to the questions in *Teaching and You* represent your current beliefs, she was describing her beliefs about knowledge and truth and what she thought was right. Although his beliefs and conclusions were different, Brad was pursuing the same goal. This is why philosophy is important for you.

Revisiting My Beliefs

This section addresses the first item in *This I Believe*, "The purpose of educational philosophy is to help me and other prospective teachers understand how past experts have thought about teaching." This statement is only partially true. A philosophy of education goes well beyond helping you and other prospective teachers understand the thinking of past experts; it also guides us as we work in our classrooms and provides a framework for thinking about educational issues (Conroy, Davis, & Enslin, 2008).

Philosophy and Teacher Professionalism

In their conversation, Allie and Brad expressed different views, but their contrasting positions have common features, and these positions are closely related to different dimensions of teacher professionalism (see Figure 5.1). For instance, decision making and reflection are illustrated in their conversation. Reflecting on our practice not only helps us develop a coherent **philosophy of education**, it also makes us more aware of who we are as teachers and the directions we want to pursue as we develop as teachers (Schussler, Stooksberry, & Bercaw, 2010).

Teacher professionalism requires that teachers are able to explain why they teach the way they do.

Allie and Brad both reflected on their practice and made decisions about what topics and learning objectives were most important and how to best help students reach those objectives. Allie, for example, said, "[T]here's real, practical stuff out there that kids need. They have to be good readers, they need to be able to write and do math, and they need to understand this stuff, the science I'm teaching." Based on her reflection, she decided to emphasize

FIGURE 5.1 Elements of Professionalism in Allie's and Brad's Philosophies

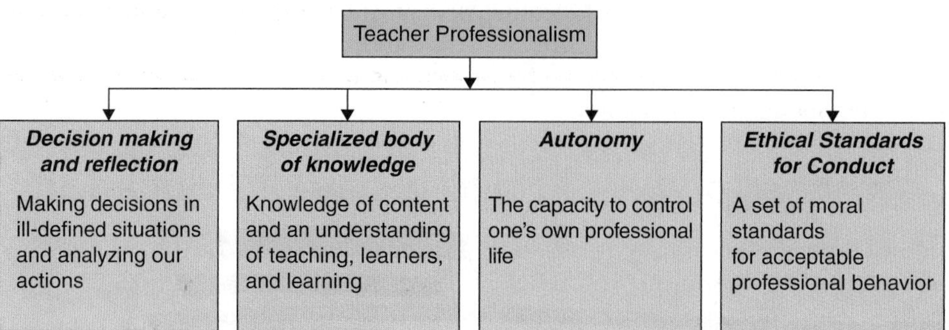

what she believed was essential knowledge, and she further decided to frequently assess her students to help them acquire this knowledge. Brad's reflection led him to different conclusions. He concluded that directly involving students in problem solving and decision-making activities was more important.

A specialized body of knowledge is also a component of teacher professionalism, and both Allie and Brad based their philosophical decisions on research. For example, Allie said, "Everything I read in journals talks about how important background knowledge is for new learning." She didn't base her decisions on intuition or whim; rather, she grounded them in professional knowledge. The same was true for Brad: "Everything I read says that kids need lots of experience in making decisions and solving problems." He disagreed with Allie, but his decisions were also based on knowledge.

You will do the same when you begin teaching. You will make decisions about what you believe is most important to teach and what is the best way of helping your students learn. Educational philosophy can help you make these decisions.

The Relationship Between Philosophy and Theory

Philosophy and theory overlap in many ways, and the distinction between the two is often blurred (Stewart, Blocker & Petrik, 2013). They're not identical, however. A **theory** is a set of related principles that are based on observation and are used to explain the world around us. The term *explain* in the definition is important: The primary function of theories is to help us understand and explain events we observe in our day-to-day lives.

For example, Allie's emphasis on knowledge is based on theories of learning that suggest, "Everything we learn depends on what we already know." Her philosophy goes beyond theory, however. Instead of explaining the way things *are*, as a theory would do, philosophy suggests the way things *ought to be*, and also analyzes theories, ideas, and beliefs. Allie, for example, suggested that schools should emphasize knowledge and understanding, whereas Brad thought they should focus on problem solving and decision making. Allie also expressed the belief that kids need extensive background knowledge to learn new ideas, whereas Brad believed that experiences with problem solving and decision making were more important. In this regard, both Allie and Brad stepped beyond theory into the realm of philosophy.

People in other professions also use philosophies to direct their actions. In medicine, for example, one school of thinking suggests that the medical profession should emphasize prevention through healthy lifestyles, whereas another focuses on healing through medication and other treatments. A description of the way something ought to be—such as the way teachers, physicians, or other professionals ought to practice—is called a **normative philosophy** (Stewart et al., 2013).

Check Your Understanding

1.1. Define philosophy and normative philosophy, and explain how they differ from theory.
1.2. To which part of teacher professionalism is philosophy most closely related? Explain.
1.3. What's the major difference between Allie's and Brad's normative philosophies?

For feedback, go to the appendix, *Check Your Understanding*, located in the back of this text.

Branches of Philosophy

Philosophy is a broad discipline that encompasses a number of different questions or concerns. Four of the major areas include:

- Epistemology
- Metaphysics
- Axiology
- Logic

We examine each in the sections that follow.

Epistemology

Teaching and You

How do we resolve controversies in our lives? For example, consider global warming. Do you believe global warming exists? If you do, why? If you don't, why not?

Think about the questions we asked in *Teaching and You* here. The answers to these questions relate to **epistemology,** the branch of philosophy that deals with knowledge and questions such as, "How is knowledge acquired?" and "How do we know what we know?" For instance, if you don't believe in global warming, what led you to that conclusion? On the other hand, if you argue that a great deal of scientific evidence suggests that global warming does indeed exist, you are also dealing with epistemology because evidence and the scientific method address the question, "How do we know what we know?"

Epistemology was involved in Allie and Brad's discussion. For instance, Allie said, "And there's real, practical stuff out there that kids need. . . . And practice, thorough assessment, and detailed feedback are some of the best ways we have of getting them to learn. That's reality." She argued that practice and assessment with feedback are important ways students come to know the ideas they learn.

A variety of ways of knowing exist. The scientific method (testing a problem by systematically collecting facts through observation and experimentation) is one; experience, intuition, relying on the knowledge and expertise of others, and even divine revelation are others.

Epistemology is important for all of us because our beliefs about how students learn influence how we teach. For instance, many experts answer the question, "How is knowledge acquired?" by suggesting that students, and people in general, don't passively receive and store information from others, as a video recorder would do. Instead, they mentally process the information in an attempt to make sense of it, and then construct their own understanding (Eggen & Kauchak, 2013). If you adhere to this belief, you will provide a variety of experiences for your students and then structure lessons and lead discussions that help them make sense of their experiences.

On the other hand, if you believe that knowledge is acquired by listening to a knowledgeable expert, you will be more likely to lecture to students and expect them to reproduce what they've heard on tests. These are ways that epistemology influences our teaching.

Metaphysics

Epistemology examines *how* we know, and **metaphysics** is a branch of philosophy that considers *what* we know. Metaphysics considers questions of reality and ultimately attempts to answer the question "What is real?" (Jacobsen, 2003). For instance, if you don't believe that global warming exists, your thinking is in the context of metaphysics, because you're making a decision about reality, and it's still in the realm of metaphysics if you have the opposite view.

With respect to metaphysics, Allie and Brad are far apart. Brad argued, "Reality is, in fact, what you perceive it to be, and there's no objective source out there to decide which view is the 'right one,'" to which Allie countered, "Look at that oak tree outside the window. You can perceive it to be anything you want, but it's still an oak tree. And it doesn't matter what anybody thinks: Two plus two is four—not three, not five, not anything else." Allie believes in a reality independent of our perception, but Brad believes that perception and reality are inextricably intertwined.

Our metaphysical beliefs influence both the way we teach and our goals for our students. For instance, we've all heard the question, when encountering a partially filled glass of liquid, "Is the glass half empty or half full?" Optimists say half full, while pessimists say half empty. In a similar way, teacher optimism, in the form of positive expectations for our students, can influence how we teach; teachers who have positive expectations for their students, who believe they can learn, try harder and refuse to let students fail (Good & Brophy, 2008). When we believe the glass is half full, we try harder to challenge our students and are less likely to give up on them when they struggle. Optimism is important in teaching, and our views of reality have direct consequences for our teaching.

Axiology

Axiology is a third branch of philosophy that considers values and ethics, issues now prominent in American education. For example, surveys indicate that as many as three fourths of students admit to cheating on tests, and cheating appears to be on the rise at all levels of education (C. Doyle, 2010). Also, large numbers of students in schools express concerns about being bullied, a moral problem that involves a misuse of power (Josephson Institute Center for Youth Ethics, 2010).

Revisiting My Beliefs

This discussion addresses the second item on *This I Believe*, "Children should learn morals in the home. Teaching morals in school is not part of my job." But this is not the prevailing opinion in our country today (Bushaw & Lopez, 2010).

Outside of schools, political corruption and scandals that led to the economic downturn in the latter part of the last decade have sent shock waves through our financial system and American society in general. The American public is increasingly looking to education for solutions to problems such as these (Bushaw & Lopez, 2010).

How might axiology influence your own teaching? Let's look again at Allie and Brad's conversation. Allie argued, "I'm not doing my job if I don't get them to learn as much as possible"; Brad retorted, "I would be doing the kids, their parents, and ultimately our whole society a disservice if I didn't try to prepare them for life outside school." Both argued that they wouldn't be behaving ethically if they weren't true to their beliefs about what's important for students to learn. Axiology is involved whenever we examine our values to decide what's best for our students.

Logic

Teaching and You

You comment to a friend, "I'm going to ace my next test," to which your friend responds, "How can you be so sure?" You reply, "Hard work is the key to success, and I've been studying hard."

Logic is the fourth branch of philosophy and influences how we think about the world. To see how, let's look at the example in *Teaching and You*. You made the comment, "I'm going to ace my next test," and when challenged by your friend, you responded, "Hard work is the key to success, and I've been studying hard." In making these statements, you demonstrated **logic,** the branch of philosophy that examines the processes of deriving valid conclusions from basic principles.

In making your conclusion, you demonstrated a form of logic called *deductive reasoning*. It begins with a proposition, called a *major premise,* which can be a principle or generalization such as "Hard work is the key to success." The major premise is followed by a fact or observation, called a *minor premise,* such as "I've been studying hard," and the process ends with a conclusion that follows from the two premises. In your case the conclusion was, "I'm going to ace the next test."

Allie also demonstrated deductive reasoning in asserting that she was promoting learning in her students.

Although these aren't her exact words, the following statements represent her sequence of thoughts:

Practice, assessment, and feedback promote learning (her major premise).

I am providing my students with practice, and I'm assessing their learning and providing them with feedback (her minor premise).

Therefore, I am promoting learning in my students (her conclusion).

Inductive reasoning, the counterpart to deductive reasoning, begins with specific facts or observations and ends with a conclusion that pulls them together. For instance, let's say you're an elementary teacher, and you have your students plant seeds under a variety of growing conditions, such as differing amounts of sunlight. Your students find that seeds placed in bright sunlight grow faster than those in either moderate or dim light. Based on these specific instances, your students then make general conclusions about sunlight and plant growth, such as, "The more sunlight plants receive, the faster they grow."

Logic helps us promote clear thinking in our students. For instance, in social studies, we help students see that if we stereotype a specific cultural group based on the behavior or appearance of a few members of the group, we're using faulty inductive reasoning. Similarly, many controversies in education and other aspects of life occur because proponents and critics disagree on the validity of conclusions derived from deductive reasoning. For example, some educational reformers believe that test-based accountability—holding teachers and students accountable by using standardized tests to measure student learning progress—is an effective way to improve education in our country (Sparks, 2011a). This is a major premise. And because standardized testing has become a major part of schooling (a minor premise), education should be improving (conclusion). On the other hand, critics cite evidence that runs counter to that conclusion, and they also question the validity of the major premise (Hout & Elliot, 2011). Instead, critics believe that an overemphasis on testing actually detracts from learning—a different conclusion based on a different major premise. Other controversies in education involve similar disagreements between premises and conclusions.

Check Your Understanding

2.1. Describe each of the major branches of philosophy.

2.2. Allie said, "I'm not doing my job if I don't get them to learn as much as possible." This comment best illustrates which branch of philosophy? Explain your answer.

2.3. Two teachers are in a discussion, and one says, "Everything we know depends on experience. So, the key is providing lots of experiences in the classroom. If we provide them with enough experiences, they'll learn." To which branch of philosophy is this person's statement most closely related? Explain your answer.

2.4. "That doesn't quite make sense," a teacher diplomatically comments to a colleague. "You said that your kids are so unmotivated, but last week you said that kids basically want to learn. . . . Those two don't fit." To which of the branches of philosophy is this person's comment most closely related? Explain your answer.

For feedback, go to the appendix, *Check Your Understanding,* located in the back of this text.

Philosophies of Education

Teaching and You

Think back to when you were in elementary, middle, and high school. What courses did you find most valuable, and why do you think they were most useful? Who were your best teachers, and why do you believe they were the best?

Think about the questions we asked in *Teaching and You*. Your answers to these questions are important because they provide insights into your own philosophy of education. The different philosophies of education that we describe in this section help answer these and other questions about schooling, the curriculum (what you study), and instruction (how you teach) by providing different perspectives on school quality. In this section we examine four educational philosophies that are prominent in schools today:

- Perennialism
- Essentialism
- Progressivism
- Social reconstructionism

Perennialism

What kinds of classes are most valuable? You might have answered the first question in *Teaching and You* by saying that your high school literature courses were most valuable, because you studied important novels, such as *To Kill A Mockingbird,* which examined family, loyalty, racism, and a belief in human goodness in the face of evil and adversity. You've found that dealing with time-honored issues, such as questions about right and wrong, the human condition, and the purpose of life were most valuable and important to you.

If you feel this way, your thinking is consistent with **perennialism**, an educational philosophy suggesting that nature—including human nature—is constant and schools should teach content and topics that have withstood the test of time. The term *perennial* is an adjective meaning "perpetual" or "long lasting." Consistent with beliefs in the constancy of nature, perennialists believe in a rigorous curriculum that is essentially the same for all students and remains the same over time. For them, education should provide a solid foundation that prepares students for future life. If students find that the topics they study are relevant to their present lives, so much the better, but this isn't the most important goal of schooling.

In addition to great literature, such as *To Kill a Mockingbird,* perennialists believe that the curriculum should emphasize math and science courses because they expose students to the rigors of logical thought and develop students' intellect.

Our country's founding fathers held perennialist views, and historically, perennialism has been an important educational philosophy in our country. It was prominent until the early 20th century, when the thinking of Thomas Dewey (1902, 1906, 1923, 1938) encouraged teachers to focus more on problem solving, applications to the real world, and the importance of experience in learning. (We discuss Dewey's work later in this section.)

Perennialism experienced a brief renaissance in the 1980s with the publication of Mortimer Adler's (1982) *The Paideia Proposal: An Educational Manifesto.* Adler advocated a general curriculum for all students that included math, science, history, geography, literature, and fine arts. However, the goal in studying these topics was more the development of intellectual skills, such as writing, speaking, computing, and problem solving than the topics themselves. The content, together with these skills, would lead to higher levels of thinking, reflection, and personal awareness.

Adler's ideas received considerable attention from the popular press and several people prominent at the time, such as William Bennett, the secretary of education from 1985 to 1988, and Allan Bloom, author of the bestseller, *The*

Closing of the American Mind, published in 1987. Bennett and Bloom claimed that American education had abandoned its historical ideals and was largely responsible for the lax social and sexual habits of modern students and their focus on materialism as evidence of success.

Adler's suggestions were controversial, however. Critics argued that his proposals were elitist, aimed primarily at students with the highest ability (Ozmon, 2012). Critics also questioned the value of distant and abstract ideas for students who lacked school-related experiences and were often poorly motivated. Even though not prominent in education today, Adler's efforts remain alive. His book was reissued (Adler, 1998), and interest in student discussion and dialogue as a vehicle for learning continues to be prominent today.

Perennialism in Classrooms

Jacob Wallace has his students involved in reading and analyzing Nathanial Hawthorne's *The Scarlet Letter* (1850). This classic American novel set in Boston in the 1600s describes a tragic and illicit love affair between the heroine (Hester Prynne) and a minister (Arthur Dimmesdale). The novel's title refers to the letter *A*, meaning *adulterer,* which the Puritan community makes Hester wear as punishment for her adultery.

"Surprisingly, the kids love it," Jacob comments. "Everyone has heard of the Puritans, and we use their intolerance and repressiveness as a metaphor for issues in today's society, such as gay and lesbian rights, cohabitation outside of marriage, and the counterculture of the 1960s. Then, we consider the concept of evil, and we ask which is more evil, Hester's and Dimmesdale's love affair, the Puritans' humiliating Hester by making her wear the *A*, or her husband's attempted revenge directed toward her and Dimmesdale? . . .Then, as we discuss evil in a more general sense, the kids realize that it isn't as cut-and-dried as they previously thought. . . . Once we get past some of the stilted language, they really get into it, and I've even had to stop them from yelling at each other and remind them that attempting to shout each other down is just another form of repression. . . . It's great."

Jacob's efforts are consistent with perennialism. The concepts of *good* and *evil, sin,* and *repression* are ideas that have been examined throughout history, and they're as timely today as they have ever been. The ideal perennialist curriculum would have students examine these and other important concepts through the study of classic literature, analyzing and evaluating the ideas presented in them, as Jacob did with his students.

Essentialism

To begin this section, think again about *Teaching and You* in the previous section, where we asked which courses were most valuable in your elementary, middle, and high school experiences. When we asked our students the same question, many said the reading courses they took when they were young, or the math courses they took throughout their schooling because they provided the skills they needed to succeed in college and ultimately in the world at large.

If you feel the same way, your thinking is consistent with **essentialism**, an educational philosophy suggesting that specific knowledge and skills exist that all people should possess. We've all heard of "back to the basics" movements, proponents of which argue that learning should focus on basic skills, such as reading, writing, mathematics, science, and social studies. Essentialists argue that the purpose of schooling is to advance society by providing a curriculum that includes the skills needed to function effectively in today's world, and teachers should play a central role in directing classes to help students acquire these skills (Null, 2007). Unfortunately, many of our students aren't mastering the "essentials" in many of these areas. For example, only 12% of American 12th graders scored well enough on the National Assessment of Educational Progress to be considered "proficient" in American history, and most couldn't identify the country aiding North Korea in the Korean War (China) (National Center for Education Statistics, 2010g).

Many of the educational reform efforts in our country over the last 30 years have arisen from essentialist views. In the 1980s, for example, reform was spurred by *A Nation at Risk* (National Commission on Excellence in Education, 1983), the widely publicized report recommending that all high school students master core requirements in five "basic" areas—English, math, science, social studies, and computer science. The *No Child Left Behind* act of 2001, which mandated state-generated standards and tests designed to determine if these standards were met, was another effort at reform that focused on "basics," primarily reading and math. The emphasis in today's schools on high-stakes tests to hold teachers and students accountable for meeting predetermined standards is largely a reflection of essentialist views of teaching.

Revisiting My Beliefs

This discussion addresses the third item in *This I Believe*, "As a teacher, my primary goal should be to help students master essential content rather than to help them develop emotionally and socially." Essentialists would strongly agree with this statement.

Essentialism and perennialism share the view that knowledge and understanding are crucial, and both are wary of educational trends, such as learner-centered approaches to education, integrated curricula, and a focus on learner self-esteem. Essentialists don't share perennialists' emphasis on universal truths through the study of classical literature, however; instead, they emphasize knowledge and skills that are useful in today's world.

Because of its emphasis on practical, usable knowledge, the essentialist curriculum is more likely to change than the perennialist curriculum. For instance, because technology has become such an important part of our lives in the 21st century, technological literacy is now viewed as a basic skill, and schools across the country are struggling to prepare students for the technological world they'll live and work in (Roblyer & Doering, 2013).

Essentialism has also influenced teacher education programs around the country. As our society becomes more diverse and researchers better understand how diversity affects learning, teacher preparation programs are placing increased emphasis on working effectively with learners from diverse backgrounds. This means you'll likely take a course in multicultural education, and topics in this area will be included in other courses as well. This emphasis reflects the belief that understanding learner diversity is now an essential part of being an effective teacher, a shift in emphasis reflecting essentialist thinking.

Essentialism in Classrooms

Essentialism plays a central role in American education today, and this is reflected in Allie's comment, "There's real, practical stuff out there that kids need. They have to be good readers, they need to be able to write and do math, and they need to understand this stuff, the science I'm teaching." She believes a body of knowledge and skills exist that all students should master, and it's her job to be sure they do.

Essentialist philosophy has also influenced teacher education programs in the form of testing and accountability. As a prospective teacher, you will be required to take a specified sequence of courses, and you'll likely be expected to demonstrate mastery of essential teaching skills on a standardized test, either the Praxis Series™ or a state-specific test (Hightower, 2012).

This emphasis is also reflected in the design of this text. For instance, we list important learning outcomes at the beginning of each chapter, and include *Check Your Understanding* questions throughout each chapter to help you determine the extent to which you've reached the objectives. *Important Concepts* are also placed in bold print, listed at the end of each chapter, and defined in the glossary. These features reflect our belief that important knowledge exists that all professionals should master and understand.

Progressivism

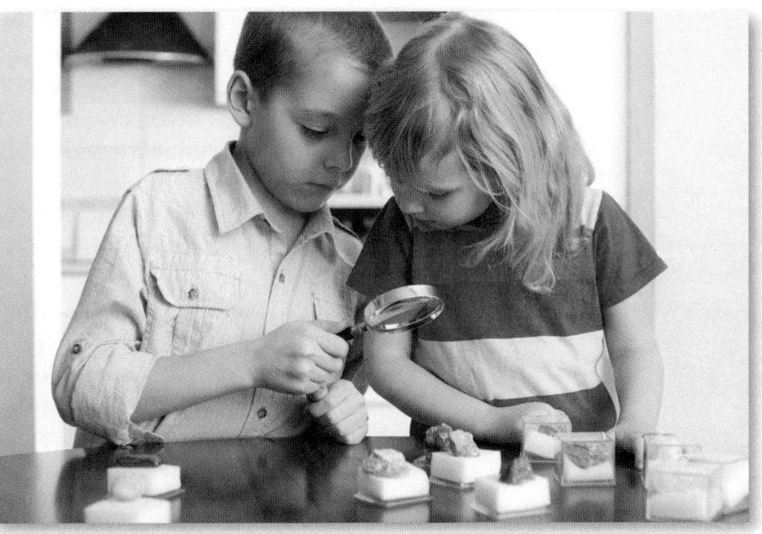

Progressivism focuses instruction on real-world problem solving and individual development.

Consider again the question that we asked in *Teaching and You* about which courses were most valuable to you as you progressed through school. Many of our students answered this question by saying that their best courses were those that had them work on projects (e.g., science projects) that allowed them to solve problems that were interesting to them or to write about topics that were important to them.

If this is how you responded, your thinking reflects **progressivism**, an educational philosophy emphasizing real-world problem solving and individual development. Progressivists believe the purpose of schooling is to develop students as completely as possible—physically, intellectually, socially, and emotionally. The curriculum should be composed of experiences applicable in today's world. Teachers should be caring individuals, and instead of relying primarily on lecture as a teaching method, they should use questioning and discussion to guide students as they search for meaning in the world and their lives.

Brad's educational philosophy is aligned with progressivism. In his conversation with Allie, he commented:

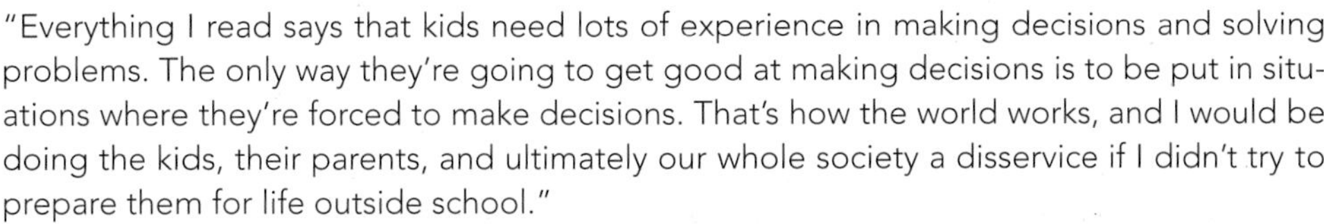

"Everything I read says that kids need lots of experience in making decisions and solving problems. The only way they're going to get good at making decisions is to be put in situations where they're forced to make decisions. That's how the world works, and I would be doing the kids, their parents, and ultimately our whole society a disservice if I didn't try to prepare them for life outside school."

Progressivism has been enormously influential in American education, and it continues to be debated today (T. Johnson & Reed, 2012). Because of its influence, let's briefly look at how the progressive movement developed in this country.

The Progressive Era in American History

From 1890 to 1920, American education experienced dramatic growth (Pulliam & Van Patten, 2013). School enrollments, fueled by accessibility and compulsory attendance laws, increased 70%, and the number of teachers grew by 80%.

During this period of growth, educators reexamined schooling practices and began to question the value of students' studying topics that had few direct relationships to their present-day lives. John Dewey (1859–1952), an American philosopher and educational reformer was at the center of this movement. Dewey (1923, 1938) wrote extensively on education, and his work has had more impact on American education than any other philosopher. His ideas continue to be actively debated by educators today (e.g., Isaac, 2011; Pope & Stenhagen, 2011).

Dewey first encountered progressive teaching practices through his children, who attended a lab school in Chicago that was experimenting with hands-on experiential learning. He became so fascinated with student-centered teaching that in 1896 he established his own lab school connected to the University of Chicago, where he worked. The school became the birthplace of progressive education, which gained prominence during the early to mid-20th century. For Dewey, classrooms should become microcosms of our democratic society: What students learn in school should help them in the real world. Goals such as personal growth and preparation for participation in a democracy are met through an activity-oriented curriculum. Content, which historically was an end in itself, now became a tool to solve real life problems.

Dewey's ideas created both excitement and criticism. To some, seeing learners actively involved in solving real-world problems was exciting. To others, progressive education deemphasized important content and catered to student interests and whims.

Interest in progressive education waned after the mid-20th century, caused in part by a well-intentioned but misguided attempt at fostering life-adjustment courses such as "Developing an Effective Personality" and "Marriage and Living," which were attacked by critics as lacking in content and academic rigor (Norris, 2004). These criticisms increased as a result of the furor caused by Russia beating our country into space with its launching of the Sputnik satellite in 1957. Losing this race symbolized a weak American educational system, critics asserted; the public agreed, and the progressive movement declined.

Dewey's defenders argue that critics either misrepresent or don't understand him (Fallace, 2011). Dewey didn't deemphasize knowledge and understanding in favor of student interests, his defenders assert. To Dewey, asking, "Which is more important: the interests of the child or the knowledge of subject matter?" was a dumb question. Both are equally important.

Many aspects of progressive education, such as problem-based instruction, cooperative learning, and guided discovery are alive and well today. And you and your peers in teacher preparation programs are encouraged to connect the topics you teach to the real world and actively involve your students in learning activities. You are also encouraged to help your students develop not only intellectually but also personally, socially, morally, and physically. These are all progressivist ideas.

Revisiting My Beliefs

This section addresses the fourth item in *This I Believe*, "Our nation's schools should focus on teaching students to think and solve problems in the real world." People with a progressivist philosophy would agree with this statement. Progressivists believe our schools and classrooms should prepare students for life by immersing them in real-world applications.

This discussion also relates to the second question we asked in *Teaching and You* in this section: "Who were your best teachers, and why do you believe they were the best?" Most believe their best teachers were those who cared about them, both as an individual and as a student, and actively involved them in learning activities. These beliefs are consistent with progressivism.

The progressive movement in education recently experienced a boost with increased interest in **21st-century skills** (Partnership for 21st Century Skills, 2011), a reform movement focusing on the development of cognitive skills that students need to survive and succeed in a rapidly changing technological world. These skills emphasize technology as well as analytical and communication skills, and teachers are encouraged to use open-ended problem-based and project-based instruction that places students in small groups to work on real-world problems (Sawchuk, 2009a). Not surprisingly, perennialists and essentialists criticize this movement for its lack of emphasis on content (Sawchuk, 2009b).

Progressivism in Classrooms

To see how progressivist philosophy can influence your teaching, let's join a group of urban middle school teachers as they talk over lunch.

"I'm having a heck of a time with my students," Kelly Erhardt, a first-year English teacher, confesses. "They simply couldn't care less about learning to write or learning grammar or punctuation".

"Welcome to middle school teaching," Dan Shafer, a geography teacher and "veteran" of 3 years, smiles. "These kids have to see how the stuff they study applies to their lives. No magic solution exists, but here's what I did with my geography kids, and it went really well.

"I told them we'd be working with maps all year, so understanding scale was important, both in class and in life outside of school. I showed them a map of our state and talked about scale. Then, I broke students into pairs, and each pair had to decide on a scale, construct a map of the room, and present it to the class. Some were a little disorganized, but gradually they did okay, and they're learning to work together. Tomorrow, we're going outside to make a map of the school grounds—to scale."

"That does sound like fun," Kelly responds. "I wish we had done something like that when I studied maps. All we did was listen to the teacher talk."

"Can't do that, or you'll lose them," Mary Burbank, the science teacher and a 10-year veteran, joins in. "I'll offer another example that you might consider. . . . Yesterday, I started class by swinging a pair of athletic socks tied to a string around my head and then letting it go. I asked them what they observed and led them to notice that the socks traveled in a straight line after I let go of the string and they kept on going until the wall of the room stopped them. So, then I asked them what happens when they ride in a car and go around a curve. They said they were 'thrown' against the door of the car. So, then we got to the idea that being 'thrown' against the door was our bodies' tendencies to travel in a straight line as the car rounded the curve. We also talked about why we wear seatbelts, and they got the idea that when we slam on the brakes, our bodies tend to keep going, so we wear seatbelts to keep us from getting hurt. I finally described what we were discussing as the concept *inertia,* and not only did they get it, they liked it.

Like Dan just said, they have to see how ideas relate to their lives. If I started out lecturing about inertia, they'd drift off in 5 minutes. You have to figure out how to connect English to them right now. . . . You're a smart kid; you'll figure it out."

Think for a minute about the advice Kelly's colleagues gave her. None of their recommended activities involved students' simply listening while teachers lectured; instead, the teachers involved students in learning activities that related to their personal lives. These activities reflect the emphasis placed on learner thinking and involvement that we see in many classrooms today and are examples of a progressivist philosophy (Eggen & Kauchak, 2013).

Social Reconstructionism

Think about our world today. Our students and the society they live in have changed. Too many students use drugs, engage in irresponsible sexual behavior, and bully other students. Many of them live in poverty, and some are homeless. In the world outside of school, maintaining a clean, healthy environment and having adequate supplies of water for growing populations are receiving increasing attention.

Social reconstructionism focuses students on critical problems in today's society.

Social reconstructionists believe schools and teachers should be addressing these problems. **Social reconstructionism** is an educational philosophy asserting that schools, teachers, and students should take the lead in addressing social problems and improving society. Social reconstructionists answer the question, "What is the purpose of schooling?" by responding that schooling should be used to eliminate social inequities by creating a new and more just society. The curriculum would include topics that reflect social issues, and discussion would be a primary teaching method.

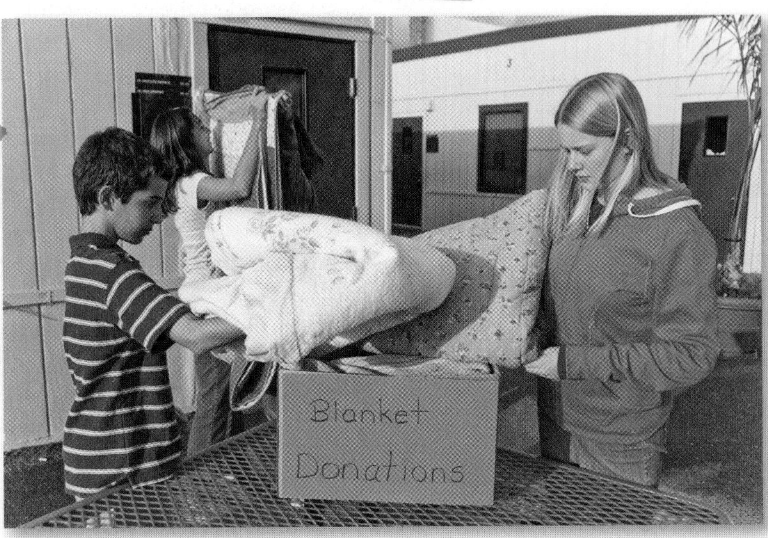

The roots of social reconstructionism in our country are often traced to American philosopher and educator Theodore Brameld (1904–1987). Influenced by the thinking of

John Dewey (1923, 1938) and affected by the horrors of World War II, Brameld believed that the human race possessed the potential either to annihilate itself through conflict and weapons such as the atomic bomb or to create a humane and just society through the use of technology and compassion. Teachers and schools, he believed, should serve as the agents for creating this just society.

Paulo Freire (1921–1997), a Brazilian philosopher and educator whose concerns for the poor and underprivileged were colored by his personal experiences with poverty and hunger during the Great Depression of the 1930s, also influenced social reconstructionist thinking in this country. He believed that schools are institutions that dominant groups in specific cultures use to maintain social inequities (Freire, 1989). For example, many suburban schools in our country are modern, roomy, positive environments where teachers have access to adequate resources. Many urban schools, by contrast—with students who are overwhelmingly members of cultural minorities—are often old, overcrowded environments where not even enough textbooks are available (Kozol, 1991, 2005). Social reconstructionists such as Friere would cite these facts as evidence for their position.

Social reconstructionism is also related to **social justice,** a movement in education that emphasizes human rights, fairness, and equity in the opportunities available to all members of society (Grant & Agosto, 2008). Social justice focuses on the fair and equal treatment of all groups, and opposes discrimination on the basis of race, class, gender, sexual orientation, and ability. In the classroom, social justice translates into instructional practices that allow all students to succeed. It can also mean helping our students become more aware of the inequities currently existing in our society.

Revisiting My Beliefs

This section addresses the fifth item in *This I Believe*, "I should encourage my students to think about their personal role in making the world a better place." Social reconstructionists believe this statement is true and recommend teaching students about how they can make a difference through their actions.

Social justice can be controversial. Critics claim that it equates with socialism and property and wealth distribution, and warn that schools shouldn't be advocating these politically laden actions (Gollnick, 2008). Proponents claim that social justice is nothing more than good teaching that makes students aware of the plights of others and examines ways to make our democracy more equitable and fair. Given the current political polarization in our country, this controversy is likely to continue.

Social Reconstructionism in Classrooms

Emma Wilkenson, a high school biology teacher, has her students read *The Ripple Effect: The Fate of Fresh Water in the 21st Century* (Prud'homme, 2011), a book that describes the ways Americans use and abuse water, raises questions about future water supplies, and asserts that access to clean water will be one of the most important issues of this century.

As part of their study, students examine basic issues around water such as molecular structure and the hydrologic cycle as well as the issues raised in the book, and Emma directs a discussion that leads to conclusions about what they personally, at this point in their lives, can do to ensure that we will have access to adequate water supplies in our future.

Jeremy Stevens, an American history teacher, uses the Internet to have his students watch Martin Luther King's famous "I Have a Dream" speech. In the speech, delivered on the steps of the Lincoln Memorial in Washington, DC, King describes his desire for a future where blacks, whites, and other races would coexist harmoniously as equals.

"This speech was a defining moment of the American civil rights movement," he explains to his students.

The next day, he displays the following paragraphs from the speech:

I have a dream that one day on the red hills of Georgia, the sons of former slaves and the sons of former slave owners will be able to sit down together at the table of brotherhood.

I have a dream that my four little children will one day live in a nation where they will not be judged by the color of their skin but by the content of their character.

He reminds students that the speech was given in 1963 and asks them why the speech in general, and the two paragraphs in particular, were so significant at the time. He then

TABLE 5.1 Classroom Applications of the Educational Philosophies

Philosophy	Educational Goal	Curriculum	Teaching Methods	Learning Environment	Assessment
Perennialism	Train the intellect	Focus on enduring ideas	Lecture; questioning; discussion	High structure; strong focus on academic work	Frequent assessment and feedback
Essentialism	Acquire the basic skills needed to function in today's world	Essential knowledge and basic skills	Lecture; questioning; practice and feedback	High structure; strong focus on essential knowledge and skills	Frequent objective and performance assessments and feedback
Progressivism	Develop problem solving, decision making, and other life skills	Practice in problem solving and other life skills	Emphasizes applications in problem-based learning, cooperative learning, and guided discovery	Democratic; collaborative; emphasis on learner responsibility	Ongoing informal assessment
Social Reconstructionism	Contribute to the creation of a just society	Social issues	Discussion; collaboration; student projects	Model for equity and justice	Examination of written products; informal observation

asks, "To what extent do you believe that racial injustice and inequality have been overcome in our country and in the world?" The question sparks hot debate among students, and Jeremy reminds them that if they're practicing justice and equality in their classroom, all opinions are allowed and respected, no matter how strongly they disagree with each other.

The class closes the discussion by creating a list of things they can do to promote justice and tolerance for dissenting opinions in their own school and how they can promote them in their lives outside of school.

Emma and Jeremy both taught topics traditionally included in biology and American history. In addition, however, they examined issues influencing the world both today and in the future, and they encouraged students to make commitments to make the world a better place in which to live. Emma and Jeremy's efforts are applications of social reconstructionist philosophy.

Social reconstructionism is politically controversial (Manzo, 2008). For example, conservative critics argue that social reconstructionists have abandoned intellectual pursuits in schools and instead use schools for political purposes. Critics further contend that social reconstructionism is as controlling as more conservative philosophies, such as perennialism and essentialism; it merely establishes controls more to proponents' liking (Ozmon, 2012). Advocates respond that making and acting on moral decisions are an essential part of being a good citizen in our democracy. Filling students' heads with abstract ideas without encouraging them to develop a moral compass for their actions leaves them adrift in an amoral and even immoral world.

Classroom applications of the major educational philosophies are summarized in Table 5.1.

TECHNOLOGY and TEACHING: Educational Technology and Philosophy

Technology is everywhere, and it is transforming classrooms, too. But what role should technology play in classroom teaching? The proper place of technology in teaching and learning has been discussed and debated, essentially from the time that it has come into widespread use. Philosophy, which helps us sort out our priorities in other educational domains, can also help us think about the most productive ways to use technology in our classrooms.

In this section we consider four different perspectives on the role of educational technology and analyze them in terms of the four different educational philosophies. Let's look at them.

Educational Technology as a Tool for Producing Technologically Literate Citizens

Without question, we live in a technological world, and technology is shaping virtually every aspect of our lives. For all intents and purposes, technological literacy is nearly as much a basic skill as reading, writing, and math. Students who acquire these basic skills—including technology—will be better equipped to function effectively, both in school and in the world outside of school.

Consistent with essentialist educational philosophy, this view suggests that students should be taught technological skills such as word processing and the use of spreadsheets, presentation software such as PowerPoint, and the ability to access information on the Internet. An essentialist perspective suggests that you should teach your students technology skills and provide them with sufficient practice to allow these essential skills to develop.

In addition, a progressivist philosophy suggests that schools should prepare students for the challenges they'll encounter in the real world outside of school. One of the major challenges they'll face is to learn about and become proficient with the technologies they'll need to survive in a technological world when they graduate. The best place to learn about these technologies, progressivists assert, is in school, where learning tasks can be aligned to match the realities of out-of-school tech demands.

Technology as a Tool for Delivering Information

The perspective that technology is a tool for delivering information grew out of a movement that began in the 1930s, when experts proposed that media such as slides and films should be used to deliver information in more concrete and effective ways than could be done with books and lectures. This view of educational technology continues to be prominent today, as evidenced by the popularity of PowerPoint presentations and by the use of technology to teach ideas that are difficult to illustrate directly (Roblyer & Doering, 2013).

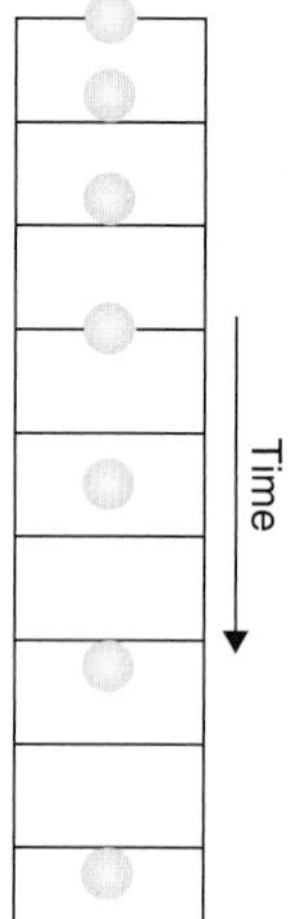

For instance, look at the time-lapse image of a falling ball that you see here. It's easy to illustrate the force of gravity; simply drop a ball, and students can see it fall to the floor. However, directly observing acceleration caused by gravity is much more difficult, if not impossible. In the time-lapse image, each of the rectangles represents the same amount of time. You can see that images of the ball are farther and farther apart, which concretely illustrates the ball's acceleration. Without technology, it would be impossible to show students how acceleration operates on a falling object.

This perspective on educational technology borrows from both essentialist and progressivist educational philosophies. The more realistically content can be represented for learners, the more likely they are to acquire the skills needed to function in life after school. This is the essentialist aspect. In addition, progressivism suggests that the most meaningful learning occurs when school experiences mirror the real world, and technology has the power to bring almost faithful reproductions of the real world into classrooms.

Technology has a long history of use as a tool for accurately and vividly presenting information, and this function will certainly continue long into the future.

Technology as an Instructional System

Beyond technological literacy and a tool for presenting information more effectively, some suggest that technology can be used to effectively deliver instruction and literally replace teachers (Cuban, 2001). Drill-and-practice software, tutorials, and simulations are examples of this view. When using drill-and-practice software, students respond to items, such as math facts (e.g., 6 × 9 = ?), and receive immediate feedback that can range from a simple "OK" or "No, try again," to elaborate animated displays or verbal explanations.

Tutorials are designed to be self-contained and include an entire instructional sequence, such as units on learning rules for punctuation or rounding numbers. As opposed to drill-and-practice software, which is designed to supplement other instruction, tutorials are intended to be true stand-alone teaching materials, and the best are highly interactive.

Simulations allow students to physically manipulate processes represented on the screen. For example, students might be shown a variety of chemicals, told to arrange them in various combinations, and observe and explain the results. Or students can dissect a frog in a simulation, avoiding the mess and bother and also sparing the life of a frog.

Historically, quality of the software has been a problem in the use of technology as an instructional supplement. For example, some critics argue that drill-and-practice software programs are little more than electronic flash cards (Roblyer & Doering, 2013). And the promise (or threat) of technology replacing teachers hasn't been fulfilled. Technology can be a valuable tool for supplementing instruction, but a long and expanding body of literature continues to confirm that the most important factor in influencing student learning is you—the teacher.

How do these instructional uses of technology relate to educational philosophies? First, because it has the potential to make our instruction more effective, technology complements both perennialist and essentialist philosophies, which stress the importance of knowledge acquisition. In addition, instructional technology also fits well with progressive philosophies because it emphasizes the integration of technology into classrooms and our lives. If students are going to learn how to use technology efficiently and wisely, they need to see this happen in the classroom.

Technology as a Tool for Communication and Creating Social Change

In the last few years, the power of technology as a communication tool and for creating social change has grown. Born into the world of laptops, cell phones, and texting, some estimates suggest that our students spend an average of 8½ hours each day exposed to digital technologies (Hicks, 2010). One survey found that a typical American teenager sends and receives 50 or more text messages per day, or 1,500 per month; 31% of teenagers send and receive more than 100 messages per day, or more than 3,000 per month (Pew Charitable Trust, 2010)! Our students live in a world in which they are constantly bombarded by technology, and some experts wonder whether this is having adverse effects on students' cognitive and social development (M. Jackson, 2009; Small & Vorgan, 2008.)

Progressivists see a major role for schools in helping students understand the role of technology in their lives. If we expect students to use new technologies wisely, schools need to provide guidance in this domain. Currently, too many schools respond to this onslaught of new technologies by barring the doors and prohibiting students from accessing technology in classrooms. As an alternative, many schools are experimenting with social websites that allow students to communicate and share their ideas with students across the country (Flanigan, 2012). Progressivists see this as essential for managing and directing technological change, as opposed to ignoring or fighting it.

Technology is also being seen as a vehicle for social change. For example, social media is given considerable credit for what has become widely known as the "Arab Spring" of 2011, which brought down dictators in countries such as

Egypt, Tunisia, and Libya. Without the capacity for almost instant communication available through social media, such as Facebook, these revolutions would have been unlikely.

This role of technology as an agent of social change wasn't planned; instead, it was thrust on technology. Leaders didn't decide in advance that technology should be a tool for producing social change, a view that would be consistent with social reconstructionist philosophies. Rather, protesters and rebels sought freedom and change, and they capitalized on technology to bring it about. As leaders, and people in general, come to better understand the power of technology for creating social change, it could become a tool to improve the human condition, and in that regard, it can become a true application of social reconstructionist educational philosophy.

As with many changes and innovations, a downside exists, however. Cyberbullying is a concrete example and is particularly pernicious, because a single keystroke can send hurtful and damaging messages across the Internet. Leaders are attempting to respond. For instance, in a widely publicized incident that occurred in 2010, Tyler Clementi, a Rutgers University student, committed suicide after his roommate used a webcam to record Clementi kissing another man, shared the video with others, and made plans to host a "viewing party" of the incident. In 2012, the roommate was convicted of a hate crime and invasion of privacy (Zernike, 2012). The prominence of social media is likely to make cyberbullying incidents such as this more common, with more complex legal issues.

As with all tools, technology has the potential for both good and bad. It is up to all of us as educators to ensure that it is used for the good of our students.

Philosophies of Education and Cultural Minorities

The philosophies we've examined in this chapter are "Western," meaning their origins are European or American. Two principles undergird this Western orientation: The preeminence of the individual and an emphasis on rational thought. The first is seen in the emphasis on the individual's growth of knowledge in both perennialism and essentialism and the interaction of the individual with the environment in progressivism. The second is reflected in the emphasis on objectivity, science, and the scientific method. Essentialism and progressivism both emphasize clear, rational thinking and science as a way of knowing.

Teachers need to be sensitive to the philosophies and world views that different students bring to their classrooms.

Some philosophers criticize this emphasis on science and objectivity and point to its undesirable consequences in American life. Americans are working more hours per week than they ever have in the past, technology dominates our lives, and we are chronically sleep deprived, for example. Critics of this Western orientation assert that valuable alternatives can be found in the philosophies of other cultures.

Some philosophies, such as those embedded in certain Native American cultures, use the shared folklore of elders and knowledge that comes from the heart as their sources of wisdom (Starnes, 2006). Because people in these cultures have a long history of living in harmony with the land, their philosophies emphasize ecological balance and interpersonal cooperation; this emphasis results in valuing individual achievement primarily as it contributes to the group's overall well-being. Competition and individual displays of achievement are frowned upon. Understanding these differences can help explain why Navajo students shun competitive classrooms and are sometimes reluctant to participate in the competitive verbal give-and-take of fast-paced questioning sessions that require individuals to demonstrate how much they know (Starnes, 2006).

Similarly, for some African cultures, feelings and personal relationships, as ways of knowing, are as important as or more important than science and rational thought (Nieto & Bode, 2012). Further, in many African cultures, art and music are important means not only of expression but also of seeking knowledge. This philosophical view helps explain why music was such a prominent part of slaves' lives in America, why African Americans have made such a strong contribution to modern and impressionistic art, and why African influences can be seen in much of the contemporary music in Europe and the Americas.

Many Asians also value harmony. The desire to balance life, family, society, and nature leads to reverence for elders, respect for authority, and adherence to traditions. Because cooperation is so important, being polite is highly valued, and feelings and emotions are controlled to maintain order and proper social relationships (Fong, 2007). Awareness of these perspectives could help teachers understand characteristics commonly attributed to Asian American students. For instance, they're often described as shy, reluctant to speak out in class, and restrained in their nonverbal behavior, which sometimes makes reading their nonverbal cues difficult.

EXPLORING DIVERSITY: Philosophy and Cultural Minorities

The personal philosophies many of our students bring to our classrooms often differ from ours and mainstream America's and can influence their perspectives on life. You should be sensitive to your students' varying beliefs, but you should also be cautious about drawing conclusions and making individual decisions about students on the basis of group descriptions. Critics argue that these descriptions are little more than stereotypes that grossly oversimplify the complexities of alternative philosophies (Sternberg, 2007). For example, some Americans simplistically think of Africa as a country, not realizing that it's a vast continent more culturally and linguistically diverse than North or South America. In a similar way, the term *Asian* encompasses students from a number of diverse countries and cultures, including China, Japan, Vietnam, and Korea. To speak of a singular "African philosophy"—or Native American or Asian philosophy—does an injustice to diverse groups of people and their philosophies (Ngo & Lee, 2007). Further, people are people, and categorizing them on the basis of sweeping and uncertain philosophical generalizations is questionable at best and perhaps even potentially damaging.

Rather than viewing students as Hispanic, Native American, or African American, or as representative of any other cultural or ethnic group, we should see students as individuals. Concluding that a boy named Ted Chang, for example, doesn't speak out in class solely because of the influence of his Chinese culture is unwise. Getting to know Ted as an individual will better help you understand why he's quiet and will help you find ways to involve him in learning activities, just as you would involve any student in your classes.

Respecting and valuing cultural differences is a good idea; making decisions that may detract from learning, based on overgeneralizations about these differences, is not. Realizing that not all people have the same philosophical orientations will help you be more sensitive to important individual differences in your students.

DIVERSITY AND YOU

Philosophy and the Classroom

Four middle school teachers are discussing their students during their weekly pod meeting in which they share ideas about their curriculum and discuss the 110 students in their pod. Their school recently instituted these pods or teams of teachers to create a more personal learning experience and to better track each student's academic progress.

"I'm concerned about Roberto," Jim Hansen begins. "He shuffles into class and seems to try to hide behind Jerry, one of the biggest boys in my class. He hasn't done his math homework for the second time this week. When I asked him about it, he said that the 12 problems I assigned were too many. He mumbled, 'I hate math,' as I walked back to the front of the room to greet the other students as they came into the room.

Roberto is a recent immigrant from Nicaragua, and his English is limited. Some of the other students frown when he talks, because they can't understand his broken English; he often doesn't fully understand my explanations. At lunch, if his friend Raul isn't there, he eats alone. He seems so alone and is struggling both academically and socially."

"I've noticed the same problems in my class," Caitlin Connors adds. "His background knowledge is a problem, and I can't really blame him. How would you like to try and remember all those names and places in American history? It's a lot to learn even for someone with a background in our history"

"You think that's a problem. Try teaching science to someone who struggles with English," Shanda Meyers replies. "My regular students complain about our textbook. . . . They say it's too hard. Roberto's having trouble just keeping up with what's going on much less putting all the information together in his head."

"Okay, we agree that Roberto needs help," Rasheen Wallace, the language arts teacher on the team, interjects. "But the big question is, what are we going to do about it?"

"He's lacking the basics," Jim Hansen offers. "We need to try and get him up to speed on all the stuff he's missed. We could take turns meeting with him early in the morning to help him catch up. I could start with basic math facts like addition and subtraction, and then progress to decimals and fractions."

"That's a start, but I'm not sure the problem is just basics. He really seems to have a motivation problem in my class," Rasheen interjects. He just seems to be floating, going through the motions in my language arts class. He doesn't seem to understand what grammar and punctuation have to do with his life. Maybe I need to do more writing and applied stuff. I could find out if he still has relatives back in Nicaragua and help him write letters to his friends and family back there. My Spanish isn't great, but I think I remember enough to be dangerous."

The other teachers nod and offer their own suggestions about possible solutions to the problem.

QUESTIONS TO CONSIDER

1. Consider Jim Hansen's suggestion for helping Roberto. What educational philosophy are his ideas based on?
2. What about Rasheen Wallace's suggestion to help Roberto? What educational philosophy are her ideas based on?
3. Which of the four educational philosophies—perennialism, essentialism, progressivism, or social reconstructionism—would be most effective for working with students who are cultural minorities? Least effective? Why?

Go to *Diversity and You* in the MyEducationLab™ *Book Resources* that accompany this text to log your thoughts and receive feedback from your authors.

Check Your Understanding

3.1. What are the major philosophies of education?

3.2. Because students must be able to function effectively in, and adapt to, a changing world, a teacher emphasizes the "whole person"—physical, social, emotional, and intellectual—in her students. She stresses and models physical fitness, involves her students in discussions to help them practice social skills and perspective taking, and involves them in problem solving about modern-day topics. To which of the educational philosophies are the teacher's efforts most closely related? Explain.

3.3. You visit a school, and you overhear a conversation between two teachers. One says, "I love teaching Shakespeare. His work has been studied for hundreds of years, and it's as timely now as it was then." Which educational philosophy is best illustrated by the teacher's comment? Explain.

3.4. A teacher who wants her students to examine racism and injustice involves them in a unit on nonviolent noncooperation using a study of Gandhi's struggles against racism in India as an example. She further illustrates the ideas with a study of Martin Luther King's nonviolent protests against American racism. To which of the educational philosophies are the teacher's efforts most closely related? Explain.

For feedback, go to the appendix, *Check Your Understanding*, located in the back of this text.

ISSUES YOU'LL FACE IN TEACHING

The Essential Knowledge Debate

Americans in general, and American students in particular, are repeatedly criticized for their lack of knowledge and skills. For example, as you saw earlier in the chapter, students at all levels have only a rudimentary understanding of American history (National Center for Education Statistics, 2010g). And concerns about American's lack of knowledge have become prominent enough that a feature article in the March 28, 2011, issue of *Newsweek* raised the question, "How dumb are we?" (A. Romano, 2011). Similar concerns have been raised about math and science, where international comparisons indicate that American students lag behind many of their counterparts in other countries (Cavanagh, 2012a).

This issue has spawned books such as *The Dumbest Generation* (Bauerlein, 2008), and social critics' comments, such as "We are becoming the stupid giant of planet Earth: richer than Midas, mightier than Thor, dumber than rocks" (Pitts, 2008). The issues have even made their way into late-night comedy, such as The Tonight Show's segment "Jaywalking" in which host Jay Leno asks people on the street basic questions such as, "Who are the people on Mount Rushmore?" which they can rarely answer.

In response to criticisms about American students' lack of knowledge, educators have written standards in virtually every content area. Experts call standards, "essential questions: doorways to understanding" (Wiggins & McTighe, 2005, p. 105). Every state has specified standards, and to hold students and schools accountable, they have created tests to measure the extent to which the standards are being met. In addition there is a national movement to create uniform standards for all 50 states (Gewertz, 2011c). Standards apply to teachers as well: Virtually all states now require teachers to pass some type of exam in order to be licensed (Hightower, 2012).

THE QUESTION

Are standards, and the accompanying high-stakes tests that are used to measure the extent to which the standards are met, the answer to the problem of students' lack of knowledge and skills? Here are arguments on both sides of the issue of the standards controversy.

PRO

- All people should master certain well-defined skills and bodies of knowledge, a view grounded in essentialist educational philosophy.
- Standards are a relatively simple way of describing what students should learn, and the public as well as parents deserve to know what our students are learning.
- Specifying standards and then using high-stakes testing of students to ensure that the standards are being met are an effective way to ensure that students are acquiring essential knowledge and skills.
- Research on learning indicates that prior knowledge is essential for understanding new content (Bruning, Schraw, & Norby, 2011; Eggen & Kauchak, 2013). For instance, to understand the civil unrest in the United States during the 1960s, students need to understand the relationships among the Vietnam War, the Civil Rights Movement, and people's growing distrust of government and authority.

CON

- Personal motivation and the ability to use strategies to acquire knowledge are better predictors of later success than the accumulation of facts (Kuhn, 2007).
- It's difficult to determine what knowledge is "essential." For example, is it more important to remember that Christopher Columbus "discovered America" in 1492 or that his voyage precipitated huge social and cultural changes that are still being felt today? These questions continue to be debated.
- The sheer amount of knowledge called for by standards is overwhelming. One testing expert commented, "Even if a modest number of super-general content standards are being used, beneath these standards there are still way too many curricular aims for teachers to successfully promote in a given year. Similarly, there are way too many curricular aims to assess in the hour or so available for the administration of any standards-based test" (Popham, 2004, pp. 77–78).
- Accountability and high-stakes testing aren't working (Sparks, 2011a). A blue-ribbon committee undertook a decades-long study of test-based incentive systems and found these systems had little positive effect on student learning (Hout & Elliot, 2011).

YOU TAKE A STAND

Now it's your turn to take a position on the issue. Is the emphasis on essential knowledge, standards, and high-stakes testing a productive way to promote learning, or do other philosophical positions offer a more promising perspective?

Go to *Issues You'll Face in Teaching* in the MyEducationLab™ *Book Resources* that accompany this text to log your thoughts and receive feedback from your authors.

Developing Your Philosophy of Education

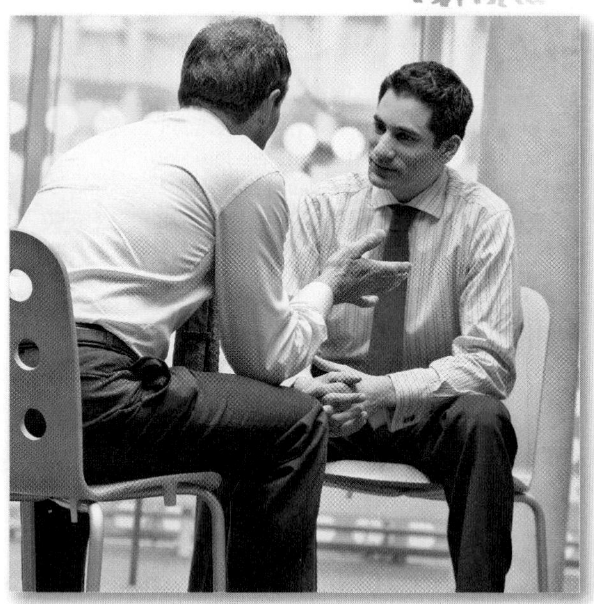

Dialoguing with other teachers can help beginning teachers shape their personal philosophy of education.

The philosophies you've studied in this chapter will help you make one of the most important decisions of your professional life: deciding what kind of teacher you want to become. This decision will influence the content you select, the teaching strategies you'll use, and the criteria you use to analyze, reflect on, and improve your teaching (see Figure 5.1). This decision will be strongly influenced by your philosophy of education.

Professionals are able to articulate what they're doing and why. For instance, if you walk into classrooms, see students involved in basic skills activities, and ask the teachers why they selected these activities, professionals can give you clear and specific answers. If they hold an essentialist philosophy, for example, they might suggest that the activities will help the students acquire core knowledge and skills that learners need to function effectively in the world. Some teachers, however, do activities simply because the activities are next in their textbooks or curriculum guides or because they did the activities last year; these are inadequate and unprofessional reasons.

If you're clear about your own philosophy, you will be able to make systematic changes when you conclude your instruction needs improvement. If your philosophy isn't clear, you'll be less likely to make needed changes, or you might make changes at random and hope everything improves. In either case, student learning suffers and professional growth doesn't occur. This is why philosophy is so important for all of us—for you and others just beginning their careers, and for those of us who are veterans and want to continue to grow professionally.

As you begin to form your personal philosophy, keep three ideas in mind. First, every teacher's philosophy is evolving and dynamic and will change and be refined as you gather experiences and learn. So don't be concerned if your current philosophy is initially murky and unclear; it will crystallize and become clearer as you think about and use it. Second, your personal philosophy is likely to include elements of more than one of the educational philosophies. For example, both Don and Paul, your authors, have strong essentialist philosophies with respect to knowledge. However, we believe in progressivist teaching methods equally strongly. And aspects of both perennialism and social reconstructionism also have merits for us. Third, be open to other perspectives; changing your views as you grow as a professional is an indicator of the open-mindedness necessary for personal and professional growth.

The Role of Beliefs in a Philosophy of Education

To begin establishing your own philosophy of education, first try to identify your own beliefs, because these exert a powerful influence on how you'll teach (Speer, 2008). Allie and Brad both did a good job of describing their beliefs about teaching and learning. Here is a summary of Allie's beliefs:

"Everything we learn depends on what we already know."

"There's real, practical stuff out there that kids need. They have to be good readers, they need to be able to write and do math, and they need to understand this stuff, the science I'm teaching."

"Practice, thorough assessment, and detailed feedback are some of the best ways we have of getting them to learn. That's reality."

And here is a summary of Brad's beliefs:

"The only way [kids are] going to get good at making decisions is to be put in situations where they're forced to make decisions. . . . That's how the world works."

"Being put in situations where they have to practice making decisions is 'real, practical, stuff.'"

"Reality is, in fact, what you perceive it to be, and there's no objective source out there to decide which view is the 'right one.'"

You can see that Allie's and Brad's beliefs are quite different, but both had thought about what they believed and were able to clearly state their positions.

The following questions can help you get started in identifying your own beliefs.

- What's the purpose of schooling? For example, should students focus on content, or is the development of self-concept, interpersonal skills, and other personal qualities more important?
- Is my role as a teacher to pass knowledge on to students, or should I guide students as they learn on their own?
- How do students best learn? Do frequent tests and quizzes promote learning, or should students have opportunities to explore topics without the threat of evaluation constantly?
- Is motivating students part of my job, or should motivation come from within students? Should I push them, or should they be left largely on their own?

Examining Your Beliefs

Our beliefs influence and ultimately shape the philosophies that we carry into our classrooms. To assess your developing beliefs about education, respond to the following statements, and then answer the questions that follow. Use this scale in making your responses:

Teaching and You

Which of the educational philosophies make the most sense to you? To examine your beliefs about schools, and teaching, and learning, respond to the questions that follow and see how your own beliefs mesh with these different philosophies.

5 = strongly agree
4 = agree
3 = neither agree nor disagree
2 = disagree
1 = strongly disagree

1. Schools should emphasize important knowledge more than students' personal interests.	1	2	3	4	5
2. Teachers should emphasize interdisciplinary subject matter that encourages project-oriented, democratic classrooms.	1	2	3	4	5
3. Schools should emphasize each student's responsibility in making the world a better place.	1	2	3	4	5
4. The primary aim of education is to develop a person's intellectual capacity.	1	2	3	4	5
5. Schools should emphasize basic skills more than humanistic ideals.	1	2	3	4	5
6. Teachers should guide student's investigations about the physical and social world around them.	1	2	3	4	5
7. The best teachers lead students in discussions about important social issues.	1	2	3	4	5

8. The goals of education should be the same for everyone: All students should understand the important literature, mathematics, and science of Western civilization. 1 2 3 4 5

9. The purpose of schools is to ensure practical preparation for life and work more than personal development. 1 2 3 4 5

10. Curriculum should emerge from students' needs and interests; it *should not* be prescribed in advance. 1 2 3 4 5

11. The best education emphasizes the great works in the arts and humanities. 1 2 3 4 5

12. It is more important for teachers to involve students in activities that analyze and criticize society than to have them accumulate a lot of information. 1 2 3 4 5

13. Education should enhance personal growth through problem solving in the present rather than emphasizing preparation for a distant future. 1 2 3 4 5

14. Human nature's most distinctive quality is the ability to reason; therefore, the intellect should be the focus of education. 1 2 3 4 5

15. Schools should take the lead in combating racism and sexism camouflaged as traditional values. 1 2 3 4 5

16. Teachers should help students learn a common core of useful knowledge, *not* experiment with their own views about curricula. 1 2 3 4 5

Now add up your responses using the following scale:
Strongly Disagree = 1; Disagree = 2; Agree/Disagree = 3; Agree = 4; Strongly Agree = 5.

Perennialism:
Item #4 ____ + #8 ____ + #11 ____ + #14 ____ = ____

Essentialism
Item #1 ____ + #5 ____ + #9 ____ + #16 ____ = ____

Progressivism:
Item #2 ____ + #6 ____ + #10 ____ + #13 ____ = ____

Social Reconstructionism
Item #3 ____ + #7 ____ + #12 ____ + #15 ____ = ____

What did the totals of your responses tell you about your own beliefs about teaching? Did the tallies confirm what you believe your philosophy of education is at this point in your studies, or were they inconsistent with what you previously thought your philosophy of education was? Don't worry if an inconsistency exists. Remember, you're only beginning your journey as a teacher, and your beliefs will evolve and become more crystallized as you gain experience and develop. Let's turn now to the process of forming your philosophy of education.

Forming a Philosophy

All new knowledge depends on what we already know. So, my job is to help kids learn as much as they can about the topics I teach, and that's what I try to do every day. I know that

TABLE 5.2 An Analysis of Allie's Philosophy of Education

Belief Statement	Component of Her Philosophy
"Everything we learn depends on what we already know."	"My job is to help kids learn as much as they can about the topics I teach, and that's what I try to do every day."
"There's real practical stuff out there that kids need. They have to be good readers, they need to be able to write and do math, and they need to understand this stuff, the science I'm teaching."	"I'm going to be sure that the kids learn the real, practical stuff they need to function in today's world."
"Practice, thorough assessment, and detailed feedback are some of the best ways we have of getting them to learn. That's reality."	"I'm going to give them lots of practice; I'm going to quiz them thoroughly and often, and I'm going to give them detailed feedback about the quizzes."

I can get them to learn. The best way to get kids to learn is to have them practice and then provide them with feedback. So, I'm going to give them lots of practice; I'm going to quiz them thoroughly and often, and I'm going to give them detailed feedback about the quizzes. If I do my job, they'll learn.

What you've just read is a succinct description of Allie's philosophy of education: It's clear, well-articulated, and consistent with her beliefs. The relationships between her beliefs and components of her philosophy are outlined in Table 5.2.

Because Allie's philosophy is well-articulated, she can use it to guide her thinking as she defines her goals and designs learning activities and assessments. It helps ensure that all three—goals, learning activities, and assessments—are consistent with one another. You may or may not agree with Allie's goals or the rationale for them, but the fact that she's clear in her thinking increases the likelihood that her students will reach the goals, and she'll be more likely to make conscious choices to change and improve her teaching when she sees evidence that change is needed.

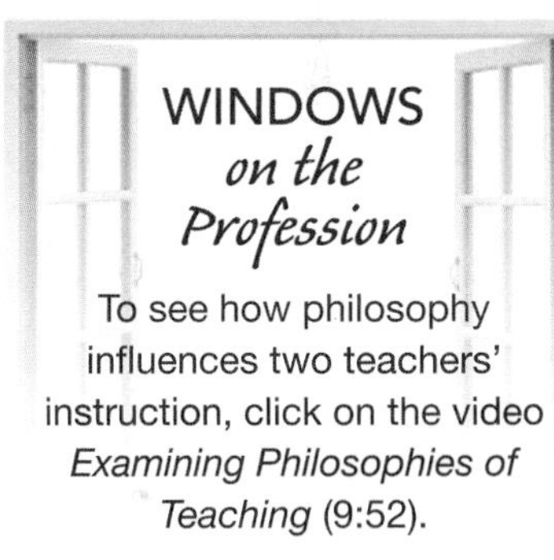

To see how philosophy influences two teachers' instruction, click on the video *Examining Philosophies of Teaching* (9:52).

Armed with your analysis of your beliefs, and a description of Allie's philosophy, you should now be ready to create your personal philosophy that can guide your thinking and actions.

URBAN EDUCATION: Philosophy of Education in Urban Environments

Forming a coherent philosophy of education is important for all teachers; for new teachers in urban classrooms, it's crucial. The philosophy that you develop will help you understand your role in urban classrooms and how you can best help urban students learn and develop (Hollins, 2012).

Examining Your Beliefs About Urban Learners

Understanding your own beliefs in forming your personal philosophy of education is particularly important when you work in urban settings. Answering the question, "What do I believe about urban learners and working in urban schools?" is essential, and becoming aware of your beliefs will strongly influence how you approach your work with urban students. For instance, consider the following contrasting beliefs.

- Urban students are much like all students: They want to learn, but they need some help and encouragement.
- Homework is as important a part of instruction when working with urban students as it is with all students.

- Urban students need caring and supportive teachers, as do all students.
- Working in an urban setting is much like working in any other school.
- Working in an urban setting is dangerous, and teachers must be vigilant to prevent possible personal harm.
- Urban students don't want to learn, and they're in school only because they're required to be there.
- Urban students believe respecting and liking teachers are viewed as a sign of weakness.
- There is little point to assigning homework to urban students, because they won't do it.

Though only examples, you can see how these different beliefs could influence the way you approach your work with urban students. For example, if you believe that—at a basic level—urban students want to learn, and their acting as if they don't is more an effort to protect their sense of self-worth than a true disinterest in learning, you will make a greater effort to help them understand the topics you're teaching than if you believe that they genuinely don't want to learn. Similarly, if you believe that working in an urban setting is much like working in any other school, you will interact with students differently than if you believe that urban environments are dangerous, where you must "watch your back."

Developing a Philosophy for Urban Settings

As with forming a philosophy of education in general, constructing a philosophy that guides your actions in urban settings begins with a careful examination of your beliefs. However, the process of identifying and articulating your beliefs with respect to urban settings requires additional study, reflection, and perhaps some soul searching, because many negative stereotypes exist about urban schools and urban students. If you're uninformed, it's easy to slip into accepting a stereotype as true. When this happens, your negative beliefs will detract from your effectiveness in working with urban students.

Urban classrooms are challenging, and we're not suggesting that a set of positive beliefs will make your work with urban students simple and easy. However, a well-formed philosophy that you can reflect on can serve as a powerful foundation as you teach and interact with your urban students.

We hope this chapter provides you with the professional knowledge needed to begin your journey toward developing a personal philosophy and that it encourages you to think about teaching in different ways. At this point, you won't have all the answers you'll need to decide what education should be and how you can help make it that way. But if you're now able to begin asking some important questions, then our goal for the chapter has been fulfilled. Good luck.

Check Your Understanding

4.1. Why is a personal philosophy of education important?
4.2. Describe the three essential steps involved in forming a philosophy of education.
4.3. Look again at Brad's thinking, as indicated by his conversation with Allie. Based on this information, what is his philosophy of education? Explain how his philosophy is based on his beliefs.

For feedback, go to the appendix, *Check Your Understanding*, located in the back of this text.

VOICES from the CLASSROOM

"I teach because I believe in children and in their deep desire to learn and grow as the best people that they can be."

KRISTEN BRUMMEL, 2011 Teacher of the Year, Hawaii

CHAPTER 5 Summary

1. Define philosophy, and explain the difference between philosophy and theory.
   - Philosophy is a search for wisdom. A normative philosophy describes the way something ought to be, such as the way educators ought to teach and treat their students. In forming a philosophy, a professional teacher searches for the wisdom to maximize learning for all students.
   - Philosophy provides a framework for thinking and guides our practice. Philosophy and theory overlap but are not the same. Theories are used to explain events and behavior as they are, whereas philosophies go further to suggest the way events and behaviors ought to be.
2. Describe each of the branches of philosophy, and identify examples that illustrate each.
   - Epistemology is the branch of philosophy that describes how we know what we know. It's important for teachers because it influences how we teach and our choice of teaching methods.
   - Metaphysics considers what we know and addresses questions of reality and, ultimately, what is real. Our beliefs about reality influence our goals for our students, as we help them discover their own realities.
   - Axiology considers values and ethics and examines questions and issues involving decisions about right and wrong. Axiology is important because schools play an important role in shaping students' values and, ultimately, their moral behavior.
   - Logic is the process of deriving valid conclusions from basic principles. Effective teachers help students understand the logic of different arguments and also how to think clearly about ideas.
3. Describe the major educational philosophies, and identify examples that illustrate each.
   - Perennialism focuses on time-honored absolutes. Because truth doesn't change, a teacher's responsibility is to expose students to time-tested knowledge and truth. Assigning students to read Shakespeare's works because they focus on the human condition is an example.
   - Essentialism suggests that a critical core of information exists that all people should possess, schools should emphasize basic skills and academic subjects, and students should master these subjects. A curriculum that emphasizes reading, writing, and a deep understanding of math is consistent with essentialism.
   - Progressivism views goals as dynamic and evolving and emphasizes that learning should be experience based and relevant to students' lives. A teacher involving students in problem-based learning activities is applying progressivist philosophy.
   - Social reconstructionism sees schools and other social institutions in need of restructuring, with marginalized people and their works elevated to more prominent positions in the content of schooling.

4. Explain why a personal philosophy of education is important, and describe the steps involved in forming one.
   - A personal philosophy of education is important because it guides your instructional decisions and specifies criteria you can use to reflect on and analyze your teaching.
   - A personal philosophy also helps you explain and defend your educational goals.
   - Developing a personal philosophy begins with a description and an analysis of your beliefs and continues with an internally consistent articulation of your philosophy.
   - Developing a personal philosophy of education increases your professionalism by providing a concrete frame of reference for both action and reflection.

Important Concepts

axiology
epistemology
essentialism
logic
metaphysics
normative philosophy
perennialism
philosophy
philosophy of education
progressivism
social justice
social reconstructionism
theory
21st-century skills

Portfolio Activity

Assessing Your Philosophy of Education

InTASC Principle 9: Professional Learning and Ethical Practice

The purpose of this activity is to help you begin to develop a philosophy of education. Review your responses to the questions we asked in the section *Examining Your Beliefs*.

1. Do you think your responses accurately reflect your philosophy of education? Why or why not?
2. Which educational philosophy was most congruent with your current beliefs about education? Least?
3. How will your responses to this survey influence your teaching at your projected first teacher assignment (e.g., first grade or middle school math teacher)?
4. Now, using your scores on the survey as a basis, write a short one- or two-page summary of your developing philosophy of education.

Portfolio Activities similar to this one and related to chapter content can be found at MyEducationLab™.

Educational Philosophy and Your Teaching

Go to the topic *History and Philosophy of Education* in the MyEducationLab (www.myeducationlab.com) for *Introduction to Teaching*, where you can:

- Find learning outcomes for *History and Philosophy of Education,* along with the national standards that connect to these outcomes.
- Complete *Assignments and Activities* that can help you more deeply understand the chapter content.
- Apply and practice your understanding of the core teaching skills identified in the chapter with the *Building Teaching Skills and Dispositions* learning units.
- Access video clips of CCSSO National Teachers of the Year award winners responding to the question, "Why Do I Teach?" in the *Teacher Talk* section.
- Check your comprehension on the content covered in the chapter with the *Study Plan.* Here you will be able to take a chapter quiz, receive feedback on your answers, and then access *Review, Practice, and Enrichment* activities to enhance your understanding of chapter content.
- Check the *Book Resources* to find opportunities to share thoughts and gather feedback on the *Diversity and You* and *Issues You'll Face in Teaching* features found in this chapter.

MyEducationLab™

After lunch Randi gathers her class on a carpet in the front of the room and points to the following words she has written on the board:

party was times good
wonderful house

it ______________ a ________ w ______________ p ____ t ____ filled with g ____ d t ____ m ____ s and good friends at the animal h ____ se

She begins by having the children pronounce each of the words—*party, was, times, good, wonderful,* and *house*—in unison. She then guides them to complete the missing parts of the sentence, so ultimately it appears as follows:

It was a wonderful party filled with good times and good friends at the animal house.

The lesson is dynamic and interactive, with both group and individual responses, and the children are remarkably attentive.

Randi then has the students practice combining words. She gives them a beginning, such as *ye,* and an ending, such as *ll,* and the students say, "Yell." She repeats the process with several more words. As part of the activity, the children have to determine whether each word is real. For instance, when they combine *yo* and *oith, they* conclude that "yoith" is not a real word.

As Randi works with the majority of the class, the special educator takes a group of five students to a table at the back of the room where she can provide more personalized support.

To conclude the lesson, they gather the children back into a whole group, where they practice pronouncing words such as *mouth, playground,* and *enough.*

Finally, they sing a song as they line up to go outside for recess.

"Wow, noon. I need to get going," Chris Lucio, a junior high teacher, says to his colleague, April Jackson, as he finishes the last bite of his lunch and jumps up from the couch in the teacher's lounge. "My kids will be chomping at the bit trying to get into the room."

Chris hurriedly leaves the lounge, stops by the main office to check his box, and then walks across the courtyard to his building.

Chris's school is organized into six periods a day, and he teaches five sections of seventh-grade geography, two advanced and three standard. Chris has planning sixth period. He has 28 students in his standard third-period geography class, which begins right after lunch.

When the bell rings, Chris's students are in their seats and facing the screen at the front of the room where Chris has displayed the images shown here on his document camera.

"Okay, everyone, look carefully at what you see on the screen," Chris says. "Today, our goal is to identify similarities and differences in what we see here, try to figure out why

Rocky Mountains

Appalachian Mountains

they exist, and see what influence the differences have on our lives. . . . What do you notice in the two pictures? . . . Sophia?"

With Chris's guidance, his students make a series of observations, in the process noticing how much higher and sharper the peaks in the Rocky Mountains are, and how much more rugged the Rockies are in general. As the lesson progresses, Chris guides them to understand that the differences are related to the difference in age between the two mountain ranges, with the Rockies being young mountains, and the Appalachians being mature. They also discuss how the differences influence different aspects of our lives, such as recreation and the use of natural resources.

Chris teaches the same lesson in each of his standard classes. His advanced students have moved through the curriculum more quickly, so he has his students in the two advanced classes examine the influence of geography on the economies of different regions of the country.

As you can see, there are similarities and differences between teaching at different levels. All teaching involves working closely with students, but how we interact with them and the challenges and rewards we'll encounter differ significantly from level to level. Our goal in this chapter is to help you understand how schools at different levels are organized and to provide you with information that will help you make a good decision about the grade level that's best for you. But, before you begin, please respond to the items in the *This I Believe* feature that follows. We address each item in the chapter.

This I Believe

CHOOSING A SCHOOL TO BEGIN MY CAREER

For each item, circle the number that best represents your belief. Use the following scale as a guide:

4 = I strongly believe the statement is true.
3 = I believe the statement is true.
2 = I believe the statement is false.
1 = I strongly believe the statement is false.

1. My school principal is the person who will have the ultimate responsibility for the successful operation of my school.

   1 2 3 4

2. If I decide to teach in an elementary school, I'll have to choose between promoting my students' social and emotional development versus preparing them for standardized tests.

   1 2 3 4

3. Middle and junior high schools are essentially the same but are given different labels.

   1 2 3 4

4. Larger schools generally provide students with better educations, because they have better facilities and can provide a wider variety of programs.

   1 2 3 4

5. If some of my students fail to master the content at the grade level I'm teaching, retaining the students in that grade is the best way to ensure that they will acquire the knowledge and skills needed to succeed at the next grade.

   1 2 3 4

MyEducationLab™

Visit the MyEducationLab for *Introduction to Teaching* to enhance your understanding of chapter concepts with a personalized *Study Plan.* You'll also have the opportunity to hone your teaching skills through video and case-based *Assignments and Activities* and *Building Teaching Skills and Disposition* lessons.

How Do Schools Function?

Think about the schools you attended before coming to your college or university. If you're typical, you first went to an elementary school, which began with kindergarten or pre-kindergarten, then to a middle or junior high school, and finally to a high school. This is the way schools are typically organized in our country. In this section of the chapter, we look at why American schools are organized this way, and what implications this organization might have for your choice of a school, as we discuss each of the following:

- What is a school?
- School personnel
- The physical plant
- Organization of the curriculum

What Is a School?

We can think about schools in several different ways. Most important for you, schools are places where you'll find your first job, learn to teach, and develop as a professional. At another level, a school is a physical place where teachers teach and students learn. Metaphors for schools include factories, shopping malls, and even prisons. The factory metaphor considers students as raw material and turns them into finished products whose quality is measured by scores on standardized tests (Cuban, 2003). Thinking of schools as shopping malls focuses on the broad array of offerings in many of them, where choice and personal preference are emphasized. Harsh critics use the prison metaphor: Students are required to attend until the age of 16, and their freedoms are severely limited while they're "incarcerated" in school.

Many teachers and educational leaders like to think of schools as extended families, learning communities where young people can learn and develop personally, socially, and intellectually. This happens in the best schools, but it can be lost in others. (We examine key differences between more- and less-effective schools later in the chapter.)

Finally, we can think of schools as **social systems**, organizations with established structures and rules designed to promote certain goals (Lezotte & Snyder, 2011), and this is the way we'll describe schools in this chapter. John Goodlad, one of education's most important thinkers of the past half century, identified four major goals for schools (Goodlad, 1984). They're outlined in Figure 6.1.

These goals are significant because they shape the ways our schools are organized and how this organization will influence your teaching. Three factors are involved. First, both parents and students have historically believed that each

FIGURE 6.1 Goals of Schools

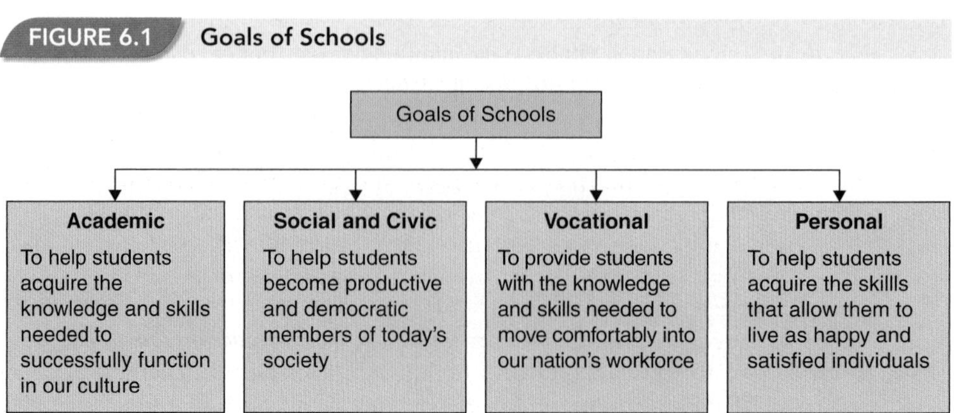

Goals of Schools
Academic
To help students acquire the knowledge and skills needed to successfully function in our culture
Social and Civic
To help students become productive and democratic members of today's society
Vocational
To provide students with the knowledge and skills needed to move comfortably into our nation's workforce
Personal
To help students acquire the skillls that allow them to live as happy and satisfied individuals

goal is important (Goodlad, 1984), so you'll be expected to address each as you work with your students. Second, the goals sometimes compete, and conflicts can occur. For example, academics are strongly emphasized in today's schools, as indicated by the current focus on standards and high-stakes testing. Critics, who include many teachers, argue that this emphasis narrows the curriculum and shortchanges the personal and social growth of students (Amrein & Berliner, 2003; Common Core, 2011). Third, the relative emphasis placed on each goal varies with grade level. Elementary schools, for example, place greater emphasis on personal and social development than high schools, where the focus is more on academic and vocational goals.

Social systems function effectively when their components work together to meet their goals. In schools important components include:

- *School personnel:* The people who make schools work—administrators, support staff, and teachers
- *The physical plant*: The school building or buildings, playgrounds and playing fields, and parking lots
- *The curriculum:* Everything teachers teach and students learn in the school

Let's see how these components affect the effectiveness of a school.

School Personnel

School personnel include all the people—the administrators, the support staff, and the teachers—who help make a school effective. When you teach, your success will depend in part on the other people in the school. In essence, you're part of a team, and the team's success depends on how well everyone works together.

Administrators and Support Staff

Elementary, middle, junior high, and high schools all have **administrators**, people responsible for the day-to-day operation of a school. The **principal** is the most important administrator, because he or she is given ultimate administrative responsibility for the school's operation. As with expert teachers, the best principals understand the process of teaching and learning and how schools can promote healthy learning and development in students (Bryk et al., 2010).

The size of a school and the wealth of a district determine the way they're administratively organized. For instance, Oak Creek, Randi's school, is large and has two "administrative support" people who assist the principal, one handling student behavior issues, and the other in charge of the curriculum.

Lakeside Junior High, Chris's school, also has two administrators who support the principal—a vice principal and an assistant principal. The vice principal's duties include scheduling, record keeping—collecting student records from teachers and keeping master records for the school—and maintaining communication with district-level administrators and parents. The assistant principal is in charge of the physical plant, which includes all maintenance and construction, as well as the process of ordering and distributing textbooks.

In many cases, schools will also have guidance counselors and may also have school psychologists, who are often shared with other schools. Oak Creek, for example, has one full-time and one part-time guidance counselor. Lakeside has two full-time guidance counselors, one for seventh and the other for eighth grade. Guidance counselors' duties commonly include scheduling, coordinating statewide assessment tests, and providing information to students about course offerings and career options.

School psychologists assist by administering group and individual tests to place students in the right classes and make decisions about whether students qualify for special education or programs for the gifted and talented. They also

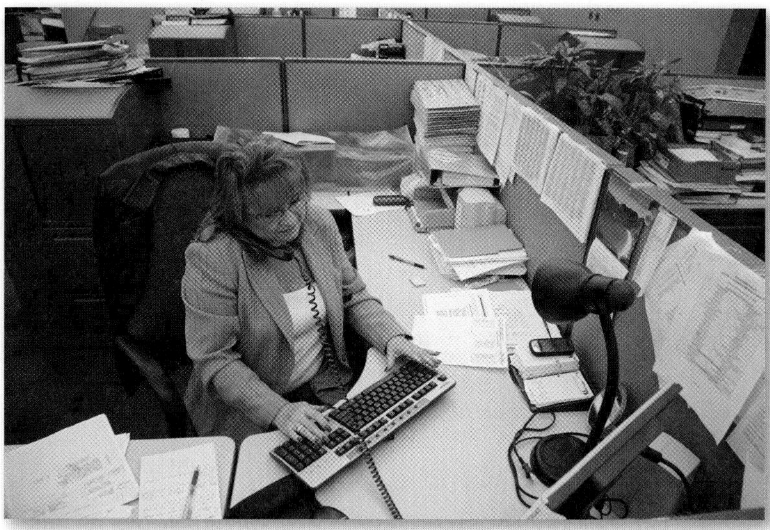

The central office is the school's nerve center; the office staff plays an important role in greeting guests and assisting teachers as well as students.

provide individual counseling for students having emotional problems and make recommendations for further mental health assistance.

Lakeside also has a full-time licensed practical nurse who maintains all student health records, serves students who need immediate care, dispenses all prescribed medications to students, and is trained in CPR. Students at Lakeside aren't allowed to take even an over-the-counter painkiller, such as aspirin, on their own, and teachers may not give students any form of medication.

Lakeside is among the 45% of public schools in our country that have a full-time, on-site nurse, which means that the majority of schools share health professionals, sometimes with several schools. And 25% have no nurse at all. With the cutbacks in educational funding in recent years, this shortage is likely to get worse before it gets better (Mithers, 2011).

In addition, all schools have support staff who keep the school running smoothly. They include:

- Secretaries and receptionists, who answer phones and greet visitors to the school
- Administrative and instructional support staff, who complete paperwork for the principal and other administrators, duplicate tests and handouts for teachers, maintain payroll records, and generally keep the school running
- Media center specialists, who manage different forms of technology as well as books
- Physical plant staff, such as custodians, who clean the rooms and buildings, and cafeteria workers, who prepare school lunches

Our descriptions of Oak Creek and Lakeside are merely examples; schools vary in the labels they use for different administrators and the duties they perform. For instance, Oak Creek uses the label "administrative support" to describe duties that might be assigned to a vice principal or assistant principal in another school. So, the labels and duties for administrators and support staff in schools that you visit, or the school in which you take your first job may differ from our examples here. But the functions remain the same; administrators and support staff ensure that the school runs smoothly.

Why do you need to understand school personnel and their roles? A school is a complex social system, and all the people working in it contribute to making it run smoothly. For example, if you have a student who is chronically disruptive, you'll need the support of the administrator in charge of student discipline, and the student may need counseling with a school psychologist.

As another example, experienced teachers commonly joke that school secretaries are the ones who really "run" a school. They know where things are and how to get things done. The way you and other teachers treat support staff helps set the tone for a positive school climate and will also influence how cooperative they are and how much help they give you. For example, requesting—instead of demanding—services, such as having a test duplicated, communicates to support staff that you value their contributions to the overall functioning of the school. The most effective schools are those in which all personnel work together for the benefit of students.

As a professional, your ability to work with other school personnel will influence how effective you and the school will be. School leaders often describe the ability to work with others as one of the most important characteristics they look for in new teachers (Lezotte & Snyder, 2011; Van Houtte & Van Maele, 2011).

Teachers

Although school principals have ultimate administrative responsibility for the school's operation, teachers are at the heart of any effective school. This means you. *No organization, system, institution, or enterprise is any better than the people in it,* and the same applies to schools. The quality of a school is determined by the quality of its teachers. You will be the most important factor influencing your students' learning! Surprisingly, only recently have educational researchers and leaders begun to understand and appreciate this fact (Thomas & Wingert, 2010). And the American public agrees. According to an annual poll of the public's attitudes toward public education, "Americans singled out improving the quality of teachers as the most important action for improving education" (Bushaw & Lopez, 2010, p. 15). Helping you develop into the kind of teacher our country's students need is the goal of this text.

Revisiting My Beliefs

This section addresses the first item in *This I Believe:* "My school principal is the person who will have the ultimate responsibility for the successful operation of my school." This statement is true: Principals are given the legal responsibility for running a school and have a major influence on its effectiveness.

The Physical Plant

In addition to the people who work in it, a school is also a physical place. Schools have classrooms, hallways that allow students to move from one room to another, central administrative offices, and other large rooms, such as auditoriums, gymnasiums, music rooms, and cafeterias. Most schools have a relatively simple boxlike structure, with hall upon hall of separate cells, or classrooms, which critics argue isolates teachers and fragments the curriculum.

Your classroom will, however, offer you privacy and a sanctuary from the hectic pace of school life. When you go into your classroom and close the door, you control essentially everything that goes on in there. Beginning in the late 1960s, schools experimented with open classrooms that had large, movable walls, but they became unpopular because of noise and lack of privacy, and by the late 1970s interest in the "open classroom" model had waned (Cuban, 2004b).

What will the physical arrangement of your school mean for you when you take your first job? The physical condition of a school says much about the public's support for education, and it can have a powerful effect on teacher morale (Brimley et al., 2012; Kozol, 2005). Both teachers and students are affected by the physical environment of a school, and your first look at a school provides you with some indication of how well the school is run.

The division of schools into separate, isolated classrooms has both advantages and disadvantages. On the one hand, your classroom will be your own domain, where you can define yourself as a teacher and operate according to your own professional judgment. On the other, it separates you from your colleagues. When you're in your classroom and you shut the door, as many teachers do, you'll be on your own. You'll be responsible for 20 to 30 kindergarteners or first graders, for example, all day, every day, as is the case with Randi. Or, if you teach in middle or high school, you'll spend most of your workday in your classroom, where you'll be responsible for the education and safety of five or six different classes of students every day—the situation Chris is in. And, although your primary responsibility will be promoting your students' learning and development, you'll also be expected to carry out noninstructional activities in other areas of the school. If you teach in an elementary school, for example, you'll be expected to escort your students to and from the cafeteria or the media center and periodically supervise them on the playground. If you're a middle or high school teacher, you'll monitor students as they move through the corridors, and you'll be expected to attend nonacademic events, such as assemblies and pep rallies. You may also be asked to sell tickets at football games, attend track meets, and go to band concerts. These responsibilities broaden your focus and integrate you into the workings of the whole school.

Organization of Schools and the Curriculum

The **curriculum**, everything that teachers teach and students learn in schools, is a third major component of every school (Wiles & Bondi, 2011). In today's schools, the formal curriculum is organized around **standards**, essentially statements of learning goals, which describe what students should know or be able to do after a prescribed period of study. For example:

- Students will recognize the letters of the alphabet.
- Students will write short paragraphs using correct organizational structure.
- Students will use the correct order of operations to simplify expressions such as $9 + 4(7 - 3)/2$.
- Students will solve problems involving the relationships between force, mass, and acceleration.

Historically, educators decided that the most efficient way to help students reach goals such as these is to organize the curriculum according to grade levels and into subject matter areas. For instance, the first goal targets children in kindergarten; third graders would be expected to reach the second goal; middle school pre-algebra students the third; and high school physics students the fourth. Standards for different grade levels and subject matter areas are part of the school's general curriculum, and these goals provide you and other teachers with direction as you decide what to teach.

How should teachers and students be physically organized to help students most effectively reach goals such as these? For example, are students most likely to reach the goals by having kindergarteners, third graders, middle school students, and those taking advanced high school courses all in the same building? Most educators don't believe so. For instance, how would 6-year-old children likely feel walking down a hall and bumping into 17-year-olds, many of whom are as big and strong as adults? Even seemingly minor concerns, such as the size of desks and the height of drinking fountains and toilets are considerations.

Because of these factors, schools are typically organized into three levels: elementary schools for young children, middle or junior high schools for beginning adolescents, and high schools for later adolescents. Considerable variation exists at each level, however, and some of the most common configurations are outlined in Table 6.1. Some school districts are even experimenting with schools

TABLE 6.1 **Common Ways to Organize Schools**

School Level	Grade Ranges
Elementary school	K–2
	K–3
	K–5
	K–6
	K–8
Middle/junior high school	5–8
	6–8
	7–8
	7–9
	8–9
High school	9–12
	10–12

that include grades 7–12, or even K–12 (J. Brown 2011), but they are much less common than those you see in Table 6.1.

What factors do educational leaders consider when making decisions about grouping students into grade levels? For example, why are grades K–5 common in elementary schools, and 6–8 or 7 and 8 common in middle schools? Two factors are most prominent: (1) the developmental characteristics of students and (2) economics and politics.

Developmental Characteristics of Students

Development refers to the physical changes in children as well as changes in the way they think and relate to their peers that result from maturation and experience. For example, 10th graders are bigger, stronger, and more coordinated than 5th graders; they're physically more developed. Similarly, 10th graders think differently from 5th graders, who also think differently from kindergarteners. And differences also exist in social development—differences in students' abilities to relate to their peers and work collaboratively in groups.

These developmental differences influence how schools are organized. For example, students in elementary schools, and particularly in kindergarten and first grade, are typically assigned to one teacher who monitors the cognitive, social, and emotional growth of students in their classroom. In some schools, **looping,** the practice of keeping a teacher with one group of students for more than a year, is used to help teachers better nurture the development of individual students. Older students are more capable of learning on their own and fending for themselves, so they are assigned a number of teachers who also serve as subject matter specialists. This is the common arrangement in middle, junior high, and high schools.

Revisiting My Beliefs

This section addresses the second item in *This I Believe,* "If I decide to teach in an elementary school, I'll have to choose between promoting my students' social and emotional development versus preparing them for standardized tests." This statement isn't true. Your students will indeed be expected to perform on tests, but the goals need not compete. You can do both to a greater extent than many people believe.

Economics and Politics

"Why school districts house certain grades together under one roof is often a matter of practical necessity rather than instructional intent" (Burkam, Michaels, & Lee, 2007, p. 288). For example, both economics and politics influenced the development of Lakeside, Chris Lucio's school, first created as a middle school and later converted to a junior high.

At the time Lakeside was built, elementary schools in the district had become overcrowded because of rapid population increases, and the process of building additional elementary schools couldn't keep up with demand. Creating middle schools temporarily solved the problem, because sixth graders could be moved into these schools. This was a decision based on economics.

Also, the middle school movement was gathering momentum at this same time, and Mary Zellner, Lakeside's first principal, was an outspoken proponent of middle schools. She was a respected leader in district politics, and because of her influence, Lakeside was built according to middle school philosophy. This philosophy deemphasized competition among students, and as a result, the school didn't have competitive athletics, which was the reason the school originally didn't have a gymnasium.

Issues then became complicated. Coaches at the local high school complained that potential athletes came to them from middle schools without the athletic experiences students from competing schools enjoyed. (These pressures aren't unusual: Many middle-level schools in the United States offer organized competitive sports.) The fact that the high school, the only high school in the district, had become overcrowded presented an additional problem. District officials solved both problems by converting the middle schools into junior highs, moving ninth graders from the high school to the junior highs, and sending sixth graders back to elementary schools. By this time, the elementary schools were able to handle the additional students, because a number of new elementary schools had been built. The decision to convert the middle school to a junior high was based on both economics and politics; it had little to do with the developmental needs of students.

Organizational changes such as these, driven by economics and politics, are common in education. As another example, to accommodate exploding enrollments, a small district in Utah decided to change its grade-level alignments to elementary (K–4), intermediate school (5–6), junior high (7–8), and high school (9–12) (Smart, 2008). District officials estimated that these realignments would save tens of millions of dollars in new construction costs.

Check Your Understanding

1.1. Schools are described as social systems. Define a social system, explain how a school is a social system, and give another example of a social system in our society.
1.2. What are the major components of a typical school organization?
1.3. Most school systems are organized into three levels; describe each.
1.4. Identify three factors that influence the way schools are organized.

For feedback, go to the appendix, *Check Your Understanding*, located in the back of this text.

School Levels

Teaching and You

We have all attended schools, but how much thought have you given to the way schools are organized? Why for example, do most school districts have elementary, middle or junior high, and high schools? Why don't they just have "schools?" What are the rewards and challenges that exist at each of these levels, and which level is best for you?

In the previous section, we saw how the developmental needs of students at different grade levels influence how schools are organized into elementary, middle or junior high, and high school levels. In this section, we take a closer look at the various ways schools meet students' needs and how these differences will influence your life when you begin your career. We begin with early childhood programs.

Early Childhood Programs

To see how teaching changes at different grade levels, click on the video *Classrooms in Action: The Real World of Teaching* (24:50).

Visitors to Randi's kindergarten classroom at Oak Creek are sometimes struck by what appears to be chaos. Students around her classroom are working on a number of seemingly unconnected tasks. Randi circulates among the groups, asking questions and offering suggestions.

Closer examination of the room reveals clusters of activity organized around centers. One center has a tub of water where students measure water in different-sized cups and also determine which kinds of objects sink and float. Another has a table with an assortment of plastic geometric blocks and shapes that children are using to construct things. A third has different costumes and clothing together with two telephones that students use for pretend conversations and dialogues. A fourth contains a variety of picture books that require different amounts of expertise with letters and words. As children circulate among these centers, Randi keeps track of who has been to which center and completed different tasks.

Paul, the second author of your text, went to a very small school in a rural area, and no early childhood programs existed in his district. This has largely changed in our country, but given the proven benefits of early education programs, participation is still much too low. For example, nationally, fewer than 50% of 3- and 4-year-olds attend preschool programs, and less than 80% are enrolled in kindergarten (Hightower, 2012). Although both figures are projected to increase in the future, students who miss out on these opportunities are likely to fall farther behind their more fortunate peers in school performance (National Center for Education Statistics, 2010b).

Early childhood education is a general term describing a range of educational programs for young children. It includes infant intervention and enrichment programs, nursery schools, public and private prekindergartens and kindergartens, and federally funded Head Start programs. Early childhood education in the United States is a mid-20th-century development, although its philosophical roots go back two and a half centuries. The French philosopher Rousseau, for example, gave this advice about educating young children:

> Do not treat the child to discourses which he cannot understand. No descriptions, no eloquence, no figures of speech. . . . In general, let us never substitute the sign for the thing, except when it is impossible for us to show the thing. . . . Things! Things! I shall never tire of saying that we ascribe too much importance to words. (Rousseau, quoted in Compayre, 1888)

Rousseau argued that young children need to play and work with concrete objects ("Things! Things!"), rather than being taught with a lot of abstract words, and this is what we saw in Randi's classroom. This approach is consistent with the need for concrete experiences that the famous developmental psychologist Jean Piaget (1952, 1970) emphasized, and it's at the philosophical core of developmentally appropriate early childhood programs.

Developmental programs accommodate differences in children's development by allowing them to acquire skills and abilities at their own pace through direct experiences. These programs are heavily influenced by the **Montessori method**, an approach to early childhood education inspired by Maria Montessori (1870–1952), an innovative Italian educator. Montessori believed that children develop at their own rate and personal qualities such as individual discipline and self-confidence come from exploring a classroom environment that provides options and choices. Visitors to a developmental classroom are likely to see learning centers around the room such as those in Randi's classroom. Unlike traditional teacher-centered instruction, where the teacher spends most of the time talking or asking questions, the teacher's role is to provide experiences for children and encourage exploration (Schulz & Bonawitz, 2007).

Because of the emphasis on standards and high-stakes testing in our country today, early childhood programs have become more "academic," meaning they are focusing more strongly on basic skills that prepare children to perform on standardized tests (Russell, 2011). We saw this in Randi's lesson, where the focus was on language arts skills such as phonemic awareness, spelling and comprehension skills. In fact, some now describe kindergarten—with homework, testing, and full-day classes—as "the new first grade" (Schoenberg, 2010). This creates a dilemma for teachers in early childhood programs.

> As 46 states and the District of Columbia work this year to put the new curricular guidelines in place, preschool and early-childhood educators are determining how to balance the common standards' emphasis on increasing and measuring academic rigor with research findings on young children's developmental needs, which place a high value on play, the arts, social skills and integrated instruction. (Zubrzycki, 2011a, p. 1)

Many teachers disagree with this trend toward more "academic" early childhood programs, but it is likely to continue, and if you choose to work in a pre-K or kindergarten classroom, you will likely feel pressures to emphasize academic skills with your students.

Although the skills Randi taught in her lesson reflected this emphasis, Randi managed to include developmentally appropriate experiences for her students as well, and you can too. It will take planning, effort, and creativity, but it is a goal well worth pursuing.

The need for learning-related experiences early in life is well documented (Berk, 2012), and the benefits of effective intervention programs at the early childhood level are long lasting. For example, research indicates that students who read well by third grade are much more likely to graduate from high school and attend college, and students who are behind in reading in the third grade are four times more likely to leave high school without a diploma than are their more skilled peers (Center for Public Education, 2011). And children who attend early childhood programs (pre-K and kindergarten) are more likely to have the necessary reading skills by third grade. The impact of quality early childhood experiences is greatest for Hispanic and black children, English learners (ELs), and children from low-income families (Center for Public Education, 2011).

Additional research indicates that children who attend early childhood programs not only are prepared academically but also are better adjusted socially and emotionally (Lasser & Fite, 2011); are healthier (Neugebauer, 2011); and even earn more money throughout their lifetimes and are less likely to be involved in crime (Frede & Barnett, 2011).

As full-time early childhood programs become increasingly common, job opportunities in these areas will continue to grow, so if you're planning to teach in an elementary school, you might consider working in a pre-K or kindergarten classroom.

Self-contained elementary classrooms are designed to meet young students' development needs.

Elementary Schools

As with early childhood programs, elementary classrooms are typically self-contained, so if you choose to work in an elementary school, you will have a great deal of personal autonomy in scheduling your day and emphasizing areas and topics you feel are important. To illustrate this idea, let's look at the schedules of a first-grade and a third-grade teacher outlined in Table 6.2. What do you notice? Your observations might include:

- Both teachers are responsible for all the content areas, such as reading, language arts, math, science, and social studies.
- The teachers' schedules are quite different. Although both teach young children, Sharon begins with language arts, and Susie begins by having the children practice skills they learned the previous day.
- The amount of time each teacher allocates to the content areas varies considerably and is a personal, professional decision. Sharon devotes 50 minutes to math, while Susie teaches math for 75 minutes a day.

Both teachers noted that the schedules in Table 6.2 were approximate and often changed, depending on their perception of students' needs and the day of the week. For example, if students were having trouble with a math topic, they might devote more time to math on a given day. This level of teacher freedom and autonomy is characteristic of elementary schools and is a major reason many people in your position choose to become elementary teachers.

Why are elementary schools organized to provide teachers with flexibility and autonomy and students with the continuity and security of one teacher? History and precedent are part of the answer. Until about the mid-1800s, elementary teachers taught all grade levels and all subjects; schools weren't organized into grade levels. This structure was born out of necessity rather than philosophy.

TABLE 6.2 Schedules for Two Elementary School Teachers

Sharon's First-Grade Schedule		Susie's Third-Grade Schedule	
8:30 AM	School begins	8:30 AM	School begins
8:30–8:45	Morning announcements	8:30–9:15	Independent work (practice previous day's language arts and math)
8:45–10:30	Language arts (including reading and writing)	9:15–10:20	Language arts (including reading and writing)
10:30–11:20	Math	10:20–10:45	Snack/independent reading
11:20–11:50	Lunch	10:45–11:15	Physical education
11:50–12:20	Read story	11:15–12:15	Language arts/social studies/ science
12:20–1:15	Center time (practice on language arts and math)	12:15–12:45	Lunch
1:15–1:45	Physical education	12:45–2:00	Math
1:45–2:30	Social studies/science	2:00–2:30	Spelling/catch up on material not covered earlier
2:30–2:45	Class meeting	2:30–2:45	Read story
2:45–3:00	Call buses/dismissal	2:45–3:00	Clean up/prepare for dismissal

Most small towns could afford only one teacher, who was expected to teach everything and everyone (Pulliam & Van Patten, 2013). With improved transportation and consolidation, one-room schools gradually waned, though some still exist today in remote rural areas (Pulliam & Van Patten, 2013).

The developmental characteristics of students also influence the organization of elementary schools. You saw earlier that young children look, think, and interact with their peers differently from older students. Educators have historically believed that young children need the stability of one teacher and a single classroom to function most effectively in school. Schools can be frightening places for little children, and self-contained classrooms provide emotional security. Further, simply moving from room to room, as middle and secondary students do, can be challenging for young children (Black, 2008); imagine, for example, a first grader going to Room 101 for math, 108 for language arts, and so on. Rotating schedules, which change from day to day and are popular in middle and high schools, would be even more confusing.

Some educators question the efficacy of a single classroom and teacher. Expecting one teacher to be knowledgeable enough to teach all the subjects in the elementary curriculum—reading, language arts, math, science, social studies, art, music and physical education—effectively is asking the impossible, they say (Wiles & Bondi, 2011). As a result, teachers commonly deemphasize some content areas, such as science, social studies, art, and music. Both Sharon and Susie acknowledge that they strongly emphasize reading, language arts, and math and de-emphasize other areas, even though these other content areas appear on their schedules (see Table 6.2).

In response to these issues, beginning in grade 3 or 4, many elementary schools do a form of specialization, or departmentalization. For example, two teachers might work as a team, with one teaching reading and writing and the other focusing on math and science. The reading/writing teacher teaches one class in the morning while the math/science teacher teaches the other; then in the afternoon, they switch classes.

Educators and parents face a dilemma: Are social and emotional well-being more important than content for elementary students? Historically, the answer has been yes. But tensions between these two positions will increase as efforts to document student academic growth through testing continue to grow.

Junior High and Middle Schools

To see differences between elementary schools and middle, junior high, and high schools, compare Sharon's and Susie's experiences to Chris's, the middle school teacher in our chapter's opening case study. Elementary teachers typically teach all or most of the content areas and set their own schedules. In contrast, as a middle school teacher, Chris teaches only one subject (geography), and he (along with all the other teachers in his school) follows a predetermined schedule. The lengths of class periods are uniform for all teachers, and the beginnings and endings are signaled by a bell. Because of these predetermined periods, junior high and middle school teachers have less control over their daily schedules.

Why are upper-level schools organized in this way? The answer centers on the same tensions between content acquisition and the developmental needs of children. Historically, views about educational goals have shifted over time. In colonial times, the goal was for students to be able to read and understand the Bible. Much later—near the end of the 19th century—promoting mental discipline and assimilating a large influx of immigrants into American society were major goals. To reach those goals, educators believed that college-bound and non-college-bound students should take the same curriculum.

As educational thinking evolved, leaders believed that society needed citizens well schooled in a variety of specific academic subjects, such as math, science, and history. This emphasis resulted in the departmentalization found in the middle or junior highs and high schools that you attended and is typical of secondary schools throughout our country.

But conflicts still exist between this emphasis on content and meeting the development needs of students. Let's see how this conflict affected the organization of junior high and middle schools.

The Development of Junior Highs

Schools in the early 20th century were typically organized into eight elementary and four high school grades. But this 8–4 organization changed when emphasis shifted away from learning basic skills, such as reading and math, and toward more intensive study of specific content areas, such as science, history, and literature. This intensive study required teachers who were subject matter experts. In addition, educators began to recognize the unique needs of early adolescents, and the modern "junior" high school was developed.

Most **junior high schools** today have a variety of offerings, although not as comprehensive as those in high schools, and they include competitive athletics and a multitude of other extracurricular activities. Although initially designed to help students make the transition between elementary and high schools, they are in every sense of the word "junior" high schools, with a clear emphasis on academic subjects.

The Development of Middle Schools

This emphasis on content, however, failed to address the developmental needs of early adolescents as was originally intended when junior highs were first developed. Think back to your friends from sixth, seventh, or eighth grade: Some of the girls were literally young women, whereas others were still little girls. Some boys needed to shave, but others looked like fifth graders. Boys and girls were becoming physically attracted to each other, and in many cases they didn't know why. This was the transitional and often tumultuous period of early adolescence (Berk, 2012).

Because of these rapid physical, emotional, and intellectual changes, early adolescence is a unique period in a child's development. Bodies are changing, hormones are surging, and adolescents are trying to figure out what to do with their developing bodies and minds. As a result, many educators believe that schools for young adolescents should be organized to meet their unique needs (Schwerdt & West, 2011).

This thinking, along with the inability of junior highs to address early adolescents' developmental needs, led to the formation of **middle schools**, schools specifically designed to help students through the rapid social, emotional, and intellectual changes characteristic of early adolescence. They typically include some combination of grades 6–8.

What is teaching like in an ideal middle school? Let's look again at Chris's experience.

Chris is a member of a four-person team that includes, in addition to himself, a math, science, and English teacher. They have a common planning period, and they teach the same group of students. Planning periods are often spent discussing the students and the topics they're teaching. Many of their students aren't native English speakers, and their discussions often center on what can be done to help those who struggle with language. In addition, Chris has four students with learning disabilities in his classroom. Whenever possible, the teachers integrate topics across as many of the four areas as they can.

"Can you help me out with anything on graphing?" Maria, the math teacher on the team, asks the others one Monday. "The kids just see graphs as some meaningless lines. I explain the heck out of them, but it doesn't seem to help all that much."

"I know what I can do," Chris offers, after thinking for a few seconds. "We've been talking about global warming and climate change for the past week, and we've looked at some temperature trends in our country as well as around the world—especially in the Arctic and in Antarctica. We've looked only at raw data but haven't graphed any of it. How about I give you some of the figures—you know, dates and temperatures—and you can graph them in math. Let me know when you do, and I'll talk about the graphs the next day in geography.

"This all sounds good," Keith, the science teacher offers. "I can change my schedule a little, and we can discuss the science behind global warming."

"And, I'll make the topic of my next essay some aspect of it," Sarah, the English teacher adds. "By the way, how is Emma Williams doing in math?"

"Not so good," Maria responds. "In fact, I was going to ask you all about her. She hasn't been turning in her homework, and she seems only 'half there' in class."

"Same thing for me," Keith, who is also the student's homeroom teacher, adds. "We'd better see what's going on. . . . I'll call her parents tonight."

As you saw with Chris and his team, the best middle schools follow a different approach from junior highs, and they make adaptations, such as the following (Carjuzaa & Kellough, 2013):

- They organize teachers and students into interdisciplinary teams: For example, Chris, Maria, Keith, and Sarah instruct the same group of students and work together to coordinate topics.
- They strive to create and maintain long-term teacher–student relationships with attention to the importance of emotional development. "Issues like a student's ability to feel safe, resolve conflicts, self-regulate impulses, and trust adults all have a relationship with attendance and disciplinary problems, which in turn affect academic outcomes" (Lowe, 2011, p. 40).

- They use interactive teaching strategies to involve all students: Teachers are encouraged to move away from the lecture-dominated instruction so common in high schools and toward instruction based on student involvement. In addition, teachers place greater emphasis on teaching study strategies, such as note taking, outlining, and time management.
- They eliminate activities that emphasize developmental differences, such as competitive sports: In middle schools, everyone is invited to participate in intramural sports and clubs.

When done well, these changes have a positive influence on students (Sparks, 2011a). For instance, interdisciplinary teams allow teachers to efficiently plan for the integration of topics across different content areas, so students can see how the information they're learning applies to different content areas. And when teachers have the same students, they can more closely monitor their progress, as the team did with Emma. Forming relationships with students helps them adjust to an atmosphere less personal than in their elementary schools. And eliminating competitive sports encourages greater participation in athletic activities and minimizes the advantages early-maturing students have over their later-developing classmates.

Interactive teaching strategies, such as developing lessons with questioning and involving students in cooperative learning activities, are particularly important in middle schools. These strategies actively involve students in learning activities and can also develop their thinking and social interaction skills. Motivation often drops during the early adolescent years, and researchers believe this drop is partially due to increased use of lecture as a teaching strategy (Schunk, Pintrich, & Meese, 2008).

Chris's meeting with his team describes what should happen in an "ideal" middle school, and you may not see these modifications in the schools you visit. Many are middle schools essentially in name only, and they have characteristics, such as competitive sports and no interdisciplinary teams, that are much more like junior highs. This is unfortunate, because a sharp drop in the academic performance of many students occurs when they make the transition to middle school (Schwerdt & West, 2011). In fact, researchers found that students who remain in K–8 schools perform better academically than do students moving to middle schools in the 6th grade, a finding that corroborates the importance of emotional support on academic performance (Lowe, 2011). About 6,000 schools nationwide are structured in the K–8 configuration, whereas about 8,000 are 6–8.

Don's (your book's first author) first teaching job was in a K–8 school in the Midwest, and he discovered that this organizational structure had both advantages and disadvantages:

Classes in the upper grades were departmentalized, so these students had teachers who were subject matter experts. Also, because they stayed in the same school, students didn't seem to suffer from the notorious "middle school slump" that afflicts so many young adolescents (Lowe, 2011). Because we were housed with the lower grades, we used our own clocks to signal class changes, and if teachers needed extra time for an involved lesson, they just worked with other teachers to adapt the schedule so they had an extra 10 or 15 minutes to complete a lesson.

This arrangement also had disadvantages, however. Our teaching environment felt like an extended elementary school, and I wondered if my students would encounter culture shock when they entered the neighboring large high school. Also, extracurricular options were limited, and students didn't have access to clubs and activities that allowed them to explore and develop socially and creatively.

So, what does all this mean for you if you choose to teach in a middle school or junior high? Obviously, you can't create an interdisciplinary team if it doesn't already exist in your school, for example. You can, however, develop your interactive teaching skills to involve all students, instead of merely lecturing to your students. And in addition to academic outcomes, you can also make the development of student responsibility and self-regulation important goals for your classroom. You can also design a classroom management system that helps create a safe emotional environment in your classroom and promotes a learning community in which you and all the students work together to help everyone learn. It won't be an ideal middle school, but it will do a great deal to promote both the emotional well-being and development of your students and their academic performance.

Revisiting My Beliefs

This section addresses the third item in *This I Believe,* "Middle and junior high schools are essentially the same but are given different labels." In an ideal middle school, this statement is false: These schools have different philosophies and view students differently. In the real world, however, the statement is often true.

High Schools

You all attended high school, and some of you graduated within the last year or two. Most of you probably graduated from a **comprehensive high school**, a secondary school that aims to meet the needs of all students. Let's examine this unique American innovation more closely.

The Comprehensive High School

In *The American High School*, James Conant (1959) argued persuasively that the most effective high schools offer a variety of academic courses and facilities to meet the needs of all students. In attempting to meet this goal, most high schools organize students into tracks to meet their learning needs and aspirations (Oakes, 2008). For example, students in the college-preparatory track take courses designed to prepare them for college-level work. This track might include Advanced Placement or dual-enrollment classes in core subject areas. **Advanced Placement (AP) classes** are courses taken in high school that allow students to earn college credit, making college less time-consuming and expensive. **Dual-enrollment** courses are closely related—but not identical to—AP classes. For example, with dual enrollment, students are literally enrolled in college classes while in high school, whereas they are not with AP classes. And students in AP classes take a mandatory final test at the end of the course to receive college credit, but students in dual enrollment don't. Many colleges and school counselors believe that AP courses are more effective logistically and instructionally (D. Brown, 2011). Across the country more than 18% of high school students take AP courses, but cultural minority students are under-represented, even when teachers recommend them for the courses (Adams, 2012). Teachers can address this problem by explaining the program in classes and personally talking to eligible students.

Extracurricular activities provide valuable learning opportunities not typically tapped by traditional classrooms.

Students of average ability, who may or may not go to college, are often tracked into "standard" classes, and they may take some vocational courses, such as word processing, designed to provide practical skills they can use immediately after graduating. A vocational track specifically targets students not going to college, preparing them for careers in such areas as automobile repair or technology.

Criticisms of the Comprehensive High School. Can a comprehensive high school be all things to all students? Critics say no and focus on four issues:

- problems with tracking
- size
- departmentalization
- lack of academic rigor (Cuban, 2010)

Different tracks, designed to present quality alternatives, have become a paradox of the comprehensive high school because they often produce exactly the opposite of what is intended. Instead of providing freedom and choice, tracking limits choices and segregates students, often leaving many with substandard educational experiences (Oakes, 2008). Students who come from low-status (SES) families, who are lower achieving, or who are members of cultural minorities are often steered into vocational or lower-level tracks, with poor instruction and a less-challenging curriculum that often doesn't prepare them for the world of work. Because of these deficiencies, some critics charge that tracking should be eliminated completely (S. Kelly & Price, 2011).

School size, which exceeds 1,500 students in many comprehensive high schools, is a second problem (Cuban, 2010). As schools become larger, they also become more impersonal and bureaucratic. This problem is particularly acute for lower achievers, who often get lost in the shuffle and fail to receive a quality education.

Departmentalization, the organization of teachers and classes into separate academic areas, is a third problem with comprehensive high schools, critics contend. Departmentalization fragments the curriculum and interferes with learning:

> While the adults organize as separate departmental entities isolated from one another, however, their teenage students seek interconnectedness and relevancy in their school experience. What they get instead is math with no relationship to social studies, science without any connection to literature, and so forth. This relevancy-starved approach continues year in, year out with no alternatives, and any "reforms" seen in public education are invariably found at the elementary or middle school level. (Cooperman, 2003, p. 30)

Fragmentation in the curriculum also comes from the schedule itself, which breaks the day into 50-minute periods that many think are too short to pursue topics in depth. **Block scheduling**, in which students spend more time in classes but meet less frequently during the week—such as 90 minutes every other day—is one attempt to solve this problem (J. Anderson, 2011). Block scheduling is quite common, and you're likely to encounter it as you visit high schools.

Block scheduling is controversial with some teachers. Some, such as those in science, like the extra time it provides for labs, but music and foreign language teachers are less enthusiastic, because the schedule doesn't provide for the daily practice they believe is important.

One factor is certain, however. If you plan to be a high school teacher, and you work in a block schedule, you'll need to adapt your instruction. It's literally impossible to lecture for 90 to 100 minutes to any group and have them pay attention, let alone students who may not always be interested in the topic you're teaching.

Lack of academic rigor is an often cited fourth criticism of comprehensive high schools. In an attempt to be all things to all students, high schools neither challenge students nor provide them with the job skills needed for a technologically oriented modern society, critics claim. Reformers promote high-stakes testing, end-of-course exams, and more rigorous graduation requirements as solutions to this problem (Cuban, 2010).

Alternatives to Comprehensive High Schools. One concrete solution to the problem of large high schools is to create "smaller learning communities" within large schools. This allows students to keep the same guidance counselor throughout high school and offers opportunities for students and teachers to get to know one another. We discuss these ideas in more depth later in the chapter.

Career technical schools designed to provide students with education and job skills that enable them to get a job immediately after high school are a second alternative to large, comprehensive high schools (Bottoms, Presson, & Han, 2004). In more than 1,000 vocational centers nationwide, students attend part of the day or evening in specialized programs and then attend their "home" high school for academic or general education courses during the other part of the day. In addition, about 250 career or specialty high schools in the United States focus on preparing students for work in a particular occupation or industry but also offer academic and general courses at that school. Students attend these career technical schools full-time.

Career academies, a variation of career technical schools, combine career education and the school-within-a-school movement. Career academies are small learning communities (typically 200 or fewer students) working with the same groups of teachers in career-oriented areas such as health and bioscience, business and finance, architecture and construction, education and child development, and information technology (Hoye & Stern, 2008). Applied classes are supplemented with field trips, job shadowing, and internships that provide realistic introductions to the world of work. Students in these academies are more likely to stay in school, attend more classes, and progress more efficiently toward graduation (Viadero, 2008a). In addition, graduates earn 10% more money than nonacademy students after graduation, a figure comparable to the benefits of attending a community college for 1 or 2 years. The benefits are especially strong for students considered to be at high risk for dropping out of school.

As with many other aspects of education, career technical education is going through a process of reform. Most of the reforms are aimed at increasing academic standards and related general educational knowledge, together with teaching students all aspects of an industry rather than focusing on a specific job skill. The federal government contributes over $1 billion annually to these programs to encourage modernizing and focusing academic programs on essential job skills (Cavanagh, 2006a). However, interest in these programs continues to decline as more and more students opt for college-prep programs (J. Newman, 2006).

This section addresses the questions in *Teaching and You* that asked why differences in grade levels exist and how they will influence your teaching and ultimately your career satisfaction. There is no doubt that teaching at different grade levels requires different instructional skills and different ways of interacting with and managing students. We've worked with teachers who have changed grade levels in the same school, and they unanimously attest to the fact that differences exist and these present both challenges and rewards. Don experienced this personally this past year. He had tutored successfully for 4 years at first-, second-, and third-grade levels. He was satisfied with the progress he was able make with the students he taught. Then he switched to kindergarten. Rough transition—either they weren't ready for him, or he wasn't ready for them. "Fun" activities, such as using dice games to reinforce math facts, or role-playing dialogues in stories, that were quite successful with older students, didn't work with kindergartners. (They didn't know any math facts to reinforce, and they couldn't read stories to act them out.) Fortunately, Don was working with an experienced teacher who helped him out and basically saved the day.

What are the implications of all this for you? Actively seek experiences in schools at different levels and especially at the levels you're tentatively targeting. If you're undecided, consciously try to work in as many grade levels as you are considering. Don't just rely on clinical experiences provided by your classes. Volunteer work and substitute teaching can provide you with valuable experiences that will help you find the right professional niche for you. This will take time and effort but will pay off in the long run.

TECHNOLOGY and TEACHING: Distance Education Redefines Our Definition of a School

When most people think of a school, they imagine a building with teachers and students. **Distance education,** a catch-all term used to describe organized instructional programs in which teachers and learners, though physically separated, are connected through technology, is changing that view (Newby et al., 2011). Distance learning attempts to meet student learning needs in three ways (Simonson, Smaldino, Albright, & Zvacek, 2012). First, it offers students in rural communities courses in specialized areas, such as advanced physics or Japanese, for which a local teacher is unavailable. Second, it provides instruction for nontraditional students, such as teenage young mothers who can't attend classes during the day or other students who are homebound because of physical conditions. Third, it can deliver a class to students over a broad geographic area where driving to a central location is not possible.

Correspondence courses in which students read books, answered questions, and received feedback from instructors through the mail were the earliest efforts at distance education. Currently, distance education includes a number of options:

- Videoconferencing, which allows learners and teachers from various sites to ask and answer questions face-to-face over great distances.
- Computer conferencing that allows students and teachers the opportunity to interact via the Internet. Like bulletin boards and chat rooms, these interactions can provide either simultaneous or synchronous interaction.
- Web-based systems that allow learners not only to watch instructional programs on television but also to access information for research. For example, in one program, students across the country viewed the Gettysburg battlefield, heard profiles of individual soldiers, and were directed to websites where they could find additional information for study.

Research suggests that the type of distance learning employed is not as important as the quality and organization of the course and the availability of the instructor for answering questions and providing feedback (Roblyer & Doering, 2013). The most effective online courses provide students with flexibility and choices in terms of when and how to work on assignments and opportunities to interact with other students. Younger students, English-language learners, and students with exceptionalities present special challenges; students in online courses need to be constantly monitored; and instruction needs to be modified to meet the needs of these students (Quillen, 2011a, 2011b).

Higher and postsecondary education have shown the greatest interest in distance education; most American colleges and universities presently offer some type of distance learning program, and these numbers are growing (Roblyer & Doering, 2013). And distance education is also growing in K–12 education; in 2008 more than one million students took on-line courses, a nearly 50% increase over 2006 (M. Davis, 2010a). Distance education has also entered the teacher education arena, offering courses and degrees at both the pre-licensure and master's levels (Sawchuk, 2009c). Flexibility and convenience are major attractions, but courses vary widely in their quality, so teachers should investigate thoroughly before enrolling (Ash, 2011).

Virtual schools are also appearing around the country, providing alternatives to standard attendance at brick and mortar schools. These schools offer comprehensive K–12 courses that connect teachers and students over the Internet. In the 2010–2011 school year, 93 virtual schools enrolled 116,000 students, up 43% from the previous year (J. Anderson, 2012). The Virtual High School, which first offered courses in 1997, currently offers more than 200 courses to more than 5,000 students in courses ranging from basic courses to 15 AP courses (Virtual High School, 2009). Although most common at the high school level, virtual courses are also appearing in elementary and middle schools. Most popular with homeschooled students, virtual courses also provide students in rural areas with access to education and students in all areas with courses in hard-to-teach areas such as advanced mathematics or some languages.

Experts caution that students, when first introduced to online instruction, may need assistance in learning how to learn from these courses (Roblyer & Doering, 2013). Also, critics warn against relying too heavily on this technology, arguing that the lack of social interaction may result in decreased social development and ultimately even learning (Monke, 2005/2006).

The effectiveness of online schools is uneven and mixed at best. Research on the achievement of students enrolled in privately managed, for-profit virtual schools found that fewer than a third achieved "adequate yearly progress," a benchmark required by No Child Left Behind, compared to over half for students enrolled in traditional, brick-and-mortar schools (J. Anderson, 2012). Whether this disturbing achievement gap is due to problems with online learning itself or the quality of instruction delivered by for-profit companies is not clear, but the growing use of online education suggests the pressing need for additional research.

As distance education grows, there is a good possibility that you'll be asked to teach courses like these in the future, and some states are considering requiring additional certification for those who teach these courses (Quillen, 2012). Teachers who have done so tell us that the experience is both enlightening and frustrating. Designing distance education courses requires teachers to re-analyze what they are doing. For example, when you don't have immediate access to students and they to you, creating learning experiences in which students succeed poses additional challenges. Interaction and feedback are essential. Teaching these courses can also be frustrating; many students aren't ready to assume responsibility for their own learning and often fall behind because they fail to complete assignments conscientiously or on time.

Check Your Understanding

2.1. Describe two ways in which teaching in an elementary school differs from teaching in a middle school, junior high, or high school.

2.2. What are four differences between effective middle schools and junior highs?

2.3. What is a comprehensive high school? How does a comprehensive high school differ from a vocational high school?

For feedback, go to the appendix, *Check Your Understanding*, located in the back of this text.

Finding a Good School

The quality of the school in which you'll work will be a major factor influencing your satisfaction with your first job—and the jobs you hold throughout your career. But, what is a good, effective, high-quality school, and what is it like to teach in one? We address these questions in this section.

Although the public commonly refers to schools as *good* or not so good, as in "Woodrow Wilson is a very good elementary school," researchers use the term *effective* instead. An **effective school** is one in which learning for all students is maximized. If students are learning, other factors associated with your job satisfaction will fall into place. For instance, successful students

Teaching and You

Were the schools you attended as a P–12 student "good schools"? Were they effective? How did you know? What criteria do you use in judging the quality of a school? How will you know if a school you're considering working in the future is a good school?

FIGURE 6.2 Characteristics of Effective Schools

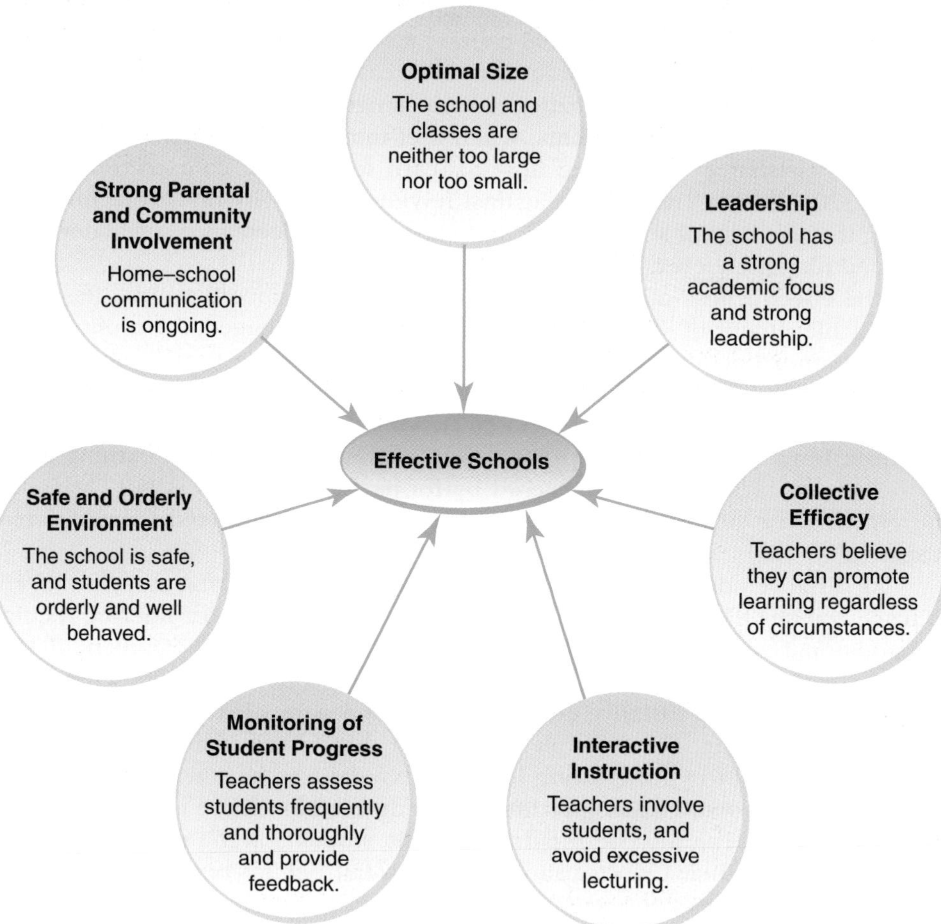

create fewer classroom management problems than students who aren't, and they also tend to be more motivated. It's a pleasure to work with motivated and well-behaved students, so it's easy to see why working in an effective school is satisfying.

When experts talk about a good or effective school, they aren't just focusing on academic success. Other factors also enter into the picture. Effective schools also nurture students' personal and social development and help them develop into emotionally healthy and happy individuals. Absentee, dropout, and graduation rates, incidents of crime, violence, and drug use, and the number of students who go on to college, all provide different measures of how well a school serves its students. These statistics not only tell us how the students in a school are doing, they also tell us how effective a school is. Effective schools focus on students' total development and establish policies that protect students and help them develop into healthy individuals.

Research has identified several essential characteristics of effective schools (Bryk et al., 2010; Lezotte & Snyder, 2011). They are outlined in Figure 6.2 and discussed in the sections that follow.

Teaching and You

How large were the schools you attended? Were they too big, too small, or just the right size? How did the size of the schools you attended influence the quality of experiences you had? How does school size influence student learning, and how will it affect your life as a teacher?

Optimal Size

Size—both the size of the school and the size of classes—can strongly affect students' learning experiences and your satisfaction with your job. Let's see how.

School Size

Paul went to a small, rural high school in Montana. When he told Don he was the valedictorian of his high school class, Don (who went to a much larger high school near Chicago) replied, "Big deal! I could have been a valedictorian, too, if my graduating class was 16!"

Are small schools better than big ones, or is the reverse true? As it turns out, the relationship between size and quality isn't that simple. Schools must be large enough to provide an adequate variety of curricular offerings, resources, and facilities, but not so large that they lose the human, personal dimension students so badly need (Lowe, 2011; Ready & Lee, 2008).

How big is too big? The largest high school on record, DeWitt Clinton High School in the Bronx, housed 12,000 students in 1934 (R. Allen, 2002). (How do you suppose ninth graders felt walking into that school on the first day of the school year?) One-room elementary schools are at the other end of the spectrum; for example, one elementary school in Nevada had one teacher and six students (one fifth grader, four fourth graders, and a first grader) in 2009 (Friess, 2009). Imagine being that teacher!

School size is also correlated with level; elementary schools tend to be the smallest and high schools the largest. The average size of elementary schools is 470 students; for secondary schools this figure is 704 (U.S. Bureau of Census, 2012). But averages are deceiving; 18% of high school students attend rural schools with enrollments of less than 100 students, while some attend urban schools that have enrollments over 3,000 students.

The ideal size for a high school isn't clear, but an experiment in New York City schools found that reducing student numbers to around 400 resulted in both academic gains and higher graduation rates, and these benefits were especially pronounced for students who were cultural minorities or low SES (H. Bloom & Unterman, 2012). When schools are either too large or too small, learning decreases, especially for low-SES students (C. Howley & Howley, 2004). This is ironic, because a disproportionate number of low-SES students attend either very small or very large high schools. Examples include small rural schools in sparsely populated states, such as Wyoming or Montana, and large urban schools in cities such as New York, Chicago, or Los Angeles.

Advantages and disadvantages exist in both small and large schools, however. For example, Paul's high school had a total enrollment of 46—that's 46 total students in grades 9–12. Because of its small size, most of the students in the school participated in a wide range of extracurricular activities. Paul, for instance, played football, basketball, baseball, and ran track. He played in the band, sang in the chorus, worked on the school newspaper, and was on the yearbook staff. This variety of experiences would have been impossible in a large school. On the other hand, the curriculum offerings were very limited. For example, neither chemistry nor physics were offered in his high school, so he had to work extra hard when he took them in his first year of college.

His first teaching job was also in a small school—a total enrollment of 150 in grades 9–12. He taught general math, earth science, physics, algebra, and geometry; was assistant football, basketball, and track coach; and drove the team bus to games and track meets.

Virtually the opposite issues exist in very large schools. If you teach in a large school, the likelihood of having 5 different preparations, as Paul experienced his first year, is low. On the other hand, you will probably have large classes, many more than the average of 11 per class that he had in his first year.

Size, itself, doesn't detract from a school's effectiveness; instead, it influences other factors. For example, as schools become larger, it's more difficult to create learning environments in which students feel physically and emotionally safe (J. Feldman et al., 2006). Also, education is less personal in large schools, because it's harder for teachers and students to get to know one another and to work together.

Both parents and teachers want smaller schools, but the cost of building them deters taxpayers. In a national survey, parents said they believed their children received a more rigorous and personalized education in smaller schools, and teachers said that smaller schools prevented students from "falling through the cracks" (Public Agenda, 2002). Research also supports smaller schools: They have significantly higher graduation rates, and experts believe this is due to increased opportunities for teachers and students to interact in meaningful ways, which lead to fewer discipline and safety issues (Sparks, 2012).

Creating **schools within schools**, smaller learning communities within larger schools where both teachers and students feel more comfortable, is one solution to the problem of school size (Ready & Lee, 2008). For example, Kernan Middle School in Jacksonville, Florida, has more than 1,200 students, more than experts recommend for any school, and especially for a middle school.

To address the issue of school size, Kernan students are grouped within "houses" of approximately 400 students each at the start of sixth grade. Students stay in these houses through eighth grade, enabling them to get to know the adults in their building. They deal with a small front office managed by an assistant principal, who, for all intents and purposes, is the principal of this mini school. The students get to know all the teachers in the hallway as well as the other students who are part of their houses. The goal is for each student to be well known by at least one adult. Students are at ease in making the transition to the next grade level because they're familiar with the house and all its components (people, rules, procedures). When asked, a student will typically identify himself or herself as a "house A student" or a "house B student," for example. At the end of the middle school experience, students will hopefully have formed meaningful, personal relationships with more people than they would in a typical arrangement. Similar examples exist in many parts of the country.

In *Teaching and You* at the beginning of this section, we asked how school size affected your own experiences in school. When we asked the same question to our students, most students thought that small to intermediate schools felt the best—neither too small nor too large. Our students wanted a school that was big enough to offer social and academic variety, but not so large that they felt like a number. Their reactions corroborate the research we discussed in this section.

Class Size

Class size also influences a school's effectiveness, as well as the students and teachers in a class. Classes of 20 or fewer students are considered optimal, but many are much larger, particularly in middle, junior high, and high schools. Don recently worked with a health teacher who had 47 students assigned to one of her classes. If all her students show up for class, there aren't enough desks. The **teacher–student ratio**, the number of students taught by one teacher, is one commonly used measure of class size. This ratio can be misleading, however, because districts typically include administrators and other district-level personnel in the computation, which makes the teacher/student ratio appear better than it actually is. Critics often argue that class size doesn't matter or that reducing class size isn't worth the cost, but research suggests otherwise. And the effects are particularly pronounced in the lower grades and for students at risk (Viadero, 2008b).

Reductions in class size can have both short- and long-term effects. In Tennessee, for example, where average class sizes were reduced from 25 to 15 students, researchers found immediate gains in reading and math scores. Follow-up studies revealed that the positive effects lasted through 12th grade; low-SES students who participated in the program for 4 years were twice as likely to graduate from high school as their counterparts in larger classes. Students in the smaller classes also took more challenging courses later in school and were more likely to attend college than those in larger classes. These positive effects were especially strong for low-SES and African American students (Konstantopoulos, 2008).

Smaller class sizes will also make your life easier. When first-year teachers were asked what would help improve the quality of teaching, a whopping 97% identified reduced class sizes as a major factor (Rochkind, Ott, Immerwahr, Doble, & Johnson, 2008). If you're fortunate enough to have small classes, you won't have to spend as much time on classroom management, you'll have fewer papers to grade, your record keeping will be less demanding, and getting to know your students will be easier. Teachers' morale and job satisfaction increase when class sizes are reduced. Now, the trick is to convince both politicians and the public that reducing classes will improve both learning and teaching.

Revisiting My Beliefs

This section addresses the fourth item in *This I Believe*, "Larger schools generally provide students with better educations, because they have better facilities and can provide a wider variety of programs." This statement is true up to a point: Schools need to be large enough to provide adequate offerings, but when they're too large, students can become lost and the human dimension suffers.

Leadership

Just as you influence the learning that occurs in your classroom, your principal will set the academic tone for the first school in which you'll teach.

> In [an] effective school, the principal acts as an instructional leader by persistently communicating the mission to the staff, students, parents, and larger community. The principal understands the principles of effective instruction and uses that knowledge in the management of the instructional program (Lezotte & Snyder, 2011, p. 51)

Teaching and You

What will be the most important factor influencing your satisfaction with teaching? What should you look for when you make decisions about accepting your first teaching position?

Effective principals consistently communicate their school's mission to you and your colleagues; they create a climate that makes student learning the core goal of the school. They emphasize that high expectations are important for all students, and they try to create a teaching environment that will allow you to maximize your instructional time. The best principals are also instructional leaders who can advise staff and serve as a resource to parents and students. Faculty meetings focus on instructional issues, and learning and effective teaching are continually discussed topics (Sergiovanni, 2009a, 2009b).

An array of clubs, sports, and other extracurricular offerings exist and are important in effective schools, but they don't take precedence over learning. For example, classes aren't canceled so students can attend sporting events, and class time isn't used for club meetings.

This discussion has implications for you when you interview with a principal for your first job. For example, think about the kinds of questions he or she asks. Are the questions specific, and do they focus on student learning? And you can ask questions of your own, such as:

- What do you believe are the most important characteristics of an effective teacher?
- What do you look for when you're observing in a teacher's classroom?
- What learning challenges exist in your school, and how do your effective teachers meet them?

The principal of a school provides academic leadership and also helps create a productive work environment for teachers.

If the principal's answers are vague, or they focus on trivial items, such as whether or not you have an up-to-date "word wall" or samples of student work on your bulletin board, you might—assuming you have other options—think carefully about whether you want to work in that school. We don't object in the least to "word walls" or displays of student work, but the question we should always be asking is, "What impact does this have on student learning?" The way you manage your classroom, the way you present your content, and the way you treat your students, such as we saw with Randi and Chris (and his team), are much more important, as are your beliefs about teaching and learning, which we examine next.

At the beginning of this section, we asked what factor would most influence your satisfaction with your first job and throughout your career. When we ask this same question to the teachers we work with in schools, they are almost unanimous in their response—their principal! School principals can have an almost magical effect on a school. When they are good, they boost morale and make the teachers in that school feel like they're doing a good job and making a difference in students' lives. Unfortunately, the opposite is also true.

Earlier we suggested that you directly ask prospective principals strategic questions about their knowledge of and attitudes toward good teaching. We also suggest that you ask teachers in that school how they like working for that principal. Their answers could make an important difference in your first years of teaching.

Collective Efficacy

High collective efficacy, teachers' beliefs in their schools' ability to promote student learning regardless of external conditions, is pervasive in an effective school (Lezotte & Snyder, 2011). When teachers believe in their school's ability to help students, good things happen. Morale increases, teachers teach more energetically, and student learning increases.

High collective efficacy begins with **personal teaching efficacy**, each teacher's belief that he can promote learning in all students, regardless of their backgrounds or home conditions. High-efficacy teachers take personal responsibility for the success of their students (Bruning, Schraw, & Norby, 2011). If students aren't learning, rather than blaming students' lack of intelligence, poor home environments, uncooperative administrators, or some other cause, high-efficacy teachers conclude that they need to do a better job and look for ways to improve student learning.

Two aspects of high-collective-efficacy schools are important. First, students from all SES levels learn more in them than in schools where collective efficacy is lower. This, in itself, isn't surprising; it makes sense that the harder teachers work to promote learning, the more students learn. Second, low-SES students in high-collective-efficacy schools have achievement levels nearly equal to those of high-SES students in low-collective-efficacy schools. High-collective-efficacy schools help reduce achievement differences between groups of students who typically benefit quite differently from schooling (Goddard, Hoy, & Hoy, 2004).

How do high-efficacy teachers and high-collective-efficacy schools accomplish these results? A number of factors contribute, but two are essential: (1) interactive instruction and (2) frequent monitoring of student progress.

Interactive Instruction

Imagine walking through the hallways of a school; the doors of classrooms are open so you can glance inside. Can you determine anything about the effectiveness of the school with a simple glance? The answer is yes, as this principal found.

Cassie Jones, principal of an urban middle school, walks through the halls, and listens to the sounds coming from the different classrooms. As she walks by Ben Carlson's social studies class, she hears him say, "Yesterday we talked about the strengths and weaknesses of the North and South at the outbreak of the Civil War. Who remembers one of these?"

As she moves down the hall, she stops in front of Sarah McCarthy's science class. Sarah is at the front of the room swinging a set of keys from a piece of string. "Hmmm," Cassie thinks, "no wonder her class is so quiet—she's got them hypnotized." As she listens further, she hears Sarah say, "This is a simple pendulum, just like the one we find in grandfather clocks. Who can tell me what factors influence the rate at which a pendulum swings?"

"Good question," thinks Cassie. "Maybe that's why her kids are so quiet."

When Cassie turns the corner, she is greeted by a steady stream of student voices arguing about something.

"I don't care what you say, stealing is wrong."

"But his family didn't have enough to eat. They were hungry, and he couldn't let them starve!"

"What's Hector up to today?" Cassie thinks as she listens more closely to Hector Sanchez's English class.

"Listen, everyone," Hector breaks in with a strong voice, "it's not enough just to disagree with your partners. You have to explain why. Remember, one of the reasons we read books like *Sounder* is to help us understand our own lives. So, you have three more minutes in your discussion groups to explain why the father was right or wrong to steal food for his family. Be sure that you've written your reasons on your papers to be turned in."

Cassie chuckles as she hears Hector's class rejoin the battle. "He's sure got them stirred up today. I'm lucky to have such a talented teaching staff that has so many different strengths."

Teachers in effective schools involve students in learning activities, and you also saw how interactive Randi and Chris were in the lessons we used to introduce the chapter. If most teachers in the school are asking large numbers of questions and students are involved in discussions, the likelihood that the school is effective increases (Lemov, 2010). On the other hand, if teachers are mostly lecturing, or students are spending large amounts of time doing seat work, the school is likely to be less effective. Evaluating schools in this way is admittedly simplistic, and other factors influence how much students learn, but interaction between teacher and students and between students is an essential ingredient for learning (Eggen & Kauchak, 2013). And interactive instruction is also important for motivation (Schunk, Pintrich, & Meece, 2008). Students at all levels prefer challenging, interactive activities to sitting passively, listening to teacher lectures (Brophy, 2010). Effective schools provide opportunities for students to become actively involved in their learning.

Monitoring of Student Progress

In effective schools, teachers frequently assess their students and provide them with continual feedback about learning progress. Effective learning environments are assessment centered, providing both students and teachers with information about learning (Stiggins & Chappuis, 2012). "Assessment centered" means that assessment isn't tacked on at the end of an instructional period, such as a test at the end of a unit or term; rather, it's an integral part of the entire teaching–learning process. Teachers in effective schools gather large numbers of work samples; they give frequent quizzes and tests; and their assessments measure more than recall of facts. They return quizzes and assignments shortly after they're given, and they thoroughly discuss test items to provide students with feedback about their responses (Stiggins, Arter, Chappius, & Chappius, 2010). The need for assessment-centered classrooms also helps us understand why interactive instruction is so effective—it allows you to gather a great deal of information about your students' understanding by listening to their responses to questions as they attempt to describe their developing thinking.

Safe and Orderly Environment

Students at all grade levels need to feel safe and secure. Many are concerned about school safety issues, such as fighting, bullying, and classmates who are disruptive. Schools, which should be sheltered communities for learning, often mirror the problems of society. "Academic success isn't just about instruction: It's about safe campuses, good nutrition, and mental and physical health" (Lowe, 2011, p. 40).

The need for safe and orderly schools is supported by both research and theory. Researchers found effective schools to be places of trust, order, cooperation, and high morale (Koth, Bradshaw, & Leaf, 2008). Students need to feel emotionally safe in school for healthy learning and development to occur.

Theories of learner development suggest that people prefer to live in an orderly rather than a chaotic world (Piaget 1952, 1970). In addition, the psychologist Abraham Maslow (1968), who described a hierarchy of human needs, argued that only the need for survival is more basic than the need for safety. Studies of classroom management also confirm the need for order: Orderly classrooms are important for student learning and motivation, as well as healthy development (Emmer & Evertson, 2013; Evertson & Emmer, 2013).

You can do much to promote safe schools by your actions, both within your classroom and around the school. In your classroom you can create a haven in which students feel safe, secure in the knowledge that this is a place where bullying and harassment won't be tolerated. You can also set a positive and proactive tone in hallways and playgrounds by requiring students to treat each other with courtesy and respect. Let's look at an example.

Allen, a rambunctious sixth grader, is running down the hall toward the lunchroom. As he rounds the corner, he bumps Alyssia, causing her to drop her books.

"Oops," he replies, continuing his race to the lunchroom.

"Hold it, Allen," Chris [our middle school teacher in this chapter], who is monitoring the hall, says. "Go back and help her pick up her books and apologize."

Allen walks back to Alyssia, helps her pick up her books, mumbles an apology, and then returns. As he approaches, Doug again stops him.

"Now, why did I make you do that?" Doug asks.

"'Cuz we're not supposed to run."

"Sure," Doug says evenly, "but more important, if people run in the halls, they might crash into someone, and somebody might get hurt. . . . Remember that you're responsible for your actions. Think about not wanting to hurt yourself or anybody else, and the next time you'll walk whether a teacher is here or not. . . . Now, go on to lunch."

In this brief episode, Chris helped promote a safe environment and gave Allen a lesson in responsibility. You can do the same when you begin teaching. And as with efficacy, when teachers band together collectively to make their school safe, students feel the difference.

Strong Parental and Community Involvement

Schools, no matter how well they're organized, can't be effective if parents aren't involved in their children's education (O'Connor, Dearing & Collins, 2011). Learning is a cooperative venture, in which you, your students, and their parents work together.

Home and school cooperation occurs at two levels (Bryk et al., 2010). At the classroom level, you and other teachers can actively enlist the help of parents in helping their children learn. At the community level, an effective school reaches out to the immediate neighborhood and becomes a center for help and assistance.

School management and planning teams that combine school personnel with community leaders provide valuable feedback about current efforts and guidance for future directions. Medical clinics address community health care needs. In many urban and rural areas where these services are scarce or lacking, the school becomes an oasis where parents and their children can come for help and assistance.

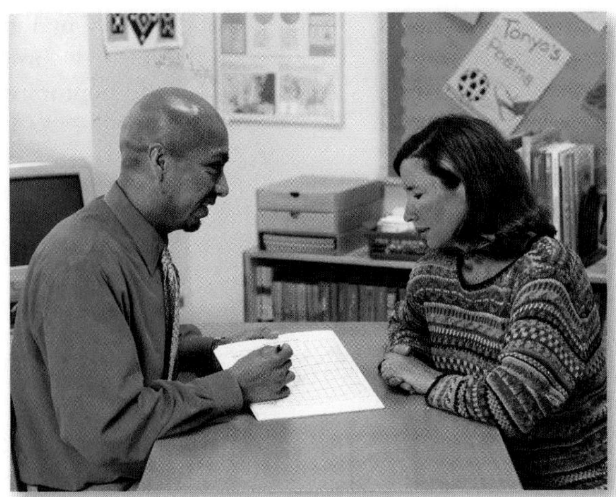

Effective schools develop mechanisms to allow parents and teachers to work together.

Students benefit from home–school cooperation in a number of ways:

- Students exhibit more positive attitudes and behavior.
- Students achieve more, regardless of SES, ethnic/racial background, or the parents' levels of education. The more extensive the parental involvement, the higher the student achievement.
- Students earn higher grades and test scores, attend school more regularly, and complete homework more consistently.
- Student alcohol use, violence, and antisocial behaviors decrease as parental involvement increases.
- Educators hold higher expectations for students whose parents collaborate with teachers. They also have higher opinions of those parents (Sheldon, 2007).

To summarize, "Decades of research have shown the value of parent involvement, revealing a consistent, positive relationship between parents' engagement in their children's education and student outcomes. . . . This relationship holds true regardless of race, SES, or gender (Lezotte & Snyder, 2011).

TABLE 6.3 Implications of Effective Schools for You as a Teacher

Effective Schools Dimension	Implication for You
Optimal Size The school and classes are neither too large nor too small.	Do everything you can to personalize your classroom to make students feel a part of it. Learn all of your students' names as quickly as possible, and address them by name both in and out of class.
Leadership The school has a strong academic focus and strong leadership.	Consider the kinds of questions your potential principal asks you during your interview. Are they academically focused, and do they indicate a thorough understanding of teaching and learning?
Collective Efficacy Teachers believe they can promote learning regardless of circumstances.	Talk to teachers when you interview, and try to gauge the climate of the school. Are the teachers upbeat, and do they make generally positive comments about the school and students? If they do, it is likely that the work environment will also be positive.
Interactive Instruction Teachers involve students and avoid excessive lecturing.	Observe and talk to expert teachers, and ask them how they involve students. Learn about effective teaching strategies, and practice basic teaching skills, such as questioning, until they become essentially automatic.
Monitoring of Student Progress Teachers assess students frequently and thoroughly and provide feedback on learning progress.	Make assessment an integral part of your instruction. Give frequent quizzes, measure understanding above the recall of factual information, and discuss all assessments with your students after they've been given.
Safe and Orderly Environment The school is safe, and students are orderly and well behaved.	Create a classroom learning community that involves all students. Design a system of rules and procedures to help maintain order in your classroom. Require that students respect each other, and refrain from all forms of hurtful comments.
Strong Parental and Community Involvement Home–school communication is ongoing	Begin communication immediately with a letter home to parents describing your classroom goals and how they can help their children learn. Continually send work samples home so parents are aware of their child's learning progress. Call parents at the first sign of either behavioral or academic problems.

Parental involvement takes work and may not happen naturally. You'll need to be proactive in reaching out to parents and other care givers. This starts with a letter at the beginning of the school year that describes your class and how parents can contribute to their child's education. Parent–teacher conferences provide opportunities to reinforce that message. Send work samples home frequently; some teachers do this as a regular routine every Friday. When learning or management problems surface, contact parents immediately; they love their children and want them to succeed in school. Often all they need are encouragement from you and concrete suggestions about how they can help their child with schoolwork at home.

Table 6.3 (on previous page) summarizes the implications effective schools have for you when you begin your career and as you move through it.

ISSUES YOU'LL FACE IN TEACHING

Grade Retention

Our schools are organized to teach students increasingly complex ideas as they move from one grade to the next. In addition, ideas learned in one grade build on one another as students master content in each grade. But what happens when students aren't ready for, or don't master, course content at a specific grade level?

Some school systems have implemented the policy of **grade retention**, the practice of requiring students to repeat a grade if they don't meet certain criteria (Van Horn, 2008), and you will likely be faced with this issue at some point in your career. You will be asked to provide input as to whether some of your students should be retained in a grade to give them more time to master essential content.

The elimination of **social promotion**, the process of promoting low-achieving students to the next grade so they can be with their age-similar peers—even if they're failing—has become an important policy suggestion in many reform efforts. This stand is particularly popular with politicians (Medina, 2010).

The issue of grade retention is not new, but with calls for higher standards and greater accountability, reformers have reasserted arguments supporting it. In 2010, nationwide nearly one million students were retained, over 2.3% of the student population (Robelen, Adams & Shah, 2012). Several states, including Texas, Louisiana, and Florida, require students to pass a standardized test before they are promoted to the next grade. Recent research shows that cultural minorities are retained at a much higher rate than other students; for example, in 2010, black students were three times more likely to be retained than white students (Robelen et al., 2012).

Delaying kindergarten entry for children whose birthdays are near the cutoff date or who are developmentally immature is a variation on grade retention. Advocates suggest that giving students, and especially boys, an extra year to mature and develop enhances chances for success and minimizes the risk of failure due to developmental lags.

At the middle and secondary levels, as an alternative to making students repeat courses they've failed, some districts around the country have implemented a policy called **grade recovery,** where failing students are allowed to improve their grades to as high as a C by using online programs designed to improve their understanding and skills (Franco & Patel, 2011). This policy is controversial, however, with many teachers complaining that students realize that they can use it to "beat the system." They make little effort during the year, teachers complain, and then work for as little as 3 days on a grade-recovery program to change a failing grade to a C (T. Sanders, 2011).

THE QUESTION

Is grade retention an effective educational policy? What are the long-term ramifications for students who are retained in a grade? Are students retained in grade more or less likely to be personally, socially, and academically successful later in their schooling? These questions are controversial, and arguments on each side of the issue are outlined below:

PRO

- Retaining students in a grade until they've acquired the knowledge and skills for that level makes sense, and promoting students who lack the skills sets them up for future failure (Greene & Winters, 2006).
- Spending a second year in a grade gives learners another chance to acquire the necessary understanding and skills and sends the message that schoolwork is important.
- Social promotion communicates to students that they can "get by" without working hard, forces teachers to deal with underprepared students while simultaneously trying to teach students who are prepared, and gives parents a false picture of their children's progress.
- Some research at the lower elementary level indicates that grade retention in kindergarten, first, or second grade results in higher test scores on high-stakes tests in third grade (Hughes, Chen, Thoemmes, & Kwok, 2010).

CON

- A long history of research on grade retention doesn't support the practice (Van Horn, 2008). Students retained in grade perform lower on subsequent achievement tests than their nonretained classmates (Jimerson, Pletcher, &

Graydon, 2006), and they are much more likely to later drop out of school. In fact, grade retention is the strongest predictor of later dropping out (Powell, 2010/2011).

- Students who have been retained in grade are much less likely to participate in postsecondary education, and later retention (between fourth and eighth grades) was linked more strongly to lower rates of postsecondary education than retention between first and third grades (Ou & Reynolds, 2010).
- Grade retention can cause emotional problems (Berk, 2012). One study found that going blind or losing a parent were the only two life events that children felt were more stressful than being retained (Shepard & Smith, 1990). The psychological effects of grade retention are especially acute in adolescence, when physical size differences and peer awareness exacerbate the problem (Jimerson, Pletcher, & Graydon, 2006).
- Better and less expensive alternatives to both grade retention and social promotion exist (Powell, 2010/2011; Van Horn, 2008). Before- and after-school tutoring, summer school programs with reduced class sizes, instructional aides who work with low-achieving children, and peer tutoring are all possibilities.

YOU TAKE A STAND

So, is grade retention an effective way to help struggling students? Or, if at all possible, should students be moved to the next grade level, even if their achievement doesn't meet prescribed standards?

Go to *Issues You'll Face in Teaching* in the MyEducationLab™ *Book Resources* that accompany this text to log your thoughts and receive feedback from your authors.

EXPLORING DIVERSITY: School Organization and the Achievement of Cultural Minorities

Since about the 1970s, African American and Hispanic students have made considerable progress in narrowing the achievement gap separating them from their white and Asian peers. Wide disparities still exist, however, and some evidence suggests that their progress has leveled off or may even be declining (Viadero, 2009a). For example, statistics gathered from the National Assessment of Educational Progress—often called "The Nation's Report Card"—indicate that African American and Hispanic students still trail their white peers by an average of about two grade levels. Further, while more than 80% of Asian students and nearly 80% of white students graduated on time in 2008, this figure was less than 60% for African American and Hispanic students and only slightly more than 50% for American Indian students (National Center for Education Statistics, 2011g).

Revisiting My Beliefs

This discussion in Issues You'll Face in Teaching addresses the fifth item in *This I Believe*, "If some of my students fail to master the content at the grade level I'm teaching, retaining the students in that grade is the best way to ensure that they will acquire the knowledge and skills needed to succeed at the next grade." As you see, experts disagree, and you now have the opportunity to weigh in on the issue.

Researchers have identified several factors to explain differences in achievement between white and minority students, including poverty, negative peer pressure, and parental values (Ogbu, 2003). Each is a possibility, but two other factors—tracking and class size—have also been identified, and they both relate to the way schools are organized.

Tracking and Members of Cultural Minorities

Earlier in the chapter, you saw that comprehensive high schools often practice tracking, despite evidence that the educational experiences in lower-level tracks are often substandard (Oakes, 2008). This problem is particularly critical for members of cultural minorities because they tend to be overrepresented in lower-level tracks and underrepresented in higher-level ones. For instance, white and Asian students are about twice as likely to be enrolled in rigorous, college-preparatory oriented courses as African American and Hispanic students (National Center for Education Statistics, 2009).

Tracking and minority achievement have a form of negative synergy: Student achievement in low-level classes is reduced compared to the achievement of students of comparable ability in high-level classes. Because decisions about tracking are based on records of students' past achievement, minority students continue to be placed in lower-level tracks, and the negative relationship between achievement and tracking is magnified. Unfortunately, school leaders haven't identified a satisfactory solution to this problem.

Cultural Minorities and Class Size

The relationship between class size and minority achievement is more encouraging. Earlier you saw that student achievement is higher in smaller classes. This research is important, because the effects of reducing class size are especially beneficial for cultural minorities (P. Smith, Molnar, & Zahorik, 2003).

Two studies are particularly significant. First, assessments of a major Tennessee project for reducing class size found the following (J. Finn, Gerber, & Boyd-Zaharias, 2005):

- Children in small classes (about 15 students per class) consistently outperformed children in larger classes.
- Inner-city children (about 97% of whom were members of cultural minorities) in small classes closed significant parts of the achievement gap between themselves and nonminority children that exists in larger classes.
- Children in small classes outperformed children in larger classes, even when teachers in the large classes had support from aides.

In the second study, a 4-year experiment with reduction in class size in Wisconsin, researchers found the achievement gap between minorities and nonminorities shrank by nearly 20% in smaller classes, whereas in comparable regular classrooms, it grew by nearly 60% (Molnar, Percy, Smith, & Zahorik, 1998). In addition to narrowing the achievement gap between minority and nonminority students in first grade, the program also prevented it from widening when students in the smaller classes progressed to second and third grades. When class sizes are reduced, teachers have more personal contacts with individual students and can design more effective learning activities to engage students (Blatchford, Bassett, & Brown, 2005).

DIVERSITY AND YOU

Making Urban Schools and Classrooms Effective

You have just graduated, and you quickly find that the job market is tight. You've been offered a job in a large urban high school with a student body that is overwhelmingly minority.

You've visited the school, seen that the resources are decent, and think that the administration is supportive and effective. But two factors disturb you. The school is heavily into tracking, and because you are new, you're assigned many of the basic or remedial classes. In addition, class sizes are large, averaging over 30 students.

QUESTIONS TO CONSIDER

1. What can you personally do to minimize the negative effects of tracking?
2. What can you do to reduce the effects of the large classes that you will be teaching?

Go to *Diversity and You* in the MyEducationLab™ *Book Resources* that accompany this text to log your thoughts and receive feedback from your authors.

Check Your Understanding

3.1. Describe characteristics of an effective school.

3.2. What is the most distinguishing characteristic of effective instruction in effective schools?

3.3. Why is frequent monitoring of student progress essential for an effective school?

For feedback, go to the appendix, *Check Your Understanding*, located in the back of this text.

VOICES from the CLASSROOM

"I believe it's through the instructional and emotional nurturing of our youngest students that our school, our community, and our world are most positively affected. . ."

KRISTI LUETJEN, 2010 Teacher of the Year, Connecticut

CHAPTER 6 Summary

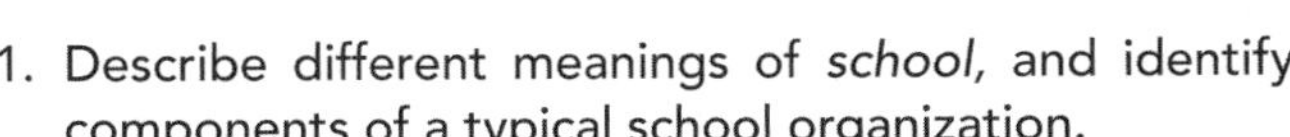

1. Describe different meanings of *school*, and identify components of a typical school organization.
   - One definition describes schools as places where young people go to learn and develop intellectually, personally, and socially. Another describes a school as a place—a building or set of buildings. Schools are also social institutions, organized to promote student growth and development as well as the welfare of society. This is the definition used in this text.
   - Personnel—the school principal and other administrators, support staff, such as custodians and cafeteria workers, and teachers—are the most important component of an effective school.
   - The physical plant—buildings that house classrooms, the library, the cafeteria, and other support functions—make up a second component. The physical plant reflects a school's educational priorities and influences the activities in that school.
   - The curriculum, what is taught in school, is a third component, and it is typically organized into grade levels, with content intended to be taught to students of different ages.
2. Describe important differences among schools at different levels.
   - Early childhood programs describe a number of educational options serving young children and include infant intervention and enrichment programs, nursery schools, and public and private pre-kindergartens and kindergartens.
   - Elementary schools are organized so that a single teacher is responsible for all of the instruction in the different content areas. Elementary teachers arrange their own schedules and typically emphasize reading, language arts, and math in their instruction while de-emphasizing content areas such as science, social studies, and the arts.
   - Middle schools, junior highs, and high schools differ from elementary schools in that they're organized into different content areas and have specified periods of time devoted to each.
   - Effective middle schools differ from junior highs in four ways: (1) Unlike junior highs, middle schools organize teachers and students into interdisciplinary teams, where all teachers on a team have the same group of students. (2) Middle schools place greater emphasis on students'

emotional development than do junior highs. (3) Teachers in effective middle schools emphasize interactive teaching strategies that involve students. (4) Middle schools eliminate activities in which developmental differences among students are emphasized, such as competitive athletics.

- A comprehensive high school aims to meet the needs of all students through differentiated offerings, which means it provides offerings for students who are likely to attend college as well as students who will be entering the job market after graduation.

3. Identify characteristics of a good or effective school.
   - Optimal size is one characteristics of a good or effective school. Effective elementary schools keep class sizes below 20 students per class, and effective high schools struggle to maintain enrollments that allow personalization and attention to every student.
   - Effective schools are safe and orderly, they're academically focused, they actively involve parents, and they have strong leadership from the principal. Teachers in effective schools take responsibility for student learning, use interactive instruction with students, and continually monitor student progress.
   - Grade retention requires students who haven't mastered grade content to repeat the grade. Advocates claim it promotes content mastery and eliminates social promotion; critics counter that it damages students developmentally and emotionally.

Important Concepts

administrators
Advanced Placement (AP) classes
block scheduling
career academies
career technical schools
comprehensive high school
curriculum
departmentalization
development
developmental programs
distance education
dual enrollment
early childhood education
effective school
grade recovery
grade retention
high collective efficacy
junior high schools
looping
middle schools
Montessori method
personal teaching efficacy
principal
schools within schools
social promotion
social system
standards
teacher–student ratio
virtual schools

Portfolio Activity

Choosing a School

InTASC Core Teaching Standards 9: Professional Learning and Ethical Practice

The purpose of this activity is to help you begin thinking about the grade level in which you will be most effective and happy working. On a sheet of paper or online, create four columns with the headings "Elementary Teachers," "Middle School/Junior High Teachers," "High School Teachers," and "Me." Think about the effective teachers you've known, and list their characteristics in the appropriate columns. In the last column, list the personal strengths that you think you'll bring to the teaching profession. Compare this personal list with the school-level ones, and decide which educational level best fits your personal strengths.

Portfolio Activities similar to this one and related to chapter content can be found at MyEducationLab™.

Choosing a School

Go to the topic *School Organization* in the MyEducationLab (www.myeducationlab.com) for *Introduction to Teaching*, where you can:

- Find learning outcomes for *School Organization,* along with the national standards that connect to these outcomes.
- Complete *Assignments and Activities* that can help you more deeply understand the chapter content.
- Apply and practice your understanding of the core teaching skills identified in the chapter with the *Building Teaching Skills and Dispositions* learning units.
- Access video clips of CCSSO National Teachers of the Year award winners responding to the question, "Why Do I Teach?" in the *Teacher Talk* section.
- Check your comprehension on the content covered in the chapter with the *Study Plan.* Here you will be able to take a chapter quiz, receive feedback on your answers, and then access *Review, Practice, and Enrichment* activities to enhance your understanding of chapter content.
- Check the *Book Resources* to find opportunities to share thoughts and gather feedback on the *Diversity and You* and *Issues You'll Face in Teaching* features found in this chapter.

MyEducationLab™

CHAPTER 7

Governance and Finance: Regulating and Funding Schools

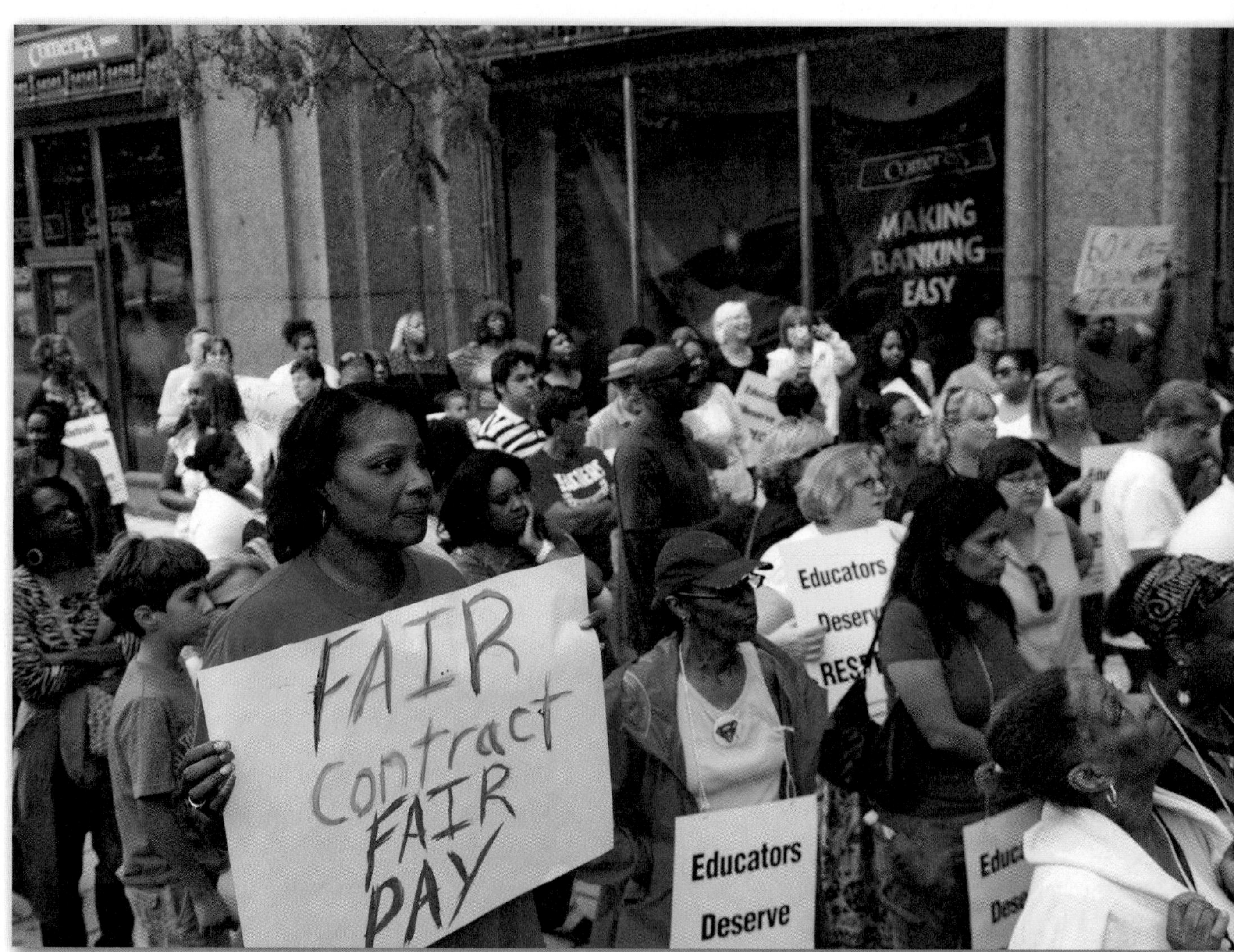

VOICES from the CLASSROOM

". . . and what I want from my students is that when they leave my care for the year, that they were changed for the better, so that the use of the time that we had together was worth it for them and for me, so that I can say that they were changed for the better and that my life was different as well. And that's why I teach."

JAY MAEBORI, 2011 Teacher of the Year, Washington

CHAPTER OUTLINE

LEARNING OUTCOMES

After you have completed your study of this chapter, you should be able to:

1. **Describe the major educational governance structures at state and local levels.** InTASC Core Teaching Standard 9, Professional Learning and Ethical Practice
2. **Explain the different sources and targets of educational funding.** InTASC Core Teaching Standard 9, Professional Learning and Ethical Practice
3. **Describe major current issues in school governance and finance.** InTASC Core Teaching Standard 9, Professional Learning and Ethical Practice.

School governance and school finance may seem irrelevant to you right now as a pre-service teacher, but veterans know better. The way your school is run and the way your school district uses money will make a big difference in the quality of your professional life. And the major budget cuts that occurred in the recession that began in 2008 have resulted in thousands of cuts in teacher positions, which will make the job market for you even more challenging. As you read the following case study, think about how governance and finance influence Carla Buendia, an elementary teacher in a large district in the Midwest.

Carla sits at her desk, looking at the pile of books and papers covering it. "I better get this one right, as it'll be our only chance," she thinks to herself. Carla is a member of Unified Metropolitan School District's Elementary Math Steering Committee, which has been meeting regularly over the last 2 years to study the elementary math curriculum in the district. Test scores have been declining, especially in the areas of applications and problem solving, and the committee has been asked to make a recommendation to the district's school board. Tonight is the night.

Don't be nervous," Carla tells herself, but her advice isn't working. She's been to school board meetings as a spectator when teacher salaries and contracts were being discussed, and she's clearly uneasy about being in front of the hundred or more people who will be in attendance. "Why did I ever say I'd do this?" she thinks. "Too late for that. I just better have my act together when it's my turn to speak."

Carla's work involves governance issues as well as finance issues if her school board decides to adopt her committee's recommendations. We'll return to Carla's work with the math steering committee as the chapter unfolds, but for now, imagine taking a tour of several schools that are only a few miles from each other. The experience can be unsettling. One is bright, cheerful, and clean, with student projects and works of art prominently displayed; the other is dark and depressing, and the hallways are cluttered with trash. These differences often can be traced to the ways the schools are governed and financed.

School governance and finance will also influence the resources available to you when you begin your teaching career. As an example, drive across the state line from New York, where the average spending per pupil in 2011 was $17,750, to Ohio, where it was $9,512 (National Education Association, 2011). The disparity will make a difference in many factors that ultimately will influence learning.

This I Believe

GOVERNANCE AND FINANCE AND MY LIFE AS A TEACHER

For each item, circle the number that best represents your belief. Use the following scale as a guide:

4 = I strongly believe the statement is true.

3 = I believe the statement is true.

2 = I believe the statement is false.

1 = I strongly believe the statement is false.

1. All states govern education in basically the same way.

   1 2 3 4

2. The state office of education in each state is responsible for setting rules and regulations.

   1 2 3 4

3. In the past, the federal government has provided the largest source of educational funding.

   1 2 3 4

4. Most of a district's budget goes to funding instructional activities.

   1 2 3 4

5. Students in different districts across states are provided with approximately the same amount of money to fund their education.

   1 2 3 4

Some politicians argue that money doesn't influence the quality of education, but evidence suggests otherwise (Brimley, Verstegen, & Garfield, 2012). Money buys paper, supplies, and equipment and allows students to *do* science experiments instead of reading about them. Money also allows districts to hire new teachers.

Before continuing, take a few minutes to respond to the survey in the accompanying *This I Believe* feature. We discuss each of the items as the chapter unfolds.

MyEducationLab™

Visit the MyEducationLab for *Introduction to Teaching* to enhance your understanding of chapter concepts with a personalized *Study Plan.* You'll also have the opportunity to hone your teaching skills through video and case-based *Assignments and Activities* and *Building Teaching Skills and Disposition* lessons.

Governance: How Are Schools Regulated and Run?

In a few short years, you will walk into your own classroom, look around, and think, "At last, it's all mine." That's a good feeling, and it will be all yours—sort of. Although you will have considerable autonomy in implementing your own vision of good teaching, you also operate within a specified governance framework.

Governance: A Legal Overview

Unlike many other countries, where the national government is responsible for schools, in the United States the Tenth Amendment to the Constitution clearly assigns legal responsibility for education to the 50 states. Because the states differ significantly in geography, history, economics, and politics, you might think that they would also differ in their approaches to governing education. But in fact, they're surprisingly similar in the way they're organized. These organizational structures are outlined in Figure 7.1 and described in the sections that follow.

FIGURE 7.1 State Administrative Organizational Structure

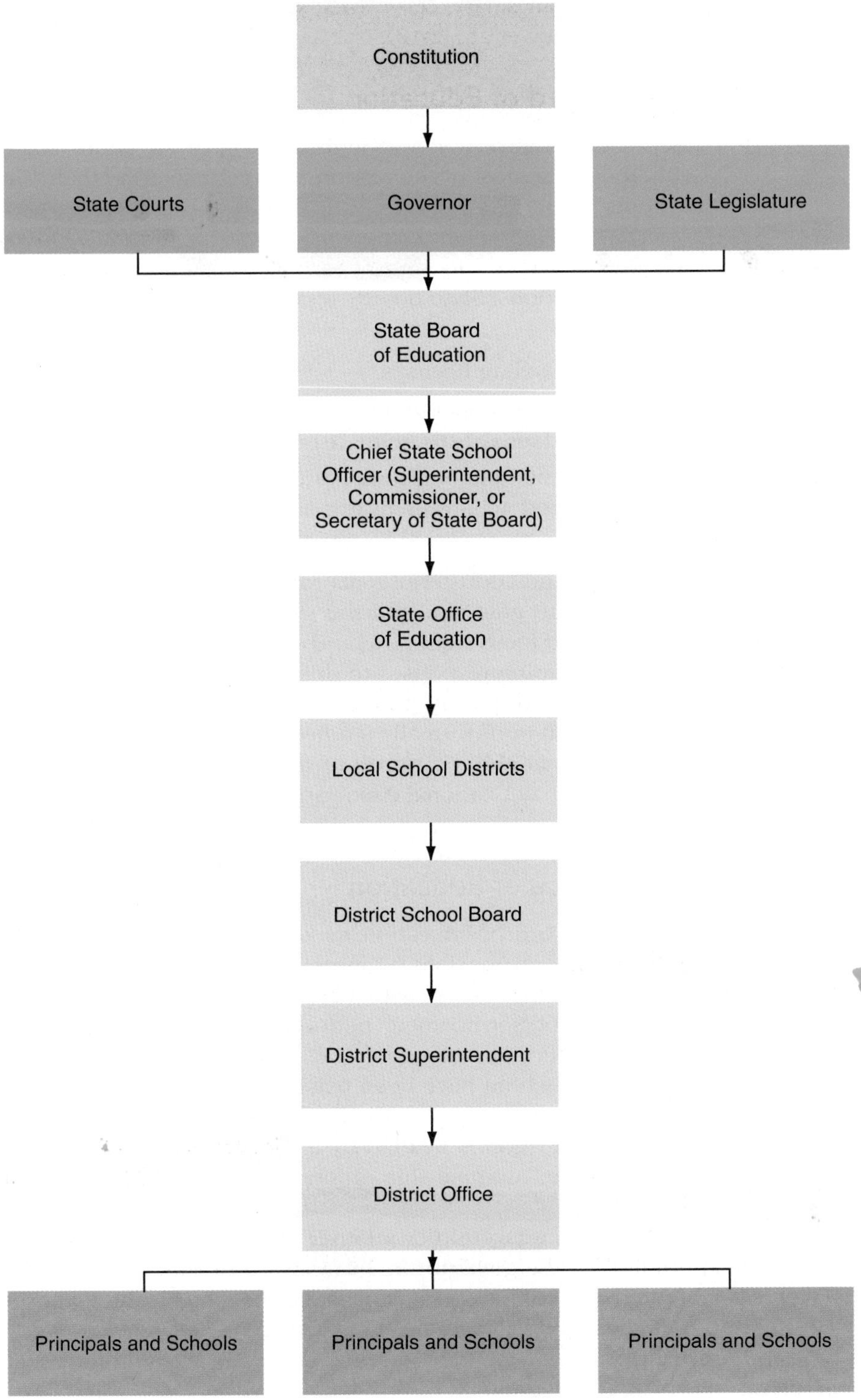

State Governance Structures

In every state, a constitution outlines the roles and responsibilities of state education officers. Governors focus public attention on educational issues and solicit public support for educational funding. State legislatures meet annually to debate school finance and other issues. These legislative sessions are important to

Revisiting My Beliefs

The information in this section answers the first item in *This I Believe*, "All states govern education in basically the same way." This statement is essentially true. Despite some variation in views about the ways schools should educate children, most states govern education in basically the same way.

you and other teachers because states supply almost half of a district's education budget, and legislative actions (or inactions) influence your salary, class sizes, supplies, and available equipment (Brimley et al., 2012).

State Board of Education

Because the governor and legislators have an entire state to run, they turn most of the responsibility for steering their state's schools to the **state board of education**, the legal governing body that exercises general control and supervision of the schools in a state. State boards are similar in purpose to district school boards and perform both regulatory and advisory functions. State boards regulate education in four major ways:

- Issuing and revoking teaching licenses
- Establishing the length of the school year
- Publishing curriculum standards to guide teachers' instruction
- Developing and implementing uniform systems for gathering education data, such as standardized achievement test scores, enrollment trends, and demographics

State boards set long- and short-term goals for their states and help create an educational agenda for the governor and the state legislature. For example, national standards are a major focus right now, and state boards are assisting governors and legislatures in shaping responses to this initiative (Gewertz, 2011c).

State board members are typically people outside professional education, meaning most haven't worked in or formally studied education. They are usually appointed by the governor, but about a fourth of the states elect these officials, who typically serve without pay (National Association of State Boards of Education, 2007).

Teaching and You

How will the state office of education assist you as you begin your teaching career? How will it influence your life as a teacher?

State Office of Education

The state board of education makes policy; the **state office of education** is responsible for implementing that policy on a day-to-day basis. In contrast with state boards, which are composed of lay members who meet periodically to discharge their duties, state offices of education are staffed by full-time education professionals, virtually all of whom have been teachers and most of whom have advanced degrees in education.

Each state office of education is headed by a chief state officer, with titles that differ from state to state. In some this officer is called *superintendent,* in others, *commissioner* or *secretary of the state board*. Chief state officers are appointed by the state board of education or another board in 23 states, elected in 14 states, and appointed by the governor in 13 (McNeil, 2008a). The state office implements teacher and administrator licensing, supervises curriculum, approves school sites and buildings, and collects statistical data. As a new teacher, you will apply to the office of education in your state for an initial teaching license, the requirements of which are determined by the state board.

A state office of education influences the curriculum (what is taught) in a state in two important ways: state standards and textbook approval. Let's look at them.

State Standards. State standards, statements specifying what students should know and what skills they should have after completing an area of study, is one of the most important ways state offices of education influence curricula. Currently, all 50 states have written standards, most commonly in reading and math, but often in other areas such as science and social studies as well (Gewertz, 2010). Currently there is a move to make these standards the same in all 50 states, but the ultimate outcome of this reform is unclear at this time (Gewertz, 2011c). State offices of education are also responsible for administering statewide testing programs based on standards, and these tests can influence what and how you teach.

Textbook Approval. Textbook approval is a second way state offices of education influence curriculum. The textbooks you will use in your classroom must be on a state-approved list; states usually offer districts a choice of several acceptable text series for a given grade level. The textbook selection process can be highly politicized when controversial topics, such as evolution in science or problem-based versus computationally oriented approaches to math, are involved. In this chapter's opening case, Carla's steering committee began its search for a math series by looking at the state-approved list. The committee then conferred with the state's math specialist to evaluate the options.

Revisiting My Beliefs

This section addresses the second item in *This I Believe*, "The state office of education in each state is responsible for setting rules and regulations." The statement is technically false, because the state board of education is the legally responsible body. But many decisions about implementing rules are left to the state office of education, so, in practice, the statement is true in some cases.

The state office of education will influence your own life in several important ways. First, you will seek licensure from the state office of education in your state. In addition, because it controls both textbooks and standards, the state office will also affect your teaching. Make sure when you first start teaching that you consult your state office's website for both guidance and support.

Although state boards and state offices of education influence teaching and learning, for the most part they do so at arm's length; the day-to-day responsibility for educating students falls to the districts. This is why Carla's experience at a district school board meeting is relevant. Let's look at districts' roles in governing education.

School Districts

The school district in which you teach will have a powerful influence on your first teaching job. A **school district** is an administrative unit within a state that is defined by geographical boundaries and is legally responsible for the public education of children within those boundaries. With respect to educational governance, it's where the action is: School districts hire and fire teachers, and they determine the content that students learn (the curriculum) and, to a certain extent, the kinds of learning experiences (instruction) students have in schools. That's why Carla was making her presentation to the district school board. She was involved in decisions about the district's elementary math curriculum. Decisions such as these are usually made at the district level; school districts also determine what books will be used and make them available to you and your students at the beginning of the school year.

School districts differ dramatically in number and size. For example, there are about 14,000 school districts in the United States, and if they were divided equally among the states, each state would have about 300 (Brimley et al., 2012). States also differ dramatically in the number and size of their school districts. For example, the whole state of Hawaii constitutes one school district, but Texas and California each have more than 1,000 districts. The New York City School District has more than a million students, but almost half of the districts enroll fewer than 1,000 students per year. The largest 100 districts have an average of 673 schools and enroll more than 22% of our nation's students (National Center for Education Statistics, 2011g).

Historically, the trend has been toward consolidating schools into fewer, larger districts. For instance, in 1932, the United States had more than 127,000 school districts, but 80 years later, it had only about 14,000 (Brimley et al., 2012). Efficiency is the primary reason for consolidation: Larger districts can offer broader services and minimize duplication of administrative staff. For example, one medium-sized district with a superintendent and a district staff of 10 people is more efficient than two small districts that require a superintendent and a staff of 6 to 8 people each. However, parents often resist consolidation because of loyalty to high school athletic teams and longer bus rides for their children.

What's it like to learn and teach in a small district? Marathon School District in Texas has 56 students (M. Smith, 2011). Class sizes, an issue that continually plagues larger districts, are so small that grade levels are often combined. The competition for valedictorian wasn't intense, because there was only one graduating senior. Even though the district has to share special education services with other districts and sports and extracurricular activities are limited, town residents are fighting to keep their district. "If you close the school, you close the town," residents warn.

So what district size is best for you as a beginning teacher? Small and large districts have both advantages and disadvantages. If you choose to work in a small district, you will often be able to rely on face-to-face contacts to make things happen quickly. On the other hand, these districts often lack resources and instructional support staff. For example, Carla teaches in a large district, and as the committee did their work, they were assisted by a district math coordinator, a testing specialist, and technology experts who helped them evaluate the claims of different commercial math programs. This type of assistance doesn't exist in small districts.

Large districts also have problems. They tend to be hierarchical and bureaucratic, and getting things done takes time. Teachers sometimes feel like nameless and faceless cogs in large, impersonal organizations. And decision making in large districts is placed in the hands of sometimes-contentious committees. The ideal district has an administrative structure that is supportive and responsive to teachers but also leaves them alone to do what they love most—work with their students.

Every school district has a local school board, a superintendent, and central staff. These are the people who make the district-level decisions about teaching and learning in your classroom. Let's see how they will influence your life as a teacher.

The Local School Board

A **local school board** is a group of elected lay citizens responsible for setting policies that determine how a school district operates. With respect to governance, what kinds of rules and regulations do school boards pass? Who are the members of these boards? How are school board members selected? Because these questions will influence your life as a teacher, you should know the answers to them.

Teachers often appear in front of local school boards to explain existing programs and seek funding for new ones.

What Do School Boards Do? School boards serve five important functions, outlined in Figure 7.2 and discussed in the paragraphs that follow.

Working with the district budget is the most important, and often most contentious, school board function. School boards are responsible for raising money through taxes and for disbursing funds to the schools within the district. They also make decisions about various district services, such as providing buses and maintaining lunch programs. Your school board will directly influence you by making decisions about salary increases and benefits, such as health care and retirement packages.

They also affect you indirectly by making budget decisions that affect class size and the amount of instructional materials that are available (S. Dillon, 2011a). Wrestling with each year's budget occupies a major part of a school board's time and energy; it's a continual process that begins in the fall and ends in the spring.

FIGURE 7.2 Functions of Local School Boards

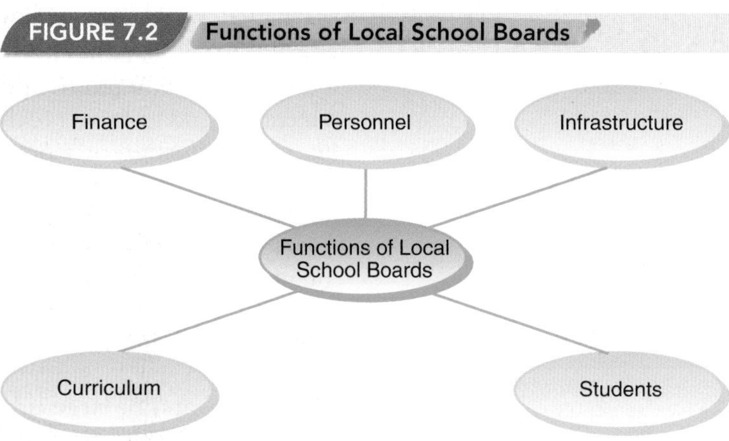

Personnel responsibilities are closely aligned with financial decisions. School boards are legally responsible for hiring and firing all school personnel, including teachers, principals, custodians, and school bus drivers. Your teaching contract will be offered by your district school board, which has the legal authority to hire and fire teachers.

The curriculum—everything teachers teach—is a third area of school board jurisdiction. Your school board, assisted by district administrators, will be responsible for defining the curriculum and implementing the standards developed by your state. In virtually all districts, teachers are consulted about the curriculum; in the better ones, teachers are directly involved in curriculum decisions. For example, Carla's committee helped decide what math curriculum the district would adopt.

Decisions that affect students are also made by school boards. They set attendance, dress, grooming, conduct, and discipline standards for their districts. For example, issues such as school uniforms or effective math programs are debated at district, state, and national levels, but the decision—sometimes after contentious debate—is ultimately made by local school boards.

School boards also determine extracurricular policies—from the mundane to the controversial. For example, some districts require students to maintain a certain grade-point average to participate in sports, a policy that critics contend doubly punishes struggling student athletes by first failing them in the classroom and then preventing them from participating in sports. Supporters of no-pass/no-play policies argue that they improve motivation to learn by providing incentives for academic success.

The question of whether to grant gay and lesbian clubs equal status with other school-sponsored organizations is another topic that has generated controversy at school board meetings. As you would expect, attendance at these meetings increases when controversial issues are on their agendas.

Finally, school boards make decisions about district infrastructure. For example, they ensure that school buildings and school buses are maintained and safe, and they approve plans and hire contractors when new schools are built.

In recent years, school closings, consolidation, and other budget-related issues have become the primary concerns of school board members, along with reform efforts aimed at increasing student achievement (Samuels, 2012a). Interestingly, during the late 1980s, student achievement wasn't even listed in school board members' top concerns. Budget issues and the national trend toward greater school accountability have powerfully affected the ways school boards operate.

Members of School Boards and Their Selection. Who serves on school boards, and how do they get there? These are important questions because school board members create an important link between schools and the people they serve (Resnick & Bryant, 2010; Usdan, 2010). Most school boards elect their members for 3- or 4-year terms; in the remainder, members are appointed by large-city mayors or city councils.

School board elections can be controversial for two reasons. First, the voter turnout for most school board elections is embarrassingly low. As few as 5% to 10% of eligible voters often decide school board membership. Critics contend that this fact results in boards that don't represent the citizens in the district (Hess, 2010b). Second, the question of whether school board membership should be at-large or limited to specific areas within a city is often contentious. At-large elections tend to favor wealthy, white-majority candidates who have more money to run a campaign or who benefit from white-majority voting pools. In a limited-area election, only citizens who live in a specific part of the city are allowed to vote for candidates representing that area. Area-specific elections provide greater opportunities for minority candidates to represent local, ethnic-minority neighborhoods.

Who serves on school boards? The typical school board member is male, white, older, and wealthy, although membership is slowly becoming more diverse. For example, surveys have found that more than 44% of board members are female, and in large urban districts 22% are African American and 6% Latino. In addition, 75% have at least a bachelor's degree, with many possessing higher professional degrees (National School Boards Association, 2011).

Despite progress in recent years, disparities still exist in the composition of school board members and the people they're elected to serve. For example, although the number of minority school board members has risen in recent years, the percentage still lags behind student percentages in most urban school districts. School board elections serve as a major obstacle to greater minority involvement because they require major outlays of money and time. Critics contend that wealthy school board members can't empathize with the financial hardships that teachers and community members often experience. Critics also question the ability of male-dominated school boards to effectively represent the teaching force, which is predominantly female.

The Superintendent

The school board makes policy, and the **superintendent**, the school district's head administrative officer, along with his or her staff, implements that policy in the district's schools. The division of labor between the board and the superintendent isn't simple and well-defined, however (Darden, 2008a). Because most board members have little or no background in professional education, the superintendent often plays a central role in leading the board and helping set agendas.

Historically, superintendents have been hired by school boards and have held an advanced degree in education, but some districts are now looking outside the field of education to find superintendents. For example, Joel Klein, the former chancellor of the massive New York City school system, was a lawyer and politician who worked in the Justice Department in the Clinton administration (Fertig, 2009). And Arne Duncan, the former superintendent of the Chicago school system and President Barak Obama's Secretary of Education, graduated from Harvard with a degree in sociology.

As with school boards, women and minorities are underrepresented as superintendents (Kowalski, McCord, Peterson, Young, & Ellersen, 2011). Three quarters of the teaching force and slightly more than half of the general population are women, but they make up only 24% of superintendents. Similarly, members of cultural minorities make up a third of the student population and more than 10% of teachers, but they account for only a small percentage of superintendents (less than 10%).

When power and authority are shared, as is the case with school boards and superintendents, conflicts are inevitable, and when they occur, the superintendent usually loses. In large urban districts, the average tenure for superintendents is 3.5 years (Council of the Great City Schools, 2009). Accountability, in the form of student test scores, and the challenges of balancing budgets in tough economic times are major reasons that superintendents' tenure is so short.

Disputes with school boards, politics, and budget shortfalls are major challenges superintendents face (Samuels, 2012a). When controversy flares over issues such as student drug use, school violence, desegregation, and lagging student achievement, a community looks to the superintendent for answers. Superintendents often get caught in the crossfire of politics and public opinion and, unable to quickly solve these problems, are either terminated or feel obliged to resign (Cuban, 2008).

What are superintendents paid for this frustrating and insecure job? Pay varies considerably with both location and district size; the average 2010 salary for a superintendent in districts larger than 25,000 students was $225,897, but competition for superintendents in larger urban districts has resulted in salaries that are considerably higher (Winters, 2010). For example, the recently appointed superintendent of the Los Angeles school district, the second largest in the country, received an annual salary of $330,000 plus benefits, more than the governor of the state (Samuels, 2011).

To hear one school superintendent describe the different challenges facing other superintendents, click on the video *Challenges Facing Superintendents: One Superintendent's Perspective* (3:28).

Must have handbook

The District Office

The district office assists the superintendent in translating school board policies into action and provides a link between you and your school board (see Figure 7.1). It also coordinates the myriad curricular and instructional efforts within the district. The district office is responsible for these tasks:

- Ordering textbooks and supplies
- Developing programs of study
- Ordering, distributing, and analyzing standardized tests
- Evaluating teachers and assisting those with difficulties

The district office is instrumental in translating abstract state and school board mandates into reality. How it does this can give teachers a sense of empowerment or make them feel like hired hands.

The district office will also play an important role in helping you get started in your first job. It will provide a new-teacher orientation that will likely include an overview of the district's curriculum, any district-wide instructional initiatives, and your district's assessment program. These policies and procedures are important for you because they frame the district's professional expectations for its new teachers. In addition, the central office will coordinate a mentoring program that will help you make the transition from university student to working professional.

Teaching and You

How important will the first principal you'll work for be? How much difference will a good or bad principal make in your job satisfaction? What factors should you consider when you interview with the principal of a school?

The School Principal

The school **principal**, the person given the ultimate administrative responsibility for a school's operation, is the district administrator who will have the greatest impact on your life as a teacher (D. Boyd, Grossman, Ing, Lankford, Loeb, & Wyckoff, 2011). The principal is the person who hires and sometimes fires teachers, and who plays a major role in establishing both the academic and the work climates of a school.

A demographic profile of principals (see Table 7.1) mirrors that of school board members: Most are white, and males are still in the majority in middle and high schools. Principals almost always have classroom experience, and most have at least a master's degree.

As the person who oversees the everyday operation of the school, the principal has wide-ranging responsibilities, and teacher selection and evaluation are two of the most important

Principals are crucial in creating well-run, learning-oriented schools.

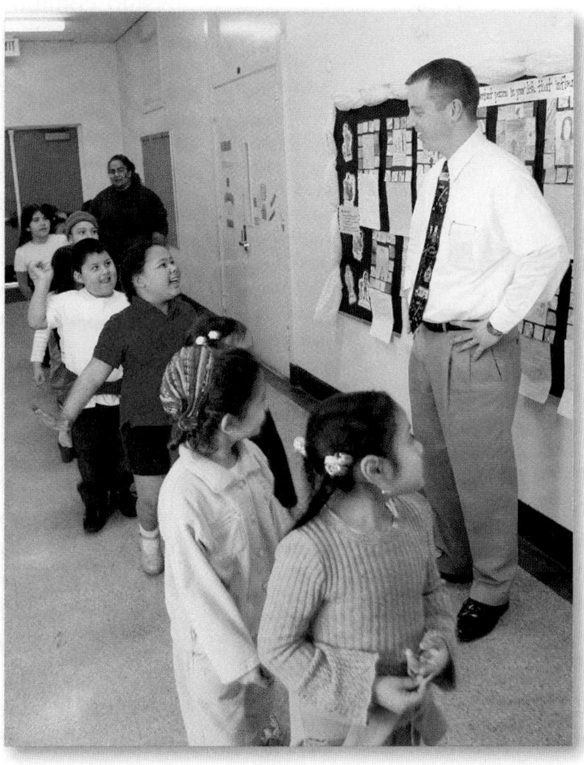

TABLE 7.1 Profile of School Principals

	High School Principals (%)	Middle School Principals (%)	ElementarySchool Principals (%)
Sex			
Male	70.6	66.8	40.1
Female	29.4	33.2	59.9
Ethnic Background			
White	85.0	83.0	80.7
African American	9.2	10.5	10.1
Hispanic American	4.1	5.1	7.0
Asian American	0.4	0.7	0.9
Native American	0.4	0.8	0.6
Other	0.7	–	0.6
Highest Degree Earned			
Bachelor's	3.3	1.8	7.6
Master's	60.8	55.5	59.4
Professional diploma	26.6	33.6	25.3
Doctorate	9.3	9.1	7.7
Salary (12-month)	**$89,700**	**$87,866**	**$80,500**

Sources: Bureau of Labor Statistics (2009); U.S. Department of Education (2008, 2010).

(Sergiovanni, 2009a, 2009b). The principal's interview will be a crucial factor in determining whether or not you get the job, and it will also give you an opportunity to learn about the person you'll be working for and the kind of school you'll be working in. During an interview, you should try to determine the principal's views about your role as a teacher and how the administrator runs the school.

The principal is also responsible for school-level curricular and instructional leadership, community relations, and the coordination of pupil services provided by school counselors, psychologists, nurses, and others. Principals also implement and monitor the school budget and ensure that the school's physical facilities are maintained. It's not easy being a principal; the job is both challenging and stressful, and many teachers choose not to become principals because the problems outweigh the benefits.

Experienced teachers want principals who are instructional leaders and who take a hands-on approach to the teaching–learning process. This leadership is especially important for beginning teachers, who need support, mentoring, and feedback. Because of their busy schedules, however, many principals become managers who focus primarily on the day-to-day operation of the school and forget that their most important role is to support teaching and learning.

In *Teaching and You* at the beginning of this section, we asked how important principals will be for you in your first teaching job. Very! Principals are the most important people in the district's administrative structure because they work directly with you and your students. Effective principals can transform a mediocre school into a positive and productive learning environment, but the opposite is also true; an ineffective principal can make a school an unpleasant place in which to work (D. Boyd et al., 2011). Your first principal can make a huge difference in your first year of teaching, so for your interviews, make sure you find out as much as you can about the principals, the schools, and what each principal expects from you. Go into your interviews with important questions you want answered, and be sure to ask them during the interview. In addition to providing you with valuable information, your questions will show that you are knowledgeable about the teaching profession and sincerely interested in the position.

Check Your Understanding

1.1. Who is legally responsible for governing education in the United States?
1.2. Describe the educational governance structure at the state level.
1.3. Describe the governance structure at the local, district level.

For feedback, go to the appendix, *Check Your Understanding*, located in the back of this text.

WINDOWS *on the Profession*

To hear a superintendent describe characteristics of effective principals, click on the video *Effective Principals: A Superintendent's Perspective* (3:50).

School Finance: How Are Schools Funded?

To understand how school finance affects your life as a teacher, let's return to Carla's work on her school's Elementary Math Steering Committee.

"And based on our analysis of math programs around the country, we believe this one is best for our children. . . . Any questions?" Carla asks as she concludes her presentation to the school board.

"Let me make sure that I'm clear about this," one board member responds. "In addition to the texts themselves, students will need manipulatives. . . . I'm sorry, but I'm not sure exactly what 'manipulatives' are."

"Manipulatives are concrete objects, such as cubes that could be put in a box to help kids understand the concept of volume, and plastic squares that could be used to illustrate area. The success of this program depends on students seeing math ideas in action."

"Thank you. . . . And teachers will need additional in-service training to bring them up to speed on how to use these new materials. Is that right?"

"Yes. What we've read and heard is that teacher in-service is essential to the success of this program," Carla replies, as her fellow committee members nod in agreement.

"What seems clear to me," the chair of the school board adds, "is that this program, along with our technology initiative and the changes in our language arts program, is going to need additional funding. We need to make sure that the public understands how and why taxes are going to go up next fall. We've all got a big job ahead of us—selling, no, explaining, why our schools need additional monies."

Money is important in education. It will determine your salary, professional-development opportunities, and access to resources, such as computers, lab supplies, supplementary texts, and a host of other materials. It also influences the quality of schools by allowing districts to do such things as reduce class sizes and recruit and retain qualified teachers. From 2003 to 2011, the general public, in national polls, said that lack of financial support and funding for education was a major problem facing local schools; another major problem was overcrowded schools, an issue closely related to financial support (Bushaw & Lopez, 2011). In 2010, nearly 50 million students were attending public schools at a cost of $540 billion dollars; education is a big business, and this money has attracted lots of attention from business, both good and bad (National Center for Education Statistics, 2011a). In this section, we look at where this money comes from and how it will influence your life as a teacher.

School Funding Sources

Local, state, and federal sources all provide money for education. Let's see how these funds are raised at each level of government and how they make their way to your classroom. These revenue sources are outlined in Figure 7.3 and discussed in the sections that follow.

Revisiting My Beliefs

The information in Figure 7.3 indicates that the third statement in *This I Believe*, "In the past, the federal government has provided the largest source of educational funding," is clearly false, because both state and local shares have been considerably larger.

FIGURE 7.3 Education Revenues from Local, State, and Federal Sources

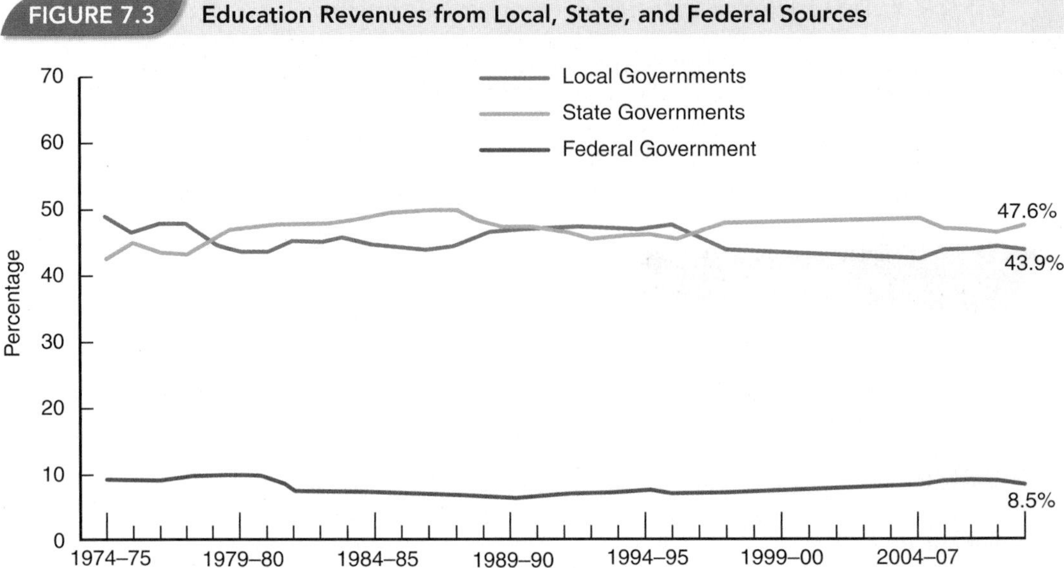

Source: Data from National Center for Education Statistics (2010f).

State Revenue Sources

As you see in Figure 7.3, states contribute the largest source of educational funding, accounting for nearly half of the monies that go into schools. State income taxes and sales taxes are the two largest sources of state income, each contributing about one third of all state revenues. Sales taxes are regressive, however, meaning they take proportionally more from lower-income families who spend a larger portion of their income on necessities, such as food, clothing, and housing. Progressive states provide some relief by excluding food from items that are taxed. Personal income tax accounts for another third of state revenues. The remaining third comes from other sources such as taxes on liquor and tobacco, oil and mining revenues, and corporate income taxes.

Recently, state lotteries and gambling have become major sources of revenue, and they were often promoted to skeptical taxpayers as new sources for school funding. But education is often the victim of a zero-sum shell game, in which increased funding from lottery monies is balanced by decreasing monies from other sources, such as sales taxes. While most states (42) have lotteries, fewer than half allocate profits directly to education, and the percentage of income taxes going to education in these states varies considerably (Brimley et al., 2012). Also, lotteries are an inefficient way to collect money; states spend 30 cents of every lottery income dollar on expenses, including advertising and commissions to stores that sell lottery tickets (Stodgill & Nixon, 2007). Another problem with lotteries is that these gambling ventures generally attract participants who are poor and have had little schooling, and 10% to 15% of players account for 80% of lottery sales (Brimley et al., 2012). (Given the terrible odds of winning, some call lotteries "taxes on stupidity.") Unfortunately, cash-strapped states are increasingly turning to "sin taxes" that target gambling, tobacco, and alcohol, and place more of the funding burden on the poor and uneducated (Trinko, 2010).

Disparities among different states' support for education can also be striking. Let's look at one teacher's experience.

Nikki, Paul's daughter, began her teaching career in a middle school in a state and district with generous education funding. Her average class size was 16, with a maximum of 22. Her district employed a full-time math supervisor for her middle school and another person, whose full-time job was to support math instruction in two middle schools! As we might predict, her students were very high achievers, and often won state math competitions. Student motivation and classroom management problems were virtually nonexistent.

She then moved to a different state where state support was much lower, and took a teaching position in a high school where 31 was her average class size, with as many as 40 in some classes. "I had basically good kids, but I had too many of them, and we never had the materials we needed to make the content interesting." Student achievement, motivation, and classroom management were always undercurrents that caused both stress and frustration.

We're not suggesting that more money would have solved all of Nikki's problems in her second school, but claiming that funding has no influence on educational quality is nonsense fomented in the interest of political expediency.

Local Funding

As we saw earlier in our discussion of school governance, financing education at the local level is the responsibility of local school boards, which is why Carla made her presentation to her local board, and the need for increased funding was one of the implications of her presentation. At the local level, most funding for schools comes from **property taxes**, which are determined by the value of property in the school district (Brimley et al., 2012). Other local revenue sources include income taxes, fees for building permits, traffic fines, and user fees charged to groups that hold meetings in schools. In collecting property taxes, local authorities first assess the value of a property and then tax the owner a small percentage of the property's value (usually less than 1%).

Differences in property values among districts affect the quality of life and resources available to teachers as well as students.

Funding education through local property taxes has disadvantages; the most glaring are inequities between property values and resources in different districts. Wealthier cities or districts have a higher tax base, so they're able to collect (and spend) more money for their schools. Poorer rural and urban school districts find themselves on the opposite end of this continuum, with a lower tax base, resulting in lower revenues. Property taxes also place an unfair burden on older taxpayers, whose homes may have increased in value while their ability to pay taxes has remained constant or decreased. In addition, many older taxpayers resist these charges because they no longer have children in school and don't see the immediate benefit of increased spending for schools.

The property-tax method of financing schools also has a political disadvantage (Brimley et al., 2012). Unlike sales taxes, which taxpayers pay in small, continual, and almost unnoticed increments, property taxes are more visible targets for taxpayer dissatisfaction. Statements arrive once a year with a comparison to the previous year, and property-tax increases are discussed in public forums whenever school boards ask their taxpayers for increased funding.

Dissatisfaction with this method of funding reached a head in California in 1978, when voters passed an initiative called Proposition 13, which limited property taxes in the state. By the 1990s, 45 other states had passed similar measures (Brimley et al., 2012). The effect on educational funding has been chilling: Schools and school districts have had less to spend and have had to fight harder when requesting new funds from taxpayers.

Federal Funding for Education

The federal government is the third, smallest, and most controversial source of educational funding. From 1920 to 1980, the federal share increased from virtually nothing to a peak of nearly 10%, declining in the 1980s to less than 7% before rising to its current level of 8.5%. Though the amount spent on education has increased steadily over the years, the total still accounts for only about 2% of all federal expenditures (National Center for Education Statistics, 2011b). Nearly half of federal funds for education are channeled through the U.S. Department of Education, with the next largest proportion—about 20%—coming from the Department of Health and Human Services, which oversees Head Start as well as national drug prevention programs.

Although the percentage of education funds contributed by the federal government has been small, the impact has been considerable, largely because of the use of **categorical grants**, federal grants targeted for specific groups and designated purposes. Head Start, aimed at preschoolers, and Title I, which benefits economically disadvantaged youth, are examples of categorical aid programs targeting specific needs or populations. Because the funds must be used for specific purposes, categorical grants have strongly influenced local education practices.

During the 1980s, categorical funds were replaced by **block grants**, federal monies provided to states and school districts with few restrictions for use. Begun during the conservative Reagan administration (1981–1989), block grants purposely reduce the federal role in policy making, in essence giving states and districts more control over how monies are spent. Proponents contend this makes sense—who knows local needs better than local educators? But critics contend that funds are often misspent or spent in areas where they aren't needed (Brimley et al., 2012).

Variations in School Funding Over Time

State and local shares of school funding have remained fairly steady over time, ranging from between 40% and 50% since 1990. These figures are national averages, and the federal, state, and local proportions can vary significantly from state to state. For example, none of Hawaii's school budgets came from local sources, whereas in some states, local funds account for more than 40% of school funding (Brimley et al., 2012).

Shifts in education funding patterns reflect changing views about education throughout the history of our country. In early America, education was a local responsibility with virtually no involvement by the federal government. In sharp contrast, 20th-century leaders saw a direct connection between education and the country's political and economic well-being. Quality schools and a well-educated workforce became national concerns, and the federal government's role in education increased. Similarly, states began to recognize the importance of education in attracting high-tech industries and high-paying jobs.

Federal funding of education is controversial. Proponents of a greater federal role believe that education is essential for the country's continued progress in the 21st century and that the federal government should continue to exert leadership (and provide funds) in this area. Critics warn of increased federal control over what they believe should be a local responsibility. Political conservatives also argue against the expansion of what they consider to be an already bloated federal bureaucracy. For these critics, less is better when it comes to federal funding. In contrast, local funding, they say, makes schools more efficient and responsive to local needs and wishes.

The public has consistently believed that adequate educational funding is important but is undecided about the relative amounts that local, state, and federal governments should contribute. In earlier polls, more than 20% of those polled favored a greater role for local funding through property taxes, a third favored state sources, and slightly more than a third favored greater reliance on federal taxes (Rose & Gallup, 1998). More recent polls indicate that the public still views lack of funding as a serious problem but remains undecided about where additional money should come from (Bushaw & Lopez, 2011).

Recent Trends in Educational Funding

Educational funding depends on taxes, and tax revenues fall when an economic recession hits the U.S. economy. In recent years, the U.S. economy experienced a major downturn, and both schools and teachers have suffered. Teaching positions have been cut, teacher salaries frozen, class sizes increased, and students have been increasingly asked to pay for extracurricular activities, ranging from athletics to academic clubs. The impact of the recent recession was exacerbated by the sharp drop in property values in many states, a major source of educational funding (Cavanagh, 2012b).

One of the worst cutbacks in educational funding occurred in Texas, where legislators cut $5.4 billion from the state's education budget (Fernandez, 2012). Districts had to cut bus funding, and teachers were asked to clean and sweep their rooms to make up for janitor positions that were eliminated to save money. This harkens back to the 1700s and 1800s, when teachers were expected to clean rooms, chop wood, and haul in water for one-room schoolhouses. But this is the 21st century. Hundreds of school districts have sued the state, saying that the state's current school finance system fails to adequately and equitably fund public education.

The federal government tried to ameliorate these negative trends with the passage of the $787-billion **American Recovery and Reinvestment Act** designed to provide an economic stimulus to a faltering U.S. economy (McNeil, 2009). New federal aid to education in that bill totaled $115 billion, with major chunks distributed in the following ways:

- State stabilization funds to prevent teacher layoffs and cuts to programs in education ($53.6 billion)
- Additional funds for Title I programs targeting disadvantaged students ($13 billion)
- Increased funding for special education services ($12.2 billion)

In addition, new, one-time funds also targeted specific areas such as Head Start, homeless children, and teacher quality initiatives emphasizing performance pay (D. Hoff, 2009a; McNeil, 2009). But these funds have dried up, and states are faced not only with tight budgets but also lawsuits, challenging whether states are meeting their educational responsibilities (Cavanagh, 2012b).

What are the implications of these changes for you as a beginning teacher? In the near term, the competition for jobs might be tighter; long-term, the prospects are more optimistic, as the student population continues to increase and teachers retire (Hussar & Bailey, 2011). Increased competition means that you'll need to adjust accordingly; the best teacher candidates will get the best jobs. Take your teacher education seriously, and look for ways to distinguish yourself from the competition. Good grades are important, but just as important will be the breadth and quality of your experiences in schools as well as recommendations from your instructors.

Teaching and You

Where do you plan to teach when you graduate? Do different states spend different amounts of money on education? Do a particular state's expenditures on education matter?

Educational Revenues: Where Do They Go?

The largest part of states' total budget expenditures go to education, with more than a third spent on P–12, and more than 10% going to higher education (Brimley et al., 2012). In 2010–2011, the 50 states and the District of Columbia spent an average of $10,826 per pupil, but as you see in Table 7.2, spending varied considerably from state to state. New York spent the most ($17,750), and Arizona spent the least ($6,448). The data in Table 7.2 also reveal regional trends. Most of the higher per-pupil expenditures are found in the Northeast and upper Midwest, with lower expenditures in the South and the West.

A significant portion of a district's budget goes to transportation, building maintenance, and food services.

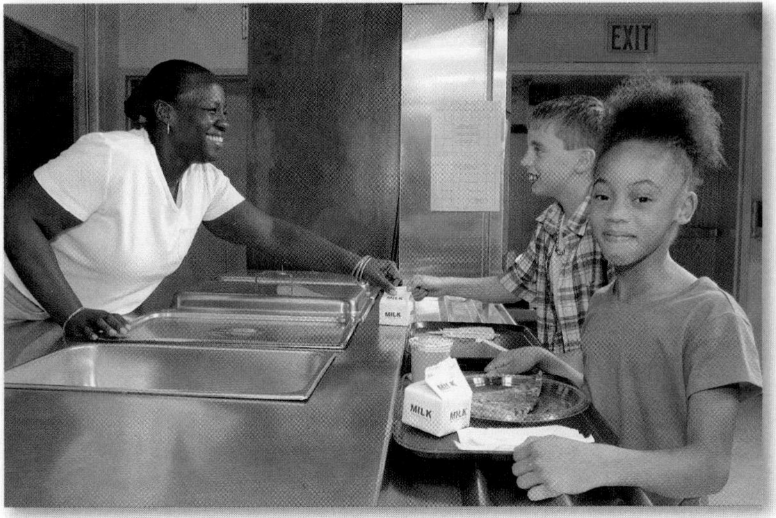

TABLE 7.2 State-by-State Spending per Student

State	Spending Rank	Annual $ per Student
New York	1	17,750
New Jersey	2	17,717
Vermont	3	17,447
Wyoming	4	16,066
Rhode Island	5	15,803
Maryland	6	15,268
Maine	7	15,032
Connecticut	8	14,989
Massachusetts	9	14,828
Delaware	10	13,960
District of Columbia	11	13,803
New Hampshire	12	13,797
Pennsylvania	13	13,334
Michigan	14	12,015
Arkansas	15	11,999
Minnesota	16	11,905
Illinois	17	11,896
Hawaii	18	11,819
Wisconsin	19	11,791
Virginia	20	11,753
West Virginia	21	11,369
New Mexico	22	11,346
Alaska	23	11,147
Georgia	24	10,971
Oregon	25	10,959
Louisiana	26	10,578
Nebraska	27	10,452
Indiana	28	10,390
Washington	29	10,367
Montana	30	9,973
Iowa	31	9,856
South Carolina	32	9,616
Kentucky	33	9,612
Colorado	34	9,588
Ohio	35	9,512
Alabama	36	9,483
Missouri	37	9,422
South Dakota	38	9,310
Kansas	39	9,254
Texas	40	9,128
Florida	41	9,124
North Dakota	42	8,880
California	43	8,689
Tennessee	44	8,393

State	Spending Rank	Annual $ per Student
Oklahoma	45	8,311
North Carolina	46	8,303
Idaho	47	8,101
Nevada	48	8,089
Mississippi	49	8,003
Utah	50	7,056
Arizona	51	6,448
U.S and DC Average		**10,826**

Source: National Education Association. (2011). *Rankings and estimates (2010–2011)*. Retrieved from http://www.nea.org/assets/docs/HE/NEA_Rankings_and_Estimates010711.pdf

It's tempting to conclude that a state's commitment to education can be judged by its per-pupil spending, but some states are wealthier than others, and the number of children per taxpayer varies, so they have a greater capacity to fund education. Funding differences between states are also influenced by the cost of living and the number of children who need to be educated. Utah, for example, which has the second lowest per-student spending in the country ($7,056), also has the highest birth rate in the nation—about 1.5 times the national average—so whatever funds are available must be divided among more children.

The effects of funding on excellence in education are controversial, with early research concluding that the amount spent has little or no influence on achievement (Hanushek, 1996). More recent research, however, finds that higher per-pupil expenditures can result in higher achievement, if funds are used wisely and strategically (B. Baker, 2012). Increased expenditures seem to have their greatest effect on low-income and minority students.

The relationship between funding and learning isn't simple or precise, however. Achievement tests—the most commonly used measure of student learning—focus on core academic areas, such as reading, math, and science, and not every dollar spent on education goes to teaching these basic subjects. Some monies go to art and music, for example, which are valuable areas of the curriculum, but increased expenditures in these areas won't be directly reflected in higher test scores. Furthermore, as you see in Figure 7.4, only about 61% of the money allocated to education is spent on instruction, most of which goes to teacher salaries. The rest is spent on areas that affect achievement only indirectly.

In addition to the more than 60% that directly supports instruction, 13% of school district funds go to instructional assistance needs, such as student services, teacher professional advancement, and curriculum development (Figure 7.4). Another 8% goes to administration. Approximately one third of administration funding is spent on the central district office, with the other two thirds going to schools, primarily for principals' salaries. Maintenance of school buildings and grounds (physical plant) takes up another 10% of the budget. Transportation (school buses) and food services (cafeteria lunches) each account for another 4%.

To understand the magnitude of transportation expenditures, consider these national figures: In an average school year, 500,000 yellow school buses travel 4.4 billion (billion, not million!) miles, providing rides to millions of K–12 students (Brimley et al., 2012). Student activities add 5 million trips. Schools provide transportation to 55% of the nation's student population at a cost of $779 per student.

FIGURE 7.4 Educational Expenditures on Different District Programs

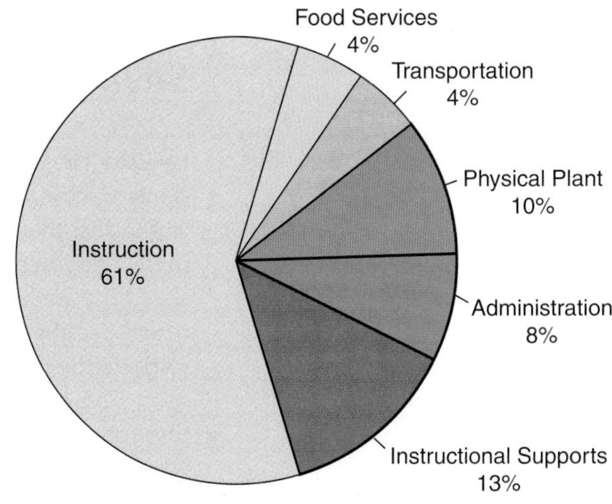

Sources: Based on information from Brimley et al. (2012); National Center for Education Statistics (2010f).

Revisiting My Beliefs

This section addresses the fourth item in *This I Believe*, "Most of a district's budget goes to funding instructional activities." This statement is true: The average U.S. district spends more than 60% of its budget on instruction.

The recent surge in fuel costs has resulted in scheduling changes and cutbacks in bus services for students. A number of smaller, rural districts are experimenting with 4-day school weeks, and other districts have changed the requirements for bus services, limiting access to younger students who live more than 2 miles from school (D. Turner, 2010). Critics question whether these changes will result in more accidents and deaths from students driving and walking on dangerous streets; about 800 students die each year going to and from school (Purdom, 2008). Of these, only about 2% are school bus related, making this one of the safest ways for students to get to school.

Critics often decry the large amount of monies (nearly 40%) spent on areas other than academics and have initiated national efforts to mandate that a minimum of two thirds of education funds go to instruction—teachers and textbooks. But school finance experts point out, that expenditures for school nurses, school buses, and school lunches, for example, are all part of the total education process, and no research evidence links higher spending on instruction to increases in student achievement. In addition, experts note that the amounts schools spend on administration and maintenance of the physical plant compare favorably with those spent in industry (Brimley et al., 2012). This may be a classic case of micromanaging, in which legislators want to influence education without spending more money.

Check Your Understanding

2.1. What are the major sources of educational funding?
2.2. How are educational revenues spent?

For feedback, go to the appendix, *Check Your Understanding*, located in the back of this text.

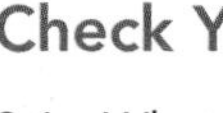

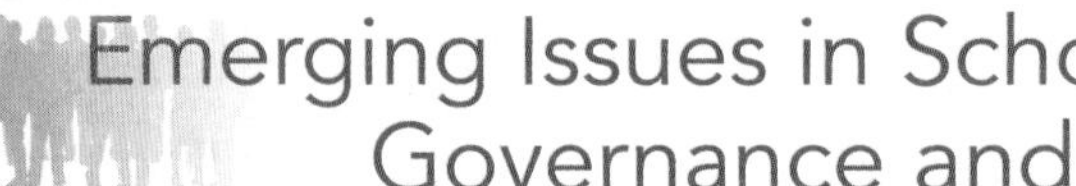

Emerging Issues in School Governance and Finance

Teaching and You

How important will the finances and administration of the first district you work in be to your professional life? What are some indicators of healthy and well-financed districts? What are some signs that a district is having problems, either administratively or financially?

As schools confront the challenges of the 21st century, they face two major issues in the areas of governance and finance:

- Equity in funding, one of the most fundamental issues facing education
- The governance of struggling urban schools

Let's look at these challenges.

Savage Inequalities: The Struggle for Funding Equity

Lakesha Lincoln walks into Andrew Jackson Middle School among a horde of other students. Jackson is a 72-year-old urban school in a large northeastern city. She doesn't react to the fact that three of the five lights down the long main hall are out, and that the hall badly needs a paint job, because they have been that way for a long time.

She walks by the girls' bathroom, where a sign on the door says, "Bathroom out of order. Use the bathroom on the second floor." She decides she'll wait and get permission to go to the bathroom during her first-period class.

She enters her homeroom and sits down. She has barely enough room to squeeze through the rows of desks, because there are 38 students in her homeroom, and the room was built for 30. Discarded paper sits on the floor from yesterday, and the boards haven't been cleaned from the last class of the previous day.

Students are milling around the room as the bell rings, and Mr. Jensen, her homeroom teacher, tries his best to get them to settle down. He is struggling, because he has had no professional training, and he is doing his best to feel his way through his first year of teaching.

Dawn Johnson walks into Forest Park Middle School, which is in the suburbs. It was built in 2008, and it's roomy, well lit, and pleasant. Dawn enters her homeroom, which is spotless, with ample equipment and materials to support instruction. Her room is comfortable, with plenty of space available for her and 22 classmates.

The last of the students slide into their chairs as the bell rings, and Mrs. August is standing in front of the room ready to begin. She is a 10-year veteran, with a reputation for being demanding but fair. Students agree that they learn a lot from her.

Disparities in property tax revenues can result in dramatic differences in funding for schools that are quite close geographically.

As you saw earlier, significant differences in per-pupil expenditures exist, both between and within states. Jonathan Kozol describes this issue in his influential book, *Savage Inequalities*:

> Americans abhor the notion of a social order in which economic privilege and political power are determined by hereditary class. Officially, we have a more enlightened goal in sight: namely, a society in which a family's wealth has no relation to the probability of future educational attainment and the wealth and station it affords. By this standard, education offered to poor children should be at least as good as that which is provided to the children of the upper-middle class. (Kozol, 1991, p. 207)

This standard of equality is not what Kozol found when he visited schools across the country. Instead, he found that many urban schools around the country were like Lakesha's—dirty and run down with peeling paint, broken toilets, antiquated or missing textbooks, and teachers who were uncertified or lacked experience or both. Only miles away, suburban schools such as Forest Park Middle, where Dawn attends, featured new, well-maintained, attractive buildings that were inviting learning environments. And teachers were generally seasoned, knowledgeable professionals. These stark contrasts gave Kozol's book its title.

In 1968, Demetrio Rodriguez, a sheet-metal worker in a poor suburb of San Antonio, Texas, looked at the schools his children were attending, compared them with schools in wealthier districts only 10 miles away, and found similar discouraging contrasts between his children's schools and those of neighboring districts. The primary problem was that property taxes for his district produced only $37 per student compared to $412 per student for the wealthier suburb. These differences aren't unusual: In Texas during the 1980s, for example, the 100 most affluent districts in the state spent an average of $7,233 per student, whereas the poorest 100 averaged $2,978! Faced with these inequities, Mr. Rodriguez sued, contending that his children were being penalized by where they lived (Brimley et al., 2012).

Revisiting My Beliefs

This section addresses the fifth item in *This I Believe*, "Students in different districts across states are provided with approximately the same amount of money to fund their education." This statement isn't true: Large disparities in the property tax base that provides funds for schools result in widely varying resources for students and their teachers.

Nationally, wealthy districts in some states spend 56% more on their more affluent students than do poorer ones; in Alaska, for example, the gap between high- and low-spending districts was $13,730 in 2011 (Cavanagh, 2010; Edwards, Chronister &

Bomster, 2012). This doesn't make sense, because poorer students, or those in poverty, require more help than richer ones. Despite efforts to alleviate these inequalities, substantial within-state differences continue to exist between districts serving low- and high-income families. For example, in Kansas, per-pupil expenditures vary from $5,655 in the poorest district to $16,969 in wealthier ones, a difference of over 3 to 1; in Illinois some wealthier districts have $18,000 more per pupil to work with than poorer ones (Brimley et al., 2012).

Legal challenges over funding equity have increased. The battle lines for these cases were drawn in California in 1971, when the California Supreme Court ruled in a 6 to 1 vote that the use of property taxes to fund education resulted in unconstitutional funding inequities in the state (*Serrano v. Priest*, 1971). At the time per-person educational expenditures in wealthier districts were 6 times more than those in poorer districts. To reduce these funding inequities, the state's share of education funding rose from 40% to 70%.

The *Serrano v. Priest* lawsuit went all the way to the U.S. Supreme Court. Based on the California decision, many believed that the Supreme Court would find the spending patterns in Texas unconstitutional. However, in a 5 to 4 vote, it did just the opposite, ruling in 1973 that the U.S. Constitution does not guarantee citizens a right to an education. The Court did point out, however, that funding inequities might violate state constitutions, many of which do guarantee citizens that right.

The Supreme Court ruling on the Rodriguez case sent the issue back to state courts, and many other state suits followed. By 2010, 44 of the 50 states had lawsuits challenging existing funding formulas, and courts overturned existing systems in eight states and upheld others in nine states, with other cases still pending (Brimley et al., 2012). Differences in state rulings are primarily the result of differences in the wording of state constitutions: Some constitutions are quite specific in guaranteeing "equal education for all," whereas others are vague in specifying that educational opportunity should be "ample" or "efficient." When rulings favored the plaintiffs, inequities were reduced, and decreasing or eliminating reliance on the property tax was a primary factor.

Funding inequities are complicated by the fact that not all districts in a state have the same needs. Some have a higher proportion of low-income children, nonnative English speakers, or children who need special education services. These students require extra resources and are more expensive to educate. Reformers are calling for funding formulas that go beyond simply equalizing dollars; they want plans that meet the needs of all students (McNeil, 2008b). These proposed reforms are expensive and controversial, however, because many parents from wealthier districts object to having their local taxes used to fund distant schools across the state. In addition, the problems involved in quantifying educational needs in terms of dollars and cents are complex (Cavanagh, 2010).

Efforts have been made to change funding practices within rather than between districts (Fiske & Ladd, 2010). The **weighted student formula** allocates resources within a district to schools on a per-school basis according to student needs. Instead of every school in a district getting the same per-pupil amount, the weighted student formula provides more funds to schools that have more special education students or other students requiring additional services. Several U.S. urban school districts, such as Chicago, Denver, Houston, Los Angeles, and Seattle, are experimenting with this change. Advocates claim that it's a fairer way of distributing funds and that it decentralizes educational decision making by allowing individual schools to decide how education dollars will be spent. Comprehensive research is still needed to see if this change will work in other, smaller districts where increased funding for some schools could mean decreased, and potentially crippling, funding for others.

URBAN EDUCATION: Takeovers as Alternatives to Local Control

Governance by local school boards is the predominant pattern in U.S. education, but what happens when local control doesn't work? Twelve of the largest cities answered this question by authorizing the mayor to take over the running of their city's schools; this occurred in Boston in 1991, in Chicago in 1995, and in New York in 2002 (Medina, 2009a; Viteretti, 2009a). Mayoral takeovers occur because of either fiscal mismanagement or academic underachievement of students in a school system. In addition to mayoral takeovers in large urban cities, states have authorized similar moves in smaller districts, removing local school boards and replacing them with a new management team.

Mayors of large cities, seeing education as central to their cities' economic growth, have taken this drastic action in an attempt to turn their educational systems around (Samuels, 2012b). How bad does it have to get to trigger these actions? Consider the case of Detroit (Winerip, 2011c). In 2009, math scores were the lowest in 21 years; the district had a budget deficit of $200 million and was losing students at a rate of 8,000 students per year. For each student who left, the district lost $7,300 in state funds—an annual loss of $58 million. After 2 years of fiscal reform, the budget continued to hemorrhage to a $327 million deficit, and enrollments continued to fall from 104,000 in 2007 to 74,000 in 2011 (McClatchy-Tribune, 2011). Something had to be done. Changes in governance included balancing districts' budgets, closing neighborhood schools, improving the facilities of the ones that remained, and renegotiating with unions. Mayors in other cities have also experimented with educational reform, expanding choice options through charter schools, creating smaller, thematic high schools, and attempting to tie teacher and principal pay to student achievement (Medina & Gootman, 2008).

One of the more controversial takeovers occurred in Washington, DC, where the mayor's newly appointed superintendent attempted to replace tenure with offers of higher teacher pay (S. Dillon, 2008b). The new superintendent believed that tenure was a major obstacle to removing incompetent teachers and offered significant pay raises (as much as $40,000 per year) for teachers who were willing to forgo tenure. Teachers were offered a choice between the old system with tenure and the new one without, but Washington DC Teachers Union members viewed the proposal with mixed reactions and voted it down, fearing the loss of the political and job protection afforded by tenure.

Experts give takeovers a mixed, but generally positive, report card (S. Dillon, 2008b; Stover, 2008). Schools tend to be run more efficiently, and budgets are balanced. But student achievement, the bottom line for many critics, has shown only modest gains. Critics charge that these takeovers place too much power in the hands of one person, eliminating the democratic influence of elected school boards (Ravitch, 2010b). Proponents counter that mayors are elected by more people than typically occur in school board elections and that administrative changes are a necessary precursor to educational reform, which can't occur if districts are poorly managed (Viteretti, 2009b). School district takeovers, as one solution to the problems of failing urban school districts, are probably here to stay. Their success will ultimately be judged by their ability to improve teaching and learning in urban classrooms.

Earlier we asked in *Teaching and You* how important finances and administration will be to your professional life. The answer is considerably; how a district is run and how educational funds are allocated and used will have a major effect on you and your classroom. Unfortunately, it is often difficult to get an accurate reading on these factors. Here are two suggestions. First, talk to the teachers you meet when you interview at a school. Ask them how they like teaching in that district and whether they feel supported and appreciated. You can also Google the district to see what issues have been in the public eye in recent years.

Privatization and Commercialization: Are Our Schools for Sale?

Education is a big business; total money spent on education in 2009 was $591 billion (Hu & Gebeloff, 2011). When that amount of money is spent on anything, business and industry are sure to be interested. Often this interest is beneficial, such as when corporations take the lead as advocates for a better-educated citizenry or workforce. Sometimes, however, the profit motive encourages corporations to engage in educational pursuits that may or may not benefit students or their parents. In this section, we look at privatization and commercialization, two trends that are reshaping the schools and classrooms in which you'll be teaching.

Privatization

Privatization, the move to outsource educational services to corporations, is one by-product of school choice. Schools are multibillion-dollar enterprises, and corporations have always looked at education as a possible place to make money. Both textbooks and standardized tests generate billions of dollars for corporations (Molnar et al., 2009, 2010).

Historically, corporate activities in schools have taken three basic forms: (1) selling to schools (vending); (2) selling in schools (books, computers); and more recently, (3) selling of schools (Molnar et al., 2010). The move toward school choice has accelerated this last option with privately run, for-profit schools. Modeled after HMOs (health maintenance organizations), EMOs (education maintenance organizations) manage and run either whole districts or specific schools within a district. In addition, the No Child Left Behind legislation, specifying that students in failing schools be provided with supplemental tutoring, has opened the door to a billion-dollar tutoring industry for private corporations (Stover & Hardy, 2008).

Certain aspects of school privatization aren't new. Schools have been outsourcing contracts for support services, such as school lunches and transportation, for years. In addition, districts typically hire companies such as IBM and Hewlett-Packard to provide technology support. What is new is the idea of handing over control of a whole school or district to a private corporation.

Corporations such as Edison Schools, Inc., and Sylvan Learning Incorporated are leaders in the school privatization movement. Edison began in 1992 and made its stock public in 1998 with an initial Wall Street offering of $18 per share; optimism soon doubled share prices. Chris Whittle, its founder, predicted that by 2020, Edison would run 1 of every 10 schools in the United States, but so far the company has grown slowly, and its stock sank to $2 in 2001. In 2005, Edison ran 136 schools across the country, serving 53,500 students (Reid, 2005). Its most visible challenge came when the School District of Philadelphia, a floundering system suffering from perennial low student achievement, offered Edison a 5-year, $60 million contract to manage 20 of its schools.

Critics make a number of arguments against privatization (Molnar et al., 2009, 2010). They question the ability of a corporate efficiency model to work in education and assert that corporate strategies will adversely affect both teachers and students. Further, they contend, privatized schools have a dual mission—improving test scores and making a profit—and corporate profits and education don't mix. Attention to the bottom line means that student welfare may be sacrificed to make money. Critics also identify a narrow focus on the basics, as well as neglect of nonnative English speakers and students with special needs as additional problems.

Support for the critics' position can be found in Edison's efforts in Philadelphia, where controversy existed from the beginning. The district's initial call for outside help was based on an evaluation conducted by Edison itself and not sent out for competitive bids (Gewertz, 2002). In essence, the state of Pennsylvania hired Edison to conduct a study, completed in 2 months, for $2.7 million (Bracey, 2002). Not surprisingly, the Edison report concluded that external help should be sought, and the district authorized the creation of 20 Edison charter schools. After less than 1 year of operation, the School District of Philadelphia, citing budget considerations, decided to shift $10 million of the next year's $20 million contract from Edison and other private companies to other reform projects (Gewertz, 2003). One disillusioned parent commented, "I don't consider putting 15,000 students with a company that can't guarantee operations next year reform. It's not just a stock game, this is my child's life" (M. Saltman, 2005, p. 154).

Teacher morale and lagging student performance in Edison schools have been persistent problems. For example, in an Edison-contracted San Francisco elementary school, approximately half of the teachers left in each of Edison's first 2 years of operation, citing problems with long work hours, a regimented curriculum, and overemphasis on preparing students for tests. There were also claims that students with academic or behavioral difficulties were "counseled out" of the school in hopes of raising test scores (Woodward, 2002). San Francisco canceled its contract with Edison, but under a renewed charter contract with the state of California, the Edison school's test scores remained low, ranking last among scores from San Francisco's 75 elementary schools.

Privatization advocates argue that these problems are exceptions, that Edison works in some of the most challenging schools in the country, and that the public shouldn't expect miracles overnight (Chubb, 2007). They also assert that competition from the corporate sector is good because it encourages public schools to reexamine unproductive practices. In addition, advocates claim, the same business efficiencies that have made the United States a world leader can also work in schools, and a focus on performance (as measured by standardized tests) can provide schools with a clear mission to increase student achievement.

Research has found some benefits of privatized schools. They are typically cleaner and more efficiently run than public schools (Reid, 2005). Technology is frequently emphasized, and more attention is given to individualized instruction. However, companies have not provided clear evidence that students learn more in privately run schools, a core assertion of privatization advocates. Some research shows improved achievement, but other research shows either no gain or declines (P. Campbell, 2007a, 2007b). Unfortunately, the research on achievement gains in privatized schools is murky, clouded by the sponsors—either privatization backers or critics—who seem to produce results that bolster their position.

Commercialization

Commercialization involves corporations using schools as avenues or arenas for advertising and other business ventures. Many school districts currently engage in some type of business partnership with corporations. At one time, school–business partnerships often consisted of corporations buying a football scoreboard or placing an ad in the school newspaper, and currently a number of states are considering making school buses traveling ads for businesses (Jennings, 2011).

School commercialization takes many forms, but all are intended to increase sales and brand children to a product at an early age. One of the most common, embedded advertising, promotes a product as part of a plot line. We've all seen actors and actresses in movies drinking a certain soft drink or beer, and while seemingly harmless, these ads must be effective, as evidenced by the billions of

growth. Jason talks about the initiative in class, explaining how it will help the environment. He mentions that he is head of a local action committee and that interested students can receive extra credit for passing out fliers after school.

Some parents complain to Jason's principal, claiming that he shouldn't be spending school time on political activity. His principal calls him in to discuss the parents' concerns, and during the meeting, Jason adamantly argues that he has the right to involve students in local politics, claiming that a part of every course should to be devoted to civic awareness and action. His principal points out that Jason was hired to teach science, not social studies, and that parents' concerns are important.

Sasha Brown looks at the two folders in front of her and frowns. Her job is to recommend one of two students from her school for a prestigious science and math scholarship to the state university. Although the decision will ultimately be made by a committee, she knows that her recommendation will carry considerable weight because she is chair of the math department.

Brandon, one of the candidates, is a bright, conscientious student who always scores at the top of his class. The son of a local engineer, he has a good grasp of mathematical concepts. Sonia, the other candidate, is not as strong conceptually but often solves problems in creative ways. The fact that she is female is also an issue, because a female hasn't won the award in its 6-year history. In addition, Sasha knows that Sonia comes from a single-parent family and needs the scholarship more than Brandon does.

MyEducationLab™

Visit the MyEducationLab for *Introduction to Teaching* to enhance your understanding of chapter concepts with a personalized *Study Plan.* You'll also have the opportunity to hone your teaching skills through video and case-based *Assignments and Activities* and *Building Teaching Skills and Disposition* lessons.

What would you do in Jason's position? In Sasha's? Do guidelines exist to help you, and how do these dilemmas relate to teacher professionalism? We address these issues in this chapter.

Before you begin your study, please respond to the items in the *This I Believe* feature.

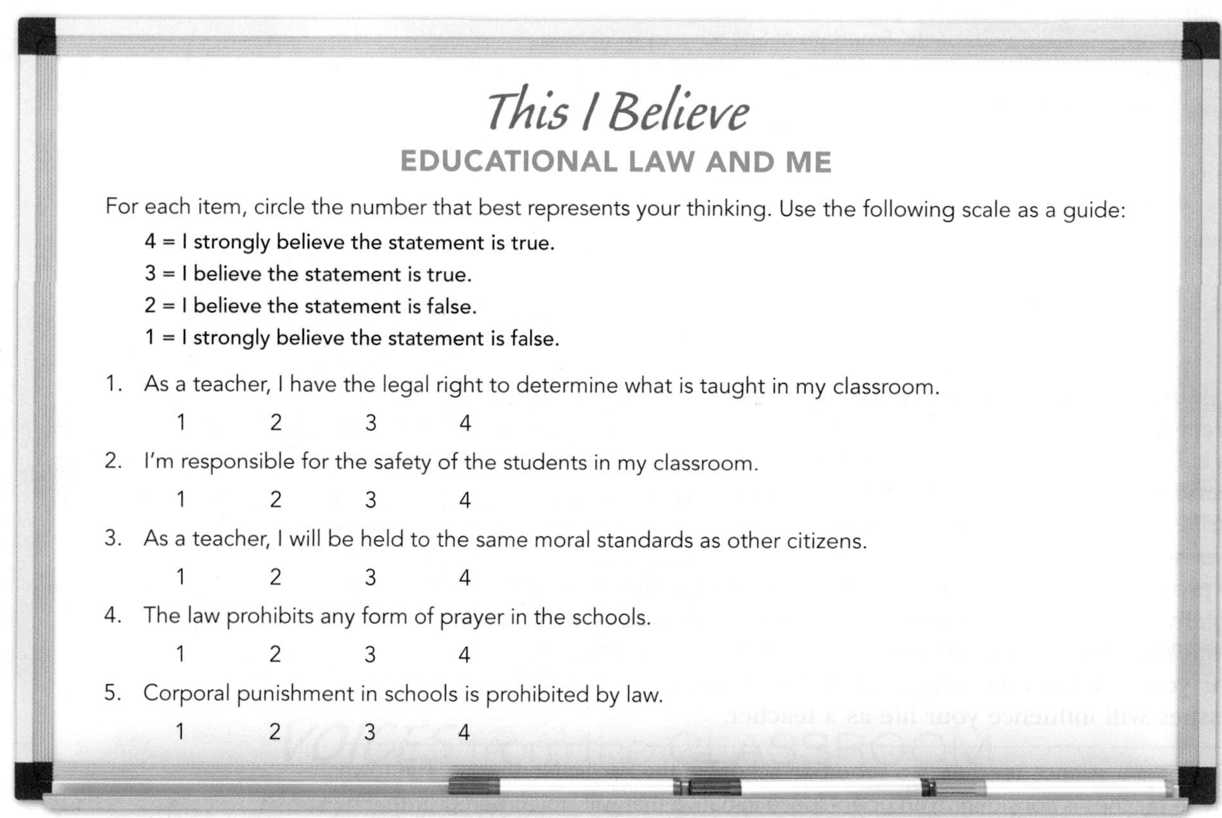

This I Believe

EDUCATIONAL LAW AND ME

For each item, circle the number that best represents your thinking. Use the following scale as a guide:

4 = I strongly believe the statement is true.
3 = I believe the statement is true.
2 = I believe the statement is false.
1 = I strongly believe the statement is false.

1. As a teacher, I have the legal right to determine what is taught in my classroom.
   1 2 3 4
2. I'm responsible for the safety of the students in my classroom.
   1 2 3 4
3. As a teacher, I will be held to the same moral standards as other citizens.
   1 2 3 4
4. The law prohibits any form of prayer in the schools.
   1 2 3 4
5. Corporal punishment in schools is prohibited by law.
   1 2 3 4

Law, Ethics, and Teacher Professionalism

As a professional, you are responsible for making decisions in ill-defined situations, you have the autonomy to do so, and you'll use your professional knowledge to make those decisions. Understanding the legal and ethical aspects of your profession is an important part of this knowledge. However, if you're typical, you may lack professional knowledge in these areas, leaving you unprepared to deal with legal and ethical issues when they arise (Schimmel, Militello, & Eckes, 2011). Not surprisingly, students are also often unaware of their legal rights and responsibilities. In this chapter we discuss the law and how it can influence your professional decision making. We begin by putting the legal aspects of teaching into a larger context.

Limitations of Laws

Teaching and You

You're working in a middle school, and you see a fight between two students on the playground. Does the law address your responsibilities in a situation like this?

The answer to the question we asked in *Teaching and You* here is unequivocally yes. You're responsible for the safety of children in your classroom as well as your school, so you can't ignore the fight. In fact, parents have the right to sue teachers if they can demonstrate that they are negligent by failing to protect students from injury. Are you required to physically break up the fight, or can you simply report it to the administration? As with many other situations, the law is imprecise and doesn't specify an exact response.

Laws regulate your professional rights and responsibilities, but two limitations affect the extent to which they can guide your professional decisions. First, laws are purposely general, so they can apply to a variety of specific situations. For example, regarding the protection of students from injury, teachers not only are required to break up fights on a playground, they also need to supervise chemistry experiments, maintain order at school assemblies, and stop horseplay in locker rooms.

Jason's dilemma is another case. The law generally protects a teacher's freedom of speech, but does it allow him to campaign in his classroom and present issues that may not be part of the assigned curriculum? The answers to these questions are not explicitly described in laws, so your professional decision making is crucial.

A second limitation of laws is that they were created in response to problems that existed in the past, so they don't provide specific guidelines for future decisions. New situations often raise new legal questions. For example, the use of technology raises a number of questions: In what ways are students' e-mails and Facebook messages restricted? Are your professional e-mails protected by privacy clauses, or are they public domain? What kinds of materials can you legally download from the Internet? What can you legally copy? Experts are wrestling with these issues, and preliminary guidelines have appeared, but you will often have to make decisions based on your knowledge of the law as it exists and your own professional judgment. This again illustrates why professional knowledge is so important.

Professional ethics provide broad guidelines for teachers as they make decisions in complex situations.

Ethical Dimensions of Teaching

The law tells teachers what they can do (their rights) and what they must do (their responsibilities); however, laws don't tell us what we should do. For information on appropriate conduct, we need to turn to ethics, the discipline that examines values and offers principles that can be used to decide whether acts are right or wrong (Gladding, 2007).

Professional ethics are a set of moral standards for professional behavior. For example, the Hippocratic Oath guides the medical profession; in taking the oath, physicians pledge to do their best to benefit their patients, to tell the truth, and to maintain patients' confidences. Other professions have similar ethical codes, which are designed to guide practitioners and protect clients.

You were introduced to the National Education Association's (NEA) code of ethics in Chapter 1 when you studied teacher professionalism (see Figure 1.7). The NEA code provides guidance to teachers in ambiguous professional situations such as those described at the beginning of the chapter.

As with the law, codes of ethics are limited; they provide only general guidelines for professional behavior (Warnick & Silverman, 2011). To see why, let's look again at Jason's dilemma. Under Principle I of the NEA Code of Ethics, Item 2 states that "the educator . . . shall not unreasonably deny the student access to varying points of view." Has Jason been balanced and fair in presenting both sides of the environmental and political issue? A code of ethics isn't, and never can be, specific enough to provide a definitive answer. Jason must answer the question for himself based on his personal philosophy of education and, within it, his personal code of ethics.

The limitations of the NEA code are also illustrated in Sasha's case. Item 6 of Principle I cautions teachers not to discriminate "on the basis of race, color, creed, [or] sex," but it doesn't tell Sasha which student to choose. Judged strictly on academics, Brandon appears to be the better candidate. If Sasha believes that Sonia is less talented than Brandon, choosing her because she is female would be granting her an unfair advantage. On the other hand, Sasha may believe that Sonia's math talents are different from—but equal to—Brandon's and that it's ethically valid to consider her financial need and the good that might result from giving recognition to a female in a male-dominated area of the curriculum.

In response to these complexities, teachers are often encouraged to "treat all students equally." But even this edict isn't as simple as it appears on the surface. Effective teachers purposely call on shy students to involve them in lessons, sometimes avoid calling on assertive students who tend to dominate discussions, and give students who are struggling with English more time to answer questions and finish tests. Teachers treat students differently depending on their individual needs; professional ethics direct teachers to treat all students equitably, but not always equally.

These examples illustrate why developing your personal philosophy of education is so important. A philosophy of education provides a framework for thinking about educational issues and guides your professional practice. Your personal philosophy will guide you as you make decisions about what's important and what's fair. Because the law and professional codes of ethics can provide only general guidelines, a personal philosophy is essential in helping you make specific decisions each day.

Check Your Understanding

1.1. Explain the differences between legal and ethical influences on the teaching profession.

1.2. What are two limitations of using existing laws as the basis for professional decision making?

For feedback, go to the appendix, *Check Your Understanding*, located in the back of this text.

The U.S. Legal System

When making professional decisions, you will be influenced by the legal system in the United States, which is a complex web of laws that originate from federal, state, and local laws. Laws regulating schools and teachers are part of this larger legal system, which uses peoples' rights and responsibilities as the basis for defining fairness.

Federal Influences

Through amendments to the Constitution and specific laws enacted by Congress, the federal government plays a central role in defining the rights and responsibilities of teachers and students.

Constitutional Amendments

> **Teaching and You**
>
> How much freedom do you have in selecting topics to teach? Are you limited in what books and articles you can ask your students to read? Can you publicly criticize the administrators and school boards you work for? How much freedom do students have in running their school newspapers and yearbooks?

The First Amendment to the Constitution guarantees freedom of speech to all of our country's citizens, but where is the line drawn with respect to the questions we asked in *Teaching and You* here? You can't have your students read *Playboy* magazine, but how about *Catcher in the Rye*, a classic coming-of-age novel with explicit sexual references? Legal uncertainties also exist with respect to the second and third questions.

The Fourth Amendment protects citizens from unreasonable searches and seizures. To what extent does this amendment protect you and your students? For instance:

- Can school officials search students' backpacks and purses when they're on school property?
- Are students' lockers considered personal property, or can they be searched if school officials suspect drugs or weapons are in them?

The Fourth Amendment provides general guidelines about search and seizure but doesn't specifically answer these questions.

The Fourteenth Amendment states, "nor shall any State deprive any person of life, liberty, or property without due process of law." What does "due process" mean in the context of schools? For example:

- Can you be fired without a formal hearing?
- Can students be expelled from class without formal proceedings?
- How long can a student be suspended from school, and what kinds of deliberations need to precede such a suspension?

Again, the Constitution provides general guidelines about due process, but specific decisions are left to you and other educators.

Federal Laws

Federal laws passed in Congress also influence education. For example, the Civil Rights Act of 1964 states, "No person in the United States shall on the grounds of race, color, or national origin, be excluded from participation in or be denied the benefits of, or be subjected to discrimination under any program or activity receiving federal financial assistance." This law helped end school segregation in our country. Similarly, Title IX, passed in 1972, prohibits discrimination on the basis of gender and has been instrumental in helping equalize the resources provided for boys' and girls' sports.

State and Local Influences

States also influence education by passing laws regulating teachers' qualifications, working conditions, and legal rights (Zirkel, 2009). For example, most states require a bachelor's degree to teach, and many are now requiring a major in an academic area.

States also create departments of education with a variety of responsibilities, such as determining the length of the school year and approving textbooks. They also pass laws creating local school districts, which are then legally responsible for the day-to-day functioning of schools.

The Overlapping Legal System

Overlapping levels in the legal system correspond to different responsibilities, but conflicts sometimes occur. When they do, the system attempts to resolve disputes at a lower level before sending them to a higher one. Let's look at two examples.

Brenda Taylor has been hired to teach American history at a rural high school. Three days before the school year begins, her principal informs her that she will be the debate team sponsor. She objects, saying she knows nothing about debate. When the principal insists, she looks into her contract and finds that a description of her duties includes the phrase "and related extracurricular activities." It doesn't mention the debate team. She complains again to her principal, but he is desperate to find someone and insists that it be Brenda. She writes a letter to the school board, which appoints a grievance committee. The committee rules in the district's favor. Brenda, not willing to back down, hires a lawyer, and her case goes to a state court.

Henry Ipsinger likes his job in a suburban middle school but disagrees with the school's priorities. A strong proponent of middle school philosophy, he believes that middle schools are supposed to be for all kids, not just the academically and athletically talented. He especially objects to his school's participation in Academic Olympics, an interschool academic competition, and the school's emphasis on competitive football and basketball.

Henry isn't afraid to express his opinions, and, to the consternation of his principal, frequently does so at faculty meetings. When his concerns aren't addressed, he takes his complaints to school board meetings. His complaints fall on deaf ears, though they raise a number of eyebrows. He then tries politics, openly backing opposition candidates to the school board. His involvement in local politics was the final straw: At the end of the school year, he is cited for insubordination, and his contract isn't renewed.

Livid, Henry hires a lawyer, claiming his First Amendment right to freedom of speech has been violated. The case works its way through the court system all the way to the U.S. Supreme Court.

Can you be asked to perform duties beyond your teaching responsibilities? Can you be fired because of your professional opinions? Both questions fall into a gray area called *school law* and are addressed by different court systems.

Brenda's and Henry's cases both started at the local level, but Brenda's complaint moved to state courts because her suit involved conditions of employment, which are state responsibilities. Henry's case went to federal courts because freedom of speech is a right guaranteed by the Constitution.

In the next section, we examine your rights and responsibilities, probably the most important dimensions of school law for teachers.

Check Your Understanding

2.1. Describe how the legal system at the federal level influences education.
2.2. How do state laws influence education policies and practices?
2.3. What is the educational significance of the overlapping legal system in the United States?

For feedback, go to the appendix, *Check Your Understanding*, located in the back of this text.

Teachers' Rights and Responsibilities

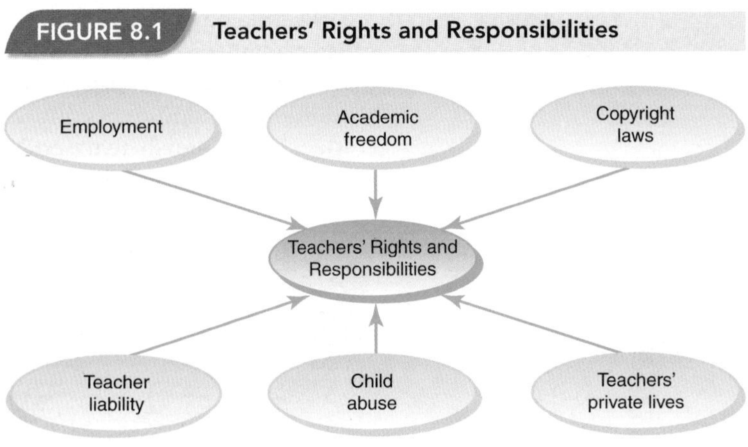

This section of the chapter is about you, and it contains one of the most important topics you'll study in this book. It describes your rights and responsibilities, and your understanding of the information here can prevent you from being sued or even fired.

As citizens, teachers enjoy the same legal safeguards as all Americans, including freedom of speech and the right to due process. But because you're a professional entrusted with the care of children, you have responsibilities beyond those of other citizens. These rights and responsibilities exist in six areas, which are outlined in Figure 8.1 and discussed in the sections that follow.

Teacher Employment and the Law

How you get and keep a job is one of the first things you'll think about as you join the teaching profession. Legal guidelines influence the process and can guide your efforts.

Licensure

Licensure is the process by which a state evaluates your credentials as a prospective teacher to ensure that you have achieved satisfactory levels of teaching competence and are morally fit to work with young people. Every state has licensure requirements, which typically include a bachelor's degree from an accredited college or university with a minimum number of credit hours in specified areas, such as those required for a teaching major or minor.

In addition, prospective teachers are screened for felony arrests or a history of abusing or molesting children. Applicants who fail these screens usually have the right to petition before a state professional practices board that will hear their individual cases.

Teachers are increasingly being asked to pass competency tests that measure their ability to perform basic skills (reading, writing, and mathematics); their background in an academic area, such as biology, history, or English; and their understanding of learning and teaching. These tests are controversial, but when properly developed and validated, they have been upheld in courts (Schimmel, Stellman, & Fischer, 2011). If you meet these requirements, you'll receive a teaching license that makes you eligible to teach but doesn't guarantee you a job.

Contracts

A **teaching contract** is a legal employment agreement between you and a local school board. In issuing contracts, school boards must comply with laws that prohibit discrimination on the basis of sex, race, religion, or age, and contracts are legally binding for both parties. School boards can be sued for breaking a contract without due cause, and you must also honor a signed contract. Many states permit a teacher's certificate to be revoked for breach of contract, a practice growing more common as the competition for teachers increases.

As a new teacher, you should carefully read your contract and any district policies and procedures manuals covered by it. Extracurricular assignments, such as sponsoring school clubs or monitoring sports events, may not be specified in detail in an initial contract but can be required later. This is what happened to Brenda Taylor when her contract said, "and related extracurricular activities." Courts have generally upheld districts' rights to require these additional responsibilities, but have also said that a reasonable connection must exist between additional assignments and a teacher's regular classroom duties. So, for example, speech or English teachers may be required to sponsor a debate club but not have to coach an athletic team if they have no corresponding experience.

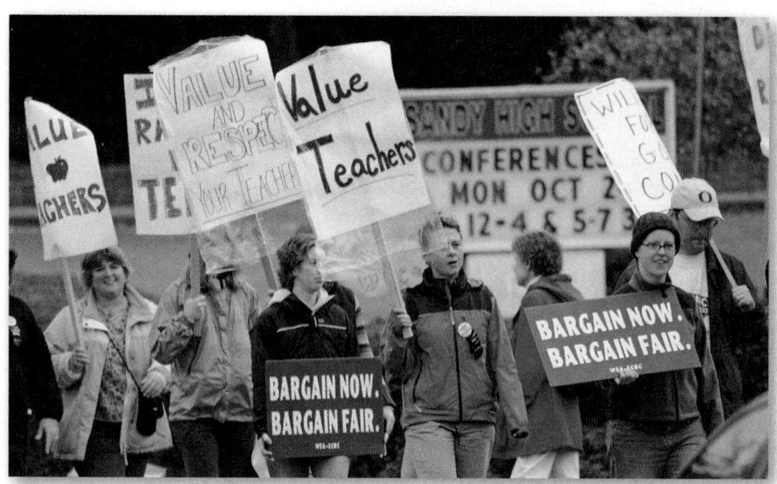

Collective bargaining between professional organizations and school districts determines teachers' salaries and working conditions.

Collective Bargaining

Many details of your contract, such as working conditions, class size, salaries, benefits, and transfer policies, will be determined by collective bargaining agreements between your school district and the local professional organization. Most teachers belong to either the NEA or the American Federation of Teachers (AFT), and the power of collective bargaining is a major reason they do.

Collective bargaining occurs when a local chapter of a professional organization negotiates with a school district over the rights of teachers and the conditions of employment. Legally, teachers have a constitutional right to join a professional organization but cannot be forced to do so (Schimmel, Stellman, et al., 2011). In most states, the law requires the local school board to negotiate with whatever professional organization represents the largest number of teachers in that district. The final agreement applies to all teachers in the district.

If teachers believe that a school district isn't meeting the terms of the contract they signed or believe that they are given unreasonable responsibilities or work conditions, they can file a grievance. A **grievance** is a formal complaint against an employer alleging unsatisfactory working conditions. When a teacher files a grievance, she is usually arguing that a working condition, such as class size or a teaching assignment, violates the teacher's contract. You cannot be dismissed for filing a grievance, and the professional organization that negotiates the contract with the district will usually provide legal counsel.

Teachers also have a limited right to strike in about half of the states. In the others, state legislatures group teachers with other employees such as police officers and firefighters, believing that the public welfare would suffer from a strike. Because of the variability between states related to strikes and items covered by collective bargaining, you should become familiar with the laws governing these issues. Professional organizations in your area are helpful in this regard.

Collective bargaining has become a political hot potato, with several states passing legislation to ban teachers from using it to bargain with school districts (Sawchuk, 2011c). Conservatives claim that collective bargaining was responsible for budget shortfalls in many districts; professional organizations such as NEA and AFT counter that collective bargaining is a necessary safeguard to ensure teacher rights and obtain a decent working wage. Lawsuits are now blocking the bills that have been passed, and the future of collective bargaining in some states is in question.

Tenure

Tenure is a legal safeguard that provides job security by preventing teacher dismissal without due cause. Tenure is designed to protect teachers from political or personal abuse and to ensure the stability of the teaching force. It's grounded in the principle asserting that teachers should be hired and fired on their professional merits and not because of personal connections or political views. Tenured teachers can be dismissed only for causes such as incompetence, immoral behavior, insubordination, or unprofessional conduct.

When any of these charges are filed, due process must be observed, and the teacher must be provided with the following (Sanchez, 2009):

- A written description of the charges and adequate time to prepare a rebuttal to them
- Access to evidence and the names of witnesses
- A hearing conducted before an impartial decision maker
- The right to representation by legal counsel and the opportunity to introduce evidence and cross-examine witnesses
- A school board decision based on the findings of the hearing
- A written record of the hearing and the right to appeal an adverse decision

These safeguards, guaranteed by the Fourteenth Amendment, provide you with the same constitutional protections enjoyed by the population at large.

Like collective bargaining, teacher tenure has also come under attack in several states (Sawchuk, 2011c). Critics claim that tenure has been used to protect incompetent teachers; proponents counter that it is necessary to protect teachers' job security and their ability to express opinions on controversial topics in the classroom. The public is divided on the topic of teacher unionization, with nearly half (47%) believing that it has hurt the quality of public education (Bushaw & Lopez, 2011). Much of the public's ambivalence toward unions can be traced to negative press about tenure and its perceived ability to protect teachers who aren't doing their jobs.

Dismissal

You'll work hard to become licensed and perhaps even harder to get a teaching position. You obviously won't want to lose your job, so it's important to understand your rights in the unlikely event that this occurs.

Most districts require a probationary period before tenure is granted—commonly 3 years. During this time, beginning teachers have a yearly contract, and you can be dismissed for a variety of reasons, such as overstaffing, reduced school enrollments, or evidence of incompetence. Although uncommon, some states require districts to provide a formal hearing on demand when a nontenured teacher is dismissed. If you're uncertain about your rights during this period, you should check with your district, state office of education, or professional organization.

Dishonesty on a job application can also result in a new teacher's dismissal. Students close to obtaining their degrees are sometimes offered positions during their internships. In some cases they agree but, because of unforeseen circumstances, are unable to graduate or obtain a license. When districts discover the problem, they can either dismiss the teachers or lower their status to substitute teacher, resulting in lower pay and loss of benefits.

Reduction in Force. Because of budget cuts, declining student numbers, or course or program cancellations, districts are sometimes forced to dismiss teachers. **Reduction in force**, or "riffing," as it's called in industry, is the elimination of teaching positions because of declining student enrollment or school funds. Typically, districts dismiss teachers with the least seniority; the last in are the first out. Fortunately, "riffing" occurs relatively infrequently as increasing numbers of students enter our educational system, but it can occur during difficult economic times, such as during the recent recession. Educational funding decreased in a number of states, as well as at the federal level, resulting in increased class sizes, as well as some teacher layoffs (Cavanagh, 2011b; Klein, 2011). When it is time to look for a teaching position, investigate the funding picture in your state or local district to make sure that your job will be secure in the future.

Reduction in force can involve both tenured and nontenured teachers and is regulated either by state law or by collective bargaining agreements (Schimmel, Stellman, et al., 2011). If you're faced with this possibility, you should consult representatives from your local professional organization.

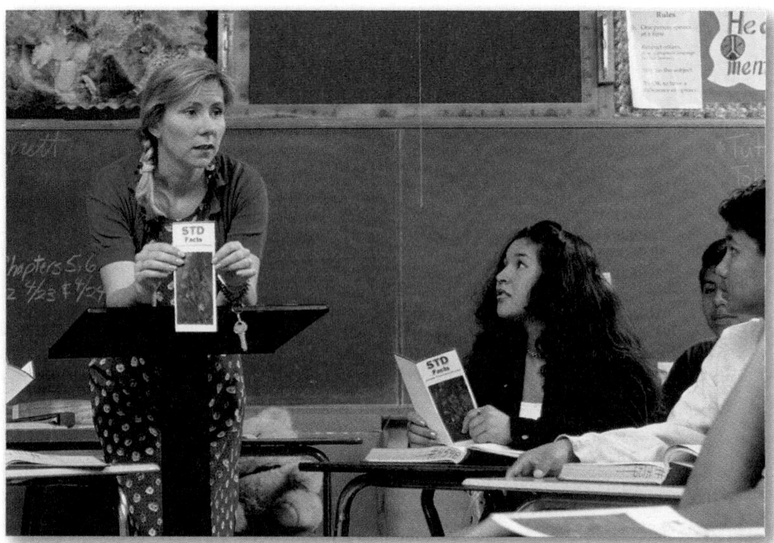

Academic freedom protects teachers' rights to choose both content as well as teaching methods.

Academic Freedom

Academic freedom refers to your right to choose both content and teaching methods based on your professional judgment. Freedom of speech is protected by the First Amendment, but academic freedom has limits. What are they? Consider these actual cases:

In an attempt to motivate his students, a teacher organized his classroom around a sports-competition theme called "Learnball." Dividing his students into teams, the teacher instituted a system of rewards that included playing the radio and shooting foam basketballs. His principal objected, and when the teacher refused to change his methods, he was fired. He sued to get his job back, claiming his freedom of speech had been violated. (*Bradley v. Pittsburgh Board of Education*, 1990)

An eleventh-grade English teacher was leading a discussion on taboo words. To illustrate his point, he wrote the four-letter slang word for sexual intercourse on the board. Parents complained, and the teacher was dismissed. He sued to get his job back, claiming his freedom of speech had been curtailed. (*Mailloux v. Kiley*, 1971)

Teaching and You

Most of us went into teaching because we wanted to help others grow and develop or because we wanted to share our love of a content area with our students. But what legal restrictions are there in terms of what we can discuss with our students?

You will be hired to teach a specific age group or curriculum, such as first grade, middle school science, or high school English. State and district curriculum frameworks exist to guide you, and they often identify required textbooks. Within this general framework, teachers are free to teach topics as they see fit. Sometimes these topics and methods are controversial and may result in a teacher's being disciplined or even dismissed, as in the cases you just saw.

In resolving disputes about academic freedom, the courts consider the following:

- Your goal in discussing a topic or using a method
- The age of the students involved
- The relevance of the materials to the course
- The quality or general acceptance of the questioned material or methods
- The existence of policies related to the issue

In the case of the teacher using the *Learnball* format, the courts upheld the district's dismissal. The court concluded that this teaching strategy was not widely accepted and that the teacher had been warned repeatedly by the administration to stop using it.

The opposite occurred in the case of the English teacher. The teacher's job was reinstated because the court upheld the importance of two kinds of academic freedom: (1) the "substantive" right to use a teaching method that serves a "demonstrated" purpose and (2) the procedural right not to be discharged for the use of a teaching method not prohibited by clear regulations. The teacher's goal was for his students to understand taboo words and how they influenced literature, a topic that fell under the broad umbrella of the English curriculum. Had this not been the case, or if the teacher had been clearly warned against using this strategy, the outcome would likely have been different.

When considering the discussion of controversial topics or the use of controversial methods, you should try to decide whether they fall within the scope of your assigned curriculum. In essence, teachers need to determine if they are speaking as public employees educating students (which is legal) or private citizens advocating a particular position (which is questionable). If you choose to move forward, you should have clear goals in mind and be able to defend them if objections arise (Berlin, 2009). Academic freedom protects knowledgeable, well-intentioned teachers working within their assigned responsibilities, but the legal process of defending the inclusion of questionable topics can be long and demanding (Zirkel, 2007). If you're uncertain about an issue that might involve academic freedom, you should check with your principal or other school administrator.

Grades and grading are also covered under academic freedom. In general, you are free to assign the grades you deem appropriate, with two caveats. First, your grading system should be consistent with accepted practice in the school and district, and second, you should be able to justify the grade with evidence based on student performance. If these requirements are met, courts rarely intervene in issues involving grading (Zirkel, 2008a).

Revisiting My Beliefs

This section addresses the first item in *This I Believe*, "As a teacher, I have the legal right to determine what is taught in my classroom." This statement is true: Academic freedom allows teachers to select content for their classrooms if the content is appropriate for their students and teaching assignment.

Copyright Laws

As teachers, we want to share the most current information with our students. This can involve copying information from newspapers, magazines, books, and even television programs. Sometimes, however, doing so can violate copyright laws (Schimmel, Stellman, et al., 2011).

Copyright laws are federal laws designed to protect the intellectual property of authors, which includes printed matter, videos, computer software, and other types of original work. Just as patents protect the intellectual work of inventors, copyright laws protect the work of print writers, filmmakers, software creators, songwriters, and graphic artists. Federal guidelines have been developed to balance the rights of authors with the legitimate needs of teachers and learners.

Fair-use guidelines are policies that specify limitations in the use of copyrighted materials for educational purposes. For example, you may make a single copy of a book chapter, newspaper or magazine article, short story, essay, or poem for planning purposes, and may copy short works (poems that are less than 250 words or prose that is less than 2,500 words) for one-time use in the classroom. However, you may not create class anthologies by copying material from several sources or charge students more than it cost them to copy the materials. In addition, pages from workbooks or other consumable materials may not be copied.

Videotapes and computer software pose unique challenges. They, too, were created by and belong to someone, and fair-use guidelines also apply to them. For example, you may record a television program, but you must use it within 10 days. You may show it again for reinforcement but must erase the recording after 45 days. One copy, and no more, of software may be made as a "backup." Materials on the Internet may not be copied unless specific permission is given or unless the document is published by the federal government.

These guidelines restrict teachers, but the restrictions are not usually a major handicap. You should also share the principle of fair use with your students as they work on projects in which they download materials from the Internet (D. Saltman, 2011). This can provide a "teachable moment" to help them understand its purpose and the ways that copyright laws help protect people.

Teacher Liability

Teaching and You

Have you ever been asked to care for a younger brother or sister? Or babysit someone else's child? Did you ever have to worry about their health or safety, or do something to ensure that the children in your care would be safe? How is that similar to what you'll encounter as a teacher?

An elementary teacher on playground duty was mingling with students, watching them as they ran around. After the teacher passed one group of students, a boy picked up and threw a rock that hit another boy in the eye, causing serious injury. The injured boy's parents sued the teacher for negligence. (*Fagen v. Summers*, 1972)

A teacher was taking a group of first graders on a school-sponsored field trip to the Oregon coast. While some of the students were wading in the water, a big wave rolled in, bringing a big log with it, and one of the children was seriously injured. The parents sued the teacher for negligence. (*Morris v. Douglas County School District*, 1965)

We don't typically think of schools as dangerous places, but large numbers of children in small spaces combined with youthful exuberance and energy can result in falls, scrapes, and accidents. And field trips, science labs, woodworking shops, and physical education classes pose special risks.

You are legally responsible for the safety of children under your supervision. The courts employ the principle of **in loco parentis**, which means "in place of the parents," in gauging the limits of teacher responsibility. In loco parentis requires teachers to use the same judgment and care as parents in protecting the children under their supervision. **Negligence** is a teacher's or other school employee's failure to exercise sufficient care in protecting students from injury. If negligence occurs, parents may bring a liability suit against you or your school district. Liability suits are a major concern of experienced teachers that influences their day-to-day professional decision making (Public Agenda, 2004).

In attempting to define the limits of your responsibilities as a teacher in liability cases, the courts consider whether you do the following:

- Make a reasonable attempt to anticipate dangerous conditions
- Take proper precautions, and establish rules and procedures to prevent injuries
- Warn students of possible dangerous situations
- Provide proper supervision

In applying these principles to the rock-throwing incident, the courts found no direct connection between the teacher's actions and the child's injury. The teacher was properly supervising the children, and events happened so quickly that she was unable to prevent the accident. Had she witnessed, and failed to stop, a similar incident, or had she left the playground for personal reasons, the court's decision would probably have been different.

Field trips pose special safety and legal challenges because of the dangers of transportation and the increased possibility of injury in unfamiliar surroundings. Many school districts ask parents to sign a consent form to inform them of the trip and release school personnel from liability in case of injury. These forms won't protect you from liability, however; even with signed forms, teachers are still responsible for the safety of the children in their care. The courts ruled in favor of the parents in the Oregon case, because this type of accident is fairly common on beaches along the Oregon coast. The teacher, they ruled, should have anticipated the accident and acted accordingly.

As you supervise, you need to consider the ages and developmental levels of students, as well as the type of classroom activity. Young children require more supervision, for example, as do some students with special needs. Science labs, cooking classes, use of certain equipment, and physical education classes pose special safety hazards. Professional organizations, such as the National Science Teachers Association, provide guidelines to help teachers avoid liability-causing situations in their classroom, and beginning teachers should be familiar with their guidelines. In addition, you should carefully plan ahead, anticipate potential dangers, and teach safety rules and procedures to all students.

In spite of conscientious planning, accidents can and do happen. Beginning teachers should consider the liability insurance offered by professional organizations, which provides legal assistance to members who are sued. In addition, new teachers should check with the districts that employ them for liability coverage. It's a good idea for all teachers, and if you're teaching in riskier areas such as science, vocational education, or sports, it's even more important.

Revisiting My Beliefs

This section addresses the second item in *This I Believe*, "I'm responsible for the safety of the students in my classroom." This statement is true. In loco parentis suggests that teachers are indeed responsible for the students in their care. Factors such as the age and intelligence of the students, as well as dangers inherent in a particular situation, should guide your actions as you work to protect the welfare of your students.

Child Abuse

Jimmy is a quiet, shy fourth grader. He rarely volunteers in class and seems to withdraw from interactions with the rest of the children. He is underweight, and efforts to sign him up for federally financed lunches have been rebuffed by his parents, who assert they don't need help from anyone.

One day you notice a bruise on Jimmy's face. When you talk to him at lunch break, he says he fell while playing, but there aren't any scrapes or abrasions typically associated with a fall. You ask him how things are at home, and his eyes fill with tears. You ask him if he wants to talk about it; he just shakes his head no. When you ask him if someone hit him, he blurts out, "Please don't say anything, or I'll get in trouble."

What are your responsibilities in this situation? The student begged you to say nothing; do you honor his request? The answer is no. All 50 states and the District of Columbia have laws requiring educators to report suspected child abuse (Schimmel, Stellman, et al., 2011). In addition, teachers are protected from legal action if you act in "good faith" and "without malice." If you suspect child abuse, you should immediately report the matter to school counselors or administrators. All schools have established procedures for dealing with cases of suspected child abuse, and these guidelines help you understand your role in the process.

Teachers' Private Lives

Mary Evans has taught in Chicago for more than 8 years and doesn't mind the long commute from the suburbs because it gives her an opportunity to "clear her head." She has been living with her boyfriend for several years, and everything has seemed fine until one day she discovers that she's pregnant. After lengthy discussions with her partner, she decides to keep the baby but not get married. When her pregnancy becomes noticeable, her principal calls her in. She affirms that she isn't married and doesn't intend to be. He asks for her resignation, suggesting she is a poor role model for her students.

Gary Hansen has lived with the same male roommate for several years. They are often seen shopping

Teachers have a right to their own private lives but must meet community standards of acceptable conduct.

together in the local community, and they even attend social events together. Students and other faculty "talk," but Gary ignores suggestions that he's homosexual until the principal calls him into his office, confronts him, and threatens dismissal.

Teaching and You

Have you ever done anything crazy, risky, or even illegal that you didn't want other people to know about? Most of us have. If these actions were to become common knowledge or widespread in your community, what effect would they have on your teaching career?

An individual's right to "life, liberty, and the pursuit of happiness" is one of our country's founding principles. What happens, however, when your lifestyle conflicts with those of the community where you work? Is your private life really "private," or can you be dismissed for what you do in your free time?

In answering these questions, the courts have relied on a definition of teaching that's broader than classroom instruction. Teachers do more than help students understand English and history, for example; they also serve as role models. As a result, teachers are scrutinized more closely than people in general. Other professionals, such as attorneys or physicians, might be able to lead lifestyles at odds with community values, but teachers might not. What are teachers' rights with respect to their private lives?

Clear answers don't exist. Morality and what constitutes a good role model are contextual. For example, in the 1800s, women's teaching contracts often required them to

- abstain from marriage
- be home between the hours of 8:00 P.M. and 6:00 A.M. unless attending school functions
- and wear dresses no more than 2 inches above the ankle

More recently, pregnant teachers were required, even if married, to take a leave of absence once their condition became noticeable. Obviously, views of morality change. As the California Supreme Court noted, "Today's morals may be tomorrow's ancient and absurd customs" (Schimmel, Stellman, et al., 2011, p. 278).

Moral standards also vary among communities: What's acceptable in large cities may not be in the suburbs or rural areas. Cities provide a measure of anonymity, and notoriety is one criterion courts use to decide whether your private activities damage your credibility as a role model. **Notoriety** describes the extent to which a teacher's behavior becomes known and is controversial. For example, many young people are choosing to live together as an alternative to marriage, and this lifestyle is obviously less noticeable in a large city than in smaller communities.

Where does this leave you? Generalizations such as "Consider the community in which you live and teach" provide some guidance, as do representative court cases. The law isn't clear and specific, however, with respect to teachers' private lives.

The issue of homosexuality illustrates how schools can become legal battlegrounds for people's differing values and beliefs. Some people believe that homosexuality is morally wrong and that people who are homosexual shouldn't be allowed to work with young people; others believe that whether a person is homosexual is irrelevant to schools and teaching. When the issue has gone to courts, they have generally ruled in favor of homosexual teachers. In a landmark California case, a teacher's homosexual relationship was reported to the state board of education, which revoked his license. The board argued that state law required teachers to be models of good conduct, and that homosexual behavior is inconsistent with the moral standards of the people of California (*Morrison v. State Board of Education,* 1969). The California Supreme Court disagreed, concluding that "immoral" was broad enough to be interpreted in a number of ways and stating that no evidence existed indicating that Morrison's behavior adversely affected his teaching effectiveness.

In other cases involving criminal or public sexual behavior, such as soliciting sex in a park, courts have ruled against teachers (Schimmel, Stellman, et al., 2011). Notoriety was a key element in these cases.

The case involving the unwed mother further illustrates the murkiness of school law. A case in Nebraska resulted in the dismissal of an unwed mother because the school board claimed there was "a rational connection between the plaintiff's pregnancy out of wedlock and the school board's interest in conserving marital values" (*Brown v. Bathhe,* 1976). In other cases, however, courts have ruled in favor of pregnant unwed teachers, including one in Ohio who became pregnant through artificial insemination (Schimmel, Stellman, et al., 2011).

Although the law is ambiguous with respect to teachers' private sexual lives, it is clear regarding sexual relations with students. Teachers are in a position of authority and trust, and any breach of this trust will result in dismissal. When teachers take sexual advantage of their students, they violate both legal and ethical standards.

Other teacher behaviors can also jeopardize your job. Drug offenses, excessive drinking, driving under the influence of alcohol, felony arrests, and even a misdemeanor, such as shoplifting, can result in dismissal (Schimmel, Stellman, et al., 2011). In *Teaching and You* we asked if you had ever done anything crazy, risky, or illegal. Hopefully if your answer was yes, that kind of behavior is in your past, because legal problems can jeopardize your teaching career. The message is clear: You are legally and ethically required to be a good role model for your students.

Revisiting My Beliefs

This section addresses the third item in *This I Believe*, "As a teacher, I will be held to the same moral standards as other citizens." This statement isn't true: You are, in fact, held to higher moral standards because you serve as a role model for your students.

One additional warning: Teachers should be aware that their classroom is considered part of the workplace; it isn't considered to be private property by the courts (Sanchez, 2009). If school officials have reason to suspect illegal activity, such as drug use, they can search your desk or file cabinets without a search warrant. Courts take student safety very seriously and are willing to allow districts wide latitude in ensuring that schools are safe places for students to learn.

Technology presents new challenges to teachers' rights in terms of their personal lives.

Teachers with AIDS

In determining the rights of teachers with AIDS (acquired immune deficiency syndrome) or HIV (human immunodeficiency virus) infections, the courts have used nondiscrimination as the legal principle guiding their decisions. The foundation for this principle was established in a case involving a Florida teacher with tuberculosis (*School Board of Nassau County, Florida v. Arline,* 1987). The courts' dilemma involved weighing the rights of the individual against the public's concern about the possible spread of disease. The U.S. Supreme Court ruled in favor of the teacher, considering the disease a handicap and protecting the teacher from discrimination because of it.

The Florida decision set a precedent for a California case involving a teacher with AIDS who had been removed from the classroom and reassigned to administrative duties (*Chalk v. U.S. District Court Cent. Dist. of California,* 1988). The court ruled in favor of the teacher, using medical opinion to argue that the teacher's right to employment outweighed the minor risk of communicating the AIDS virus to children.

Check Your Understanding

3.1. How are teacher employment issues influenced by the law?
3.2. What is academic freedom, and why is it important to teachers?
3.3. How do copyright laws influence teachers' practices?
3.4. What is teacher liability, and how does it influence teachers?
3.5. How are teachers' rights regarding their private lives similar to and different from those of the general public?

For feedback, go to the appendix, *Check Your Understanding,* located in the back of this text.

Teaching and You

Have you ever posted or written something on the Internet that you wished you hadn't? How hard was it to correct your mistake?

ISSUES YOU'LL FACE IN TEACHING

Technology and Restrictions on Teachers' Freedom to Communicate with Students

Technology opens doors for teachers, both personally and professionally. It allows us to communicate with friends, colleagues, and students easier than we ever have in the past. But recent legislation and court cases have raised a number of red flags about your rights and responsibilities in terms of your use of technologies such as the Internet and cell phones.

Technology is everywhere; Facebook announced its 500-millionth user in 2010, and 73% of American teenagers report using some form of social networking websites (Davis, 2010b). Teachers, as well as students, are also using Facebook to connect with others. But the openness of technologies such as Facebook to public scrutiny has raised questions about teacher privacy and their rights as employees.

In the past, students' peeks into their teachers' lives were running into them at the local grocery store. Now, students only have to log onto their computers to find their teachers' Facebook profiles, "Tweets," or personal blogs, and inappropriate information in these postings can cause problems when searching for, or trying to keep, jobs. Experts in this area advise, "Don't post anything that you wouldn't want on the front page of a newspaper" (A. Manning, 2010). One Massachusetts administrator was forced to resign after describing residents of her community as "snobby and arrogant" on her Facebook site. Interactions with parents may have led her to feel that way, but we're sure she didn't intend the whole world, including the parents she worked with, to know how she felt.

Teacher–student communications are another area of concern. In the past, teachers could talk openly one-to-one with students, only needing to keep the door to your classroom open to avoid any hint of impropriety. Cell phones and the Internet have changed that, providing opportunities for inappropriate relationships between teachers and their students.

State lawmakers have responded. In Louisiana, the legislature passed a law requiring teachers to document within 24 hours any electronic interaction with individual students through a non-school-issued device, such as a personal computer or cell phone (Ash, 2009). Missouri passed a similar law limiting teacher–student messaging, but repealed it months later after critics warned of legal and logistical problems (Associated Press, 2011c). Other states are considering similar restrictions on teacher's private text messages to students and social networking interactions between teachers and students (Gutierrez, 2012).

THE QUESTION

Are these recent legal restrictions on teachers' use of technologies beneficial, or even necessary, for teacher–student communication? Here are arguments on both sides of this complex legal issue.

PRO

- These laws provide both teachers and students with clear guidelines about appropriate and inappropriate teacher–student interactions.
- Parents want and need safeguards for their children's safety.
- The laws only target individual messages to students and allow group messages in which teachers can clarify assignments or provide group feedback about homework.

CON

- These laws create an atmosphere of fear and mistrust between teachers and students, and professional codes of ethics already address this issue.
- Laws such as these inhibit legitimate one-to-one communication between teachers and their students. The burden of documenting such interactions discourages teachers from communicating with their students.
- Coaches and sponsors of extracurricular activities, who often use their personal cell phones to coordinate last-minute logistical concerns, will be hampered by these restrictions.

YOU TAKE A STAND

Are legal attempts to restrict teachers' one-to-one communications with students a good idea or a step backward for the teaching profession?

Go to *Issues You'll Face in Teaching* in the MyEducationLab™ *Book Resources* that accompany this text to log your thoughts and receive feedback from your authors.

Religion and the Law

Religion provides fertile ground for helping us understand how conflicting views of education can result in legal challenges. Religion plays an important role in the lives of Americans. For example, 9 of 10 people claim a preference for some religious group, and nearly 6 of 10 regard their religious beliefs to be very important to them (Rose & Gallup, 2006; Winseman, 2005).

The First Amendment to the Constitution establishes the principle of separation of church and state:

> Congress shall make no law respecting an establishment of religion, or prohibiting the free exercise thereof; or abridging the freedom of speech, or of the press; or the right of the people peaceably to assemble, and to petition the Government for a redress of grievances.

Teaching and You

How religious are you? Do you ever discuss your religious beliefs with your friends? What will you do if one of your students asks, "Do you believe in God?" or "Do you go to church?"

Two of the clauses of this amendment present an important legal principle with implications for you as a teacher. The **establishment clause** prohibits the establishment of a national religion. The words "or prohibiting the free exercise thereof" is the **free exercise clause**, which prohibits the government from interfering with individuals' rights to hold religious beliefs and freely practice religion. The interpretation of both of these clauses has led to legal battles (McCarthy, 2009).

Because religion is central to people's lives, the issue of religion in schools is legally contentious, and educators are often caught in the crossfire. Important questions that have arisen include the following:

- Are students and teachers allowed to pray in schools?
- Can religion be included in the school curriculum?
- Are religious clubs allowed access to public school facilities?

We answer these questions in the sections that follow.

Although the Constitution forbids establishment of any particular religion in schools, a number of complex issues make this a controversial topic.

Prayer in Schools

In the past, prayer and scripture reading were common in many, if not most, schools. In fact, they were required by law in some states. For example, Pennsylvania passed legislation in 1959 that required daily Bible reading in the schools but exempted children whose parents didn't want them to participate. The law was challenged, and the U.S. Supreme Court ruled that it violated the First Amendment's establishment clause (*Abington School District v. Schempp,* 1963). Nondenominational or generic prayers designed to skirt the issue have also been outlawed. In a New York case, the Supreme Court held that generic prayers also violated the establishment clause (*Engle v. Vitale,* 1962). Neither schools nor teachers can officially encourage student prayer; prayer is permissible, however, when student initiated and when it doesn't interfere with other students or the functioning of the school (LaMorte, 2012).

The law also forbids the official use of religious symbols in schools. For example, the courts ruled that a 2-by-3-foot portrait of Jesus Christ displayed in the hallway next to the principal's office was unconstitutional (Schimmel, Stellman, et al., 2011). Also, the U.S. Supreme Court struck down a Kentucky law requiring that the Ten Commandments be posted in school classrooms (*Stone v. Graham,* 1981).

These cases illustrate a clear legal trend: Officially sanctioned prayer and religious symbols—whether they come from school boards, principals, or teachers—violate the principle of separation of church and state and are not allowed in public schools (Sorenson, 2007). Students may be Christians, Jews, Muslims, Buddhists, Hindus, or members of other religions. Imposing a particular form of prayer or religion on children in a school is both illegal and unethical, because it can exclude children on the basis of religion. On the other hand, schools cannot—nor should they want to—prohibit students from praying in private.

Although the courts have been clear about denying prayer as a regular part of schools' opening ceremonies, the issue of prayer at graduation and other school activities is less clear, however. In a landmark case, a high school principal asked a clergyman to provide the graduation invocation and also suggested the content of the prayer. The U.S. Supreme Court ruled that this was a violation of separation of church and state (*Lee v. Weismann,* 1992). The school's involvement in the prayer was the key point; it is uncertain whether the Court would have banned the prayer if students or parents had initiated it. The Supreme Court also voted 6–3 against student-led prayers at football games in Texas (Walsh, 2000); the Court concluded that students would perceive the pregame prayer as "stamped with the school's seal of approval," thus violating separation of church and state.

In a recent twist on the school prayer issue, several states have instituted mandatory moments of silence in schools (Zirkel, 2010b). Critics contend these pauses are nothing more than veiled attempts to institute a minute of prayer; advocates say they are designed to help students relax and focus on the day ahead. Courts have used the "Lemon" test to judge the legality of these moments of silence, named after a landmark legal case in this area (*Lemon v. Kurtzman,* 1971). In applying the test, the courts ask these questions:

- Is there a secular purpose to the practice?
- Is the primary effect to advance or inhibit religion?
- Does the practice avoid excessive government entanglement in issues of religion?

When applying these criteria to state laws, the courts look to the reasons behind the laws (Darden, 2008a). If the reasons are secular, the laws are allowed to stand; if religious intents are involved, the laws are ruled unconstitutional.

Revisiting My Beliefs

This section addresses the fourth item in *This I Believe*, "The law prohibits any form of prayer in the schools." This statement isn't true. The law doesn't prohibit prayer in the schools per se. Students can legally pray in school, but neither school officials nor teachers can lead or sanction organized prayer in schools.

Religious Clubs and Organizations

Organized prayer in schools is illegal, but it may be legal for extracurricular religious clubs to meet on school grounds. In one instance, a student in Omaha, Nebraska, requested permission to meet with her Bible study group before school. Officials refused, concerned about the possibility of undesirable groups, such as the Ku Klux Klan, using the case as precedent. The U.S. Supreme Court ruled in the student's favor, stating that schools must allow religious, philosophical, and political groups to use school facilities in the same ways as other extracurricular organizations (*Board of Education of the Westside Community School v. Mergens,* 1990). The fact that the club was not school sponsored or initiated was central to the Court's argument.

Religion in the Curriculum

A high school biology teacher prefaces his presentation on evolution with a warning, stating that it is only a "theory" and that many theories have been proven wrong in the past. He encourages students to keep an open mind and offers creationism, or the Biblical version of the origin of the world, as an alternative theory. As part of his presentation, he holds up a pamphlet, published by a religious organization; the pamphlet refutes evolution and argues that creationism provides a more valid explanation. He offers the pamphlets to interested students.

Where does religion fit in the school curriculum? Can a well-intentioned teacher use the classroom to promote religious views? Given court decisions on school prayer, "no" or "never," is the simple answer. But this issue isn't that simple.

Evolution is an example. Concern over this issue dates back to the famous 1925 "Scopes Monkey Trial," in which a high school teacher, John Scopes, was prosecuted for violating a Tennessee state law that made it illegal to teach any theory that denied the Bible's version of divine creation. Scopes argued that the law violated his academic freedom, contending that the theory of evolution had scientific merit and should be shared with his high school biology students. In a highly publicized trial, Scopes was found guilty of violating the state law and fined $100, but the decision was later reversed on a technicality.

Several states have since attempted to use legislation to resolve the evolution issue (Schimmel, Stellman, et al., 2011). In the 1960s, the Arkansas legislature passed a law banning the teaching of evolution in that state. The U.S. Supreme Court declared the law unconstitutional, because it violated the establishment clause of the First Amendment. In 1982, the Louisiana legislature, trying to create a middle ground, passed a "Balanced Treatment Act," requiring that evolution and creationism be given equal treatment in the curriculum. The U.S. Supreme Court also threw this law out, arguing that instead of being balanced, it was designed to promote a particular religious viewpoint.

In a more recent case involving religion in the public schools, a federal judge in Pennsylvania ruled that intelligent design did not qualify as a scientific theory (Cavanagh, 2006b). *Intelligent design* is the belief that the complexity we see in living things, including humans, is the result of some unnamed guiding force. The Dover, Pennsylvania, school board voted to require that intelligent design be taught as an alternative to evolution. Parents in the district sued, claiming that intelligent design was an attempt to interject religion into the public schools. The courts agreed, concluding, "The overwhelming evidence at trial established that ID [intelligent design] is a religious view, a mere relabeling of creationism, and not a scientific theory" (Cavanagh, 2006b, p. 10). Although the court's ruling had legal standing only in the U.S. District Court for the Middle District of Pennsylvania, legal experts predict that the legal precedent it established will carry considerable weight in future cases involving intelligent design.

The broader issue of religion in the curriculum has also surfaced in several other court cases. In Tennessee, fundamentalist parents objected to including literature such as *The Wizard of Oz, Rumpelstiltskin*, and *Macbeth* in the curriculum, arguing that these works exposed children to feminism, witchcraft, pacifism, and vegetarianism. A lower court supported the parents, but a higher federal court reversed the decision, asserting that accommodating every parent's religious claims would "leave public education goals in shreds." It supported the right of districts to use religiously controversial materials if they were useful in achieving important educational goals (*Mozert v. Hawkins County Public Schools*, 1987, 1988). Comparable cases in Alabama (*Smith v. Board of School Commissioners of Mobile County*, 1987) and Illinois (*Fleischfresser v. Directors of School District No. 200*, 1994) resulted in similar outcomes. When schools can show that learning materials have a clear purpose, such as exposing students to time-honored literature, parental objections are usually overridden.

EXPLORING DIVERSITY: Teaching About Religion in the Schools

Unfortunately, legal controversies have had a dampening effect on teaching about religion in schools (Hutton, 2008). Here we emphasize the difference between teaching *about different religions* and *advocating a particular one*. Religion has had an enormous impact on art, literature, and history (e.g., the Crusades, New World exploration). Avoiding the study of religion leaves students in a cultural vacuum that shortchanges their education.

But how can schools teach about religion without provoking religious controversies? Educators across the country wrestled with this problem and developed the following guidelines (Haynes, 2008):

- Teachers and administrators in public schools should not advocate any religion.
- Public schools should not interfere with or intrude on a student's religious beliefs.
- Public schools may teach about the history of religion, comparative religions, the Bible as literature, and the role of religion in the history of the United States and other countries.

Experts caution that the Bible should not be used as a history textbook, should not be taught exclusively from a Christian perspective, and should not be used to promote the Christian faith or Christian values (Hutton, 2008). In addition, a student paper in a comparative religions class can include religious references and opinions, but it would be inappropriate for that student to present that paper to promote one religion over another (Berlin, 2009). To address this issue, the First Amendment Center, a national organization promoting free speech, published the guidelines *The Bible and Public Schools: A First Amendment Guide* (First Amendment Center, 1999). The guidelines, endorsed by the NEA, the AFT, and the National School Boards Association, recommend using secondary sources to provide additional scholarly perspectives with respect to the Bible as a historical document. These guidelines seem straightforward, but future legal battles over this emotion-laden issue are likely.

DIVERSITY AND YOU

Religion and the Community in Which You'll Teach

The English department in a rural high school is in the middle of their monthly departmental meeting. After a review of next year's budget issues and scheduling problems, the chair of the department asks if anyone has questions or problems they'd like to discuss. You're a first-year teacher and just had an unpleasant discussion with a parent on the phone. You had just begun a unit on American novels, and in your overview of the subject, you brought in a Bible, held it up, and discussed how it had influenced works such as *Moby Dick*, *The Scarlet Letter,* and even *To Kill a Mockingbird.* The parent was irate about the use of the Bible in a public school class, claiming it had no place in the curriculum. You ask for advice. The chair looks around the room with a smile and asks, "Any advice for the newest member of our faculty?"

"Welcome to Greensburg," Harry, a grizzled veteran of 30 years, replies. "We should have warned you. A third of the parents don't want any religion in the school, a third want their religion, and a third don't care. I steer away from any mention of religion in my literature classes. It's just not worth the hassle."

"Oh, Harry," Karen responds with an exasperated sigh. "What kind of advice is that for a new teacher? Anyone who knows anything about American literature knows that religion played a major role in shaping its themes. You can't do an honest analysis of any major work without discussing the cultural context of the times."

"Yeah, but good luck if you try," Steve, a 4-year veteran, interjects. "When we studied English literature, and I talked about King Arthur and the Crusades, I thought it would be useful if the students know a little about the Muslim religion and conflicts with Christianity over the years. I received several irate calls from parents about promoting Islam. You'd think I was trying to start a mosque here in Greensburg. Luckily, our principal covered my back, but we both concluded that this might not be the best topic to teach right now, especially with all the 9/11 stuff and the wars in Iraq and Afghanistan."

QUESTIONS TO CONSIDER

1. What is the legal status of teaching about religion in the schools?
2. What other factors might influence the advice you give to this first-year teacher about teaching about religion and literature?

Go to *Diversity and You* in the MyEducationLab™ *Book Resources* that accompany this text to log your thoughts and receive feedback from your authors.

Check Your Understanding

4.1. Describe the legal implications of religion in the schools.
4.2. What is the legal status of prayer in schools?
4.3. Can a school allow religious clubs or organizations to meet on school grounds?
4.4. What is the legal status of religion in the curriculum?

For feedback, go to the appendix, *Check Your Understanding*, located in the back of this text.

Students' Rights and Responsibilities

The law also helps define students' rights and responsibilities, and understanding them can guide you in your work with students. Students' rights and responsibilities fall into seven general areas, outlined in Figure 8.2 and discussed in the sections that follow.

Students' Rights in Speech and Dress

Many parents in an urban middle school are advocating mandatory school uniforms. They believe that wearing uniforms would reduce classroom management problems, discourage the display of gang colors, and minimize social comparisons between wealthy students and those less fortunate. The school administration supports the proposal.

The student editors of the school newspaper hear of this proposal and conduct a poll of students, which indicates that a majority is opposed to uniforms. The editors want to publish these results along with an editorial arguing for student choice in what to wear. The principal refuses to let them print the article. What are students' rights in this matter?

As you've seen throughout this chapter, the First Amendment guarantees citizens freedom of speech, and we want our students to understand and appreciate this right as they prepare to be responsible citizens. Do they retain this right when

FIGURE 8.2 **Students' Rights and Responsibilities**

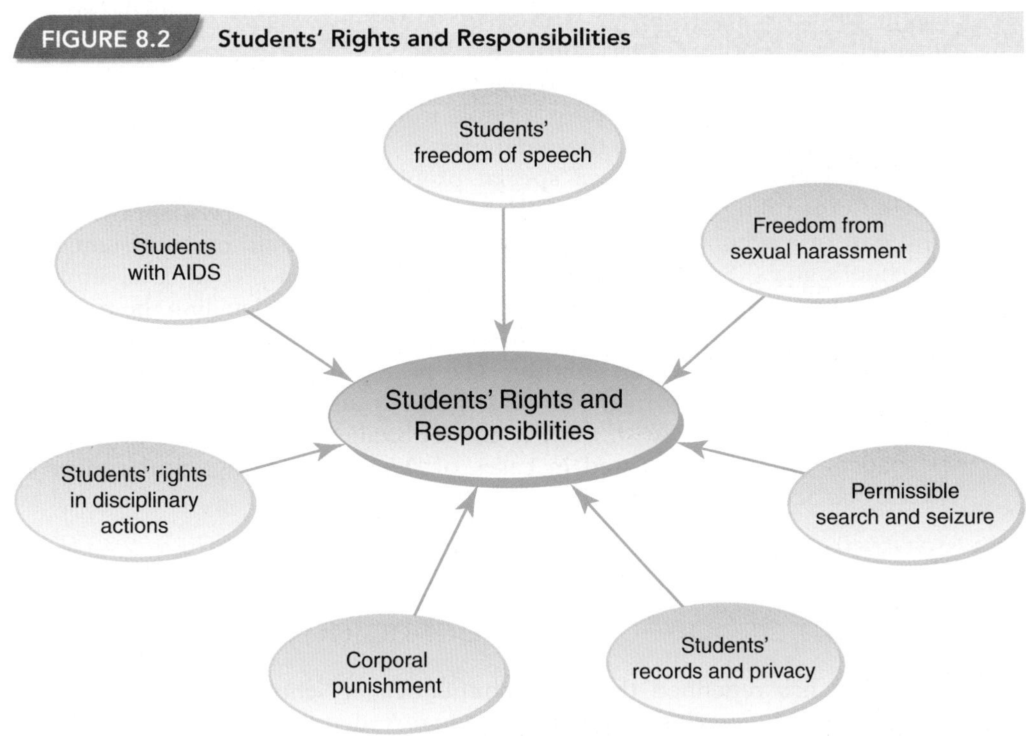

they enter schools? The answer is *yes*, but within limits: They have the right to express themselves in schools provided doing so doesn't interfere with learning.

A landmark case in this area occurred during the peak of the controversial Vietnam War. As a protest against the war, three high school students wore black armbands to school, despite the school's ban on such protests (*Tinker v. Des Moines Community School District*, 1969). When the students were suspended, they sued the district, arguing that the suspensions violated their freedom of speech. The case went all the way to the U.S. Supreme Court, which ruled in favor of the students. The Court ruled that freedom of speech is a right of all citizens, and students' freedom of expression should not be curtailed if it isn't disruptive and doesn't interfere with the educational mission of the schools (Cambron-McCabe, 2009; Fossey & Russo, 2008).

Students' freedom of speech was tested again in 1986. During a high school assembly held to nominate student government leaders, a student made a speech that contained an explicit metaphor comparing a candidate to a male sex organ. Not surprisingly, students in the audience hooted, made sexual gestures, and became disruptive. The student was reprimanded, and he sued, claiming his freedom of speech had been curtailed. This case also went to the U.S. Supreme Court, which ruled that "schools . . . may determine that the essential lessons of civil, mature conduct cannot be conveyed in a school that tolerates lewd, indecent or offensive speech" (*Bethel School District No. 403 v. Fraser*, 1986). In this instance, the court ruled that the school didn't violate the student's freedom of speech because the speech interfered with learning (Cambron-McCabe, 2009).

In a more recent, and bizarre, case involving student freedom of expression, a student unfurled a banner announcing "Bong Hits for Jesus" while his high school was given released time to watch a parade carrying the Olympic torch to the 2002 Winter Olympics. The banner made national news, and school officials, embarrassed by the unwelcome publicity, suspended the student for 10 days for actions advocating drug use (Greenhouse, 2007). The student sued, claiming this was only a prank to get on TV, and that the school was unlawfully limiting his freedom of speech. After several lengthy court cases, the issue landed in the U.S. Supreme Court, which ruled in a 6–3 vote that the school district had acted legally in reprimanding the boy. Justice Roberts, speaking for the majority, noted that the principal who suspended the student acted properly, and "[F]ailing to act would send a powerful message to the students in her charge . . . about how serious the school was about the dangers of illegal drug use." He added, "The First Amendment does not require schools to tolerate at school events student expression that contributes to those dangers."

School newspapers pose a special problem with respect to freedom of speech. Court rulings usually reflect the idea that a school newspaper is an integral part of a school's extracurricular activities and should be consistent with the school's goals (Schimmel, Stellman, et al., 2011). In a pivotal case, students working on a newspaper wanted to print two articles, one detailing the personal stories of three anonymous, pregnant teenage students, and the other dealing with the effects of divorce on children. The principal objected, arguing that the students in the first story might be identified because of details in the articles. The newspaper authors sued, but the U.S. Supreme Court decided that school newspapers could be regulated in cases of "legitimate pedagogical concerns" (*Hazelwood School District v. Kuhlmeier*, 1988).

TECHNOLOGY and TEACHING: Students' Freedom of Speech and Technology

Technology has redefined the legal boundaries of schools' control over student speech and behavior. In years past, when students left school grounds, the influence of district policies ended at school boundaries, superseded by home and parents. The introduction of cell phones and the Internet has erased that boundary and made legal issues surrounding students' freedom of speech more complex.

Our students live in a world of social technology; most teenagers consider the Internet and texting as a normal, if not essential, part of their everyday lives. But these changes in society have also resulted in new definitions of students' rights. These changes are evident in three major areas: freedom of speech, sexting, and cyberbullying.

Students' Freedom of Speech

Student freedom of speech is protected by the First Amendment, but what happens when student electronic messages hurt others or disrupt school functioning? Two recent court cases illustrate the complexity of the issues.

Students in two different Pennsylvania schools created mock MySpace profiles featuring profiles of their principals. Both contained outrageous and unbelievable statements about the principles (e.g., one called the principal a "big whore," and "sex addict," and the other claimed the principal was "big marijuana-smoking steroid freak"). Students in both incidents, who at the time thought this was pretty funny, were suspended and subsequently took their cases to court, claiming their First Amendment rights were violated.

What would you do if you were the judge on these cases? Interestingly, separate courts delivered two different opinions (Paulson, 2010; Zirkel, 2010a). One U.S. Circuit Court of Appeals concluded that the schools could legally suspend the students because these actions were necessary to preserve the principal's authority and avert future disruptions. The other court reached just the opposite conclusion, protecting the student's First Amendment rights and asserting that the school had failed to prove that the posting had significantly disrupted the teaching environment. These contradictory rulings confirm that the whole issue of student freedom of speech on the Internet is currently murky, uncertain territory (Walsh, 2012).

A second case involving electronic freedom of speech focused on the issue of school safety.

Six middle school girls in Nevada posted an "Attack a Teacher Day" message on a Facebook page. The students claimed it was just meant as a joke, but they were suspended from school and arrested on the same day that a teenage student in Omaha, Nebraska, fatally shot an assistant principal, wounded the principal, and then took his own life (Associated Press, 2011b).

The ultimate outcomes of these legal actions were not known at the time this edition of your book was published, but they point to the complexities of issues surrounding the incidents. Can schools control the contents of students' private e-mail messages, and what are the limits to students' freedom of speech? Future court decisions will help answer these questions.

Cyberbullying

Bullying has always been a problem in our schools, but technology has added a new dimension to the problem. A recent informal poll of seventh graders revealed that 45% had been cyberbullied (Hoffman, 2010). Adjectives like "ho," "skank," and "fat bitch," appear frequently in students' postings about other students, and both parents and school officials are taking action. Cyberbullying becomes a serious problem when it places other students' mental health or lives at risk.

In a well-publicized case of cyberbullying involving a gay college student, a roommate secretly videotaped a homosexual encounter and posted the video on the Internet. The student was so devastated by the "outing" that he committed suicide by jumping off a bridge 200 feet into the Hudson River (Hampson, Leinwand, & Marcus, 2010). Other cyberbullying incidents at the middle and high schools levels have resulted in similar teen suicides.

Cyberbullying hurts, but what schools and teachers can legally do about it is not clear. Schools can regulate school computer use, but their control over students' personal computers is marginal at best (Schimmel, Stellman, et al., 2011). Courts are increasingly skeptical about limiting students' freedom of speech in the absence of clear evidence that a particular behavior is disrupting the school's normal functioning. However, individual teachers can help address this problem by the stance they take in their classrooms, both toward bullying and cyberbullying. You can make clear your feelings about the negative effects of both and about how bullying, in whatever form, negatively affects everyone in your classroom. If enough teachers do this, bullying in schools can be reduced.

Sexting

Sexting, in which students send sexual photos, videos, or texts from one cell phone to another, presents another challenge related to the limits of student free speech. A first question to ask about sexting is, "Why would anyone in their right mind want to broadcast naked pictures of themselves?" The simple answer is they don't, and the key idea is "broadcast." Typically, these pictures are sent to one person, and the person sending them either doesn't realize or doesn't think about the fact that they might be shared with the world at large. Surveys vary about the prevalence of sexting; one found that 5% of teenagers had sent such messages (Hoffman, 2011), whereas another reported a figure as high as 20% (Manzo, 2009a).

In addition to the personal embarrassment involved, sexting can also become a form of cyberbullying. One Ohio teenager committed suicide after the nude photos she sent her boyfriend via her cell phone were shared with classmates (Manzo, 2009a).

Again, the limits of student free speech and schools' abilities to limit it are being tested. School authorities, interested in protecting students from harm, actively discourage the practice but are sometimes hesitant to become involved in personal matters affecting students' mental health and their lives. Unfortunately, students often don't realize that these messages can go viral, can spread all over the Internet (and their school), and can qualify as child pornography, if the subject is under 18.

Student Dress Codes

Look around you as you go to class, and notice the different ways that students dress. How we dress is often an expression of who we are, but is student dress an aspect of free speech covered by the First Amendment? The answer is complex, as you saw in the case involving student protests against the Vietnam War. Recognizing the complexity of the issue and the need for local norms, the Supreme Court has repeatedly refused to become embroiled in issues such as hair and skirt length, leaving them to lower courts instead (LaMorte, 2012). As a result, whether dress is considered a form of student expression depends on the state and its circuit court.

The dress code issue actually has two sides, clothing that is prohibited, and clothing, such as uniforms, that is required (Darden, 2008b). Schools have banned clothes such as tank or tube tops; ripped, baggy, or saggy pants; pajama tops or bottoms; sweat pants; hats; hooded sweatshirts; and athletic wear associated with local gangs. Courts usually ask if the restrictions contribute to positive school learning environments when considering whether they're legal. For example, student dress that is sexually suggestive can be banned because it can distract other students.

Messages and images on T-shirts have also raised the issue of students' freedom of speech. In one case, a Virginia middle school banned a T-shirt with a National Rifle Association Shooting Sports Camp logo on the back containing three figures holding or shooting guns. The parents of the student objected, and the courts agreed, saying there was no link between the T-shirt and the district's ability to run safe and manageable schools (Galley, 2004). In a second case, schools banned a student from wearing a T-shirt with the message "Homosexuality is shameful." A federal court upheld the ban, arguing that schools can limit a student's right to free speech when the content of that speech harms other students (Trotter, 2006). This means that schools can prohibit students from saying things at school that demean students who are members of particular groups, such as gay, Black, Islamic, and Jewish (Mercurio & Morse, 2007). School officials should protect students' freedom of speech but must also protect the rights of others and maintain the efficient operation of their schools.

School Uniforms

Largely in response to students' wearing gang colors, a growing number of public schools are requiring school uniforms. Proponents claim that gang clothing and designer sports clothes contribute to violence and delinquency. Initial experiments in Baltimore and Long Beach, California, were promising, resulting in better student behavior. A number of districts, including those in New York, Chicago, Miami, and Phoenix, allowed schools to require uniforms (Konheim-Kalkstein, 2006).

Proponents of school uniforms argue that they contribute to improved classroom behavior and respect for teachers, increased school attendance, better academic performance, lower clothing costs, reduced social stratification, and lower rates of crime and violence (Konheim-Kalkstein, 2006). Although uniforms are popular with parents and administrators, critics counter that requiring them violates students' rights, students will find other ways to compete, and uniforms have minimal effect on either behavior or achievement. Instead, they argue, the positive effects are due to greater parental involvement in the school and a visible and public symbol of commitment to school improvement and reform (DeMitchele, 2007).

Currently, half the states have at least one district that requires school uniforms, and the figure is likely to increase in the future (LaMorte, 2012). The courts have generally supported the use of mandatory school uniforms, concluding that they contribute to improved student behavior (Schimmel, Stellman, et al., 2011).

The complex issue of students' rights with respect to freedom of speech can become an effective framework for teaching students about the law. But what, exactly, should you strive for when you teach your students about freedom of speech? At one level you want to them to express their opinions about controversial topics, because the discussions promote learning and because the process prepares them to take stands and describe their views later in life. But students also need to understand that individual freedoms have limits; for example, they don't have the right to infringe on the rights of others. By encouraging open exchange of ideas while reminding students of their responsibilities to one another, you can create a classroom that becomes a model of democracy. This is a powerful and worthwhile ideal.

Sexual Harassment

One right that all students should have is freedom from unwanted and unwelcome sexual behavior that interferes with their lives. Unfortunately, sexual harassment is common on many school campuses, and students and their parents have resorted to courts to curtail the problem.

A landmark case involving sexual harassment in Georgia made its way to the U.S. Supreme Court (Schimmel, Stellman, et al., 2011). Parents of a fifth-grade student sued the school district after several months of repeated warnings from the parents failed to eliminate unwanted touching and sexual comments. The Supreme Court ruled that the district was liable for damages because it had failed to address the problem.

You are central to addressing this problem, because you are in a position to monitor student actions, both in your classrooms and hallways. You should clearly communicate that sexual harassment in any form will not be tolerated and that that the school you work in is a safe place for all students.

School officials may search student lockers if they have probable cause to believe these contain something illegal or dangerous.

Permissible Search and Seizure

Students' rights are important, but what happens when these rights conflict with school safety issues? The Fourth Amendment to the Constitution protects citizens from unlawful search and seizure, and warrants are required before a person or that person's property can be searched. How do these protections apply to students? Again, educators face dilemmas. We don't want to run our schools like prisons or teach students that personal privacy is not a right. But because drug and alcohol use and violence on school campuses remain persistent problems, many leaders feel compelled to search students and their property or even use entryway metal detectors and surveillance cameras to maintain safe schools (Warnick, 2007). Where do courts draw the line on the issue?

The issue of unlawful search and seizure surfaced in New Jersey in the 1980s when a teacher discovered two girls smoking cigarettes in a high school restroom. When questioned by the vice principal, one admitted smoking, and the other, T.L.O., denied the charge. The vice principal opened T.L.O.'s purse and found both cigarettes and rolling papers, which prompted him to empty the purse, where he discovered marijuana, a pipe, empty plastic bags, a number of dollar bills, and a list titled "People who owe me money" (*New Jersey v. T.L.O.*, 1985). T.L.O. confessed that she had been selling marijuana at school and was sentenced to a year's probation by the juvenile court.

T.L.O. appealed the ruling, claiming that she was the victim of an illegal search. The U.S. Supreme Court reviewed the evidence and upheld both the verdict and the legality of the search, concluding that school searches are legal if they target a specific problem. But schools must have probable cause to conduct the search; that is, they must have a reasonable suspicion that the student being searched deserves the treatment (Berlin, 2009).

In addition to probable cause, the nature of the search is important: Does it involve passing through a metal detector or opening a school bag, or is it more intrusive? The courts have consistently upheld the legality of metal detectors at school entrances, asserting that such searches are nonintrusive (Schimmel, Stellman, et al., 2011).

More intrusive strip searches, however, are generally considered illegal. In one case, a high school student was strip-searched after a police dog mistakenly identified her as carrying drugs. (Authorities later found that the dog was drawn to the girl because earlier in the day she had been playing with her dog, which was in heat.) The school district was required to pay damages to the girl's family (*Doe v. Renfrow*, 1980). In a more recent case, high school students were required to strip to their underwear in an attempt to recover missing money ($364). A federal circuit court found the search unconstitutional, concluding that the missing money did not justify the intrusiveness of the search (Hendrie, 2005a). While condoning searches for probable cause, the courts remain sensitive to the rights of students (Zirkel, 2009). School lockers, however, are considered school property and may be searched if reasonable cause, such as suspicion of drug or weapon possession, exists.

The use of urine tests to detect drug use illustrates how legal issues can become convoluted. In one case, the Supreme Court held that random drug testing for student athletes was legal, arguing that the safety of students and the importance of a drug-free school environment outweighed the privacy rights of student athletes who were participating voluntarily (*Board of Education of Independent School District No. 92 of Pottawatomie County v. Earls*, 2002). Despite this ruling, which involved students in voluntary school activities, the courts have been unanimous in prohibiting school-wide drug testing (Underwood & Webb, 2006).

In a twist on the issue of student monitoring, several Texas districts are using micro computer chips embedded in name tags to keep track of students while they're in school (Radcliffe, 2010). School officials claim these tracking devices make keeping student attendance records more efficient and can also help find missing students during emergencies such as fires. Critics, however, question whether these tags could be illegally hacked into by predators and whether these devices violate students' privacy, a topic we'll explore in the next section.

Student Records and Privacy

Students' records—grades, standardized test scores, teacher comments, and letters of recommendation—can determine whether they are admitted to special programs or colleges of their choice. School records can also influence students' ability to get jobs. What legal safeguards guide the creation and use of these records?

In 1974, Congress passed the Family Educational Rights and Privacy Act (FERPA) as an amendment to the Elementary and Secondary Education Act of 1965. Also called the **Buckley Amendment**, FERPA is a federal act that makes school records accessible to students and their parents. Under this act, schools must:

1. Inform parents of their rights regarding their child's records.
2. Provide parents access to their child's records.
3. Maintain procedures that allow parents to challenge and possibly amend information that they believe is inaccurate.
4. Protect parents from disclosure of confidential information to third parties without their consent.

The law doesn't guarantee access to all student records, however. For example, you may jot down notes during a busy school day, such as reminders about a student's behavior that will help you decide whether to refer a child for special education testing; these notes can't be made public without the your consent. Also, a teacher's letter of recommendation may remain confidential if students waive their rights to access. To protect teachers in these situations, the Buckley Amendment excludes teachers' private notes, grade books, or correspondence with administrators.

A court case in Oklahoma further defined the types of information protected by the Buckley Amendment (LaMorte, 2012). A mother objected to the practice of having her children's papers graded by other students and the results called out in class; she claimed this violated her children's rights to privacy, and a federal circuit court agreed. But in a unanimous decision, the Supreme Court overturned the lower court's decision, concluding that the term *education records* didn't cover student homework or classroom work.

Administrators and teachers have mixed feelings about the Buckley Amendment because of the extra effort and paperwork required to put the procedural safeguards into place, and because of potential encroachments into teachers' private records. The law has improved parents' access to information, however, and it has made school officials more sensitive to the importance of confidentiality in dealing with students' and parents' needs for information.

Corporal Punishment

In a Pennsylvania elementary school, a 36-year-old, 6-foot, 210-pound school principal paddled a 45-pound first-grade boy four times during one school day for a total of 60 to 70 swats. After the incident, the boy needed psychological counseling, cried frequently, and had nightmares and trouble sleeping. (*Commonwealth of Pennsylvania v. Douglass,* 1991)

The Fayette County Board of Education in Tennessee specified in 1994 that any paddles used to discipline students must be

- Not less than 3/8 inch or more than 1/2 inch thick
- Free of splinters
- Constructed of quality white ash
- Three inches wide (except the handle) and not more than 15 inches long for grades K–5
- Three and a half inches wide (except the handle), and not more than 18 inches long for grades 6–12

Students could receive a maximum of three swats with these district-approved paddles. (R. Johnston, 1994)

Fortunately times have changed. **Corporal punishment**—the use of physical, punitive disciplinary actions to correct student misbehavior—is highly controversial, because of the legal issues involved and the questionable effects of using physical punishment as a disciplinary tool. In a 1977 landmark case, the Supreme Court ruled that corporal punishment isn't a violation of the Eighth Amendment to the Constitution, which prohibits cruel and unusual punishment. The Court further ruled that states may authorize corporal punishment without either prior hearing or prior permission of parents (*Ingraham v. Wright*, 1977). In the 2007 school year, corporal punishment was used with almost a quarter of a million students and is much more common in the South, where it is embedded in the cultural and social fabric (Frosch, 2011). It is currently prohibited in 30 states and the District of Columbia, which means the door is left open for the use of corporal punishment in the remaining 20 states. Unfortunately, research also indicates that where it is legal, corporal punishment is more than twice as likely to be used on cultural minorities, such as black and Native American students, than on those who are white (Quaid, 2008). So where does all this leave you?

In states where corporal punishment is permitted, legal guidelines suggest teachers may use corporal punishment under the following conditions:

- The punishment is intended to correct misbehavior.
- Administering the punishment doesn't involve anger or malice.
- The punishment is neither cruel nor excessive and doesn't result in lasting injury.

However, if you're considering this disciplinary option, you should ask yourself several questions:

- Is this the best way to teach students about inappropriate behavior?
- Would other options be more effective in encouraging students to consider their behaviors and the effects of those behaviors on others?
- What does corporal punishment teach children about the use of force to solve problems?

Psychologists disapprove of the use of corporal punishment, both because negative side effects, such as modeled aggression, can occur and because there are more effective alternatives (Berk, 2012). For example, properly administered detention is an effective form of punishment and doesn't include negative side effects. Because of both legal and psychological issues, we recommend that you avoid corporal punishment.

Revisiting My Beliefs

This section addresses the fifth item in *This I Believe*, "Corporal punishment in schools is prohibited by law." This statement isn't true. As you saw, the majority of states (30) prohibit the use of corporal punishment, but it is legal in 20 others.

Students' Rights in Disciplinary Actions

Jessie Tynes, a sixth-grade teacher, turns around just in time to see Billy punch Jared.

"Billy, what did I tell you about keeping your hands to yourself?" Jessie demands. "There's no room for this nonsense in our school and our classroom! You're out of this class until I meet with your parents. Come with me to the principal's office, where you'll sit until we can solve this problem of keeping your hands to yourself."

Sean, a high school junior, is walking to his locker when someone reaches in from behind to knock his books on the floor. When he turns around, he sees Dave standing behind him with a smirk on his face. Losing his temper, Sean pushes Dave. A scuffle begins, but it is broken up by Mr. Higgins, the vice principal. Both students receive 10-day suspensions.

How are the two incidents similar and different? Both involve infractions of school rules, but they differ in the severity of the problem and resulting actions. These differences are important when the courts consider due process. The Fourteenth Amendment to the Constitution states that no "state shall deprive any person of life, liberty, or property without due process of law." **Due process** is a key element related to students' rights in disciplinary matters.

Students have a right to an education, and courts specify that limiting this right can occur only when due process is followed. The courts, however, also acknowledge the rights of schools to discipline students in the day-to-day running of schools.

In our first example, suspending Billy is generally considered an internal affair best resolved by his teacher, his parents, and Billy himself. Unless a suspension lasts longer than 10 days or results in expulsion, teachers and administrators are usually free to discipline as they see fit, assuming the punishment is fair and equitable. The exact definition of due process varies from state to state, so you need to understand the specifics of the law in your state (Schimmel, Stellman, et al., 2011).

Zero-tolerance policies are often a major factor in many student suspensions (LaMorte, 2012). Zero-tolerance policies, which often result in immediate suspensions, became prevalent following the Columbine High tragedy that left 14 students and a teacher dead, and target weapons, drugs, or school fights. The purpose of these policies is to send a clear message about the importance of school safety. Although courts have generally upheld the legality of these policies, critics, including the American Bar Association, question whether this one size fits all approach to school discipline is an effective legal way to prevent school violence (American Bar Association, 2010).

Actions that lead to suspension, such as the incident between Sean and Dave, and that lead to entry on a student's record or permanent expulsion require more formalized safeguards. These include the following:

1. A written notice specifying charges and the time and place of a fair, impartial hearing
2. A description of the procedures to be used, including the nature of evidence and names of witnesses
3. The right of students to legal counsel and to cross-examine and present their own evidence

4. A written or taped record of the proceedings as well as the findings and recommendations
5. The right of appeal

As this list indicates, the procedures involved in long-term (longer than 10 days) suspensions and expulsions are detailed and formal. Because these actions consume considerable amounts of time and energy, schools generally use them only as a last resort.

Disciplinary Actions and Students with Exceptionalities

Students with exceptionalities are provided with additional legal safeguards under the Individuals with Disabilities Education Acts (IDEA) of 1997 and 2004. These laws were passed to ensure students with exceptionalities access to an education, while safeguarding the rights of other students (Hardman, Drew, & Egan, 2011; Heward, 2013). IDEA 1997 enabled school administrators to discipline students with disabilities in the same way as students without disabilities but required schools to review any change of placement, suspension, or expulsion that exceeded 10 days. The purpose of this special review was to determine whether the student's behavior was related to a disability, such as a behavior disorder. If the review determined that the student's behavior wasn't related to the disability, the same disciplinary procedures used with other students could be imposed, but schools were required to continue to provide educational services in the alternative placement.

IDEA 2004 revised these discipline procedures to make it easier to remove a student with disabilities under special circumstances, such as bringing a weapon to school; possessing, using, or selling illegal drugs at school; or inflicting serious injury to someone at school. Under these circumstances, school officials can remove a student with disabilities to an interim alternative educational setting for up to 45 school days, regardless of whether the misconduct was related to the child's disability. This provision was designed to ensure the safety of other students and teachers.

Students with AIDS

AIDS became a major health and legal issue in the schools in the 1980s. Previously thought to be limited to sexually active gay men and drug users who shared hypodermic needles, AIDS entered the school-age population through contaminated blood transfusions.

Battle lines were quickly drawn. Concerned parents worried that the AIDS virus would be spread in school through either casual contact or the sometimes rough-and-tumble world of children on playgrounds. Parents of children with AIDS wanted their children to have access to as normal an education as possible. The courts were soon drawn into the fray.

A landmark and precedent-setting case occurred in St. Petersburg, Florida, in 1987 and involved 7-year-old Randy Ray, a hemophiliac infected with the AIDS virus through a blood transfusion. Because of his condition and fears about possible spread of the disease, school officials refused to allow Randy and his two brothers, who also were infected, to attend school. His parents first reacted by moving elsewhere, but when that failed to open school doors, they moved back to St. Petersburg and sued the school district.

A U.S. district court ruled that the boys should be allowed to attend school with special safeguards, including special attention to the potential hazards of blood spills (*Ray v. School District of DeSoto County*, 1987). Subsequent cases involving other students with HIV/AIDS have been similarly resolved, with courts holding that these children are protected by federal laws that prohibit discrimination against individuals with disabilities. Central to the courts' decisions have been the potential negative effects of exclusion on the social and emotional well-being of the child. The courts have been clear in rejecting exclusion as the automatic solution to the problem of dealing with HIV-infected students and instead have required schools to address the specific risk factors involved in each case.

In this chapter, we've seen that laws are designed not only to protect the rights of individuals but also to further the good of society; eliminating barriers to cultural minorities is a case in point. But federal efforts to eliminate the problem of racial segregation have thrust the U.S. legal system into controversy.

Check Your Understanding

5.1. What are students' rights with respect to freedom of speech?
5.2. Describe students' rights with respect to permissible search and seizure.
5.3. What is the Buckley Amendment? Why is it important to both schools and teachers?
5.4. Is corporal punishment legal in schools?
5.5. Describe students' rights with respect to disciplinary actions.
5.6. Describe the legal rights of students with AIDS.

For feedback, go to the appendix, *Check Your Understanding*, located in the back of this text.

VOICES from the CLASSROOM

"I want to be able to inspire them, to motivate them, and to help them through whatever it is they need. In my classroom, I teach my students that it is okay to ask questions, it is okay to be creative, and it's okay to make mistakes."

RAENA BERMUDES, 2011 Teacher of the Year, Northern Mariana Islands

CHAPTER 8 Summary

1. Explain the differences between legal and ethical influences on the teaching profession.
   - Both laws and ethical codes provide guidelines as teachers make professional decisions. Laws specify what teachers must and can do. Codes of ethics provide guidelines for what teachers should do as conscientious and caring professionals. Professional organizations such as the National Education Association (NEA) and American Federation of Teachers (AFT) publish codes of ethics for teachers.
   - Two major drawbacks to using both laws and ethical codes to guide professional decisions are (1) they are general, lacking in specificity, and (2) they were created to address problems in the past and, consequently, may not be relevant to current issues.
2. Describe how the legal system at the federal, state, and local levels influences education.
   - The U.S. legal system is a complex web of interconnected bodies. At the federal level, the U.S. Constitution provides broad guidelines for legal issues, and Congress passes laws that affect education.
   - Most of the direct legal responsibility for running schools belongs to states and local school districts. The U.S. Constitution gives states the legal rights to govern education, and many day-to-day responsibilities are passed on to districts.
   - The overlapping U.S. legal system places the legal responsibility for specific issues or cases at different levels depending on the particular issue involved.

3. Explain how factors such as teacher employment, academic freedom, liability, and teachers' personal lives are influenced by the law.
   - Teachers have rights and responsibilities as professional educators. Licensure provides them with the right to teach; a teaching contract specifies the legal conditions for employment. Most new teachers are hired on probationary status. Once granted tenure, teachers cannot be dismissed without due process.
   - Teachers' academic freedom is guaranteed by the First Amendment to the Constitution. But in deciding on issues of academic freedom, the courts examine the educational relevance of the content or method involved and the age of the students.
   - Copyright laws, designed to protect the property rights of authors, provide restrictions on teachers' use of others' original materials. New questions about fair use are being raised by the increased use of videotape and DVDs and material presented on the Internet.
   - Liability poses unique challenges to teachers. The courts hold that teachers act in loco parentis, and when they fail to protect the children under their charge, they can be sued for negligence. When deciding on issues of liability, the courts take into account the age and developmental level of students as well as the kinds of risks involved in an activity.
   - Teachers' private lives aren't as private as some would wish. Teachers are expected to be role models to students, so their activities in their hours away from school are often scrutinized and, if illegal, can result in dismissal.
4. Describe the legal implications of religion in the schools.
   - Because of differing beliefs about the proper role of religion in education, religion provides a legal battleground in the schools. Organized or school-sponsored prayer is banned in schools, but students' right to pray in school is protected by law.
   - Courts have approved religious clubs and organizations and private expressions of student religious beliefs. Religious clubs are provided the same legal safeguards as other extracurricular organizations.
   - Although the courts disapprove of religious advocacy, teaching about religion is legal when it can be justified educationally.
5. Describe students' legal rights and responsibilities.
   - Many of the same issues of rights involving freedom of speech and due process that affect teachers also pertain to students. Students' right to freedom of speech is protected by the courts, but the expression of free speech must not interfere with the school's or the teacher's instructional agenda.
   - Students are protected by the U.S. Constitution from unreasonable search and seizure. Lockers are considered school property, however, and students and their belongings may be searched if school officials have a reasonable suspicion about the possession of drugs or dangerous weapons.
   - Students' education records are protected by federal legislation called the Buckley Amendment. The main thrust of this law is to protect the privacy of students' educational records.
   - Corporal punishment is legally allowed in a number of states. Those laws contain safeguards against injury and anger or malice.
   - Because the courts view attending public schools as a legal right, school officials must conduct student expulsions from school in a prescribed manner that makes the process transparent to parents or guardians.
   - The educational rights of students with AIDS are protected by law. School officials must address specific risk factors to other students when excluding children with AIDS from educational activities.

Important Concepts

academic freedom
Buckley Amendment
collective bargaining
copyright laws
corporal punishment
due process
establishment clause
fair-use guidelines
free exercise clause
grievance
in loco parentis
licensure
negligence
notoriety
professional ethics
reduction in force
sexting
teaching contract
tenure

Portfolio Activity

Deepening Your Knowledge of Legal Issues

InTASC Principle 9: Commitment

The purpose of this activity is to encourage you to deepen your understanding of one aspect of school law. Choose a topic from this chapter, and research it further. (*Teachers and the Law,* by Schimmel, Stellman, et al., 2011, is an excellent source.) In a short paper, describe the issue and implications it might have for you as a teacher.

Portfolio Activities similar to this one and related to chapter content can be found at MyEducationLab™.

School Law: Ethical and Legal Influences on Teaching

Go to the topic *Ethical and Legal Issues* in the MyEducationLab (www.myeducationlab.com) for *Introduction to Teaching*, where you can:

- Find learning outcomes for *Ethical and Legal Issues,* along with the national standards that connect to these outcomes.
- Complete *Assignments and Activities* that can help you more deeply understand the chapter content.
- Apply and practice your understanding of the core teaching skills identified in the chapter with the *Building Teaching Skills and Dispositions* learning units.
- Examine challenging situations and cases presented in the IRIS Center Resources.
- Access video clips of CCSSO National Teachers of the Year award winners responding to the question, "Why Do I Teach?" in the *Teacher Talk* section.
- Check your comprehension on the content covered in the chapter with the *Study Plan*. Here you will be able to take a chapter quiz, receive feedback on your answers, and then access *Review, Practice, and Enrichment* activities to enhance your understanding of chapter content.
- Check the *Book Resources* to find opportunities to share thoughts and gather feedback on the *Diversity and You* and *Issues You'll Face in Teaching* features found in this chapter.

MyEducationLab™

CHAPTER 9

The School Curriculum in an Era of Standards

VOICES from the CLASSROOM

"Great teaching isn't magic, but it creates magic moments, and it's through those magic moments that I truly love my profession."

STEFANI COOK, 2011 TEACHER OF THE YEAR, IDAHO

CHAPTER OUTLINE

LEARNING OUTCOMES

After you've completed your study of this chapter, you should be able to:

1. **Describe different definitions of curriculum, and explain how curriculum and instruction are related.** InTASC Core Teaching Standard 7, Planning for Instruction
2. **Explain how the explicit curriculum, the implicit curriculum, the null curriculum, and the extracurriculum are different.** InTASC Core Teaching Standard 7, Planning for Instruction
3. **Identify different forces that influence the curriculum, and explain how each exerts its influence.** InTASC Core Teaching Standard 7, Planning for Instruction
4. **Describe prominent controversial issues in the curriculum.** InTASC Core Teaching Standard 7, Planning for Instruction

Think about the question we asked in *Teaching and You.* In your work as a teacher, you'll ask yourself many questions, but as you plan, three of the most important will be: "What topics should I teach?" "Why am I teaching them?" and "How will I help my students understand them?" These questions are so basic that we often forget that a great deal of thought and decision making (and sometimes controversy) go into answering them. Let's look in on one teacher involved in this process.

Teaching and You

You're working in your room as you plan for your next week. What questions will you ask yourself as you begin to plan?

It's Saturday afternoon, and Suzanne Brush, who teaches second grade, is planning for her coming week. She examines her state math standards, and finds the following:

> **Data Analysis and Probability**
>
> Standard 1:
>
> The student understands and uses the tools of data analysis for managing information. (MA.E.1.1)
>
> 1. displays solutions to problems by generating, collecting, organizing, and analyzing data using simple graphs and charts. (Florida Department of Education, Sunshine State Standards, Mathematics PreK–2, 2007, p. 2)

"Okay, . . . they need to be able to collect data and analyze it using graphs and charts," she thinks.

She also goes online and looks at some sample test bar graph items from the state high-stakes test to see how her students' understanding of the standard will be measured.

Based on the standard and the test item, she decides on an activity in which students try different flavors of jellybeans, pick their favorites, and

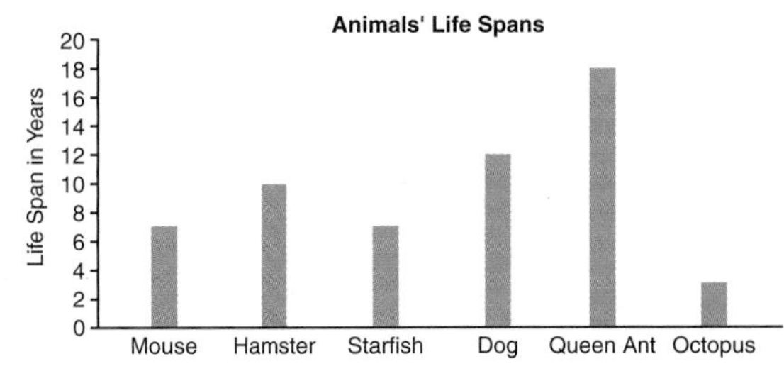

How much longer is the life of a dog than an octopus?

a. 4 years c. 9 years
b. 6 years d. 12 years

Source: Based on Florida Comprehensive Assessment Test (2007). *Mathematics Sample Test Book.* Tallahassee: Florida Department of Education.

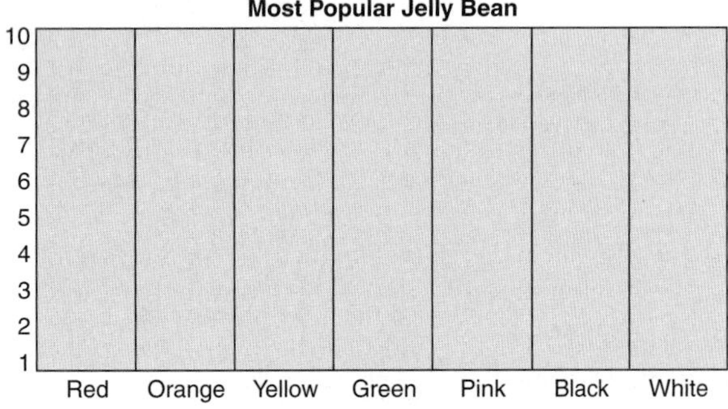

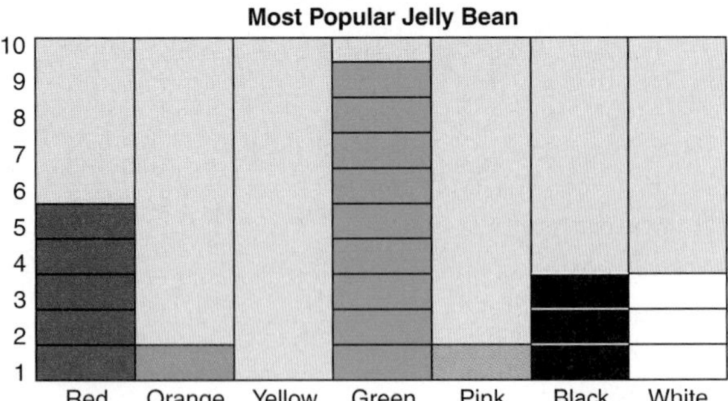

chart their preferences on a bar graph. "I'll do it Monday—it should be a great way to start the week," she thinks to herself, and she then prepares plastic bags with an assortment of jellybean flavors in each.

On Monday, she begins, "I'm planning a party for our class, and I want to have some jellybeans for prizes, but I don't know what your favorite flavor is." After several suggestions from students, the class decides to give everyone different-flavored jellybeans, have them taste them, and choose their favorite flavor.

Suzanne passes out the plastic bags with jellybeans, students taste them, and when they're finished, she continues, "We have an empty graph in the front of the room," as she moves to the front and displays the outline of a graph that appears as you see here.

Suzanne then explains that she has some colored cardboard pieces for the graph that match the colors of the jellybeans. She directs students to come to the front of the room and paste the colored piece that represents their favorite jellybean on the graph.

When the students are done, the graph appears as the one you see here.

Suzanne then reassembles the class and says, "We collected the information and organized it up here on the graph. Now we need to look at it and analyze it."

We'll rejoin Suzanne's lesson later, but before we do, please respond to the items in the *This I Believe: Curriculum Decisions and My Classroom* feature. We address each in the chapter.

This I Believe

CURRICULUM DECISIONS AND MY CLASSROOM

For each item, circle the number that best represents your belief. Use the following scale as a guide:

4 = I strongly believe the statement is true.
3 = I believe the statement is true.
2 = I believe the statement is false.
1 = I strongly believe the statement is false.

1. Because it is important to remain objective about what students should learn, I should be careful to avoid letting my attitudes and values influence decisions about what I teach.

   1 2 3 4

2. Decisions I make about what *not to teach* are sometimes as important as the decisions about what to teach.

   1 2 3 4

3. School activities, such as clubs and sports, can provide positive outlets for students and are an essential part of schooling.

   1 2 3 4

4. Because standards and accountability are so important in today's schools, the most important decisions about what I will teach are now out of my hands.

   1 2 3 4

5. Sex education should be taught in the home, and it should not be a topic that is addressed in schools.

   1 2 3 4

What Is Curriculum?

Let's look at the various decisions Suzanne made as she planned. She first decided that her students needed to understand how to collect data and analyze it using graphs and charts. In making that decision, she consulted math standards, her students' math textbook series, as well as math methods texts from her undergraduate program. She then decided that she would use her jellybean activity to help them understand how data can be represented in charts and graphs. Her first decision was about *curriculum*, and the second was about *instruction*.

Educational theorists offer a variety of definitions of curriculum, and no single one is generally accepted (Wiles & Bondi, 2011). Some common definitions include:

- The subject matter taught to students
- A course of study, or a systematic arrangement of courses
- The planned educational experiences offered by a school
- The process teachers go through in selecting and organizing learning experiences for their students

Also, definitions of curriculum and instruction often overlap, and in some cases curriculum subsumes instruction, because one of our planning decisions is what instructional strategy to use to accomplish our learning goals. We avoid these issues and simply define **curriculum** as everything that teachers teach and students learn in schools, and **instruction** as the strategies teachers use to help students reach their learning goals in the curriculum. For example, Suzanne wanted her second graders to understand that graphs help us represent information; her learning goal was based on a curriculum decision. To reach the goal, she had her students sample a variety of jellybeans, pick their favorite flavors, represent their preferences on a large graph, and analyze the information mathematically. These were decisions about instruction. Instead, for instance, she could have simply explained why graphs are valuable, modeled the process for creating graphs, given her students some information, and had them graph and analyze it. That would have been a different decision about instruction.

The curriculum you construct as a teacher means different things to different people. For the students, it's a roadmap for learning, telling them what they will do in class and what you expect of them. For parents, your curriculum tells them what their child will be learning. For your principal, it provides a concise and succinct description of what you'll be doing in your classroom as you teach. Most importantly, the curriculum you create says a lot about you as a teacher. It describes the topics and ideas you think are important. It communicates your ability to connect ideas in a coherent fashion. It also communicates, though sometimes implicitly, whether you are demanding and challenging and that your classroom is rigorous and engaging, or whether the content you're teaching is easy or even irrelevant to students' lives. In short, the curriculum you create and present to students reflects who you are as a teacher.

Once we construct our curriculum, we typically share it with others. On Back-to-School Night at the beginning of the school year, we provide parents with an overview of the topics we'll be covering and how we plan to help students learn these. For older students, we typically summarize our curriculum in a syllabus that provides a shorthand overview of our course. For younger students, we often share parts of the curriculum at the beginning of a lesson to tell them what they'll be learning that day. Sometimes we even share our curriculum with other teachers so we can coordinate our efforts and provide students with a coherent menu of ideas. The curriculum you create is important because it allows you to put your ideas about teaching and learning down on paper to share with others.

MyEducationLab™

Visit the MyEducationLab for *Introduction to Teaching* to enhance your understanding of chapter concepts with a personalized *Study Plan.* You'll also have the opportunity to hone your teaching skills through video and case-based *Assignments and Activities* and *Building Teaching Skills and Disposition* lessons.

To see how schools use standards to describe and communicate the curriculum, click on the video *Communicating Standards to Parents* (3:16).

Check Your Understanding

1.1 Describe four definitions of curriculum.

1.2 Identify one important difference between the definition of curriculum used in this text and the definitions described in item 1.1.

1.3 How are curriculum and instruction related?

For feedback, go to the appendix, *Check Your Understanding,* located in the back of this text.

Components of the Curriculum

Describing the curriculum as "everything that teachers teach and students learn in schools" makes the concept very broad. It includes content, such as the geography and climate of a certain region, and skills, such as being able to solve math problems. It also includes personal and social development and the attitudes and values that students acquire as part of their day-to-day school experiences. Experts use four aspects of curriculum to describe how schools help students acquire these abilities, attitudes, and values (Eisner, 1993; Schubert, 2008):

- The explicit curriculum
- The implicit, or "hidden," curriculum
- The null curriculum
- The extracurriculum

The Explicit Curriculum

The **explicit curriculum**, or *formal curriculum*, is the stated curriculum found in textbooks, curriculum guides, and standards, as well as other planned formal educational experiences (Oliva & Gordon, 2013). It includes everything you're expected to teach, everything students are expected to learn, and what schools are held accountable for. Suzanne's lesson on graphing was part of the explicit curriculum.

The explicit curriculum at the elementary level is quite different from its counterpart in middle, junior high, and high schools. We look at these differences in the following sections.

Curriculum in Elementary Schools

The elementary curriculum focuses strongly on basic skills, such as reading, writing, and math, and if you're planning on teaching in elementary schools, you'll have considerable autonomy in determining how topics in these areas are taught as well as how much time you'll devote to different topics. To see how this plays out in the classroom, let's look at two elementary teachers' schedules. Sharon is a first-grade teacher, and Susie teaches third grade. Their schedules are outlined in Table 9.1.

Both teachers are responsible for all the content areas, such as language arts, math, and science, and the amount of time they devote to the different areas—a curriculum decision—is a personal decision made by each teacher.

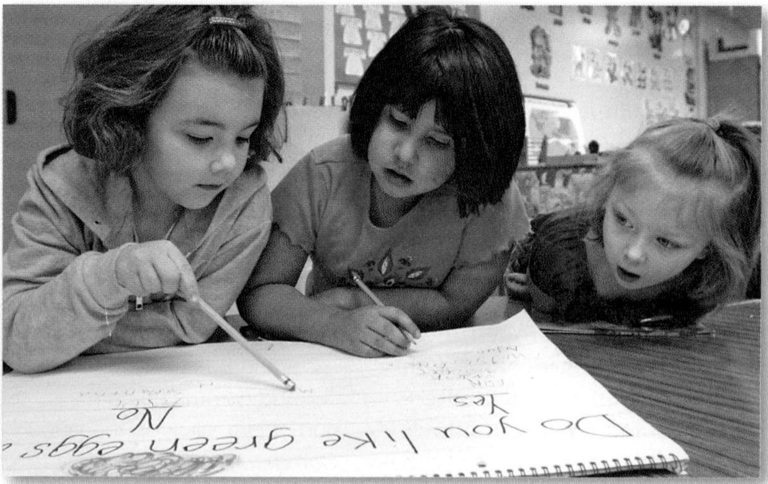

The elementary curriculum is heavily influenced by language arts and reading.

TABLE 9.1 Two Elementary Schedules

Sharon's First-Grade Schedule		Susie's Third-Grade Schedule	
8:30 AM	School begins	8:30 AM	School begins
8:30–8:45	Morning announcements	8:30–9:15	Independent work (practice previous day's language arts and math)
8:45–10:30	Language arts (including reading and writing)	9:15–10:20	Language arts (including reading and writing)
10:30–11:20	Math	10:20–10:45	Snack/independent reading
11:20–11:50	Lunch	10:45–11:15	Physical education
11:50–12:20	Read story	11:15–12:15	Language arts/social studies/science
12:20–1:15	Center time (practice on language arts and math)	12:15–12:45	Lunch
1:15–1:45	Physical education	12:45–2:00	Math
1:45–2:30	Social studies/science	2:00–2:30	Spelling/catch up on material not covered earlier
2:30–2:45	Class meeting	2:30–2:45	Read story
2:45–3:00	Call buses/dismissal	2:45–3:00	Clean up/prepare for dismissal

Though the specific details of these schedules are different, they reveal two important patterns in the elementary curriculum. First, most elementary schools focus heavily on reading, writing, and math. For example, in a 6-hour teaching day (subtracting the time for lunch), Sharon devotes 1 hour and 45 minutes and Susie a minimum of 1 hour and 35 minutes to language arts (including spelling). Both teachers schedule additional time for reading stories.

Second, more time on reading and math means less for social studies, art, music, and other areas, such as physical education. Also, in spite of the widespread impact of technology on our daily lives, and even though most classrooms have computers in them, elementary school teachers place little emphasis on computer use and computer skills.

Beginning in the second or third grade, many elementary schools specialize their instruction. For example, one teacher might be assigned to teach language arts, while another focuses on math. They might also switch for science and social studies or music and art. Reduced planning and preparation time is one advantage of specialization; the disadvantages include logistical and coordination problems and spending less time with your own students.

If you observe in elementary classrooms, you'll probably see schedules that vary from those in Table 9.1. But even with these differences, you'll likely see primary emphasis placed on reading, writing, and math. We'll see why when we look at forces influencing the curriculum later in the chapter.

Curriculum in Middle Schools

Middle schools are specifically designed to help early adolescents make the sometimes-difficult transition from elementary to high school. The curriculum is organized around specific content areas, and, unlike in elementary schools, the content areas are each allocated the same amount of time (the length of one class period).

If a middle school designs its curriculum in a way that is consistent with "middle school philosophy," the school also focuses on real-life issues that concern middle school students, and an effort is made to connect different content areas (National Middle School Association, 2010). Let's look at a team of middle school teachers helping students make these connections.

Carrie Fisher is an eighth-grade American history teacher in an urban middle school. She and her team members have a common planning period each day when the students go to P.E. During this period, they generally discuss the topics they're teaching and the students they share in their classes. The students are heterogeneously grouped and vary widely in ability.

To begin today's meeting, Carrie announces, "I'll be starting the Civil War in about 3 weeks. At the end of the unit, each group will have to make a report on some aspect of the war. Is there any way I can connect with what you're doing in the curriculum?"

"I could have them read Crane's *The Red Badge of Courage*. That's on the district's optional list and really does a good job of communicating the realities of the Civil War," Jim Heath, the language arts teacher, offers.

"That would be great," Carrie replies. "That's just what they need—something to help them understand that history is about real people. How about you, Jacinta? Any links to math?"

"Well, we're just starting to work on different kinds of data such as nominal, ordinal, and interval data. If you can give me some different kinds of data from the Civil War, I can use them to illustrate how different kinds of data provide different kinds of information.

These teachers are working to make the curriculum meaningful for middle-school students by helping them see connections across disciplines. Although these connections are valuable at any level, they are particularly emphasized in elementary and middle schools.

Again, this is what you'll see if the middle school in which you observe attempts to apply a middle school philosophy. Many, however, are middle schools in name only, and, in fact, they look more like junior highs than middle schools.

Curriculum in Junior High and High Schools

The organization of junior high schools is similar to that of high schools—hence the name *junior high*—and this organization influences the curriculum. Whereas one team of teachers in middle schools often have the same group of students, as you saw with Carrie and her colleagues, no such coordination exists in the curriculum for most junior high and high schools. The curriculum in those schools focuses on separate disciplines and becomes more specialized. Some say it also becomes more fragmented.

Integrated Curriculum

The emphasis on content in junior and senior high schools has implications for students' learning experiences. For example, a high school student might study geometry from 9:20 to 10:10, English from 10:15 to 11:05, and so on through the rest of the day. Critics argue that compartmentalizing the curriculum in this way detracts from learning, because teaching and learning bear little resemblance to the world outside school. Instead, they argue, schools should offer an **integrated curriculum** (also referred to as an *interdisciplinary curriculum*), in which concepts and skills from various disciplines are combined and related (Wiles & Bondi, 2011). Different forms of integration occur informally in many elementary classrooms. For example, teachers might have students read about a science topic and then conduct an experiment or interview someone who has expertise in the area. As a culminating activity, students write about the topic, thus integrating science with language arts.

In middle and secondary schools, efforts have been made to formally integrate topics within a content area. For example, in middle schools, students typically take general science in sixth grade, life science in seventh, and physical science in eighth. Some schools integrate these content areas by having students study related topics from earth, life, and physical science in each of the middle school years. For example, using energy as a focal point, students might study the sun as an energy source in earth science, food as a source of energy in life science, and nuclear power in physical science.

An integrated curriculum has the following potential benefits:

- It increases the relevance of content by making connections among ideas explicit.
- It improves learning by increasing motivation.
- It promotes collaborative planning, which increases communication among teachers.

Even the most ardent proponents acknowledge, however, that the process of integrating curriculum is very demanding and time-consuming, and few teachers have the knowledge of content in different disciplines that is required to create effective integrated units. Also, in attempts to create links across content areas, teachers are often unable to help students develop a deep understanding of important concepts and bodies of knowledge in individual areas.

Curriculum integration is most popular at the elementary level, where a single teacher can relate several topics, and at the middle school level, where teams of teachers periodically meet to interconnect content areas. It's least common at the high school level, where a disciplinary approach to the curriculum is entrenched. The emphasis on standards and accountability that is so prominent in today's schools is likely to reduce the interest on integrating curriculum at all levels.

TECHNOLOGY and TEACHING: What Role Should Technology Play in the Curriculum?

Technology is playing an increasingly powerful role in our daily lives, but what role should it play in the explicit curriculum? Not surprisingly, the answer to this question has changed over time to reflect changes in technology. During the 1980s, for example, the call was for computer literacy. Stand-alone desktop computers were finding their way into homes and workplaces, and society asked schools to respond with a curriculum that taught students how to word process and use the computer for basic literacy and computing tasks (Roblyer & Doering, 2013).

Rapid technological change occurred, and the Internet, hand-held computers, and social networking sites such as Facebook and Twitter soon produced students who were not only computer literate but also tech-savvy. Often students knew more about computers than their teachers, and keeping technology from distracting students while they were learning other content became the challenge. Bans on cell phones and hand-held computers in classrooms quickly followed.

But educators still wondered if this informal, society- and media-driven exposure to technology was preparing students for the 21st century. Advocates of a curriculum reform movement called 21st-Century Skills began to recommend a major revamping of our current curriculum offerings to meet the need for technology-savvy students who could function in the rapidly changing economic landscape. Manufacturing and rust-belt industries were dying, and future workers needed to be prepared to compete in a global economy (Partnership for 21st Century Skills, 2009). The **21st-Century Skills** movement promotes technology expertise as well as global awareness, civic literacy, critical thinking, and communication skills that people need to function effectively in the 21st century. Advocates continue to embrace core content in math, reading, writing, science, and social studies, but they also endorse more emphasis on learning skills, such as problem solving and critical thinking, and life and career skills, such as personal responsibility, initiative, and self-direction. Social and cross-cultural awareness are also important because of our country's rapidly increasing diversity and the need for people who can function in a global economy. Technology permeates all the other components. A number of corporations, including Apple, Microsoft, and Intel, support these skills, believing they will make future workers more productive.

Recognizing the magnitude of the task ahead of them, promoters of 21st-Century Skills are recommending a multipronged curriculum reform strategy that targets new standards, instruction, assessment, and professional-development opportunities for teachers. Their goal is to reorient the curriculum so that it prepares students for a technological future.

But major obstacles to this technology-driven reform effort exist. The philosophical question of what knowledge is most worth learning is one. Critics assert that these skills are nothing more than frills that distract teachers from helping students learn basic skills in reading, writing, and math, and important content that all students should know in other areas, such as science and social studies (Mathews, 2009). Critics also argue that 21st-century skills aren't viable curriculum goals, asserting that the skills can't be effectively taught in the absence of content (Sawchuk, 2009b).

A second obstacle is the current accountability movement, which attempts to define the curriculum in terms of standards (Roblyer & Doering, 2013). *What gets tested gets taught* is a curriculum truism, and advocates for a larger role of technology in classroom learning are worried that other content-related standards will push technology out of the curriculum. Who will be responsible for teaching these technology skills? Language arts teachers as part of the writing process, science teachers as part of scientific literacy, or stand-alone classes that focus specifically on technology skills?

Critics also question whether it is possible to create a coherent, technology-driven curriculum, given the rapid pace of technological change (C. Doyle, 2011). Preparing students for the future should be the major thrust of any technology curriculum. But given the rapid, almost revolutionary, changes that have occurred in technology in recent years, who can predict the technological future? For example, 20 years ago, innovations such as Blackberries, iPads, and other mobile computing devices were only being talked about in development labs. How can we develop a curriculum to prepare students for a technological future if we don't know what that will be?

Despite these questions and concerns, technology will play an increasingly large role in our nation's economy and our students' futures. How to address the challenges that arise from these changes will continue to be a curriculum question and controversy in the explicit curriculum.

The Implicit Curriculum

Think about the questions we ask in *Teaching and You* here. Your answers relate to the **implicit curriculum**, which includes the unstated and sometimes unintended aspects of the curriculum. It consists of the hidden messages you and your school send as children participate in school activities, and it will be heavily influenced by your attitudes and actions (Oliva & Gordon, 2013). Also called the *hidden curriculum* (Feinberg & Soltis, 2004) or the *informal curriculum* (McCaslin & Good, 1996), the implicit curriculum is reflected in the way you present your content, the classroom management routines and rules you establish, the way you treat students, the general climate of your classroom, and the unstated values and priorities that shape the school day (E. Margolis & Romero, 2009). For example, if a teacher only calls on students with their hands up, shy or reluctant students quickly learn that the way to avoid being called on is to hunker down in their seats and make themselves invisible. Lessons may run more smoothly, but the implicit message is that only "smart" or verbally assertive students participate in lessons—an unintended consequence of the implicit curriculum.

Teaching and You

Do students learn more and retain information longer if you guide your students in learning activities and help them acquire ideas on their own, or is it more efficient and effective to simply explain topics to them? Why do you think so?

Revisiting My Beliefs

This section addresses the first item in *This I Believe*, "Because it is important to remain objective about what students should learn, I should be careful to avoid letting my attitudes and values influence decisions about what I teach." This statement isn't true, and more importantly, it's impossible for you to avoid having your attitudes and values influence your teaching.

A great deal of learning takes place through the implicit curriculum, and it begins when children are very young. Students, even those of so tender an age, learn early what it takes to "do school." They learn early what a teacher does in a classroom. They learn early how they must behave in order to get on. (Eisner, 2003, p. 648)

As another example of how the implicit curriculum influences students, let's return to Suzanne's work with her second graders. They had represented their jelly bean preferences on the large bar graph at the front of the room, and Suzanne had reassembled them and said, "We collected the information and organized it up here on the graph. Now we need to look at it and analyze it." We rejoin her class now.

"Tell us what we know by looking at this graph. . . . Candice, what do we know?" she asks, walking toward the middle of the room.

"People like green," Candice answers.

"Candice said most people like the green jellybeans. . . . Candice, how many people like green?"

". . . Nine."

"Nine people like green. . . . And how did you find that out? Can you go up there and show us how you read the graph?"

Candice goes up to the graph and moves her hand up from the bottom, counting the green pieces as she goes.

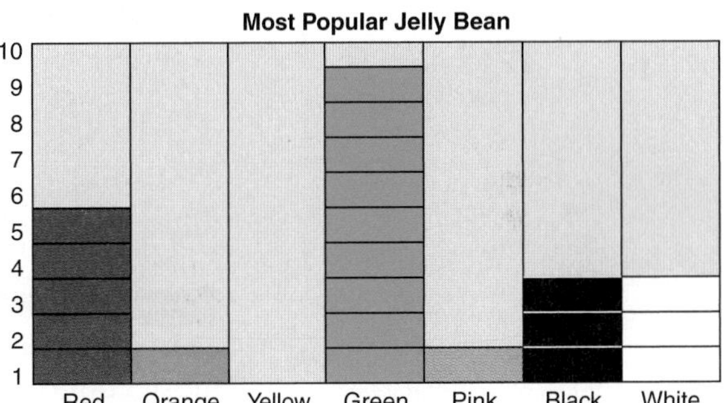

Suzanne has her students make several more observations of the information on the graph and then says, "Okay, now I'm going to ask you a different kind of question. . . . How many more people liked the green jellybeans than the red? Look up at the graph. Try to find the information, set up the problem, and then we'll see what you come up with. . . . I'm looking for a volunteer to share an answer with us. . . . Dominique?"

"Nine plus 5 is 14," Dominique responds.

"Dominique says 9 plus 5 is 14. Let's test it out." (She asks Dominique to go up to the graph and show the class how she arrived at her answer.) "We want to know the difference. . . . How many more people liked green than red, and you say 14 people, . . . 14 more people liked green. Does that work?"

"I mean 9 take away 5," Dominique says after looking at the graph for a few seconds.

"She got up here and she changed her mind," Suzanne smiles warmly. "Tell them."

"9 take away 5 is 4."

"9 take away 5 is 4. So how many more people liked green than red? . . . Carlos?"

"Four."

"Four, good, four," Suzanne again smiles. "The key was you had to find the difference between the two numbers."

Suzanne then has students work at a series of centers, such as graphing the months in which the students' birthdays fall, the most common ways students get to school, and the hair color of each student. After students finish their work, she reviews what they've done and closes the lesson.

What did Suzanne's students learn from this brief episode? The following are possibilities:

- Math is more than simply memorizing basic facts.
- Making mistakes is a normal part of learning.
- Learning is an active process of applying what we know in our daily lives.

These are powerful and positive messages of the implicit curriculum.

Students learn from the implicit curriculum in many ways. For instance, if you use classroom management to create classroom environments in which experiences make sense to your students, they will be more likely to accept responsibility for their own behavior (Emmer & Evertson, 2013; Evertson & Emmer, 2013). If you call on all students even if they don't have their hands raised, students learn that all are welcome and expected to participate and learn

(Lemov, 2010). These messages reflect the implicit curriculum and are important parts of students' total learning experiences.

The implicit and explicit curricula sometimes conflict. For example, some historical research indicates that students who have independent and questioning minds, who are assertive, who challenge authority, and who insist on explanations are sometimes rejected by teachers (Kedar-Voivodas, 1983). This results in a clash between the explicit curriculum, which focuses on learning and mastery of content, and the implicit curriculum, which rewards docile students and conformity. What do students learn when they're expected to listen passively as teachers lecture, or if competition for grades is emphasized? They likely learn that "playing the game" and "beating the system" are more important than hard work and mastery of content. These are not messages we want to send.

With awareness, you can help ensure that the implicit and the explicit curricula of your classroom are consistent. Making learning the focal point of your teaching, modeling your own interest in the topics you teach, respecting students, and expecting them to respect you and each other all communicate important, positive values and are part of the implicit curriculum. Some of the most important learning experiences that students take away from schools are the result of it.

The Null Curriculum

A third dimension of the curriculum focuses on topics that are ignored or left unexamined. The decisions you make about what you won't teach are often as important as what you do teach. Topics left out of the course of study are referred to as the **null curriculum** (Kridel, 2010). You don't have time to "cover" everything, so you choose topics you consider most important or that you feel most comfortable with. For example, if you're an American history teacher, you'll cover the events of the American Civil War, but you may be uncomfortable dealing with controversial factors in the war, such as slavery and racism. So, you slide over them briefly even though they're an important part of our country's history. They then become part of the null curriculum.

You demonstrate your professionalism when you think carefully about the topics you choose to emphasize and those you choose to leave out. As with the implicit curriculum, important messages about learning are tacitly communicated through the null curriculum.

Revisiting My Beliefs

This addresses the second item in *This I Believe*, "Decisions I make about what *not to teach* are sometimes as important as the decisions about what to teach." This statement is indeed true.

Recess: The Missing Fourth "R"?

Recess, a topic receiving increased attention today, is thought by many to be a crucial fourth "R," and is considered a prime example of the null curriculum (Parker-Pope, 2009). Estimates suggest that 30% to 40% of elementary classrooms have cut back on or eliminated recess time, and developmental psychologists are worried that young children are missing out on an essential component of the curriculum. Free play during recess can provide students with crucial experiences needed for cognitive, social, and emotional development (Adams, 2011). In addition, lack of time for free play has been linked to a number of childhood problems, ranging from obesity to anxiety and hyperactivity (Ridgers, Carter, Stratton, & McKenzie, 2011). One study involving more than 11,000 children linked recess to fewer behavioral problems in the classroom (Samuels, 2009b).

Given these positive benefits, why is recess becoming part of many elementary classrooms' null curriculum? Time, precious time, is the answer, because many schools are feeling pressures to spend more time on subjects that are the focus of high-stakes tests (Thacher, 2010). However, these decisions may be having adverse effects on children's learning and development.

If your school doesn't have recess, there isn't much you can do. However, if the issue is discussed in your school, you can emphasize that research consistently suggests that recess is important, and you can advocate for including it in the school day. You can also periodically have your students get out of their desks for a few minutes to simply stretch, move around, and relax. Even these short and simple breaks can have learning benefits (Thacher, 2010).

The Extracurriculum

Extracurricular activities provide valuable learning opportunities for students as well as teachers.

The **extracurriculum** consists of learning experiences that extend beyond the core of students' formal studies. The extracurriculum includes clubs, sports, school plays, and other activities that don't earn students academic credit.

Although outside the explicit curriculum, extracurricular activities provide valuable learning experiences. Research indicates that a well-developed extracurricular program is an integral part of an effective school, and students who participate in extracurricular activities derive a number of benefits (S. Turner, 2010):

- Higher academic performance and attainment
- Reduced dropout rates
- Lower rates of substance abuse
- Less sexual activity among girls
- Better psychological adjustment, including higher self-esteem and reduced feelings of social isolation
- Reduced rates of delinquent behavior

Research also indicates that low-ability students, members of cultural minorities, and students who are at risk for failing to complete high school are less likely to participate in extracurricular activities, which can lead to feelings of alienation toward the school (Covay & Carbonaro, 2010). Many low socioeconomic status (SES) high school students are forced to work after school to make ends meet, a practice that not only competes with participation in extracurricular activities but also can have adverse effects on school success in general (H. Marsh & Kleitman, 2005).

Sports, one form of extracurricular activity, can be an important positive influence on students, especially for members of cultural minorities. Participation in sports can reduce behavior problems and increase positive attitudes toward school. Studies of the effects of participation in sports indicate that girls involved in sports have lower teen pregnancy rates, are less likely to be sexually active, and have fewer sexual partners (Parker-Pope, 2010). Sports provide students with alternative outlets for healthy development and help girls cut loose from the conventional form of femininity that encourages them to establish self-worth mainly in terms of sexuality and heterosexual appeal. Sports also provide opportunities for students to make friends and excel in areas not typically tapped by the regular curriculum.

School leaders wanting to help students develop in healthy ways in this sometimes confusing world might look more closely at extracurricular activities for answers. Given what we know about the benefits of extracurricular activities, schools should take a more proactive role in recruiting students for extracurricular activities by making them aware of the activities available. This is especially important for students at risk, members of cultural minorities, and students with exceptionalities, groups that traditionally have been underrepresented in extracurricular activities.

Revisiting My Beliefs

This information relates to the third item in *This I Believe*, "School activities, such as clubs and sports, can provide positive outlets for students and are an essential part of schooling." This statement is most definitely true.

Extracurricular activities also offer you and other beginning teachers opportunities for professional growth. Sponsoring clubs and coaching teams can provide you with both a salary supplement and chances to interact with your colleagues at a personal level. Working with students in these activities can be emotionally rewarding and can provide you with insights into students' personalities and lives. Don and Paul, your authors, both coached sports and sponsored clubs when we taught in public schools and found the experience time-consuming and demanding but very rewarding. We were able to get to know students in ways not possible in the regular classroom.

Check Your Understanding

2.1. What is the difference between the explicit and the implicit curricula?

2.2. How is the null curriculum different from both the explicit and the implicit curricula?

2.3. Compare the extracurriculum to other curricula.

For feedback, go to the appendix, *Check Your Understanding*, located in the back of this text.

Forces That Influence the Curriculum

Teaching and You

When you begin your career, you'll make a great many decisions about what you teach and how you'll teach it. What will you use to help you make these decisions?

To this point, we've examined the curriculum as it currently exists in schools. But what forces shaped it in the past and are shaping it today? Answers to these questions can be found both in society at large and in educational reforms, and they answer the question we asked in *Teaching and You*. These forces will influence the decisions you make about what to teach and, to a certain extent, even how to teach. They are outlined in Figure 9.1 and discussed in the sections that follow.

The Teacher

The most powerful and important force influencing the curriculum is you, the classroom teacher. Ultimately, you determine the learning experiences that occur in your classroom.

FIGURE 9.1 Forces that Influence the Curriculum

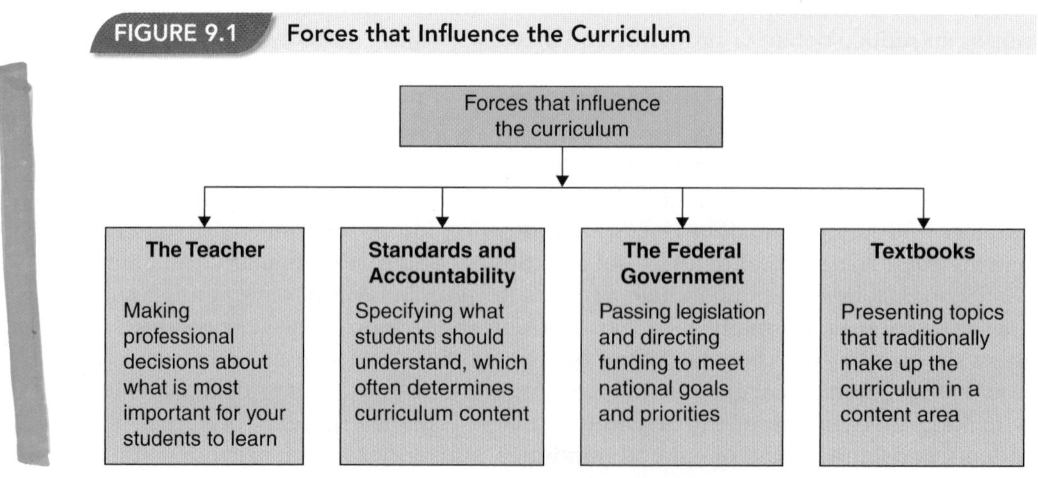

Forces that influence the curriculum
The Teacher
Making professional decisions about what is most important for your students to learn
Standards and Accountability
Specifying what students should understand, which often determines curriculum content
The Federal Government
Passing legislation and directing funding to meet national goals and priorities
Textbooks
Presenting topics that traditionally make up the curriculum in a content area

The curriculum you create reflects your learning goals. Because time doesn't allow us to teach all goals, you'll have to make decisions about priorities. For instance, of the following goals, which do you consider to be most important?

- Thoroughly understand traditional content, such as important concepts and ideas from literature, science, history, and advanced mathematics.
- Develop basic skills, such as the ability to read fluently, write effectively, and complete mathematical tasks.
- Develop workplace skills, such as the ability to work with others and solve problems.
- Develop learner self-esteem and the motivation to be involved in learning for its own sake.

Answers to this question vary. Some educators suggest that the last goal is most important, arguing that intrinsically motivated people will adapt and acquire the skills needed to function effectively in a rapidly changing world. The development of the individual is preeminent in their view. Others suggest that society needs people who can solve problems and function well in groups, the third goal. Still others advocate the first or second goals, asserting that academic skills, knowledge, and understanding are the keys to expertise and the ability to solve today's complex problems.

These arguments are grounded in different philosophical positions, and each of these positions has both strengths and weaknesses, as outlined in Table 9.2.

Many of today's curriculum controversies are rooted in these different philosophical positions. For example, today's reform movements, including accountability and high-stakes testing, have resulted from widespread complaints about young people entering the workforce without the basic knowledge and skills needed to function effectively in today's society (Hirsch, 2001, 2011). These current reforms are based on essentialist philosophical positions.

Others argue that our young people lack even the most basic concepts and language needed to deal with moral issues that they'll face in their later lives, and without this moral compass, our society will inevitably decline (C. Smith, Christoffersen, Davidson, & Herzog, 2011). Cheating, bullying, and drug use are

TABLE 9.2 Philosophical Foundations of the Curriculum

Basis for Curriculum	Dominant Educational Philosopy	Advantages	Disadvantages
Needs of individuals	Progressivism	• Concern for individuals is placed at the heart of curriculum development.	• Efforts to respond to the special needs of each individual are virtually impossible.
		• Learner motivation is promoted.	• Students may not be the best judges of their long-range needs, opting for shallow learning experiences.
Needs of society	Progressivism Social Reconstructionism	• Students learn to integrate information from a variety of sources.	• Society's needs change rapidly, often making curriculum obsolete.
		• Curriculum is relevant, contributing to learner motivation.	• Learners may be steered into career choices too early, limiting long-range opportunities.
Academic disciplines	Essentialism Perennialism	• Research indicates that expertise and problem solving ability depend on knowledge (Eggen & Kauchak, 2013).	• Academic disciplines tend to artificially "compartmentalize "what students learn.
		• Schools and teachers are being held accountable and accountability depends on discipline-based tests.	• Students complain that traditional subjects are irrelevant.

symptoms of this lack of moral direction. These concerns reflect a social reconstructionist philosophy, which tries to change society through curricular interventions. The philosophical positions you embrace and believe in will determine, in large part, the curriculum you design for your students.

Standards and Accountability

A second major factor influencing the curriculum is the current emphasis on standards and accountability. Over the last several years, a great deal has been written about American students' lack of knowledge. For example, a report from the National Assessment of Educational Progress in 2010 found that only 12% of American 12th graders scored well enough to be considered "proficient" in American history (National Center for Education Statistics, 2010g), a result significant enough to be covered on the national news (S. Dillon, 2011b). Concerns about American's lack of knowledge have become prominent enough that a feature article in *Newsweek* raised the question, "How dumb are we?" (A. Romano, 2011).

In response to these concerns about students' lack of knowledge, educators have established academic **standards**, statements that describe what students should know or be able to do at the end of a prescribed period of study. All the states and the District of Columbia have established standards, and your school will be held accountable for the extent to which students meet the standards prescribed by your state. **Accountability** is the process of requiring students to demonstrate understanding of the topics they study as measured by **high-stakes tests**, standardized tests that can determine whether or not students are promoted to the next grade level, or even graduate from high school with a standard diploma. (If performance on a test can determine whether or not a student is allowed to graduate from high school, for example, the "stakes" are very high, which is the source of the term "high-stakes tests.")

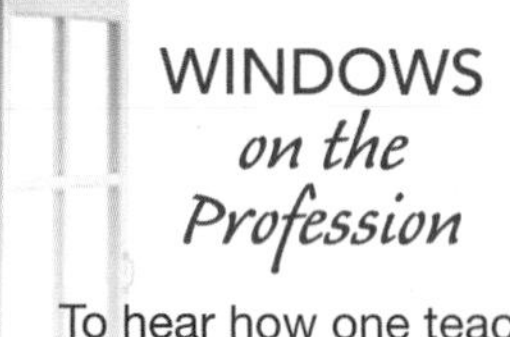

To hear how one teacher integrates standards into the curriculum, click on the video *Standards and Accountability: Using Standards to Guide Instruction* (7:57).

Standards have a powerful influence on the curriculum. To see how, think again about the emphasis placed on reading, writing, and math that we saw earlier in our discussion of the elementary curriculum. The high-stakes tests in most states focus on these content areas, so this is what schools emphasize in the curriculum. "What gets tested gets taught," and standards may be the most powerful force influencing the curriculum today. For example, whether a content area like science is emphasized will depend on whether it is included on the high-stakes test for a particular state; some states include science on their high-stakes tests but others do not. Content areas such as social studies, art, and music are rarely covered on high-stakes tests, so they are receiving little emphasis in the curriculum.

You also saw the influence of standards and accountability on curriculum decisions illustrated in our opening case study. In planning her lesson, Suzanne consulted her state's standards and even looked for a sample test item to ensure that her lesson would be consistent with the standard and the high-stakes test her students would take.

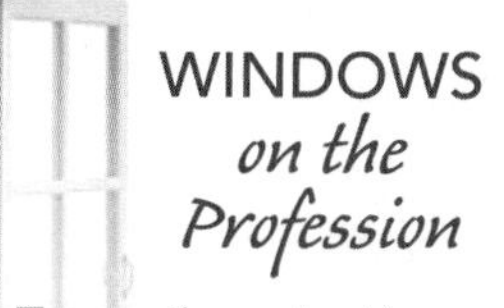

To see the actual lesson built around these state standards, click on the video *Curriculum, Standards, & Accountability* (10:24).

The influence of standards, accountability, and high-stakes tests is so powerful that some districts create teacher guides that specify topics, performance tasks, and even the number of class periods that should be devoted to specific topics. And teachers are told to avoid deviating from the prescribed curriculum (S. Schellenberg, Personal Communication, January 15, 2012). As you would expect, these practices are highly controversial (Nichols & Berliner, 2008; Popham, 2011). Adding to the problem is that fact that beginning teachers, like you, often feel inadequately prepared to deal with the new assessment roles required of them by the accountability movement (Stiggins & Chappuis, 2012).

Regardless of the state in which you teach, standards, accountability, and high-stakes testing will be a part of your professional life.

The Federal Government

Even though the leaders who originally framed our country's constitution gave control of education to the states, our federal government has a long and rich history of involvement in education, and this role has increased rather than decreased over time. The No Child Left Behind (NCLB) Act of 2001, a key educational mandate of the George W. Bush administration, is one example of this increased federal role. Another example is the Race to the Top Program, a $4.35 billion initiative created by the Obama administration and designed to spur reforms in state and local district K-12 education (U.S. Department of Education, 2009a).

The federal government's efforts to influence school curricula dramatically increased in the 1950s when people began to view education as an important vehicle for accomplishing national goals. Table 9.3 outlines some of the major pieces of federal legislation that have influenced both the curriculum and other aspects of schools.

As you see in Table 9.3, federal legislation has led to significant changes in U.S. classrooms. The Individuals with Disabilities Education Act (IDEA), federal legislation passed in 1975, requires that all students have access to the regular curriculum. As a result, it's almost certain that you'll have learners with exceptionalities, such as students with learning disabilities, in your classroom. The National Defense Education Act (passed in 1958) resulted in much greater emphasis on math, science, and foreign languages, particularly in high schools. Although this emphasis has varied somewhat over the years, well-qualified math, science, and foreign language teachers continue to be in high demand.

TABLE 9.3 The Federal Government's Influence on the Curriculum

Act	Date	Impact on Curriculum
National Defense Education Act	1958	Made math. science, and foreign language high priorities.
Economic Opportunity Act	1964	Increased emphasis on vocational training and teaching marketable skills.
Civil Rights Act	1964	Prohibited discrimination on the basis of race, color, or national origin. Intended to provide all students with equal access to the curriculum.
Elementary and Secondary Education Act	1965	Created Title I, designed to help disadvantaged children acquire basic skills.
Billingual Education Act	1968	Provided for teaching the curriculum in students' native languages as they gradually learned English.
Title IX	1972	Increased girls' participation in physical education and sports.
Individuals with Disabilities Education Act (IDEA)	1975	Increased participation of learners with exceptionalities in the regular curriculum.
Environmental Education Act	1991	Stimulated the modern environmental education movement.
Goals 2000: Educate America Act	1994	Established goals to be met by American education by the year 2000.
No Child Left Behind Act	2001	Requires states to establish standards for what learners should know and be able to do in different subjects and holds them accountable for student performance on tests linked to these standards.
Race to the Top	2009	Part of the American Recovery and Reinvestment Act, it is designed to spur reforms in state and local district K–12 education.

More recent federal legislation has the potential to have an even greater influence on your own teaching. For instance, one of the provisions of the Race to the Top program stipulates that students' test scores will be an important factor in teachers' evaluations. This stipulation is highly controversial.

> Evaluating teachers in relation to student test scores will have many adverse consequences. It will make the current standardized tests of basic skills more important than ever, and even more time and resources will be devoted to raising scores on these tests. The curriculum will be narrowed even more than under George W. Bush's No Child Left Behind, because of the link between wages and scores. There will be even less time available for the arts, science, history, civics, foreign language, even physical education. Teachers will teach to the test. There will be more cheating, more gaming the system. (Ravitch, 2011, para. 4)

We are not presenting this information to scare or discourage you. Rather, it's a reality in today's schools, and the more knowledgeable you are about this reality, the better prepared you'll be to deal with these forces when you take your first job. (We offer some suggestions for adapting to these issues at the end of this section of the chapter.)

Despite questions about quality, most teachers rely on textbooks for their instruction.

Textbooks

You're a beginning teacher, and you're thinking about what you'll teach during the next week. Where will you turn for help? If you're typical, you'll reach for the textbook you're using.

Textbooks are part of teaching life. In the United States, districts spend more than $5.5 billion per year on textbooks (Sporkin, 2011). Teachers depend heavily on them to select content, sequence topics, and locate instructional activities. In some of your education classes, you may be encouraged to set textbooks aside or at least not depend heavily on them. But research suggests that if you're typical, you probably won't do so (Zahorik, 1991). Other than standards, many experts believe that textbooks will be the most powerful influence on your curriculum decisions (C. Marsh & Willis, 2007).

Textbooks can be valuable resources, and we're not suggesting that you abandon them. Instead, we recommend that you use them strategically, deemphasizing—or even eliminating—some topics and chapters in textbooks while including other valuable topics not in them. Reasons for using textbooks selectively include:

- *Student needs*: The topics presented in textbooks may not be consistent with the specific needs of your students, school, or district. Following a textbook too closely then fails to meet these needs.
- *Scope*: To appeal to a wide market, textbook publishers include a huge number of topics (Aarons, 2010). Texts and curriculum guides often contain twice as much material as students can learn in the time available, and curriculum experts recommend that teachers select the most important concepts and skills to emphasize and concentrate on the quality of understanding rather than on the quantity of information presented (Patton & Roschelle, 2008).
- *Quality*: Textbooks sometimes are poorly written, lack adequate examples, are superficial, or even contain errors of fact (V. R. Lee, 2010). Following textbooks too closely can lead to superficial understanding or even faulty ideas that detract from learning.

On the other hand, innovative textbooks and other curriculum materials can be positive catalysts for change, and they can encourage you to rethink what and how you teach. In addition, because of the current emphasis on standards, most publishers now key objectives in their textbooks to state standards, making them useful planning tools.

Adapting to the Forces Influencing the Curriculum

Earlier in this section, we said that you are the most powerful factor influencing the curriculum in your classroom, despite the influence of other factors like standards and textbooks. This is as it should be, because you are a professional and know what's best for the children you teach. However, these forces will certainly have an impact on your teaching. We also believe, however, that the impact is often overstated. While ensuring that your students are prepared for the high-stakes tests that they'll be required to take, you'll have a great deal of latitude and autonomy in deciding how much time to devote to different standards and how you'll prepare your students for relevant tests. Let's look at an example.

Mike Durant is a biology teacher in a large high school in Texas. He looks at his state's standards for biology, one of which says:

> Science concepts. The student knows that interdependence and interactions occur within an environmental system. The student is expected to:
>
> [C]ompare variations and adaptations of organisms in different ecosystems.
>
> (Texas Education Agency, 2011)

"I'll use my skull and these pictures," Mike thinks to himself, referring to the skull of an American bison and some photographs of bison in the wild that he has saved for just this occasion. "We'll examine the structure of the skull and I'll have the kids make some conclusions about its size, what kind of environment this animal lived in, what its primary food sources were, and we'll even see if we can figure out what it's most common enemies were."

Mike organizes his class into groups of three and has students make conclusions about the animal based on what they observe about the skull and the photographs, and they examine each group's findings in a whole-class discussion. With Mike's guidance they conclude that the animal was an herbivore, because it had large, flat-surfaced teeth that would be effective for grinding food, such as grass; the size of the skull suggested that it was a large animal; and the fact that it was an herbivore probably meant it lived in herds to protect itself from predators.

After they've finished, Mike has the students think about themselves, and how we, as humans, have adapted to our environments.

Mike's curriculum planning decisions are significant for several reasons. First, he was well aware of the standard his students were expected to meet, and his lesson was consistent with the standard. However, the standard had a minimal effect on the way he approached the topic. The standard provided some direction with respect to the curriculum, but it had little effect on his planning and ultimately his teaching.

Second, Mike used his textbook to supplement his activity, rather than use it as the primary source of information for his students. In fact, he had his students read about organisms and the way they adapt to their environments *after*, rather than before, he conducted his activity. Because of the experience they had investigating the skull, their reading was more meaningful, and the likelihood that the students would actually do their assigned readings increased.

Third, guiding a learning activity, such as this one, is very professionally satisfying. Seeing students actually thinking about what they're studying and making connections to their lives is one of the most rewarding experiences we have when we teach.

Mike demonstrated the characteristics of a pro. He helped his students reach a standard mandated by his state, and he did it in a creative, professionally satisfying, and time-efficient way. This is how you can adapt to the forces influencing the curriculum.

Revisiting My Beliefs

The information in this section addresses the fourth item in *This I Believe*, "Because standards and accountability are so important in today's schools, the most important decisions about what I will teach are now out of my hands." This statement isn't true: Standards present general frameworks for you, but the most important decisions about curriculum and instruction remain in your hands.

We also see this form of creative professional adaptation illustrated in Suzanne's work. For example, she used her state's standards as a guide, but the decisions about how to plan and present the content were hers and hers alone. She relied on her professional knowledge in designing the learning activity to promote students' involvement and interest. There is no substitute for this knowledge and professionalism.

You are essentially "alone" as a professional when you shut your classroom door. Closing the door is symbolic, representing your professional control over the curriculum and how it's taught.

Check Your Understanding

3.1 Identify four forces that influence the curriculum.

3.2 How does each of the forces in 3.1 exert its influence on the curriculum?

3.3 Why is teacher professionalism so important in making curricular decisions?

For feedback, go to the appendix, *Check Your Understanding*, located in the back of this text.

ISSUES YOU'LL FACE IN TEACHING

A National Curriculum?

The leaders who drafted our country's constitution placed curriculum decisions directly in the hands of the states by passing the Tenth Amendment, and the principle of state control of curricula has been in place since that time.

Today, this principle is being questioned by many who advocate national standards, and by extension, a national curriculum (D. Hoff, 2009b; Porter, 2011). And the politics of this controversy have become blurred. Historically, political liberals have advocated a strong federal role in education, whereas conservatives have supported states' rights and have advocated a smaller federal presence. However, the NCLB legislation was a massive federal intervention and was promoted and passed by the conservative Bush administration. Though it still left control of the curriculum in states' hands, NCLB exerted a powerful federal influence on how different states implement and test for these standards. For some, a national curriculum with mandated federal testing is a logical next step.

THE QUESTION

Is the idea of national standards leading to a national curriculum a good idea? Arguments for and against a national curriculum include the following:

PRO

- The rigor of standards varies significantly from state to state; some states have much lower standards and levels of achievement than others. A national curriculum would create uniform standards for all and help raise achievement for low SES and cultural minority students in all states (C. Finn & Petrilli, 2009).
- Students in countries such as Germany and Japan, which have national standards and national exams, achieve higher than American students (National Center for Education Statistics, 2011e).
- A national curriculum would provide stability and coherence. The population in the United States is highly mobile: Twenty percent of Americans relocate every year, some urban schools have a 50% turnover rate during the school year, and by the end of third grade, 1 of 6 children has attended three or more schools (Hartman, 2006). Teachers working with new students from different districts or states often can't tell what they have or haven't already studied.

CON

- It will create a massive and unwieldy federal bureaucracy, which will also weaken local control and accountability.
- A national curriculum won't be responsive to regional differences and will ignore the needs of diverse students in different parts of the country.
- The national standards being proposed are no more rigorous than existing ones and won't provide the rigor that is frequently lacking in current state standards (Porter, 2011).

YOU TAKE A STAND

Now it's your turn to take a position on the issue. Should our country have national standards and a national curriculum, or should curriculum decisions be left in the hands of the states?

Go to *Issues You'll Face in Teaching* in the MyEducationLab™ Book Resources that accompany this text to log your thoughts and receive feedback from your authors.

Controversial Issues in the Curriculum

At one level, the curriculum seems straightforward; we teach our students the knowledge and skills they need to succeed in college or function in their lives after school. However, as the questions in *Teaching and You* reveal, it isn't that simple, and a number of controversies exist with respect to decisions about what we should teach. For instance:

> **Teaching and You**
>
> During a health lesson it becomes obvious that several students are confused about factual issues relating to birth control. Should you clear up the misconceptions and address the topic as part of the curriculum or leave this topic as something students should discuss with their parents? Another student comments that cheating isn't that big a deal, because everyone cheats. How should you respond to this comment?

- Should sex education be part of the curriculum, which relates to the first question we raised in *Teaching and You*?
- Should teaching values and morals be part of the curriculum—the second question we asked?
- If you're preparing to become a science teacher, should you offer disclaimers about the theory of evolution, suggesting that it is only one explanation for the makeup of our natural world?
- Should you be allowed to have your students read anything that your professional judgment dictates, or should limits be placed on what students can read in school?

The answer to each question is controversial, and they have implications for you as you attempt to implement the curriculum in your school. We examine these issues in this section.

Sex Education

Sex education has been a long-term controversial curriculum issue. Back in 1969 an article in *Time* magazine claimed, "Sex education has become the most hotly debated topic in American elementary education" (*Time Magazine U.S.*, 1969, para. 1), and it's as hotly debated today as it was back then.

Sex education is controversial for several reasons. First, people can't agree on whether it should even be included in the school curriculum. Many, including religious, social, and political conservatives insist that it should be the responsibility of families or churches. They contend that sex is inextricably connected with personal, moral, and religious values, and the proper place for sex education is the home, where parents can embed it in a larger moral framework.

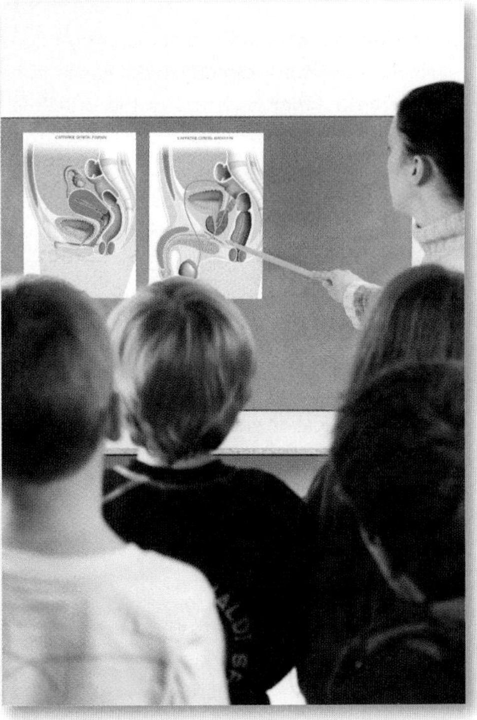

Sex education, although controversial, has become a common curriculum component in many school districts.

Proponents of sex education counter with statistics, such as the following:

- By their 19th birthday, 7 of 10 teenagers of both sexes have had sexual intercourse (Abma, Martinez, & Copen, 2010), and 6% have had sexual intercourse before age 13 (National Campaign to Prevent Teen Pregnancy, 2010).
- Although teens in the United States and Europe have similar levels of sexual activity, those in Europe are more likely to use effective contraceptive methods, so they have substantially lower pregnancy rates (Ventura & Hamilton, 2011).
- The U.S. teen pregnancy rate continues to be one of the highest in the developed world and more than twice as high as in Canada and Sweden (Guttmacher Institute, 2011c).

If parents and churches are responsible for sex education, they're doing a poor job, proponents of sex education contend. Additional evidence indicates that parents' knowledge about contraception and other health topics is often inaccurate or incomplete, and the same is true for information on the Internet; research indicates that nearly half of the websites teens turn to for sexual health information contain errors of fact (Guttmacher Institute, 2011b).

Advocates also argue that schools are responsible for ensuring that all students have access to accurate information about their bodies and their developing sexuality, and courts have upheld school districts' rights to offer sex education courses (Schimmel, Stellman, & Fischer, 2011). Parents who object are free to take their children out of the classes or programs.

Further, polls indicate that the majority of parents and the population at large favor some type of sex education. For example, polls indicate that more than 9 of 10 parents of middle and high school students favor sex education and believe that their children should be given information to protect themselves from unplanned pregnancies and sexually transmitted diseases (Kaiser Family Foundation, 2004).

Polls indicate that students also feel the need for accurate information about sex. In one survey, 17-year-olds expressed a pressing need for sex education, and they also believed that boys and girls should be taught in nonsegregated groups, men and women should cooperate in leading classes, enrollment in classes should be voluntary, and a variety of viewpoints should be presented (Michener, 2006).

The content of sex education courses is also controversial, and it's highly politicized. Religious and social conservatives support abstinence-only programs and strongly oppose any other form of sex education, including discussion of contraception. They argue that it encourages sexual promiscuity and is fundamentally dangerous to the well-being of our young people and society in general (Dimick & Apple, 2005). The administration of George W. Bush supported conservative groups and promoted these programs. Liberal groups have been equally adamant, arguing that conservatives are doing a disservice to children, including their own.

What does research say? Research on abstinence-only programs is mixed (Jemmott, Jemmott, & Fong, 2010; Sessions-Stepp, 2007). One study that tracked teenagers 4 to 6 years after these programs found no differences between students who participated in abstinence-only programs and those who didn't (Mathematica Policy Research, 2007). In addition, research indicates that teenagers who took virginity pledges had the same number of sexual partners and had sex at around the same age as students who didn't (Samuels, 2009a). One author summarized the research on abstinence-only programs in this way: "Abstinence-only programs show little evidence of sustained (long-term) impact on attitudes and intentions. Worse, they show some negative impacts on youth's willingness to use contraception, including condoms, to prevent negative sexual health outcomes related to sexual intercourse" (Hauser, 2008, para. 19). The best available evidence indicates that the most effective programs combine abstinence education with information about birth control and the development of refusal and other communication skills (Berk, 2012).

Revisiting My Beliefs

This section addresses the fifth item in *This I Believe*, "Sex education should be taught in the home, and it should not be a topic that is addressed in schools." This statement remains controversial, but research indicates that most parents and citizens in general advocate some form of sex education in our nation's schools.

Moral and Character Education

Now, let's consider the second question we asked in *Teaching and You*. How should you respond to a student who says that cheating is no big deal? It's a specific example of a bigger question: Should your primary focus as a teacher be making students more knowledgeable and academically skilled, or should it also include making them "better" people through moral or character education? As with sex education, the place of values and moral education in the curriculum is also controversial (Gauld, 2012). Most educators, and the public at large, agree that some type of moral education should be part of the curriculum, but they disagree about the form it should take.

One position, called **character education**, suggests that moral values and positive character traits, such as honesty, tolerance and fairness, should be explicitly taught, emphasized, and rewarded. Proponents believe that right and wrong do exist and that parents and schools have a responsibility to teach students to recognize the difference (Ornstein, Pajak & Ornstein, 2011). Character education emphasizes the study of values, practicing these values both in school and elsewhere, and rewarding displays of these values when they occur. If you take a character education position, you would respond to your student in no uncertain terms that cheating is wrong, it will not be tolerated in your classroom, and if someone is caught cheating, they will be appropriately punished.

Moral education, by contrast, is more value free, emphasizing instead the development of students' moral reasoning. Moral education uses moral dilemmas and classroom discussions to teach problem solving and to bring about changes in the way learners think about moral issues. Teachers implementing this approach would use characters in books and current events to discuss and investigate moral issues. If you took a moral education position in responding to your student, you would raise questions about the short- and long-term impact of cheating, what the world would be like if all students held similar views, and how the issue of cheating relates to the functioning of our society.

Critics of character education argue that it indoctrinates rather than educates; critics of moral education assert that it has a relativistic view of morals, with no right or wrong answers (Ornstein et al., 2011). Character education's strengths lie in its emphasis on explicitly promoting core values, such as honesty, caring, and respect for others that virtually all people believe are necessary and good. And research indicates that character education programs are effective for developing both students' social skills and their academic abilities (Nucci, 2009). However, emphasizing moral student thinking and decision making is important as well, and this is the focus of the moral education perspective.

The classroom environment you create and your own leadership in this area are more important than the specific approach you use to promote your students' moral development. You set the moral tone for your classroom with your actions and words. You help all your students feel as if they are welcome and belong in school, that they will be respected, and that they can offer their views without fear of embarrassment or ridicule. Other than parents, you're the most powerful factor influencing the development of caring and responsible young people.

Service Learning

Cindy Lloyd's students at Somerset Intermediate School in Westover, Maryland, conducted a grocery drive called Harvest for the Hungry. In addition to collecting and distributing food for the poor, they studied the effects of malnutrition in science. In social studies, they learned about the economics and politics of food distribution. They read novels and poetry about poverty, wrote newspaper articles about their campaign, and toured a food bank. (Based on F. Smith, 2006)

Service learning attempts to promote students' moral development by combining service to the community with content-learning objectives. It blends civic action with academic subjects to provide students with an appreciation of the academic disciplines, while enhancing their sense of civic responsibility

Service learning teaches values by actively involving students in community-based service projects.

(Hart, Donnelly, Youniss, & Atkins, 2007). It is grounded in the belief that providing service changes both the provider and the recipient of the service.

Examples of service-learning programs include environmental education projects designed to encourage people to recycle, volunteer work in hospitals, and projects aimed at getting people out to vote. They also include internships and field-based programs that allow students to see academic concepts applied in real-world situations. One innovative service-learning project encouraged students to focus their efforts on their own school (Taines, 2012). Participants could see the fruits of their efforts on a daily basis as the school environment improved.

Because of the emphasis on application, service learning can also be motivating. One urban high school student commented,

> Every Wednesday we go out for the entire day and do community service, and it's really made a big difference to me. In our building, we have Early Head Start, where moms drop their babies off, and I go down there and help. That's really made me want to go to school on Wednesdays, getting to loosen up and have a little bit of fun. . . . (Cushman, 2006, p. 37)

Some advocates of service learning connect it to the goal of social justice, which attempts to create a society in which all of our citizens have equal access to opportunities (Hansen, Anderson, Frank, & Nieuwejaar, 2008). By working with diverse members of the community, students become more aware of the adverse conditions that prevent all members of our society from leading productive lives. In addition, service learning provides students with a concrete way to address the inequities found in our society. This is another way that service learning combines action with learning.

The popularity of service-learning programs has grown over the years, and a national service-learning clearinghouse exists to provide resources and promote service-learning projects (ETR Associates, 2011).

Whether service learning should be voluntary or required is an important policy question. Not all parents support service-learning requirements, but courts have upheld the legality of these courses, noting that they promote habits of good citizenship and introduce students to the idea of social responsibility (Schimmel, Stellman, et al., 2011).

Intelligent Design

Where did we come from, and how did we get here? These questions have intrigued people since the beginning of time and are central issues in most religions. More directly, what role should schools play in helping students deal with these questions?

Intelligent design is a theory suggesting that certain features of the universe and of living things are so complex that their existence is best explained by an intelligent cause, rather than an undirected process such as natural selection or evolution. Proponents of intelligent design argue that it's a scientific theory that stands on equal footing with, or is superior to, evolution as an explanation for the existence of life.

Opponents argue that intelligent design is little more than **creationism**, a religious view suggesting that the universe was created by God as described in the Bible, framed in terms designed to make it appear scientific. And the overwhelming majority of the scientific community views intelligent design as unscientific, pseudoscience, or junk science (Attiel et al., 2006). The U.S. National Academy of Sciences has taken the position that intelligent design and other claims of supernatural intervention in the origin of life are not science, because they can't be tested by experiment, don't generate any predictions, and propose no new hypotheses of their own (Steering Committee on Science and Creationism, 1999).

Public opinion polls are interesting. For example, in spite of overwhelming evidence suggesting that the earth and humans have a long history, one poll suggested that 4 of 10 people believe that God created humans in their present form within approximately the last 10,000 years, and another 4 of 10 believe that humans have evolved, but God has guided the process (Gallup, 2011).

Intelligent design is intensely controversial and highly politicized, and the issue has even gone to court. In the first direct challenge to a Pennsylvania school district's requirement that science classes teach intelligent design as a viable alternative to evolution, a U.S. federal court ruled that the requirement was a violation of the establishment clause of the First Amendment to the U.S. Constitution (*Kitzmiller et al. v. Dover Area School District*, 2005).

Controversies over intelligent design are not likely to diminish. For example, in 2009, the controversy reemerged in Texas, as its State Board of Education heard impassioned testimony from scientists and social conservatives on revising the science curriculum (McKinley, 2009). This debate centered on language in the state's curriculum that said students should explore "the strengths and weaknesses" of all theories, including evolution. Critics—essentially the entire scientific community—argue that the phrase "strengths and weaknesses" is a strategy religious conservatives are using to embed creationism in the curriculum. Advocates of the language argue that they are simply fighting for academic freedom and against what they see as fanatical loyalty to Darwin and evolutionary biologists. Several other states have considered legislation requiring classrooms to be open to discussions about the strengths and weaknesses of evolution (McKinley, 2009).

The issue is broader than just language in state standards. For example, business leaders have argued that Texas would have trouble attracting highly educated workers and their families if the state's science programs were seen as a laughingstock among biologists (McKinley, 2009).

This issue isn't going away, and if you're preparing to become a science teacher, you will probably encounter it in some form or other in your classroom when you begin teaching. If you do, consult with your department head and other school leaders to understand how the controversy is playing out in your community.

Censorship

What do the following books have in common?

Of Mice and Men, by John Steinbeck
The Diary of a Young Girl, by Anne Frank
The Adventures of Huckleberry Finn, by Mark Twain
To Kill a Mockingbird, by Harper Lee

In addition to being recognized as quality works of literature and mainstays of many school reading lists, each has, at various times, been targeted to be banned from the public school curriculum. The language arts curriculum has often been controversial because of the issue of **censorship**, the practice of prohibiting objectionable materials from being used in academic classes or, in some cases, from even being placed in libraries.

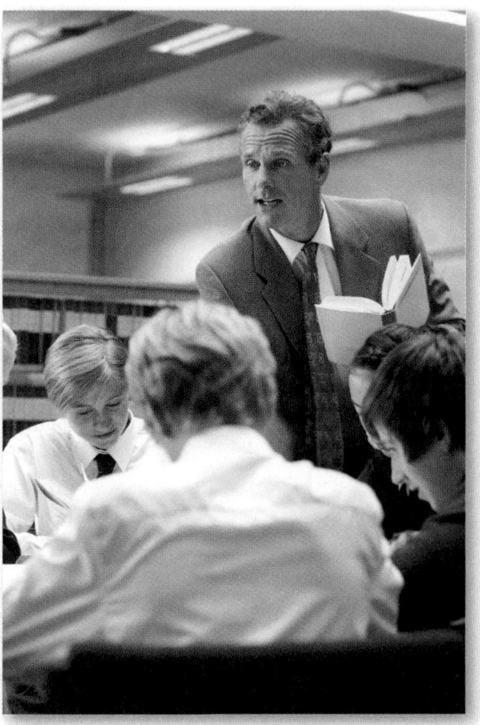

Censorship influences teachers' ability to use controversial materials and books in their classrooms.

Issues of censorship have existed throughout history and are likely to continue in the future. These issues are even more prominent and politicized now with ongoing concerns about the fight against terrorism, moral values, and the rights of gays and lesbians, together with the increased political power of religious conservatives in the United States. For example, in 2005, Oklahoma legislators urged libraries to limit students' access to books with gay themes (Oder, 2005), and librarians in Arkansas were pressured to remove books with similar themes from school libraries (Weiss, 2005). In Miami, Florida, the federal courts became embroiled in a censorship battle over the book, *A Visit to Cuba*, which critics believed painted too rosy a picture of communist Cuba (Banning Books in Miami, 2009).

What books and what content students should be allowed, or required, to read in schools is a question that remains unanswered. For instance, J. K. Rowling's wildly popular Harry Potter series has raised censorship questions because of issues with magic and the supernatural. Defenders of Rowling argue that the books encourage young people to read and examine moral themes, their messages are quite harmless, and censorship is not an appropriate response to controversial literature (Glanzer, 2005). Critics argue that these books send the wrong message to young adults. The fact that this series is very popular with young people only fuels the controversy.

Censorship in the curriculum also raises questions about other issues in education. For instance, to what extent should parents have control over the books their children read? And how much autonomy should you have in selecting books that, in your professional judgment, are important for promoting your students' learning and development?

The courts have generally opposed censorship of books, ruling that schools and teachers have a right to expose students to different ideas and points of view through literature (Schimmel, Stellman, et al., 2011).

TECHNOLOGY and TEACHING: The Controversy over Internet Censorship

The Internet can be a powerful learning tool, but students' ability to access information from it at the click of a button also raises concerns about the kinds of materials available to children. Internet filtering via software programs can be used to block out entire lists of web pages based on specific, predetermined categories, or people can use certain words to limit access to sites. States typically use filters to prevent students from accessing information in five broad categories: criminal skills, hate speech, drugs, gambling, and sex. In addition, some districts have tried to block access to games and social media sites such as Facebook and Twitter, claiming they present distractions to students during school time (Hu, 2011).

This practice is, as you would expect, controversial. The first is the issue of free speech. Free speech advocates contend that such filtering is unconstitutional, violating students' rights to access to information and free speech. The American Association of School Librarians has weighed in against the practice, comparing banned websites to banned books (Hu, 2011).

Censorship results in the exclusion of many interesting and educationally defensible sites (Callister & Burbules, 2004). For example, one sex screen banned the Declaration of Independence (presumably because it calls for citizens to violently overthrow their government, if necessary). Critics contend that this indiscriminate screening not only robs students of important information but also may be politically biased, as is the case with Marxism.

The United States is not unique in attempting to censor Internet use. For instance, the "Arab Spring" of 2011—when populations in countries such as Tunisia, Egypt, Libya, and Syria rose up against their totalitarian leadership—has been largely attributed to the virtually instant access to information. As we would expect, each country's leadership attempted to suppress Internet access.

This is virtually impossible, however, which leads to an additional issue with respect to Internet access: accuracy of information. For instance, in 2011, a You Tube video portrayed Miss USA candidates as not "believing in" math and being opposed to teaching math in schools. By the end of January 2011, it had been viewed by more than 1.3 million people (You Tube, 2011). This video was clearly a hoax and largely harmless, but it illustrates the fact that anything can be placed on the Internet, whether or not any evidence exists to support the information. Hoaxes are common, and they're not all as harmless as this example. If people fail to examine information critically, potential for harm exists.

The Internet is ubiquitous, and its impact will continue to increase. As it does, issues such as censorship and accuracy of information will also increase. Perhaps most important for you, as you work with your students, is the need to remind them to examine everything they see on the Internet with a critical eye before they accept the information as accurate. And as you use the Internet in your classes, you'll need to be aware of your state's and district's Internet policies.

EXPLORING DIVERSITY: Women and Minorities in the Curriculum

Critics have targeted the U.S. curriculum because they believe it has failed to adequately represent the contributions of women and cultural minorities (Ornstein et al., 2011). For example, until the 1960s and 1970s, the majority of the works included in junior high and high school literature books were written by white men, such as William Shakespeare, Mark Twain, and Robert Frost, with only a few marginal contributions by white women.

Recognition of the historical contributions of minorities was similarly lacking. For example, Dr. Charles Drew (1904–1950), an African American, developed the procedure for separating plasma from whole blood, an enormous contribution that unquestionably saved many soldiers' lives in World War II. Dr. Charles Norman (b. 1930), another African American, was the first person to implant an artificial heart in a human. Historically, most history books have ignored contributions of individuals who are members of cultural minorities. In response to critics, this situation is changing. For example, a postage stamp was issued in Drew's honor in 1981, and science fiction writer Isaac Asimov, a friend of Norman's, based his novel *Fantastic Voyage* on work done in Norman's laboratory. History texts have been expanded to include the contributions of women and minorities. School literature books also have changed: Many now include works written by members of various cultural minority groups, such as Maya Angelou, Sandra Cisneros, Gary Soto, and Toni Cade Bambara.

The issue is controversial, however, and critics charge that cultural minorities' works continue to be underrepresented in the curriculum (Banks & Banks, 2010). Because more than a third of our schoolchildren are members of cultural minorities, and the proportion is increasing, critics argue, the curriculum should be broadened to better reflect minority members' contributions and presence in our society. In addition, they assert, some time-honored literature, such as Mark Twain's *The Adventures of Huckleberry Finn*, portrays characters in ways that promote racial stereotypes and prejudice.

Some critics even argue that entire curricula should be oriented to specific ethnic groups. For instance, to help African American students understand and appreciate their cultural heritage, proponents of an "Afrocentric" curriculum advocate focusing on the achievements of African cultures, particularly ancient

Egypt. Students who study the contributions of people with ethnicities similar to their own will gain in self-esteem, motivation, and learning, they contend. A number of urban school districts have experimented with an Afrocentric curriculum (Gollnick & Chinn, 2013). The effectiveness of this approach has yet to be thoroughly examined by research.

As you would expect, these positions have critics of their own. Some educators and social commentators question the accuracy and balance of the content and whether the emphasis on differences leads to racial and ethnic separatism (Hirsch, 1987; Ravitch, 2000). They also argue that schools have gone too far in emphasizing cultural differences, resulting in the reduction or elimination of works that focus on some of the great contributions to literature, such as those of Shakespeare. Further, we are all Americans, they maintain, and overemphasis on diversity has resulted in the failure of students to develop a common cultural heritage and shared national identity.

The role of women in the curriculum is also controversial. For example, many feminist groups contend that women continue to be both underrepresented and misrepresented in the curriculum, arguing that students read too many books that portray men as doctors, lawyers, and engineers, and women as nurses, teachers, and secretaries. A study of California's history–social science standards found that of the 96 Americans mentioned in the standards, only 18% were female (Sleeter, 2005). When this occurs, they assert, girls are sent messages about appropriate roles and careers for them. In response to criticisms, a strong and systematic national effort has been made to address the needs of girls and women in the curriculum (Helgeson, 2012). Some people contend that the emphasis on girls' needs has gone too far, which is the argument made in *The War Against Boys*, the provocative book by Christine Hoff Sommers (2000). Nearly 15 years later, the debate continues as hotly as ever, and the controversy is likely to remain in the future.

DIVERSITY AND YOU

Controversies and the Curriculum

You're sitting in the teachers' lounge and are drawn into a discussion about the "sanitized" version of *The Adventures of Huckleberry Finn*, the version published in early 2011, in which the N-word, which occurred 219 times in the original version, was replaced by the word *slave*. Ken, one of your colleagues, strongly disagrees with this "sanitizing" process, arguing that the original version presents an accurate picture of racism and racist attitudes at that time, and a significant portion of the book's message is lost in the revision. Further, he contends, today's rappers continue to liberally use the N-word in their lyrics.

Joan, another of your colleagues, and an English teacher, takes the opposite view, arguing that the original version of the novel has fallen off many reading lists, substantively because the use of the N-word remains as vitriolic today as has ever been. "I don't use it in my classes anymore," she notes. "I just don't want to deal with the controversy, which detracts from the text's literary message. It got almost explosive in one of my classes last year, and I don't want to go through that again."

"What do you think?" they ask simultaneously, seeing that you're obviously interested in the conversation.

QUESTIONS TO CONSIDER

1. Knowing that it can be highly emotional and potentially controversial, should a book, such as *The Adventures of Huckleberry Finn,* be included as part of the school curriculum? If so, is a "sanitized" version preferable to the original?
2. Some authors, and teachers, argue that classics, such as Harper Lee's *To Kill a Mockingbird,* and Steinbeck's *Of Mice and Men,* in addition to *The Adventures of Huckleberry Finn,* no longer belong in the curriculum because the content is dated, and more recent novels with similar themes are more motivating to today's students (Foley, 2009). Do you agree or disagree with this position? Explain why.

Go to *Diversity and You* in the MyEducationLab™ *Book Resources* that accompany this text to log your thoughts and receive feedback from your authors.

Check Your Understanding

4.1 How do issues involving sex education and moral development differ in their influence on the school curriculum?

4.2 Describe the concept of intelligent design, and explain how it could influence curriculum decisions.

4.3 How could issues involving censorship influence your curriculum decisions?

For feedback, go to the appendix, *Check Your Understanding*, located in the back of this text.

VOICES from the CLASSROOM

"I don't always succeed in unlocking the potential in every one of my students; but it is this challenge that keeps me in education..."

JESSICA GARNER, 2010 Teacher of the Year, North Carolina

CHAPTER 9 Summary

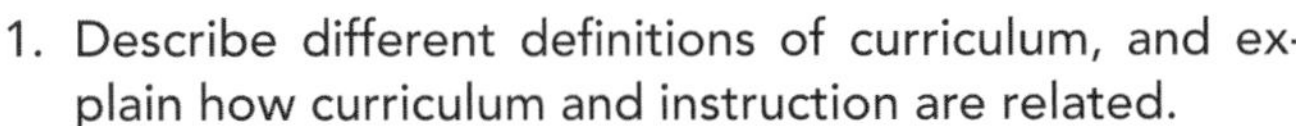

1. Describe different definitions of curriculum, and explain how curriculum and instruction are related.
   - *Curriculum* is defined in a variety of ways, such as the subject matter taught to students, a systematic arrangement of courses, the planned educational experiences offered by a school, experiences students have in school, and the process teachers go through in selecting and organizing learning experiences for their students.
   - In this chapter, *curriculum* is defined as everything teachers teach and students learn in school, and instruction is described as the strategies teachers use to help students reach the goals established in the curriculum.
2. Explain how the explicit curriculum, the implicit curriculum, the null curriculum, and the extracurriculum are different.
   - The *explicit curriculum* is the curriculum found in standards, curriculum guides, textbooks, and other formal educational experiences.
   - The *implicit, or hidden, curriculum* is reflected in the unstated values and priorities of the school and the classroom, along with the general climate of our classrooms. It differs from the explicit curriculum in that it isn't specifically prescribed and, in some cases, is out of the teachers' conscious awareness or control.
   - The *null curriculum* differs from the explicit and the implicit curricula in that they both reflect what is taught, whereas the null curriculum reflects what is not taught.
   - The *extracurriculum* includes learning experiences that extend beyond the core of students' formal studies. Participation in extracurricular activities correlates with a number of positive outcomes, including increased achievement and more positive attitudes toward school.
3. Identify different forces that influence the curriculum, and explain how each exerts its influence.
   - A teacher's general philosophical views of teaching and learning as well as standards and accountability, the federal government, and textbooks all influence the curriculum.
   - Teachers' philosophies influence the curriculum because philosophy is grounded in beliefs; professionals teach what they believe is important, and they use approaches they believe are most effective.

- Standards and accountability influence the curriculum because standards specify what students should be learning, and what is tested often becomes what is taught.
- The federal government influences curriculum through its legislative mandates as well as through the programs it supports financially.
- Textbooks influence the curriculum because many teachers use textbooks as a primary source for their curricular decisions about what to teach.

4. Describe prominent controversial issues in the curriculum.
   - Sex education, education in morals and values, intelligent design versus evolution, censorship, and the underrepresentation of women and minorities in the curriculum are controversial issues facing today's teachers. These issues are likely to remain unresolved in the near future.
   - These controversial issues influence the curriculum because they affect what topics are or are not taught and how they are presented to students.

Important Concepts

21st-Century Skills
accountability
censorship
character education
creationism
curriculum
explicit curriculum
extracurriculum
high-stakes tests
implicit curriculum
instruction
integrated curriculum
intelligent design
moral education
null curriculum
service learning
standards

Portfolio Activity

Making Curriculum Decisions

InTASC Core Teaching Standard 7: Planning For Instruction

The purpose of this activity is to help you begin the process of making decisions about curriculum. (You will have an opportunity to refine your portfolio entry when you study the process of instruction in more detail.)

1. Go to the Internet, and identify two of your state's standards for your content area or teaching level. For example, if you're preparing to be an elementary teacher, identify a reading and a math standard for the grade level you want to teach. If you're preparing to be a middle or secondary teacher, identify two content-related standards.
2. Write one or more learning goals that best represent your interpretation of each standard.
3. Then describe a learning activity designed to help students reach the learning goal or goals for each standard.

Portfolio Activities similar to this one and related to chapter content can be found at MyEducationLab™.

The School Curriculum in an Era of Standards

Go to the topic *Assessment, Standards, and Accountability* in the MyEducationLab (www.myeducationlab.com) for *Introduction to Teaching*, where you can:

- Find learning outcomes for *Assessment, Standards, and Accountability*, along with the national standards that connect to these outcomes.
- Complete *Assignments and Activities* that can help you more deeply understand the chapter content.
- Apply and practice your understanding of the core teaching skills identified in the chapter with the *Building Teaching Skills and Dispositions* learning units.
- Examine challenging situations and cases presented in the IRIS Center Resources.
- Access video clips of CCSSO National Teachers of the Year award winners responding to the question, "Why Do I Teach?" in the *Teacher Talk* section.
- Check your comprehension on the content covered in the chapter with the *Study Plan*. Here you will be able to take a chapter quiz, receive feedback on your answers, and then access *Review, Practice, and Enrichment* activities to enhance your understanding of chapter content.
- Check the *Book Resources* to find opportunities to share thoughts and gather feedback on the *Diversity and You* and *Issues You'll Face in Teaching* features found in this chapter.

MyEducationLab™

CHAPTER

10 Classroom Management: Creating Productive Learning Environments

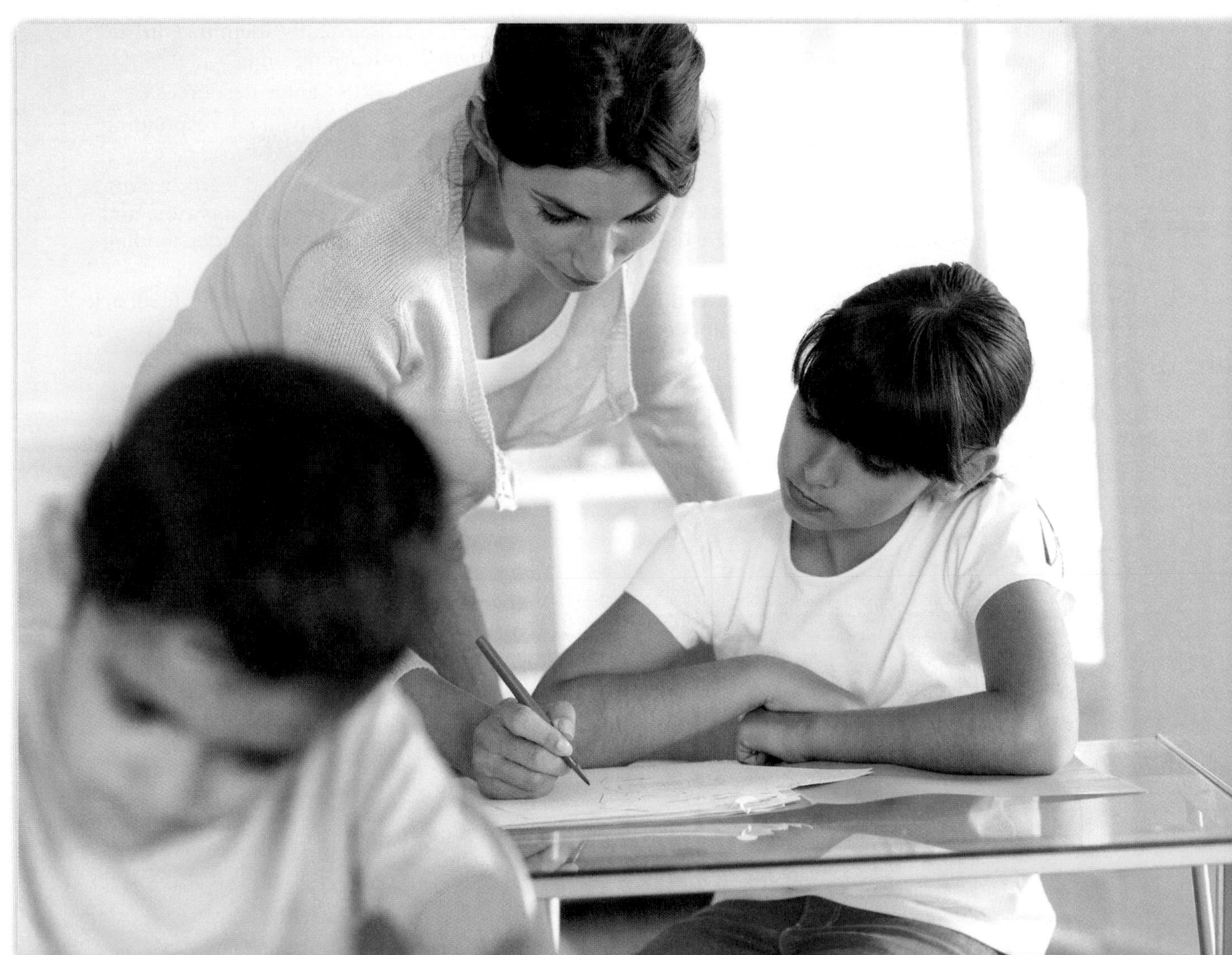

VOICES from the CLASSROOM

"For so many of our students, school is the one place that they know they can come to that's safe . . . I teach to make a difference in the life of a child."

MEGAN ALLEN, 2010 Teacher of the Year, Florida

CHAPTER OUTLINE

LEARNING OUTCOMES

After you've completed your study of this chapter, you should be able to:

1. **Describe productive learning environments, and explain how they contribute to learning.** InTASC Core Teaching Standard 3, Learning Environments.
2. **Identify the processes involved in creating a productive learning environment.** InTASC Core Teaching Standard 3, Learning Environments.
3. **Explain how involving parents contributes to a productive learning environment.** InTASC Core Teaching Standard 3, Learning Environments.
4. **Describe how effective teachers intervene when misbehavior occurs.** InTASC Core Teaching Standard 3, Learning Environments.

Teaching and You

As you anticipate your first teaching position, what is your greatest concern? Why do you feel that way?

Classroom management is a topic of ongoing concern for teachers, administrators, and the public, and it directly relates to the question we asked in *Teaching and You*. If you're typical, the answer is classroom management. It was for both of us (Don and Paul, your authors) as we started our first jobs, and most beginning teachers perceive it as their most serious challenge (D. Kaufman & Moss, 2010). It's also a major cause of teacher burnout and job dissatisfaction for veteran teachers, and public opinion polls identify it as a primary problem for our schools (Bushaw & Lopez, 2010).

As you read the following case study, think about the classroom management challenges facing Shannon Brinkman, a first-year, fifth-grade teacher.

Shannon Brinkman, an elementary teacher in an urban school in the Southwest, looks up as the last of her fifth graders file out the door on the last day of the school year.

"Phew!" It's been a tough year for this first-year teacher. It seemed like her class was in constant turmoil, as she struggled to figure out who she was and what to expect from her fifth graders. Every day presented new management challenges, and Shannon struggled to just keep her head above water.

Her kids weren't bad as individuals; in fact, she grew attached to each and every one of them individually. But as a group, they took on a different character and seemed to constantly resist her efforts to teach.

Shannon doesn't know if she can take another year like this one. Maybe she isn't cut out to be a teacher.

With a sigh, she looks out the window and resolves to seek help from other experienced teachers. Next year just has to be different.

This I Believe

CLASSROOM MANAGEMENT AND MY CLASSROOM

For each item, circle the number that best represents your belief. Use the following scale as a guide:

4 = I strongly believe the statement is true.

3 = I believe the statement is true.

2 = I believe the statement is false.

1 = I strongly believe the statement is false.

1. The best way I can maintain an orderly classroom is to quickly stop misbehavior in my students whenever it occurs.

   1 2 3 4

2. The best way to increase the amount my students learn about a topic is to allocate more time to that topic.

   1 2 3 4

3. Showing that I care about students is important if I plan to teach elementary students, but it is less important if I plan to teach middle or high school students.

   1 2 3 4

4. It is important that I involve my students' parents in their children's education.

   1 2 3 4

5. If some of my students are involved in a fight or a scuffle, I am required by law to intervene.

   1 2 3 4

Shannon's experience is not unusual. Many beginning teachers struggle with classroom management, and it's a major reason many new teachers leave the profession. We'll return to Shannon's work with her students, but before we do, please respond to the items in the *This I Believe: Classroom Management and My Classroom* feature here. We address each in the chapter.

MyEducationLab™

Visit the MyEducationLab for *Introduction to Teaching* to enhance your understanding of chapter concepts with a personalized *Study Plan.* You'll also have the opportunity to hone your teaching skills through video and case-based *Assignments and Activities* and *Building Teaching Skills and Disposition* lessons.

What Is a Productive Learning Environment?

Creating a productive learning environment in your classroom is central to effective classroom management, but what exactly is a productive learning environment? The term **productive learning environment** *seems* somewhat remote and abstract, but in fact it's very simple—it's a classroom that is safe and orderly and focused on learning. In it students feel physically and emotionally safe, and the daily routines, learning activities, and standards for appropriate behavior are all designed to promote learning and development. In productive learning environments, students are well behaved, but the emotional climate is relaxed and inviting. They understand that learning is the highest priority, they're respectful of others, and they accept responsibility for their actions. Teachers rarely have to raise their voices, and the focus is on helping everyone learn.

This may seem idealistic, but with time and effort, it's possible in most classrooms. **Classroom management**, all the actions teachers take to create an environment that supports academic and social-emotional learning, is essential for creating this ideal. Let's see why it's so important.

Why Classroom Management Is so Important

Classroom management is important to everyone associated with education. For our students' parents, school leaders, and the public at large, effectively managed classrooms suggest that schools and teachers are in charge and know what they're doing (Bushaw & Lopez, 2010).

For those of us who teach, classroom management contributes to learning and development—our primary goals in classrooms—in multiple ways. Students are more motivated to learn, and they learn more in well-managed classrooms (Good & Brophy, 2008). They learn more when the environment is safe, secure, and inviting, so we strive to make our classrooms emotionally safe (Emmer & Evertson, 2013; Evertson & Emmer, 2013). We emphasize respect and responsibility because they promote our students' personal, social, and moral development. We avoid criticizing students because criticism detracts from learning. We create systems of rules and procedures because they help students develop a sense of personal responsibility for their actions.

Goals of Classroom Management

Successful classroom management begins with goals; they guide our actions and provide structure to our classroom. Let's see how Shannon Brinkman, the fifth-grade teacher in our opening case, changes her goals to make her classroom management more effective and her classroom a more inviting place to learn.

After several weeks of much-needed vacation, Shannon decides she needs to make some changes in her classroom. She just can't take another year like her first one. She meets with several of the teachers in her school that seem to have their act together; they enjoy teaching, and kids like to be in their classrooms. She even digs out her notes from her old classroom management class and rereads some of the chapters from management texts she used. As she reads and thinks about the advice from others, a plan starts to emerge. She not only has to change her management goals for the next year but also how she structures her classroom and interacts with students. This year is going to be different.

As Shannon prepares for her second year of work, she spends several days preparing her room. She tapes posters and pictures on the walls and labels the clock, windows, door, and other common objects with signs in both Spanish and English.

As her students enter her classroom on the first day, she greets them at the door and tells them to find their names on the desks. Shannon has 14 girls and 10 boys in her class, and 8 of them speak Spanish as their first language. As soon as her students are settled, she asks them to introduce themselves and describe their families, some of their favorite activities, and anything else they think might be interesting.

After they're finished, Shannon comments, "We are going to have a great year. I asked you to introduce yourselves because we're all going to work together to help each other learn and grow. Our classroom is like a family, and in families, people help each other.

"To be sure we all help each other and learn as much as we can, we need some guidelines that will make our classroom run smoothly," she continues, and then asks her students to make suggestions that will help them all be comfortable and will keep the classroom safe and orderly. They discuss the suggestions, and Shannon makes notes to be sure she remembers what they've said. After the discussion, she takes a picture of each student with her digital camera.

She prints the pictures that evening and, based on their discussion, also creates a poster describing class rules and procedures. Before school the next morning, she displays the pictures on a bulletin board under a sign that says, "Our class," and she places the rules and procedures where everyone can see.

Her first day has been demanding, but she feels ready to jump into the year.

Revisiting My Beliefs

This discussion addresses the first item in *This I Believe*, "The best way I can maintain an orderly classroom is to quickly stop misbehavior in my students whenever it occurs." This statement isn't true; prevention, not intervention, is the key to effective classroom management.

Some of the earliest research on classroom management was done by Jacob Kounin (1970), who helped us understand the difference between classroom management and **discipline**, teachers' responses to student misbehavior. Kounin found that the key to an orderly classroom is the teacher's ability to prevent management problems from occurring in the first place, rather than handling misbehavior once it occurs. His findings have been consistently corroborated over the years (Reupert & Woodcock, 2010).

Classroom management is much more than simply keeping students quiet and in their seats. It's a process that, when effectively implemented, contributes to learners' academic, personal, and social development. In designing an effective classroom management system, we have four primary goals:

- Creating a positive classroom climate
- Creating a community of learners
- Developing learner responsibility
- Maximizing time and opportunity for learning

Creating a Positive Classroom Climate

A **positive classroom climate** is an environment in which learners feel physically and emotionally safe, personally connected to both their teacher and their peers, and worthy of love and respect (O'Connor, Dearing, & Collins, 2011). In a positive classroom climate "[S]tudents can afford to be emotionally vulnerable, and . . . that vulnerability extends to the student's willingness to risk engagement in acts of kindness and concern for others" (Nucci, 2006, p. 716). Aggressive acts such as name-calling, bullying, putdowns, and other forms of hurtful interactions are forbidden because they detract from feelings of safety and the willingness of students to be open to others. A positive classroom climate is essential because students learn more when the emotional climate is supportive.

Effective classroom management creates a community of learners in which students learn personal responsibility.

Shannon promoted a positive classroom climate in several ways. First, as she planned for her year, she created displays and placed pictures on her classroom walls to make her room physically attractive. Second, because she knew that a number of her students were native Spanish speakers, she labeled objects around the room in both English and Spanish. Third, as her students came into the room the first day, she greeted them at the door and had them introduce themselves to their classmates. She took their pictures, which she displayed on a bulletin board before the students came in the second day. Each of these actions helped to make her classroom warm and inviting.

Creating a Community of Learners

A positive emotional climate allows you to create a **learning community** in your classroom, a place where you and your students all work together to help everyone learn (Mason, 2007). In a learning community, you and all your students—high and low achievers, members and nonmembers of cultural minorities, students with and without exceptionalities, boys and girls—work together. Everyone participates in learning activities, supports each other's learning efforts, and believes they can succeed. You facilitate this process by treating your students as individuals, refusing to allow members of cultural minorities to cluster in groups at the back of your classroom, involving everyone in learning activities, and calling on all your students as equally as possible. Each of these actions makes your students feel as if they belong and are welcome in your classroom.

Shannon began this process by having her students offer suggestions for making their classroom a better place to learn. She didn't impose classroom rules on her students; the class collaborated in developing them. Her efforts helped students believe that they had a personal investment in the class and a role in making it a productive place to learn.

Respect for all is an integral part of a learning community. You are courteous and attentive in your interactions with your students, and you require the same in return. When you speak, your students show respect by listening, and they also listen when a classmate has the floor. Learning to respect the rights of others advances personal and social development, and it extends well beyond school. People who are sensitive to the thoughts and feelings of others are much more successful in life than those who haven't developed this essential trait (Berk, 2012).

Helping your students learn to be respectful will obviously be a challenge, particularly in some environments, and you will have a few students who are disrespectful regardless of what you do. However, with time and effort, you can make important strides toward this essential goal, and for the students you reach, you will have made an invaluable contribution to their lives, both in and beyond school.

Developing Learner Responsibility

"My kids are so irresponsible," Kathy Hughes, a colleague and friend of Shannon's grumbles in a conversation after school. "They don't bring their books, they forget their notebooks in their lockers, they come without pencils. . . . I can't get them to come to class prepared, let alone get them to read their assignments."

"I know," Shannon responds, smiling sympathetically. "Some of them are totally spacey, and others just don't seem to give a rip."

Teachers frequently lament students' lack of effort and willingness to take responsibility for their own learning, and this feeling of frustration is also common among beginning teachers.

Helping students learn to be responsible is one of the biggest challenges you'll face. Classroom management provides you with excellent opportunities to teach students about personal responsibility, not only to their own schoolwork, but also to other students. You can promote responsibility by talking about it, explicitly teaching it, and helping students understand the consequences for behaving irresponsibly.

To see how we might reach this goal, let's return to Shannon's work with her students.

On the second day of school, Shannon begins, "To learn as much as possible, we need to work together and support each other in all our efforts. For instance, I need to plan for what we're trying to accomplish, and I need to bring the examples and materials that will help you understand our topics. . . . That's my part. . . . So, what is your part?"

With some guidance from Shannon, the students conclude that they should bring their books and other materials to class each day, they need to be in their seats when the bell rings, and they need to understand their homework instead of merely getting it done. They also decide that they need to listen until their classmates finish talking, and they need to be supportive of their classmates' efforts.

"Now, who is responsible for all this?" Shannon asks.

"We are," several students respond.

"Yes. . . . I'm responsible for my part, and you're responsible for your parts.

"Now, let's see what happens when people aren't responsible," Shannon continues, displaying the following on the document camera:

> *Josh brings all his materials to school every day, and he carefully does his homework. He has a list that he checks off to be sure that he has each of the items and that he understands his homework. If he's uncertain about any part, he asks the next day. He participates in class discussions and is supportive when his classmates talk.*
>
> *Josh is learning a lot, and he says his classes are interesting. His teachers respect his effort.*
>
> *Andy gets in trouble with his teachers because he often forgets to bring his book, notebook, or pencil to class. He sometimes forgets his homework, so he doesn't get credit for the assignment, and he isn't learning very much. Andy also snaps at his classmates in discussions, and sometimes hurts their feelings. Now, some of the other students don't want to talk to him.*
>
> *Andy's teacher called his mom to discuss his behavior and lack of responsibility, and now Andy can't watch TV for a week.*

"What are some differences you notice between Josh and Andy?" Shannon asks after giving students a minute to read the vignettes.

The students make several comments, and in the process, Ronise concludes, "It's his own fault," in response to someone pointing out that Andy isn't learning very much and not getting along with the other students.

"Yes," Shannon nods, "if we don't take responsibility for ourselves and control our own actions and emotions, whose fault is it if we don't learn?"

"Our own," several students respond.

"Yes," Shannon emphasizes. "We're all responsible for ourselves."

Interestingly, students often don't understand how their actions affect learning and influence others, so Shannon taught the idea of responsibility by illustrating it with an example (Josh) and nonexample (Andy)—which is the way we teach any concept. By illustrating the consequences of being—or not being—responsible, Shannon helped promote awareness and understanding in her students (Charles & Senter, 2012).

Shannon further contributed to the process by explaining how she tried to be responsible herself, "I need to plan for what we're trying to accomplish, and I need to bring the examples and materials that will help you understand our topics. . . . that's my part." In doing so she modeled responsibility and illustrated the respect for others that is so essential for creating a learning community and developing a positive classroom climate.

Students obviously won't learn to take responsibility for their actions in one lesson, but with ongoing effort throughout the school year, you can make a difference with many of them. And the benefits can be enormous. Your job will become easier, and students develop a sense of personal satisfaction, accomplishment, and autonomy when they see that they are in charge of their own behavior. Even difficult and hard-to-reach students can be taught to accept responsibility for their own actions and behaviors.

Maximizing Time and Opportunities for Learning

Creating a positive classroom climate and a community of learners will help your students learn to accept responsibility for their own actions, and disruptions and misbehavior will decrease, so you will have more time to devote to teaching and learning, the fourth important goal of classroom management.

But "time" isn't as simple as it appears on the surface, and different dimensions exist (Weinstein, Romano, & Mignano, 2011):

- **Allocated time**—the amount of time a teacher or school designates for a content area or topic, such as elementary schools' allocating an hour a day to math or middle and secondary schools' having 55-minute periods.
- **Instructional time**—the time left for teaching after routine management and administrative tasks are completed.
- **Engaged time**—the amount of time students are paying attention and involved in learning activities.
- **Academic learning time**—the time students are successful while engaged in learning activities.

When reformers suggest lengthening the school day or year, they're suggesting an increase in allocated time (Ubinas & Gabrieli, 2011). Comparisons with other countries reveal that students in our country have significantly less time allocated to their studies than do students in other countries (Gewertz, 2008). Critics say this is a major reason U.S. students don't perform as well as their international counterparts.

Time's value, however, depends on how efficiently it's used. Let's look at how two teachers use their allocated time.

Shannon has a warm-up exercise on the board when her students come back to her room after lunch and get ready for math. She completes routine tasks while they finish it, and she then moves immediately into her math lesson. When the lesson is finished, she gives an assignment and monitors the class while they work on it.

Donna Burroughs, who teaches in the room next to Shannon, completes routine tasks while her students talk among themselves. After a few minutes, she begins her math lesson and finishes with 10 minutes left in the time she has allocated for math, during which she again lets her students talk quietly.

These examples illustrate differences in the teachers' instructional time, and if they represent patterns, Donna will lose nearly 40 hours of this precious time over the course of a school year! The obvious result is less student learning.

The benefits of increased allocated time are reduced if instructional time is spent on noninstructional activities, as you saw in the example with Shannon and Donna. Engaged time is lost if students aren't paying attention, and academic learning time decreases if students are confused and unsuccessful.

These different dimensions of time help us understand why classroom management is so essential for learning. In classrooms where students are engaged and successful, achievement is high, learners feel a sense of accomplishment, and interest in the topics increases (Good & Brophy, 2008).

The ideal to strive for is to maximize instructional, engaged, and academic learning time so that all our allocated time is devoted to learning. Although teachers need to spend some time on routine activities, such as taking roll and collecting homework, we should try to come as close as possible to this ideal.

Revisiting My Beliefs

This discussion addresses the second item in *This I Believe*, "The best way to increase the amount my students learn about a topic is to allocate more time to that topic." This statement isn't true: The best way to increase student learning is to involve them in learning activities in which they're successful.

Check Your Understanding

1.1. What is a productive learning environment?

1.2. Explain why effective classroom management is so important for creating a productive learning environment.

1.3. Describe the goals of classroom management.

For feedback, go to the appendix, *Check Your Understanding*, located in the back of this text.

FIGURE 10.1 Creating Productive Learning Environments

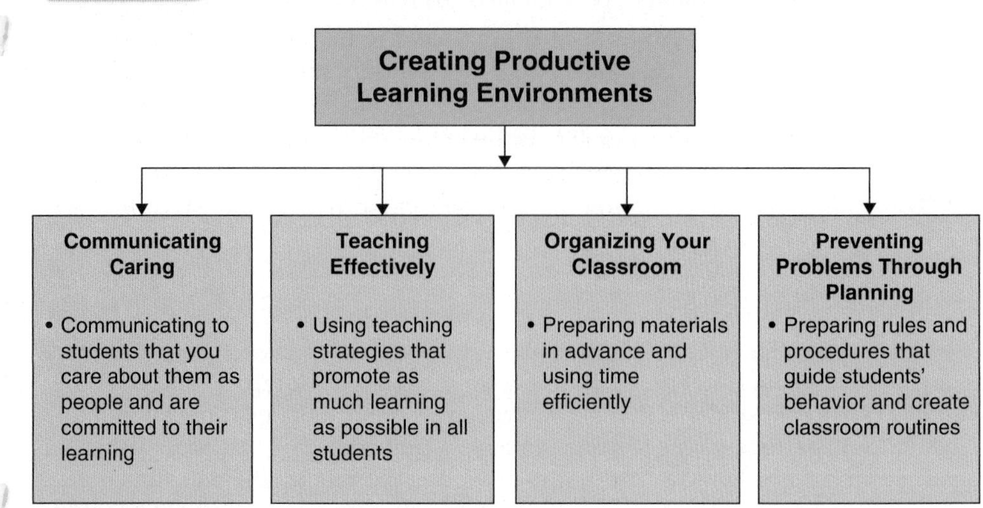

Creating a Productive Learning Environment

A productive learning environment is a classroom that is orderly and focused on learning. But how specifically can you create one in your own classroom? In this section we describe what you can do to create this type of environment in your own classroom, beginning with your personal role as a teacher.

Your role in creating a productive learning environment is essential. You set the emotional tone for the classroom and create an atmosphere that can be positive and inviting, neutral, or even threatening. (As a student, Don—one of your authors—entered his high school biology class and was greeted with, "My name is Isabel Wilharm, and the name means exactly what it says. Step out of line and I *will harm*." Ugh!) You also design learning activities that engage all of your students and ensure that none are ignored or distanced emotionally. You are the key to determining how your classroom feels.

Creating productive learning environments includes four processes. They're outlined in Figure 10.1 and discussed in the sections that follow.

Teaching and You

Think back to your time in elementary, middle, and high school, and ask yourself which of your teachers you remember most positively. What do you remember about them?

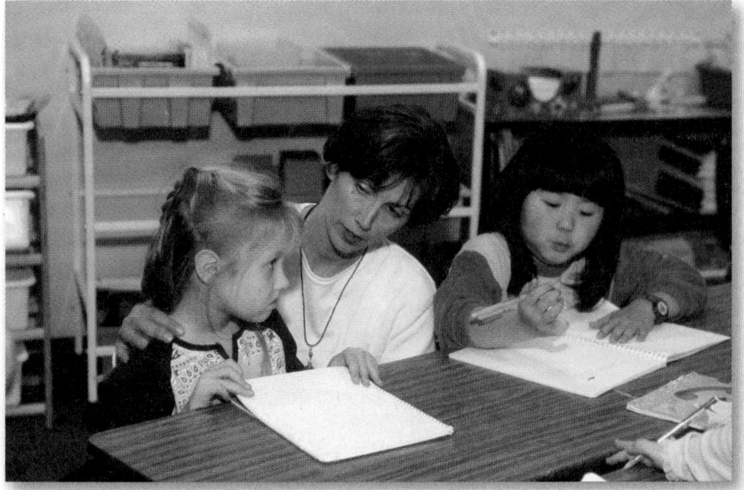

Caring, an essential component of a productive learning environment, connects teachers with students on a human level.

Communicating Caring

To begin, let's consider the question we asked in *Teaching and You*. If you're like the students we asked in our classes, believing that they cared about you as a person and were committed to your learning was most important. **Caring** refers to a teacher's investment in the protection and development of young people, and a caring teacher is at the heart of a productive learning environment (Noddings, 2005, 2010a). The importance of caring is captured by one fourth grader's comment: "If a teacher doesn't care about you, it affects your mind. You feel like you're a nobody, and it makes you want to drop out of school" (Noblit, Rogers, & McCadden, 1995, p. 683). Research supports this fourth grader's feelings.

> Students who perceived that teachers cared about them reported positive motivational outcomes such as more prosocial and social responsibility goals, academic effort, and greater internal control beliefs. It appears that students want teachers to care for them both as learners and as people. (Perry, Turner, & Meyer, 2006, p. 341)

Additional research indicates that students are more motivated and learn more in classrooms where they believe their teachers like, understand, and empathize with them (O'Connor et al., 2011). Students who believe they're wanted and who receive personal support from their teachers also are more interested in their class work and describe it as more important than do students whose teachers are distant. A supportive classroom environment, where each student is valued regardless of academic ability or performance, is essential for both learning and motivation for all students.

Revisiting My Beliefs

This discussion addresses the third item in *This I Believe*, "Showing that I care about students is important if I plan to teach elementary students, but it is less important if I plan to teach middle or high school students." The first part of this statement is true, but the second isn't: A caring teacher is important for students at all grade levels, and its importance doesn't diminish as students grow older.

Showing Them That We Care

How do we communicate that we care about our students? Several concrete suggestions that you can use in your own classroom include:

- Learn students' names quickly, and call on students by their first name.
- Greet students every day, and get to know them as individuals.
- Use "we" and "our" instead of "you" and "your" in reference to class activities and assignments.
- Use personal nonverbal communications such as eye contact and smiling.
- Spend time with students before and after school and during lunch breaks.
- Hold students to high standards.

We want to particularly emphasize the last two items. We all have 24 hours in our days—no more, no less—and the way we choose to allocate our time is the truest measure of our priorities. Helping students who have problems with an assignment or calling a parent after school hours communicates that you care about your students' learning. Spending a moment to ask a question about a baby brother or to compliment a new hairstyle communicates caring about a student as a human being.

The idea that holding students to high standards is an indicator of caring may seem surprising. But as one motivation expert suggested, teachers demonstrate that they care for students in the following ways:

> [N]ot accepting sloppy, thoughtless, or incomplete work, by pressing them to clarify vague comments, by encouraging them not to give up, and by not praising work that does not reflect genuine effort. Ironically, reactions that are often intended to protect students' self-esteem—such as accepting low quality work—convey a lack of interest, patience, or caring. (Stipek, 2002, p. 157)

This view is corroborated by research. When junior high students were asked, "How do you know when a teacher cares about you?" they responded that paying attention to them as human beings was important, but more striking was their belief that teachers who care are committed to their learning and hold them to high standards (B. Wilson & Corbett, 2001).

Teaching Effectively

Think about the question we asked in *Teaching and You*. We're most likely to drift off, text, or talk to a neighbor if our instructor stands at the front of the class droning on in a boring lecture. This was certainly true when we—Don and Paul—were students, and it's true in all teaching situations. It's impossible to create a productive learning environment without effective teaching.

Teaching and You

Think about your own experiences as a student. In which classes are you most likely to drift off, perhaps text a friend, or even chat with the person next to you?

The close link between management and instruction has been consistently corroborated by research, and it is true whether you plan to teach in elementary, middle, or high schools.

> Without question, the most essential classroom management tool is a rigorous and relevant curriculum. Walk the halls of any school, and you'll find that it's not the strictest teacher with the most rules, but the personable teacher with the most interesting and challenging lesson plan that has the best-behaved students. (Kraft, 2010, p. 45)

This suggests that when you plan for classroom management, you should simultaneously plan for effective instruction.

Organizing Your Classroom

We've probably all said at some point in our lives, "I need to be better organized." This usually means that we don't have routines for where we put personal items, such as our keys, aren't able to easily access important papers and other materials, or a have tendency to just waste time.

The same idea applies in classrooms. **Classroom organization** is a professional skill that includes:

- Preparing materials in advance
- Starting classes and activities on time
- Making transitions quickly and smoothly
- Creating well-established routines

As with effective instruction, it's impossible to create a productive learning environment if teachers are fumbling around for materials, if they waste time at the beginning or end of their allocated class time, or if they lack procedures for routine activities. Organization is essential for effective classroom management, and it's one of the first aspects you'll consider as you plan.

As an example, let's look again at Shannon and her work with her students.

Shannon has a warm-up exercise on the board when her students come back to her room after lunch and get ready for math. She completes routine tasks while they finish it, and she then moves immediately into her math lesson. When the lesson is finished, she gives an assignment, and monitors the class while they work on it.

Shannon was well organized. She had an exercise prepared and waiting for her students as they entered the room, so instruction began the instant the bell rang. By planning a warm-up activity as she did, having your materials prepared in advance, and beginning your instruction immediately, you can eliminate "dead" time, when disruptions are most likely to occur.

Transitions from one activity to another, such as from whole-class instruction to group work and back again, are also important. Providing clear and precise directions for group work helps make transitions quick and smooth and reduces the opportunities for disruptions.

Well-established routines, such as procedures for turning in papers, going to the bathroom, and lining up for lunch, are essential as well. When students perform routines, such as turning in papers, automatically, management problems are reduced and opportunities for teaching and learning are maximized, because you don't have to spend time and energy explaining or reminding students of what to do.

To see how a teacher uses organization and effective teaching skills to minimize management problems, click on the video, *Essential Teaching Skills in Urban Classrooms* (13:43).

Preventing Problems Through Planning

In a productive learning environment, management is nearly invisible. The atmosphere is calm but not rigid, movement around the classroom and interactions in lessons are comfortable, and students work quietly. Learning is taking place.

You will have to give few directions that focus on behavior, you will reprimand students infrequently, and your reprimands will rarely intrude on learning. This is an ideal, but in most cases you can make it happen. How?

The key is careful planning. Some classes are tougher to manage than others, and if you anticipate a challenging class, it simply means that you'll need to plan even more carefully. In most cases creating an orderly classroom is possible, but beginning teachers often underestimate the amount of time and energy it takes.

Developmental Differences in Students

As you begin your planning, you first need to consider the developmental level of your students; if you're a first-grade teacher, you will plan differently than if you're a middle or high school teacher. For instance, first graders are typically compliant and eager to please their teachers, but they also have short attention spans and tire easily (Evertson & Emmer, 2013). If you're teaching first grade, you'll need to carefully model simple procedures, such as how to turn in papers, and you'll need to provide your students with concrete examples that illustrate each of your classroom rules.

In comparison, middle schoolers often test their developing independence, they're sometimes rebellious and capricious, and they're sensitive about teachers who have "favorites" or "pets." So, if you're a middle school teacher, you will need to be judicious in consistently and dispassionately enforcing your rules (Emmer & Evertson, 2013). However, students at all levels need caring teachers who have positive expectations for them and hold them to high standards.

Creating Procedures and Rules

Having considered how to organize your classroom, and keeping your students' developmental needs in mind, you are now ready to make decisions about the procedures and rules you'll implement in your classroom. They will be the cornerstone of your classroom management system.

Procedures are the routines students follow in their daily learning activities, such as how they turn in papers, sharpen pencils, and make transitions from one activity to another. For instance, Shannon's students turn in their papers from the ends of the rows, with each student putting her paper on the top of the stack as it moves forward. This allows Shannon to collect the stacks from the first student in each row, and when she returns the papers, she simply gives the stacks to those same students, who take their papers off the top and pass the stacks back to the students behind them. Simple procedures such as these both create a sense of order for students and will save you time and energy.

You should create procedures for activities such as the following:

- Entering and leaving the classroom
- Handing in and returning papers
- Accessing materials such as scissors and paper
- Sharpening pencils
- Making trips to the bathroom
- Making up work after an absence

After planning and teaching students about procedures, effective teachers then have their students practice until they can follow the procedures virtually without thinking about them.

Rules, such as "Listen when a classmate is talking," are guidelines that provide standards for acceptable classroom behavior (Emmer & Evertson, 2013; Evertson & Emmer, 2013). When consistently enforced, clear, reasonable rules not only reduce behavior problems that interfere with learning but also promote a feeling of pride and responsibility in the classroom community. Perhaps surprisingly, students also see the enforcement of rules as evidence of caring: "Students also say that they want teachers to articulate and enforce clear standards of

TABLE 10.1 Examples of Classroom Rules

First-Grade Teacher	Seventh-Grade Teacher	Tenth-Grade Teacher
• We raise our hands before speaking. • We leave our seats only when given permission by the teacher. • We stand politely in line at all times. • We keep our hands to ourselves. • We listen when someone else is talking.	• Be in your seat and quiet when the bell rings. • Follow directions the first time they're given. • Bring covered textbooks, notebook, pen, pencils, and planner to class every day. • Raise your hand for permission to speak or to leave your seat. • Keep hands, feet, and objects to yourself. • Leave class only when dismissed by the teacher.	• Do all grooming outside class. • Be in your seat before the bell rings. • Stay in your seat at all times. • Bring all materials daily. This includes your book, notebook, pen/pencil, and paper. • Give your full attention to others in discussions, and wait your turn to speak. • Leave when I dismiss you, not when the bell rings.

Source: Reprinted from Eggen, P., & Kauchak, D. (2013). *Educational psychology: Windows on classrooms* (9th ed.). Upper Saddle River, NJ: Merrill/Prentice Hall.

behavior. They view this not just as part of the teacher's job but as evidence that the teacher cares about them" (Brophy, 2010, p. 24).

Examples of rules at different grade levels are found in Table 10.1. Note that some rules occur at all levels, such as students' staying in their seats and waiting for permission to speak. Other rules are specific to a grade level and reflect the developmental needs of students at that level.

Guidelines for creating and implementing effective rules include:

- State rules positively.
- Emphasize rationales for rules.
- Minimize the number of rules.
- Monitor rules throughout the school year.

To see how one teacher establishes rules and procedures at the beginning of the school year, click on the video, *Establishing Rules and Procedures at the Beginning of the School Year* (11:00).

Stating rules positively communicates desirable expectations for students and sets a positive emotional tone. Providing rationales for rules is perhaps the most essential guideline because students are much more likely to accept responsibility for their own behavior and obey rules when they understand the reasons for them. Also, students want rules to make sense, and providing rationales helps meet this need. Keeping the number small helps prevent students from breaking rules simply because they forget. And finally, in spite of your best efforts during planning and the initial teaching of rules, your students will need periodic reminders throughout the year.

URBAN EDUCATION: Effective Classroom Management in Urban Environments

Urban classrooms provide unique challenges to teachers attempting to create productive learning environments. Consider the case of Mary Gregg, a first-grade teacher in an urban school in the San Francisco Bay Area.

> Mary's classroom is a small portable room with a low ceiling and very loud air fans. The room has one teacher table and six rectangular student tables with six chairs at each. Mary has 32 first graders (14 girls and 18 boys). Twenty-five of the children are children of color; a majority are recent immigrants from Southeast Asia, with some African Americans and Latinos, and seven European Americans. (LePage, Darling-Hammond, & Akar, 2005)

Research on teaching in urban contexts reveals three themes. First, students in urban schools come from very diverse backgrounds (Macionis & Parrillo, 2010). As a result of this diversity, their prior knowledge and experiences vary, and what they view as acceptable patterns of behavior also varies, sometimes dramatically. Second, urban classes are often large; Mary had 32 first graders in a room built for 25. Third, and perhaps most pernicious, negative stereotypes about urban students create the perception that developing a productive learning environment through classroom management is difficult, if not impossible.

Two of the most common urban stereotypes are "Students can't control themselves" and "Students don't know how to behave because their parents don't care." In response to these stereotypes, urban teachers often "teach defensively," "choosing methods of presentation and evaluation that simplify content and reduce demands on students in return for classroom order and minimal student compliance on assignments" (LePage et al., 2005, p. 331).

This defensive approach to classroom management and instruction results in lowered expectations and decreased student motivation. Students who aren't motivated to learn are more likely to be disruptive because they don't see the point in what they're being asked to do, a downward spiral of motivation and learning occurs, and management issues become increasingly troublesome.

It doesn't have to be this way. In spite of diversity and large numbers of students in a small classroom, effective urban teachers create active and orderly learning environments. Let's look at Mary Gregg's classroom management during a lesson on buoyancy.

> Once into the science activity, management appears to be invisible. There is, of course, some splashing and throwing things into the water, but as the lesson progresses, the teacher engages in on-the-spot logistical management decisions. For instance, everyone is supposed to get a chance to go to the table to choose objects to be placed in cups. After choosing the first one to go, Mary sets them to the task. Very quickly, it is the second person's turn and the students do not know how to choose who should get the next turn. At first she says "you choose," then foresees an "It's my turn. No it's my turn" problem and redirects them with a counterclockwise motion to go around the table. (LePage et al., 2005, pp. 328–329)

Although challenging, classroom management in an urban environment doesn't have to be overrestrictive or punitive. How is this accomplished? Research suggests four important factors:

- Caring and supportive teachers
- Clear standards for acceptable behavior
- High structure
- Effective instruction

Caring and Supportive Teachers

Teachers who care are important in all schools but are critical in urban classrooms. When students perceive their teachers as uncaring, disengagement from school life occurs, and students are much more likely to misbehave than their more involved peers (Charles & Senter, 2012).

Clear Standards for Acceptable Behavior

Because they bring diverse backgrounds and experiences to class, urban students' views of acceptable behaviors often vary. As a result, being clear about what behaviors are and are not acceptable is essential in urban classrooms. As we saw earlier in the chapter, students interpret clear standards of behavior as evidence that the teacher cares about them. One urban student had this to say about clear behavioral expectations:

> She's probably the strictest teacher I've ever had because she doesn't let you slide by if you've made a mistake. She going [sic] to let you know. If you've

made a mistake, she's going to let you know it. And, if you're getting bad marks, she's going to let you know it. She's one of my strictest teachers, and that's what makes me think she cares about us the most. (Alder, 2002, pp. 251–252)

The line between clear standards for behavior and an overemphasis on control is not cut-and-dried. One important difference is that in productive urban classrooms, order is created through "the ethical use of power" (Alder, 2002, p. 245). Effective teachers are demanding but also helpful; they model and emphasize personal responsibility, respect, and cooperation; and they're willing to take the time to ensure that students understand the reasons for rules (Weinstein et al., 2011). Further, in responding to the inevitable incidents of students' failing to bring needed materials to class, talking, or otherwise being disruptive, effective teachers in urban schools enforce rules but provide rationales for them and remind students that completing assigned tasks is essential because it helps develop the skills needed for more advanced work. In contrast, less-effective teachers tend to focus on negative consequences, using threats such as, "If you don't finish this work, you won't pass the class."

High Structure

Students in urban schools sometimes come from environments where stability and structure may not be a regular part of everyday life, making order, structure, and predictability even more important (Whitcomb, Borko, & Liston, 2006). Procedures that lead to well-established routines are important, and predictable consequences for behaviors are essential. A predictable environment leads to an atmosphere of order and safety, which is crucial for developing the sense of attachment to school essential for learning and motivation.

Effective Instruction

If students aren't learning and aren't actively involved in classroom life, management problems are inevitable. Classroom management and instruction are interdependent, and, unfortunately, students in urban classrooms are often involved in low-level activities such as listening to lectures and doing seat work that isn't challenging. This type of instruction contributes to low motivation and disengagement, which further increase the likelihood of management problems.

Check Your Understanding

2.1. Describe the four processes involved in creating productive learning environments.
2.2. Describe the two planning elements that help create productive learning environments.
2.3. What makes classroom management in urban classrooms unique?

For feedback, go to the appendix, *Check Your Understanding*, located in the back of this text.

Creating Productive Learning Environments: Involving Parents

Learning is a cooperative venture: You, your students, and their parents are in it together. Students must be cooperative and motivated to learn if a learning environment is to be productive, and parental support is essential for promoting this cooperation and motivation (O'Connor et al., 2011).

Benefits of Parental Involvement

Students benefit from parental involvement in several ways:

- More positive attitudes and behaviors
- Higher long-term achievement
- Greater willingness to do homework
- Better attendance and graduation rates
- Greater enrollment in postsecondary education (Anfara & Mertens, 2008)

These outcomes result from parents' increased participation in and understanding of school activities, higher expectations for their children's achievement, and teachers' increased understanding of learners' home environments. Deciding how to respond to a student's disruptive behavior is easier, for example, when you know that his mother or father has lost a job, his parents are going through a divorce, or a family member is ill.

Parent–teacher collaboration can also have benefits for you as a teacher. For example, teachers who encourage parental involvement report more positive feelings about teaching and their school and rate parents higher in helpfulness and follow-through (Weinstein et al., 2011).

WINDOWS *on the Profession*

To see how one teacher effectively interacts with a parent during a parent–teacher conference, click on the video *Working with Parents: A Parent–Teacher Conference* (8:15).

Strategies for Involving Parents

Virtually all schools have formal communication channels, such as open houses (usually occurring within the first 2 weeks of the year, when teachers introduce themselves and describe general guidelines); interim progress reports, which tell parents about their youngsters' achievements at the midpoint of each grading period; parent–teacher conferences; and, of course, report cards. Although these processes are school wide and necessary, you can do more to involve parents:

Revisiting My Beliefs

This discussion addresses the fourth item in *This I Believe*, "It is important that I involve my students' parents in their children's education." This statement is most definitely true: Involving parents can have a number of benefits, and increased achievement is one of the most important.

- Send a letter home to parents within the first week of school that expresses positive expectations for students and solicits parents' help. The letter Shannon sent home with her students appears in Figure 10.2. You might also include an extra copy of the guidelines for parents' future reference, and send home a follow-up letter to parents who forgot to return the letter the first time.
- Maintain communication by frequently sending home packets of student work, descriptions of new units, and other information about academic work.
- Emphasize students' accomplishments through newsletters, e-mails, or individual notes.

All forms of communication with parents should be scrupulously clean and free of spelling, grammar, and punctuation errors. First impressions are important and lasting; your communications create perceptions of your competence, and errors detract from your credibility. Take the extra time to proof all your memos to parents.

Calling parents is one of the most effective ways to involve parents (Longfellow, 2008). Talking to a parent allows you to be specific in describing a student's needs and gives you a chance to again solicit support. If a student is missing assignments, for example, you can alert the parent, ask for possible explanations, and encourage parents to more closely monitor their child's study habits.

When you talk to parents, make an effort to establish an initial positive, cooperative tone that lays the foundation for joint efforts. Consider the following:

"Hello, Mrs. Hansen? This is Shannon Brinkman, Jared's teacher."

"Oh, uh, is something wrong?"

"Not at all. I just wanted to call to share with you some information about your son. He's a bright, energetic boy, and I enjoy seeing him in class every day. But he's been having some problems handing in his math homework assignments in my class."

FIGURE 10.2 Letter to Parents

August 28, 2013

Dear Parents,

I am looking forward to a productive and exciting year, and I am writing this letter to encourage your involvement and support. You always have been, and still are, the most important people in your child's education. We cannot do the job without you.

For us to work together most effectively, some guidelines are necessary. With the students' help, we prepared the ones listed here. Please read this information carefully, and sign where indicated. If you have any questions, please call me at Southside Elementary School (555-5935) or at home (555-8403) in the evenings.

Sincerely,

Shannon Brinkman

Shannon Brinkman

AS A PARENT, I WILL TRY MY BEST TO DO THE FOLLOWING:

1. I will ask my child about school every day (evening meal is a good time). I will ask about what he or she is studying and try to learn about it.
2. I will provide a quiet time and place each evening for homework. I will set an example by also working at that time or reading while my child is working.
3. Instead of asking if homework is finished, I will ask to see it. I will ask my child to explain some of the information to me to check for understanding.

Parent's Signature ________________________

STUDENT SURVIVAL GUIDELINES

1. I will be in class and seated when the bell rings.
2. I will follow directions the first time they are given.
3. I will bring homework, notebook, paper, and a sharp pencil to class each day.
4. I will raise my hand for permission to speak or leave my seat.
5. I will keep my hands, feet, and objects to myself.

HOMEWORK GUIDELINES

1. Our motto is, I WILL ALWAYS TRY. I WILL NEVER GIVE UP.
2. I will complete all assignments. If an assignment is not finished or ready when called for, I understand that I get no credit for it.
3. If I miss work because of an absence, it is my responsibility to come in before school (8:15–8:45) to make it up.
4. I know that I get one day to make up a quiz or test or turn in my work for each day I'm absent.
5. I understand that extra credit work is not given. If I do all the required work, extra credit isn't necessary.

Student's Signature ____________________________

Please return when signed. Thanks, Shannon

"I didn't know he had math homework. He never brings any home."

"That might be part of the problem. He just might forget that he has any to do. I have a suggestion. Let's try to set up a system that will help him remember. I always have the class write down their math homework in their folders every day. Please ask Jared to share that with you every night, and make sure that it's done. When it's done, please initial it so I know you and he talked. I think that will help a lot. How does that sound?"

"Sure. I'll try that."

"Good. We don't want him to fall behind. If he has problems with the homework, have him come to my room before or after school, and I'll help him. Is there anything else I can do? . . . If not, I look forward to meeting you soon."

This conversation was positive, and it created a partnership between home and school. In addition, it created a specific plan of action.

Calling parents is admittedly time-consuming, but it can pay major dividends. Also, because you're allocating some of your 24 hours to that individual student, it communicates better than any other way that you care about your students.

Economic, Cultural, and Language Barriers to Communicating with Parents

Home–school partnerships create effective communication links with parents, increasing learning while decreasing management problems.

Economics, culture, and language can all create barriers that limit the involvement of minority and low- socioeconomic status parents in school activities. Low-SES parents frequently lack resources—such as child care, transportation, Internet access, and even telephones—that would allow them to become involved in school activities. Multiple jobs often prevent parents from volunteering at school and even helping their children with homework.

Cultural differences can also be misinterpreted (Hu, 2008). Because of their respect for teachers, for example, some Asian and Hispanic parents hesitate to become involved in matters they believe are best handled by the school, but teachers sometimes misinterpret this deference to authority as apathy (Weinstein et al., 2011).

Language can be another barrier: Parents of bilingual students may not speak English, which leaves the child responsible for interpreting communications sent home by teachers. Homework also poses a special problem because parents can't interpret assignments or provide help, and schools sometimes compound the difficulty by using educational jargon when they send letters home.

Involving Minority Parents

You can narrow the home–school gap by offering parents specific strategies for working with their children (Cavanagh, 2009). Let's see how one teacher does this:

Nancy Collins, a middle school English teacher, has students who speak five native languages in her class. During the first 2 days of school, she prepares a letter to parents, and with the help of her students, translates it into their native languages. The letter begins by describing how pleased she is to have students from varying backgrounds in her class, saying that they enrich all her students' education.

She continues with a short list of procedures and encourages the parents to support their children's efforts by:

1. Asking their children about school each night
2. Providing a quiet place to study for at least 90 minutes a day
3. Limiting television until homework is finished
4. Asking to see samples of their children's work and grades they've received

She tells her students that the school is having an open house and that the class with the highest attendance will win a contest. She concludes the letter by reemphasizing that she is pleased to have so much diversity in her class. She asks parents to sign and return the letter.

The day before the open house, Nancy has her students compose a handwritten letter to their parents in their native languages, asking them to attend. Nancy writes "Hoping to see you there" at the bottom of each note and signs it.

Nancy's letter was effective in three ways. First, writing it in students' native languages communicated sensitivity and caring. Second, the letter included specific suggestions, which provide parents with concrete ideas for helping their children. Even parents who can't read a homework assignment are more involved if they ask their children to explain their schoolwork. The suggestions also let parents know they're needed. Third, by encouraging parents to attend the school's open house, Nancy increased the likelihood that they would do so. If they did, and the experience was positive, their involvement would likely increase.

TECHNOLOGY and TEACHING: Using Technology to Communicate with Parents

Communication is an essential step in home–school cooperation, but parents' and teachers' busy schedules are often obstacles. Technology can help make home–school links more effective (Bitter & Legacy, 2008). Voice mail and e-mail can help overcome these obstacles by creating communication channels between parents who work and teachers who are busy with students all day.

A growing number of teachers use websites that describe current class topics and assignments. In addition, students and parents are now able to monitor missing assignments, performance on tests, and current grades via e-mail and websites (Gronke, 2009). Schools also use electronic hotlines to keep parents informed about current events, schedule changes, lunch menus, and bus schedules. However, many parents still prefer traditional information sources such as newsletters and open houses. This may be because some households don't have access to the Internet and e-mail, as well as because of the instinctive desire for the face-to-face contact that exists in open houses.

One innovative program teaches first graders to Tweet their parents about current classroom activities (Manchir, 2012). The program has two benefits. Parents like being informed about classroom activities, as it gives them something to talk about with their children. In addition, students are learning to communicate effectively with social media, and can see how technology can be a valuable tool in their learning and their lives.

Another innovation uses the Internet to provide parents with real-time images of their children, and increasing numbers of preschool and day-care programs are installing cameras and Internet systems that provide parents with secure-access websites they can use to monitor their children during the day.

Check Your Understanding

3.1. Explain how involving parents contributes to productive learning environments.
3.2. What strategies are available to communicate with parents?

For feedback, go to the appendix, *Check Your Understanding*, located in the back of this text.

Intervening When Misbehavior Occurs

Despite caring about your students, planning carefully, and teaching effectively, you will still have students who periodically misbehave or fail to pay attention. It happens in all classrooms. Let's see how Shannon, our fifth-grade teacher, deals with misbehavior during a lesson in which she's reviewing decimals and percentages.

"What kind of problem is this, . . . Gabriel?" she asks as she walks down the aisle and points to a problem on the overhead.

". . . It's a percentage problem," Gabriel responds after thinking for a few seconds.

As soon as Shannon walks past him, Kevin sticks his foot across the aisle, tapping Alison on the leg with his shoe while he watches Shannon's back. "Stop it, Kevin," Alison mutters, swiping at him with her hand.

Shannon's experience illustrates why classroom management can be vexing for teachers. She planned carefully and taught effectively, but she still had to deal with Kevin's and Alison's behaviors. And doing so requires making immediate and judicious decisions. For instance, if an off-task behavior is brief and minor, such as a student asking another student a quick question, you can usually ignore it. But if the behavior has the potential to disrupt the learning activity, such as the one involving Alison and Kevin, you'll need to intervene. And you'll need to make a decision about whether or not to intervene on the spot and instantly.

Teaching and You

What would you do in this situation? What options do you have? What are the advantages and disadvantages of each?

Intervening Effectively

An **intervention** is a teacher action designed to increase desired behaviors or to eliminate student misbehavior and inattention. Teachers use a variety of interventions, such as moving near or calling on inattentive students to bring them back into the lesson, simply telling a student to stop talking, or, in extreme cases, removing a disruptive student from the classroom. Let's see how Shannon reacts to the misbehavior in her classroom.

Hearing the disruption behind her, Shannon turns, comes back up the aisle, and continues, "Good, Gabriel," and standing next to Kevin, asks, "And how do we know it's a percentage problem. . . Kevin?" looking directly at him.

"Uhhh . . . ."

"What words in the problem give us a clue that it's a percentage problem, Kevin?"

". . . 'Which is the better buy?'" Kevin answers, pointing at the sales numbers from the two stores. "We have to figure out which store sale saved us more. That's a percentage problem."

"Good," Shannon replies, moving to the overhead and displaying additional word problems involving percentages.

"Go ahead and do the first problem," Shannon directs. "Be sure you're able to explain your answer."

She watches as students work on the problem and then moves over to Sondra, who has been whispering and passing notes to Nicole across the aisle. "Move up here," she says quietly, nodding to a desk at the front of the room.

"What did I do?" Sondra protests.

"When we talked about our rules at the beginning of the year, we agreed that it was important to listen when other people are talking and to be quiet when others are working," Shannon whispers.

She watches as Sondra changes seats. Then, tapping her knuckle on the overhead, Shannon says, "Okay, let's see how we did on the problem. Explain what you did first, . . . Juanita."

Effective management interventions stop the undesired behavior while still maintaining a human link between the teacher and student.

When intervening, you have three goals: (1) stop the misbehavior quickly and simply; (2) maintain the flow of your lesson; and (3) help students learn from the experience. But emotional factors often complicate the process.

Emotional Factors in Interventions

Have you ever been chewed out in front of other people or been in a losing argument in public? How did it make you feel, and how did you feel afterward? We all want to avoid being humiliated in front of our peers, and the same applies in classrooms. The emotional tone of your interventions influences both the likelihood of students complying with them and their attitudes toward you and the class afterward. Loud public reprimands, criticism, and sarcasm reduce students' sense of safety and are particularly destructive in elementary schools, where children are vulnerable and strongly seek the approval of their teachers. In middle and secondary schools, they create resentment, detract from classroom climate, and lead to students finding creative ways to be disruptive without getting caught.

Similarly, arguing with students about the interpretation of a rule or compliance with it also detracts from the emotional climate of classrooms. You never "win" an argument with students. You can exert your authority, but doing so is not sustainable throughout a school year, resentment is often a side effect, and the encounter may expand into a major incident (Pellegrino, 2010).

Consider the following incident that occurred after a teacher directed a chronically misbehaving student to move:

Student: I wasn't doing anything.

Teacher: You were whispering, and the rule says listen when someone else is talking.

Student: It doesn't say no whispering.

Teacher: You know what the rule means. We've been over it again and again.

Student: Well, it's not fair. You don't make other students move when they whisper.

Teacher: You weren't listening when someone else was talking, so move.

The student knew what the rule meant and was simply playing a game with the teacher, who allowed herself to be drawn into an argument. Now, let's compare this with an alternative approach.

Teacher: Please move up here (pointing to an empty desk in the first row).

Student: I wasn't doing anything.

Teacher: One of our rules says that we listen when someone else is talking. If you would like to discuss this, come in and see me after school. Please move now (turning back to the lesson as soon as the student moves).

This teacher maintained an even demeanor and didn't allow herself to be pulled into an argument or even a brief discussion. She handled the event quickly and efficiently, offered to discuss it with the student later, and immediately turned back to the lesson.

Students' inclination to argue with teachers depends, to a large extent, on the emotional climate of the classroom. If rules and procedures make sense to students, and if they're enforced consistently and fairly, students are less likely to argue. When students break rules, simply reminding them of the rule and why it's important, and requiring compliance, are as far as minor incidents should go. (We examine serious management issues, such as defiance and aggression, later in the chapter.)

Helping Students Understand Our Interventions

We have two major goals when we intervene: To stop the misbehavior and to help students grow and develop as responsible members of our classroom community. To be effective, our rules and procedures should be understood by our students, and we want our interventions to make sense to them as well. If they do, the likelihood of future management problems is reduced, and students learn about the connection between their actions and your interventions. Interventions that help students make sense of their actions are outlined in Figure 10.3 and discussed in the sections that follow.

FIGURE 10.3 Helping Students Understand Your Interventions

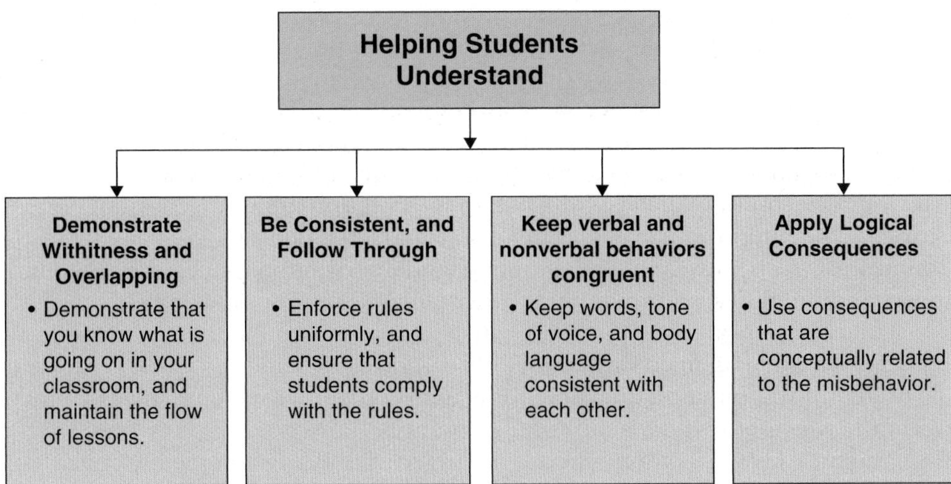

Demonstrate Withitness and Overlapping. Effective interventions need to be based on accurate information. **Withitness** is a teacher's awareness of what's going on in all parts of the classroom at all times and communicating this awareness to students. It's an essential component of successful interventions, and expert teachers describe withitness as "having eyes in the back of your head."

Shannon demonstrated withitness in three ways:

- She identified the misbehavior immediately, and quickly responded by moving near Kevin.
- She correctly identified Kevin as the cause of the incident. If, in contrast, she had reprimanded Alison, she would have left students with a sense that she didn't know what was going on.
- She responded to the more serious infraction first. Kevin's poking was more disruptive than Sondra's whispering, so she first called on Kevin, which drew him back into the activity and made further intervention unnecessary, and then she moved over to Sondra to stop her whispering and note passing.

Withitness involves more than dealing with misbehavior after it happens. Teachers who are withit also watch for the initial signs of inattention or confusion; they approach, or call on, inattentive students to bring them back into lessons; and they respond to signs of confusion with questions such as "Some of you look puzzled. Do you want me to rephrase that question?" They are sensitive to students and make adjustments to ensure students are involved and successful.

Shannon also managed to eliminate Kevin's, Sondra's, and Nicole's misbehavior while simultaneously maintaining the flow of her lesson. This skill is called **overlapping**, the ability to attend to two issues simultaneously. Overlapping allows you to maintain the flow of your lesson while stopping the misbehavior, two major goals of interventions.

Lack of withitness and overlapping is often a problem for beginning teachers (Wubbels, Brekeimans, den Brok & van Tartwijk, 2006). Teachers have so much to think about that they sometimes simply don't notice misbehavior when it occurs. They tune it out because they're concentrating on the lesson and where it's headed. The best solution to this issue is well-established routines and carefully planned instruction that simplify the amount you have to think about.

Be Consistent, and Follow Through. "Be consistent" is recommended so often that it has become a cliché, but it is essential nevertheless. If one student is reprimanded for breaking a rule and another is not, for example, students will notice the inconsistency. They are likely to conclude that the teacher doesn't know what's going on or has "pets," either of which detracts from classroom climate.

Although consistency is important, achieving complete consistency in the real world is virtually impossible, and even not desirable. You should adapt your interventions to both the student and context. For example, most classrooms have a rule about speaking only when recognized by the teacher, and as you're monitoring seat work, one student asks another a question about the assignment and then goes back to work. Failing to remind the student that talking is not allowed during seat work is technically inconsistent, but an intervention in this case is both unnecessary and counterproductive. On the other hand, a student who repeatedly turns around and whispers becomes a disruption, and intervention is necessary. Students understand the difference, and the "inconsistency" is appropriate and effective.

Following through means doing what you've said you'll do. Without follow-through, your management system will break down because students learn that you aren't fully committed to maintaining an orderly environment. This is confusing and leaves them with a sense of uncertainty.

The first few days of the school year are crucial. Being completely consistent and following through during this time will set the tone for the rest of the year.

Keep Verbal and Nonverbal Behaviors Congruent. For interventions to make sense to your students and be effective, your verbal and nonverbal behaviors need to be congruent. When messages are inconsistent, people attribute more credibility to body language and tone of voice than to spoken words (Aronson, Wilson, & Akert, 2010).

Shannon's actions were congruent. For example, when she moved over to Kevin and called on him, she looked him directly in the eye, and she watched as Sondra changed seats. Her nonverbal behavior communicated that "she meant what she said." If Shannon had glanced over her shoulder at Kevin instead, her communication might have been confusing; her words would have said one thing, but her body language would have said another.

Research supports these contentions. When teachers make more eye contact with their students, for example, their students are more likely to believe that they're withit and in charge of their classes (Wubbels et al., 2006).

Beginning teachers often have difficulty in this area.

> There appeared a distinct difference between beginning and experienced teachers' nonverbal behavior that may be an important cause for the unsatisfying relationships of some beginning teachers with their students. Behaviors that facilitated visual contact (looking to students) and signaling withitness and overlapping were demonstrated by experienced teachers almost twice as much as by student teachers. (Wubbels et al., 2006, p. 1180)

Our nonverbal behavior sends powerful messages about our intentions. Be aware of your nonverbal behavior and the messages you're sending; strive to keep your verbal and nonverbal behavior consistent.

Apply Logical Consequences. Logical consequences are outcomes that are conceptually related to misbehavior; they help learners make sense of an intervention by creating a link between their actions and the consequences that follow. For example:

Allen, a rambunctious sixth grader, is running down the hall toward the lunchroom. As he rounds the corner, he bumps Alyshia, causing her to drop her books.

"Oops," he replies, continuing his race to the lunchroom.

"Hold it, Allen," Doug Ramsay, who is monitoring the hall, says. "Go back and help her pick up her books and apologize."

Allen walks back to Alyshia, helps her pick up her books, mumbles an apology, and then returns. As he approaches, Doug again stops him.

"Now, why did I make you do that?" Doug asks.

ISSUES YOU'LL FACE IN TEACHING

The Role of Punishment in Classroom Management

Have you ever gotten a speeding ticket? What happened to your subsequent driving behavior—at least for a while? Most of us can attest to the idea that punishment works—at least in the short run. But then what?

Teachers, in general, and beginning teachers in particular, worry about whether they will be able to maintain order in their classrooms. Many turn to **punishment**, the process of decreasing or eliminating undesired behavior through some aversive consequence. But punishment as a management tool is controversial. Advocates say it's sometimes necessary, but critics say it's ineffective and counterproductive. The role of punishment, both in classroom management and in child raising, has been debated for centuries (e.g., "Spare the rod and spoil the child."), and this debate continues today.

Punishment can range from a teacher action as simple as saying, "Andrew, stop whispering," to **corporal punishment**, the use of physical actions, such as paddling students, to eliminate undesirable behavior. The use of punishment in classrooms usually occurs in the form of simple desists, time-out, or detention. **Desists** are verbal or nonverbal communications teachers use to stop a behavior (Kounin, 1970), such as telling a student to stop whispering, or putting fingers to the lips to signal "Shh." **Time-out** involves removing a student from the class and physically isolating him in an area away from classmates. **Detention**, most commonly used with older students, is similar to time-out, and involves taking away some of students' free time by keeping them in school after regular dismissal times.

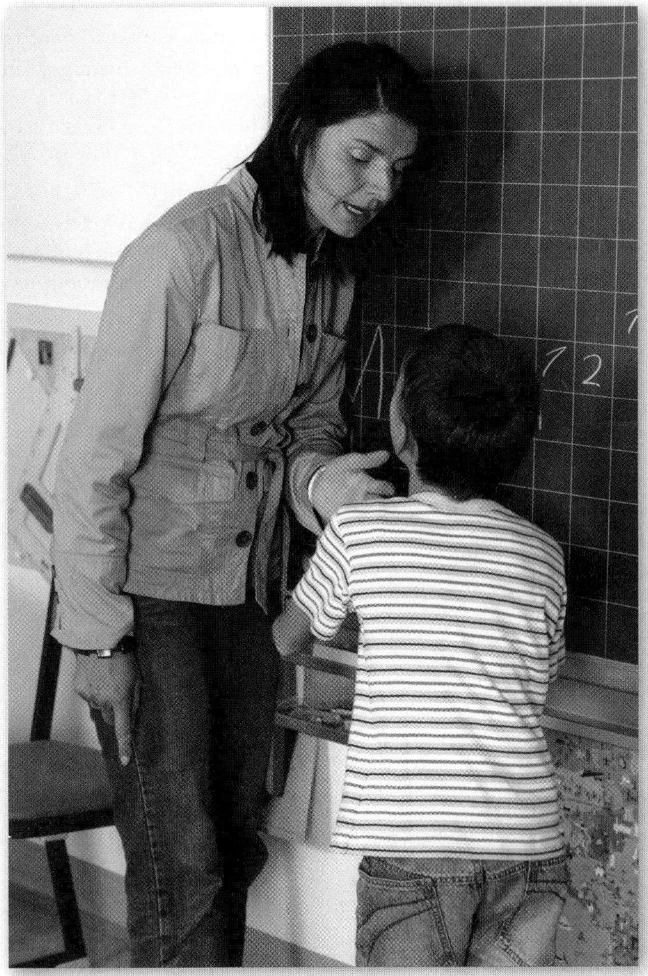

Punishment as a classroom management tool is controversial and should be used sparingly.

THE QUESTION

So, is punishment an effective tool for promoting order in our classrooms? Arguments both for and against the use of punishment can be made.

PRO

- Research supports the use of desists and time-out. For instance, desists, when administered immediately, briefly, and unemotionally, can effectively reduce misbehavior (Emmer & Evertson, 2013; Evertson & Emmer, 2013), and time-out is effective for a variety of disruptive behaviors (Alberto & Troutman, 2013).
- Additional research suggests that punishment is sometimes necessary; when all negative sanctions are removed, some students become more disruptive (Alberto & Troutman, 2013).
- Veteran teachers believe punishment is acceptable when the severity of the punishment matches the severity of the misbehavior (Cowan & Sheridan, 2003).
- When paired with explanations about the undesired behavior, punishment can actually be humane because it helps unruly students learn new, more acceptable behaviors quickly (Alberto & Troutman, 2013).

CON

- Some critics suggest that punishment should never be used in classrooms because it damages the relationship between you and your students (e.g., Kohn, 1996). Punishment can have unintended consequences, such as resentment and hostility, and can damage teachers' efforts to create a positive classroom climate.
- Critics also argue that the use of punishers to maintain an orderly classroom overemphasizes control and obedience rather than emphasizing that students are responsible for their actions—an outcome that contributes to personal development (Freiberg, 1999).
- Punishing students for simple acts, such as talking without permission, fails to examine possible causes for the behavior, such as ineffective instruction or not understanding why it's important to give everyone a chance to speak (Alberto & Troutman, 2013).

- Research indicates that systems based on reinforcing positive behavior are more effective than those using punishment (Nelson, Young, Young, & Cox, 2010).

YOU TAKE A STAND

Now it's your turn to answer the question: Is punishment effective, and should it be a part of classroom management systems?

Go to *Issues You'll Face in Teaching* in the MyEducationLab™ *Book Resources* that accompany this text to log your thoughts and receive feedback from your authors.

"Cuz we're not supposed to run."

"Sure," Doug says evenly, "but more important, if people run in the halls, they might crash into someone, and somebody might get hurt. . . . Remember that you're responsible for your actions. Think about not wanting to hurt yourself or anybody else, and the next time you'll walk whether a teacher is here or not. . . . Now, go on to lunch."

Doug used a logical consequence in this incident to help Allen understand how his actions affect other people. Having to pick up Alyshia's books after bumping her and causing her to drop them made sense to Allen, and this is our goal in applying logical consequences. They help students understand the effects of their actions on others and promote the development of responsibility (Weinstein et al., 2011).

Although serious management problems are rare and infrequent, teachers need to be prepared to handle them quickly and efficiently.

Handling Serious Management Problems: Violence and Aggression

If you answered yes to our question in *Teaching and You* (that appears below), you're like many other preservice and beginning teachers. Many preservice teachers think—and worry—about incidents of school violence and even the possibility of being assaulted by a student. However, incidents of defiance and aggression toward teachers are rare in schools; you are much more likely to encounter the everyday management problems we've been discussing (Moriarity, 2009). However, these incidents do happen, and you need to be aware of the possibility and be prepared to deal with an incident in the unlikely event that it occurs.

Responding to Defiant Students

Teaching and You

We've all heard about highly publicized incidents of school shootings and other stories about teachers being assaulted by students. How likely are events such as these? Do you worry about these possibilities as you anticipate your first teaching job?

Tyrone, one of your students, has difficulty maintaining attention and staying on task. He frequently makes loud and inappropriate comments in class and disrupts learning activities. You warn him, reminding him that being disruptive is unacceptable, and blurting out another comment will result in time-out.

Within a minute, Tyrone blurts out again.

"Please go to the time-out area," you say evenly.

"I'm not going, and you can't make me," he says defiantly. He crosses his arms and remains seated at his desk.

What do you do when a student like Tyrone says, "I'm not going, and you can't make me?" Experts offer two suggestions (Moriarity, 2009). First, remain calm and avoid a power struggle. A natural tendency is to become angry and display a show of force to demonstrate to students that they "can't get away with it." Remaining calm gives you time to control your temper, and the student's mood when facing a calm teacher is likely to change from anger and bravado to fear and contrition (Good & Brophy, 2008).

Second, if possible, give the rest of the class an assignment, and then tell the student calmly but assertively to step outside the classroom so you can talk. Communicate an assertive, but not threatening, tone.

Defiance is often the result of negative student–teacher relationships, and incidents of defiance occur most often with students who are aggressive or impulsive and display temper tantrums (Emmer & Evertson, 2013). When a problem occurs with such a student, it's important to let the student say everything that is on her mind in a private conference, such as outside the classroom, before responding. Finally, arrange to meet with the student before or after school, focus on the defiance as a problem, and attempt to generate solutions that are acceptable to both of you.

In the case of a student who refuses to leave your classroom, or one who becomes physically threatening, immediately send someone to the front office for help. Defiance at this level requires extra help and long-term intervention from a mental health professional.

Responding to Fighting

As you work with a small group of your fourth graders, a fight suddenly breaks out between Trey and Neil, who are supposed to be working on a group project together. You hear sounds of shouting and see Trey flailing at Neil, who is attempting to fend off Trey's blows. Trey is often verbally aggressive and sometimes threatens other students.

What do you do?

Incidents of student aggression toward each other are much more common than threats to teachers; about 10% of all public schools had one or more serious violent crimes, such as physical attack, sexual battery, or suicide, with the vast majority of the incidents being physical attacks or fights without a weapon (M. Kelly, 2011).

In a situation such as the one involving Trey and Neil, you are required by law to intervene. If you don't, you and the school can be sued for **negligence**, the failure to exercise sufficient care in protecting students from injury (Schimmel, Stellman et al., 2011). However, the law doesn't require you to physically break up the fight; immediately reporting it to administrators is acceptable. Your immediate goal when incidents like this occur in your classroom is to protect the victim and other students.

An effective response to fighting involves three steps: (1) Stop the incident (if possible), (2) protect the victim, and (3) get help. For instance, in the case of the classroom scuffle, a loud noise, such as shouting, clapping, or slamming a chair against the floor, will often surprise the students enough so they'll stop (Evertson & Emmer, 2013). At that point, you can begin to talk to them, check to see if the victim is all right, and then take the students to the main office, where you can get help. If your interventions don't stop the fight, you should immediately send an uninvolved student for help. Don't attempt to separate the students unless you're sure you can do so without danger to yourself or them. You are responsible first for the safety of the other students and yourself, and second for the involved students.

Breaking up a scuffle is, of course, only a short-term solution. Whenever students are aggressive or violent, experts recommend involving parents and other school personnel (Good & Brophy, 2008). Parents want to be notified immediately if school problems occur. In addition, school counselors, school psychologists, social workers, and principals have all been trained to deal with these

> **Revisiting My Beliefs**
> This discussion addresses the fifth item in *This I Believe*, "If some of my students are involved in a fight or scuffle, I am required by law to intervene." This statement is true, and failure to intervene can result in you and the school being sued for negligence.

problems and can provide advice and assistance. Experienced teachers can also provide a wealth of information about how they've handled similar problems. No teacher should face serious problems of violence or aggression alone. Further, excellent programs are available to teach conflict resolution and to help troubled students (D. Johnson & Johnson, 2013). If teachers can get help when they first suspect a problem, many incidents can be prevented.

Responding to Bullying

Matt, one of your seventh graders, is shy and a bit small for his age. As he comes into your class this morning, he appears disheveled and depressed. Concerned, you take him aside and ask if anything is wrong. With some prodding he tells you that he repeatedly gets shoved around on the school grounds before school, and two boys have been taunting him and calling him gay. "I hate school," he comments.

How do you respond?

Bullying, a form of peer aggression that involves a systematic or repetitious abuse of power between students, is a serious management problem in our schools. In a survey of more than 43,000 high school students, half admitted they had bullied someone in the past year, and nearly the same percent said they had been bullied, teased, or taunted (Josephson Institute Center for Youth Ethics, 2010). Forty-four states have passed antibullying laws, and many districts have implemented zero-tolerance policies. Unfortunately, these laws and policies have been largely ineffective in reducing incidents of bullying (Graham, 2010; Walker, 2009).

Bullying is a serious management issue because it threatens students' feelings of safety and security in schools and classrooms. In addition, serious psychological problems for both perpetrators and victims can be long-term side effects. Bullies learn maladaptive ways of relating to others, and victims often suffer from anxiety and depression (Berk, 2012).

Teachers are central to schools' efforts to eliminate bullying, so you play an important role in the process. "Children's school behavior is greatly shaped by their school's culture, climate, and more specifically, the attitudes and behaviors of teachers" (Hyman, Kay, Tabori, Weber, Mahon, & Cohen, 2006, p. 869). The most effective responses to bullying are school-wide and include communication with parents, close adult supervision, talking with bullies after bullying incidents, and immediate, appropriate, and consistent consequences for bullying acts (Sherer, & Nickerson, 2010). Near term, when you see a case of bullying, you should intervene immediately and apply appropriate consequences for the perpetrators. Trey, for example, must understand that his aggressive actions are unacceptable and won't be tolerated.

Long-term, you can use the incident as a teachable moment, in which you discuss ideas about right and wrong, appropriate treatment of others, tolerance for differences, and abuse of power (Graham, 2010). These discussions won't produce immediate results, but in time they can make a difference. For the students you reach, the results can be increased personal responsibility and healthier social development.

EXPLORING DIVERSITY: Adapting Classroom Management to Diverse Populations

Learner diversity presents a unique set of challenges for classroom teachers. A long history of research suggests that discrepancies exist in disciplinary referrals and punishment for students who are members of cultural minorities (Noguera, 2012). For example, African American boys are referred for behavior problems at a much higher rate than their peers, and they also receive harsher punishments (LaMarche, 2011).

Further, research indicates that European American students are disciplined for infractions that could be described as objective, such as smoking, leaving school without permission, or profanity. By comparison, African American students are more commonly disciplined for infractions that require a teacher's interpretation, such as disrespect, defiance, or class disruptions. And subsequent punishments for African American students are more severe.

> Fear may . . . contribute to overreferral [among students of color]. Teachers who are prone to accepting stereotypes of adolescent African American males as threatening or dangerous may overreact to relatively minor threats to authority, especially if their anxiety is paired with a misunderstanding of cultural norms of interaction. (Skiba, Michael, Nardo, & Peterson, 2002, p. 336)

Additional evidence suggests that communication breakdowns between teachers and students who are English learners (ELs) sometimes result in students' being punished for what teachers thought they heard and not for what children actually said (Kirylo, Thirumurthy, & Spezzini, 2010). Some researchers believe this miscommunication occurs because most teachers are middle class, female, and white, whereas students who are ELs are cultural minorities and are often from families with lower SES.

Culturally responsive classroom management, which combines cultural knowledge with teachers' awareness of possible personal biases, can help

DIVERSITY AND YOU

Classroom Management in Diverse Environments

You're a beginning sixth-grade world history teacher in an urban middle school with a highly diverse student population. You're having a difficult time maintaining order in your classroom. You're starting a study of factors leading up to World War I, and you explain that one of the factors was increased nationalism—loyalty to a country's language and culture. As you're explaining, some of the students talk openly to each other, and a few even get out of their seats and sharpen pencils in the middle of your presentation. You point to the rules on the bulletin board, but this seems to work only for a while. You threaten them with referrals and other punishments, which work briefly, but the disruptions soon recur.

Other students are listless and make little effort to pay attention; some even put their heads down on the desk during the lesson. You try interventions, such as walking around the room as you talk, and standing near the inattentive students, but neither strategy works well.

You decide to address the issue directly. You walk up to the front of the room and say in a loud voice, "Class, this content is really important. It will help you understand why we continue to have conflict in the Middle East." As you conclude, you hear a barely audible "Who cares?" from one of the students.

QUESTIONS TO CONSIDER

1. Based on the information in the vignette, it appears that you have two primary problems. What are they?
2. With respect to instruction, what can you do to help solve your problem?
3. With respect to classroom management, what can you do to solve your problem?

Go to *Diversity and You* in the MyEducationLab™ *Book Resources* that accompany this text to log your thoughts and receive feedback from your authors.

overcome some of these problems. Culturally responsive classroom management designed to address this problem has five elements:

- Become personally aware of possible cultural biases.
- Learn about students' cultural heritage.
- Learn about students' neighborhoods and home environments.
- Create caring learning environments.
- Develop culturally responsive classroom management strategies. (Milner & Tenore, 2010)

As teachers become aware of their own possible fears and biases and come to understand students' interaction patterns, they often realize that student responses that appear threatening or disrespectful often are not intended that way. Increased awareness and knowledge, combined with culturally responsive classroom management strategies, can contribute a great deal toward overcoming racial discrepancies in classroom management issues (McCurdy, Kunsch, & Reibstein, 2007). These strategies include, to a large extent, those we've discussed in this chapter, such as working to create a positive classroom climate, promoting student responsibility, and establishing clear expectations for behavior. Combined with conducting highly interactive lessons and providing students with specific and nonjudgmental feedback about their behavior and learning progress, these strategies are effective with all students, and they're particularly important for students from diverse backgrounds. As with all strategies, they won't solve every problem, but they can contribute to your students' academic and social–emotional learning.

Check Your Understanding

4.1. Describe how effective teachers intervene when misbehavior occurs.

4.2. What actions, both short-term and long-term, should teachers take when encountering incidents of violence and aggression?

For feedback, go to the appendix, *Check Your Understanding*, located in the back of this text.

VOICES from the CLASSROOM

"I love my classroom; I'm happy in my classroom. Students are funny; they make me laugh. New best practice for teachers: you must laugh with your students at least once a day. Because smiling is contagious, and students will thrive in the positive energy of your classroom."

CHANDRA EMERSON, 2008 Teacher of the Year, Kentucky

CHAPTER

10 Summary

1. Describe productive learning environments, and explain how they contribute to learning.
   - A productive learning environment is a classroom that is orderly and focused on learning. The emotional climate is positive, and all the routines are designed to maximize learning for each student.
   - Classroom management is important because orderly classrooms communicate to parents, school leaders, and the public at large, that schools and teachers are in charge and know what they're doing.
   - Classroom management is also important because a strong link exists between orderly classrooms and student learning and motivation.
   - The goals of classroom management include creating a positive emotional classroom climate, developing a community of learners, promoting learner responsibility, and maximizing time and opportunities for learning.
2. Identify the processes involved in creating a productive learning environment.
   - Teachers who create productive learning environments care about their students as people and are committed to their learning.
   - Teachers who create productive learning environments teach effectively; they create learning activities in which students are involved in experiences that are meaningful.
   - Teachers in productive learning environments are well organized. They have their materials ready; they begin classes on time; they make transitions quickly and smoothly, and they have well-established routines.
   - Planning for classroom management involves considering the developmental characteristics of students and creating a clear and comprehensive system of procedures and rules.
3. Explain how involving parents contributes to a productive learning environment.
   - Students whose parents are involved in their education have better attitudes toward school, learn more, and are more likely to cooperate in class and do their homework.
   - Teachers who encourage parental involvement also feel more positive about teaching and their school, and they have higher expectations for parents.
   - Teachers can involve parents by sending samples of student work home, emphasizing student accomplishments, and contacting parents by phone or e-mail.
4. Describe how effective teachers intervene when misbehavior occurs.
   - Effective interventions are designed to stop misbehavior quickly and efficiently, maintain the flow of instruction, and help students learn from the intervention.
   - Teachers who intervene effectively avoid loud, public, demeaning interventions, and help maintain students' emotional safety.
   - Teachers who intervene effectively demonstrate withitness, an understanding of what's going on at all times in their classrooms, and overlapping, the ability to deal with two issues at once.
   - Teachers who intervene effectively are consistent in their interventions, follow through to ensure compliance, keep their verbal and nonverbal communication congruent, and apply logical consequences when consequences are necessary.
   - Serious management problems, although rare, can occur in classrooms, and teachers are required by law to intervene in cases of fighting and scuffling.
   - Effective teachers in urban environments are caring and supportive, establish clear standards for behavior, provide structure in their classrooms, and use effective instruction to complement their classroom management.

Important Concepts

academic learning time
allocated time
bullying
caring
classroom management
classroom organization
corporal punishment
culturally responsive classroom management
desist
detention
discipline
engaged time
instructional time
intervention
learning community
logical consequences
negligence
overlapping
positive classroom climate
procedures
productive learning environment
punishment
rules
time-out
withitness

Portfolio Activity

Classroom Rules and Procedures

InTASC Principle 3: Learning Environments

The purpose of this activity is to encourage you to begin thinking about classroom rules and procedures and how they will help you create a productive learning environment in your classroom. On the basis of the content in this chapter, interviews with teachers, other texts, and classroom discussion, what rules and procedures will you implement in your classroom? How do they reflect the specific age group that you'll be teaching? How do they reflect the specific content area you'll be teaching?

Portfolio Activities similar to this one and related to chapter content can be found at MyEducationLab™.

Classroom Management: Creating Productive Learning Environments

Go to the topic *Managing the Classroom* in the MyEducationLab (www.myeducationlab.com) for *Introduction to Teaching*, where you can:

- Find learning outcomes for *Managing the Classroom,* along with the national standards that connect to these outcomes.
- Complete *Assignments and Activities* that can help you more deeply understand the chapter content.
- Apply and practice your understanding of the core teaching skills identified in the chapter with the *Building Teaching Skills and Dispositions* learning units.
- Access classroom management simulations to practice the skills you're learning in the chapter.
- Access video clips of CCSSO National Teachers of the Year award winners responding to the question, "Why Do I Teach?" in the *Teacher Talk* section.
- Check your comprehension on the content covered in the chapter with the *Study Plan.* Here you will be able to take a chapter quiz, receive feedback on your answers, and then access *Review, Practice, and Enrichment* activities to enhance your understanding of chapter content.
- Check the *Book Resources* to find opportunities to share thoughts and gather feedback on the *Diversity and You* and *Issues You'll Face in Teaching* features found in this chapter.

MyEducationLab™

around themes that capture student interest and draw them into learning activities (Brophy, 2010). Suggestions for doing so include the following:

- Use lesson introductions to attract and maintain students' attention throughout lessons.
- Personalize content by focusing on real-world applications and linking topics to students' lives.
- Promote high levels of student involvement in learning activities.

Attracting and Focusing Students' Attention

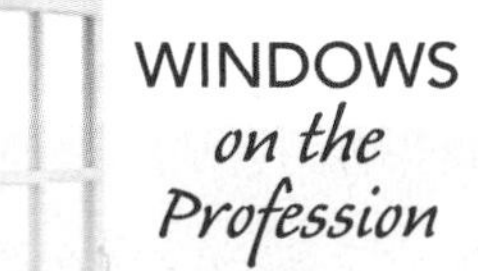

To see an elementary teacher using effective examples to motivate her students during a science lesson, click on the video *Applying the Motivation Model: Studying Arthropods* (12:29).

Even though not intentional, students' attention often wanders during lessons. You can address this issue by consciously planning to attract their attention at the beginning of a lesson. For example, an elementary teacher begins her discussion of arthropods by showing students a live lobster (We illustrate this lesson with a case study later in the chapter). A high school history teacher begins a study of the American Revolution by announcing that the school is short of money and is going to place a surtax on the students for attending. Shirley planned to begin her lesson by showing students her cardboard pizzas as an attention getter.

Beginning lessons with attention-grabbing activities need not take a lot of extra work. For example, as an introduction to the concept *adverbs*, having a student run across the front of the classroom quickly and then slowly and then asking his classmates to describe how he moved takes little extra time and no extra work, but it can make a significant difference in students' attentiveness. The same is true for the history teacher's comment about a surtax, and it's also true for the other topics we teach.

Personalizing Content Through Real-World Applications

Have you ever said to yourself, "I don't get it; I can't see how all of this applies to me"? You can address this problem in your teaching by linking content to your students' lives (Brophy, 2010). For example, when students understand that wearing seatbelts in their cars is an application of the law of inertia in science, or that when they listen politely while a classmate is speaking, they are applying the principle of freedom of speech—part of the First Amendment to our country's Constitution—their interest in the topics is likely to increase. Keeping the question, "How can I relate this topic to my students' interests and experiences?" in mind as you plan can make an important difference in their motivation and learning.

Shirley used her pizzas and cakes to illustrate fractions, and the teacher focusing on arthropods had her students squeeze their own legs to remind them that our skeletons are inside our bodies, as opposed to arthropods' exoskeletons. As other examples, a language arts teacher inserts students' names in examples of well-written paragraphs, and a geography teacher begins a study of landforms by having students describe the area where they live. And like attention getters, personalizing content doesn't have to take a lot of extra time on your part. Experienced, effective teachers constantly think about ways to personalize content and integrate this strategy into their teaching.

Involving Students

Involvement, the extent to which students are actively participating in a learning activity, is a third way to increase interest and learning. Think about your own experiences with friends at lunch or at a party. When you're talking and actively listening, you're more interested in the conversation and attentive than if you're uninvolved or on its fringes. The same applies in classrooms.

Questioning and group work are two powerful tools you have at your disposal for promoting your students' involvement. We examine both of these later in the chapter.

This discussion addresses the question in *Teaching and You* at the beginning of the section where we asked you to identify your best teachers and classes. When we asked the same question to our students, they said their best teachers involved them in their lessons, attracted and maintained their attention throughout the lesson, and connected the topics to real-world applications. In short, these teachers were motivating.

Understanding factors that increase students' motivation allows you to consciously plan learning activities that promote your students' motivation. We discuss planning for instruction in the next section of the chapter.

Revisiting My Beliefs

This section addresses our first item in This I Believe, "Some students are more motivated to learn than others, and I can do little about those who aren't motivated." This statement isn't true: Some students are indeed more motivated to learn than others, but we can do a great deal to increase motivation in our students.

WINDOWS *on the Profession*

To see different ways that teachers integrate motivation into their lessons, click on the video *Motivation* (10:36).

Check Your Understanding

1.1 Define motivation, and describe the difference between intrinsic and extrinsic motivation.

1.2 Describe the relationship between motivation and student achievement.

1.3 Describe three factors within teachers' control that can increase students' motivation to learn.

For feedback, go to the appendix, *Check Your Understanding*, located in the back of this text.

Planning for Effective Teaching

Planning is important for two major reasons. First, it makes us more effective as teachers. Effective teaching doesn't just happen; we all need to carefully think about and plan for it. A second reason that planning is so important for beginning teachers is that good planning helps relieve the anxiety that inevitably comes with our initial teaching efforts. This doesn't mean that you won't be nervous when you first teach, but careful planning will do much to ensure that you have a decent night's sleep before you teach your first lesson and will also contribute to the lesson's effectiveness.

Careful planning helps teachers define their goals and ensures that instructional activities are aligned with these goals.

Effective teaching only begins with planning. After planning we then implement our plans and also need to assess whether our lesson was successful. These processes are outlined in Figure 11.1, and we discuss them as the chapter unfolds.

All good teaching begins with planning, and as we plan, we make a series of decisions. For example, as she planned for her lesson on fractions, Shirley made a series of decisions that included:

- Selecting a topic she believed was important for her students to study
- Specifying learning objectives related to the topic
- Preparing and organizing learning activities to help students reach her objectives
- Create assessments to determine if students reached the objectives
- Ensuring that her instruction and assessments were aligned with her learning objectives

Teaching and You

Imagine that you're sitting in your room and planning for the first lesson that you'll teach in your first job. What will you think about, and how will you begin?

FIGURE 11.1 Processes Involved in Effective Teaching

Processes Involved in Effective Teaching
Planning for Instruction
• Select topics
• Specify objectives
• Prepare learning activities
• Prepare assessments
Implementing Instruction
• Conduct learning activities that help students reach learning objectives
• Employ essential teaching skills
Assessing Student Learning
• Informally assess learning during instruction
• Formally assess learning after instruction

These planning decisions address the questions we asked in *Teaching and You*. When you plan, you'll need to think about each of these five areas of decision making, which typically begins with the topic you want to teach.

Select Topics

Determining what is important for students to learn is important because it frames all your other planning decisions (L. Anderson & Krathwohl, 2001). Standards, such as the one Shirley used, as well as textbooks, curriculum guides, and your own personal philosophy are all sources you can use in helping you make this decision.

Your knowledge of content is particularly important in deciding which topics are important to teach, because there isn't enough time to teach everything. The more knowledgeable you are, the easier it will be for you to decide what is most important for your students to learn. Many beginning teachers turn to the Internet or their old college textbooks to help them in this process.

Specify Learning Objectives

After identifying a topic, you'll next need to decide what, specifically, you want your students to know or be able to do with respect to the topic—your **learning objectives**. Shirley's learning objectives, for example, were for her students *to understand equivalent fractions* and *to be able to add fractions with unlike denominators*. Clear learning objectives are essential because they guide the rest of the decisions you will make as you plan. Clear objectives will also guide you as you implement your plans. Lack of success with a lesson can often be traced back to teachers' not being clear about what they wanted students to learn.

Let's look at Shirley's objectives again. Her first was for her students to understand equivalent fractions, and her second was for them to be able to add fractions with unlike denominators, which requires first creating equivalent fractions. Both involved equivalent fractions, but each required different thinking of her students.

To respond to these differences, experts developed a system to classify objectives, questions, and assessment items. The result was the famous "Bloom's Taxonomy," which has been basic professional knowledge for all teachers for more than a half century (B. Bloom, Englehart, Furst, Hill, & Krathwohl, 1956). The categories in the system include:

- *Knowledge*: Knowledge of facts, definitions, and other forms of memorized information, such as knowing the definition of equivalent fractions
- *Comprehension*: Understanding information, such as the ability to state a problem in one's own words or identify an example of a concept, such as understanding equivalent fractions (Shirley's first objective)
- *Application*: Using what one knows to solve an original problem, such as adding fractions with unlike denominators (Shirley's second objective)
- *Analysis*: The ability to break information into component parts and provide evidence to support conclusions, such as explaining why adding one set of fractions requires forming equivalent fractions, but adding another set does not
- *Synthesis*: Combining information to create an original process or product, such as constructing a unique process for finding a solution to a problem

FIGURE 11.2 A Taxonomy for Learning, Teaching, and Assessing Based upon Cognitive Science

	The Cognitive Process Dimension					
The Knowledge Dimension	1. Remember	2. Understand	3. Apply	4. Analyze	5. Evaluate	6. Create
A. Factual knowledge						
B. Conceptual knowledge						
C. Procedural knowledge						
D. Metacognitive knowledge						

Source: "A Taxonomy for Learning, Teaching, and Assessing" from *A Taxonomy for Learning, Teaching, and Assessing: A Revision of Bloom's Taxonomy of Educational Objectives Abridged Edition* (1st ed.), by L. Anderson & D. Krathwohl. Copyright © 2001 by Anderson/Krathwohl/Cruikshank/Mayer/Pintrich/Raths/Wittrock. Printed and electronically reproduced by permission of Pearson Education, Inc., Upper Saddle River, NJ.

- *Evaluation*: Making judgments about validity or quality of work based on a set of criteria, such as determining which of two approaches to solving a problem is more efficient

To reflect our increased understanding of teaching and learning since the middle of the 20th century, when the original taxonomy was published, it has been revised. This new taxonomy describes objectives in terms of students' cognitive (thought) processes, and uses the term *knowledge* to identify the content students should know or acquire. The result is a matrix with 24 cells that represent the intersection of four types of knowledge with six cognitive processes (L. Anderson & Krathwohl, 2001). This revised taxonomy appears in Figure 11.2.

To understand this matrix let's look at Shirley's objectives again. They were: (1) *to understand equivalent fractions* and (2) *to add fractions with unlike denominators*. *Equivalent fractions* is a concept, so her first objective would be classified into the cell where *concepts* intersects with the cognitive process *understand*. Adding fractions involves the application of a procedure, so her second objective would be classified into the cell where *procedural knowledge/skills* intersects with the cognitive process *apply*. Using the taxonomy during planning allows us to see what types of knowledge and cognitive processes we're emphasizing in our teaching, and it also reminds us that we want our students to do more than just remember factual knowledge. Unfortunately, schooling often focuses more on this most basic type of learning than it does on the other 23 cells combined. These other forms of knowledge and more advanced cognitive processes are even more important now in the 21st century, as student thinking, decision making, and problem solving are increasingly emphasized as our tech-immersed world becomes more complex.

Prepare and Organize Learning Activities

Having identified her learning objectives—what she wanted her students to understand and be able to do—Shirley then prepared and organized her learning activities. Two steps are involved in this process: (1) creating or finding high-quality examples or problems to illustrate the topic, and (2) sequencing the examples to be most meaningful to students.

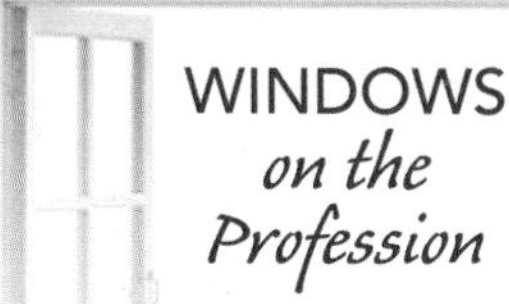

To see how teachers use high-quality examples to teach concepts, click on the video *Constructing Concepts: Using Concrete Examples* (9:07).

High-quality examples are representations of content that ideally have all the information in them that students need to learn a topic, and their importance in promoting learning cannot be overstated. Shirley's cardboard "pizzas" and "cakes" were the examples she used to help her students understand equivalent fractions and how to add fractions with unlike denominators. They were high quality because her students *could see* that her "pizzas" were divided into eight equal parts, so they *could see* why adding two fractions, such as 2/8 and 3/8 would be 5/8. She then planned to use her "cakes" to build on this knowledge and to help her students learn how to create equivalent fractions. (You'll see how Shirley used them in the next section of the chapter when we discuss implementing instruction.)

Shirley's examples were in elementary math, but high-quality examples are essential for teaching topics at all grade levels. For instance, if you're planning to teach language arts, you might use actual student writing samples to provide examples of good organization, grammar, and punctuation. If you're teaching science you might swing a cup of water tied to the end of a string around your head, and use this simple demonstration to illustrate the concept of *inertia*. If you're teaching music, you might use popular recordings to help your students learn ideas such as *melody* and *rhythm,* and if you teach geography, you could download colored pictures of the Glacier National Park and the Great Smokey mountains from the Internet to illustrate young and mature mountain ranges. It would be impossible to teach these topics effectively without these high-quality examples. While essential for all learners, high-quality examples are even more important for members of cultural minorities or students who are not native English speakers, because they help accommodate differences in students' prior experiences and knowledge (Echevarria & Graves, 2011).

FIGURE 11.3 Sample Assessment Items from Shirley's Planning

Part I

Look at the drawings of pairs of fractions below. Circle the pairs that are equivalent, and explain why they are equivalent in each case.

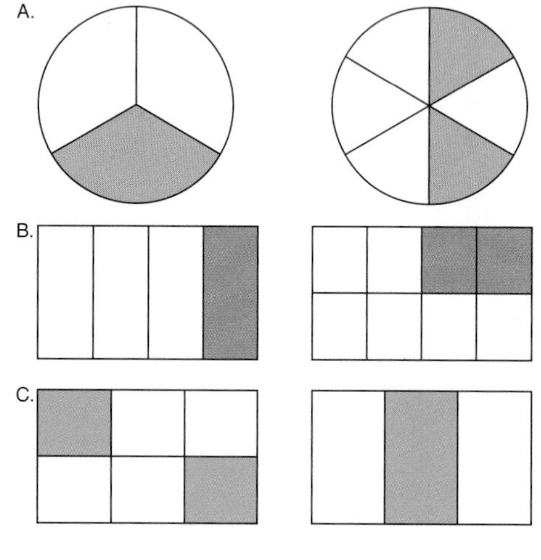

Part II

Add the following fractions.

$\frac{1}{5} + \frac{2}{5} =$ ______ $\frac{2}{7} + \frac{4}{7} =$ ______

$\frac{1}{3} + \frac{1}{2} =$ ______ $\frac{3}{4} + \frac{1}{8} =$ ______

Create Assessments

Think about the classes you're now in. In which do you study the hardest, and in which do you learn the most? If you're typical, it's classes in which you're frequently and thoroughly assessed. **Assessment** is the process we use to gather information and make decisions about students' learning, and unfortunately we tend to think of it as a process that comes after a lesson has been taught. Quizzes and tests are the most comment forms of assessment, and indeed, we give them after we teach lessons. However, to assess most effectively, we should think about assessment during our initial planning (Stiggins & Chappuis, 2012).

Effective assessments answer two questions: (1) How will I know if my students have reached my learning objectives? (2) How can I use assessment to increase my students' learning? Shirley considered assessment when she said, "I'll give them a quiz Friday, so I can see how well they understand equivalent fractions and adding fractions with unlike denominators." This helped answer the first question. Her decision, "If they don't do well, I'll give them some more practice," addressed the second. Sample assessment items that Shirley used are illustrated in Figure 11.3.

Assessment is an interesting educational phenomenon. Somehow, historically, it has been perceived negatively and even as punitive in some cases. And students sometimes protest that they would study just as hard if they weren't assessed. However, this negative perception of assessment is a misconception that can detract from learning, and students' suggestion that they would study as hard if they weren't assessed isn't supported by research (Stiggins & Chappuis, 2012). In fact, the exact opposite is true (Carey, 2010; Rohrer & Pashler, 2010). "Testing has such a bad connotation; people think of standardized testing or teaching to the test. Maybe we need to call it something else, but this is one of the most powerful learning tools we have" (Carey, 2010, para. 28). Expert teachers, such as Shirley, assess frequently during instruction, using both questioning and in-class exercises to provide students and themselves with ongoing information about learning progress (Stiggins & Chappuis, 2012).

Making decisions about assessment during planning is also important because it helps ensure that your learning activities and assessments are aligned with your learning objectives. Let's see what this means.

Revisiting My Beliefs

This section addresses the second item in *This I Believe*, "Because assessing students with quizzes and tests uses instructional time, students who are frequently assessed learn less than those assessed less frequently." Exactly the opposite is true: The process of assessment makes a major contribution to learning, and it is one of the most valuable uses of our instructional time.

Ensure Instructional Alignment

Thinking about assessment during planning helped Shirley answer an additional question: "How do I know if my instruction and assessments will help my students reach my objectives?" The answer to this question describes **instructional alignment**, the match between learning objectives, learning activities, and assessments.

Alignment is an essential component of effective instruction.

> Without this alignment, it is difficult to know what is being learned. Students may be learning valuable information, but one cannot tell unless there is alignment between what they are learning and the assessment of that learning. Similarly, students may be learning things that others don't value unless curricula and assessments are aligned with learning goals. (Bransford et al., 2000, pp. 51–52)

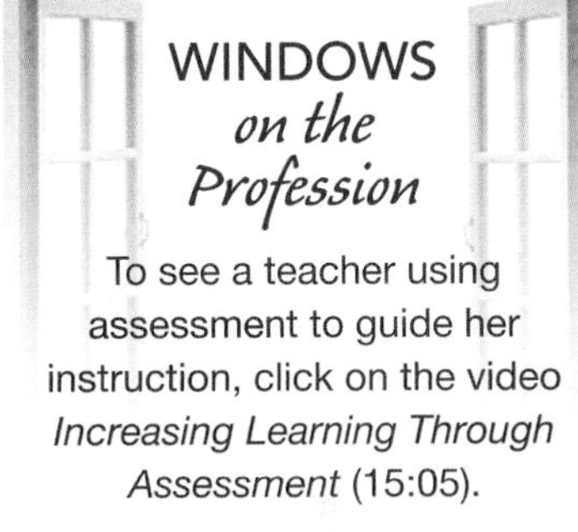

To see a teacher using assessment to guide her instruction, click on the video *Increasing Learning Through Assessment* (15:05).

Shirley's objectives were for students to understand the concept *equivalent fractions* and to add fractions with unlike denominators; her instruction focused on these objectives, and the quiz items in Figure 11.3 directly addressed these objectives. So, her instruction was aligned.

Alignment isn't as easy as it appears. For instance, if a teacher's objective is for students to be able to write effectively, yet learning activities focus on isolated grammar skills, the instruction is out of alignment. It is similarly out of alignment if the objective is for students to apply math concepts to real-world problems, but learning activities have students practice computation problems. Instructional alignment encourages us to ask ourselves, "What does my objective actually mean, and do my learning and assessment activities truly lead to the objective?"

Planning in a Standards-Based Environment

In response to concerns about students in our country lacking the knowledge and skills they need to compete successfully in today's world, educators have established academic **standards**, statements that describe what students should know or be able to do at the end of a period of study. Every state has written standards in virtually all content areas, so regardless of the state in which you teach, standards will be a part of your professional experience.

Standards are labeled in different ways, such as "Essential Knowledge and Skills" (Texas Education Agency, 2008a), "Learning Standards" (Illinois State Board of Education, 2008a), "Content Standards" (California State Board of Education, 2008a), or "Sunshine State Standards" (Florida Department of Education, 2010). To access your state's standards, click on the following link: http://www.education-world.com/standards/state/index.shtml. Then, click on the pull-down menu and select your state.

Standards are essentially statements of learning objectives, but they're written with varying degrees of specificity (Swanson, 2008). (Notice that our definition of *standards* is similar to the definition of learning objectives that we presented earlier in the chapter.) So, before you can design learning activities to help your students meet a specific standard, you'll need to interpret the meaning of that standard. If you're unclear about what a standard is asking, a good idea is to check with the sample assessment items that accompany standards. These are specifically designed to provide you with a clear idea of what your students will face on a standards-based exam. Then, having first interpreted the standard, you can plan as we described the process in this section.

To illustrate, let's return to Shirley as she planned for her lesson. She began her planning by referring to her state standards for fourth-grade math. One standard looked like this:

> Generate equivalent fractions and simplify fractions. (Florida Department of Education, 2010)

Shirley translated this standard into the following learning objectives: (1) *to understand equivalent fractions* and (2) *to be able to add fractions with unlike denominators.* She then designed her instruction to help her students understand equivalent fractions and to be able to add fractions with unlike denominators.

You'll follow the same process when you plan. You'll first interpret the standard; the interpretation of the standard will be your learning objectives; and you'll then plan learning activities and assessments aligned with the objectives.

Revisiting My Beliefs

This section addresses the third item in *This I Believe*, "Planning for instruction primarily involves identifying the topics that are important for my students to learn." This statement isn't true: While planning does involve identifying topics, it is much broader and includes other activities to ensure that instructional activities result in student learning.

Check Your Understanding

2.1 What are the five essential steps in planning for instruction?

2.2 Planning in a standards-based environment involves an additional step beyond the planning steps described in this section of the chapter. What is this additional step?

2.3 Classify the following objectives into one of the cells of the taxonomy table in Figure 11.2, and explain your classification. (1) Students will identify examples of figures of speech such as similes, metaphors, and personifications in written paragraphs. (2) They will write original paragraphs that include those figures of speech.

For feedback, go to the appendix, *Check Your Understanding,* located in the back of this text.

Implementing Instruction: Essential Teaching Skills

When we implement instruction we put the plans we made into action. It involves all the decisions you make as you work with students, and it's the second phase of instruction (see Figure 11.4).

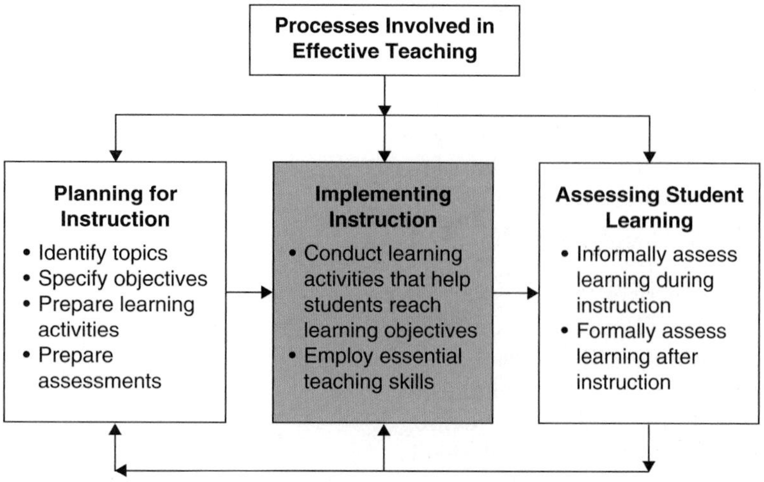

Every lesson is different, but the good ones share characteristics that are common to all. **Essential teaching skills** are the abilities that all teachers, including those in their first year of teaching, demonstrate as they help their students learn. For instance, regardless of the grade level or the topic you're teaching, you'll need to be well organized and be able to ask strategic questions to guide your students' learning. *Organization* and *questioning* are two essential teaching skills we describe in this section. They are derived from a long line of classroom research, and their importance for promoting learning is well documented (Good & Brophy, 2008). These essential teaching skills are outlined in Table 11.1, and we illustrate them with Shirley's work in the sections that follow.

FIGURE 11.4 Implementing Instruction

Processes Involved in Effective Teaching
Planning for Instruction
• Identify topics
• Specify objectives
• Prepare learning activities
• Prepare assessments
Implementing Instruction
• Conduct learning activities that help students reach learning objectives
• Employ essential teaching skills
Assessing Student Learning
• Informally assess learning during instruction
• Formally assess learning after instruction

TABLE 11.1 Essential Teaching Skills

Essential Teaching Skill	Description	Purpose in Promoting Learning
Teacher beliefs and behaviors	Teachers' beliefs and actions that influence the learning environment	Create a classroom environment that promotes student motivation and learning
Organization	Teacher actions that include: (1) starting lessons on time, (2) having materials prepared in advance and ready for use, (3) making smooth transitions from one activity to another, and (4) having well-established routines	Maximize the amount of time available for instruction
Focus	Concrete objects, pictures, models, and other examples teachers use to illustrate their topics	Attract and maintain learners' attention, and provide them with the experiences they used to reach teachers' learning objectives
Review	Discussion and clarification of previously taught content	Help students recall prior knowledge to which new content can be connected
Questioning	The process of (1) using many questions during instruction, (2) calling on students as equally as possible, (3) giving them time to think about their responses, and (4) providing cues and prompts when they're unable to answer	Promote the active involvement of students, and encourage them to think about the topic being taught
Feedback	Communicating with students about their learning progress	Provide students with the information they need to confirm or increase their understanding
Closure and Application	Summary at the end of a lesson and practice with the content	Help students confirm their understanding and use their knowledge in new contexts

Teacher Beliefs

Admittedly, teacher beliefs are not "skills," but they are indeed *essential*. Effective teaching begins with who you are—your beliefs about students and learning and how you interact with students as you work with them. Your beliefs about students and learning set the stage for everything else that occurs in your classroom (Torff, 2011). They include:

- caring
- personal teaching efficacy
- high expectations
- enthusiasm and modeling

Let's look at them.

Caring

A caring teacher is at the heart of every effective classroom. **Caring** refers to a teacher's investment in the protection and development of young people, and a caring teacher is essential for effective teaching.

> Students who perceived that teachers cared about them reported positive motivational outcomes such as more prosocial and social responsibility goals, academic effort, and greater internal control beliefs. It appears that students want teachers to care for them both as learners and as people. (Perry, Turner, & Meyer, 2006, p. 341)

You can communicate your care for your students in several ways:

- Learn your students' names quickly, and call on them by their first names.
- Greet them each day, and get to know them as individuals.
- Use personal nonverbal communications such as eye contact and smiles to establish human contact.
- Use "we" and "our" instead of "you" and "your" in reference to class activities and assignments.
- Spend time with them.
- Hold them to high standards.

We want to particularly emphasize the last two suggestions. We all have 24 hours in our days—no more, no less—and the way we choose to allocate our time is the truest measure of our priorities. Helping students who have problems with an assignment or calling a parent after school hours communicates that you care about your students and their learning. Spending a moment to ask a question about a baby brother or to compliment a new hairstyle communicates caring about a student as a human being.

The idea that holding students to high standards is an indicator of caring may seem surprising. But as one motivation expert suggested, teachers demonstrate that they care for students by:

> [N]ot accepting sloppy, thoughtless, or incomplete work, by pressing them to clarify vague comments, by encouraging them not to give up, and by not praising work that does not reflect genuine effort. Ironically, reactions that are often intended to protect students' self-esteem—such as accepting low quality work—convey a lack of interest, patience, or caring. (Stipek, 2002, p. 157)

Personal Teaching Efficacy

Before we can become effective, we have to believe in ourselves. **Personal teaching efficacy** describes teachers' beliefs in their abilities to help students learn, regardless of students' home lives, the conditions of the school or the support of the school administration (Bruning, Shraw, & Norby, 2011).

To illustrate this idea, let's look at a brief exchange between Shirley and Jim Fantini, one of her colleagues.

"My students didn't score as well as I would have liked on the math part of the Stanford Achievement Test last year, and I promised myself they were going to do better this year," Shirley comments as she glances through a set of math quizzes.

"But you said your students aren't as sharp this year," Jim responds.

"That doesn't matter. I need to push them harder. I think I can do a better job than I did last year. They're going to be so good at fractions that they'll be able to do the problems in their sleep."

"You never give up, do you?" Jim smiles, shaking his head.

Shirley's comments "I think I can do a better job than I did last year" and "They're going to be so good at fractions . . ." reflect her belief in her ability to help all her students learn. When students aren't learning, high-efficacy teachers don't blame it on lack of intelligence, poor home environments, uncooperative administrators, or some other external cause. Instead, they redouble their efforts, persevere with low achievers, emphasize praise rather than criticism, and maximize the time available for instruction.

Low-efficacy teachers, in contrast, spend less time on learning activities, "give up" on low achievers, and are more critical when students fail. Not surprisingly, students taught by high-efficacy teachers learn more than those taught by low-efficacy teachers.

High Expectations

A time-honored maxim states, "People tend to rise to the expectations of others," and it applies to classrooms as well. The more we expect of our students, the more we'll get out of them. It's true that some students have more ability than others, but most are capable of learning much more than they often do. Shirley's comment, "I need to push them harder," captures the spirit of high expectations. When we have high expectations for our students, effort and learning increase, and the opposite is true if our expectations are low.

Unfortunately, teachers treat students for whom they have high expectations differently than those for whom they have low expectations. These differences exist in four areas (Good & Brophy, 2008):

- *Questioning*: Teachers tend to call on perceived high achievers more often, they allow these students more time to answer, and they prompt perceived high achievers more often when they don't respond.
- *Teacher effort*: Teachers give perceived high achievers more thorough explanations, their instruction is more enthusiastic, and they require more complete and accurate student answers.
- *Feedback*: Teachers praise perceived high achievers more and criticize them less. They also offer perceived high achievers more complete and lengthier feedback.
- *Emotional support*: Teachers interact more with perceived high achievers, make more eye contact, stand closer, and orient their bodies more directly toward these students.

Teachers are typically not aware of the fact that they treat perceived high achievers better than lower achievers (Stipek, 2002), and this is the reason we're discussing these patterns. If you understand that you might—without realizing it—unconsciously treat your higher- and lower-achieving students differently, you can make a conscious effort to treat all your students as equitably as possible and hold appropriately high expectations for each one.

Enthusiasm and Modeling

Enthusiasm is contagious. If we see someone behave enthusiastically, we tend to become more enthusiastic ourselves, and the same applies in teaching. If your instructors demonstrate interest in the topics they're teaching, you're more likely to become more interested in them as well. This occurs through **modeling**, the tendency of people to imitate others' behaviors (Bandura, 2001, 2004).

Your modeling can have a powerful influence on both your students' motivation and their learning. For example, imagine how you would feel if one of your instructors said, "I know this stuff is boring, but we have to learn it anyway," compared to "Now this idea is interesting and important; it will help us understand how our students think and learn." Obviously, you're more likely to be interested in the second topic. As another example, if you want your students to be courteous and respectful to you and each other, you'll need to treat them with the same courtesy and respect. If you want them to be responsible and conscientious, you'll need to model these same characteristics by returning their papers promptly, having your instructional materials organized and ready to use, and using your instructional time effectively.

As we said at the beginning of this section, effective teaching begins with you, the teacher, and caring, personal teaching efficacy, positive expectations, and teacher modeling and enthusiasm are all essential for promoting your students' learning.

Teaching and You

Have you ever misplaced your keys and spent a frustrating amount of time looking for them? Have you ever said, "I've got to get organized; this chaos is driving me crazy."?

Organization

Organization is important in our personal lives, and it's no less so for effective teaching. To see how, let's join Shirley's class on Monday morning just before math, which she schedules each day from 10:00 A.M. to 11:00 A.M.

Shirley walks up and down the aisles, placing sheets of paper on each student's desk as students finish a writing assignment in language arts.

At 9:58, she says, "Quickly turn in your writing assignment, and get out your math books."

Her students stop writing and pass their papers forward, putting their papers on the top of the stack. Shirley puts the papers in a folder and at 10:01 pulls out her cardboard pizzas and says, "Let's see what we remember about adding fractions. Look at these pizzas. We'll use them to review what we've learned about fractions."

Shirley scheduled math from 10:00 to 11:00 and announced that it was time for math at 9:58. By 10:01 her students had turned in their papers and were ready, so she made the transition from language arts to math in 3 minutes. In addition, she had her cardboard pizzas and cakes already prepared and at her fingertips and placed the sheets of paper on students' desks as they turned in their language arts papers. Also, she had taught her students routines that they followed essentially without thinking about them, which saved both time and energy. For instance, they placed their papers on the top of the stacks as they were passed forward, without being reminded to do so.

These examples illustrate **organization**, the set of teacher actions that maximizes the amount of time available for instruction. Teacher actions that promote organization are outlined in Table 11.2.

Teachers who aren't as organized spend more time in transitions from one activity to another, so they don't start lessons when they're scheduled, they use valuable class time accessing materials, and lose valuable instructional time because their routines aren't well established. The result is fewer minutes available for teaching and student learning.

Focus

You care about your students and have high expectations for them. You believe you can get them to learn regardless of their circumstances, and you're enthusiastic about what you're teaching. And you're well organized.

Now, we focus on the actual lesson. What should occur first? Attention is the beginning point for all learning, so it makes sense to attract their attention as the lesson begins; students need to pay attention to you so they can understand the topic you're teaching. Earlier in our discussion of motivation, you saw that the

TABLE 11.2 Teacher Actions that Promote Organization

Teacher Action	Example
Starting on time	Shirley's students had their math books out and were waiting at 10:01.
Making smooth transitions	Shirley made the transition from language arts to math in 3 minutes.
Preparing materials in advance	Shirley had her cardboard pizzas and cakes easily accessible.
Establishing routines	At Shirley's signal, the students put their papers on the top of the stack without being told specifically to do so.

ability to attract and maintain students' attention is important for increasing motivation and interest, and it's equally important for learning.

This is accomplished with a form of **focus**—concrete objects, pictures, models, materials displayed on the document camera, and even information written on the board that help attract and maintain attention during learning activities. Some experts use the term *hook* to describe this attention-attracting function (Lemov, 2010).

High-quality examples, such as those Shirley used in her lesson, are excellent forms of focus. Building lessons around examples provides students with experiences that they can use to develop their understanding, so, in addition to helping maintain attention, the examples also serve as the raw material for constructing their understanding of the topic.

Review

Once we have our students' attention, we need to encourage them to think about the topic and connect it to information they already know. Let's rejoin Shirley's lesson to see how she does this.

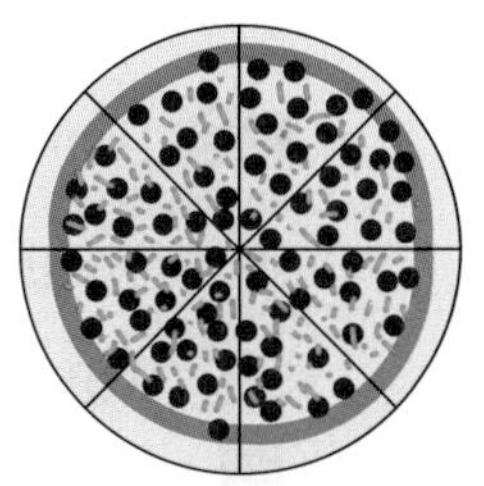
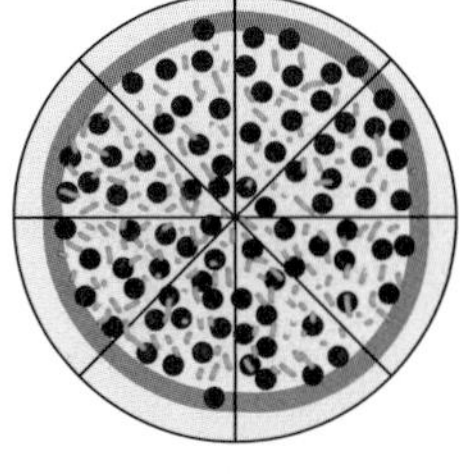
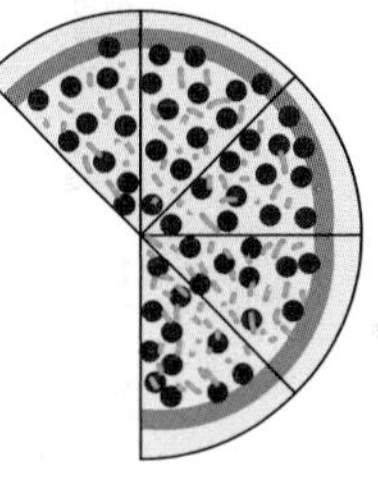
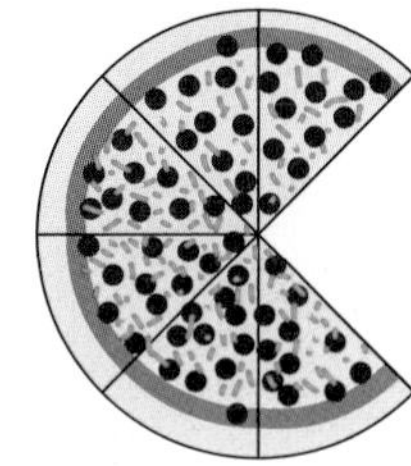

"Let's see what we remember about adding fractions," she says, displaying the pizzas as shown here.

She then removes three pieces from the first and two pieces from the second so they appear as shown here.

She continues, "What fraction of one whole pizza did we eat?"

After giving her students several seconds to think about their answers, she asks, "How many pieces of the first pizza did we eat? . . . Jacob?"

"Three."

"And how about this pizza? How many pieces did we eat? . . . Emma?"

"Two."

She then writes 3/8 + 2/8 on the board and, pointing to these numbers, asks, "Why did I write 3/8 here and 2/8 there? . . . Aiden?"

"You have eight pieces in each pizza, and you ate three of them in that one," Aiden responds, pointing to the one on the left.

"Good," Shirley smiles. "And what about the second one? How many pieces of that pizza did we eat? . . . Sophia?"

"Two."

"So what fraction of a total pizza did we eat altogether? . . . Mason?"

"Five eighths of a pizza?" Mason responds after thinking for a few seconds.

"Good, Mason. . . . And why is it 5/8 . . . Claire?"

". . ."

"How many pieces altogether in each pizza?"

"Eight," Claire answers.

"Good, and how many did we eat, altogether?"

"Five."

"Yes," she smiles at Claire, "so we ate 5/8 of one pizza."

Shirley then writes these problems on the board: 3/7 + 4/7 = ?, 2/5 + 1/5 = ?, and 4/8 + 2/8 = ? and reviews them as she did with her pizzas.

"Now remember," she emphasizes, "in each of these problems, the two fractions have the same denominator. . . . Be sure to keep that in mind as we continue our study of fractions.

Reviews help students recall the prior knowledge they need to understand the content of the current lesson, and effective lessons begin with a review. For example, Shirley reviewed adding fractions with like denominators to prepare them for understanding equivalent fractions and adding fractions with unlike denominators. Presenting concrete examples, such as her "pizzas," during the review increased its effectiveness by providing additional links to what her students already knew.

Questioning allows teachers to guide student learning while gauging learning progress.

Questioning

Think again about student motivation, focus, and Shirley's review. In our discussion of motivation, we found that involvement is important for increasing student interest, and students learn more if they are involved and paying attention.

> Teachers who elicit greater achievement gains spend a great deal of time actively instructing their students. Their classrooms feature more time spent in interactive lessons featuring teacher–student discourse and less time spent in independent seatwork. . . . Most of their instruction occurs during interactive discourse with students rather than during extended lecture-presentations. (Brophy, 2006, p. 764)

Questioning is the single most effective way that you have to promote your students' involvement (Lemov, 2010). Shirley conducted her entire review with questioning, and a large body of evidence suggests that guiding students with questioning produces much more learning than simply explaining topics to them (Good & Brophy, 2008).

With respect to questioning, expert teachers excel in four areas:

- Frequency
- Equitable distribution
- Wait-time
- Prompting

Frequency

Frequency simply refers to the number of questions teachers ask during lessons, and expert teachers ask many more questions than do teachers who are less skilled. Questioning involves students, and their answers—or inability to answer—provide us with valuable information about their understanding, information we can't get if we simply explain the content to them.

Shirley's review illustrates this point. Let's see how Shirley used questioning to involve and assess her students.

Shirley:	So what fraction of a total pizza did we eat altogether? . . . Mason?"
Mason:	Five eighths of a pizza?
Shirley:	"Good, Mason. . . . And why is it 5/8 . . . Claire?"
Claire:	". . ."
Shirley:	How many pieces altogether in each pizza?"
Claire:	Eight.
Shirley:	Good, and how many did we eat, altogether?
Claire:	Five.
Shirley:	Yes [smiling at Claire], so we ate 5/8 of one pizza.

Claire's inability to respond to the question, "Why is it 5/8?" indicated that she didn't fully understand the process of adding fractions, so Shirley intervened by asking her additional questions. Shirley wouldn't have realized that she needed to intervene if she had merely explained or talked about the process.

Equitable Distribution

Let's look at Shirley's review again. It took only several minutes, and in that short time she called on Jacob, Emma, Aiden, Sophia, Mason, and Claire—six different students, and all by name. Her actions illustrate **equitable distribution**, the practice of calling on all students—both volunteers (students who have their hands raised) and nonvolunteers (those who don't)—as equally as possible (Kerman, 1979). To emphasize that we should call on all students regardless of whether they have their hands raised, some experts use the term *cold call* when describing equitable distribution (Lemov, 2010).

Equitable distribution sends an important message to your students. By calling on them as equally as possible, you're communicating:

I don't care whether you're a boy or girl, member of a cultural minority or a nonminority, high achiever or low achiever. I want you in my classroom, and I want you involved. I believe you're capable of learning, and I will do whatever it takes to ensure that you're successful.

Earlier we saw how important high expectations are for promoting student learning. Nothing communicates high expectations better than the practice of equitable distribution. In classrooms where it's practiced, student achievement rises, and classroom management problems decrease (Good & Brophy, 2008). When students know that they'll be called on, they are more alert and involved in the lesson and learning follows.

Wait-Time

If we want students to answer questions that require them to think and do more than just remember factual information, we need to give them time to think. To illustrate this idea, let's think again about the dialogue between Shirley and her students. In each case, after asking a question, she paused briefly and gave the whole class several seconds to think before she called on someone. Then, after calling on a student, she briefly paused again to give the student additional time to answer. This period of silence after a question is asked and after a student is called on is called **wait-time**. Giving students a few seconds to think about their answers makes sense, but in most classrooms, wait-times are very short, often 1 second or less (Good & Brophy, 2008). Increasing wait-time to about 3 to 5 seconds results in higher-quality student responses, greater participation from all students, and ultimately increased learning (Rowe, 1986).

Prompting

At this point you might be thinking to yourself, "All this sounds fine, but what do I do if a student can't respond? **Prompting**, providing additional questions and cues when students fail to answer correctly, is the answer. To see how prompting works, let's look again at the dialogue from Shirley's review.

Shirley: Why is it [the fraction of the pizza they ate] 5/8? . . . Claire?
Claire: ". . ."
Shirley: How many pieces altogether in each pizza?
Claire: Eight.
Shirley: Good, . . . and how many did we eat, altogether?
Claire: Five.

When Claire didn't respond to her first question, Shirley asked, "How many pieces altogether in each pizza?" This was a prompt, and it helped Claire respond successfully.

Revisiting My Beliefs

This section addresses the fourth item in *This I Believe*, "The best way I can teach effectively is to clearly explain the content I'm teaching to my students." Quite the opposite is true: You will be most effective if you can involve your students in lessons with your questioning.

The value of prompting is well documented (Good & Brophy, 2008). As with equitable distribution, it communicates positive expectations—that you believe students are capable, and you want and expect each to answer successfully.

Less-effective teachers tend to turn an unanswered question to another student instead of prompting. For example, Shirley could have asked, "Can someone help Claire out?" when Claire didn't answer, but this would have communicated that she didn't believe Claire was capable of answering and didn't expect her to do so—not a message we want to send our students.

WINDOWS *on the Profession*

To see a high school English teacher using questioning to involve her students in a lesson, click on the video *Scarlet Letter* (15:42).

In this section we emphasized using questioning to involve your students in your learning activities. This doesn't suggest that you should never explain an idea to your students, because clear explanations are also a part of good teaching. What we are suggesting, however, is that you will be more effective if—instead of relying on explaining as your primary teaching method—you guide your students' evolving understanding with questioning. It will take time and practice, but the more skilled at questioning you become, the more successful and rewarding your teaching will be.

Feedback

We've all had experiences similar to those in *Teaching and You*. We've been uncertain about our learning progress because of the absence of **feedback**, information about current understanding that can be used to promote new learning. Feedback has a powerful effect on student learning, and some experts suggest you should never give a quiz or test without providing your students with feedback. *Never* is an absolute term, but in this case it might be appropriate; if we give students a quiz or test, we need to grade them and give students feedback as quickly as possible (Hattie & Timperley, 2007).

Teaching and You

Have you ever been in a class where you handed in assignments and had to wait weeks before they were graded and returned? Or where you had to wait until the midterm exam to find out how you were doing? How did you feel in each case?

You can provide feedback in a number of ways. You can grade homework and assignments individually and then discuss them as a group activity in which you analyze troublesome items. You can also use classroom time to discuss frequently missed items on quizzes, and tests, and then allocate more instructional time for the items that caused the most problems, or you can use that extra time to help struggling individual students while the majority of your class is doing seat work. You can also provide feedback as you question your students. If they answer correctly, you acknowledge the answer with a simple, "Good" or "Well done." Or, if the student answers correctly, but appears uncertain, you can provide additional information to confirm the response. Ongoing feedback through questioning is one of the most effective ways to promote students' learning.

Closure and Application

Just as lessons need clear beginnings, they also need closure to pull all the ideas in the lesson together. Let's rejoin Shirley's lesson once more to see how she develops it and brings it to closure. Notice as you read the case study how she continues to use questioning to encourage student involvement.

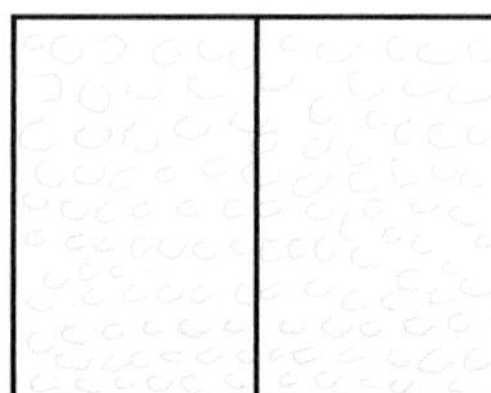

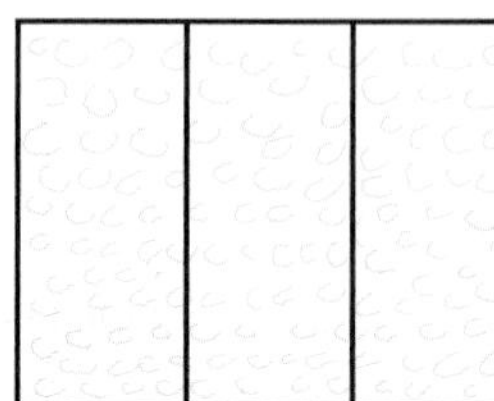

After completing her review, Shirley continues, "Now, I have a different kind of problem," as she pulls out the two cardboard cakes as shown here.

"I'm eating cake, and I eat this piece," she says, pointing to a third, "and then I eat this piece," she adds, pointing to one of the halves. "How much cake have I eaten?"

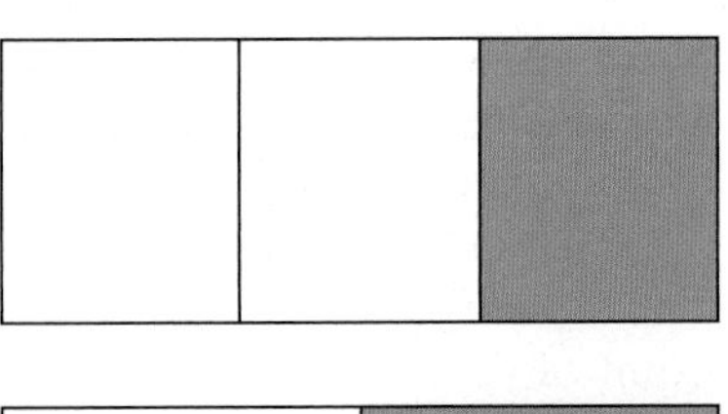

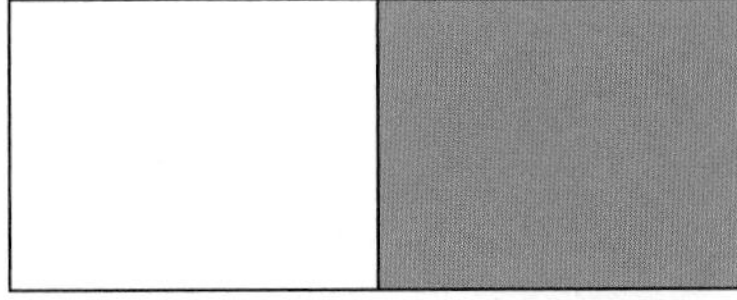

Her students offer several ideas ranging from 2/3 to 2/5, and Shirley then says, "Take the sheets of paper that I gave you, and fold them like our cakes here."

She helps them fold one of the papers into thirds and the other in half and tells them to shade one section of each as you see to the right.

She continues, "How much cake do we have here? . . . Ethan?" pointing at the paper divided into thirds.

"A third."

"Good," Shirley smiles. "Now, let's all fold our paper this way," and she shows the students how to fold the paper, so it appears as you see here.

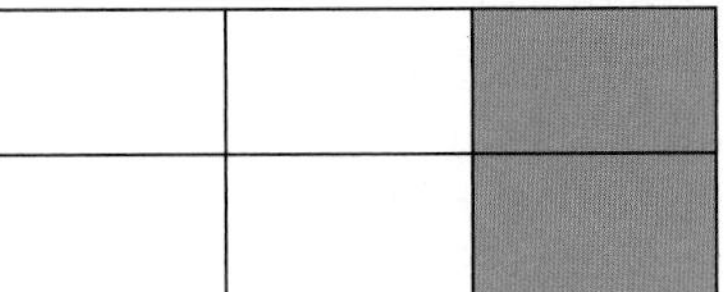

"How many pieces do I have now? . . . Emily?"

". . . Six."

"So what portion is now shaded? . . . Logan?"

"Two sixths."

"Good, Logan," and she moves to the board and writes 1/3 = 2/6.

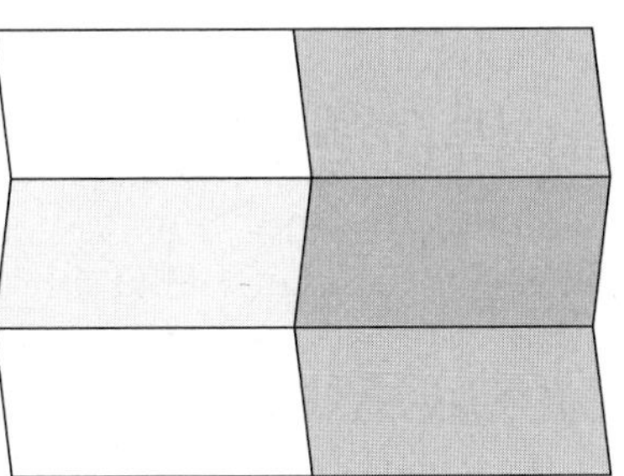

"Now, how do we know that the 1/3 and the 2/6 are equal?"

"It's the same amount of cake," Noah responds.

"Exactly," Shirley smiles. "They're called *equivalent fractions*."

Shirley then has the students divide the other paper in thirds, so it appears as shown here:

"What do we see here?"

". . . They both have the same number of pieces," Olivia observes.

"And all the pieces are the same size," Isabella adds.

"I know!" Adam says excitedly. "We've eaten 5/6 of one cake."

"Please explain that for us," Shirley requests.

"It's like the pizza. We have two pieces there, and three pieces there, so it's 5/6 of one cake."

Shirley then models a process for finding equivalent fractions by multiplying the numerator and denominator by the same number, and guides students through two more problems.

"Now, what have we been doing here? . . . Liam?" Shirley asks.

". . . We're finding equivalent fractions."

"And why do we want to find them? . . . Jackson?"

". . . So we can add fractions when the denominators aren't the same."

Shirley praises the class for their good work, gives them a sheet of practice problems, and says, "Everyone, let's do the first one on your sheet. What do you get when you add 2/3 and 1/4?"

As her students work the problem, Shirley walks up and down the rows to check their progress and offer brief suggestions.

After they have finished the problem, Shirley discusses it, and repeats the process with a second and a third problem. She then has them work independently on additional problems for the remainder of their time in math. As the majority of the students work independently, she calls Heather, Harper, Mandi, and Mason to a table at the back of the room, where she provides them with some extra assistance.

Finally, seeing it is 10:59, Shirley says, "It's nearly time for our break. As soon as you've cleaned up around your desks, we'll go."

In this segment of the lesson, Shirley helped her students understand the concept *equivalent fraction* and how to add fractions with unlike denominators. She then

summarized the lesson and brought it to **closure**, a form of review at the end of lessons designed to help students organize what they've learned into a meaningful idea. Closure pulls the different ideas in a lesson together and signals the end of a lesson.

Shirley achieved closure by having her students explicitly state the main point of the lesson. Let's see how she did this.

Shirley: Now, what have we been doing here? . . . Liam?

Liam: We're finding equivalent fractions.

Shirley: And why do we want to find them? . . . Jackson?

Jackson: So we can add fractions when the denominators are not the same.

Then, she had her students apply their understanding of equivalent fractions by giving them a worksheet with a series of new problems to solve. As they worked on the problems, she carefully monitored their progress for signs of confusion or off-task behavior. Teachers who are less effective give students seat-work assignments and then sit at their desks and do work of their own. Without question, teaching is demanding and teachers are very busy, but students need careful monitoring during seat-work activities to prevent confusion or frustration.

The essential teaching skills described in this section are important in all classrooms. You will, however, adapt them to meet the specific learning needs of your students. In the next section, we examine adaptations for students in urban classrooms.

EXPLORING DIVERSITY: Effective Instruction in Urban Classrooms

Urban classrooms are unique in several ways. First, urban students tend to come from diverse backgrounds, which presents challenges when we try to accommodate differences in background knowledge. Second, many urban learners struggle in school, and so ensuring success in our instruction is especially important. Third, crowded classrooms, less experienced teachers, and inadequate funding and facilities exacerbate problems. These differences have implications for your teaching if you take a job in an urban school.

The Need for Examples

High-quality examples are important for all learners, but because of the diversity of urban students' prior experiences, they are critical when teaching in urban classrooms. Examples help accommodate differences in urban students' backgrounds by providing them with common experiences that they can think about and you can talk about during your lessons. For example, a science teacher explaining the concept of *density* might use the following examples:

- A clear plastic glass filled with cotton that can be compressed to show how density changes when mass doesn't, as you see here

- Several pieces of screening that are the same size area-wise, but have different numbers of meshes in them

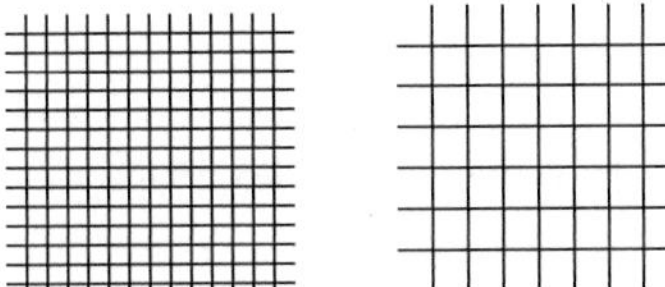

- Several different-sized groups of students standing in the same area of the classroom, as shown in the figure

In addition to examples, graphs, models, concrete objects, pictures, and other visuals are valuable learning aids for English learners who struggle with both content and language (Echevarria & Graves, 2011).

To be most effective, connect your examples to situations your students can identify with, which isn't as hard to do as it might seem. For example, if you're a geography teacher working on longitude and latitude, you might begin a lesson by asking your students to describe the precise location of their school or a popular hangout. Or if you're a language arts teacher working on grammar skills, you could present a paragraph about your class, or a sporting event at the school. With a little thought, you can do the same with most of the topics you teach.

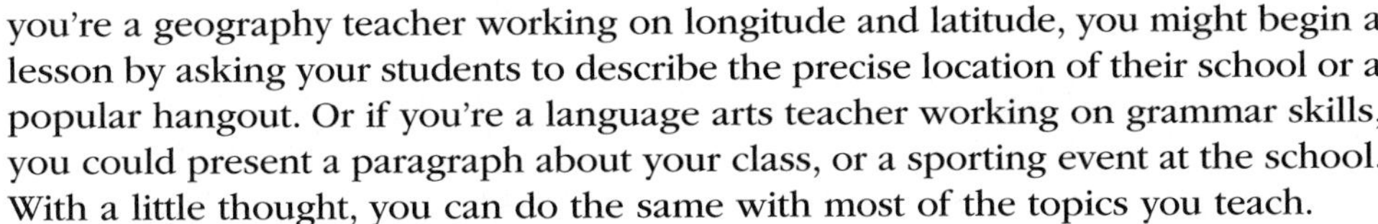

Urban students, like students in general, sometimes wonder how abstract ideas relate to their lives; by making explicit links between new content and their day-to-day experiences, you can increase both their motivation and their learning.

The Need for Interactive Instruction

When working in challenging environments, teachers tend to revert to instructional strategies that afford them the most control. This often results in inordinate amounts of passive learning activities such as lecture and seat work (Good & Brophy, 2008). One urban high school student complained,

> In my chemistry class, the teacher just keeps going and going and writing on the board. She never stops to ask the class, "Is everyone with me?" She's in her own little world. She never turns around, she just talks to the board, not to us. (Cushman, 2003, p. 8)

Exactly the opposite is needed; students need to be actively involved in learning activities with their teachers instead of spending excessive amounts of time doing seat work (Brophy, 2010). In a study of urban elementary classrooms, more-effective teachers interacted with their students nearly 50% more than less-effective ones (Waxman, Huang, Anderson, & Weinstein, 1997). Interacting with students is important for all students; for those in urban schools, it's essential.

Equitable distribution is also important during interactive lessons in urban classrooms. Making distribution the prevailing pattern in your classroom communicates your belief that all your students can learn and that you expect them to do so. It also actively involves large numbers of students in your lesson.

The Need for Feedback and Application

To work effectively with students in urban classrooms, you also need to provide your students with opportunities to test their developing ideas and receive feedback. The knowledge urban students develop is likely to vary considerably because their background experiences are so diverse. This means that detailed discussions of assignments, homework, and quiz and test results are essential when working with urban students.

DIVERSITY AND YOU

Teaching in Urban Schools

You're in a conversation with one of your classmates, and you comment, "I think we all need to be thinking about working in urban environments. . . . Education is being cut back, so jobs are going to be tight, and this is where we, as first-year teachers, will have the best chance of getting a job. It also is where we can do the most good.

"No way," your classmate responds. "I'm not going to work in an urban school. Those kids are simply too hard to teach. I'd have to learn a whole new set of techniques to work with them."

"That isn't true," you counter. "The skills and strategies you use with urban kids are the same ones you use with kids in general."

"I don't believe it," your classmate retorts. "I've heard horror stories about trying to teach in those schools. I'm going to hang in until I can get a job in a suburban school."

QUESTIONS TO CONSIDER

1. In your conversation you asserted, "The skills and strategies you use with urban kids are the same ones you use with kids in general." How valid is your assertion? Why is there an achievement gap between students in urban schools and those in suburban schools, and why is so much written about teaching and learning in urban schools?
2. Your classmate seemed adamant about not working in an urban school, and commented, "I've heard horror stories about trying to teach in those schools." How valid are the "horror stories" likely to be?

Go to *Diversity and You* in the MyEducationLab™ *Book Resources* that accompany this text to log your thoughts and receive feedback from your authors.

Student success is essential in the process (Brophy, 2010). Because urban students often lack a history of successful school experiences, they can quickly become frustrated and give up. Experiencing success is the only long-term solution to this dilemma.

Check Your Understanding

3.1 What are the essential teaching skills that all teachers should possess?

3.2 As U.S. history students walk into their classroom, they see a large matrix comparing the climate, geography, and economies of the northern and southern states before the Civil War. As soon as the bell stops ringing, the teacher says, "Write a minimum of two differences each in the geography, climate, and economy columns of the chart." Students begin, and as they're writing the teacher takes roll. Which of the essential teaching skills does this example best illustrate? Explain.

3.3 Shirley used her cardboard "pizzas" in her review and used her "cakes" to introduce the topic of equivalent fractions. Which essential teaching skill did the use of these materials best illustrate? Explain.

For feedback, go to the appendix, *Check Your Understanding*, located in the back of this text.

Instructional Strategies

An understanding of different instructional strategies will help you answer the questions we asked in *Teaching and You*. **Instructional strategies** are prescriptive approaches to teaching designed to help students acquire a deep understanding of specific forms of knowledge. In this section, we examine four of the most popular instructional strategies that are used in schools today:

- Direct instruction
- Lecture–discussion
- Guided discovery
- Cooperative learning

Teaching and You

"What is the best way to teach?" and "What kind of teacher do I want to be?" We know you are just beginning your teacher preparation program. However, even at this early point, these two questions are important, because they'll influence your growth as a professional.

Direct Instruction

Direct instruction provides students with opportunities to practice new knowledge and skills.

Direct instruction, a teaching strategy designed to teach essential knowledge and skills needed for later learning, is one of the most widely used instructional strategies in today's classrooms. It is straightforward and widely applicable (Eggen & Kauchak, 2012; Kauchak & Eggen, 2012), and it's particularly effective for working with struggling students and learners with exceptionalities (Turnbull, Turnbull, & Wehmeyer, 2013). Historically popular, the current emphasis on accountability and the high-stakes testing of basic skills has increased its use even further.

Creating equivalent fractions and adding fractions with both like and unlike denominators, the focus of Shirley's lesson, are examples of skills that can be effectively taught with direct instruction, as are punctuating in writing, balancing equations in chemistry, and using longitude and latitude to pinpoint locations in geography.

Direct instruction occurs in three phases, outlined in Table 11.3 and discussed in the following sections.

Let's see how Shirley applied each of these phases as she used direct instruction to teach about equivalent fractions.

Introduction and Review

To attract her students' attention, provide focus, and increase their interest, Shirley used her cardboard pizzas to introduce her lesson. She then reviewed by having them add fractions with like denominators. Although the importance of focus and review seems obvious, teachers often begin their lessons with little attempt to attract attention or activate students' relevant prior knowledge (Brophy, 2010).

Developing Understanding

In the developing understanding phase of direct instruction, you help your students acquire a thorough understanding of the skill. It's the most important phase of the strategy and, ironically, it's the one teachers often rush through and perform least well (Monte-Sano, 2008). Instead of focusing on understanding, they often emphasize memorization, fail to ask sufficient questions, or move too quickly to practice.

TABLE 11.3 The Phases of Direct Instruction

Phase	Purpose
Introduction and review: Teachers begin with a review of previous work.	• Attract students' attention. • Access learners' prior knowledge.
Developing understanding: Teachers describe and model the skill or guide students to an understanding of the concept. Teachers use many examples and emphasize high levels of student involvement.	• Develop students' understanding of the concept or skill.
Practice: Students practice the skill or identify additional examples of the concept, and the teacher provides guidance and detailed feedback. During independent practice, students practice on their own.	• Increase students' expertise with the concept or skill, and develop students' understanding to the point that they can identify examples of the concept or perform the skill with little effort.

Shirley avoided these pitfalls. She began with her "cakes" and involved her students by asking a great many questions. She continued providing additional examples and then modeled the process for finding equivalent fractions by multiplying the numerator and denominator by the same number. She didn't move to the practice phase until she was confident that most of her students understood the process, which is essential for student success during the next phase (Eggen & Kauchak, 2012; Kauchak & Eggen, 2012).

Practice

When students learn a new skill, they need opportunities to practice it by applying it to new problems. Once Shirley felt most students understood the concept of *equivalent fractions* and how to create them, she assigned additional problems. As they worked, she carefully monitored their progress and then provided detailed feedback about the first problem before asking them to solve the second. She repeated this process with two more problems, and if her students had struggled with either one, she would have had them continue to practice under her guidance until she believed they were ready to practice on their own.

Homework is often used for additional practice, and when properly used, it can reinforce students' developing understanding of the new skill (H. Cooper, Robinson, & Patall, 2006). "Properly used" means that you assign homework that is an extension of content your students have studied and practiced in class; in other words, it's aligned with your learning objectives and activities. Although grading homework can be time-consuming, you'll need some mechanism for providing feedback and giving students credit, or they won't take it seriously.

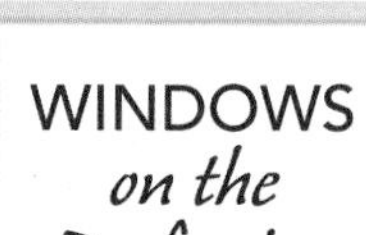

To see a teacher using direct instruction in an elementary language arts lesson, click on the video *Applying Cognitive Motivation Theory: Writing Paragraphs* (13:06).

Strengths and Weaknesses of Direct Instruction

As you'll see when you observe and work in classrooms, direct instruction is one of the most widely used teaching strategies in our schools today, and this is probably for good reason; a large body of research attests to its effectiveness (Hattie, 2009; Rosenshine, 2008). Direct instruction also "feels" right when you do it effectively, and your students are successful. Because you're constantly interacting with your students, you can see their competence and confidence grow as they learn new ideas and acquire new skills. It's a good feeling for both them and you.

Direct instruction is somewhat controversial, however. Critics point out that, because the teacher controls the flow and direction of lessons, it isn't effective for promoting self-regulated learning in students. And evidence suggests that the development of self-regulation is one of the most valuable outcomes of learning (Berk, 2012). Critics also assert that the strategy is overused, and that it can result in a "drill-and-kill" mentality that reduces learning to a form of rote practice (Ryder, Burton, & Silberg, 2006).

All approaches to instruction have strengths and weaknesses, and teachers who are most effective know and use a repertoire of strategies. That's why we introduce you to different strategies in this section.

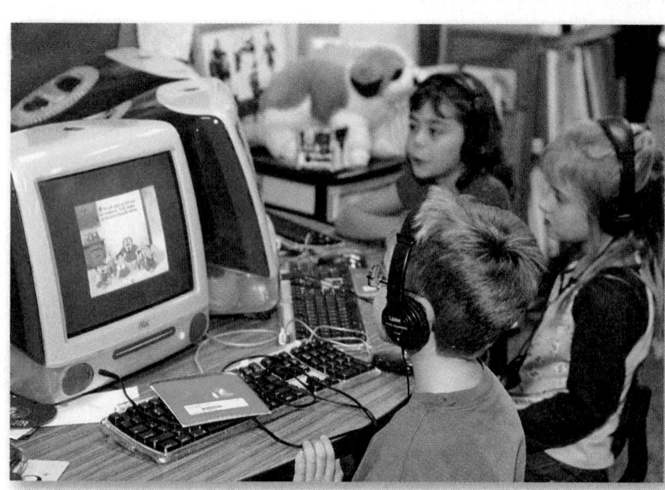

Technology can provide an effective way for students to practice skills with immediate feedback.

TECHNOLOGY and TEACHING: Capitalizing on Technology to Teach Basic Skills

For direct instruction to be effective, students need to practice the skills they're learning. But this takes time, and being able to provide sufficient practice time for your students can be a challenge. Here is where technology can be a valuable tool.

Drill and Practice Software

Historically, students used worksheets and flash cards to practice basic skills, such as phonetic analysis in reading or addition and multiplication facts in math. As we've moved past the first decade of the 21st century, technology is rapidly replacing worksheets, and experts estimate that 85% of existing educational software emphasizes skill learning (Tamim, Bernard, Borokhovski, Abrami, & Schmid, 2011).

Let's look at an example (adapted from Math.com, 2010). You're practicing rounding numbers, and you log onto a rounding numbers program.

You open the program, and the following appears:

When you click on "New Problem," a problem, such as you see here, is displayed.

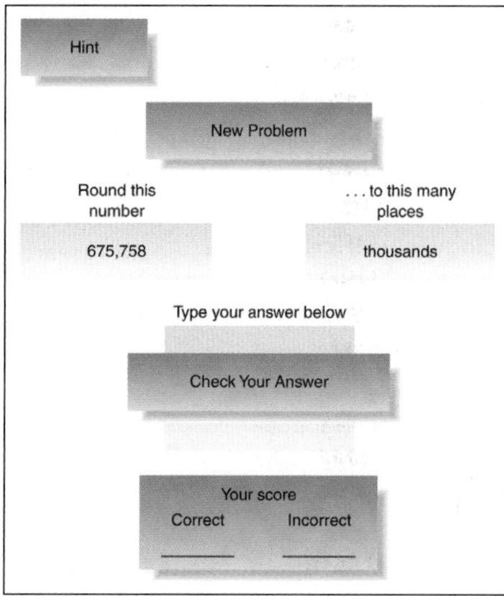

You type in 675,000.

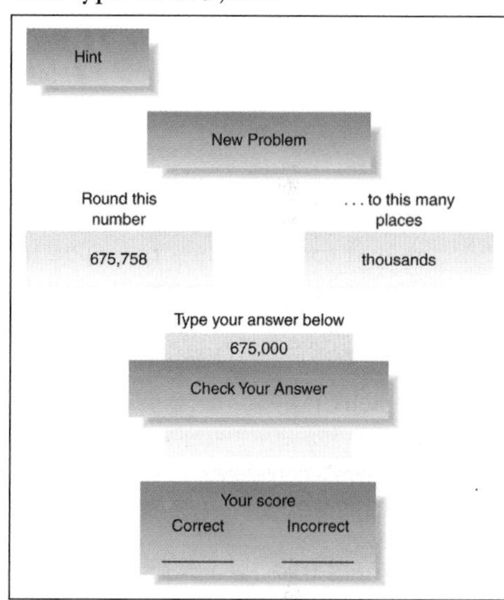

When you click on "Check Your Answer," "No, try again," pops up in a separate box. A bit uncertain about why your answer is incorrect, you click on "Hint" which tells you, "Look to the digit to the right of the rounding place. Is it 5 or greater?" Using the hint, you type in 676,000, and "Correct!" pops up. Had you answered incorrectly a second time, "Sorry, here is the answer," would have been displayed, and you would have been given the answer.

You can use software applications such as these with your students in a variety of areas; the most common are drill-and-practice exercises in math, reading, and science.

Many programs provide more detailed feedback than simple hints, such as "Look to the digit to the right of the rounding place. Is it 5 or greater?" and they can also be designed to increase learner interest and motivation. Some software asks students to enter information about themselves, such as their names, friends, parents, and their teacher into the program, and it then personalizes problems. For instance, consider this elementary math problem:

> There are four objects, and each one is cut in half. In all, how many pieces will there then be?

Now, compare it to the one below, personalized for a student named Zach, whose teacher is Mrs. Alvarez.

> Mrs. Alvarez surprised Zach with a treat for his good behavior by giving him four small candy bars. He wanted to share them with his friend, Devin, so he cut each one in half. How many pieces does Zach now have?

The program took the information Zach had previously entered and inserted it into the problem. Software that personalizes problems in this way increases both learning and motivation (Kartal, 2010).

ISSUES YOU'LL FACE IN TEACHING

Technology in Your Classroom

Saying we live in a technological world is a vast understatement. It has become such a part of our everyday lives that we almost forget how pervasive it is.

Technology is increasingly finding its way into classrooms; in many schools in our country, technology is now an integral part of instruction (Metiri Group, 2009; Nagel, 2009), and **virtual schools**, schools that offer courses through the Internet are increasing in number (Barbour & Reeves, 2009). If you haven't already, you will probably encounter online courses as you move through your teacher preparation program. When you begin your career, you will likely experience at least some pressure to include technology in your instruction, and you may be encouraged, or even required, to teach online courses.

Technology has enormous, and obvious, benefits, such as being a time-saving tool and providing virtually unlimited access to information. However, in spite of the benefits, technology has also become controversial. Proponents claim that technology improves student learning, and school leaders who are investing large amounts of money in technology and encouraging its use are making wise decisions (Metiri Group, 2009; Nagel, 2009). Critics counter that technology is expensive and its benefits are still unproven (Hubbard & Mitchell, 2011). The issue has become politicized, with critics claiming that improper business practices exist, with corporations pushing technology to make money and not necessarily to help teachers teach better or students learn more (Collins, 2011; Quillen, 2011c).

Even technology commonly used in classrooms has become controversial. For example, PowerPoint presentations have become increasingly popular, particularly in middle and secondary schools (Isseks, 2011). However, some experts, school administrators, and teachers themselves have begun to question the effectiveness of PowerPoint presentations, suggesting that they are inconsistent with efforts to involve students in learning activities and teach higher-order thinking. Others go even further and suggest that the technology is an impediment to using student-centered forms of instruction, such as guided discovery and problem-based learning (Langenegger, 2011).

> The root problem of PowerPoint presentations is not the power or the point, but the presentation. A presentation, by its very nature, is one-sided. The presenter does everything—gathers information, eliminates extraneous points, and selects the direction and duration of the presentation. (Isseks, 2011, pp. 74–75)

THE QUESTION

Is the emphasis on technology in today's schools an effective way to improve teaching and increase learning?

PRO

- Technological literacy has become a basic skill, so developing that literacy should be a part of every school's and classroom's curriculum (Metiri Group, 2009; Nagel, 2009).
- Some research suggests that using technology promotes learning and increases teachers' effectiveness (Nagel, 2009).
- Virtual schools provide high-quality educational opportunities as well as educational choice, and they allow students in rural and remote areas to access courses that wouldn't be available in any other form (Barbour & Reeves, 2009).

CON

- The claim that virtual schools provide high-quality educational opportunities and improve administrative efficiency is not grounded in research (Glass & Welner, 2011). A significant body of research suggests that student achievement in virtual schools is lower than in traditional schools, and students in virtual schools are losing ground academically (Hubbard & Mitchell, 2011).
- Test scores in some traditional schools that have strongly emphasized the integration of technology have stagnated in comparison to test scores in general (Richtel, 2011).
- Technology is expensive. The questionable learning outcomes that result from technology don't justify its considerable cost, and this huge amount of money could be better used to reduce class sizes or provide professional development activities for teachers (Gabriel & Richtel, 2011).

YOU TAKE A STAND

So, is the current emphasis on technology an effective way to increase student learning, or should traditional instruction be emphasized, with simple technological literacy the primary emphasis with respect to technology?

Go to *Issues You'll Face in Teaching* in the MyEducationLab™ *Book Resources* that accompany this text to log your thoughts and receive feedback from your authors.

Drill-and-practice software is controversial, with critics describing it as little more than "electronic flashcards" (Inan, Lowther, Ross, & Strahl, 2010). However, when used strategically, it can be a valuable tool to promote learning in your classroom. As you saw in the example with rounding, it provides students with individualized practice and increases time on task, because the student must answer every question to proceed. Learners like the software because they can set their own pace (if the software allows), and their answers and feedback received are private, minimizing any stigma involved in not knowing how to do something (Inan et al., 2010). And a computer, unlike a human, can be programmed to have unlimited patience.

One major caution: Drill-and-practice software can supplement your teaching, but it isn't designed to replace you. Your goal, when using direct instruction, is for the new content to make sense to them, and you, not the software, will be instrumental in ensuring that your students reach that goal. Then, you can use the drill-and-practice software to provide extra practice for students who continue to struggle. This is an effective application of technology, and used this way, it can contribute to your students' learning.

Lecture–Discussion

You're an elementary teacher, and you want your students to understand the four seasons, why they occur, and how they affect our lives. Or you're a middle school geography teacher, and you want your students to understand how landforms and climate influence the economies of different regions of the world. Or perhaps you're a high school English teacher and you want your students to understand relationships among plot, character, and symbolism in novels such as *The Scarlet Letter*, *The Red Badge of Courage,* or *To Kill a Mockingbird.*

These topics are larger and more complex than a single concept or skill. So, how would you teach one of them? If you're typical, you would explain the information you want your students to understand in a lecture, which is—together with direct instruction—one of the two most commonly used teaching strategies in schools today (Cuban, 1993; Friesen, 2011).

Strengths and Weaknesses of Lectures

We've all sat through mind-numbing lectures, and because of this, the strategy has acquired a bad reputation. Let's be honest: How many people want to sit through a "lecture?" The strategy does have strengths, however. It can be effective for helping students acquire information they would have difficulty getting on their own. It can also be effective for combining disparate items of information into a cohesive whole, such as the examples with the novels, the relationships between geography, climate, and economy, or the comparison of the four seasons. And lectures can also expose students to different points of view (Friesen, 2011).

However, lectures have significant weaknesses.

- Lectures place learners in cognitively passive roles, so they are ineffective for attracting and maintaining student attention. That's why we commented, "We've all sat through mind-numbing lectures."
- Teachers often present too much information too quickly in lectures, so much of it is lost before students can make sense of it and pull it all together.
- If you're lecturing, your communication with your students is one-way, and you have little, other than the looks on their faces, to determine whether they understand information accurately.

Overcoming the Weaknesses of Lectures with Lecture–Discussions

Lecture–discussion is an instructional strategy designed to overcome the weaknesses of lectures by making them more interactive, interspersing questions into

our presentations. Let's see how a 10th-grade American history teacher applies the strategy.

Diane Anderson is discussing the events leading up to the American Revolutionary War in her American history class. She begins with a review of their previous lesson, and then says, "I want us to understand important events that led up to the Revolutionary War, and to do so we need to back up to the early 1600s. When we're finished, we'll see that there were historical events that made the war inevitable. . . . That's why history is important . . . to see how events that happen at one time affect events even today. . . . For instance, the conflicts between the British and the French in America became so costly for the British that they began policies in the colonies that ultimately led to the Revolution."

She then begins, pointing at a large map, "We know the British established Jamestown in 1607, but at about the same time, a French explorer named Champlain came down the St. Lawrence River and formed Quebec City, here. Over the years, at least 35 of the 50 states were discovered by the French, and they founded several of our bigger cities, such as Detroit, St. Louis, New Orleans, and Des Moines.

"Now, what do you notice about the location of the two groups?"

After thinking a few seconds, Alfredo offers, "The French had a lot of Canada, . . . and it looks like this country, too," pointing to the north and west on the map.

"It looks like the east was . . . British, and the west was French," Jayden adds.

"Yes, and remember, this was all happening at about the same time," Diane continues. "Also, the French were more friendly with the American Indians than the British were. Also, the French had what they called a seigniorial system, where the settlers were given land if they would serve in the military. So . . . what does this suggest about the military power of the French?"

"Probably powerful," Josh suggests. "The people got land if they went in the army."

"And the American Indians probably helped, because they were friendly with the French," Tenisha adds.

"Now, what else do you notice here?" Diane asks, moving her hand back and forth across the width of the map.

"Mountains?" . . . Lilly answers.

"Yes, exactly," Diane smiles. "Why are they important? What do mountains do?"

". . . The British were sort of fenced in, and the French could expand as they pleased."

"Good. Now, the British needed land and wanted to expand. So they headed west over the mountains and guess who they ran into? . . . Ava?"

"The French?" Ava responds.

"Right! And conflict broke out. Now, when the French and the British were fighting, why do you suppose the French were initially more successful than the British? . . . Dan?"

"Well, they had that sig . . . seigniorial system, so they were more eager to fight, because they got land."

"Other thoughts? . . . Madison?"

"I think that the American Indians were part of it. The French got along better with them, so they helped the French."

"Okay, good thinking everyone; now let's think about the British . . . Let's look at some of their advantages." (Based on Eggen & Kauchak, 2013.)

Now, let's see how Diane used lecture discussion to involve her students in the lesson. First, she introduced the topic with a review and attempted to capture students' attention by explaining how events in the past influence the way we live today. Then, she presented information about Jamestown, Quebec, and French settlements in the present-day United States. After this brief introduction, she used questioning to encourage her students to think about the new content. To illustrate, let's briefly look at some dialogue from the lesson.

Diane:	Now, what do you notice about the location of the two groups?
Alfredo:	The French had a lot of Canada . . . and it looks like this country, too [pointing to the north and west on the map].
Jayden:	It looks like the east was . . . British, and the west was French.

Diane's questions were intended to involve her students in the lesson, check their developing understanding., and help them refine and expand on it. Satisfied with their level of understanding, she returned to presenting information when she said, "Yes, and remember, this was all happening at about the same time." She continued by briefly describing the French seigniorial system and pointing out the friendly relations between the French and the American Indians.

Then, she again used questioning to involve her students.

Diane:	So . . . what does this suggest about the military power of the French?
Josh:	Probably powerful. The people got land if they went in the army.
Tenisha:	And the American Indians probably helped, because they were friendly with the French.

In this segment, Diane guided students to a deeper understanding of the relationships between different factors, such as the seigniorial system, the partnership between the French and the American Indians, and French military power.

Diane then used the same cycle of presenting information followed by questions that helped her determine whether her students understood the new information. Her goal for the whole lesson was for her students to understand the cause–effect relationships between the French and Indian Wars and the American Revolutionary War.

Your effectiveness in using the strategy will be determined by how frequently you intersperse questions into your lesson to involve your students and help them develop a deep understanding of the content (Wittwer & Renkl, 2008). These question-driven mini-discussions allow you to informally assess your students' current level of understanding and guide them to a deeper understanding of the entire topic. In a traditional lecture, these comprehension checks and the involvement they encourage don't occur, which is why lecture–discussion is a more effective strategy.

How often should you pause from presenting information to check your students' understanding? A specific rule doesn't exist, but our experience suggests that it should be short—much shorter than we think. If your explanations are longer than a few minutes—even with older students—many are likely to begin drifting off. In general, the more often you intersperse your presentations with questioning, the better.

Guided Discovery

Providing practice and feedback and clear explanations with strategic questioning are at the heart of good teaching, but what else can you do to develop your students' thinking skills and abilities to analyze information?

Guided discovery is an instructional strategy that involves teachers providing students with information and then guiding them to an understanding of concepts and generalizations (Eggen & Kauchak, 2012). The logic behind guided discovery is simple: If we want to develop our students' thinking skills, they need to practice thinking. When you use this strategy, you will present your students with examples and then guide them as they practice searching for patterns in the examples and analyzing the information they see.

The guided aspect of guided discovery is important; this strategy differs from "pure," or unstructured discovery, where learners identify patterns and relationships on their own with little guidance from their teacher. Unstructured discovery is less effective than guided approaches because, without help, students often become lost and frustrated, and this confusion can lead to misconceptions and wasted time. As a result, unstructured discovery is rarely seen in today's classrooms, except in student projects and investigations, where students work on their own.

To see guided discovery in action, let's join Lori DuBose, a fifth-grade teacher, as she helps her students understand how arthropods, cold-blooded animals with exoskeletons, such as lobsters, crabs, insects, and spiders, differ from mammals and human beings.

Lori begins by saying, "OK everyone, reach down and grab your leg. Squeeze it and tell us what you feel. . . . Isabella?"

Her students note that their legs feel soft and warm, and that a bone is inside them.

Lori has them explain their observations with questions such as "What do you feel inside your legs?" and "Why do they feel warm?" The observations and questions also establish differences with arthropods, which are cold-blooded and have exoskeletons.

Lori then says, "Look at this," as she pulls a live lobster out of a cooler and has students observe and touch it.

The students squeal "Oooh," "Yuk," and "Gross." Lori settles them down and then says, as she circulates among students, letting them feel the lobster, "Now tell me about this. . . . Sue?"

"It has a shell on it. . . . It feels hard."

"What else? . . . Jackson?"

"It's cold," Jackson replies after placing his palm on the lobster's back.

"Good!" Lori responds as she takes a large beetle out of a plastic bag and begins the same line of questioning she has been using with the lobster. She also displays a colored picture of the beetle on her document camera for the children and tells them to look at the image on the screen when they can't see the actual animal. She then repeats the entire process with a crayfish.

She continues, "Now look at all three of these animals. What is something they all have in common? . . . Sergio?"

". . . Their all felt hard."

"And what does that tell us?"

". . . Their skeletons are on the outside!" Sergio responds after thinking for several seconds.

"Well done, Sergio. You've identified one of the important features of these animals. What else did we find was similar about the animals? . . . Ava?"

"They all felt cold."

"Excellent, Ava. How is that different from the way we feel? . . . Ethan?"

"We feel warm. We're warm-blooded!" Ethan concludes excitedly. "These animals are all cold-blooded!"

"Yes, that's outstanding thinking, Ethan," Lori responds with a smile and a wave of her hand.

Lori continues to direct students' analyses of the lobster, beetle, crayfish, and their own bodies, having them identify the jointed legs in each of the animals, and finally having them identify the segmented bodies in each. Let's see how Lori wraps up the lesson.

"Now let's look at the patterns we've found in the animals," Lori directs. "What do they have in common? . . . Christy?"

". . . They're all coldblooded."

"Yes, excellent. That's one common feature of these animals," and with that she writes "coldblooded" on the chalkboard.

"What else do they have in common? . . . Robert?"

"Skeleton on the outside," Robert replies quickly.

"Good, Robert. That's another important feature," and she writes "outside skeleton" on the board on her list of characteristics.

"Kirsty?"

". . . Their legs are jointed."

"Good! Jason?"

". . . They have segmented bodies."

"Outstanding, everyone! You've identified all the important features of this group of animals. Now does anyone know the name of this animal group?"

After hearing no response Lori says, "We call these animals *arthropods*. Everybody say that word now."

The students then respond in unison, "ARTHROPODS!"

Lori then quickly writes the word on the board and says, "Now give me a definition of *arthropods*. I'll let someone volunteer."

With some prompting, they define arthropods as animals that have an outside skeleton, jointed legs, and segmented bodies and are coldblooded.

Lori extends the lesson by showing the students a clam, a worm, a grasshopper, and even Mrs. Ramirez, their parent volunteer, asking them to tell her if they are arthropods and explain why or why not.

Let's look at Lori's lesson in more detail. She began by having students squeeze their legs to determine that their skeletons were inside their bodies and that they were warm-blooded. This brief focusing event attracted students' attention and encouraged her students to contrast these characteristics with those of arthropods.

Lori then provided high-quality examples of arthropods—the lobster, beetle, and crayfish. And she even displayed large, colorful pictures of the beetle and crayfish, in case her students couldn't see the actual arthropods. After displaying each example, Lori had her students observe and describe each animal, and she then moved the lesson to closure with questions such as, "Now let's look at the patterns we've found in the animals. . . . What do they have in common?"

After identifying common characteristics, Lori identified the animals as arthropods and then had her students apply their understanding by having them analyze a clam, a worm, a grasshopper, and Mrs. Ramirez explaining why each was or wasn't an arthropod.

Strengths and Weaknesses of Guided Discovery

As with the other strategies, guided discovery has strengths and weaknesses, and its ability to develop students' thinking and promote learning are probably its biggest strengths. "Guided discovery may take more or less time than expository instruction, depending on the task, but tends to result in better long-term retention and transfer than expository instruction" (Mayer, 2002, p. 68). When using guided discovery, you spend less time explaining and more time asking questions, so your students are more cognitively active and involved than in more teacher-centered approaches. The use of examples and students' involvement also increases their motivation, which ultimately results in increased learning—an additional advantage of the strategy.

The strategy is complex and demanding, however, and teachers used to more teacher-centered, information–giving roles often feel uncomfortable with it when they first use it. This explains why we don't see it practiced more often in schools. This complexity is both a strength and a weakness. It's harder to become proficient with it, but being able to guide students to understanding through your questions and examples can be very rewarding. It takes effort to get good at it, however, and, some of your students—who are used to teachers primarily using lecture as a teaching strategy—might be initially uncomfortable with being guided rather than being told, so they will need help getting used to the strategy as well.

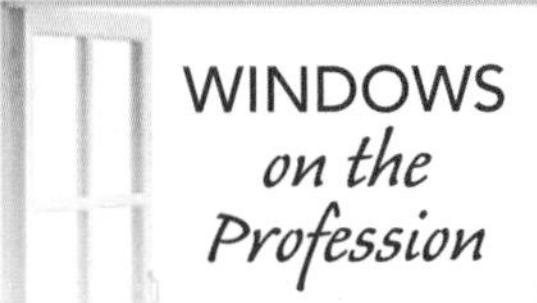

To see a teacher using guided discovery to teach students about Haiku poetry, click on the video *Guided Discovery in an Elementary Classroom* (10:01).

One other important point about these three strategies: Notice that in each of these lessons—Lori's, Shirley's, and Diane's—the teachers, although using different strategies, demonstrated the essential teaching skills that you studied in the previous section: They were all enthusiastic and well organized; they began their lessons with a focusing event; they used questioning extensively throughout to guide and involve students; and they had a form of clear closure and application. The strategies were different, but essential teaching skills supported each one.

Cooperative Learning

Whole-class instruction, such as we saw with direct instruction, lecture–discussions, and guided discovery, is effective and widely used in classrooms at all levels. But, if you have 30 or more students in your classes, the sheer numbers often make it difficult to involve all of them. Less-confident or less-assertive students may get few chances to participate, so they often drift off.

Cooperative learning activities provide opportunities for students to learn new content and develop their social interaction skills.

Cooperative learning, a set of instructional strategies used to help learners meet specific learning and social-interaction objectives, addresses this problem by breaking students into smaller groups that allow greater levels of involvement and interaction. Let's see what cooperative learning looks like at three different grade levels.

A kindergarten teacher is teaching his students basic shapes, such as square, rectangle, circle, and triangle. After explaining and illustrating each with cardboard cutouts, he divides the class into pairs and asks each group to find examples of each in their classroom. He then reassembles the class, and students share their examples.

A middle school math teacher is teaching how to solve word problems involving percent increase and percent decrease. She divides the class into teams of four and asks each team to solve the next few problems. Students in each team first solve the problems and then take turns explaining their solutions to each other. Later, the teams take turns at the board explaining to the whole class how they solved the different problems.

A senior high English teacher is reviewing different forms of figurative language, such as simile, metaphor, personification, and alliteration. He assigns a scene from Shakespeare's Julius Caesar and asks students in groups of two to identify as many of these devices as they can. The whole class then compares their findings.

Cooperative learning strategies are also widely used in today's schools, and they're popular with both teachers and students because they provide opportunities for each student to participate and share their ideas (D. Johnson & Johnson, 2013). When implemented effectively, cooperative learning involves all students, giving each of them opportunities to practice social skills such as working collaboratively with others. By participating in cooperative-learning activities, students learn to both understand the perspectives and feelings of others and how to build on others' ideas.

Cooperative learning activities typically share the following features (D. Johnson & Johnson, 2013):

- Students work together in groups—usually two to five—on a clearly assigned task.

- Learning objectives direct the groups' activities.
- Social interaction is emphasized.
- Students are held individually accountable for their learning.
- Learners depend on one another to reach objectives.

The last feature is important because it emphasizes the crucial role that peer cooperation plays in learning (D. Johnson & Johnson, 2009). Accountability through some type of follow-up activity is also essential because it keeps students focused on the objectives and reminds them that learning (not visiting) is the purpose of the activity. This follow-up activity might consist of an assignment, quiz, or project that each student must complete to provide evidence of the learning that occurred in the activity.

Introducing Cooperative Learning

Simply putting students into groups doesn't ensure either increased achievement or motivation, and this has several implications for you as you use cooperative learning with your students. First, careful planning is essential. For instance, some students tend to dominate the interaction in groups, so you will need to plan for promoting participation from all students. Simply telling your students that everyone is expected to contribute, for example, improves the interaction in groups (Saleh, Lazonder, & Jong, 2007). If explaining that you expect all students to participate doesn't work, you may need to model the process with a group, so the rest of the class understands what is expected.

Second, you'll need to make each group's assignment very clear and monitor groups carefully as they work. You can lose a considerable amount of instructional time if your students view group work as a time to socialize.

Third, groups need to be carefully organized. Suggestions for effectively organizing cooperative learning activities include the following:

- Seat group members together, so they can move back and forth from group work to whole-class activities with little disruption.
- Have learning materials ready for easy distribution to each group.
- Introduce students to cooperative learning with short, simple tasks, and make objectives and directions clear.
- Specify the amount of time students have to accomplish the task (and keep it relatively short).
- Monitor groups while they work.
- Require students to create a product as a result of the cooperative-learning activity (e.g., written answers to specific questions or a completed product).

These suggestions maximize the time available for learning and provide a focal point for students' cooperative-learning efforts.

Cooperative Learning Strategies

Different variations of cooperative learning all capitalize on social interaction, but each is designed to accomplish different objectives. Four of the most common are outlined in Table 11.4. There are other cooperative-learning strategies, and although they differ in specifics, all depend heavily on social interaction for their effectiveness.

Strengths and Weaknesses of Cooperative Learning

Research examining cooperative learning suggests that it can increase student achievement, and it can also improve problem-solving abilities, motivation, and interpersonal skills (Gao, Losh, Shen, Turner, & Yuan, 2007; D. Johnson & Johnson, 2013). Cooperative learning also provides teachers

TABLE 11.4 Cooperative Learning Strategies

Strategy	Description	Example
Reciprocal Questioning	Pairs work together to ask and answer questions about a lesson or text.	Teacher provides question stems, such as "Summarize ..." or "Why was ... important?" and students use the stems to create specific questions about the topic.
Scripted Cooperation	Pairs work together to elaborate on each other's thinking.	*Math*: First member of a pair offers a problem solution. The second member then elaborates, and the process is repeated. *Reading*: Pairs read a passage, and the first member offers a summary. The second elaborates, and the process continues.
Jigsaw II	Individuals become expert on subsections of a topic and teach it to others in their group.	One student studies the geography of a region; another, the economy; a third, the climate. Each attends "expert" meetings, and the "experts" then teach their content to others in their group.
Student Teams Achievement Divisions (STADs)	Social interaction is used to help students learn facts, concepts, and skills.	The independent-practice phase of direct instruction is replaced with team study, during which team members check and compare their answers. Team study is followed by quizzes, and individual-improvement points lead to team awards.

Revisiting My Beliefs

This section addresses the final item in "*This I Believe*," "Rather than exclusively using one particular teaching strategy, I should vary the way I teach." This statement is true. Expert teachers have a variety of teaching strategies and use them strategically when they teach.

with opportunities to use modeling during small-group discussions to teach students effective ways to interact with their peers (Jadallah et al., 2011). These are its primary strengths.

Cooperative learning also has weaknesses, however. For instance, when students are organized into mixed-ability groups, those with higher ability often feel they are being exploited by slackers and, in fact, frequently prefer to work alone instead of in groups (Su, 2007). Further, average-ability students often do not take advantage of learning opportunities in mixed-ability groups because high-ability students tend to dominate the group interaction (Saleh et al., 2007).

So, let's return to the questions we asked in *Teaching and You* at the beginning of this section: "What is the best way to teach?" and "What kind of teacher do I want to be?" The direct answer to the first question is: *There is no "best" way to teach*. Expert teachers use a variety of strategies, they vary the way they teach, and they use the strategy that best works with their students.

You must answer the second question for yourself, which is why we raise it at this early point in your teacher preparation program. You may initially be most comfortable with direct instruction and lecture–discussion, but as you acquire experience and expertise, you may use more guided discovery and cooperative learning strategies as your confidence grows. No two teachers teach the same way, and one of the challenges you'll face as a beginning teacher is to find a set of instructional strategies that works for you and your students. This will involve experimentation and some trial and error, but when you're successful, you will become a teacher with a repertoire of strategies that work for you and your students.

Differentiating Instruction

No two students learn the same way, and effective teachers adapt their instruction to meet the needs of each student. **Differentiating instruction**, the process of adapting instruction to meet the needs of students who vary in background knowledge, skills, needs, and motivations, is a response to this diversity.

Good teaching is the first step in differentiating instruction. Much of what you do when you plan carefully and effectively implement your instruction will address students' diverse learning needs. For example, simple ways to address students' diverse learning needs include:

- Plan thoroughly, and in your planning address the learning needs of all your students. For example, if some of your students are struggling with an important idea, plan for ways to spend additional time with them.
- Carefully teach essential knowledge and skills needed for further learning. This provides a foundation for future learning and minimizes the need to reteach topics later on.
- Use assessment as a tool to extend and reinforce rather than simply measure learning. Integrating assessments into your instruction provides practice for students and allows you to gauge each student's learning progress. It also provides you with information you can use to differentiate subsequent instruction.
- Vary your instruction. For example, using direct instruction in one lesson, guided discovery in another, and cooperative learning in a third, or in combination with the other strategies, helps meet students' varying needs and interests.

In addition to these general suggestions, several specific differentiation strategies are also effective (Kauchak & Eggen, 2012):

- Varying time
- Small-group support
- Multi-ability tasks

Extra Time

Time is a constant in all classrooms. You will have only so much time to teach your students, so you'll need to allocate time strategically. But learners differ in the amount of time needed to master a topic, and some may need two to four times more than others. When the amount of time available for learning is the same for all students, the gap between faster and slower students can grow wider and wider (B. Bloom, 1981). One way to accommodate these differences in learning ability is to provide extra time for students who need it.

You can provide extra time in two ways. Probably the most effective is to spend extra time with students who need it before or after school. This places extra demands on you, but it is a proven way of helping students who need more time to keep up with their classmates.

As an alternative, you can give an assignment to the whole class, such as silent reading, and then provide students who need it with extra support working on basic skills. To implement this process most effectively, you'll need to make enrichment activities available to students who complete their assignments quickly. Some suggestions are outlined in Table 11.5.

Small-Group Support

Small-group support works hand-in-glove with providing extra time for students. Providing extra instructional support for small groups of students is one of the most practical and widely used forms of differentiation. For instance, when Shirley's students began practicing finding equivalent fractions and adding fractions with unlike denominators on their own, she called Heather, Harper, Mandi, and Mason to the back of the room, where she provided additional help. Because she was working with only four students, she could modify her instruction to

TABLE 11.5 Enrichment Options for Faster Students

Enrichment Option	Description
Free reading	A shelf of books or magazines (e.g. *Ranger Rick, National Geographic World*) are kept in the back of the room for students to use.
Games	A part of the room is sectioned off for students to play academic games on the floor.
Computers	A menu of computer software games and simulations provides student choice.
Learning centers	Learning materials with objectives, directions, and learning activities guide students.
Individual research projects	Students choose long-term projects to investigate; teachers assist by helping to gather individual books and other Internet resources.
Peer tutoring	Structured learning activities help students assist each other.

meet the specific learning needs of each student. This process accomplishes two tasks. First, students who need the extra instructional support get it, and second, the students get the extra time some of them need to master the task. They then should complete the independent practice—which other students do in class—on their own after school or at home in the evening.

Effectively implementing the *developing understanding* phase of direct instruction is essential for this form of differentiation. The rest of the class needs to be able to work successfully and quietly on their own while you're helping students in the small group (Vaughn & Bos, 2012). If you have to get up to help other students or deal with off-task behaviors, your small-group support will be much less effective.

Multi-Ability Tasks

Creating multi-ability tasks that capitalize on different students' strengths is another way to differentiate instruction. **Multi-ability tasks** allow all students to succeed and develop their own unique learning strengths. As opposed to convergent tasks that have only one right answer, multi-ability tasks:

- Are open-ended, involving general answers or several ways to solve problems
- Use a variety of skills and call on a wide variety of knowledge
- Provide opportunities for different students to make different kinds of contributions
- Incorporate reading, writing, constructing and designing skills, as well as multimedia (Tomlinson, 2005)

Multi-ability tasks promote learning for all students by providing alternate ways to learn content and skills (Mastroprieri & Scruggs, 2010). For example, in one social studies unit focusing on the Aztec and Inca civilizations of the Americas, students had a number of learning options.

Different groups of students studied pictures of ruins and watched video clips portraying life in these civilizations. Others studied artifacts from the civilizations to experience the way anthropologists conduct research. One group examined a soup can commonly found in today's supermarkets to see what information the color, label, list of ingredients, and packaging suggested about our culture. Each group then reported their information and conclusions to the whole class.

Multi-ability tasks provide students with a rich menu of interesting—and hopefully motivating—options to choose from as they pursue different learning goals.

Other ways of differentiating instruction exist, such as varying learning objectives, learning materials, and assessments, but they are demanding and difficult to implement (O'Meara, 2011). If you're typical of beginning teachers, you'll probably begin with the strategies we've outlined here and, as you gain experience and confidence, experiment with different ways to adapt your instruction to meet individual student needs and interests.

Becoming an Effective Teacher: The Big Picture

Think ahead a year or two, consider your first teaching job, and ask yourself what your primary role will be. If you're like we were when we began teaching, you most likely believe it is primarily to help your students learn knowledge and skills. When we started out in teaching, Paul taught chemistry and physics in a high school and Don taught science and American History in a K–8 school. We were young and enthusiastic, we wanted our students to understand the topics we taught, and we didn't think about much else. Helping our students develop into healthy, happy adults was implicit in our interactions with them but not uppermost on our minds. In hindsight, we were missing the big picture.

Since those days we have both spent literally hundreds of hours in classrooms ranging from Pre-K through high school, and in urban, suburban, and rural environments. This experience has convinced us that helping students understand content is certainly important, but it isn't the whole picture. To see what we mean, let's look at one teacher's classroom a bit more closely.

David Hicks, a seventh-grade geography teacher has a rule, the violation of which is "punishable by incarceration" as he jokingly puts it:

You may not say or do anything at any time to one of your classmates that is sarcastic or hurtful.

"We are in this class to learn as much geography as possible," he asserts the first day. "And we're in this together. . . . We're going to help each other whenever we can, and we're going to treat each other with kindness and respect. And this also goes for when we're outside our classroom."

David conscientiously treats his students with courtesy and caring, but at the same time, "Don't mess with Hicks," is a comment his students make to each other.

"I like him," one of his students notes. "He's tough, but fair. He makes us learn, and he helps us if we need it."

What are David's students learning in his classroom? Hopefully, a considerable amount of geography, but they are also learning lessons that will serve them throughout their lives. Learning to treat others with courtesy and respect, for example, is essential. If you can't get along with other people, you're unlikely to succeed in the world of work, or in life in general.

As you progress through your teaching career, you will teach your students much more than geography, how to write coherent paragraphs, or solve math problems. You will also help them learn to accept responsibility for their actions; develop personally, socially, and morally; respect and embrace peers with different ethnic, language, and religious backgrounds; persevere in the face of frustration; and value the acquisition of knowledge and skills that may not be initially interesting to them. Ideally, you will also help them learn to delay gratification, such as foregoing an immediate pleasure like going to a movie with friends on a school night in favor of staying home and studying for an important exam. These lessons are more important than any specific content that we teach, and if we're successful, we've given students something that will serve them well throughout their lives.

When we use direct instruction to develop students' skills, we aren't just teaching content; we're also teaching students that practice and hard work are important for both learning and success in life. When we give homework, we aren't just targeting specific skills; we're also teaching students about initiative and personal responsibility. When we use lecture–discussion, we want students to understand the ideas we present, but we also want them to learn that knowledge is interconnected and organizing it in systematic ways promotes learning. Similarly, guided discovery is valuable not only because it motivates students to connect ideas, but also because it promotes critical thinking, the tendency to analyze and look for patterns in the world around us. A recent survey found that over 90% of parents, teachers, and students all thought that thinking skills such as these were crucial for preparing students for college and the world of work (MetLife, 2011). And cooperative learning teaches much more than content; it teaches students to listen to each other, to work together to reach a common goal, and to resolve conflicts in ways that will satisfy everyone.

So becoming an effective teacher is much more than just teaching content. In addition to making students more knowledgeable, we also want to help them believe in their ability to continue learning throughout their lives and thrive in the complex and often confusing world they'll grow up in. Students often forget the specifics of the content we teach, but the social skills, self-discipline, and personal growth that we help them acquire are outcomes that will remain with them forever.

Check Your Understanding

4.1 How are direct instruction, lecture–discussion, guided discovery, and cooperative learning similar and different?

4.2 Which phase of direct instruction is most important for ensuring successful practice? Why?

4.3 A teacher places her third graders in groups of four and gives each group magnets and a packet containing a dime, a spoon, aluminum foil, a rubber band, a wooden pencil, a paper clip, and nails. She directs the groups to experiment with the magnets and items for 10 minutes, look for patterns, and record these on paper. After the groups have finished, she leads a discussion in which they identify characteristics of materials that are and are not attracted to magnets. The teacher is using which strategy, or strategies, in her learning activity?

For feedback, go to the appendix, *Check Your Understanding*, located in the back of this text.

VOICES from the CLASSROOM

"It's not about the subject—it doesn't matter what I teach—it's about the students, it's about the learning. . . ."

DEBRA CALVINO, 2010 Teacher of the Year, New York

CHAPTER 11 Summary

1. Define *motivation*, and identify instructional factors that increase students' motivation.
   - Motivation is the energizing force in learning and can have a powerful effect on student success.
   - Extrinsic motivation is motivation to engage in an activity to achieve some incentive, whereas intrinsic motivation is motivation to engage in an activity for its own sake.
   - Attracting students' attention, involving students, and helping students apply their understanding to the real world are all factors that can increase motivation to learn.
2. Describe basic steps in planning for instruction.
   - Planning for instruction involves identifying topics, specifying learning objectives; preparing and organizing learning activities, designing assessments; and ensuring that instruction is aligned, that is, making sure that learning activities and assessments are consistent with objectives.
   - Finding or creating high-quality examples or problems is the most important part of preparing and organizing learning activities and is a major reason that specifying clear learning objectives is so important. If objectives are clear, then teachers know what information the examples should contain, and they can then attempt to find or create them.
   - Planning in a standards-based environment often requires teachers to first interpret the standard. Once the standard is clearly understood, the teacher can design learning activities to address that standard.
3. Describe essential teaching skills, and identify examples in classroom practice.
   - Essential teaching skills are the abilities that all teachers, regardless of topic or grade level, should demonstrate in their teaching.
   - Effective teachers are caring, have high personal efficacy and positive expectations for their students, and communicate their own genuine interest in the topics they teach.
   - Being well organized, which means that lessons begin on time, materials are prepared and ready, and well-established classroom routines exist, is essential for promoting student learning.
   - Expert teachers use focus to attract students' attention, involve students through questioning, provide informative feedback, and use reviews to activate students' prior knowledge.
   - Effective teachers help students apply their understanding in new contexts.
4. Describe instructional strategies, and identify applications of these in learning activities.
   - Instructional strategies are designed to help students reach specific learning objectives.
   - Teachers who want their students to acquire basic skills, such as adding fractions, would likely use direct instruction.
   - Lecture–discussion is an effective strategy for helping students understand the interrelationships among ideas in large bodies of knowledge, such as the relationship between geography and lifestyle in different parts of our country.
   - Guided discovery is an effective strategy for helping students understand concepts and how to form ideas on their own.
   - Cooperative learning can support the other strategies and can be effective for helping students learn social interaction skills.
   - As the backgrounds of our students have become more varied, being able to differentiate instruction to meet all students' needs is increasingly important.

Important Concepts

assessment
caring
closure
cooperative learning
differentiating instruction
direct instruction
effective teaching
equitable distribution
essential teaching skills
extrinsic motivation
feedback
focus
frequency
guided discovery
high-quality examples
instructional alignment
instructional strategies
intrinsic motivation
involvement
learning objectives
lecture–discussion
modeling
motivation
multi-ability task
organization
personal teaching efficacy
prompting
standards
virtual schools
wait-time

Portfolio Activity

Developing Teaching Expertise

InTASC Core Teaching Standards 4: Instructional Strategies

The purpose of this activity is to provide you with experience using instructional strategies, which will be a baseline you can use to measure the development of your expertise as you move through your teacher preparation program.

Get permission to teach a lesson on a topic or grade level of your choice. Use the suggestions for planning that were discussed in the chapter, and create a lesson plan. Then, teach the lesson, and have the classroom teacher record it and provide you with a copy of the recording. Have the classroom teacher provide you with feedback, then view the recording, and write an analysis of the lesson, which includes your assessment and how it compares to the classroom teacher's feedback.

Keep the recording and your analysis in your professional portfolio to be used as a comparison when you teach other lessons as you move through your program.

Portfolio Activities similar to this one and related to chapter content can be found at MyEducationLab™.

Becoming an Effective Teacher

Go to the topic *Curriculum and Instruction* in the MyEducationLab (www.myeducationlab.com) for *Introduction to Teaching*, where you can:

- Find learning outcomes for *Curriculum and Instruction,* along with the national standards that connect to these outcomes.
- Complete *Assignments and Activities* that can help you more deeply understand the chapter content.
- Apply and practice your understanding of the core teaching skills identified in the chapter with the *Building Teaching Skills and Dispositions* learning units.
- Examine challenging situations and cases presented in the *IRIS Center Resources.*
- Access video clips of CCSSO National Teachers of the Year award winners responding to the question, "Why Do I Teach?" in the *Teacher Talk* section.
- Check your comprehension on the content covered in the chapter with the *Study Plan.* Here you will be able to take a chapter quiz, receive feedback on your answers, and then access *Review, Practice, and Enrichment* activities to enhance your understanding of chapter content.
- Check the *Book Resources* to find opportunities to share thoughts and gather feedback on the *Diversity and You* and *Issues You'll Face in Teaching* features found in this chapter.

MyEducationLab™

CHAPTER 12

Educational Reform and You

VOICES from the CLASSROOM

"I teach because I want my students to use their gifts to make the world a better place. . . ."

HOLLY FRANKS BOFFY, 2010 Teacher of the Year, Louisiana

CHAPTER OUTLINE

LEARNING OUTCOMES

After you have completed your study of this chapter, you should be able to:

1. **Explain how the current reform movement has been shaped by previous efforts at reform.** InTASC Core Teaching Standard 9, Professional Learning and Ethical Practice
2. **Describe how current reform efforts that focus on the teacher will affect your life in the classroom.** InTASC Core Teaching Standard 10, Leadership and Collaboration
3. **Explain how reform efforts focusing on standards, testing, and accountability are influencing the curriculum and classroom instruction.** InTASC Core Teaching Standard 7, Planning for Instruction
4. **Describe how schools and schooling are being changed as a result of reform efforts.** InTASC Core Teaching Standard 9, Professional Learning and Ethical Practice

This chapter is about reform and how it will affect your life as a teacher. Never in its history has education been faced with so many proposals for change, and you need to understand these reforms so you can adapt to them when you enter the profession. Let's look at one teacher's experience.

Emma Harrison has landed a teaching job in a district near her home, and she's ecstatic. Her worries are over. She can begin paying off her college loans and start to "live." However, during her new-teacher orientation and conversations with experienced teachers at her school, she finds that the teaching world is quite different from what she thought it to be. She knows about *standards* because they were emphasized during her teacher preparation program, and she also encountered them during her internship. But at the time, she didn't quite realize how important they were, because they were ultimately the responsibility of her directing teacher. Now, both her principal and the district emphasize that her students will be held accountable—by having them take state-mandated tests—for meeting the standards, and her students' performance on the tests will influence her evaluations and possibly even her pay increases. And, it gets worse. These same scores will also help determine whether she will be awarded tenure in her district.

When she inquires about joining a professional organization such as the National Education Association or the American Federation of Teachers, the experienced teachers give her a funny look. Apparently she hasn't heard. The legislature in her state has eliminated collective bargaining by teachers in her state.

Emma has a lot to think about. And her students arrive next Monday.

You are likely to have experiences similar to Emma's when you begin your career. Reform means change, and sometimes change is good and sometimes it

This I Believe

EDUCATIONAL REFORM AND MY TEACHING

For each item, circle the number that best represents your belief. Use the following scale as a guide:

4 = I strongly believe the statement is true.
3 = I believe the statement is true.
2 = I believe the statement is false.
1 = I strongly believe the statement is false.

1. Educational reform in our country is a recent idea, beginning at about the turn of the 21st century.

   1 2 3 4

2. During my first years of teaching, classroom observations by my school administrators will be the most common form of evaluation that I will experience.

   1 2 3 4

3. Current proposals for merit pay will use my students' test scores as a basis for judging whether I am eligible to receive merit pay.

   1 2 3 4

4. Professional organizations such as the National Education Association and the American Federation of Teachers have led the way in the process of educational reform.

   1 2 3 4

5. In my first years of teaching, I will be expected to follow national standards in my work with students.

   1 2 3 4

MyEducationLab™

Visit the MyEducationLab for *Introduction to Teaching* to enhance your understanding of chapter concepts with a personalized *Study Plan.* You'll also have the opportunity to hone your teaching skills through video and case-based *Assignments and Activities* and *Building Teaching Skills and Disposition* lessons.

isn't. Sometimes reform is promoted for political or economic reasons, with the good of students and teachers ignored or neglected. Proponents of change paint themselves as fighting against the "educational establishment" and "educational bureaucracy" and their opponents as "obstructionist." Critics of reform counter that many reforms are poorly thought out, lack a solid research foundation, and at worst, are fronts for conservative politicians and industry backers.

The goal of this chapter is to help you understand the major changes in education that will affect your life as a teacher and help you decide how to navigate through these changes as you become a teacher. As we discuss these reforms, we'll continually ask the question, "Does reform mean better—better for the students we teach, better for the schools we teach in, and also better for teachers and the profession?" Too often, reforms are promoted by organizations that don't have these people or constituents in mind. But before we begin, please respond to the items in the *This I Believe: Educational Reform and My Teaching* feature here. We address each of the items as the chapter unfolds.

Understanding Reform

Teaching and You

As you prepare to take your first job 2 or 3 years from now, how different do you believe teaching will be compared to when you were a student in elementary, middle, or even high school? What implications will these differences have for your work as a teacher?

Reform: What Is It?

Reform means change—change to schools, change to classrooms, change for students, and change for teachers. Educational reform is designed to improve our nation's schools and make them better places to learn and work.

Reform takes many forms. It can mean changes in the way you and other teachers are screened as you enter the profession, how your teaching will be evaluated, or the way you'll be rewarded for quality work. It can also mean changes in the ways student learning is assessed, and even whether students are promoted based on these assessments.

These changes address the questions we asked in *Teaching and You*. Teaching for you will be different, and perhaps even radically different, from what it was for your teachers when you were a P–12 student. As you anticipate your first job, you'll need to understand these changes if you expect to thrive in your career. The time to begin developing this understanding is now—at the beginning of your teacher preparation program.

A Brief History of the Reform Movement

The modern reform movement began with concerns about students' lack of knowledge and skills. This movement is often traced back to 1983, when *A Nation at Risk: The Imperative for Educational Reform*, published by the National Commission on Excellence in Education (1983) appeared, and this is where we'll begin. This publication famously stated:

> If an unfriendly foreign power had attempted to impose on America the mediocre educational performance that exists today, we might well have viewed it as an act of war. As it stands, we have allowed this to happen to ourselves. We have even squandered the gains in student achievement made in the wake of the Sputnik challenge. Moreover, we have dismantled essential support systems which helped make those gains possible. We have, in effect, been committing an act of unthinking, unilateral educational disarmament. (National Commission on Excellence in Education, 1983, p. 9)

The report came at a time when other industrialized countries, such as Japan and Germany, were outcompeting us both industrially and educationally, and it struck a chord with our country's leaders; if we were to compete internationally, we needed better schools. Since 1983, public education has been immersed in a wave of efforts to address the concerns raised in *A Nation at Risk*. The most important include:

- 1989: President George H. W. Bush and the nation's governors held a national education conference to establish six broad goals to address the issues raised in *A Nation at Risk*. Their report emphasized the need for the development of student performance standards. **Standards** are statements that specify what students should know or be able to do after a prescribed period of study.
- 1993: The *National Council on Education Standards and Testing* (NCEST) was established to begin the development of national standards and testing procedures for K–12 students. This effort was ultimately unsuccessful.
- 1994: President Clinton signed the *Goals 2000: Educate America Act*, which created a special council to certify national and state standards together with state assessments.
- 1996: A *National Education Summit*, composed of the governors of more than 40 states and national business leaders, attempted to establish clear standards and subject matter content at the state and local levels.
- 1999: A second summit identified challenges facing U.S. schools in three areas—improving teacher quality, helping all students reach high standards, and strengthening accountability.

An effort to improve student learning by creating rigorous performance standards is the thread that runs through each of these efforts, and since 2001, every state in the nation has developed both standards in different content areas and tests to measure students' attainment of those standards.

Economics was the underlying theme in each of these reforms; the goal was to help make our country's economy more globally competitive. During much of the 20th century, educational reform focused on high-ability students, with the goal of producing more scientists and engineers for our growing economy (Schneider, 2011). Reformers thought of education as a pyramid, and the goal was to propel more students to the top and make these high-performing students even more proficient. Leaders didn't worry as much about lower-achieving students because they believed they would continue to find decent-paying jobs in factories.

However, technology and competition from countries such as China and India changed all that. Factory jobs disappeared, and service sector jobs, such as working in fast food restaurants, failed to provide an acceptable standard of living for those near the bottom of the educational pyramid. Our country's evolving economy no longer had workplaces for school dropouts and underachievers. Some reformers even claimed that attaining a college degree should be our goal for every student (Gewertz, 2011b; Gupta, 2011). Excellence for all became the new mantra for educational reformers, and the U.S. Congress passed legislation designed to reach that goal. This leads us to No Child Left Behind.

No Child Left Behind

The current reform movement began in 2001, with the passage of **No Child Left Behind (NCLB).** NCLB was a far-reaching federal legislative attempt to identify and serve students in all segments of our society. The impetus behind this legislation was a growing realization that many children in our poorest schools were indeed being left behind, as indicated by major achievement gaps between poor and more well-off students and between students who are members of cultural minorities and their white counterparts. Leaders concluded that requiring states to create standards in math and reading and constructing tests to measure every student's attainment of those standards was the most effective way to address these disparities. Schools that did not produce **adequate yearly progress (AYP)** in these academic areas would be subject to a variety of sanctions, including providing students with transportation to alternate schools, supplementary tutoring services, and even takeovers of the school.

As you saw in our introductory case study, when Emma took her first job, she was immediately faced with standards and their implications for both her and her students. Standards and the tests based on them are now a fact of life for teachers in our country, thanks significantly to NCLB.

This complex and comprehensive (670 pages) reform effort has been controversial from the time the legislation was first passed. On the plus side, NCLB has focused our nation's attention on the importance of education and especially on the basic skills essential for success both in school and later life. In addition, by requiring that states report the academic progress of specific subgroups, such as members of cultural minorities, it has highlighted the problem of unequal achievement in our country's students (G. Miller, 2012).

Critics of NCLB center not so much on the idea itself—that all children should succeed in school—as on the way the legislation was implemented (Alexander, 2012). For example, NCLB requires each state to design its own standards and assessments to measure the extent to which students meet those standards. This has resulted in standards and accountability systems that vary widely from state to state and, more significantly, are often inaccurate and misleading. For instance, some states, faced with the possibility of federal sanctions for not meeting their benchmarks, have "gamed the system" by lowering standards and creating lax accountability systems that reward mediocre and even poor performance (Isaacson, 2009). Requiring all students to become proficient in basic skills by 2014, a key component of the act, has been a major part of the problem. Critics assert that this requirement was as unrealistic as asking the country to do

Revisiting My Beliefs

This section addresses our first question in *This I Believe*, "Educational reform in our country is a recent idea, beginning about at the turn of the 21st century." This statement is false; educational reform has always been a part of education, but our modern reform movement dates back to 1983, when *A Nation at Risk* was published.

away with crime, poverty, or cancer by a certain date. It just can't be done, they argue (Feller & Hefling, 2012).

The future of NCLB is unclear, especially with a Congress that is strongly divided along partisan lines. There is no doubt that major provisions of the law will continue to be revised and modified, but its long-term effects on reform in general and standards and accountability in particular, will persist well into the future.

Check Your Understanding

1.1 How has the current reform movement in our country been shaped by previous efforts at reform?

1.2 What are two common themes in the current reform movement?

For feedback, go to the appendix, *Check Your Understanding*, located in the back of this text.

Reform: Focus on the Teacher

As reformers try to change our schools, they continually ask, "In order to improve our students' learning, what aspects of our schools or schooling should be changed?" The answer to this question hasn't always been obvious, and educational reformers have offered a variety of (largely unsuccessful) answers.

> For . . . roughly the last half century . . . professional educators believed that if they could find the right pedagogy, the right method of instruction, all would be well. They tried New Math, open classrooms, Whole Language—but nothing seemed to achieve significance or lasting improvements. (E. Thomas & Wingert, 2010, p. 25)

The answer, however, is simple (but admittedly not easy to implement). *No organization, system, institution, or enterprise is any better than the people in it*, and the same applies to schools. The quality of a school is determined by the quality of its teachers. *You will be the most important factor influencing your students' learning!*

Surprisingly, only recently have educational researchers and leaders begun to understand and appreciate this fact.

> . . . In recent years researchers have discovered something that may seem obvious, but for many reasons was overlooked or denied. What really makes a difference, what matters more than the class size or the textbook, the teaching method or the technology, or even the curriculum, is the quality of the teacher. (Thomas & Wingert, 2010, p. 25)

How important are teachers? Research provides answers. One widely publicized study found that students who had highly effective teachers in third, fourth, and fifth grades scored more than 50 percentile points higher on standardized math tests than those who had ineffective teachers in the same three grades (W. Sanders & Rivers, 1996). Another study revealed that 5 years in a row of expert teaching was nearly enough to close the achievement gap between disadvantaged and advantaged students (Hanushek, Rivkin, & Kain, 2005). Additional research has found that expert teachers in later grades could substantially, but not completely, make up for poor teaching in earlier grades (Rivkin, Hanushek, & Kain, 2001). One expert said it succinctly, "The teacher matters a lot, and there are big differences among teachers" (Hanushek, 2011, p. 34). A massive study goes even further.

> Elementary- and middle-school teachers who help raise their students' standardized-test scores seem to have a wide-ranging, lasting positive effect on those students' lives beyond academics, including lower teenage-pregnancy rates and greater college matriculation and adult earnings, according to a new study that tracked 2.5 million students over 20 years. (Lowery, 2012, para. 1)

The importance of teachers has even caught the attention of the popular press. "The Key to Saving American Education" was the cover title of the March 15, 2010, issue of *Newsweek,* identifying teachers as the "key" (E. Thomas & Wingert, 2010), and the *New York Times* focused a lengthy article on "Building a Better Teacher" in its March 7, 2010, issue (E. Green, 2010). One expert concluded, "Teacher quality is now a national priority" (J. Margolis, 2010, Introduction, para. 1). And the American public agrees. According to an annual poll of the public's attitudes toward public education, "Americans singled out improving the quality of teachers as the most important action education can take to improve learning" (Bushaw & Lopez, 2010, p. 15).

As reformers began to realize the centrality of the teacher to any efforts to improve our schools, they looked for ways to shape and improve the teaching force. One of these was a reexamination of teacher tenure, designed to protect teachers from undue political pressure. A second area of reform focused on teacher evaluation and asked whether our current evaluation procedures are identifying excellent teachers and culling out the bad ones. And related to teacher evaluation is the whole question of how to reward good teachers, both monetarily and professionally. Finally, what role should teacher professional organizations or unions (which negotiate wages, benefits and working conditions) play in educational reform? We examine each of these teacher-related attempts at reform in this section, beginning with teacher evaluation.

Teacher Evaluation

Teacher evaluation is the process of assessing teachers' classroom performance and providing feedback they can use to increase their expertise. Historically, this process has existed in a variety of forms, many of which continue to be used today. We outline them in Table 12.1. As you see in the table, prospective teacher candidates, such as yourself and your peers, are graded during your undergraduate course work and are required to pass tests when you enter and exit your teacher preparation program. During your internship (student teaching), you will be evaluated a number of times by your cooperating teacher and college supervisor. After completing your program and before you're employed, you will be evaluated by prospective employers who will interview you and examine your professional portfolio. When you begin teaching, and as you move through your career, you'll be observed and evaluated by your school administrators.

Critics argue that existing teacher evaluation procedures are grossly inadequate and do little to reward good teachers and eliminate those who are ineffective.

Teaching and You

Did you have any ineffective teachers when you were in school? How did you know they were ineffective? Why didn't your school do anything about them? What should schools do about teachers who aren't performing adequately?

TABLE 12.1 Current Forms of Teacher Evaluation

Type of Evaluation	When	Purpose
National (e.g., Praxis) or state competency tests	Before and after teacher preparation programs	To guarantee minimal levels of basic skills and subject matter knowledge
Grades and course work	During teacher preparation programs	To provide information about a candidate's knowledge of content and motivation and aptitude for learning
Student teaching observations	During clinical experiences	To verify a candidate's ability to perform in the classroom
Portfolios and teacher interviews	After teacher education program and before employment	To provide additional information on a candidate's qualifications
Supervisor observation	First 3 years of teaching	To make decisions about tenure
Annual supervisory observation	Typically every year	To ensure continued teacher competence and performance
Student test scores	Typically every year in some content areas and states	To corroborate and add to the information provided by other evaluations

For example, a comprehensive study of teacher evaluation practices involving 15,000 teachers across 4 different states found current teacher evaluation practices infrequent, inefficient, and ineffective (Weisberg, Sexton, Mulhern, & Keeling, 2009). Others call them "perfunctory" and haphazard (Pallas, 2010/2011), while still others question whether the instruments used accurately assess teacher quality (Goodwin, 2010).

Current models of teacher evaluation combine supervisor's observations with student test scores.

The teacher evaluation systems used in most districts today fail to differentiate between good and mediocre teachers and also fail to identify teachers needing professional help to improve their abilities. In fact, the vast majority of teachers (often more than 99%) receive "Satisfactory" ratings when they are evaluated. (When you were a student in school, did you think that 99% of your teachers were "satisfactory"?) Worse, current teacher evaluation practices rarely provide teachers with information they can use to improve their teaching. For example, in one study more than 7 of 10 teachers reported that their most recent evaluations failed to identify any areas for future improvement (Weisberg et al., 2009). It's difficult to improve without constructive feedback.

In our *Teaching and You* feature at the beginning of this section, we asked if you ever experienced any ineffective teachers. Most of us have. The prevalence of inadequate evaluation systems that fail to weed out ineffective teachers is one major reason why we all have experienced as many poor teachers as we have.

Current reforms in teacher evaluation are attempting to remedy this problem by creating more valid and reliable teacher evaluation systems and rewarding the most highly effective teachers. These systems have three goals (Pallas, 2010/2011). Certifying that a beginning teacher has the skills needed to manage a classroom and to promote student learning is the most basic goal, and verifying that veterans are doing a competent job in their classrooms is a second. If teachers in either group are found lacking, these evaluations are intended to provide feedback that can help low-performing teachers improve their practice. Identifying and rewarding exemplary performance is the third goal of these evaluation systems. These goals lead us to the idea of value-added models of teacher evaluation.

Value-Added Models of Teacher Evaluation

The basic idea behind **value-added models** of teacher evaluation is simple: assess the amount students learn—as measured by their performance on standardized tests—while in a particular teacher's classroom and recognize and reward these accomplishments (Pallas, 2010/2011). When using value-added models, researchers use statistical methods to accommodate extraneous factors, such as student background, ability, socioeconomic status (SES), and class size, in an attempt to determine how much a teacher contributes to students' learning. This contribution is then considered the "value" the teacher added. For example, if a second grader scores at the 50th percentile on a reading test at the beginning of the year and on the 60th percentile at the end of the year, researchers conclude that the gain is a result of the teacher's expertise, and value had been added.

Teaching and You

Based on your past experience with tests, how accurate are they for measuring what you've learned? How accurate do you think standardized tests would be to assess what your students have learned in your classroom? What other factors might influence your students' test performance?

This process isn't as simple as it appears on the surface, however, and value-added models are controversial (Martineau, 2010). First, critics question the assumption that tests accurately measure what teachers are accomplishing in their classes. If the tests aren't valid, then the value-added measure is also invalid (Papay, 2011). Second, can test results capture important learning outcomes that may not show up immediately? We've all had teachers who presented intriguing ideas and asked thought-provoking and even puzzling questions that only made sense to us later, sometime even years later. And we've also had teachers whose inspiration had a long-term impact on our motivation and even career choice. Value-added models can't capture these important, long-term outcomes, critics assert. Also, value-added models can't measure important dimensions of professional competence, such as collaborating with colleagues, demonstrating leadership, and working with parents (Pallas, 2010/2011).

Adding to the controversy is a movement to publish the results of teacher evaluations based on students' test scores and to make these evaluations open to the public, with listings of the scores and names of individual teachers in newspaper articles (Sawchuk, 2012a). (How would you like to have your evaluations made public during your first year of teaching?) Currently, this is legal in 18 states under the mantle of parents' rights to know who is teaching their children. However, experts caution that multiple years of data are often necessary to make valid conclusions about a teacher's performance, and publishing these data indiscriminately could damage individual teachers as well as schools (Darling-Hammond, 2012).

In addition, there are practical concerns about value-added evaluation procedures. One of these is the absence of valid and reliable tests for many subjects outside the traditional ones typically used to evaluate elementary teachers: math, reading, and sometimes science. Experts estimate that between 50% and 70% of teachers work in areas not currently covered by standardized tests (Gratz, 2010; Springer & Gardner, 2010). An unanswered question is how to evaluate the large numbers of teachers who work in areas such as art, speech, music, physical education, and preschool programs where no valid tests exist. Further, many students transfer in and out of classrooms, so teachers have limited amounts of time to prove their effectiveness.

Finally, value-added models have special significance for you as a beginning teacher. You will learn a great deal in your first year of teaching, and you will almost certainly possess more expertise at the end of your first year than you had at the beginning. How can a model that uses a standardized test to take a snapshot of student achievement provide an accurate picture of your developing expertise? And value-added models provide no information about how to solve problems—such as less-than-expected student performance on the tests—if problems are identified.

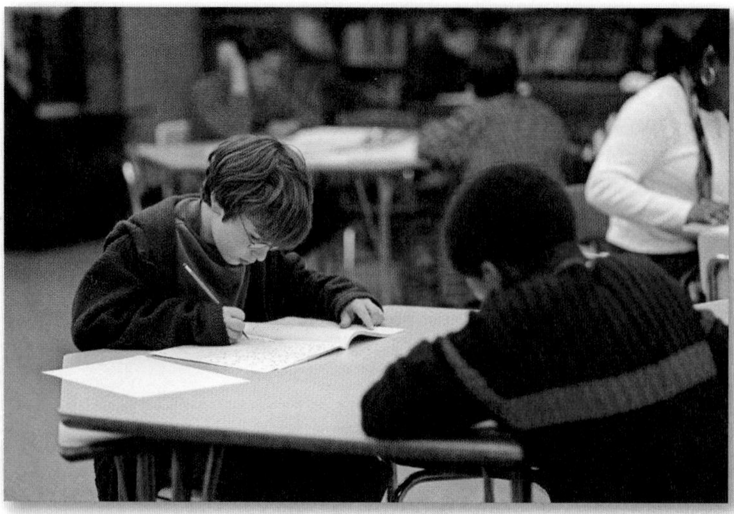

Value-added models of teacher evaluation use student gains on standardized achievement tests to measure a teacher's effectiveness.

In spite of these conceptual and logistical problems, value-added models are being implemented in hundreds of school systems across the country, including those in Chicago, New York, Los Angeles, and Washington, DC (S. Dillon, 2010). Student test scores are then added to classroom observations and principals' judgments of a teacher's contributions to the school community (Pallas, 2010/2011).

In a sign of changing times, the **National Education Association (NEA)**, the nation's largest professional teacher organization, which historically has resisted attempts to assess teacher competency through standardized tests, issued a policy statement stating that teachers should be required to demonstrate their impact on student learning—exactly what value-added models attempt to do (Sawchuk, 2011a). Bowing to external political pressure, the NEA now recommends combining student achievement measures with classroom observations to achieve a composite picture of teacher competence. In addition, the **American Federation of Teachers (AFT)**, the second-largest teacher professional organization, has participated in several pilot teacher evaluation projects where the emphasis is on group or school-level incentives, rather than individual teacher-based plans (Springer & Gardner, 2010).

What are the implications of these changes for you when you begin teaching? First, realize that you will be immersed in some form of teacher evaluation throughout your teaching career. Second, thoroughly understand how you will be evaluated and learn to "play the game." If you're going to be observed, ask to see the observation instrument and familiarize yourself with its categories and weightings. For instance, if the instrument has a category saying, "Learning objectives are displayed for students," be sure to write your learning objectives on the board before you're observed. If student involvement is going to be evaluated, then plan an activity in which all of your students are actively involved. Think of teacher evaluation as an opportunity to demonstrate your knowledge and skills, and then do your homework so your evaluations will allow you to shine.

It is likely that you'll be faced with value-added models when you begin teaching. In other words, the way your students perform on standardized tests will be considered in evaluations of your teaching. Even here you can take steps to perform well. For instance, become familiar with the content measured on the tests, as well as test formats, and do everything you can to ensure that your students have mastered the content and are familiar with test formats and procedures. (This suggestion differs from "teaching to the test," which focuses on specific test items and instead provides practice with those item formats.)

In *Teaching and You* at the beginning of this section, we asked about the ability of tests to capture how much students have learned. This is the essence of value-added models of teacher evaluation, and their ability to gauge teacher performance depends on the validity of the tests used; if the tests don't accurately assess what students learn, then the system is invalid. In addition, many other factors, such as students' home backgrounds, as well as their past experiences in school, also influence test performance.

Having considered how you will likely be evaluated when you begin your career, we turn now to a discussion of the monetary rewards you might expect for exemplary performance.

Revisiting My Beliefs

This section addresses the second question in *This I Believe*, "During my first years of teaching, classroom observations by my school administrators will be the most common form of evaluation that I will experience." The truth of this statement depends on the state and district where you teach. Many states are experimenting with value-added models of teacher evaluation, but in other states, observation continues to be the most common form of teacher evaluation.

Pay for Performance

As a beginning teacher, you will certainly want to know how much you'll be paid and how your pay increases over the years will be determined. Emma Harrison asked these questions early, and the answers she got influenced her actions over the course of her first year of teaching. Historically, salary increases have largely been based on years of experience and the number of graduate and in-service credit hours that teachers earn. This is represented by the "traditional" wing on the left side of Figure 12.1. If you're involved in a traditional plan, for example, you can expect a "step" increase in salary each year that you teach, and you will receive an additional increase if you take additional course work or earn a master's degree.

Teaching and You

Do you think all teachers should receive the same raises every year? Should teachers in high-need areas, such as special education, receive higher salaries? Should teachers receive incentive pay for working in challenging schools? Would you be willing to be involved in a teacher reward system that is riskier but offers the potential for bigger raises if you qualify?

Most districts also include **pay-for-performance plans**, which offer teachers higher salaries and bonuses for taking on extra responsibility, working in high-need areas, or performing in an exemplary way, and they address the questions we asked in *Teaching and You* here. For example, if a pay-for-performance system

FIGURE 12.1 Different Teacher Compensation Plans

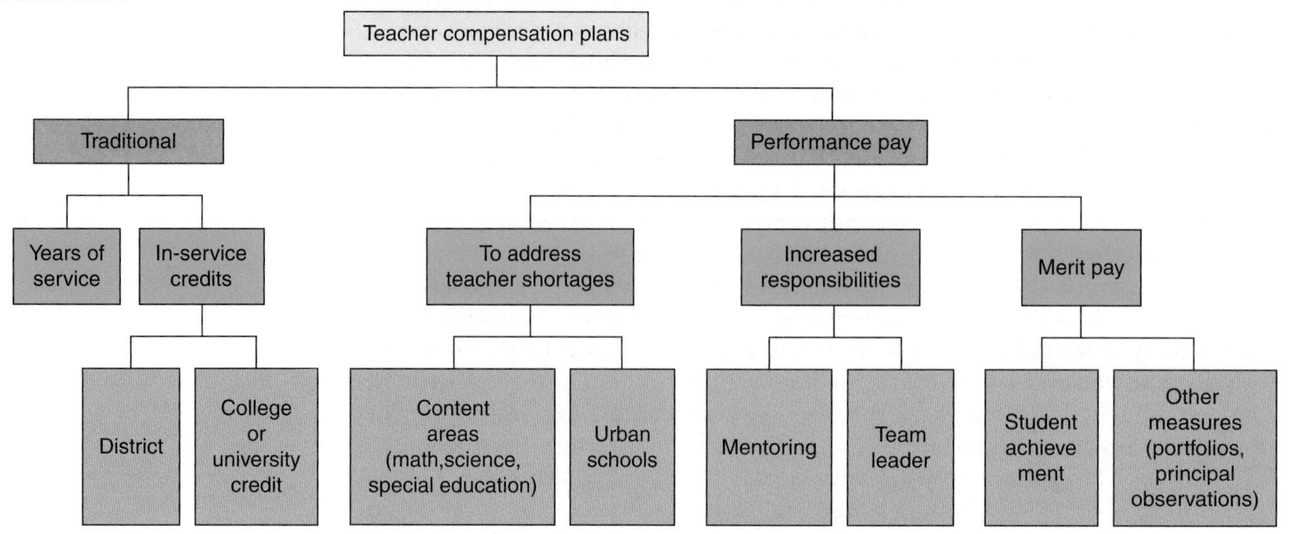

exists in your district, would you be eager to participate? In districts that use these systems, teachers receive a salary supplement for coaching, such as athletics or debate, serving as a team leader or grade chairperson in an elementary school, or a department head in a middle or secondary school. Some districts offer teachers incentive pay for working in urban schools and other hard-to-staff environments. And some districts pay teachers higher salaries for working in high-need areas, such as math, science, special education, or foreign language. Each is a form of pay-for-performance, as is paying teachers bonuses if their students perform well on standardized tests. As you move through your career, you will probably encounter some of these options, such as serving as a grade-level chair or department head, not only for the professional challenges, but also for the extra pay.

Merit Pay

Merit pay, a supplement to a teacher's base salary used to reward exemplary performance, is a type of pay for performance (see Figure 12.1). Why shouldn't we pay good teachers more if they do a better job? This seemingly simple question is at the heart of a controversial and contentious reform proposal that is being considered across the country.

Merit pay differs from other pay-for-performance plans in two ways. First, it is available to all teachers, not just those who take on extra responsibilities, such as being a team leader. Second, it is based entirely on exemplary performance, which is usually determined by student test scores and/or observations by school administrators. Interest in merit pay has existed for many years, but it got a major boost when the Obama administration targeted part of the $4.35 billion Race to the Top funding to support its development. This funding required successful competitors to develop merit pay plans in their states (Springer & Gardner, 2010).

True merit pay, sometimes referred to as "differentiated pay" or "cash incentives," takes several different forms. Some systems reward individual teachers based on their students' performance on tests; others reward them based on administrators' observations or on teaching artifacts such as exemplary lesson plans or student work. A third rewards entire schools for student test performance. Rewarding exemplary or meritorious performance is the common factor in each of these plans.

The U.S. public is generally in favor of most incentive proposals. In a 2008 poll, for example, 76% of the general public supported incentive pay for teachers; for those who had children in school, this figure rose to 79% (Bushaw & Gallup, 2008).

However, merit pay is highly controversial. Proponents argue that rewarding exemplary teaching performance makes sense and that money can provide incentives for teacher excellence (Honawar & Olson, 2008). Advocates also claim that effective merit pay systems would encourage brighter and more competent people to consider teaching as a career and will also encourage the best and brightest teachers to remain in the profession. Some advocates further argue that evidence from student achievement data supports the process (Jason, 2011).

Critics make precisely the opposite arguments. They contend that while superficial examinations suggest that merit pay systems make sense, a closer look shows that they are ineffective (Strauss, 2011). For instance, a merit system in the New York City schools was permanently discontinued because research indicated that it failed to produce gains on student achievement (E. Green, 2011; Otterman, 2011). Critics also contend that merit pay is divisive, damages morale, and makes teachers less likely to cooperate with each other (J. Marsh & McCaffrey, 2011/2012). They also question the assumption that teachers will work harder for more pay.

> To believe that teachers will try harder if offered a financial incentive is to assume that they aren't trying hard now, that they know what to do, but simply aren't doing it, and that they are motivated more by money than by their students' needs. These are unlikely and unsupported conclusions, which teachers find insulting rather than motivating. (Gratz, 2009, p. 40)

Critics also contend that merit systems are often too complex and fail to address the need for higher base salaries for all teachers (Koppich, 2010). In addition, critics assert that many merit-pay systems are put into place without clear guidelines, agreed-upon and objective measures of teacher performance, or effective processes for identifying high-performing teachers. They contend that teachers won't buy into a system if they don't understand it, if they believe it's unfair, or if it doesn't truly reward the best teachers (Hulleman & Barron, 2010). Finally, research—in addition to the study in New York City schools, just mentioned—has failed to find a strong link between merit-pay systems and increased student learning, the ultimate criterion for any educational reform (Honawar, 2008).

Teachers' attitudes toward merit pay have historically been mixed. For instance, a poll taken in the early 1980s found that 63% of teachers favored merit pay, but by the middle of the decade a different poll indicated that 64% opposed it (Goldhaber, DeArmond, & DeBurgomaster, 2011). A poll taken in 2003 found that more than 60% of teachers supported higher salaries for their colleagues who work in challenging schools with low-performing students, but only 38% supported merit pay systems based primarily on student test scores (Public Agenda, 2003). More recent surveys indicate that teachers' attitudes toward merit pay continue to be mixed (Goldhaber et al., 2011). So if you talk to two different groups of teachers, you may get views that directly contradict each other.

In spite of mixed research results and widely varying teacher attitudes toward the practice, the trend in our country is toward merit pay programs. For instance, the National Governors Association, a group that advises America's governors on policy decisions, has recommended a move toward merit pay (Koebler, 2012). In the Washington, DC, school system, a program has been implemented so that teachers rated "highly effective" for 2 years in a row are eligible for large bonuses. One, for example, received bonuses totaling $30,000 over a 2-year period, an amount virtually unheard of in education (S. Dillon, 2011b).

But several important questions about merit pay remain unanswered:

- Does it work? Will merit pay encourage teachers to work harder or differently?
- Will merit pay based on student achievement encourage teachers to focus on some aspects of student learning (i.e., aspects that are tested and rewarded) while neglecting others?

- Are individual or group awards, such as rewarding an entire school for achievement gains, more effective?
- What are the long-term effects on student achievement, teacher morale, and teacher recruitment?

Obviously, increased research is needed to accompany development efforts in this area. But unfortunately, reformers aren't waiting for this research to be done before implementing merit pay plans. Tennessee and Idaho are two good (or bad) examples. Tennessee implemented a statewide system in the 2011–2012 school year with only 3 months of field testing (Heiten, 2011). In addition to tightening tenure laws, the new legislation also created a merit system in which half of a teacher's evaluation would be based on student achievement measures and half based on principal observations. Teachers in nontested areas such as music and art receive value-added scores that are not based on their students' performance but on school-wide math and reading scores. One first-grade teacher for whom no achievement scores were available had to use fifth-grade language art scores; a high school math teacher had to use her school's writing scores (Winerip, 2011e). When no standardized scores are available for a specific teacher, he or she is given a choice, and the game becomes one of choosing an area where a teacher thinks the school will do well.

Understandably, teachers are upset, not only about being evaluated on the merits of someone else's work, but also for the extensive amounts of time required to prepare for principal observations. Will Shelton, an experienced middle school principal commented, "I've never seen such nonsense. This destroys any possibility of building a faculty atmosphere. It causes so much distrust." One of his teachers concurred, replying, "Will, morale is in the toilet" (Winerip, 2011f, p. A16).

In Idaho, the situation was even worse. Teacher bonuses in over two-dozen districts were based to some degree on how well teachers engage parents (Bonner, 2011). One district required teachers to make contact with parents at least twice every 3 months; another based up to 70% of potential bonuses on parents' attendance at parent–teacher conferences. Teachers who have taught for a number of years will tell you that many factors besides a teacher's eagerness and receptivity to meeting with parents determine attendance rates at parent–teacher conferences; low-SES parents who are required to work several jobs or who may not appreciate or value the importance of these conferences are much less likely to attend them than their more wealthy counterparts. An additional problem with the Idaho plan was that funds for merit pay were extracted from the general funds available for education, resulting in fewer teachers and greater class sizes.

The problem is that while states and school districts are experimenting with merit pay plans, they are also playing with teachers' lives and careers. Experts are concerned that these hasty, ill-conceived experiments will poison the water for future merit pay efforts (Heiten, 2011).

Despite all these problems, some form of merit pay may await you in your first teaching job. As with teacher evaluation, you need to understand what these plans are, how they work, and what it takes to "win." Talk to experienced teachers, and find out from them how the system works and what strategies they are adopting to function in them.

In the long term, our schools need well-thought out plans that actively involve teachers in their design and that address the multitude of issues and problems currently connected to merit pay plans. One expert in this area commented, "The fix-it-now approach to pay, with its over-reliance on value-added measurements, turns a blind eye to the technical challenges involved and to the fact that reading and math scores are a profoundly limited proxy for instructional effectiveness (Hess, 2010a, p. 53).

Revisiting My Beliefs

This section addresses the third item in *This I Believe*, "Current proposals for merit pay will use my students' test scores as a basis for judging whether I am eligible to receive merit pay." This statement is likely to be true; most current proposals for merit pay include student test scores as a part of the process.

In *Teaching and You* at the beginning of this section, we asked if you would be willing to forego automatic pay increases for the possibility of larger merit ones. This is the essence of merit pay systems, which depend on teachers' confidence that effort and hard work can result in larger pay raises. In addition, their effectiveness depends on their ability to truly capture superior (and inferior) teaching performance. Our guess is that their acceptance by teachers will depend, in large part, on teachers' beliefs that a system can actually do this.

Despite mixed research results and attitudes, and a number of problems, some form of merit pay may await you when you take your first teaching job. As with teacher evaluation, you need to thoroughly understand these programs and prepare yourself to survive, and even flourish, in them.

WINDOWS *on the Profession*

To hear one superintendent's views about performance pay, and click on the video *Performance Pay: A Superintendent's Perspective* (7:20).

Professional Organizations and Collective Bargaining

Teaching and You

You've taken your first job, and you believe you're being asked to perform duties not called for in your contract. To whom can you turn? Or who can you go to for advice if one of your students is involved in an accident and you're being sued for liability?

A **professional organization** is an organization (usually nonprofit) seeking to advance a particular profession, the interests of individuals engaged in that profession, and the public interest. The two major professional organizations in education, the **National Education Association (NEA)** and the **American Federation of Teachers (AFT),** represent over 80% of our nation's public school teachers (Koppich, 2010), and understanding their role in your professional life addresses the questions we asked in *Teaching and You*. For example, you could turn to the local chapter of your professional organization if you felt you were being taken advantage of and wanted to do something about it, and you would probably do the same in the case of a lawsuit. Professional organizations also provide staff development experiences, hold conferences, and provide professional information about a variety of topics.

Educators use the terms *professional organization* or *professional association* because they emphasize the professional aspects of their jobs, but reformers and the popular press often use the term *union* instead. Educators try to avoid the term, because it conjures up the image of blue-collar workers and the sometimes negative perception of unions—corrupt, inefficient, and a form of protection for incompetent or lazy workers. When we refer to unions in this section, we will be talking about the professional organizations in education—the NEA and AFT or their local counterparts.

Reformers have taken steady aim at these organizations, claiming they are primarily concerned about teacher welfare and focus on bread-and-butter issues such as teacher salaries, pensions, and health care packages instead of making schools better places for students to learn (Cavanagh, 2011c). In addition, they claim that these organizations are obstructionist, consistently blocking efforts to modify teacher tenure laws and evaluation procedures that protect incompetent teachers and fail to reward the best teachers for their efforts (Hanushek, 2011). In short, critics claim that professional organizations (unions) are major obstacles to reform.

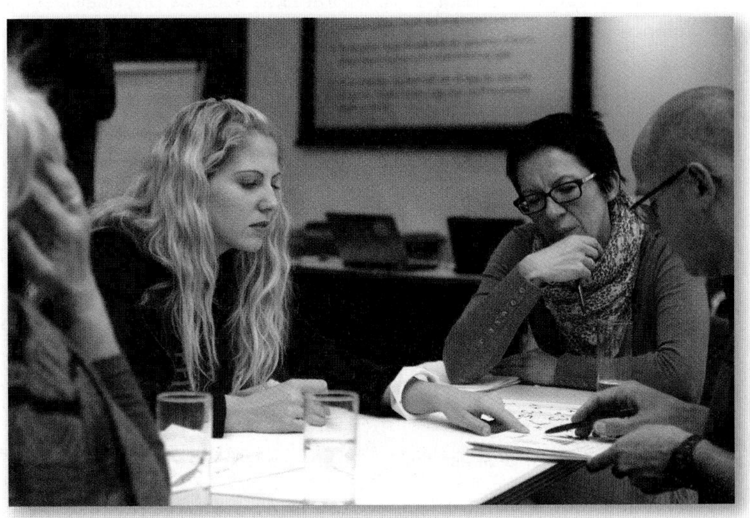

Professional organizations provide opportunities for teachers to share ideas and influence educational policy.

The NEA began in 1870 and quickly attracted members due to a number of inequities involving teacher pay and other forms of compensation (Pulliam & Van Patten, 2013). Differentiated pay scales favored secondary teachers who were

ISSUES YOU'LL FACE IN TEACHING

Teacher Tenure

Jake Kramer is a high school science teacher in a rural district. He has completed his second year of teaching and is looking forward to achieving tenure after his third year. But he's worried. He has taught a unit on global warming and has criticized the process of strip mining coal and clear cutting forests in the local area. Members of the community have complained to his school board, and word of the community's displeasure with his positions has filtered down to him through his principal. Business people in his community say he's anti-growth and that his positions will cost local jobs and hinder the local economy. He believes there's a good chance that if the controversy continues, he won't receive tenure at the end of his third year.

Teacher tenure, status granted to teachers after a probationary period (typically 3 years), indicating that employment is essentially permanent, has become a focus of reformers at every level of education, from the president of our country down to local school districts (Brill, 2009). Modeled after the tenure process found at colleges and universities, it typically requires teachers to prove their competence over a 3-year probationary period when they are subjected to scrutiny by their principal that can sometimes include student test score results.

The movement for teacher tenure began in the late 1800s, when local communities in Massachusetts decided that teachers needed protection from political reprisals and arbitrary dismissals (Chesley, 2011). New Jersey, in 1909, was the first state to establish statewide teacher tenure, and most states followed New Jersey's lead by either guaranteeing tenure by law or allowing local districts to offer it to teachers.

Tenure is designed to ensure that teachers enjoy academic freedom, protect them from political pressures or administrative heavy-handedness, and provide them with job security. Once granted tenure, teachers can be fired only for gross incompetence; felonies; immoral acts, such as physical violence or sexual advances toward students; or insubordination. For instance, if Jake were tenured, he would have the freedom to discuss politically divisive issues, such as global warming, without fearing for his job.

Currently, the wisdom of tenure is being debated nationally, with reformers calling for its elimination or radical transformation into something more manageable. As of 2011, Florida and New Jersey had essentially eliminated tenure, and a number of other states were considering significant changes in the tenure process (Rotherham, 2011). By the time you take your first teaching job, it's possible—or maybe even likely—that tenure won't exist in your state.

THE QUESTION

Should the tenure process exist, and should teachers continue to be allowed to earn tenure? Arguments exist on both sides of the issue.

PRO

- Tenure was instituted at a time when the teaching profession had limited prestige and few safeguards protected teachers from arbitrary dismissal (Pulliam & Van Patten, 2013). Since that time it has protected teachers' rights during periods of political turmoil such as the Communist witch hunts of the 1950s.
- Tenure provides job security to millions of teachers, making teaching more attractive to young people considering a career in education and encouraging practicing teachers to remain in the profession.
- Tenure isn't the problem; legal procedures are currently in place to remove incompetent teachers (Schimmel, Stellman, & Fischer, 2011). Districts need to take responsibility for this problem and do a better job of eliminating and replacing teachers who are incompetent or immoral (Zirkel, 2010c).

CON

- Earning tenure is too easy, and the time frame (typically 3 years) and criteria (infrequent principal evaluations and in rare cases student test scores) are too lax. Nationally, at least 95% (with some experts estimating a figure closer to 99%) of teachers receive tenure. This allows too many incompetent teachers to enter the profession in the first place (Weisberg et al., 2009).
- Removing tenured teachers from classrooms is an enormously expensive and time-consuming process. In New York City, for example, it costs an average of $400,000 to remove an incompetent teacher, and the process can take between 2 and 5 years for cases to be settled by an arbitrator (Brill, 2009). Joel Klein, who at the time was chancellor of the New York City schools, famously stated that death-penalty cases can be resolved faster than teacher-misconduct cases (Rotherham, 2011). And teachers in question receive full salaries and benefits during the process.
- The vast majority of teachers don't need tenure. Jake Kramer's experience, for example, is unique because secondary teachers rarely deal with controversial topics, and elementary teachers almost never do. Currently, our country's Constitution provides sufficient safeguards to make tenure laws unnecessary.

YOU TAKE A STAND

Now it's your turn to take a position on the issue. Does tenure provide a necessary safeguard for teacher security, or do the problems associated with tenure outweigh its benefits?

Go to *Issues You'll Face in Teaching* in the MyEducationLab™ *Book Resources* that accompany this text to log your thoughts and receive feedback from your authors.

primarily male, and secondary teachers were often paid twice as much as female teachers working in elementary schools. Leaders rationalized this discrepancy by arguing that secondary teaching required more knowledge and expertise, and males needed higher salaries because they were the major breadwinners in most families.

Over time, and with a great deal of struggle, salaries were equalized, and the salary schedule based on experience and degrees, which exists in today's schools, was the result. This salary schedule seemed to work well until reformers began to question whether this form of compensation was encouraging mediocrity and failing to recognize the best (and worst) teachers. In response, legislators in a number of states, including Ohio, Wisconsin, Indiana, and Idaho have passed laws aimed directly at teacher unions. These laws mandate the use of student achievement test data in teacher personnel decisions such as pay raises and tenure decisions, and they also limit teachers' collective bargaining rights (Cavanagh, 2011d). **Collective bargaining** occurs when a local chapter of a professional organization such as the NEA or AFT negotiates with a school district over the rights of teachers and the conditions of employment. This process is important because national figures show that, across the employment spectrum, jobs protected by collective bargaining pay 35% more than those that aren't (AFT, 2010).

One of the more acrimonious collective bargaining battles occurred in Wisconsin, where the conservative governor tied teacher benefits to state budget shortfalls. Proposed budget cuts of nearly 10% to state education programs included reduced pension and health care benefits to teachers (Cavanagh, 2011d). These cost-saving measures also attempted to limit teachers' collective bargaining rights, shorten teacher contracts to 1 year, and restrict the size of future teacher salary increases. Teachers responded by calling in sick, fighting the new laws in court, and attempting to defeat reform supporters in subsequent elections. In Ohio the legislature passed a similar law limiting teacher collective bargaining rights, but voters overwhelmingly rejected it in a subsequent referendum. Experts predict similar battles in other states (McNeil, 2011b).

Their reluctance to address teacher quality issues has tarnished the image of both the NEA and AFT, and their resistance to reform is slowly changing. Under pressure, the NEA has changed its position on the use of student performance data in teacher personnel decisions, but only with major caveats and calls for procedural safeguards to protect teachers (Sawchuk, 2011a). And the AFT has been involved in several innovative teacher compensation pilot projects that link school-wide bonuses (not individual teachers) to test scores (Koppich, 2010). In a sign of changing times, the AFT was integral in an innovative teacher evaluation/compensation project in New Haven, Connecticut, in which teachers traded higher pay for increased teacher evaluation (Kristoff, 2012). Initial results are encouraging, with significant numbers of ineffective tenured teachers being released with the support of both AFT and teachers in the district.

Changes such as these come at a time when the public is requiring more information about schools' and teachers' performance. In one poll, for example, more than 70% wanted more information about both teachers' performance and student academic achievement, and when parents were polled, this figure rose to 80% (Brenneman, 2011). Responding to this need for information, the *Los Angeles Times* published a database with the effectiveness ratings of 6,000 individual teachers in the L.A. district. Teachers and their professional organizations were outraged at this breach of professional information, but the paper defended its actions as part of the public's right to information about its schools (Song & Felch, 2011). Arne Duncan, the current Secretary of Education, agreed, citing parents' rights to know about the effectiveness of their children's teachers.

What are the implications of all this turmoil for you as a beginning teacher? Does it suggest that you shouldn't join a professional organization because they have failed to provide proactive leadership in issues related to teacher quality?

Probably not. From a personal perspective, professional organizations can provide you with valuable assistance on a number of important issues that could change your professional life, such as liability insurance against student lawsuits, to professional help and advice when conflicts arise over work conditions. Emma Harrison, in the case study at the beginning of the chapter, realized this when she asked about professional organizations in her state; unfortunately, her state legislature had passed a law limiting the ability of professional organizations in her state to negotiate work-related factors such as merit pay, tenure, and teacher evaluation. In the past, professional organizations played major roles in shaping decisions on these important dimensions of professional life and gave teachers a voice in the process.

How recent legislation will affect both students and the teaching profession is the larger question. One view paints an optimistic picture and sees a new era in education in which teacher salaries are tied to teacher performance and student test scores. The best teachers will be paid more, and those at the other end of the spectrum will be identified, remediated if possible, and removed from the profession if not.

A less cheery perspective views these legislative actions as threats to professional organizations, such as the NEA and AFT, and to the collective bargaining process itself. Teachers are in a unique position to understand and offer solutions to problems facing our nation's schools, union supporters contend, and refusing to involve them in the search for solutions to these problems—essentially treating them like hired underlings—defies everything we know about making workers productive (Koppich, 2010). Concerns are also being raised about whether these legislative changes will discourage bright young people from entering the profession and discourage good teachers from remaining in it. At this point, no one knows which view will prevail.

Revisiting My Beliefs

This section addresses the fourth item in *This I Believe*, "Professional organizations such as the National Education Association and the American Federation of Teachers have led the way in educational reform." This statement isn't true, and professional organizations have been criticized for dragging their feet in current reform efforts.

Check Your Understanding

2.1 How will reform efforts that focus on the teacher affect your life in the classroom?
2.2 What are the most common forms of teacher evaluation that you will encounter as a beginning teacher? How do these relate to value-added models?
2.3 What is merit pay? Why is it so controversial?
2.4 What are the two major professional associations? Why are they important to you as a beginning teacher?

For feedback, go to the appendix, *Check Your Understanding*, located in the back of this text.

Reform: Focus on the Curriculum

In addition to reform efforts aimed at improving teacher quality, reformers have also targeted the school curriculum. These efforts have centered on the process of creating standards that specify what students should know or be able to do after a period of study. In the first section of the chapter, you saw how standards have historically been a focus of reform efforts.

Standards, Testing, and Accountability

Spurred on by the NCLB Act of 2001, a major sea change has occurred in the area of curriculum. If you had been a teacher in the past, you would have been relatively free to teach what you wanted. You would have had state and district curriculum guides, and you may or may not have consulted them before you decided what was best for your students. Now, as a result of NCLB, every state has constructed standards in all content areas, and if you teach reading, math, or perhaps science, you and your students will both be held accountable for meeting them. **Accountability** means that your students will be required to demonstrate that they've met the standards, and you will be responsible for ensuring that they do.

States have also developed standardized tests to hold students (and their teachers) accountable for meeting these prescribed learning standards. In many cases, the assessments are **high-stakes tests**, standardized assessments that states and districts use to determine whether students can advance from one grade to another, graduate from high school, or have access to specific fields of study, like advanced math or science courses. For example, if graduating from high school depends on students' performance on the test, the stakes are "high," which is why the tests are described this way. In 2011, 25 states had current or planned policies to require students to pass an exit exam to receive a high school diploma (McIntosh, 2011). If you recently graduated from high school, you might have taken one of these tests yourself. When you teach, you will be on the other side of the fence; you will be responsible for preparing your students to perform well on these assessments.

Standards in Today's Schools

Though most attention has been focused on reading, math, and science, standards have also been written for a variety of content areas, such as:

- Fine arts
- Science
- Physical education
- Economics
- Agricultural science
- Business education
- Technology applications
- Trade and industrial education
- Spanish language arts and English as a second language

And even this list is not exhaustive.

Because space doesn't allow us to list examples from every state, we present representative samples for the sake of illustration. For those of you reading this text who don't live in these states, you can easily access your own state's standards by clicking on the following link:

http://www.education-world.com/standards/state/index.shtml

Then click on the pulldown menu and select your state.

What do standards from different states look like? The following is an example in fourth-grade math from the state of Texas (Texas Education Agency, 2008b).

> (4.2) Number, operation, and quantitative reasoning. The student describes and compares fractional parts of whole objects or sets of objects
>
> The student is expected to:
>
> (A) use concrete objects and pictorial models to generate equivalent fractions.

The number (4.2) identifies this as the second standard in the list of fourth-grade standards in math, and the letter (A) lists one of the ways that each student can meet that standard. Different states code their standards in different ways, but all are designed to describe learning and assessment targets for teachers and students.

As another example, the following standard is from the state of Illinois in middle school science (Illinois State Board of Education, 2008a).

Illinois Science Assessment Framework

Standard 12F—Astronomy (Grade 7)

12.7.91 Understanding that objects in the solar system are for the most part in regular and predictable motion. Know that those motions explain such phenomena as the day, the year, the phases of the moon, and eclipses.

Though the way the standard is coded differs from the codes in Texas, both describe essential knowledge to be learned and assessed on tests.

As you see from these two examples, standards are stated in different ways and with varying degrees of specificity. Many states' systems of describing standards are quite complex, and understanding and interpreting them can be challenging. For instance, what exactly does "use concrete objects and pictorial models to generate equivalent fractions" mean? And this is one of the more succinctly written standards.

Many professional organizations, such as the National Council of Teachers of Mathematics (National Council of Teachers of Mathematics, 2008), the National Council of Teachers of English (International Reading Association & National Council of Teachers of English, 2008), and others that focus on science, social studies, early childhood education, special education, the arts, health education, and bilingual education all have produced similar standards. Most of the state standards are grounded in the standards prepared by these organizations.

Standards and Assessment

Along with standards, states have also constructed tests aligned with those standards. As with standards, state tests have different labels, such as the Texas Assessment of Knowledge and Skills (TAKS) (Texas Education Agency, 2008c), the Florida Comprehensive Assessment Test (Florida Department of Education, 2008), the California Standards Test, (California State Board of Education, 2008b), and the Illinois Standards Achievement Test (Illinois State Board of Education, 2008b).

Standards, which can be accessed on the Internet, provide teachers with direction in their planning efforts.

States also vary in the way they administer their tests. For example, the TAKS is given at every grade level 3 through 10 in reading and math, science is given in grades 5, 8, and 10, and social studies is given in grades 8 and 10. On the other hand, the Florida Comprehensive Assessment Test, which also requires all students in grades 3 through 10 to take the reading and math portion, administers the science portion to students in grades 5, 8, and 11. Social studies is not measured on the exam. When you begin teaching, you will become fully aware of the testing schedule for your state.

To help teachers align their instruction with state standards, sample test items that parallel the items on the standardized assessments or older versions of the tests themselves are usually available. Both are linked to specific standards. These sample items and older versions of the tests are useful in two ways. First, as you saw in the preceding section, you must interpret the meaning of the standard, and sample items help you with this process. Second, the sample items help guide you as you prepare your students for the tests. The following are sample items that measure the extent to which students have reached standards presented earlier.

For example, a sample test item from the TAKS designed to measure the extent to which students have reached the fourth-grade math standard shown on page 397 looks like this (Texas Education Agency, 2008c).

23 The model is shaded to represent a fraction.

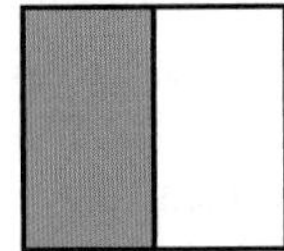

Which model below shows an equivalent fraction?

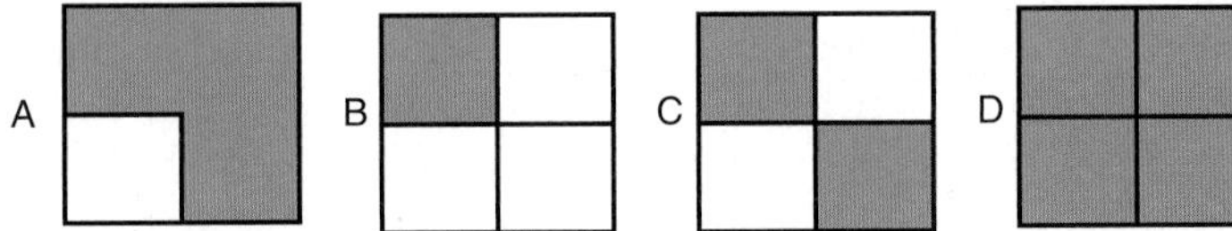

Now consider again the Illinois middle school science standard on page 398, and compare it with a corresponding assessment item from the Illinois Standards Achievement Test linked to the standard (Illinois State Board of Education, 2008c).

12.7.91

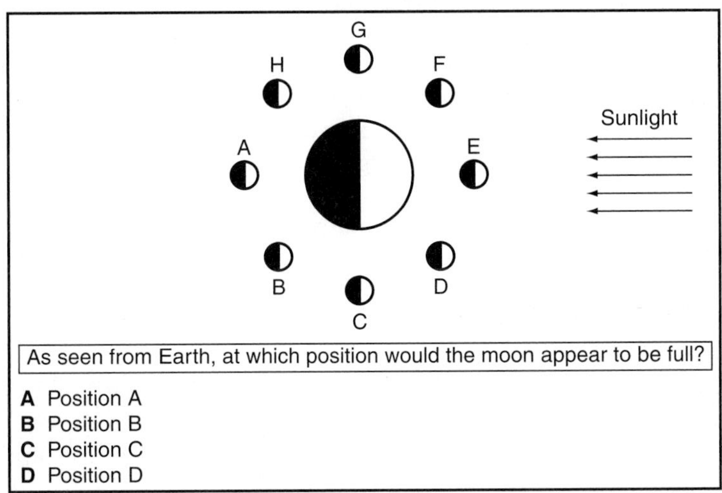

G
H
F
Sunlight
A
E
B
D
C
As seen from Earth, at which position would the moon appear to be full?
A Position A
B Position B
C Position C
D Position D

These sample standards and items are similar in two ways. First, the items measure more than students' ability to remember factual information, which is typical of many, if not most, standards. Each of the sample items goes beyond factual knowledge and measures students' understanding of conceptual knowledge. This means that when you plan your instruction to meet standards, you'll need to teach students to do more than simply memorize information, and you should also develop assessments that do more than measure their knowledge of facts.

Second, the items on the state assessment tests are written in a multiple-choice format, which both increases their reliability and makes them easier to score. The fact that these items are multiple-choice has an important implication for you; you'll need to be sure your students are comfortable with this testing format. This suggests that some of the teacher-made assessments you create should be in multiple choice as well, so your students have practice responding to this format. This is a demanding process, but one that will help prepare your students for future assessments and increase the likelihood that their test scores reflect what they actually know.

At this early point in your teacher preparation program, standards, accountability, and high-stakes testing might seem somewhat intimidating. However, as you spend time on your state's website and are provided with support from your school when you begin your first job, the task won't seem so daunting.

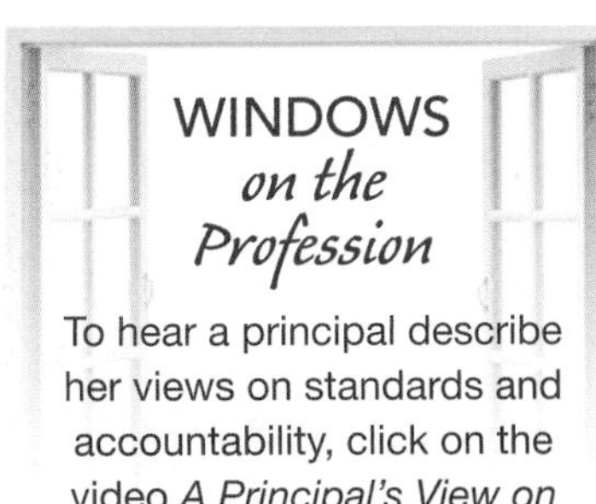

To hear a principal describe her views on standards and accountability, click on the video *A Principal's View on Standards* (4:20).

National Standards

In response to the fact that different state's standards vary widely in quality and rigor, the **Common Core State Standards Initiative (CCSSI)**, another major reform effort, was launched in 2009. This effort was designed to establish a single set of clear educational standards for all states in English-language arts and mathematics (Common Core State Standards Initiative, 2010a). By 2011 these standards had been formally adopted by 45 of the 50 states (Gewertz, 2011c). The standards are designed to ensure that students graduating from high school are prepared to go to college or enter the workforce, and that parents, teachers, and students have a clear understanding of what is expected of them. The new standards are also linked to international benchmarks designed to ensure that American students can compete in the emerging global marketplace (C. Lee & Spratley, 2010).

To illustrate, let's look at two proposed national standards. The following is an example from first-grade math.

> First grade:
>
> Number—Operations and the Problems They Solve
>
> **Addition and Subtraction**
>
> 1. Understand the properties of addition.
>   a. Addition is commutative. For example, if 3 cups are added to a stack of 8 cups, then the total number of cups is the same as when 8 cups are added to a stack of 3 cups; that is, 8 + 3 = 3 + 8.
>   b. Addition is associative. For example, 4 + 3 + 2 can be found by first adding 4 + 3 = 7 then adding 7 + 2 = 9, or by first adding 3 + 2 = 5 then adding 4 + 5 = 9.
>
> (Common Core State Standards Initiative, 2010b, p. 13)

Now, here is an example in writing for middle and high school.

> Writing Standards for History/Social Studies and Science 6–12
>
> Grades 9–10 students:
>
> 1. Write informative/explanatory texts, including the narration of historical events or scientific procedures/experiments, in which they:
>   a. Introduce a topic and organize information under concepts and into categories, making clear the connections and distinctions between key ideas; use formatting and graphics (e.g., headings, figures, tables, graphs, illustrations) as useful to clarify ideas.
>   b. Develop a topic that has historical or scientific significance using well-chosen, relevant, and sufficient facts, data, details, quotations, examples, extended definitions, or other information. (Common Core State Standards Initiative, 2010c, p. 60)

As you see, these standards are similar in format to most existing state standards. The consistency that the standards provide among the states in our country, and even with other countries, is their primary advantage, and these standards have been endorsed by most professional groups (Gewertz, 2010).

However, as with most reforms, the movement toward common standards is controversial, and critics raise a number of questions. For example, will common core standards result in lessons dictated from afar? How will the public in each state have access to and control over what is being taught in their schools? And will common standards lead to a national curriculum and a national test, something that local control advocates resist strongly (Palikoff, Porter, & Smithson, 2011)? Currently, a number of states are working on assessments that would measure students' attainment of these national standards (Gewertz, 2012b). A similar controversy over local control of schools killed national standards efforts in the 1990s (Gewertz, 2011a). Critics also contend that the new standards aren't demanding enough and overemphasize basic skills at the expense of higher-order thinking (Porter, 2011). Finally, skeptics believe many of the proposed standards are vague and wonder if they provide teachers with sufficient guidance for implementation. Model curriculum units, sample lesson plans, formative assessments, and test items linked to standards are all needed to provide teachers with more guidance and support (Gewertz, 2011c).

Despite these concerns, the common standards movement is moving forward, and you will likely encounter them when you begin teaching. The federal government has invested over $360 million in this reform, and private organizations, such as the Bill and Melinda Gates Foundation, have added millions more (Gewertz, 2011c).

Revisiting My Beliefs

This section addresses the fifth item in *Th*
"In my first years of teaching, I will be expected to follow national standards in my work with students." This statement is probably true. Most states have adopted national standards and are using them to guide instruction. You will know whether this applies in your state when you take your first job.

Controversies in the Standards Movement

Standards, accountability, and high-stakes testing are facts of teaching life, and they'll influence all aspects of your teaching. Every state has created standards in a variety of content areas, and schools, districts, and states must report the achievement of different groups of students classified by race, ethnicity, gender, and English proficiency. This requirement has focused attention on the considerable disparities in achievement between different groups of students, such as those who are members of cultural minorities.

Schools are graded—A, B, C, D, and F—depending on how their students perform, and in addition to the stigma for being in a D or F school, sanctions, such as school closings, threaten schools that fail to make adequate yearly progress with any of these student subgroups. The pressure on states, school districts, and particularly on schools and teachers within specific schools, is enormous.

Because of these pressures, accountability and high-stakes testing are controversial. Critics argue that they damage both schools and students in several ways (Heilig & Darling-Hammond, 2008). First, critics assert, because high-stakes tests focus on math, reading, and science, teachers spend the majority of their time on these subjects and de-emphasize other content areas, such as social studies, art, and music. This narrowing of the curriculum deprives students of a well-rounded education and also stifles teacher professionalism and creativity (Ravitch, 2010a).

The pressure for students to perform well on the tests can also produce unintended consequences. To avoid test-related sanctions, teachers frequently request transfers out of grades that are tested and schools that face sanctions. For example, expert teachers often ask to transfer out of urban and high-poverty schools where students often underachieve, and as a result, students are deprived of precisely the teachers they need most (Institute of Education Sciences, 2011). In addition, high school exit exams may discourage students from staying in school, so they contribute to the dropout problem. And these adverse effects are greater for members of cultural minorities or students with low SES. In Texas, for example, nearly 1 of every 6 high school seniors in 2007 didn't graduate because of low test scores, and this figure was 1 in 4 for African American and Latino students (Stutz, 2007).

Critics also contend that current tests are not adequate for making crucial decisions about students' lives and that cutoff scores are often arbitrary. For example, when the state of Virginia lowered the cutoff score for a test by 1 point, nearly 6,000 failing scores became passing (Bracey, 2003). In New York City, just the opposite happened; 82% of students passed their math tests in 2009, the next year, only 54% passed (Noddings, 2010b). Did students suddenly become dumber? Not really, school administrators just changed the cutoff passing score. Deciding student grade promotion or graduation on the basis of one score is being increasingly criticized by a number of professional organizations, both within and outside education, including the American Educational Research Association (1999) and the American Psychological Association (cited in American

Educational Research Association, 1999). Other experts also warn that high-stakes tests have negative side effects such as decreased student motivation and ultimately decreased learning (Berliner, 2009).

Finally, questions related to high-stakes testing with minority students remain unanswered. One involves test bias and whether existing tests provide an accurate picture of minority achievement, and particularly the achievement of students who are not native English speakers (Plank, 2010).

In summary, critics argue, "The pressure to score well on a single test is so intense that it leads to nefarious practices (cheating on the test, data manipulation), distorts education (narrowing the curriculum, teaching to the test) and demoralizes our educators" (Nichols & Berliner, 2008, p. 672).

However, advocates of testing, while conceding that teacher preparation, instructional resources, and the tests themselves need to be improved, argue that these tests are the fairest and most effective means of promoting success for all students (Buck, Ritter, Jensen, & Rose, 2010). Further, they assert, evidence indicates that educational systems that require content standards and use tests that thoroughly measure the extent to which the standards are met greatly improve the achievement for all students, including those from disadvantaged backgrounds (Wiggins, 2010).

Public opinion polls show that parents are undecided about both accountability and high-stakes testing. For instance, more than 4 of 10 public school parents believe there is too much emphasis on achievement testing, with only about 1 of 10 saying there is not enough. However, another 4 of 10 parents believe that the emphasis on achievement testing is about right (Bushaw & Lopez, 2011). With respect to the issue of narrowing the curriculum, parents' reactions are also mixed. When asked if they thought reduced emphasis on subjects other than reading and math—because of the reading-math emphasis—was a good or a bad thing, more than half of parents said it would be a good thing. Slightly more than 4 of 10 said it would be a bad thing, with the remainder reporting they didn't know (Bushaw & Lopez, 2011).

Check Your Understanding

3.1 Explain how reform efforts focusing on standards, testing, and accountability are influencing the curriculum and classroom instruction.

3.2 Describe the relationship between assessment, standards, accountability, and high-stakes tests.

3.3 What are national standards? How will they influence your life as a beginning teacher?

For feedback, go to the appendix, *Check Your Understanding*, located in the back of this text.

Reform: Focus on Schools

We have examined reform efforts that have focused on both teachers and the curriculum. In this section we consider reforms directed at schools themselves. We begin with the federal effort called "Race to the Top."

Race to the Top

Race to the Top was a more than $4 billion U.S. Department of Education competition, open to all 50 states, designed to spur innovation and reforms in state and local district K–12 education. Announced by President Obama and Secretary of Education Arne Duncan in 2009, the competition awarded states points for satisfying certain educational policies, such as designing performance-based standards for teachers and principals, complying with nationwide standards, promoting charter schools, and applying technology. Four states—Alaska, North

Dakota, Texas, and Vermont—chose not to participate, and 11 states and the District of Columbia ultimately won the competition and now have 4 years to implement their ambitious plans for reform (Cavanagh, 2011f).

The major goals for the program were to:

- Improve teacher and principal effectiveness through performance-based assessments (student test scores).
- Encourage the adoption of Common Core Standards and develop corresponding assessment systems.
- Target low-performing schools and either improve them or convert them to charters or privately managed schools.
- Improve existing data management systems to provide better information to teachers and decision makers.

These goals were translated into criteria for the Race to the Top competition, which encouraged 28 states to pass laws to improve teacher quality and 16 states to pass legislation to increase their ability to intervene with low-performing schools (McNeil, 2011a).

The Race to the Top program is significant for three reasons. First, it was the first large-scale attempt by the federal government to use a competition to foster educational reform. Second, like NCLB in 2001, it purposely left the specifics of reform to individual states to avoid criticisms that the federal government was being heavy-handed. Third, it sent a clear signal that the federal government was squarely behind a number of recent reform proposals, such as: (1) the use of student achievement data to evaluate schools, principals, and teachers; (2) a commitment to common-core standards and a corresponding national assessment system; and (3) a focus on low-performing schools with charters and privately managed schools as viable alternatives. Each is likely to influence you in your first teaching job.

As with all reforms, Race to the Top has critics, and the criticisms focus more on the criteria used to determine winners than on the competition itself. In fact, some districts in winning states declined to participate because program criteria were inconsistent with their own goals (Cavanagh, 2011g). Critics also argue that accountability and high-stakes testing, two integral components of Race to the Top, haven't worked in the past and are unlikely to succeed in the future (Ravitch, 2010a). Professional organizations complain that the program mandates top–down reform, focuses too narrowly on testing and accountability, favors charter schools at the expense of support for public schools, and fails to address inadequate funding for all students (N. Anderson, 2009).

School Choice

School choice is a term used to describe a variety of programs designed to give families the opportunity to choose the school their children will attend. Promoted by political conservatives who bemoan the lack of alternatives to public education, and dramatized by popular movies such as *Waiting for Superman* (Guggenheim, 2011) and *The Lottery* (Sackler, 2010), the choice movement is transforming the face of education in our country.

School choice exists when a student attends a school outside of the one they would have been assigned to by their geographic location, such as a certain section of a city. School choice encompasses open enrollment laws that allow students to attend other public schools, private schools, or charter schools. Vouchers, homeschooling, and tax credit and deductions for expenses related to schooling outside the public school system are also options offered by school choice programs. (We examine vouchers and homeschooling in more detail later in this section.)

Advocates of school choice argue that the freedom to choose is a central American value. We can choose where and how we live and the occupation in which we work, for example. Shouldn't we also have a choice in the kind of schools our children attend? As presently organized, where students go to school is largely determined by the neighborhoods in which they live. And the schools across our country are remarkably similar. For instance, walk into most public schools across the country, and you'll see teachers basically teaching the same content in the same way. Even the boxlike architecture of school buildings is nearly the same everywhere.

Critics of our existing system decry this uniformity and argue that we are a nation of 50 states with unique and distinctive histories and subcultures, and our schools ought to reflect this diversity. In addition, they assert, experimentation and innovation have been central to our nation's progress, and conformity discourages innovation. The availability of alternatives would result in healthy competition and better schools. They also argue that the public school system has become bloated, bureaucratic, and unresponsive to individual citizens' needs.

Opponents of school choice counter these arguments by saying that parents already have choices. For instance, they can move to neighborhoods served by better schools, and the quality of schools is a major factor parents consider when choosing where to live (Haughney, 2010). If parents don't like the schools in their neighborhood, they can move or send their children to private schools, and 11% of parents currently do this (Manno, 2010). Districts already allow parents who believe their local schools are subpar to send their children across town to better schools with open enrollment and magnet school programs. Doing so requires some time and expense, but parents still have choices.

But advocates of choice point out that many poor, minority, and inner-city parents don't have the resources to vote with their wallets or their cars (Goyette, 2008). They can't afford to move to better neighborhoods with better schools, send their children to private schools, or even to drive across town each day to transport their children to a non-neighborhood public school. In addition, some school districts are so bad, critics contend, that other schools in the district don't really provide viable alternatives (Kahlenberg, 2011). These parents deserve the right to choose, just as much as more wealthy parents do.

But how can parents be provided with options? School choice has resulted in two major forms of educational reform: charter schools and vouchers.

Charter Schools

Teaching and You

When you look for your first teaching position, should you consider teaching in a charter school? What are the advantages and disadvantages of teaching in one?

Charter schools are alternative schools that are publicly funded but independently operated. The charter school movement began with the belief that the best way to reform schools is to take a school out of the existing bureaucracy and completely redesign it. Charter schools typically begin when a group—teachers, community members, a private corporation, or a combination of all three—develops a plan for a school, including its curriculum, staffing, and budget. This plan, or "charter," must then be accepted by the local school board or state office of education and serves as a contract with the state.

Most school districts already have alternative schools, such as magnet schools with specialized programs and schools designed to meet the needs of students who cannot function well in regular schools and classrooms, such as young, unwed mothers or children with serious behavior or emotional problems. Charter schools are similar to other alternative schools in that they offer a different curriculum or target special populations, but they differ in that they're independently administered public schools and are subject to less regulatory control from a district's central administration.

Charter schools began in Minnesota in 1991, when the legislature approved eight teacher-created and teacher-operated schools. Since that time, 39 additional states and the District of Columbia have passed charter school legislation resulting in the creation of more than 5,000 schools with nearly 2 million students, or about 4% of the public school student population (Lake & Gross, 2012).

The focus of different charter schools varies dramatically, but most attract parents seeking smaller schools and class sizes, better instruction, or alternatives to public school curricula and environments (Ravitch, 2010a). Many—about one third of all charter schools—are designed by urban community leaders to meet the needs of inner-city youth, and nationally, more than 60% of charter students are members of racial or ethnic minority groups, compared to less than half for regular public schools (Manno, 2010). Some focus on developing students' African heritage through language instruction, literature, and the arts. Others attract parents who want a return to the basics, and still others focus on Hebrew, Arabic, and other languages that parents want to preserve and pass on to their children (Applebome, 2011).

KIPP Schools

KIPP (Knowledge Is Power Program) is a national network of free, open-enrollment charter schools that has the goal of preparing students in underserved communities for success in college and in life. KIPP schools usually target grades five through eight, and they typically have enrollments of about 300 students. In 2010 there were 99 KIPP schools in 20 states and the District of Columbia serving more than 26,000 students, and the program has recently expanded into early childhood education (Zehr, 2011b). Almost all KIPP students come from black or Hispanic families under the poverty line.

KIPP schools significantly increase the length of the school day and the school year. For example, school days are 9 and a half hours long, students attend school on every other Saturday, summer school is required, homework is a must, hard work brings special rewards such as field trips, and principals have a great deal of autonomy, such as the power to hire and fire teachers.

Some evidence indicates that KIPP students perform well academically, outperforming their peers in comparable schools in both math and reading (Zehr, 2010b), but these accomplishments are not uniform. For example, a new KIPP school in Jacksonville, Florida, scored at the bottom of all comparable schools in northeast Florida (Palka & Sanders, 2011), and other research suggests that KIPP schools have higher student attrition rates (Zehr, 2011c). Some critics contend low achievers are "pushed out" rather than remediated (Toppo, 2009), but other research has found that high attrition rates due to transfers were not a problem (Zehr, 2011d).

As with all educational reforms, the effectiveness of KIPP schools continues to be debated. And the schools' policy of lengthening the school day and school year again raises the question of whether time in school should be increased for all students and how much this increased time will cost taxpayers.

Evaluating Charter Schools

Charter schools are growing in both number and students and have received support from every American president since George H. W. Bush. In addition, they are frequent beneficiaries of philanthropic organizations, such as the Gates Foundations (Zehr, 2010d). But are they successful and an effective educational reform?

Evaluating charter schools is difficult because they vary dramatically in both mission and quality. Some are excellent. For example, one all-boys high school in Chicago serving urban African American students placed all 107 of its first graduating class in 4-year colleges, and just 4% of these students were reading at grade level when they entered as freshmen (Paulson, 2010). Effective charters provide a coherent curriculum with excellent teachers to motivated students whose families made the special effort to place them there. Often the competition for these schools is so great that lotteries are used. Desperate parents, searching for viable alternatives to dismal, inner-city options anxiously attend lottery meetings to see if their children can be admitted. *Waiting for Superman*, a documentary about a lottery for one inner-city charter, received national attention and highlighted the plight of urban schools and their patrons (Sackler, 2010). Charter schools provide one alternative in sometimes bleak and discouraging educational landscapes.

On the other hand, a variety of problems with charter schools have surfaced. Fiscal mismanagement, particularly in charter schools run by for-profit organizations, is one. For example, a state audit of California's Charter School Academy, which operated more than 50 schools, found the for-profit management company had misused more than $20 million in state and federal funds (Hendrie, 2005b). The organization abruptly closed all of its schools, leaving families, teachers, and school officials scrambling (Hutton, 2005). Between 2005 and 2009, nearly 500 additional charters closed their doors, leaving patrons stranded (Toch, 2010).

Whether charters can serve as viable prototypes for educational reform in regular public schools is another issue. For example, charters—as originally conceived—were supposed to offer parents alternatives and also promote educational innovation by becoming models or prototypes for reform in regular schools. But research suggests that most charters are very similar to regular public schools in style and format (Shah, 2011b).

In addition, some critics claim that charters succeed only because they receive extra funding from philanthropic organizations, such as the Gates Foundation (S. Dillon, 2011b; Toch, 2009/2010). Significantly higher levels of funding are unrealistic for regular public schools, but at least these successful charter schools that receive extra money provide evidence that public schools need more financial support.

Critics also contend that charter schools entice the best students away from poor-performing schools, leaving urban schools, in particular, in even worse shape (Goyette, 2008). Further, school choice can lead to segregation of students, either by income or by race.

The role that teachers play in charters also varies. Originally intended as opportunities for teachers to become actively involved in site-based management, some charters, and especially those run by for-profit management groups, discourage teacher input and initiative. Many are anti-union, because unions interfere with a top–down management style and alternative pay schedules (Zehr, 2011b).

The ultimate test for any school is student achievement; it's the bottom line. And it's also an issue. For example, charter schools in Arizona—one of the leaders in the charter school movement—have been labeled as underperforming at twice the rate of regular public schools (A. Lewis, 2008). Perhaps most significant—because of its scope and the fact that it was conducted by a neutral agency that neither advocated nor opposed charter schools—is a comprehensive study of charters in 15 states and the District of Columbia. The study found that student achievement in 17% of charter schools was superior to achievement in regular public schools, achievement was similar in about half of the charter schools, and it was inferior in 37% (Raymond, 2009).

To hear a superintendent's views about charter schools, click on the video *Charter Schools: A Superintendent's Perspective* (4:05).

In *Teaching and You* at the beginning of this section, we asked if you should consider teaching in a charter school. Charters offer alternative employment opportunities in the current tight job market, and you will want to keep your options open. Although currently small in terms of numbers, charters are likely to grow, given the public's interest and the political support they are receiving (Friedman, 2010). But investigate carefully before you sign a contract. Understand the school's philosophy, and know what is expected of you. For example, most successful charters have longer school days, and you may find that you will be expected to work from 7:30 A.M. to 5:00 P.M., for example. Some also require Saturday classes. Will you be compensated for this extra time? Also, salaries and benefits are often lower in charter schools (Zehr, 2011b). Whether you choose to work in a charter school is a personal decision, but be sure you're well informed before you make it.

Vouchers

How would you like to receive a ticket to attend any school that you choose? **Vouchers**, checks or written documents that parents can use to purchase educational services, are another approach to school choice reform. Vouchers are grounded in the belief that parents know best what their children need and should be free to purchase the best education wherever they can find it. Some voucher plans give parents the choice of either a public or a private school, whereas others limit the choice to public schools.

Political conservatives promote vouchers, arguing that public schools are a monopoly and that opening up schools to parental choice will allow market forces to improve education. Instead of being required to attend schools in immediate neighborhoods, all schools become viable alternatives. Over time, advocates argue, the best schools will attract more students and flourish, whereas weaker schools will be shut down by informed consumers and market forces.

Because of possible disruptive influences on public schools and issues with funding religious instruction, the voucher movement is highly controversial. Critics, including the NEA and the AFT, argue that vouchers increase segregation, split the public along socioeconomic lines, and drain students and resources from already struggling urban schools (N. Anderson, 2011; Maxwell, 2010).

Some advocates would also like to use vouchers for religious private schools. Why, they ask, should parents have to pay for a quality education twice—once when they pay public-school taxes and again when they pay tuition at private schools? Critics counter that this violates the principle of separation of church and state. Nationally, 75% of private schools are religiously affiliated (Manno, 2010).

In 2002 the U.S. Supreme Court, in a 5 to 4 decision, ruled that the voucher program in Cleveland, which allowed vouchers to be used for religious private schools, didn't violate separation of church and state (Schimmel, Stellman, & Fischer, 2011). The idea that voucher funds went to parents rather than directly to religious schools was central to the decision. After the Supreme Court's decision, the number of applicants for the Cleveland voucher program rose significantly, but research conducted by a Cleveland-based nonprofit organization concluded that Cleveland vouchers served more as a subsidy for students already attending private schools than as an "escape hatch" for students eager to leave the public schools (Walsh, 2002).

In 2006, the Florida Supreme Court, in a 5–2 ruling, struck down Florida's voucher system, ruling that "the diversion of money not only reduced public funds for a public education but also used public funds to provide an alternative education in private schools that are not subject to the 'uniformity' requirements for public schools" (L. Romano, 2006, p. A05). More recently, Indiana passed a voucher plan that provided vouchers to families with incomes as high as $60,000 a year (Cavanagh, 2011a). Legal battles are likely to occur in other states and may prove difficult for voucher advocates because 37 state constitutions currently prohibit state aid to religious schools (Schimmel, Stellman, & Fischer, 2011).

As with charter schools, the academic benefits of vouchers are unclear. Some research suggests that voucher programs can lead to small achievement gains, but other research indicates no achievement gains, or small gains in some populations, such as African American, but not in others (Toch, 2011/2012; Trinko, 2011).

In general, the American public does not support vouchers. For instance, in a 2011 poll of the public's attitudes toward public education, only 1 of 3 Americans supported using public dollars to allow parents to send their children to private schools (Bushaw & Lopez, 2011). But a number of states continue to pursue vouchers despite this general public opposition (R. Coyne, 2011).

State tuition tax-credit plans are a variation of school voucher programs in which parents are given tax credits for money spent on private school tuition. Tuition tax credits have emerged in some states as a more politically viable alternative to publicly financed school vouchers (Robelen, 2009). Research suggests, however, that tuition tax credits primarily benefit wealthy families who are already sending their children to private schools. In Illinois in 2000, for example, tax credits cost the state more than $61 million in lost revenues (Gehring, 2002). Taxpayers earning more than $80,000 claimed nearly half that amount, whereas less than 3% went to households making less than $20,000. A similar problem occurred in Arizona, where households earning more than $50,000 received more than 80% of the tax credits (Bracey, 2002). Given these facts, the continuation of state tuition tax-credit plans over the long term is probably unlikely.

Homeschooling provides parents with the opportunity to customize a child's education to a family's specific educational goals.

Homeschooling

Homeschooling, an educational option in which parents educate their children at home, may be the ultimate form of school choice reform. Homeschooling has increased in popularity, and estimates suggest that 1.5 million students, nearly 3% of the school-age population, are being educated at home. This figure represents a more than 70% increase from 1999 to 2009 (National Center for Education Statistics, 2009).

Parents homeschool their children for a variety of reasons (Lloyd, 2009). Most—more than 8 of 10—do so for religious reasons or concerns about the moral climate of existing schools (A. Boyd & Bichao, 2012). Others want a more academic emphasis or nontraditional educational approaches. All are seeking an alternative to existing public schools.

The governance of homeschooling occurs at the state level, and state laws regulating it vary greatly from state to state (Schimmel, Stellman, & Fischer, 2011). Forty-one states have no minimum educational qualifications for parents who homeschool their children; 8 of the remaining 9 states require at least a high school diploma (Zehr, 2004). In most states, parents must demonstrate that their instruction is equivalent to that offered in public schools. An increasing number of parents who homeschool their children are turning to cyberschooling by enrolling their children in online programs (Gaither, 2009).

Approximately half the states require homeschooled students to participate in regular standardized testing. Homeschooled students who take these tests typically do well, scoring, on average, over 30 percentile points higher than students in public schools (A. Boyd & Bichao, 2012). Whether these differences are due to the quality of instruction or self-selection (i.e., better students are being homeschooled) is not clear.

Despite its growing popularity, homeschooling has its critics. The greatest concern focuses on the lack of safeguards with respect to the quality of education provided for homeschooled children and the possibilities of neglect and even abuse (Gross, 2008). A California court recently jumped into the fray, ruling that homeschooled children must be taught by a credentialed teacher, or parents could face possible fines or criminal charges (Terwiller & Toppo, 2008). Other concerns center on whether children schooled at home will learn important social-interaction skills, and whether narrow courses of study will expose children to alternative views and perspectives (Kunzman, 2009).

EXPLORING DIVERSITY: Reform and Cultural Minorities

Reducing the achievement gap between members of cultural minorities and their white counterparts is the goal of many current reform efforts. This gap was highlighted by the NCLB legislation, which required states to report achievement scores for different cultural and ethnic groups within each school and district. We examine the effect of different reform efforts on members of cultural minorities in this section.

The standards movement has been the most pervasive reform movement in our country. As required by NCLB, all 50 states created state-specific standards, and most of the states have now adopted the national standards we discussed earlier in the chapter. Advocates argue that uniform standards and their corresponding assessments will provide more consistent information that can be used to compare the achievement of different groups of students (Cuban, 2012). In addition, advocates assert, accountability based on the standards will motivate students to master essential knowledge and skills.

Critics, on the other hand, point to data suggesting that high-stakes testing is having a negative effect on precisely the students—members of cultural minorities—that this reform is designed to help. For example, high-stakes tests have resulted in large numbers of minority students being held back a grade (Van Horn, 2008), and high-stakes graduation exams, instead of encouraging higher achievement, have discouraged students and resulted in higher dropout rates (Nichols & Berliner, 2008).

Other reform efforts have targeted the teachers of low-SES and cultural minority students. A paradox exists in our educational system: members of cultural minorities and students at risk are often taught by the least-effective teachers (Shah, 2011d) and by teachers who are inexperienced and paid less than their suburban counterparts (Sawchuk, 2011b). Ineffective teacher evaluation systems that fail to identify and remediate substandard teachers add to the problem. Reforms targeting teacher evaluation, tenure, and merit pay are intended to address these inequities, but the effectiveness of these reforms is uncertain at best (Sawchuk, 2010c; Sparks, 2011a).

Other reforms targeting low-SES and minority students are designed to use charter schools to bypass ineffective public schools altogether. Charter schools, advocates claim, can bypass the inefficient bureaucracies of large, monolithic school districts and create innovative learning environments for students. And a few achieve impressive results. But as you saw earlier in the chapter, charter schools vary dramatically in quality, and many perform no better than the schools they replace (Betts & Tang, 2011). So, with respect to diversity, reform efforts are mixed. While many of the reforms have specifically targeted underserved groups of students, actual performance results have been spotty and inconsistent.

Reform Revisited

So, how should we evaluate the recent efforts to reform our teachers and schools? Looking at results—student achievement data—is perhaps the most viable way of assessing these efforts, and these results are mixed at best. For example, comprehensive reviews of the effects of high-stakes testing on achievement have found that this approach to reform has had little or no positive effect on student learning. And in some cases, the efforts have produced negative effects by increasing student dropout rates (Sparks, 2011a). Invalid tests and inappropriate use of test results have been identified as major obstacles to the test accountability reform movement (Sparks, 2011a).

Merit pay reforms have encountered similar negative evaluations. For example, one rigorous and comprehensive study of teacher incentives on student learning in Tennessee found that this reform failed to ". . . yield consistent and lasting gains in test scores. It simply did not do much of anything" (Sawchuk, 2010c, p. 12). One critic argued that for an incentive system to work ". . . you'd have to have teachers who were saving their best strategies for an opportunity to get paid for them, and that is an absurd proposition" (Sawchuk, 2010c, p. 13). Our experience working with classroom teachers supports this view. Teachers

DIVERSITY AND YOU

Reform Strategies and Your Work with Cultural Minorities

You're a new teacher in a large urban district in the Southeast. Your district is under pressure to narrow the achievement gap that exists between more affluent and often predominantly white outer-city schools in the district and inner-city schools serving poor and minority students. The school board in your district is considering different reform proposals, and the professional organization in your district is encouraging all teachers to attend discussions of these proposals because the changes will impact their professional lives.

You attend the first meeting, and after the meeting is called to order, the chair of the committee frames the debate.

"We're here to consider proposals for changes to our district's policies that will help decrease the differences in achievement that we see among our schools and students. I believe we all agree that this is a serious problem, and our district must address it. However, considerable disagreement exists about how to address the problem. I'll open the floor to members of the school board first, and then I'll ask for opinions from other members of our community."

"I believe we're already on the right track with our new standards and tests," one school board member begins. "We've put a lot of time and effort into constructing standards for different subjects. Now we need to take the next step and put some teeth into those standards. We need to make both teachers and students accountable for these standards and basically say, 'Pass the tests, or don't advance to the next grade or graduate.' Let's send the message that we're serious about learning."

A second school board member responds, "I'm sorry to disagree, but that approach is all wrong. It's like rearranging the deck chairs on the Titanic. More standards and tests won't change anything; teachers will teach to the test, and both teachers and students will try to game the system whenever they can. Instead, we need to focus on the teacher and create better teacher evaluation and tenure systems. Until we get rid of the poor teachers in our system, nothing else will change."

"I agree with what you just said," a third board member adds, "but I don't think you've gone far enough. We need to identify the best teachers and pay them more. It's crazy to pay the best teachers the same as the worst. We need to develop an effective merit pay system."

A fourth school board member weighs in. "I agree with everything that's been said so far, but I've sat on this board for years and know that the changes you all are recommending will take time—years to implement and even more years before we see any results. I think we need something now that will change things immediately. And most of you know what I'm going to advocate: charter schools. Let's free up the chokehold of bureaucracy that is strangling our district and allow charter schools to innovate and lead the way in reform."

QUESTIONS TO CONSIDER

1. How would you respond to the school board member who advocates more testing and accountability?
2. How would you respond to the two school board members who want to target teachers as the key to reform?
3. How would you respond to the school board member advocating charters as a reform strategy?

Go to *Diversity and You* in the MyEducationLab™ *Book Resources* that accompany this text to log your thoughts and receive feedback from your authors.

aren't waiting for an incentive program to motivate their best efforts; most are already teaching as effectively as they know how.

Other states around the country, such as Texas, Washington, and Iowa, are scaling back performance-based teacher compensation plans. As with the Tennessee study, research from around the country has failed to find any significant positive benefits for reform-based teacher incentive systems (N. Fleming, 2011).

So have these various reform efforts had any effects on education at all? The answer is yes, and unfortunately, many effects on teachers themselves have been negative. As teachers have become scapegoats for many of the failures of our current educational system, teacher morale is declining (Santos, 2012). One veteran Florida teacher lamented, "The guillotine of teacher quality and merit pay is now swinging over my head" (Harper, 2011, p. 24). A principal in New York had similar concerns about a new teacher evaluation system being introduced in his state, "It's education by humiliation. I've never seen teachers and principals so degraded" (Winerip, 2011f, p. A18).

Tangible evidence of this problem exists across the country. A recent poll of teacher attitudes found a sharp decrease in teachers' satisfaction with their profession (MetLife, 2012). In Wisconsin, teacher retirements during the struggle over teachers' collective bargaining rights doubled; in Alabama, the state legislature had to call a special session to deal with high teacher turnovers linked to cutbacks in teacher benefits (Associated Press, 2011a). In their attempts to squeeze more out of teachers, state legislators send a clear message, "Do more with less, and don't depend on us for support." Ill-conceived teacher-focused reforms are likely to hinder efforts to recruit quality teachers in the future. With teacher pay being mediocre by many industry standards, job security and benefits are seen as major incentives to attract our next group of effective teachers. When these incentives are eliminated by budget-cutting and reform-minded legislatures, the prospect of future recruitment efforts is diminished.

We want to emphasize that we are not opposed to reform, just haphazard, ill-conceived reform that damages both teachers and ultimately students. In fact, reforms are, without question, needed if schools are to improve. However, to produce long-term benefits, implementation of reform efforts must be based on evidence indicating that they're effective, and how and why they're effective. This evidence doesn't exist for many current reform efforts.

To correct these problems we need well thought-out pilot programs that involve teachers from the outset. If good teachers are the key to effective school reform, we need to involve them in the design, implementation, and evaluation of future reform efforts (DeBose et al., 2012). To do otherwise will result in short-term changes that will ultimately fail to address the real problems facing our schools.

Evidence is clear about one factor; the key to improved student learning is the quality of the teacher. This means you. As we said earlier in the chapter, *no organization, system, institution, or enterprise is any better than the people in it*, and the same applies to schools. You and others like you will determine how much students in our country are learning.

Gradually, some of our nation's leaders are beginning to realize the truth of this assertion. Here's what President Obama said in his 2012 State of the Union address:

> Teachers matter. So instead of bashing them, or defending the status quo, let's offer schools a deal. Give them the resources to keep good teachers on the job, and reward the best ones. In return, grant schools flexibility: to teach with creativity and passion; to stop teaching to the test: and to replace teachers who just aren't helping kids learn. (DeBose et al., 2012)

Teachers *do* matter. None of the reform efforts we've discussed—charter schools, merit pay for teachers, the elimination of tenure, standards, accountability and high-stakes testing, or any other will work if students aren't taught by expert teachers.

Successful reform efforts must be aimed at and include you in the process of reform. Successful reform requires intelligent, motivated people who will become the professionals our schools and students need. Our goal in writing this book is to help you begin to acquire the professional knowledge that will guide your actions as you wrestle with these important changes in education.

Check Your Understanding

4.1 Explain how schools and schooling are being changed as a result of reform efforts.

4.2 What do recent federal reform efforts have in common? What do they suggest about the future of reform in U.S. schools?

4.3 In addition to reform efforts focusing on teacher tenure, teacher evaluation, merit pay, and limiting collective bargaining by professional organizations, how have states used charters to stimulate educational reform?

4.4 What are the two major forms of school choice? How are they similar and different?

For feedback, go to the appendix, *Check Your Understanding*, located in the back of this text.

VOICES from the CLASSROOM

"... but at the end of the day I would like to think that I was just working magic."

ANGIE MILLER, 2011 Teacher of the Year, New Hampshire

CHAPTER 12 Summary

1. Explain how the current reform movement has been shaped by previous efforts at reform.
   - Educational reform involves changes to current practice that will increase student learning. Current targets for reform include teacher evaluation, merit pay, teacher tenure, limits on professional organizations, standards, testing and accountability, and school choice.
   - The current educational reform movement began with the publication of *A Nation at Risk* in 1983. This report linked U.S. economic growth to education and claimed that our current educational system was substandard. More recently in 2001, reform was promoted by the No Child Left Behind (NCLB) Act, which required each state to formulate standards in basic skill areas and construct tests to measure each student's attainment of these standards.
2. Describe how current reform efforts that focus on the teacher will affect your life in the classroom.
   - Critics claim that current teacher evaluation systems are inefficient and ineffective and fail to differentiate between good and bad teachers. Reformers want to evaluate teachers on the value, or learning gains, they add in the classroom.
   - Advocates of merit pay reform believe that good teaching should be rewarded and poor teaching should be identified and dealt with, either through remediation or dismissal. Most current merit pay proposals use both classroom observation and student test scores to identify exemplary performance.
   - Tenure protects teachers from political pressures and provides job security to teachers. Critics claim that it also shields ineffective teachers and should be curtailed or eliminated.
   - Professional organizations such as the National Education Association (NEA) and American Federation of Teachers (AFT) have been thrust into the middle of reform debates in many states. Some states are attempting to limit the collective bargaining powers of these organizations. Critics claim that these organizations are obstacles to meaningful reforms and are placing teachers' welfare above students'.
3. Explain how reform efforts focusing on standards, testing, and accountability are influencing the curriculum and classroom instruction.
   - The most far-reaching reform effort to date has been the standards movement. Spurred by NCLB, the standards movement has resulted in state-level accountability tests that are often high stakes for both students and their teachers.
   - Because of enormous variability on state standards and their assessments, national standards are being formulated and have been adopted by 48 states. Advocates hope national standards will provide greater uniformity between states and ultimately lead to increased achievement for all students. Critics fear that national standards will result in a national test for all states.
4. Describe how schools and schooling are being changed as a result of reform efforts.
   - The federal government is taking a central role in reform. In the Race to the Top competition, states were asked to address the following reform topics: national standards, more rigorous performance evaluations for principals and teachers, merit pay, and charter schools. This competition encouraged a number of states to pass legislation in these areas.
   - State efforts at reform have encompassed a number of different options. The most prominent of these has been school choice in the form of charter schools, vouchers, and homeschooling. Charter schools allow individual schools to govern themselves and create viable options to existing school practices.

Important Concepts

accountability
adequate yearly progress (AYP)
American Federation of Teachers (AFT)
charter schools
collective bargaining
Common Core State Standards Initiative (CCSSI)
high-stakes tests
homeschooling
KIPP (Knowledge Is Power Program)
merit pay
National Education Association (NEA)
No Child Left Behind (NCLB)
pay-for-performance plans
professional organization
Race to the Top
reform
school choice movement
standards
state tuition tax-credit plans
teacher evaluation
teacher tenure
value-added models
voucher

Portfolio Activity

Professional Organizations

InTASC Core Teaching Standard 9: Professional Learning and Ethical Practice

The purpose of this activity is to acquaint you with the major professional teacher organizations in your state. Using the Internet, access both the NEA and the AFT sites. Compare them at the national level in terms of goals, activities, and issues. Then within each site, locate the state you'll likely be teaching in and investigate specific educational issues in that state. When you are out in the schools, talk to teachers about their experiences with either organization. Does either organization seem right for you? Summarize your decision in a one- or two-page summary.

Portfolio Activities similar to this one and related to chapter content can be found at MyEducationLab™.

Educational Reform and You

Go to the topic *Assessment, Standards, and Accountability* in the MyEducationLab (www.myeducationlab.com) for *Introduction to Teaching*, where you can:

- Find learning outcomes for *Assessment, Standards and Accountability,* along with the national standards that connect to these outcomes.
- Complete *Assignments and Activities* that can help you more deeply understand the chapter content.
- Apply and practice your understanding of the core teaching skills identified in the chapter with the *Building Teaching Skills and Dispositions* learning units.
- Examine challenging situations and cases presented in the IRIS Center Resources.
- Access video clips of CCSSO National Teachers of the Year award winners responding to the question, "Why Do I Teach?" in the *Teacher Talk* section.
- Check your comprehension on the content covered in the chapter with the Study Plan. Here you will be able to take a chapter quiz, receive feedback on your answers, and then access *Review, Practice, and Enrichment* activities to enhance your understanding of chapter content.
- Check the *Book Resources* to find opportunities to share thoughts and gather feedback on the *Diversity and You* and *Issues You'll Face in Teaching* features found in this chapter.

MyEducationLab™

teacher education courses will help you better understand learning and the teaching abilities needed to promote it. And your classes will help you benefit from your classroom experiences by making you more aware of the actions of effective teachers. You are beginning this process by taking this course and studying this book.

Item 4: *The key to finding a teaching position is to study hard and get good grades in my teacher preparation program.* That's part—but not all—of it. Doing well in your classes and getting good grades are important, but they're only the beginning. You also have to strategically plan to make yourself marketable and understand the process of getting a job. Making yourself marketable includes developing a professional reputation and also broadening your professional experiences so that prospective employers believe that you understand schools and the students in them. It also includes building a portfolio, constructing a résumé, and writing an effective letter of application—all topics we cover in this chapter.

Item 5: *The most important factor in surviving my first year of teaching is understanding the content I'll be presenting to students.* One of the most pervasive myths about teaching is the belief that knowledge of subject matter is all that is necessary to teach effectively. Knowledge of content is essential, of course, but learning to teach requires a great deal of additional knowledge—knowledge you'll acquire in your teacher preparation program (Darling-Hammond, 2008).

For instance, if you believe that teaching is essentially a process of "telling," or explaining content to students, your belief is consistent with the beliefs of many pre-service teachers—probably because this is what most of your teachers did. Research suggests, however, that lecturing to students, especially those who are young or unmotivated, is quite ineffective (Eggen & Kauchak, 2013).

Let's look at one intern's experience.

My first lesson with the kids. Chris [her supervising teacher] said I was on my own, sink or swim. I hardly slept last night, but today I feel like celebrating. The kids were so into it. I brought my Styrofoam ball and had the kids compare the latitude and longitude lines I had drawn on it and then look at the globe. I thought the first period was supposed to be Chris's lowest, but they did the best. He was impressed.

Now I understand the stuff Dr. Martinez [one of her professors] stressed so much when he was always after us to use concrete examples and question, question, question. I know I have a lot to learn. I thought I could just explain everything to them, but they got confused and drifted off so fast I couldn't believe it. As soon as I started asking questions about the lines on the Styrofoam ball, though, they perked right up. I think I can do this. It was actually a heady experience.

(Isabella, an intern in a seventh-grade geography class)

As Isabella quickly discovered, teaching is much more complex than simply explaining. And surviving your first year of teaching involves much more than simply understanding the content you're teaching. Survival skills for the first year of teaching also include becoming well organized, understanding how to manage a classroom, learning how to plan, developing skills such as questioning, getting to know your students, and learning about their needs and developing cognitive abilities.

As you saw in this section, the beliefs of beginning teachers often reveal misconceptions about teaching and learning, and these misconceptions can influence your success when you take your first job. For instance, if you retain the belief that the most effective way to help students learn something is to explain it to them, you are likely to be disappointed when you see bored looks on their faces as you lecture. Similarly, if you believe that you will learn most of what you need to know when you go into classrooms, you are likely to benefit less from your university classes than you would if you were more committed to professional growth. Understanding the beliefs of beginning teachers, and recognizing that they're often misconceptions, will help you better prepare yourself as you anticipate your first teaching position.

Having examined these beliefs, let's now look at how teachers enter the profession and how this influences your future success.

Making Yourself Marketable

Successfully navigating through your teacher education program and earning a license is an essential part of getting a teaching job, but there's more to it. In this section, we examine strategies you can use to make yourself marketable.

Teaching and You

What do prospective employers look for in a new teacher? What can you do to make yourself more marketable? When should you start thinking about this future challenge?

Developing a Professional Reputation

Because you're at the beginning of your teacher preparation program, it might appear that preparing for a job is well into the future. This isn't true. The time to begin developing a professional reputation is now. Let's look at one student's experience.

I really wish someone had reminded me of these things sooner. When I started, like a lot of others, I didn't take it all too seriously. I'd blow class off now and then, and I didn't always get there on time. I actually did study, but I guess not as hard as I should have.

When I asked Dr. Laslow for a letter of recommendation, he refused. Actually, he said he didn't know me well enough to write a good one. I couldn't believe it. He was nice about it, but he wouldn't write one, advising me to find someone who knew me better and was more familiar with my work. And a couple others were sort of lukewarm, especially in my major. I guess the classes were just too large for them to get to know me. Now it's too late. My record is a little spotty and I feel bad about it now, but I can't go back. I used to wonder why Jacob and Lucas always seemed to get all the breaks. Now I get it.

(Jeremy, a recent graduate without a job)

Do you know people who seem to get a lot of breaks? Do you get your share? Do your instructors know you, and do they respect and value your work? Students who get breaks do so for a reason. They attend all their classes, turn their work in on time, and attempt to learn as much as possible from their experiences. The quality of their work is consistently high. In other words, they behave professionally. Just as teachers in the field are expected to be professional, students are expected to as well. Professors value conscientiousness, and students like Jeremy trouble them. It's easy to understand why Jacob and Lucas got breaks but Jeremy didn't.

What can you do to develop a professional reputation? Here are several suggestions:

- Attend all your classes, and be on time. If you must miss, see your professor in advance, or explain afterward. (Don't ever miss class and then ask your professor, "Did I miss anything really important?")
- Turn in required assignments on time, and follow established guidelines or criteria.
- Study conscientiously, and try to learn as much as possible in all your classes.
- Participate in class: Offer comments and ask questions. You will enjoy your classes more and also learn more from them.
- Take every opportunity to learn something new. For example, travel, especially to other countries, provides opportunities to learn about other cultures and the ways they approach education. Trips like these also make valuable entries on your résumé (which we'll discuss shortly).
- Read and try to be well informed. Learn for the sake of learning.
- Set the goal for yourself to be the best student you can.

If you sincerely attempt to learn and grow, your professional reputation will take care of itself. But you need to begin now.

Broadening Your Professional Experiences

Broadening your professional knowledge and experience is one of the best ways of making yourself marketable. Observing and working in classrooms will help you acquire experience that will prepare you for your first job. Suggestions for broadening your professional experiences are listed in Table 13.1. Reflecting on and writing about these experiences will help make them more meaningful to you, and you can use the writings as entries in your professional portfolio. Then you can list the experiences in your résumé as a summary of your qualifications.

The first item in Table 13.1 is especially important, not only for future jobs, but also to help you decide whether teaching is a career for you. In making this decision, there is no substitute for actually getting into schools and working with students. If you have any doubts about whether teaching is for you or what level to teach at, go into schools and see what it's like. And when you do, be strategic about the kinds of schools and classrooms you visit. Targeting schools with significant populations of minority students not only will give you a realistic taste of what teaching will be like, it will also provide you with valuable learning experiences that you can talk about in interviews and highlight in your résumé.

TABLE 13.1 Broadening Your Professional Experiences

Suggested Experience	Example	Professional Benefits
Target clinical work in diverse schools and classrooms.	Request to do your clinical work in schools with high concentrations of low SES, cultural minorities, and English language learners.	You'll establish background and expertise to work in high-demand schools.
Develop a minor area of study in a high-need area.	If you're a French major, consider a minor in Spanish. If you're a biology major, consider a minor in chemistry.	You'll have more versatility in the jobs you apply for.
Tutor a child.	Become a reading tutor at a local school. Most schools welcome volunteer tutors and may also share your name with parents interested in a private tutor.	You'll gain direct experience working with children and may earn some extra money.
Seek leadership positions.	Run for a student government office.	Leadership experience on a résumé tells potential employers that you have effective human relations skills and the desire to be a lifelong learner.
Do volunteer work.	Spend a few hours each weekend helping out at the local food pantry.	Volunteer work can be enriching, and it indicates your desire to contribute to society.
Become an aide.	Ask your local school district about job openings for part-time classroom aides.	Working as an aide will give you valuable classroom experience and a part-time job.
Join professional organizations.	Join your university's chapter of the National Education Association or a student chapter of another professional organization. (Professional organizations are listed in Table 13.6.)	You'll stay up-to-date on issues in your field and expand your network of professional contacts.

Substitute Teaching

Working in classrooms and working as a substitute teacher are excellent ways to learn about teaching and develop professional experience.

One of the best ways to learn about schools and teaching and to demonstrate your developing competence is substitute teaching. Many districts continually need effective substitutes, and substituting not only provides you with valuable teaching experience but also gives you a foot in the door when you try to find a job. And you'll be paid for your efforts.

The application process for becoming a substitute teacher is similar to applying for a regular teaching job, complete with fingerprinting and a background check. School districts want to ensure that their students are in good hands. But because you might be sent to any number of schools, you probably won't be interviewed by a principal, as usually occurs with a regular teaching application. Many districts will hire people before they're licensed; others will hire substitutes who have a degree in an area but no formal teacher education course work. Local supply and demand usually determines these qualifications, and the only way to find out if you're eligible is to check with individual districts.

But be forewarned: substitute teaching can be very challenging. Teachers often leave only sketchy lesson plans, and you'll be forced to fill in details and improvise on the spot (just like teaching). We outline some additional advantages and disadvantages of substitute teaching in Table 13.2.

Building a Portfolio and Résumé

The interview was going okay, but I was uneasy. The principal I was interviewing with was cordial, but she certainly wasn't enthusiastic. "I've had it," I thought to myself. She even quit asking me questions after about 20 minutes. I really wanted the job, too.

As I was about to leave, I happened to mention, "Would you like to see my portfolio?" She looked at it for a couple minutes, and then she started asking some probing questions. When she stuck my DVD in her computer and saw me teaching, she really lit up. I got the job!

(Shelley, the new teacher at the beginning of the chapter)

Your **professional portfolio**, a collection of materials representative of your work, is an effective way to tell about yourself and document your competence and qualifications (Devlin-Scherer, Burroughs, Daly, & McCarten, 2007). Just as artists prepare a portfolio of their paintings or drawings, you will use your professional portfolio to document your developing knowledge and skills.

TABLE 13.2 Advantages and Disadvantages of Substitute Teaching

Advantages	Disadvantages
1. Gain valuable teaching experience and insights into how schools work.	1. Challenges of working in a class that knows you're just a substitute.
2. Improve future job prospects through an enhanced résumé and professional contacts.	2. Pay is lower than regular teaching, and there are no benefits like medical coverage.
3. Learn about management and students' responses to you as a teacher.	3. Facing new content each time, as well as new students, presents continual challenges.
4. Get paid while you learn and gain experience.	4. You don't get to establish meaningful long-term relationships with students and see their growth as individuals.

A **digital portfolio** allows you to compress large amounts of information into computer files, making it easy to edit and burn to a CD that can be shared with prospective employers (Zuger, 2008). We provide *Online Portfolio Activities* at the end of each chapter of this text, and *Guidelines for Beginning a Professional Portfolio* can be found on the text's website at www.myeducationlab.com.

The first item in your portfolio should be a résumé summarizing your strengths and accomplishments as a teacher. A **résumé** is a document that provides a clear and concise overview of an individual's job qualifications and work experience. It typically is the first thing a prospective employer sees, and it should make a clear and persuasive statement about your qualifications.

An effective résumé has the following components:

- Personal data
- Professional objectives
- Education
- Teaching experience
- Work experiences
- Extracurricular activities
- Honors and awards
- References

When constructing your résumé, clarity and simplicity should be guiding principles. People reading your résumé want to be able to easily find each of the items listed above.

The office of career planning and placement at your college or university will be able to help you prepare your résumé. A sample résumé containing these components is shown in Figure 13.2.

Creating a Credentials File

Your college or university has a placement center designed to help graduates find jobs. In addition to providing information about job openings, this center also serves as a repository for your **credentials file**, the collection of important personal documents you will submit when you apply for teaching positions. It typically includes your résumé, background information about you, courses you've taken, performance evaluations by your directing teacher and college or university supervisor during your internship, letters of recommendation (usually three or more), and the type of position sought. When you apply for a job, you notify the placement center, which then sends your credentials file to the prospective employer. If, after reviewing this file, the district believes there is a potential match, you'll be contacted for an interview.

Writing a Successful Letter of Application

You have written a résumé, constructed a portfolio showcasing your skills and experiences, and created a credentials file. Now, it's time to actually apply for a teaching position. School districts typically have a number of positions open before the start of the school year, so your letter of application should clearly state the kind of position you are applying for (e.g., elementary grades teacher or middle school language arts teacher). It should also highlight elements you'd like to emphasize in your résumé, and it should close with a statement detailing your availability for an interview (the topic of the next section).

Using correct grammar, punctuation, and spelling is essential in a letter of application. The letter is the first thing people evaluating you see, and even minor errors create a negative impression. Be sure to read your letter carefully before sending it, and, if possible, have a friend read it with a critical eye. (See Figure 13.3 for a sample letter of application.)

FIGURE 13.2 A Sample Résumé

Melinda Garcia

Personal Data
Address:
2647 Bay Meadows Road
Jacksonville, FL 32224

Home phone: 904-267-5943
Work phone: 904-620-6743
E-mail: mgarcia@msn.com

Professional Objectives:
Elementary Teaching Position, K–6
Elementary Title I Reading Teacher, K–6

Education:
B.A. Elementary Education, University of North Florida, June 2013
Major Area: Elementary Education, K–8
Endorsements: Reading, K–8

Teaching Experience:
Student Teaching: Paxon Elementary, Duval County School District
Cooperating Teacher: Mrs. Nola Wright
Worked in a first-grade urban classroom with seven students who were English Language Learners; assumed full control of classroom for one eight-week grading period. Also worked with Mrs. Althea Walkman, First Grade Title I Coordinator. Administered reading diagnostic tests and developed specialized reading programs for groups of students.

Math and Reading Clinical Experience: Matthew Gilbert Elementary, Duval County School District
Cooperating Teacher: Ms. Linda Gonzalez
Served as a teacher aide in a fifth-grade, self-contained classroom. Taught both small-group and whole-class lessons in reading and math.

Elementary Tutoring: Sandalwood Elementary, Duval County School District
Cooperating Teacher: Mrs. Alice Watkins
Observed and tutored third-grade students in all subject matter areas. Tutored students in reading and math one-on-one and in small groups.

Work Experience:
Counselor and Tutor: YWCA After-school Activities Program. June 2012 to present. Worked with elementary students in both academic and recreation areas.

Lifeguard, Duval County Recreation Program. Summers, 2011, 2012. Full-time summer lifeguard; also provided swimming lessons for young students (4–6 years old).

Extracurricular Activities and Interests:
Vice President, University of North Florida, Student International Reading Association
Senator, University of North Florida, Student Government Association
Member, University of North Florida Swim Team

Honors and Awards:
B.A. with Honors, University of North Florida
Florida UTEACH Scholarship Recipient, 2011–2013

References:
References and credentials file available upon request.

FIGURE 13.3 Letter of Application

Melinda Garcia
2647 Bay Meadows Road
Jacksonville, FL 32224

June 20, 2013

Dr. Robert Allington
Personnel Director
Duval County School District
2341 Prudential Drive
Jacksonville, FL 32215

Dear Dr. Allington,

I am writing this letter to apply for an elementary teaching position in your district beginning this fall. I recently graduated with honors from the University of North Florida, with a degree in elementary education and an endorsement in reading.

As my enclosed résumé indicates, I have had a number of rewarding experiences working with students in your district. Early in my elementary education program, I observed and tutored students in a third-grade classroom at Sandalwood Elementary School. I then did extensive clinical experiences in fifth-grade math and reading classes at Matthew Gilbert Elementary. During my internship at Paxon Elementary School, I was assigned to a first-grade classroom with significant numbers of Title I students and English Language Learners. During this experience, I learned a great deal about helping culturally diverse first graders become skilled readers.

As I worked toward my degree, I focused on reading as my major area of endorsement. Reading is the key to success in all other subjects, and I believe I have the knowledge and skills to help young children become successful readers. Through my extensive experiences in classrooms at different levels, I have seen how effective reading programs build on the background knowledge and skills of developing readers. Please note that I have had formal course work in reading diagnosis as well as hands-on experiences implementing different diagnostic tests. I would like to utilize this expertise in a teaching position in your district.

I have arranged for my credentials file to be sent to you from the Placement Office at the University of North Florida. Please feel free to contact me at the telephone numbers listed on my résumé for any additional information. I am available for an interview at any time this summer.

Thank you for considering my application.

Sincerely,

Melinda Garcia

Melinda Garcia

In *Teaching and You* at the beginning of this section, we asked what prospective employers look for in a new teacher and how you can make yourself marketable. They're looking for teachers who are knowledgeable and competent and who have done well in their teacher education program. In addition, they want candidates who have broad experiences working in schools with a broad range of students. The time to start thinking about these future challenges is right now, as you plan the rest of your teacher education experiences. This is why we're discussing these topics in this chapter.

Finding a Job

An important part of finding a job involves preparing yourself for the challenges of teaching. But what other factors will influence your ability to secure a teaching position? We address this question in this section.

Where Are the Jobs?

In general the job outlook is good, with P–12 enrollments projected to increase by 6% between 2007 and 2019 (Hussar & Bailey, 2011). New teacher hires were 246,000 in 2007, and this figure is projected to increase to nearly 350,000 by 2019. Student growth patterns vary by geographic area and grade level, and they reflect demographic trends in our country. The greatest enrollment increases are occurring in the South (13%) and West (12%). Experts predict, for example, that public school enrollments will increase by more than 15% in Arizona, Georgia, Idaho, Nevada, North Carolina, Texas, and Utah.

Within geographic areas, specific locations also influence job availability. Opportunities are greater in rural and urban schools than in the suburbs, and they're also greater in districts with more low-income and minority students (Kaiser, 2011). Shelley, our new teacher at the beginning of the chapter, experienced these trends:

> At first I looked for jobs in two suburban schools, but there were no openings. However, I received offers from three different urban schools. I was a little hesitant at first because I had read about the challenges of working in urban settings, especially for first-year teachers. But one of the assistant principals was great. She talked to me about the job, what it entailed, and the kind of help I'd receive in an induction program at that school. I was paired with a wonderful mentor [Mrs. Landsdorp], and I'm having a challenging but great year. I love these kids and think I'm going to make it.

Your area of specialization will also affect your chances of finding a job (Ingersoll & Merrill, 2010). The greatest areas of need are in special education, English language learning (including bilingual education and English as a second language), foreign languages (especially Spanish), math, physics, chemistry, and technology. Lower areas of teacher need include English, social studies, and physical education.

What implications do these job patterns have for you? First, if you haven't already decided on a major, don't select one based on job availability alone. To be effective (and happy), you need to be interested in and want to teach in the area you select. Don't major in chemistry, for example, if you dislike chemistry. But if you like chemistry and want to teach it, you now know that there is a high probability of getting a job in that area. Second, learn where teaching jobs exist in the areas you want to live; the career placement center at your college or university can help. You'll increase your chances of finding a job if you're flexible about where you'll teach. Your first teaching position may not be in an ideal location, but you can use it to gain experience, which can lead to other positions.

Interviewing Effectively

You're interviewing for your first job, and the principal at the school where you'd like to work asks, "You have a classroom full of unmotivated fourth graders. What would you do to increase their motivation?"

How would you respond?

Your interview is your best opportunity to show a prospective employer that you are a knowledgeable and committed professional. This is the setting that will probably determine whether you get a job. You need to shine. Some guidelines for interviewing effectively are outlined in Table 13.3.

Schools look for the following in new teachers:

- A sincere interest in making a difference in students' lives
- Knowledge of content, an understanding of how students learn, and a commitment to lifelong learning
- An understanding of how to organize and manage a classroom—beginning teachers' number-one concern
- An ability to convert state standards into meaningful learning experiences for your students
- A variety of life experiences that can contribute to your work
- The ability to work with others
- Adaptability and flexibility (Clement, 2008)

If you are genuinely interested in working with young people, and if you've been conscientious in your teacher preparation program, the interview will largely take care of itself. Nothing communicates more effectively than a sincere desire to do the job you're interviewing for.

Additional preparation can increase the positive impression you make, however. For example, how would you respond to the following questions, all of which are frequently asked in teacher interviews?

- Why do you want to teach?
- Why do you want to work in this school?
- How would you plan for classroom management?

TABLE 13.3 Guidelines for Interviewing Effectively

Guideline	Rationale
Be on time.	Nothing creates a worse impression than being late for an interview.
Dress appropriately.	Wear an outfit appropriate for an interview, and be well groomed. Shorts, jeans, and T-shirts are inappropriate, as is an eyebrow ring. You have the right to dress and groom yourself in any way you choose, but if you are serious about getting a job, you won't demonstrate your freedom of expression during a job interview.
Speak clearly, and use Standard English grammar.	Clear language is correlated with effective teaching, and your verbal ability creates an impression of professional ability.
Cell phone should be turned off.	You want to show the interviewer that this is important enough to warrant your undivided attention.
Sit comfortably and calmly.	Fidgeting—or worse, glancing at your watch—suggests either that you're nervous or that you'd rather be somewhere else.
Communicate empathy for children and a desire to work with them.	Communicating an understanding of learning, learner development, and instruction demonstrates that you have a professional knowledge base.

- How would you handle an incident of misbehavior?
- How would you motivate a class of unmotivated learners?
- How would you design your classroom for students of varying ability levels?
- What is your philosophy of education?
- How would you involve parents or caregivers in their children's education?

We suggest that you keep these questions in mind and begin to form answers to them as you go through your teacher preparation program. If you're prepared, you will also be more at ease during the interview.

The more specific and concrete your responses to questions, the more positive an impression you will make. During your interview, be specific, and use concrete examples from your own experience to illustrate your answers (Clement, 2008). For example, here is a specific response to the question about teaching philosophy:

"I believe that all children can learn, and I would try my best to make that happen by ensuring that all students are involved in the lessons I teach. Research suggests that active involvement is essential for learning. During my student teaching, I tried to get all my students involved by calling on each of them as often as possible and I used group work to develop content knowledge and social skills."

The answer communicates that you're clear about what you would try to do and why, and citing research suggests that you are knowledgeable, something all school districts value. In contrast, a vague response, such as "I am a humanistic and learner-centered teacher," leaves the interviewer with the impression that you're just saying words you learned in a class, which is much less persuasive.

Assessing Prospective Schools

Your interview is a two-way street: You are being interviewed, but at the same time you're interviewing the school. You want a job, but you also want to determine if this is the kind of place in which you want to work. Research suggests that both the upkeep and physical condition of the school as well as its professional culture will have a powerful influence on your satisfaction with a school (Donaldson & Johnson, 2011). When you interview, you should ask specific questions of the principal and other people you will work with. Doing so helps you learn about the position and communicates that you are thoughtful and serious about the job.

Teaching and You

How can you tell if a school will be a good place for a beginning teacher to work? How important is the physical condition of a school? How important will the principal be? How important will other teachers be for your future success?

Factors to consider when evaluating a school as a potential workplace include:

- *Teacher morale and efficacy*: Is teacher morale high, and do teachers believe that they make a difference in students' lives? Teaching is stressful, and school morale can make a big difference in how you feel about your job.
- *Commitment and leadership of the principal*: The principal's leadership sets the tone for the school (Ubben, Hughes, & Norris, 2011). Does the principal communicate caring for students and support for teachers? Lack of support from administrators is a major reason teachers leave a school.
- *School mission*: Does the principal communicate a clear school mission, and do teachers feel as if they're a team, all working for the benefit of students? Teachers have a strong positive effect on both teacher morale in the school and student achievement when they collectively believe they can positively influence students' lives (Woolfolk Hoy, Hoy, & Davis, 2009).

- *School climate:* Does the emotional climate of the school seem positive, and do people communicate a positive and upbeat attitude? How do office personnel treat students? Does the support staff, such as secretaries, custodians, and cafeteria workers, feel like they're part of the team? Emotional and physical workplace conditions strongly influence whether teachers remain in a school.
- *The physical plant*: Are student work products, such as art and other projects, displayed in cases and on the walls? Do posters and signs suggest that the school is a positive environment for learning? Are the classrooms, halls, and restrooms clean and free of debris and graffiti?
- *Students*: Are students orderly and polite to one another and to teachers? Do they seem happy to be at school?
- *Community support*: Do people in the community value education and support teachers? How does the school involve parents in their children's education, and do parents support school functions? The support of parents and the community strongly influences students' attitudes, behaviors, and work habits.
- *An induction program for teachers*: Does the school have a mentoring program for beginning teachers? First-year teachers who participate in mentoring programs are more likely to succeed and stay in teaching than those who don't (Ingersoll & May, 2011). (We examine induction and mentoring programs in more detail later in the chapter.)

In *Teaching and You* at the beginning of this section, we asked how you can tell if a school will be a good place for a beginning teacher to work. This is a difficult question to answer in one visit, but the answer to this question is important for your satisfaction with your first job and future development as a professional. Working conditions in schools vary dramatically, and they can make the difference between a rewarding first year and one that makes you reconsider your decision to teach.

Private School Employment

Teaching in a private school is another employment option. Nearly 6 million P–12 students attended private schools in the United States in 2010, a figure that is projected to increase by 5% over the next 10 years (Hussar & Bailey, 2011). Demand for private school teachers is also expected to increase substantially, with increases in new hires projected at over 10% (Council for American Private Education, 2011). More than 3 of 4 private schools are religiously oriented, with Catholic schools being the most common. Because of the cost of tuition, private schools attract more affluent students, and these schools generally have fewer learners with exceptionalities, members of cultural minorities, and English language learners than do public schools (Bracey, 2008). You are most likely to find private school employment in urban areas and in the South.

Starting salaries for private school teachers are usually lower than those in public schools, however, and private schools typically don't provide the same medical and insurance benefits offered in public schools. Because of these financial issues, private school teachers are more likely to leave teaching than their public school counterparts, often transferring to public schools.

Private schools sometimes waive the licensing requirements that public school teachers are required by law to meet, which can make them attractive to someone who doesn't want to spend the time and money to earn a traditional license. In addition, teachers sometimes choose private school employment because the school is dedicated to religious or intellectual

ISSUES YOU'LL FACE IN TEACHING

Traditional or Alternative Licensure?

All professionals—physicians, nurses and lawyers, for example—must be "licensed" in order to work in their occupations, and this applies to teachers as well. In education, **licensure** is the process by which a state evaluates the credentials of prospective teachers and certifies that they understand subject-area content, possess professional knowledge and skills, and are morally fit to work with young people. Teachers are required by law in all 50 states and the District of Columbia to be licensed by a state department of education before they can teach in public schools. But there are different paths to licensure, so you will have options for becoming licensed. As you study this section, think about which option may be better for you.

TRADITIONAL LICENSURE

Traditional licensure programs are housed in colleges and universities and lead to a bachelor's degree. They have a general education component that includes courses in history, English, math, and science, together with education courses designed to help you develop your professional knowledge. If you are preparing to work in a secondary school, you will also be required to earn a specified number of hours in the subject area you plan to teach, such as math or social studies. And you will be required to pass a content-area exam in this major.

ALTERNATIVE LICENSURE

Alternative licensure provides a shorter route to teaching for those who already possess a bachelor's degree. A person seeking alternative licensure must hold a bachelor's degree in a content area, such as math or English; pass a licensure exam; complete a brief, intensive teacher-training experience; and participate in a supervised teaching internship. Currently, all 50 states have alternative programs, which enroll 11% of students seeking initial licensure (Sawchuk, 2012c).

Teach for America is the best-known alternative licensure program. Founded in 1989 and claiming more than 14,000 alumni, the organization has an annual budget of $212 million and has 8,200 teachers working nationwide, mostly in hard-to-staff urban and rural schools (Rotherham, 2011). Candidates must possess a bachelor's degree and commit to 2 years of teaching; while teaching, they receive modest federal grants and college loan deferments in addition to their salaries.

THE QUESTION

Is alternative licensure better for you than the traditional route? Here are the arguments on both sides of the issue.

PRO

- Alternative licensure programs offer a shorter, less expensive, and more direct route to a teaching career.
- Because they already possess a bachelor's degree, alternative certification students have a firm content background and can concentrate on learning to teach. Also, candidates don't have to go back and worry about undergraduate degree requirements.
- These programs are especially attractive to older, more mature candidates and to members of cultural minorities, all of whom bring unique assets to classrooms.

CON

- Alternative licensure training programs are often so brief that they fail to prepare teachers for the rigors of classroom teaching. Teach for America, for example, uses 5 weeks of intensive summer training before turning candidates loose on their own classrooms (Rotherham, 2011).
- The intensive mentoring and support system that is supposed to accompany and compensate for a shorter training period often doesn't exist, resulting in a sink-or-swim approach to learning to teach (Rotherham, 2011).
- Because of the short training period and lack of support, the attrition rate for alternative licensure candidates is considerably higher than the national average for new teachers (Donaldson & Johnson, 2011). For example, only 52% of Teach for America alumni remain in the classroom after their 2-year commitment, and after 5 years, only 28% are still teaching. This compares to 50% after 5 years for teachers with traditional licensure (Donaldson & Johnson, 2011).

YOU TAKE A STAND

So, is alternative licensure for you? Your answer to this question will depend on your own unique circumstances as well as the availability of quality programs in your state.

Go to *Issues You'll Face in Teaching* in the MyEducationLab™ *Book Resources* that accompany this text to log your thoughts and receive feedback from your authors.

principles consistent with their beliefs. Communication between administrators and teachers also is easier because these schools are often smaller, and parents whose children attend private schools tend to be more involved in school activities than those with children in public schools. Deciding to teach in a public or a private school will ultimately be a decision that only you can make.

Check Your Understanding

1.1 Describe the beliefs of beginning teachers.
1.2 What are the most essential factors involved in finding a desirable job?
1.3 In which areas are teaching jobs most plentiful?

For feedback, go to the appendix, *Check Your Understanding*, located in the back of this text.

Your First Year of Teaching

Teaching and You

What are the biggest challenges you'll face as a beginning teacher? What can you do now to begin preparing for these challenges?

What will your first year of teaching be like? Let's see what one first-year teacher has to say.

Wow! Was I naive. I was tired of sitting in classes, and I wanted so badly to be finished and get out into the "real world." What I never realized was just how cushy being a student was. If I was a little tired or didn't study enough, I could just coast through class. Now, no coasting. You have to be ready every minute of every day. I've never been so tired in my life. You're in front of kids all day, and then you go home and work late into the night to get ready for the next day. They have us filling out reports, doing surveys, and everything other than teaching, so I don't get a chance to plan during the day. I can't even make a phone call unless it's during my lunch break or planning period.

And then there's my fourth-period class. They come in from lunch just wired. It takes me half the period to get them settled down, and that's on a good day.

Sometimes I just need someone to talk to, but we're all so busy. Everybody thinks they're an expert on teaching, because they've been a student. They don't have a clue. Let them try it for 2 days, and they'd be singing a different tune.

(Antonia, a first-year middle school math teacher)

About 6% of all public school teachers leave the profession each year, but the number of new teachers who leave is much higher—more than 12% after their first year, and about that amount in the second and third years (Kaiser, 2011). After the fifth year, half of new teachers have left the profession (Donaldson & Johnson, 2011).

As a new teacher, you're likely to face some or all of the following challenges:

- Disinterested and sometimes unruly students
- Unresponsive parents
- Poorly run and disorderly schools that aren't conducive to teaching and learning
- Working conditions that require so many nonteaching duties that you have insufficient time for planning and virtually no time for yourself
- Isolation and loneliness

But your first year can also be rewarding, even exhilarating. Let's look at another of Antonia's experiences:

Wow, what a day. We've been working so hard on solving equations, and all of a sudden Jeremy [one of Antonia's weaker students] bursts out right in the middle of our discussion, "Hey, I get this. It ain't all that hard." What a rush. When you see the lightbulb finally come on in a kid's head, it keeps you going for another month. And yesterday, Natalia [another struggling student] came up and said, "Miss Martinez, I used to really, really hate math, but now I actually look forward to coming to algebra." I didn't drive home after school yesterday; I flew.

Many rewards exist in teaching, and Antonia experienced some of them. It is, indeed, a heady experience to see students understand something new and know that you helped make it happen.

Stages of Teacher Development

During Don's (one of your authors) first year of teaching, his principal visited his classroom for the first time. It was early autumn, and it was hot! His class had just come in from recess, and students were sweaty and thirsty from running around on the playground.

Seeing his principal in the back of the room, Don plunged into his lesson. The room was sweltering, and students were drooping. After about 5 minutes, the principal got up quietly and opened several windows. You could feel the difference immediately. We weren't going to die in that oven!

When teachers first begin their professional careers, they are often overwhelmed with concerns about management and survival.

I was so preoccupied with making a good impression that I didn't even notice that my students were dying from the heat. Research examining the stages that teachers progress through as they develop helps us understand why I was so preoccupied and didn't even notice their discomfort (Watzke, 2007).

When teachers first begin their teaching careers, they are preoccupied with survival and making a good impression (see Table 13.4). Student behavior is uppermost in their minds, and beginning teachers often worry about losing control of their students. Paul (your other author) remembers a recurring dream he had in anticipating his first year of teaching. He dreamed that his principal was watching from out in the hall, his students were out of control, and nothing he did could bring them back. (Other teachers we've worked with have admitted the same frightening dream.) If Freud is right, our dreams provide insights into our fears and concerns. So, if you're uneasy about your first year, you're not alone. We were, and most new teachers are.

If you're typical, during this survival stage, your primary goal will be to make it through each day with minimal disruptions. Forget long-term learning goals such as making students independent learners. Forget concerns about students' social or personal development. Beginning teachers focus narrowly on getting through the day and can't wait until, exhausted, Friday comes. TGIF!

During the second stage, your confidence increases, and your focus shifts from you to your students. Classroom management is no longer your primary concern, and the content you're teaching becomes more familiar. You'll start to develop teaching strategies that work, and some of the experiences you had in your teacher education classes will make more sense now than they did then.

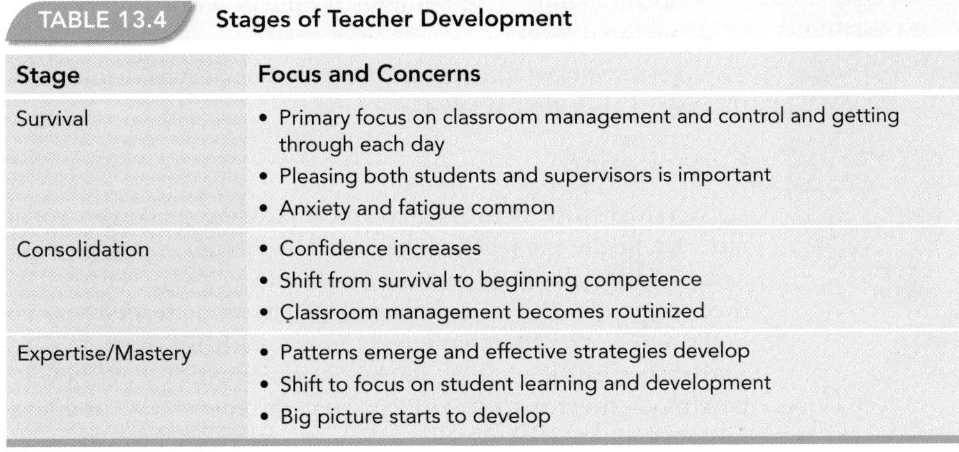

TABLE 13.4 Stages of Teacher Development

Stage	Focus and Concerns
Survival	• Primary focus on classroom management and control and getting through each day • Pleasing both students and supervisors is important • Anxiety and fatigue common
Consolidation	• Confidence increases • Shift from survival to beginning competence • Classroom management becomes routinized
Expertise/Mastery	• Patterns emerge and effective strategies develop • Shift to focus on student learning and development • Big picture starts to develop

You're not yet an expert, but you don't wake up each morning with an anxious feeling in your stomach, contemplating another day of struggle and chaos.

Gradually, as you enter the third stage, you begin to notice patterns—both in your students and the effects your teaching has on them (Darling-Hammond & Bransford, 2005). You start to figure out what works for you as well as your students. For example, when your students give you blank looks, you quickly realize you're talking too much; you change the direction of your lesson in midstream and take steps to involve your students in your learning activity. Your focus shifts to student learning and development. Your horizon is no longer surviving the next day; instead, you start to think about long-term goals, not only for them but for you. You're starting to figure out who you are as a teacher and where you want to go in the future.

Most beginning teachers go through something like this progression. We did when we worked in P–12 schools. Although these descriptions don't apply to all teachers in all situations, our students find them both reassuring and comforting. They begin to realize that they're not going crazy when they have strange dreams, and being uneasy about beginning teaching is completely normal. And they know that the first year is always the toughest and things will get better after the first year. These stages also provide guidance as you progress as a professional, knowing that a preoccupation with classroom management is not only normal but also perhaps healthy. You can't teach effectively if you're constantly struggling with management problems.

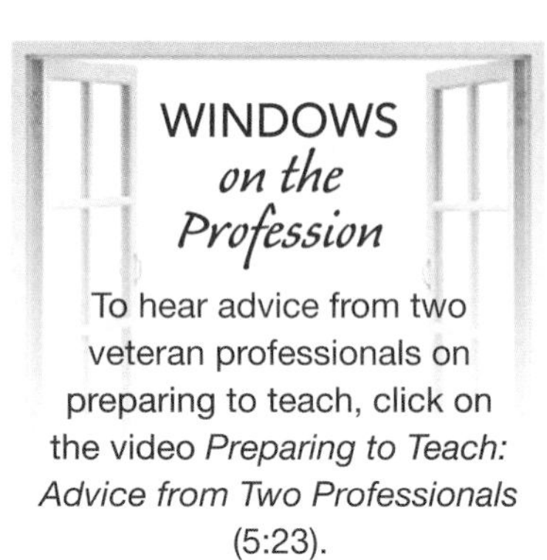

This perspective on teacher growth also reminds us of factors that produce healthy development in general. For example, background knowledge is important. Your development as a professional will largely depend on your professional knowledge and skills, so the harder you study, and the more closely you work with experienced teachers, the more ready you will be for your first teaching position. And as with development in general, the experiences you encounter as you develop as a professional will contribute to your growth. Your course work, experiences in schools, and the support of your instructors and teachers in the field will all help you "hit the ground running" when you take your first job.

Survival Skills for the First Year

You can also prepare for your first year of teaching by developing the following "survival skills":

- Organization: Use your time and energy efficiently.
- Classroom management: Create an orderly classroom environment.
- Effective instruction: Involve students in meaningful learning activities.
- Relationships with students: Connect with students at a personal level.

Let's see how these skills can help you survive—and even thrive—in your first year of teaching.

Organization can help teachers maximize the time they have for the numerous professional roles they perform.

Organization

Lack of time is one of the first and most pressing challenges you'll face as a beginning teacher. You'll feel as though you don't have a second to yourself. As Antonia commented, "I've never been so tired in my life. You're in front of kids all day, and then you go home and work late into the night to get ready for the next day." And earlier in the chapter, Shelley commented, "I can't believe how much there is to do—IEPs, progress reports, CPR training, responsibility to look for signs of abuse. When do I teach?"

Although a simple solution to this problem doesn't exist, careful organization can make a difference. Effective teachers are well organized—both in their classrooms and in their daily lives (Good & Brophy, 2008). A student in one of our classes observed the following in a first-year teacher he visited:

His desk was a mess. Books and papers piled everywhere. He couldn't find anything, and he was always shuffling through papers looking for something. He always acted like he wasn't quite ready for what was coming next.

If he couldn't find "anything," you can bet he wasted time looking for lesson plans and student papers. If you frequently, or even occasionally, lament that "I need to get organized," now is a good time to start changing your habits. Thoroughly planning your lessons, having your instructional materials stored and readily accessible, starting your lessons on time, creating procedures for routine tasks, such as turning in, scoring, and returning papers, and establishing policies for absences and making up missed work are all essential for using time effectively. These skills are automatic for expert teachers; for beginning teachers, they must be learned (Weinstein, 2007).

Classroom Management

Classroom management has historically been the primary concern of beginning teachers, and disruptive students are an important source of stress for beginners and veterans alike (D. Kaufman & Moss, 2010). It is a major reason that teachers leave the profession during their first years of teaching. Learning effective classroom management strategies will be one of the most important aspects of your teacher preparation program.

Teaching Effectively

Classroom management and instruction are interdependent; it's virtually impossible to have a well-managed classroom without effective instruction and vice versa (Eggen & Kauchak, 2013; Good & Brophy, 2008). If instruction is boring or if students don't understand what they're supposed to be learning and why, the likelihood of having classroom management problems increases dramatically. Your methods courses will help you acquire strategies for involving students in your learning activities and increasing their interest in the topics you're teaching.

Relationships with Students

Your personal relationships with your students are essential. Positive relationships with students affect students' behavior in a number of healthy ways and help to minimize behavior problems (O'Connor, Dearing, & Collins, 2011). Your students need to know that you care about their learning and about them as people, and knowing your students allows you to adjust your instruction to their needs and interests. You can begin establishing personal relationships with your students in several simple ways. For example, learn all your students' names as quickly as possible. We all like the sound of our names and being addressed by name communicates caring. Then, construct a seating chart and use it to call on all your students as equally as possible during lessons. If you miss some students one day, make it a point to call on them the following day. When you observe teachers in the field, notice the striking difference between teachers who know and address students by name and those who don't.

Knowing students' names is important, but it's only a first step. Experienced teachers often begin the school year by having students fill out a questionnaire:

- Describe three important things about yourself as a person.
- What do you want to learn from this class?
- What are your favorite topics?

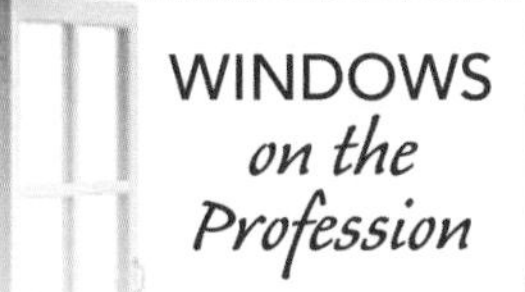

To hear a first-year teacher describe her experiences in her first year, click on the video *Succeeding in Your First Year of Teaching* (7:08).

- How do you like to learn?
- What kinds of learning activities do you enjoy?

More important than the actual questions is the fact that you care enough to ask them. It makes students feel as if you and they are working cooperatively, which is essential for your relationship with them.

In *Teaching and You* at the beginning of this section, we asked about the biggest challenges facing you as a beginning teacher. Any new job requires learning the ropes, but teaching is more challenging than most because of the complexities of classrooms. Placing 25 to 30 young people in one room for an extended period of time presents challenges that don't exist in other occupations. Being well organized, developing an effective classroom management system, teaching effectively, and developing relationships with your students are essential for a successful first year; this is why we call them *survival skills*.

Surviving Your First Day of Teaching

Teaching and You

As a student, what do you typically think about on your first day of a new class? What kinds of things are most important to you at that point in time? What do you want to hear from your instructor?

We all know that first impressions are important, and your very first day of teaching is important because it creates a first impression and sets the tone for the rest of the school year. If you're organized, together, and on top of things, students will notice. The opposite is also true, unfortunately. On your first day of teaching, you will want to start strong out of the gate and communicate to students that you are in charge and know what you're doing.

You can use the survival skills we discussed in the last section as a checklist for your first-day preparations. Get organized. No, get over-organized. Have your room set up to maximize learning. Make sure the desks are arranged so students can enter and exit efficiently and can see you and the board. Decorated bulletin boards and walls send positive subtle messages; this is your room, and it communicates who you are and what you're about.

Spend time the first day explaining your classroom-management system and what you expect from your students. For instance, explaining—and, with young children, even practicing—how they should enter and leave the room, deposit materials, and complete other routine tasks help get you off to a good start.

If you're teaching older students and decide to involve them in formulating classroom rules, begin the process on the first day. This communicates shared responsibility for your classroom and how important classroom rules are to you and your class.

Teach them something the first day; this communicates that your classroom is for learning. For older students, this might consist of providing an overview of your class with a syllabus, or with younger students an actual learning activity. Resist the urge to lecture; design an activity that actively involves each student so they know that you are serious about learning and care about every student, not just the smart ones.

Finally, immediately begin the process of learning your students' names. You might have them fold a piece of paper and write their names on it in large print, so you can then use the name plates to help you call on them by name.

There is no doubt that your first day of class will be anxiety provoking, both for you and your students. Students want to know who you are and what they'll have to do to survive in your class. They also want to know what they'll be learning about. Use student anxiety as a motivational tool; they'll be alert, wanting to know who you are and what to expect from your class. Channel your own anxiety into getting your own act together. Over prepare, and you'll sleep better the night before, and you'll likely survive—and even enjoy—your first day of teaching.

Thriving in Your New School

Thriving in your first year of teaching involves more than just teaching in your own classroom. It also involves collaborating with other teachers and working as part of a team. The help and cooperation you receive from people around you will influence your success and happiness as a beginning teacher.

Teachers often joke that the people really running a school are the secretaries. And they're probably right. If you want to know how things are done and where supplies are hidden, ask a secretary. And as with all of us, they want to feel needed and appreciated. Take the time during your first days on the job to meet the school secretaries, and get to know them as people. Don't just sign in first thing in the morning and run; take a minute to say hello and greet them as human beings. A few moments spent establishing a relationship with them will pay dividends throughout the year.

The same applies with the custodial staff. If they like you, they'll bend over backward to be helpful. They'll let you into your room when you've lost or misplaced your key; they'll come to your room and help when there's a major spill during a science experiment or a student vomits on the floor (oh, the joys of teaching!). As with other support staff, they react well to being treated with dignity and respect. Learn their names, find out about their lives outside of school, and above all, treat them as integral parts of the school team.

The other teachers are a third essential part of your school team and they collectively represent decades of experience, not only teaching but also teaching at that particular school. They can provide invaluable insights about teaching in general as well as how things work at your school. What are the kids like? How about parents? What kind of support can you expect from the principal, and what does it take to make her happy (or at least get her to evaluate you positively and leave you alone—more on that in a moment). You'll quickly find out which teachers are approachable and friendly. Many, knowing that you're a first-year teacher, will introduce themselves and offer advice and assistance early on, and they will generally be supportive of you reaching out for help. Don't be afraid to ask questions. Most experienced teachers remember what it was like to be lost and clueless.

Principals play a unique role on your school's team. In addition to being professional colleagues, they also are responsible for supervising you to ensure that you're doing a good job. They are also very busy people who wear many hats. Their primary responsibility is to ensure that their school operates efficiently and that students are learning. They will expect you to be competent and professional.

This leads us to the topic of teacher evaluation.

Teacher Evaluation

Being evaluated is another fact of professional life. You will be required to pass competency tests before you're licensed, and you will be observed several times during your first year by an immediate supervisor—principal, assistant principal, or another qualified administrator. These observations are an essential part of the evaluation process for teachers, and most states require regular evaluations of all teachers, new and experienced alike (Hightower, 2012).

Teacher evaluation exists in two forms. **Formative evaluation** gathers information and provides feedback that you can use to improve your practice, and **summative evaluation** gathers information about a teacher's competence for decision making about retention and promotion (Ubben et al., 2011). You will encounter both in your first years of teaching.

Evaluation processes vary, so you should check to see how they are handled in your state and district. Typically, they are based on theory and research that examine the relationships between teacher actions and student learning; observation instruments are then created based on the literature. For example, research indicates that effective teachers have well-established classroom routines, use instructional strategies that produce high levels of student involvement, and quickly identify and eliminate sources of disruption (Emmer & Evertson, 2013; Evertson & Emmer, 2013). Observation instruments then have observers assess elements such as:

- Whether classroom routines are in place and used effectively
- The extent to which students are attentive and involved in the lesson
- Whether the teacher can correctly identify sources of misbehavior and deal with them quickly

Observers use a similar process to evaluate skills in other domains. Most states ground their evaluation instruments in principles outlined by professional organizations, such as the Interstate Teacher Assessment and Support Consortium (InTASC). (We discuss the InTASC principles in the next section of the chapter.) The objectives at the beginning of each chapter of this book are linked to these principles.

Before being observed, you should ask to see the instrument that will be used. If you're uncertain about the meaning of any of the categories, ask an administrator or an experienced teacher to explain them. It always helps to know how you'll be evaluated, and knowing this also helps reduce the stress and anxiety that are always there when someone observes your teaching.

Induction and Mentoring Programs

Teaching and You

Where can you go for advice during your first year of teaching? What makes a good mentor? Does gender matter? What about matches with your grade level or content area?

Mrs. Landsdorp is wonderful. She is so supportive, and she is the person I always go to when I want a straight answer about what's really going on in the school and the district. She's also been very helpful in giving suggestions about how to deal with difficult parents and how I should handle myself in situations where I'm uncertain. She hasn't helped me a whole lot with nitty-gritty stuff, like planning lessons or watching me teach, but that's not her fault. She has a full teaching load, too, so she really doesn't have time. I guess what it really amounts to is that she's been a real source of emotional support, and this year is going better than I could have hoped for.

(Shelley, first-year third-grade teacher, talking about her mentor)

Mentoring and induction programs can provide you with helpful advice and support.

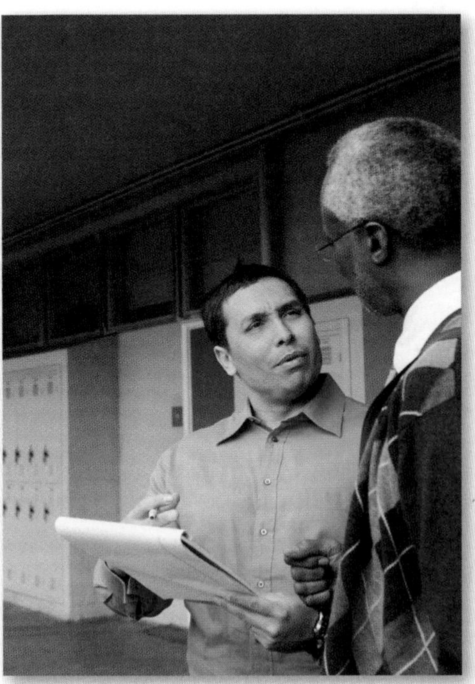

The transition to teaching is rarely as smooth as Shelley experienced. Teachers are sometimes hired at the last moment, left isolated in their classrooms, and given little help—the sink-or-swim experience of many beginning teachers. As you saw earlier in the chapter, more than a third of new teachers leave the profession by the end of their third year, and half have left within the first 5 years (Kaiser, 2011). Isolation and lack of support are major reasons for this attrition.

The stress of the first year is greatly reduced, however, if you have someone to turn to for help, and you saw how important this was for Shelley. Beginning teachers without mentors and support are twice as likely to leave as those with programs designed to help them make the transition from their teacher preparation programs to their first jobs (Kaiser, 2011).

To address this problem, many schools offer induction and mentoring programs for new teachers. **Induction programs** are professional experiences designed to help beginning teachers make the transition into teaching. These programs include structured staff development activities, such as workshops that focus on problems that first-year teachers commonly encounter; systematic efforts to provide new teachers with crucial information; and **mentors**, experienced teachers who provide guidance and support for beginning teachers. Ideally, mentors are sources of both emotional support, as Shelley reported, and technical support in planning and conducting lessons and assessing student learning. The most effective mentors match a new teacher's specific teaching assignment, so they can provide information that is both grade-level and content-area specific (Moir, 2008/2009). Effective induction and mentoring programs also significantly reduce the failure rate for beginning teachers, and they include the following elements (Ingersoll & Strong, 2011):

- A systematic attempt to provide beginning teachers with opportunities to observe and talk to experienced teachers
- Help with preparing their classes
- Feedback based on classroom observation
- Special help in linking their instruction to state and district standards
- Support with everyday problems and the process of developing a reflective professional attitude
- Professional-development activities designed to increase mentors' effectiveness
- Compensation and released time for mentors

Actual classroom observations with feedback are essential; beginning teachers provided with this help significantly improve in organizing and managing instruction, and their students are better behaved and more engaged during lessons (Strong, 2009).

Many beginning teachers, however, don't participate in anything more than perfunctory school orientations, and many mentoring programs are like Shelley's; they provide emotional support but little specific help in the process of learning to teach. Time and funding are the major reasons. In many cases, mentors also teach full time, so they have little extra time to help beginning teachers. Many mentoring programs don't compensate mentors, either financially or with release time; and with nationwide cutbacks in education, increased funding for mentoring programs is unlikely. So, at best you can probably expect a mentor who is emotionally supportive and who will offer some general suggestions. If your school has a well-designed mentoring program, you will be one of the lucky ones, and, if you have options, it should be an important factor in your decision about which position to accept.

In *Teaching and You* at the beginning of this section, we asked what makes a good mentor? Someone you can trust as a colleague and someone who will take the time to help you is the answer. Being similar in age, gender, and background are less important than their willingness to share of themselves and provide help and advice when you need it. Like finding a partner in life, there are no magical formulas, because if there were, people wouldn't spend all the time and energy in the dating scene trying to find the ideal mate. Don't be afraid to ask other teachers if you have questions; you'll soon find out who you can trust, not only for their answers, but also for their support.

EXPLORING DIVERSITY: Preparing to Teach Every Student

Diversity has always been a challenge for beginning teachers, and the challenge becomes even greater as our classrooms become more diverse. The 2010 census, for example, revealed that over 50% of the newborn infants in our country were members of cultural minorities (Tavernise, 2012b). This trend is especially pronounced in urban centers and fast-growing states such as California, Florida, and Georgia, and this trend is projected to increase across the country. In the 20 largest cities in our country, students of color make up 80% of the student population

(Macionis & Parrillo, 2010). You will, without question, work with these students when you begin teaching.

Concern over these changing demographics has resulted in efforts to recruit more teachers who are members of cultural minorities (Villegas & Davis, 2008), and Arne Duncan, the Secretary of Education in the Obama administration, made the recruitment of teachers of color a national priority.

These teachers (and you might be one of them) bring several potential assets. Students need role models who share their cultural backgrounds, and minority role models may increase minority learner motivation more effectively because students can identify more closely with them (Schunk, Pintrich, & Meese, 2008). Minority teachers can also provide culturally relevant instruction by helping bridge differences between schools and minority students' homes and cultures. Also, they can enrich a school's faculty by providing additional perspectives on effective teaching and learning practices for minority students (Villegas & Davis, 2008).

So where does this leave you as a beginning teacher? If you're not a member of a cultural minority, or if you are not a member of the same minority as your students, does it mean that you can't effectively teach minority students? Of course not; many white teachers do an excellent job of helping minority students learn and develop. But how exactly do they do this, and how can you learn to do the same?

Experts suggest a three-pronged approach to the problem (Sleeter, 2008). First, learn about your students, including the homes and communities in which they live. Talk to your students, and make a special effort to connect with them in nonclassroom settings such as lunchrooms, playgrounds, and after-school programs. Make a special effort to reach out to parents and other caregivers. This begins with back-to-school night but can also include more active outreach efforts such as spending time in the community and perhaps even home visits.

A second way to learn about the different cultures your students will bring to your classroom is through formal course work and readings. While not as direct as hands-on experience, books and articles can provide insights into the experiences of your students.

Clinical experiences in schools that serve students of color are a third and perhaps most effective way to learn about these students. If at all possible, try to arrange at least some of your classroom observations and clinical experiences in these schools. Here you can observe directly what works and doesn't work with these students. In addition, these classroom experiences also allow you to personalize this information and answer the question, "How do I want to teach when I have my own classroom?"

As you work in these classrooms, talk to the teachers about what they're doing and why. Both minority and nonminority teachers can provide valuable insights into effective teaching practices for cultural minority students.

A major question you'll need to answer is whether you need to teach in fundamentally different ways to meet the needs of minority students. Research suggests no; the same basic strategies and approaches that work with other students also work with students of color (Good & Brophy, 2008). However, research also suggests that you might have to use different motivation strategies, manage your classroom differently, and even adjust your instructional strategies to maximize learning (Emmer & Evertson, 2013; Evertson & Emmer, 2013; Schunk et al., 2008). For example, using examples from your students' own backgrounds and relating content to the experiences they've encountered in their lives can significantly increase motivation. From a management perspective, you might need to be more structured and explicit in your expectations for classroom behavior. And from an instructional perspective, actively involving students is even more important when working with members of cultural minorities. Realistically, the only way to know about these adjustments is by seeing them in action and trying them out in your own classroom.

DIVERSITY AND YOU

What Does It Take to Be Effective with All Students?

You're ecstatic! You've just been offered a contract to teach in a large urban district. Jobs are hard to find, and you think you'll like living in a large city. But after the initial euphoria, reality sets in. How are you going to prepare for the challenge of teaching in a school where the majority of your students will be members of cultural minorities? To compound the problem, you are not a minority, and you went to schools where cultural minorities were, well, minorities, comprising only a small percentage of the student population.

Over the summer you work on the problem. You talk to a friend who is in his third year of teaching in an urban school. During the week-long orientation for new teachers, you talk with other new teachers, both minority and nonminority, about their expectations for the school year. During your first month on the job, you talk to some of the veterans in the school. Here's what they tell you.

One teacher, a 20-year veteran at your school, has this advice, "Don't do anything differently. What works with most students will work with the students here. Organize your content, and teach it to them clearly. Use clear lectures and outlines to make sure they understand ideas. Tell them from the first day that you expect them all to learn, and then teach them like you mean it. You won't reach everybody, but you'll reach those who came to learn."

Another teacher, in his second year of teaching at that school, emphasizes different learning styles. "These kids are different, and they learn differently. You have to adjust your teaching to their different learning styles. I do a lot of cooperative learning, role playing, and independent projects that allow them to explore topics they're interested in."

When you ask him how he keeps track of each student's learning progress, he replies, "I don't. If they're excited about learning and are actively involved, the learning takes care of itself."

A third teacher recommends talking to and observing expert teachers in the school who are members of cultural minorities. "Find out what they do, and then use them as models. Do the same in your classroom. If it works for them, it'll work for you."

QUESTIONS TO CONSIDER

1. How do you reconcile the differing opinions of the first two teachers? Will you need to drastically alter how you teach when you work with cultural minority students?
2. Should teachers who are not minorities imitate or try to act more like their counterparts who are members of cultural minorities? What are the advantages and disadvantages of the approach?

Go to *Diversity and You* in the MyEducationLab™ *Book Resources* that accompany this text to log your thoughts and receive feedback from your authors.

Check Your Understanding

2.1 What are the three stages of teacher development?
2.2 Identify four factors that contribute to a successful first year of teaching.
2.3 What steps can you take to ensure that your first day of teaching is successful?
2.4 What else can first-year teachers do to survive and thrive in their new schools?
2.5 How are teacher evaluation systems created and used?
2.6 What are the characteristics of successful induction programs?

For feedback, go to the appendix, *Check Your Understanding*, located in the back of this text.

Career-Long Professional Development

We have discussed finding your first job and how to succeed in your first year of teaching. Now is also the time to begin thinking about your career 3 to 5 or more years down the road, because long-term professional goals can guide you during your teacher preparation program. In this section, we examine three aspects of career-long professional development:

- The **Interstate Teacher Assessment and Support Consortium (InTASC)**
- Membership in professional organizations
- Attaining certification through the National Board for Professional Teaching Standards

InTASC: A Beginning Point for Professional Development

A rapidly expanding body of research consistently demonstrates that teaching now requires professionals who are highly knowledgeable and skilled (Darling-Hammond, 2008), and the profession is responding. Created in 1987, InTASC was designed to help states develop better teachers through coordinated efforts to increase support for new teachers and create improved teacher-evaluation systems. InTASC has raised the bar by setting rigorous standards for all teachers in important areas such as planning, instruction, and assessment. "These standards. . . describe what effective teaching that leads to improved achievement looks like." (InTASC, 2011, p. 3) They also describe what you should know and be able to do when you first walk into a classroom, and they provide a concrete starting point for your own professional development.

To date, InTASC has prepared general, or "core," standards organized around 10 principles (see Table 13.5) and is preparing standards for various subject-matter areas and specific student populations. InTASC is also developing a Test for Teaching Knowledge (TTK) linked to the core principles. The learning

TABLE 13.5 InTASC Core Teaching Standards

Standard	Description
The Learner and Learning	
Standard #1: Learner Development	The teacher understands how learners grow and develop, recognizing that patterns of learning and development vary individually within and across the cognitive, linguistic, social, emotional, and physical areas, and designs and implements developmentally appropriate and challenging learning experiences.
Standard #2: Learning Differences	The teacher uses understanding of individual differences and diverse cultures and communities to ensure inclusive learning environments that enable each learner to meet high standards.
Standard #3: Learning Environments	The teacher works with others to create environments that support individual and collaborative learning, and that encourage positive social interaction, active engagement in learning, and self-motivation.
Content	
Standard #4: Content Knowledge	The teacher understands the central concepts, tools of inquiry, and structures of the discipline(s) he or she teaches and creates learning experiences that make the discipline accessible and meaningful for learners to assure mastery of the content.
Standard #5: Application of Content	The teacher understands how to connect concepts and use differing perspectives to engage learners in critical thinking, creativity, and collaborative problem solving related to authentic local and global issues.
Instructional Practice	
Standard #6: Assessment	The teacher understands and uses multiple methods of assessment to engage learners in their own growth, to monitor learner progress, and to guide the teacher's and learner's decision making.
Standard #7: Planning for Instruction	The teacher plans instruction that supports every student in meeting rigorous learning goals by drawing upon knowledge of content areas, curriculum, cross-disciplinary skills, and pedagogy, as well as knowledge of learners and the community context.
Standard #8: Instructional Strategies	The teacher understands and uses a variety of instructional strategies to encourage learners to develop deep understanding of content areas and their connections, and to build skills to apply knowledge in meaningful ways.
Professional Responsibility	
Standard #9: Professional Learning and Ethical Practice	The teacher engages in ongoing professional learning and uses evidence to continually evaluate his/her practice, particularly the effects of his/her choices and actions on others (learners, families, other professionals, and the community), and adapts practice to meet the needs of each learner.
Standard #10: Leadership and Collaboration	The teacher seeks appropriate leadership roles and opportunities to take responsibility for student learning, to collaborate with learners, families, colleagues, other school professionals, and community members to ensure learner growth, and to advance the profession.

Source: Interstate Teacher Assessment and Support Consortium. (2011). *InTASC model core teaching standards: A resource for state dialogue.* Washington, DC: Council of Chief State School Officers. Reprinted by permission.

outcomes at the beginning of each chapter in this book are keyed to InTASC standards. In addition, each of the Online Portfolio Activities found at the end of the chapters is linked to the InTASC core standards.

The InTASC standards are demanding, but they should be. If you expect to be treated as a professional, you should have the knowledge and skills that allow you to make the decisions expected of a professional. Being able to meet the InTASC standards is a good beginning.

Membership in Professional Organizations

Teaching and You

How will you keep current and up-to-date on recent changes in the profession after you graduate? What avenues exist for you to read up on changes and trends in education?

Involvement in the professional organizations in education is one of the first steps you can take to promote your professional growth. These organizations support a variety of activities designed to improve teaching and schools:

- Providing professional-development activities for teachers
- Disseminating up-to-date research and information on trends in the profession through professional publications
- Providing resources teachers can use to find answers to questions about professional issues and problems
- Holding yearly conferences that present research examining recent professional advances
- Providing politicians and policy makers with information about important issues facing education

Table 13.6 presents a list of major professional organizations, their websites, and descriptions of their missions and goals. We recommend that you join a professional organization as an integral part of your professional growth; many organizations have student memberships that allow you to become involved while still in school.

The **National Education Association (NEA)** and the **American Federation of Teachers (AFT)** are the two largest professional organizations in education. Founded in 1857, the NEA is the largest, enrolling approximately two thirds of the teachers in this country (National Education Association, 2011). Most (78%) of its members are teachers, but guidance counselors, librarians, and administrators also join. The AFT was founded in 1916 and has more than 1.3 million members who primarily teach in urban areas (American Federation of Teachers, 2011). The AFT doesn't allow administrators to join and is noted for its emphasis on better pay and better working conditions. You are likely to encounter representatives from one or both of these organizations in your first year on the job. Experienced teachers in your school will be able to give you information about the pros and cons of each.

TECHNOLOGY and TEACHING: Using Technology for Your Professional Development

Staying current as a professional will become increasingly important in this rapidly changing educational landscape. In the past, professional development looked like this:

Teachers, who have been on their feet all day, enter the classroom (usually one of their own), sit in desks designed for second graders, and listen to a speaker drone on about a topic that some already know about and others don't care. The presenter spends a considerable amount of time talking, because no one has read about the topic. At the end of the workshop, the presenter encourages everyone to apply the information they learned

TABLE 13.6 Professional Organizations for Educators

Organization and Website	Organization Mission or Goal
American Council on the Teaching of Foreign Languages http://www.actfl.org	To promote and foster the study of languages and cultures as an integral component of American education and society
American Federation of Teachers http://www.aft.org	To improve the lives of our members and their families, to give voice to their legitimate professional, economic, and social aspirations
Association for Supervision and Curriculum Development http://www.ascd.org	To enhance all aspects of effective teaching and learning, including professional development, educational leadership, and capacity building
Council for Exceptional Children http://www.cec.sped.org	To improve educational outcomes for individuals with exceptionalities, students with disabilities, and/or the gifted
International Reading Association http://www.reading.org	To promote high levels of literary for all by improving reading instruction, disseminating research and information about reading, and encouraging the life time reading habit
Music Teachers National Association http://www.mtna.org/flash.html	To advance the value of music study and music making to society and to support the professionalism of music teachers
National Art Education Association http://www.naea-reston.org	To promote art education through professional development, service, advancement of knowledge and relationship
National Association for the Education of Young Children http://www.naeyc.org	To promote excellence in early childhood education
National Education Association http://www.nea.org	To fulfill the promise of a democratic society, NEA shall promote the cause of quality public education and advance the profession of education
National Science Teachers Association http://www.nsta.org	To promote excellence and innovation in science teaching and learning for all
National Council for the Social Studies http://www.ncss.org	To provide leadership, service, and support for all social studies educators
National Council of Teachers of English http://www.ncte.org	To promote the development of literacy, the use of language to construct personal and public worlds and to achieve full participation in society, through the learning and teaching of English and the related arts and sciences of language
National Council of Teachers of Mathematics http://www.nctm.org	To provide broad national leadership in matters related to mathematics education
National Association for Bilingual Education http://www.nabe.org	To recognize, promote, and publicize bilingual education
Phi Delta Kappa http://www. pdkintl.org	To promote quality education as essential to the development and maintenance of a democratic way of life by providing innovative programs, relevant research, visionary leadership, and dedicated service
Teachers of English to Speakers of Other Languages http://www.tesol.org	To improve the teaching of English as a second language by promoting research, disseminating information, developing guidelines and promoting certification, and serving as a clearinghouse for the field

in their own classrooms. Some will, and some won't. Participants drive home tired after the workshop and think about what they'll need to do to fix dinner that night. They're tired and hungry.

But professional development has changed, and technology is the key to this change.

During the summer break, the professional-development team gives teachers a relevant and topical book to read. For some, the book is on hard copy; for others, it's on their e-readers or tablets, making it easy to read while they have a break from their summer family or job responsibilities. As they read, they are encouraged to share their thoughts with other teachers in an online discussion forum. After they return in the fall, a follow-up meeting addresses questions and concerns teachers raised on the Internet. As teachers return to their classrooms, the online discussion format allows them to share their successes and frustrations in trying to implement the reform in their classrooms.

Professional development attempts to give teachers the tools they need to improve their teaching. It has received increased attention as educational reformers realize that the key to improving education is to improve our teachers. But in the past, professional development was almost a dirty word for many teachers, characterized by workshops that were top–down, trendy, and failed to meet the actual learning needs of teachers who were at different points on the learning continuum in terms of the topic. Some needed and wanted it, while others already knew about the topic or didn't think it applied to their own unique teaching situation. Elementary teachers were thrown in with high school teachers, and math and science with art and music. Sometimes these professional development sessions worked; often they didn't.

Technology has changed that by addressing many of the concerns raised by teachers about ineffective professional-development activities (Sawchuk, 2010b). Technology has given professional-development organizers the tools to customize topics to the specific learning needs of teachers and to provide mechanisms for teachers to ask questions, raise concerns, and also share successes as they implement changes in their classrooms, the bottom line for any professional development activity.

Perhaps the most important technological change has allowed the creation of online **professional learning communities**, groups of teachers who periodically meet online to discuss and improve their teaching (Flanigan, 2011). The Internet provides a mechanism in which teachers can learn about new ideas, see them actually being used in the classrooms of other teachers via videotapes, and raise questions and concerns, not only with their counterparts in the same school or district, but also with teachers across the country. When teachers do meet face to face with other teachers, they have opportunities to discuss how the reform fits with their own unique teaching situations and students.

Experts call this blended mix of technology and face-to-face formats "hybrid" learning, because it combines the best of both face-to-face and technologically enhanced clubs, where teachers interact on the Internet, watch clips of master teachers demonstrating effective instructional strategies in video libraries, and augment these with face-to-face meetings. Researchers have found that these face-to-face meetings can still be effective as motivational tools and vehicles for teachers to share their own thoughts and experiences (Davis, 2011).

When you begin your teaching career, you will probably encounter these hybrid professional development activities in your own district. If you'd like to see what they look like now, several of them, such as Edmodo (www.edmodo.com) and Edutopia (www.edutopia.org) are available free to both teachers and their students. Teachers can access these sites and join in on professional conversations about teaching (Davis, 2011). Twitter and Facebook have also added teacher-networking sites. In addition, Edmodo provides a mechanism for teachers to link their students into online discussions with other students around the country about the topics they are studying. For example, a world civilizations website asks students to vote for the most important contribution of ancient Greek society along with its most influential figure (e.g., Alexander the Great vs. Socrates).

Technology has also affected another important dimension of professional knowledge—the content knowledge we need to accurately teach different topics. In the past, teachers had to scramble to find up-to-date information on the topics they were teaching. Trips to the library often resulted in armloads of books that teachers consulted as they planned for the next-week's lessons. Often sources were dated or unavailable. The Internet has changed all that. Search engines such as Google, Bing, and Yahoo! Search now provide a multitude of resources for teacher planning.

What are the implications of all this for you as a beginning teacher? Take the time to familiarize yourself with these teacher-networking sites, and use them to learn more about the topics you're studying in class. Confused about the national common core standards and how they'll influence your teaching? Check out www.corestandards.org/the-standards. Talk to the experienced teachers you work with, and find out which sites they like and why. A world of professional growth is literally at your fingertips.

Action Research

Understanding and critically examining research is one effective way for you to develop professionally; another is for you to conduct research in your own classrooms. **Action research** is a form of applied research designed to answer a specific school- or classroom-related question (A. Johnson, 2012; Mills, 2011). The primary goals for action research are to encourage you to become more reflective about your work and ultimately to improve your own teaching. In a sense, all expert teachers are action researchers, because they're continually examining their teaching effectiveness and seeking ways to improve. Action research formalizes and provides structure for the process.

Conducting action research typically occurs in four steps:

1. Identify a problem.
2. Plan and conduct a research study.
3. Implement the findings.
4. Use the results to generate additional research.

Let's see how Tyra Forcine, an eighth-grade English teacher, implements these steps in her classroom.

Tyra and a group of her colleagues are discussing the problems they are having with homework. Kim Brown complains that her students often "blow off assignments," and Bill McClendon reports he has so much trouble getting his students to do homework that he has stopped assigning it.

"I've heard teachers say that homework doesn't help that much in terms of learning, anyway," Selena Cross adds.

"That doesn't make sense to me," Tyra counters, shaking her head. "It has to help. The more kids work on something, the better they have to get at it."

Tyra consistently gives her students homework and checks to see if they have done it, but because of the conversation, she decides to take a more systematic look at its effects. She can't find a satisfactory answer on the Internet or in any of her college textbooks, so she decides to find out for herself.

Beginning her study at the start of the third grading period, Tyra collects homework every day and gives students 2 points for having done it fully, 1 point for partial completion, and 0 points for minimal effort or not turning it in. Each day, she discusses some of the most troublesome items on the homework. On Fridays, she quizzes students on the content covered Monday through Thursday, and she also gives a midterm test and a final exam. She then tries to see if a relationship exists between students' homework averages and their performance on the quizzes and tests.

At the end of the grading period, each student has a homework score, a quiz average, and an average on the two tests. Tyra calls the district office to ask for help in summarizing the information, and together they find a positive but fairly low correlation between homework and test averages.

"Why isn't the correlation higher?" she wonders in another lounge conversation, as she informally shares her results with other teachers.

"Well," Kim responds. "You're only giving the kids a 2, 1, or 0 on the homework—you're still not actually grading it. So I suspect that some of the kids are simply doing the work to finish it, and they aren't really thinking about it."

"On the other hand," Bill acknowledges, "homework and tests are correlated, so maybe I'd better rethink my stand on no homework. . . . Maybe I'll change what I do next grading period."

"Good points," Tyra responds. "I'm going to keep on giving homework, but I think I need to change what I'm doing, too. . . . It's going to be a ton of work, but I'm going to do two things. . . . I'm going to repeat my study next grading period to see if I get similar results, and then, starting in the fall, I'm going to redesign my homework, so it's easier to grade. I'll grade every assignment, and we'll see if the correlation goes up."

"Great idea," Kim replies. "If the kids see how important it is for their learning, maybe they'll take their homework more seriously, and some of the not-doing-it problem will also get better. . . . I'm going to look at that in the fall."

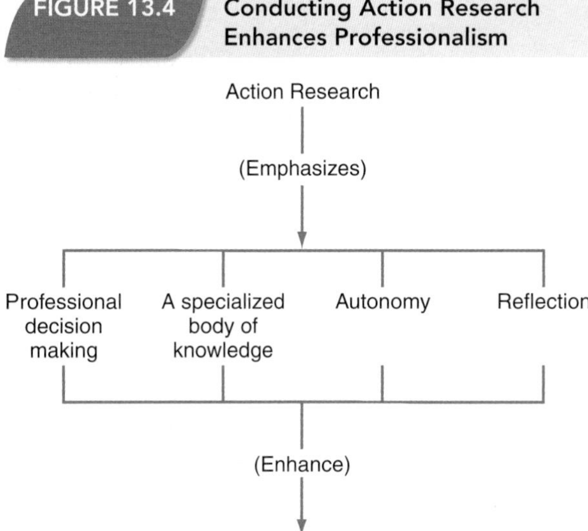

Let's see how Tyra applied the four action research steps in her classroom. First, she identified a problem central to her teaching: To what extent does homework contribute to my students' performance on quizzes and tests? This personalized approach increases teachers' motivation to do action research, because it answers questions that are important to them.

Second, she systematically designed and conducted her study, and third, Tyra and her colleagues immediately implemented the results of her project. Bill, for example, planned to give homework during the next grading period. Action research is rewarding because it addresses issues and problems that teachers really care about.

Finally, like most research, Tyra's project led to reflection about her teaching and to further experimentation in her classroom. She planned another study to see if scoring the homework more carefully would increase the correlation between homework and tests, and Kim planned to investigate the question of whether more careful scoring would lead to students' more conscientiously doing their homework.

In addition to answering questions about real classroom issues, conducting action research increases teachers' feelings of professionalism (see Figure 13.4). Contributing to a body of knowledge and making decisions based on research can help you grow both personally and professionally. Engaging in action research projects can also contribute to teachers' perceptions of their own autonomy and efficacy; as teachers investigate their own teaching, they become more aware of their own control of their teaching and their ability to change things to make their own classrooms more productive.

Attaining Certification: The National Board for Professional Teaching Standards

Licensure is the process states use to ensure that teachers meet professional standards. In comparison, **certification** is special recognition by a professional organization indicating that an individual has met rigorous requirements specified by the organization.

The **National Board for Professional Teaching Standards (NBPTS)** is one important form of certification. Created in 1987 as an outgrowth of the Carnegie Forum report *A Nation Prepared: Teachers for the 21st Century* (Carnegie Forum on Education and the Economy, 1986), the board is composed mostly of P–12 teachers but also of union and business leaders and university faculty (National Board for Professional Teaching Standards, 2011a). NBPTS seeks to strengthen teaching as a profession and raise the quality of education by recognizing the contributions of exemplary teachers, compensating them financially, giving them increased responsibility, and increasing their role in decision making.

National Board certification is based on standards that grew out of the board's policy statement, *What Teachers Should Know and Be Able to Do*

(National Board for Professional Teaching Standards, 2011b). The NBPTS summarized the professional standards contained in this report into five core propositions that describe professional teacher competencies; these propositions and how they play out in practice are outlined in Table 13.7.

National Board certification has five important elements:

- It is designed for experienced teachers. Applicants must have graduated from an accredited college or university and must have taught at least 3 years.
- Applying for National Board certification is strictly voluntary and independent of any state's licensure. The certification is intended to indicate a high level of skill and professionalism.
- National Board certification requires that teachers pass content exams in their area of specialty, such as math, science, early childhood, or physical education and health.
- Additional evidence, such as videotapes of teaching and a personal portfolio, is used in the assessment process.
- The primary control of the NBPTS is in the hands of practicing teachers, which increases the professionalism of teaching.

Because certification by the NBPTS is for veterans, you may be wondering why we provide information about it at this early point in your teacher

TABLE 13.7 Propositions of the National Board for Professional Teaching Standards

Proposition	Description
1. Teachers are committed to students and their learning.	• Accomplished teachers believe that all students can learn, and they treat students equitably. • Accomplished teachers understand how students develop, and they use accepted learning theory as the basis for their teaching. • Accomplished teachers are aware of the influence of context and culture on behavior, and they foster students' self-esteem, motivation, and character.
2. Teachers know the subjects they teach and how to teach those subjects to students.	• Accomplished teachers have a rich understanding of the subject(s) they teach, and they appreciate how knowledge in their subject is linked to other disciplines and applied to real-world settings. • Accomplished teachers know how to make subject matter understandable to students, and they are able to modify their instruction when difficulties arise. • Accomplished teachers demonstrate critical and analytic capacities in their teaching, and they develop those capacities in their students.
3. Teachers are responsible for managing and monitoring student learning.	• Accomplished teachers capture and sustain the interest of their students and use their time effectively. • Accomplished teachers are able to use a variety of effective instructional techniques, and they use the techniques appropriately. • Accomplished teachers can use multiple methods to assess the progress of students, and they effectively communicate this progress to parents.
4. Teachers think systematically about their practice and learn from experience.	• Accomplished teachers are models for intellectual curiosity, and they display virtues—honesty, fairness, and respect for diversity—that they seek to inspire in their students. • Accomplished teachers use their understanding of students, learning, and instruction to make principled judgments about sound practice, and they are lifelong learners. • Accomplished teachers critically examine their practice, and they seek continual professional growth.
5. Teachers are members of learning communities.	• Accomplished teachers contribute to the effectiveness of the school, and they work collaboratively with their colleagues. • Accomplished teachers evaluate school progress, and they utilize community resources. • Accomplished teachers work collaboratively with parents, and they involve parents in school activities.

Source: Reprinted with permission from the National Board for Professional Teaching Standards. *What Teachers Should Know and Be Able to Do*, 2011.

preparation program. We're giving you the information now for three important reasons: First, professionalism is a theme of this book, and the NBPTS is a national effort to professionalize teaching. The propositions in Table 13.7 describe the different kinds of professional knowledge emphasized. The NBPTS recognizes that increasing professionalism requires teachers who are both highly knowledgeable and skilled in their areas of specialization.

Second, National Board certification can be a long-term career goal with financial incentives. As of 2011, 42 states and nearly 200 school districts spent millions of additional dollars to reward teachers who successfully completed the process, and more than 91,000 teachers were board certified (Honawar, 2008; NBPTS, 2011). Currently, 24 states provide monetary rewards for board-certified teachers (Hightower, 2012).

Finally, some evidence indicates that National Board certification makes a difference in teacher quality. One study comparing teachers who had completed the process to non-board-certified teachers found that the board-certified teachers scored higher on nearly all measures of teaching expertise (Hakel, Koenig, & Elliott, 2008). Other studies, however, have failed to find consistent achievement differences for students taught by National Board–certified teachers (Dilworth, 2011). But the certification process does seem to encourage teachers to become more reflective about their work and their relationships with other professionals (Park, Oliver, Johnson, Graham, & Oppong, 2007). National Board certification is something for you to keep in mind as you move into your career.

Earlier we asked in *Teaching and You* how you could keep up-to-date on changes in education after you graduate. Professional organizations can provide you with current information about recent trends in education through their publications and workshops. Hopefully you'll be in education for the long haul, and a lot of changes will occur over the years. Professional organizations provide one effective way to stay current.

Check Your Understanding

3.1 What is InTASC? How has it influenced teacher preparation?

3.2 Describe two career-long professional-development opportunities available to you as a teacher.

3.3 What are five activities professional organizations support that are designed to improve teaching and schools?

For feedback, go to the appendix, *Check Your Understanding*, located in the back of this text.

VOICES from the CLASSROOM

"Every day my kids bring so much to the table and it inspires me. Their curious, open minds that love teachable moments, their perseverance in some of the toughest situations really make me appreciate what I get to experience with them every day. Every day is an exciting new journey with them. Not to mention they are hilarious to be with; they are so much fun and entertaining."

GLORIA NOYES, 2009 Teacher of the Year, Maine

CHAPTER 13 Summary

1. Describe the beliefs of beginning teachers, and identify factors involved in finding a desirable job.
   - Beginning teachers are idealistic and optimistic. They generally believe that they will be more effective than teachers now in the field. They also expect to become more confident about their ability to promote learning as they acquire experience. Unfortunately, the opposite often occurs. Beginning teachers tend to believe that they'll learn most of what they need to know to be an effective teacher from their experiences in classrooms. They also think that the key to finding a job is to get good grades in professional classes, which is just a start in the process. Finally, beginning teachers believe that the key to effective teaching is to thoroughly understand the content they are teaching. The beliefs of beginning teachers are often naive and frequently run counter to research about good teaching. Understanding these beliefs can help beginning teachers avoid potential pitfalls.
   - Making yourself marketable requires developing a professional reputation, broadening your professional experiences, building a portfolio and a résumé, creating a credentials file, and writing a successful letter of application. The sooner you begin this process, the better equipped you will be to find a job when you graduate.
   - Finding a first teaching job requires knowing where teaching jobs are available, interviewing effectively, and finding a school that will encourage professional growth.
2. Identify factors that contribute to a successful first year of teaching.
   - Teachers often proceed through three stages as they develop as professionals. In the first stage, survival is uppermost on teachers' minds; during the second, teachers develop instructional and management skills; and in the third stage, teachers continue to develop expertise and begin to focus on student learning and development.
   - Survival skills for your first year of teaching include getting organized, developing effective management and instructional strategies, and getting to know your students.
   - Surviving your first day of teaching involves conscientiously applying these survival skills in the classroom.
   - Surviving and thriving in your new school requires that you establish professional relationships with the people in your school who help make it run.
   - Evaluation is also a part of every beginning teacher's experience. Formative evaluation is designed to provide helpful feedback to teachers; summative evaluation is designed to ensure adequate performance by teachers. Research-based and standards-based teacher evaluations are two approaches that schools commonly use throughout the United States.
   - Induction and mentoring programs can help you make the transition from being a student to being an effective teacher. The best mentoring programs provide systematic help for beginning teachers, help teachers link their instruction to state and district standards, provide teachers with support in dealing with everyday problems, encourage teachers to develop a reflective professional attitude, and provide feedback based on classroom observation.
3. Describe career-long professional-development opportunities available to teachers.
   - InTASC, the Interstate Teacher Assessment and Support Consortium, was designed to help states develop better teachers. It outlines 10 basic principles that guide you as you become a new teacher.
   - Professional organizations provide a variety of services for you throughout your career. These include publications detailing current research, professional-development activities, annual conferences, and resources for teachers' questions and concerns.
   - To professionalize teaching, the National Board for Professional Teaching Standards (NBPTS) has established rigorous standards and assessments for teachers who have completed at least 3 years of successful service. Substantial financial rewards are available in many states for teachers who have completed national board certification.

Important Concepts

action research
alternative licensure
American Federation of Teachers (AFT)
certification
credentials file
digital portfolio
formative evaluation
induction programs
Interstate Teacher Assessment and Support Consortium (InTASC)
licensure
mentors
National Board for Professional Teaching Standards (NBPTS)
National Education Association (NEA)
professional development
professional learning communities
professional portfolio
résumé
summative evaluation
Teach for America

Portfolio Activity

Professional Organizations

InTASC Core Teaching Standards 9: Professional Learning and Ethical Practice

The purpose of this activity is to acquaint you with the resources that professional organizations provide. From Table 13.6, select an organization that interests you. Locate the organization's website, and explore the different services described there. Find out the membership costs and benefits. Report your findings in a one- or two-page summary.

Portfolio Activities similar to this one and related to chapter content can be found at MyEducationLab™.

Developing as a Professional

Go to the topic *Professional Development* in the MyEducationLab (www.myeducationlab.com) for *Introduction to Teaching*, where you can:

- Find learning outcomes for *Professional Development,* along with the national standards that connect to these outcomes.
- Complete *Assignments and Activities* that can help you more deeply understand the chapter content.
- Apply and practice your understanding of the core teaching skills identified in the chapter with the *Building Teaching Skills and Dispositions* learning units.
- Access video clips of CCSSO National Teachers of the Year award winners responding to the question, "Why Do I Teach?" in the *Teacher Talk* section.
- Check your comprehension on the content covered in the chapter with the *Study Plan.* Here you will be able to take a chapter quiz, receive feedback on your answers, and then access *Review, Practice, and Enrichment* activities to enhance your understanding of chapter content.
- Check the *Book Resources* to find opportunities to share thoughts and gather feedback on the *Diversity and You* and *Issues You'll Face in Teaching* features found in this chapter.

MyEducationLab™

APPENDIX

Check Your Understanding

1 Do I Want to Be a Teacher?

1.1. Identify the four most commonly cited reasons people give for entering teaching.

Results from a national poll, as well as our own informal surveys, indicate that wanting to work with young people and wanting to contribute to society are the two major reasons that people go into teaching. Our results showed that opportunities for personal growth and learning more about a content area were also important.

1.2. What are the major rewards in teaching?

The major rewards in teaching can be divided into two main categories, intrinsic and extrinsic. Important intrinsic benefits include emotional rewards, such as getting to know students on a personal level and helping young people grow and develop, and the intellectual rewards of learning new content and playing with ideas.

Extrinsic rewards include job security, frequent vacations, convenient work schedules, and the relatively high occupational status of teaching.

1.3. What are the major challenges in teaching?

The major challenges in teaching include the complexities of classrooms, which make professional decision making so difficult, and the multiple roles that teachers perform.

The first challenge—the complexity of classrooms—is described by five interrelated characteristics of teaching: It is (1) multidimensional and (2) simultaneous, meaning a number of things are going on in classrooms at the same time; (3) classroom events are pressing, requiring immediate attention from the teacher; (4) classroom events are unpredictable; and (5) finally, classrooms are public, making a teacher's decisions visible to students and even to parents and other professionals.

A second challenge facing teachers is the multiple roles they perform: Teachers are expected to create productive learning environments, work as partners with parents and caregivers, and collaborate with colleagues.

1.4. How do experienced and beginning teachers feel about the rewards and challenges of teaching? What are the implications of these findings for you as a beginning teacher?

Both experienced and new teachers feel confident about their abilities to teach and produce positive changes in their students. In addition, most feel satisfied with the career choice they made to become teachers.

We believe the two findings—high feelings of competence and positive career satisfaction—are linked. When teachers feel good about the job they are doing with students, they also feel good about their choice of a career.

So, not surprisingly, being good at teaching and being happy with a teaching career are linked. This suggests that you should make every effort to take advantage of opportunities to learn about good teaching before you enter the classroom. The knowledge and skills you gain will help you and your students.

2.1. What are the essential characteristics of professionalism?

A specialized body of knowledge that sets the professional apart from the lay public is perhaps the most important characteristic of professionalism. Autonomy, which provides the freedom to make important decisions, is a second characteristic. A specialized body of knowledge, together with autonomy, allows the professional to make decisions in ill-defined situations, and reflection helps professionals improve their decisions. Finally, ethical standards provide principles of conduct that guide professionals as they work with students and caregivers.

2.2. What are the primary arguments that teaching is a profession?

Proponents of teaching as a profession point to the growing body of research showing that effective teaching requires several kinds of knowledge and requires an extended period of training for licensure. In addition, teaching professionals engage in continuous decision making in their classrooms and reflect on the effectiveness of these decisions afterward. Teachers also have considerable autonomy in their classrooms and are guided by ethical standards for conduct.

2.3. What are the major arguments that teaching is not a profession?

Critics who claim that teaching isn't a true profession base their claims on two major points. First, they note that teaching often doesn't require rigorous training before licensure. Second, they point out that teacher autonomy is limited by curricular standards and assessment procedures.

2.4. How do the arguments for and against teacher professionalism balance each other?

Although the rigor required for teaching isn't as great as for other professions, it is increasing. In addition, although their current autonomy is restricted by standards and testing, teachers still have considerable autonomy in their classrooms. The future of the professionalization movement in teaching will be significantly influenced by current reform efforts.

3.1. Identify the different dimensions of student diversity. Explain how these dimensions will influence your work as a teacher.

Culture and ethnicity, language, religion, socioeconomic status, academic ability, physical and emotional maturity, gender, and learner exceptionalities are all sources of diversity. These different dimensions of diversity provide both challenges and opportunities to teachers. Diverse classrooms are more challenging to work in because they increase the number of decisions that teachers have to make. They also provide opportunities for both teacher and student growth. By working with diverse students, teachers learn about themselves and also have opportunities to enrich the lives of their students by helping them understand commonalities and differences in all people.

3.2. Why is an understanding of different teaching and learning environments important for beginning teachers?

Each of the different teaching and learning environments offers both opportunities and challenges to beginning teachers. Rural districts are smaller and tend to be more culturally homogeneous. Suburban districts are intermediate in size and tend to be better funded. Urban districts are larger and more culturally diverse. The number of jobs available in urban settings is increasing, and many urban districts target beginning teachers for job offers by offering a number of incentives to work in their classrooms.

4.1. How is the current reform movement in education changing the teaching profession?

The current reform movement in education is changing the profession in two major ways. First, reform initiatives that include standards, test-based accountability, and choice are changing teachers' lives. Changes are also occurring in teacher preparation: Teachers are being held to higher academic standards and are having their competency measured through state licensure exams.

4.2. Describe the major changes in teacher preparation that have resulted from the reform movement in education.

Major changes in teacher preparation primarily target higher standards for admission and higher academic standards within the programs themselves. Candidates are required to take more rigorous courses both before they enter and within teacher preparation programs. Prospective teachers also face higher licensure requirements for entering the profession, including teacher competency tests. Many teacher preparation programs are being expanded from 4 to 5 years, and experienced teachers are being asked to take more rigorous professional-development courses.

4.3. What is the Praxis Series, and how does *praxis* relate to the reform movement?

The Praxis Series™, published by Educational Testing Service, is a comprehensive battery of tests designed to ensure teacher competency. Praxis I measures base skills; Praxis II assesses teachers' knowledge of the content they'll be teaching; Praxis III is designed to assess classroom performance. The Praxis Series™ is part of a larger reform effort to improve education by improving the quality of teachers.

4.4. What are the major arguments for and against testing teachers?

Advocates of teacher testing believe this reform provides a valid, reliable, cost-effective, and bias-free method of ensuring that teachers are qualified. Critics believe that these tests aren't valid and don't predict effective teaching in the classroom. In addition, they may be biased against cultural minorities and non-English-speaking candidates.

2 Changes in American Society: Their Influences on Today's Students

1.1. Describe changes that have occurred in the American family over the last 50 years.

An increasing number of children have parents who are or have been divorced, have single parents, or have both parents working. In addition, an increasing number of families live near or below the poverty level. As a result, parents and other caregivers spend less time with their children than they did 50 years ago.

1.2. Describe the implications of the changes in American families for child care in this country.

In the 1950s, most families (57%) had a single breadwinner, and the mother stayed home to care for the children. Currently, only about 25% of young children are cared for in the home. This creates a pressing need for quality child care that not only meets children's emotional needs but also prepares them for school.

1.3. Who are latchkey children? What problems do they encounter in their homes?

Latchkey children return home after school to an empty house. They not only have less parental supervision, they also have less access to parental help with homework.

2.1. What changes have occurred in student sexuality over time? What are the implications of these changes for education?

Students are more likely to become sexually active earlier, leading to teenage pregnancies and sexually transmitted diseases. These changes suggest the need for basic sex education that can help students make informed choices.

2.2. Explain the trends in student use of alcohol and other drugs over the last several years, and describe the implications of these changes for education.

Although the use of alcohol, tobacco, marijuana, and cocaine has decreased in recent years, use among students still remains high. This suggests that students need to be educated about the legal, physical, and psychological consequences of using these drugs.

2.3. How has the rate of student obesity changed over the years? How are schools responding to this problem?

The rate of student obesity has tripled since 1980. Schools have attempted to combat this problem by banning the sale of calorie-laden soft drinks in schools. Other issues, such as exercise and healthy diets, still need to be addressed.

2.4. How have crime and violence changed in U.S. schools? What are the implications for education?

The overall rates of crime and violence in schools have decreased in recent years. They still are a reality in many schools, however, and need to be dealt with on multiple levels. At the school level, administrators need to have a comprehensive plan in place for both preventing and addressing crime and violence. Teachers also need to be aware of the possibilities for crime and violence, as well as bullying, in their classrooms and need to know how to deal with them immediately.

3.1. Define *socioeconomic status.*

Socioeconomic status is a classification system that combines parents' income, occupation, and level of education.

3.2. Explain how different socioeconomic patterns influence school success.

Socioeconomic status (SES) influences school success in several ways. First, it influences whether basic needs such as food and shelter are met. It can also influence family stability: Lower-SES families are less likely to provide safe and stable home environments. SES affects the availability of school-related experiences such as travel and going to museums and zoos. SES also influences the amount and kind of adult–child interactions in the home. Finally, SES influences parental attitudes and values about education.

3.3. How does the government define *poverty*? How does poverty influence learning?

The federal government establishes a poverty threshold, the household income level that represents the lowest level of earning needed to meet basic living needs. In 2007, the poverty level for a family of four was $20,065. Poverty influences a family's ability to meet basic needs such as food and shelter as well as educational needs such as books, and the ability to be home to supervise and help with homework.

3.4. How does homelessness influence learning?

Experts estimate that between 500,000 and 1 million children are homeless at some time during the year. Homeless children suffer from inadequate diets and medical care, frequently come from unstable families, and often don't attend school regularly.

Because their basic needs aren't met, homeless children can't take advantage of learning opportunities in school. In addition, because they don't have a stable home life to return to, they find it difficult to do homework and read at home.

4.1. What are the characteristics of students at risk?

Students at risk often come from unstable families and are often victims of high rates of poverty, violence, and alcohol and drug abuse as well as child abuse. They are often members of cultural minorities, and English may not be spoken at home.

4.2. What unique challenges do urban schools present to students at risk?

Urban schools present a number of challenges to students at risk. They tend to exist in high-poverty areas, a factor often associated with lower achievement. They are also funded less well than their suburban counterparts and have fewer experienced teachers. In addition, urban schools are often larger, making it harder for students to establish meaningful interpersonal relationships.

4.3. What can schools and teachers do to help students at risk achieve success?

Effective schools for students at risk emphasize a safe and orderly school climate, mastery of essential content, caring and demanding teachers, cooperation, student responsibility and self-regulation, and strong parental involvement.

Effective teachers for students at risk share many of the characteristics of effective schools. They are caring, have high expectations, and emphasize student responsibility. They also provide instruction that is interactive, with increased structure, support, and feedback.

3 Student Diversity: Culture, Language, Gender, and Exceptionalities

1.1. Explain how cultural diversity influences learning.

Cultural diversity influences learning through cultural attitudes, values, and interaction patterns. Some cultural attitudes and values complement classroom learning. For example, some cultures view success in school as an essential component of upward mobility and consequently emphasize the value of schoolwork as well as homework. At other times, cultural values can conflict with school success; this occurs primarily when success in school threatens the loss of the home culture. Language is a prime example here: Sometimes learning English is interpreted as also rejecting the native language.

Not all cultures have the same adult–child interaction patterns. When these interaction patterns are compatible with the rapid question-and-answer style of most classrooms, then learning is facilitated. But when the home interaction patterns differ from those in the classroom, problems can occur. Sensitive teachers are aware of this and both adapt their own interaction patterns and help students change theirs to succeed in the classroom.

1.2. Describe three ways in which effective teachers respond to cultural diversity in their classrooms.

Culturally responsive teaching has three essential components. First, effective teachers accept and value cultural differences and positively communicate this attitude to students. Second, culturally responsive teachers adapt their interaction patterns to students and also teach students about successful classroom interaction practices. Finally, effective teachers build on students' cultural backgrounds, using their neighborhood and home experiences as the foundation for classroom learning.

1.3. Describe the relationship between urban schools and cultural diversity.

Urban schools tend to have greater proportions of cultural minorities than their rural or suburban counterparts. In addition, many of these students don't speak English as their first language, requiring teachers skilled in English as a second language.

2.1. What has been the government's response to language diversity in our nation's schools?

Initially, Congress supported bilingual education with the passage of the Bilingual Education Act of 1968. This was reinforced in 1974 by a U.S. Supreme Court decision requiring districts to address the learning needs of non-English speakers. More recently, both federal and state governments have reversed these trends, emphasizing English-only approaches at the expense of bilingualism.

2.2. Bilingual education and other approaches that primarily focus on teaching English differ radically in both philosophies and practices. What are the primary differences in these two major approaches schools in working with English language learners?

The two very different approaches to dealing with ELL students differ in their emphasis on maintaining the first language. The bilingual approach aims to maintain the native language, using it as the foundation for learning English. A contrasting approach focuses exclusively on learning English. For political and practical reasons, this second approach appears to be currently dominant in the United States.

2.3. What are the major ways that teachers can adapt their instruction to meet the needs of students with varying language backgrounds?

First, teachers should strive to make their classrooms welcoming places where all students feel comfortable. Then, they should provide opportunities for students to practice their developing language skills with other students through learner-centered approaches: cooperative learning, peer tutoring, and buddy systems are all effective. Teachers should illustrate their lessons with many examples to provide concrete references for new ideas and vocabulary and frequently check for student understanding. Finally, teachers should be sensitive to embarrassing students whose language skills are still developing.

3.1. Explain how society influences gender differences in our students.

Society influences gender differences between boys and girls primarily through gender-role identity. Every society influences people's perceptions of the proper roles of males and females. Ours does as well, and students enter our classrooms with preconceived notions about how males and females should act and what careers they should select.

3.2. How should teachers respond to gender differences?

Teachers often treat boys and girls differently based on their own stereotypical views of gender roles. They should be aware of these possibilities and strive to treat boys and girls equally in learning activities. This means that they should call on boys and girls as equally as possible, give them similar amounts of time to answer, ask the same levels of questions, and provide feedback that is similarly detailed.

4.1. Define the concept of *intelligence*, and explain how the idea of multiple intelligences changes this definition.

The most widely held definition of intelligence identifies three components: the capacity to acquire knowledge, the ability to think and reason in the abstract, and the ability to solve problems. Although there are three components, intelligence is still seen as a single entity and often reported as a single score. A differing view of intelligence, based on Howard Gardner's work, suggests that it's composed of more than eight relatively independent dimensions. So, rather than a single entity, intelligence is viewed as having eight distinct capacities.

4.2. Explain the legal foundation of special education.

The legal foundation for special education was established in 1975 with the passage of the Individuals with Disabilities Education Act (IDEA), which, combined with later amendments, mandates the following: Students with exceptionalities have access to a free and appropriate public education; assessment doesn't discriminate against any students; parents are involved in decisions about their child's educational program; an environment is created that doesn't restrict learning opportunities for students with exceptionalities; and an individualized education program (IEP) of study is created for each student. Amendments to IDEA extend its provisions to children aged 3 through 5; hold states accountable for locating young children who need special education services; require districts to keep confidential records of each child and to share them with parents on request; require that methods be established to reduce the number of students from culturally and linguistically diverse backgrounds who are inappropriately placed in special education; and specify procedures that allow districts to remove students from the classroom who can potentially injure other students.

4.3. What are the major categories of exceptionalities found in classrooms?

In IDEA, the federal government specifies 13 categories of special education students. More than three fourths of these fall into four categories: learning disabilities, communication disorders, intellectual disabilities, and behavior disorders. Learning disabilities involve difficulties in acquiring and using listening, speaking, reading, writing, reasoning, or mathematical abilities. Communication disorders interfere with students' abilities to receive and understand information from others and to express their own ideas or questions. Intellectual disabilities include limitations in intellectual functioning, as indicated by difficulties in learning, and problems with adaptive skills, such as communication, self-care, and social interaction. Behavior disorders involve the display of serious and persistent age-inappropriate behaviors that result in social conflict, personal unhappiness, and school failure.

4.4. What roles do classroom teachers play in helping students with exceptionalities succeed in their classrooms?

Classroom teachers perform several important roles in ensuring classroom success for students with exceptionalities. First, they assist in identifying students who need extra help. They also collaborate with other professionals in the creation of an individualized education program (IEP), and then adapt their instruction to meet the specific learning needs of each student. Finally, they are central to monitoring the process and communicating progress to parents, administrators, and special educators.

Though the same basic instructional strategies that work with all students are also effective with students with exceptionalities, teachers also need to provide additional support. This can come from individual help or through peer tutoring. Effective teachers also teach in small steps, provide frequent feedback, model problem-solving steps, provide visual aids and increased time to complete assignments, use technology, and teach students to use strategies.

1.1. How did the diversity of the original colonies shape the educational system in the United States?

Because of cultural, geographic, economic, and religious differences in the original colonies, it wasn't possible to create a uniform, monolithic school system that would satisfy everyone. This led to state control of education, a system that survives today.

1.2. What role did religion play in colonial schools?

Religion was often the reason that many colonists came to North America, and it played a central role in colonial life. The colonists therefore included religion as a central part of each school's mission.

1.3. How did this emphasis on religion influence schools today?

The proper role of religion in schools is a contentious issue today because of differing views of the purposes of schools and schooling.

1.4. Why was the Old Deluder Satan Act of Massachusetts important for the development of our American educational system?

The Old Deluder Satan Act required every town of 50 or more households to hire a teacher to instruct the children in that town. This provided the legal foundation for public support of education.

2.1. Explain how the early national period influenced education in this country.

The early national period influenced education in this country in three important ways. First, one of the provisions of the First Amendment to the Constitution established the principle of separation of church and state. Second, legislators removed control of education from the federal government and gave it to the states. Third, with the passage of the Land Ordinance of 1785, the federal government established a role for itself in public education. These factors continue to influence today's education.

2.2. What is the Tenth Amendment to the Constitution? Why is it important for education today?

The Tenth Amendment to the Constitution mandated that responsibilities for education not explicitly assigned to the federal government would be the responsibility of each state, which put the responsibility for funding and governing education in the hands of the states. This system of state-controlled education exists today and is unique to the United States.

2.3. What was the historical significance of the Land Ordinance of 1785?

The Land Ordinance was designed to raise money through the sale of land in the territories west of the original colonies that were acquired from Britain at the end of the Revolutionary War. It specified that land was to be divided into townships consisting of 36 one-square-mile sections, with the income from one section reserved for support of public education. In passing the Land Ordinance, legislators established federal funding for public schools and introduced the idea that schools were instruments of national purpose.

3.1. Explain how the common school movement influenced education in our country today.

The common school movement influenced today's education in four important ways. First, it was during that period that states and local governments began directly taxing citizens to support public schools, a process that continues today. Second, states created departments of education and appointed state superintendents of instruction; state departments of education continue to be the institutions that oversee education in the states. Third, educators organized schools by grade level and standardized the curriculum, an organizational structure that remains today. Finally, states improved teacher preparation by creating normal schools, schools explicitly developed for the preparation of teachers. Normal schools were important because they addressed the whole issue of teacher quality, which is currently being debated in terms of fast-track and alternative certification programs.

3.2. How was the common school movement linked to the growing number of immigrants coming to the United States?

Immigrants brought with them different cultures and languages. Our country needed ways to assimilate them into the increasingly industrialized U.S. economy and to make them productive citizens. Government-supported and -run schools were seen as a way to do this.

3.3. Who was Horace Mann, and what was his contribution to education in the United States?

Horace Mann was an outspoken advocate for universal public education. He was the secretary of the Massachusetts State Board of Education from 1837 to 1848. Because of his influence, Massachusetts doubled state appropriations for education, built 50 new secondary schools, increased teacher salaries by 50%, and passed the nation's first compulsory school attendance law in 1852. He was a powerful and effective advocate for public education for everyone.

4.1. Describe the historical roots of contemporary secondary schools.

Contemporary secondary schools can be traced all the way back to the first Latin Grammar school, which was created in 1635 and focused on preparing wealthy males for the ministry or the law. In response to the narrowness of the Latin grammar schools, academies presented a more practical curriculum; both boys and girls attended, and the precedent for electives in high schools was set. The academies charged tuition, however, so English classical schools, free secondary schools designed to meet the needs of boys not planning to attend college, were created. They established the precedent of free secondary education for all students. Out of these roots, modern comprehensive high schools gradually evolved, and junior highs and middle schools further evolved as a result of criticisms suggesting that high schools didn't meet the social, emotional, and intellectual needs of young adolescents. Questions about the mission of each of these schools persist today.

4.2. How have the goals of high school education changed over time?

Initially, the predecessors of the contemporary high school were elitist and oriented primarily to preparation for college; institutions such as the Latin grammar school were strictly college preparatory. Later, schools such as Benjamin Franklin's Academy and the English classical school were reoriented to more practical subjects such as bookkeeping and surveying. Initial participation in these schools was still limited to the very wealthy or talented. The idea of a universal high school education didn't really take root until the 1900s.

4.3. How are junior highs and middle schools different from each other?

Junior highs were designed to prepare students for high school. Consequently, they focused primarily on academics and, for the most part, ignored the social and emotional needs of young adolescents. Middle schools evolved out of a growing recognition that the developmental needs of early adolescents were unique and were not being met by junior high schools. Middle school adaptations for developing adolescents included a more applied and integrated curriculum, more learner-centered instruction, and classes that allowed teachers and students to interact and get to know each other.

5.1. What are the similarities and differences in different minority groups' struggles for educational equality?

Minority groups' struggles for educational equality are similar in that they all were subjected to discrimination at different points in history. Some argue that aspects of discrimination still exist today. They are also similar in that these cultures have become integral parts of American life, but they retain elements of their native cultures, such as holidays, food, and customs.

The groups are different in their histories. First, they came to this country for different reasons. For example, Native Americans were here when the first colonists arrived; African Americans were brought over as slaves; and Asian Americans were brought to work on farms and on the transcontinental railroad.

They were also treated differently. For example, attempts were made to assimilate Native Americans into mainstream American society by having them attend boarding schools, adopt the habits of mainstream culture, and reject their native customs and habit. To a certain extent, this was true of Hispanic Americans as well. In contrast, African Americans lived under the policy of separate but equal for decades. In practice, however, the policy was separate but unequal, because the schools African American students attended were virtually always substandard and underfunded.

5.2. How does the concept of assimilation relate to Native American boarding schools?

Assimilation is the process of socializing cultural minorities so they adopt the social norms and behaviors of the dominant culture, or whites. Boarding schools attempted to speed up the process by taking Native American youth away from their families and instructing them in residential facilities. These efforts were mainly ineffective.

5.3. How does "separate but equal" relate to African Americans' educational experience in the United States?

Early attempts to educate African Americans placed them in segregated schools that purported to be separate but equal. Unfortunately, they were separate but unequal in resources and quality.

5.4. How did the process of assimilation relate to Hispanic Americans and their native languages?

In hopes of assimilating Hispanic Americans quickly, schools frequently taught classes in English only, and Spanish was forbidden. This practice not only caused the loss of the first language but also resulted in conflicts between home and school. Bilingual education aimed to retain and build on students' first language skills, but the status of bilingual education is currently in doubt because of restrictive legislation in a number of states.

6.1. How did schools become instruments for national purpose during the modern era?

Schools became instruments for national purpose during the modern era in four important ways: the Cold War, the War on Poverty, the enlistment of schools in competition for economic superiority, and the government's role in equity issues. The federal government significantly increased support for math and science during the Cold War to combat the perceived growing threat of communism. Education was seen as a tool to eliminate poverty and the economic disparities in our country in the War on Poverty. The government also passed legislation requiring the creation of learning standards in an effort to compete economically with other countries around the world, and it also passed legislation banning discrimination on the basis of culture, race, or sex.

6.2. How were federal efforts during the Cold War similar to and different from its efforts to achieve racial equality in education?

They were all similar in that both efforts viewed education as a tool for national progress. They were different in their structure. In the Cold War, for example, the government's intervention was primarily the process of providing additional resources, such as funding for the National Science Foundation. In contrast, with respect to equity issues, the intervention was in the form of legislation requiring the end of discrimination on the basis of race, culture, or sex. The Civil Rights Act and Title IX are examples of this legislation.

6.3. What are magnet schools, and how do they relate to attempts to achieve equality in our schools?

Magnet schools were created as an alternative to forced busing and integration. The goal is to achieve integration by attracting bright students from all cultural groups. The results on magnet schools are mixed. Although they do achieve integration, critics charge that they tend to steal bright minority students from their home schools and that social integration within magnet schools often doesn't occur.

6.4. What is Title IX, and how is it related to the concept of equality?

Title IX was federal legislation enacted in 1972 to eliminate gender bias in the United States. Its most dramatic influence in education has been in the area of sports, where gender-equity advocates have used it to gain equity in facilities and expenditures.

5 Educational Philosophy and Your Teaching

1.1. Define *philosophy* and *normative philosophy,* and explain how they differ from theory.

Philosophy is a study of theories of knowledge, truth, existence, and morality. Normative philosophy is a description of the way events should be, such as the way professionals should practice. A theory is a set of related principles that are based on observations and are used to explain the world. Rather than describe the way events in the world ought to be, theories simply explain why the events occur.

1.2. To which part of teacher professionalism is philosophy most closely related? Explain.

Philosophy is most closely related to a "specialized body of knowledge." All professions have specialized knowledge, and philosophy is part of this knowledge for professional educators.

1.3. What's the major difference between Allie's and Brad's normative philosophies?

First, Allie believed that essential knowledge exists, as indicated by this comment: "There's real, practical stuff out there that kids need. They have to be good readers, and they need to be able to write, and they need to understand this stuff, the science I'm teaching." She also believed that students should study, practice, and be assessed with respect to that essential knowledge. For her, study, practice, and assessment are the ways teaching and learning "ought to be." Brad, instead, believed that experiences with problem solving and decision making were the way teaching and learning "ought to be."

2.1. Describe each of the major branches of philosophy.

The four branches of philosophy are epistemology, which examines questions about how we come to know the knowledge we acquire; metaphysics, the analysis of reality and what is and is not real; axiology, the examination of matters of right and wrong; and logic, the analysis of the process of deriving valid conclusions from basic premises.

2.2. Allie said, "I'm not doing my job if I don't get them to learn as much as possible." This comment best illustrates which branch of philosophy? Explain your answer.

This comment most closely relates to axiology. Allie is saying that it would be unethical if she didn't do her best to help her students learn as much as possible.

2.3. Two teachers are in a discussion, and one says, "Everything we know depends on experience. So, the key is providing lots of experiences in the classroom. If we provide them with enough experiences, they'll learn." To which branch of philosophy is this person's statement most closely related? Explain your answer.

This person's comment most closely relates to epistemology. She is suggesting that the way people come to know what they know is through experiences.

2.4. "That doesn't quite make sense," a teacher diplomatically comments to a colleague. "You said that your kids are so unmotivated, but last week you said that kids basically want to learn. . . . Those two don't fit." To which of the branches of philosophy is this person's comment most closely related? Explain your answer.

This person's comment is most closely related to logic. He is saying that the conclusion "Kids aren't motivated" doesn't logically follow from the premise "Kids basically want to learn."

3.1. What are the major philosophies of education?

Perennialism is an educational philosophy grounded in the belief that human nature is constant, and a rigorous intellectual curriculum should exist for all students. Math, science, and literature are important, because they expose students to logical thought and ideas that have endured throughout history.

Essentialism is framed in the belief that a critical core of information exists that all people should possess. Basic skills and academic subjects would make up a curriculum based on essentialist philosophy.

Progressivism suggests that education should focus on real-world problem solving and individual development. Learner-centered curricula would be emphasized in a school grounded in progressivism.

Social reconstructionism contends that schools and teachers should take the lead in creating a better world. It suggests, for example, that issues such as racism, sexism, environmental degradation, and the exploitation of the weak by the powerful are all topics that should be addressed in the school curriculum.

3.2. Because students must be able to function effectively in, and adapt to, a changing world, a teacher emphasizes the "whole person"—physical, social, emotional, and intellectual—in her students. She stresses and models physical fitness, involves her students in discussions to help them practice social skills and perspective taking, and involves them in problem solving about modern-day topics. To which of the educational philosophies are the teacher's efforts most closely related? Explain.

This teacher is basing her work on progressivism. Her emphasis on personal growth and functioning effectively in a changing world illustrates a progressivist approach to education.

3.3. You visit a school, and you overhear a conversation between two teachers. One says, "I love teaching Shakespeare. His work has been studied for hundreds of years, and it's as timely now as it was then." Which educational philosophy is best illustrated by the teacher's comment? Explain.

The teacher is expressing views consistent with perennialism. Perennialism emphasizes thought that has endured throughout history, and the study of Shakespeare reflects this emphasis.

3.4. A teacher who wants her students to examine racism and injustice involves them in a unit on nonviolent noncooperation using a study of Gandhi's struggles against racism in India as an example. She further illustrates the ideas with a study of Martin Luther King's nonviolent protests against American racism. To which of the educational philosophies are the teacher's efforts most closely related? Explain.

This teacher is basing her work on social reconstructionism. Examining issues of injustice and making attempts to eliminate them are consistent with social reconstructionist philosophy, and using Gandhi's and Martin Luther King's works as examples to study this issue reflects this orientation.

4.1. Why is a personal philosophy of education important?

Forming a personal philosophy of education is important because your philosophy will influence the kinds of content you emphasize in your classes, the instructional decisions you make as a teacher, and the criteria you use to reflect on and analyze your teaching.

A personal philosophy is also important because it will help you explain and defend your educational goals—what you will strive to accomplish in your classroom. Your goals reflect the kind of teacher you want to be, and being able to explain and defend them means that you're knowledgeable and reflective, which are essential characteristics of professionalism.

4.2. Describe the three essential steps involved in forming a philosophy of education.

Forming a personal philosophy of education begins with a statement of beliefs about the purpose of schooling and the nature of teaching and learning. The second step involves examining those beliefs to ensure that they're consistent with each other. The third step is actually articulating your philosophy in an internally consistent statement; the statement then gives you a concrete framework that you can use to guide your actions, and because it's tangible, it can be modified when your professional knowledge expands and your beliefs change.

4.3. Look again at Brad's thinking, as indicated by his conversation with Allie. Based on this information, what is his philosophy of education? Explain how his philosophy is based on his beliefs.

Based on his conversation with Allie, Brad's philosophy of education can be described as follows:

School should be preparation for life after students leave the classroom, and the way to best prepare for life is to practice life skills, which are the abilities to make decisions and solve real-world problems instead of focusing on traditional content. For Brad, essential knowledge is the knowledge people need to make decisions and solve problems.

These views are based on the belief that the only way people learn to make decisions and solve problems is to practice both. They're also based on the belief that reality is what people perceive it to be and that it depends on the situation people are in at the time. In this regard, Brad's views are most closely aligned with progressivism.

6 Choosing a School

1.1. Schools are described as a social system. Define a social system, explain how a school is a social system, and give another example of a social system in our society.

A social system is a network of interdependent components that work together to accomplish the goals of the system. Components of a school include personnel, such as administrators and teachers; the physical plant, which includes the actual building, playgrounds, and other aspects of the physical surroundings; and the curriculum, what teachers teach and students learn. Many other social systems exist, such as city governments, churches, civic organizations, and even families. For instance, parents or other caregivers are each components of the family, as are children, and they all work together to meet family goals, such as providing for basic necessities, educating the children, and maintaining the physical and emotional health of each member.

1.2. What are the major components of a typical school organization?

The components of a typical school are personnel, the physical plant, and the organization of the curriculum. The personnel of a school include the administrative staff, vice principal, and one or more assistant principals in large schools; support staff, such as clerical workers, receptionists, and custodians; and teachers.

The physical plant often includes several buildings, such as an administrative building, classroom buildings, and a cafeteria. Most middle, junior high, and high schools also include sports facilities, such as a gymnasium, football and baseball fields, and perhaps a running track.

The curriculum is designed to teach content that is appropriate for students at different ages, which is the reason that schools are usually organized into elementary, middle or junior high, and high school levels.

1.3. Most school systems are organized into three levels; describe each.

Schools are typically organized into elementary, middle or junior high, and high school levels. Elementary schools usually house students from kindergarten, or pre-K, through the fifth or sixth grade. Middle schools usually involve some combination of fifth through eighth grades, with grades 6–8 being the most common. Junior highs most commonly house some combination of grades 7–9, and high schools typically consist of grades 9–12 or 10–12.

1.4. Identify three factors that influence the way schools are organized.

The developmental characteristics of students, economics, and politics are three factors that most commonly influence the way schools are organized. Because a typical first grader thinks differently than a typical fifth grader, for example, the curriculum is organized to accommodate those developmental differences.

Economic factors, such as tight budgets and school overcrowding, and political factors, such as high school coaches' wanting potential athletes to be prepared for high school teams, also influence the way schools are organized.

2.1. Describe two ways in which teaching in an elementary school differs from teaching in a middle school, junior high, or high school.

Elementary teachers are responsible for teaching all the content areas, such as reading, math, science, social studies, art, and music, whereas teachers at the upper levels are responsible for teaching only one area, such as math (or sometimes two, such as a combination of math and science classes). This is one important difference.

In addition, teachers in elementary schools set their own schedule; they decide how many minutes per day they will allocate to each of the content areas. At the upper levels, the time allocated for each class period is preset by school-wide schedules and bells.

2.2. What are four differences between effective middle schools and junior highs?

First, effective middle schools organize teachers and students into interdisciplinary teams, so that all the teachers on a team have the same group of students and instruction emphasizes connections between different curriculum areas. This isn't the case in junior highs. Second, middle schools more strongly emphasize long-term teacher–student relationships, with greater attention to students' emotional development, than do junior highs. Third, teachers in effective middle schools place more emphasis on interactive teaching strategies than do teachers in junior highs. Finally, middle schools eliminate activities in which developmental differences among students become apparent, such as competitive athletics.

2.3. What is a comprehensive high school? How does a comprehensive high school differ from a vocational high school?

A comprehensive high school attempts to meet the needs of all students. This means that it provides offerings for students who are likely to attend college, but at the same time meets the needs of students who will be entering the job market after graduating from high school.

Career technical schools offer a curriculum designed to provide students with education and job skills that will enable them to get a job immediately after graduating from high school.

3.1. Describe characteristics of an effective school.

Research indicates that effective schools are optimal in size—neither too small nor too large—have a clear school mission and strong leadership, maintain a solid academic focus, have high collective efficacy, employ interactive instructional strategies, monitor learning progress, have safe and orderly learning classrooms and halls, and actively involve parents in their children's education.

3.2. What is the most distinguishing characteristic of effective instruction in effective schools?

The most distinguishing characteristic of effective instruction is interactive teaching. Instead of lecturing and giving students extensive seat work, effective teachers design learning activities that actively involve students in the content they're learning.

3.3. Why is frequent monitoring of student progress essential for an effective school?

Frequent monitoring of student progress performs several important functions. First, and most important, it tells students whether they're learning important ideas and skills. It also informs teachers of learning gains, allowing them to adjust instruction to meet learning gaps. Finally, it provides helpful information to administrators and parents about children's learning progress.

7 Governance and Finance: Regulating and Funding Schools

1.1. Who is legally responsible for governing education in the United States?

The Tenth Amendment to the Constitution clearly assigns legal responsibility for education to the 50 states.

1.2. Describe the educational governance structure at the state level.

State governance of education begins with the governor and the legislature. Though they have many other responsibilities, both influence education by focusing attention on educational issues. In addition, state legislatures supply about half of a district's education budget.

The organization directly and legally responsible for governing education is the state board of education. Consisting primarily of noneducators, the state board issues and revokes teaching licenses, establishes the length of the school year, creates standards for the curriculum, and develops and implements a system for gathering educational data.

The state office of education, composed of professional educators, implements education policy on a daily basis. The state office of education is responsible for teacher licensing, curriculum supervision, approval of school sites and buildings, and collection of statistical data.

1.3. Describe the governance structure at the local, district level.

School districts are responsible for the day-to-day functioning of schools. They hire teachers and ensure that students have classrooms and books. They are governed by a local school board, consisting of elected citizens from the community. The school board sets policy; the district superintendent implements that policy. The district office, consisting of educational professionals, orders textbooks and supplies, develops programs of study, administers standardized tests, and evaluates teachers. Finally, the school principal is responsible for governing at the school level. The school principal is key to the quality of education at the school level.

2.1. What are the major sources of educational funding?

The largest percentages (49% and 43%, respectively) come from state and local sources. The remaining 8.5% comes from the federal government.

Local funding comes primarily from property taxes. State funds for education come from a variety of sources, the two largest being state income taxes and sales taxes. Smaller percentages of state education funds also come from taxes on liquor and tobacco, oil and mining revenues, corporate income taxes, and income from state lotteries and gambling.

2.2. How are educational revenues spent?

The largest percentage of the educational budget (61%) goes to instruction, including teacher salaries. Ten percent goes to instructional assistance needs such as student services, teacher professional development, and curriculum development. Another 10% goes to administration, at both the district and the school levels. Maintenance of school buildings and grounds takes up another 10%. Finally, transportation (school buses) and food services (cafeterias) each account for another 4%.

3.1. Describe the major issues in school governance and finance.

Funding inequities in different districts, alternatives to local control, and controversies related to school choice are the three most prominent governance and finance issues in today's schools.

3.2. What are the major causes of funding inequities in education? What are some proposed solutions to the problem?

Funding inequities in education result largely from unequal revenue bases. Within a state, this can result from districts that have differing property values. Because significant portions of educational funding come from property taxes, inequities between districts within a state are common. Between-state differences can also result from differences in states' tax bases. One proposed solution is a greater federal role in equalizing between-state differences. Cost and the issue of increased federal control that might go along with the funding are two obstacles to this proposal.

3.3. What are urban takeovers? What problems are they designed to address?

Urban takeovers occur when large urban districts are unable to manage their fiscal and administrative responsibilities. The primary focus of urban takeovers is monetary and administrative efficiency. They are not designed to address reform issues per se, but supporters contend that fiscal and administrative efficiencies are first steps toward reform.

3.4. How is *school privatization* similar to and different from school commercialization?

Privatization involves outsourcing educational services to private companies or corporations. This can involve hiring companies to provide services such as school lunches or transportation, or turning a whole school over to a private business. Advocates of privatization claim that competition from the private sector is good because it will encourage public schools to perform better. They also contend that the efficiencies that work in the business world will produce similar efficiencies in education. Critics point to a narrowed curriculum in privatized schools because of teaching to the test. They also point to the reduced professionalization of teachers that occurs when they're treated like employees rather than knowledgeable professionals.

Commercialization is similar to privatization in that it also involves attempts by industry to make money in schools. Commercialization is different from privatization in that it typically involves selling some product through the schools. Critics question whether schools should become supermarkets for industry ads and products.

3.5. What are pay-to-play and pay-to-learn plans? How do they affect students?

Originally, pay-to-play plans targeted school sports and asked students to pay for the right to play in sports. Recently, pay-to-learn plans also target other aspects of education, asking students to pay extra fees for classes and clubs in drama, art, music, and science. Both have a disproportionate negative effect on students who are poor or minorities, who often can't pay these fees and are discouraged from participating in the first place.

8 School Law: Ethical and Legal Influences on Teaching

1.1. Explain the differences between legal and ethical influences on the teaching profession.

Laws tell teachers what they can do (their rights) as well as what they must do (their responsibilities), but they don't tell teachers what they should do. This is the role of professional ethics, which provide guidelines for professional conduct.

1.2. What are two limitations of using existing laws as the basis for professional decision making?

One limitation is that laws are left purposely abstract and general so they can apply to a large number of cases. This makes laws vague in terms of specific instances requiring decision making. A second limitation of using laws is that they were created in response to problems that existed in the past and may not provide specific guidelines for future professional decisions.

2.1. Describe how the legal system at the federal level influences education.

Federal laws influence education primarily through three amendments to the Constitution. The First Amendment guarantees all citizens freedom of speech; this amendment forms the basis for academic freedom in the classroom, as well as issues related to students' freedom of speech. The Fourth Amendment protects citizens from unreasonable searches and seizures; this amendment protects students from unwarranted or unreasonable searches while they're on school grounds. The Fourteenth Amendment guarantees due process in issues involving deprivation of life, liberty, or property; this amendment not only protects teachers from dismissal without a formal hearing, it also protects students from expulsion or suspension from school without due process.

2.2. How do state laws influence education policies and practices?

States are legally entrusted with the education of children. States influence education by passing laws regulating teachers' qualifications, working conditions, and legal rights. They also create departments of education, which are given responsibility for formulating educational policies in the state.

2.3. What is the educational significance of the overlapping legal system in the United States?

Because different laws influencing education are created at different levels, legal issues and problems that arise from these different levels need to be resolved at the level at which the law was formed. For example, if a legal dispute involves a teacher's qualifications for being a teacher, this would go to a state court because the laws regulating teacher qualifications are formed at that level.

3.1. How are teacher employment issues influenced by the law?

Teacher employment issues are influenced in several ways by legal considerations. First, licensure is a state responsibility, and rules and regulations passed by each state determine licensure policies and procedures. Local school boards are given the legal responsibility for issuing contracts, which specify the legal conditions for a teacher's employment. Teacher tenure, which is a legal safeguard that provides job security for teachers, is determined at the state level and protects teachers from dismissal without cause. Because of these overlapping spheres of influence, teacher dismissal is a gray area that may be influenced by both state and district legal regulations.

3.2. What is academic freedom, and why is it important to teachers?

Academic freedom, which is based on the First Amendment to the Constitution, protects the right of teachers to choose both content and teaching methods based on their professional judgment. It protects teachers from undue external influences on their classroom instruction.

3.3. How do copyright laws influence teachers' practices?

Copyright laws are federal laws designed to protect the intellectual property of authors. Fair-use guidelines specify limitations on the number of copies of books that teachers can reproduce for their classrooms. They also place restrictions on the use of videotaped programs and computer software.

3.4. What is teacher liability, and how does it influence teachers?

Teachers are legally responsible for the safety of children under their care. The term *in loco parentis* means that teachers are legally expected to act in the place of parents. Failure to do so can result in negligence and a legal suit involving liability for the teacher.

3.5. How are teachers' rights regarding their private lives similar to and different from those of the general public?

All citizens of the United States are guaranteed the right to "life, liberty, and the pursuit of happiness." But because teachers, as professionals, are expected to be role models for the children they teach, their rights as private individuals may be curtailed.

4.1. Describe the legal implications of religion in the schools.

The First Amendment to the Constitution states, "Congress shall make no law respecting an establishment of religion, or prohibiting the free exercise thereof." This law has important implications for teachers. It explicitly forbids the teaching of religion in the schools, and it prohibits the government from interfering with individuals' rights to hold religious beliefs and freely practice religion. It also has implications for prayer and religious clubs in schools, which are addressed in items 4.2, 4.3, and 4.4.

4.2. What is the legal status of prayer in schools?

Neither schools nor teachers can officially encourage school prayer; however, prayer is permissible when student initiated and when it doesn't interfere with other students or the school. For example, an individual student or students saying grace before lunch in a cafeteria would be permissible under the law.

4.3. Can a school allow religious clubs or organizations to meet on school grounds?

The U.S. Supreme Court has ruled that if the school doesn't specifically sponsor the religious club or organization, it's legal to allow religious, philosophical, and political groups to use school facilities in the same way as other extracurricular organizations.

4.4. What is the legal status of religion in the curriculum?

Advocacy of religion in the schools is legally forbidden. Teachers may discuss how religion has influenced history or culture, however.

5.1. What are students' rights with respect to freedom of speech?

The First Amendment to the Constitution guarantees all U.S. citizens freedom of speech. Students in school have this same right, provided that their actions don't interfere with learning. So, for example, students can't get up in a social studies class and make a speech about their political beliefs. This doesn't mean they can't express their beliefs briefly if the context is appropriate, but in exercising free speech, they can't interfere with the teacher's (and the class's) academic agenda.

5.2. Describe students' rights with respect to permissible search and seizure.

If school authorities believe there is probable cause that a student possesses drugs or a dangerous weapon, the school may conduct a nonobtrusive search of the student and his or her possessions (nonobtrusive does not include a strip search). School lockers are considered school property and may be searched if reasonable cause of a drug or weapons violation exists.

5.3. What is the Buckley Amendment? Why is it important to both schools and teachers?

The Buckley Amendment protects a family's rights to privacy of school records. It requires schools to: (1) inform parents of their rights regarding their child's records, (2) provide parents access to their child's records, (3) maintain procedures that allow parents to challenge those records, and (4) protect parents from disclosure of confidential information. Because teachers are legal extensions of schools, they are legally bound by the same safeguards.

5.4. Is corporal punishment legal in schools?

Corporal punishment is a state-by-state legal issue. In those states that do allow corporal punishment, it must be administered to correct misbehavior, it can't involve anger or malice, and it can't be cruel or excessive or result in lasting injury.

5.5. Describe students' rights with respect to disciplinary actions.

Students have a right to an education, and this right can be abridged or changed only through due process. If school administrators plan to suspend a student for an extended period of time, they must notify the student in writing of the reasons or charges, share the legal procedures and evidence, guarantee the student access to legal counsel, and record proceedings and findings, and the student must have a right to appeal.

5.6. Describe the legal rights of students with AIDS.

Because they have a right to an education, students with AIDS cannot be automatically excluded from school activities. Schools must address specific risk factors to other students when they change the instructional activities or opportunities for a student with AIDS.

9 The School Curriculum in an Era of Standards

1.1. Describe four definitions of *curriculum*.

Curriculum has been defined in various ways: the subject matter taught to students; a course of study, or a systematic arrangement of courses; the planned educational experiences offered by a school; and the process teachers go through in selecting and organizing learning experiences for their students.

1.2. Identify one important difference between the definition of *curriculum* used in this text and the definitions described in item 1.1.

The definition used in this text is broader than those in item 1.1. It includes "everything that teachers teach and students learn in schools," which can include attitudes and values students learn that aren't formally taught. In some cases, these attitudes and values are as important for student growth as the "planned educational experiences offered by a school," which is one of the definitions outlined in this section of the chapter.

1.3. How are curriculum and instruction related?

In simple terms, *curriculum* is what teachers teach, and it includes teachers' specific learning goals. *Instruction* involves the ways teachers help students reach the learning goals.

2.1. What is the difference between the explicit and the implicit curricula?

The *explicit curriculum* is what teachers intentionally teach based on their professional judgment and textbooks, curriculum guides, standards, and other resources. In comparison, the *implicit curriculum* is the "hidden" curriculum and is influenced by the school climate and organization and teachers' attitudes and values. As a result, teachers may not be consciously aware of many aspects of the implicit curriculum.

2.2. How is the null curriculum different from both the explicit and the implicit curricula?

The *explicit* and *implicit curricula* describe what is taught, but the *null curriculum* describes what is not taught. In particular, the differences between the explicit and the null curricula reflect teachers' views about what is important to study and learn.

2.3. Compare the extracurriculum to other curricula.

The extracurriculum differs from the explicit curriculum because the extracurriculum exists outside of students' areas of formal study. It's similar to the implicit curriculum because important forms of learning result from both, but many in the extracurriculum are beyond the scope of the explicit curriculum. The extracurriculum differs from the null curriculum because it relates to what is learned (although informally learned), but the null curriculum relates to what is not learned.

3.1. Identify four forces that influence the curriculum.

The four most important forces that influence curricular decisions are you, the teacher; standards and accountability; the federal government; and textbooks.

3.2. How does each of the forces in 3.1 exert its influence on the curriculum?

The teacher is the most powerful influence on the curriculum in any classroom. Your priorities and what you believe is important for your students to learn will ultimately determine the curriculum in your classroom. We saw this in the case study with Suzanne Brush, who chose to present her topic in a certain way because of her beliefs about teaching and learning and what was best for her students. A teacher with a different philosophy and beliefs might have chosen a very different approach.

The influence of standards and accountability is illustrated by the fact that many teachers in elementary schools strongly emphasize reading/language arts and math in their teaching because these areas are measured on high-stakes tests.

The federal government's influence is illustrated in legislation such as the Individuals with Disabilities Education Act, which mandates that all students, including those with learning issues, have access to the general curriculum.

Textbooks influence the curriculum because they are a helpful resource. Unfortunately, many teachers tend to teach topics in their textbooks essentially as the textbook presents them and in the order the textbook presents them.

3.3. Why is teacher professionalism so important in making curricular decisions?

Teacher professionalism is essential, because—even though we're living in an era of reform, standards, and accountability—teachers still ultimately determine what and how students learn. You saw this illustrated in Suzanne's teaching: Although she used the standard and the sample test item as a guide, she made all the decisions about what she would specifically teach, what to emphasize, and how to best present the topic to make it meaningful to the students. This is the case for all teachers. No amount of specifying standards and accountability measures or any other mandates will ever replace the professionalism of the teacher in promoting student learning.

4.1. How do issues involving sex education and moral development differ in their influence on the school curriculum?

Issues involving sex education influence the curriculum primarily in what content should be taught. For example, some argue that students should be exposed only to curriculum that endorses abstinence from sex. Others believe that students should learn about their bodies' reproductive system and should receive information about condoms, the prevention of sexually transmitted disease, and strategies for resisting pressure to have sex.

By comparison, authorities generally agree that ethics and morals should be taught in schools, but they disagree about the approach that educators should take. So, with respect to the development of morals, the issue becomes more one of the approach to instruction than of the content to be taught.

4.2. Describe the concept of intelligent design, and explain how it could influence curriculum decisions.

Intelligent design is a theory suggesting that certain features of the universe and of living things are so complex that their existence is best explained by an intelligent cause, rather than an undirected process such as natural selection. Proponents argue that it should be taught in science classes as a viable alternative theory to the theory of evolution. Critics argue that it is not science, and although it may have a place in a social studies or literature class, it does not belong in the science curriculum.

4.3. How could issues involving censorship influence your curriculum decisions?

If certain works of literature are highly controversial, you might choose not to have your students read them, even if you believe that they would contribute to students' learning. Or those works might not be available to students because of state or district policies. You're probably more likely to make a noncontroversial decision when you begin teaching, because you'll be somewhat unsure of yourself. As you gain experience and confidence, you will be more likely to take a more controversial stand.

10 Classroom Management: Creating Productive Learning Environments

1.1. What is a productive learning environment?

A productive learning environment is a classroom that is orderly and focused on learning. In productive learning environments, students feel physically and emotionally safe, and the daily routines, learning activities, and standards for appropriate behavior are all designed to promote learning.

1.2. Explain why effective classroom management is so important for creating a productive learning environment.

Classroom management is important for two reasons. First, it is beginning teachers' number-one concern, and it's the primary factor causing teacher stress and burnout, both of which can destroy a teacher's career.

Second, classroom management, student motivation, and student learning are strongly linked. Students are more motivated to learn and learn more in well-managed classrooms.

1.3. Describe the goals of classroom management.

Effective classroom management has four goals: (1) promoting a positive classroom climate; (2) making the classroom a learning community; (3) developing student responsibility; and (4) maximizing time available for learning.

Each of these goals contributes to student learning.

2.1. Describe the four processes involved in creating productive learning environments.

Teachers who create productive learning environments first and foremost care about their students, both as people and as learners.

Second, teaching effectively is essential. It's impossible to create a productive learning environment in the absence of effective teaching.

Third, organizing your classroom is necessary so that you have your materials ready, you begin your instruction on time, make transitions quickly and smoothly, and develop well-established routines.

Finally, planning for a clear set of procedures and rules will make your classroom management system understandable and predictable.

2.2. Describe the two planning elements that help create productive learning environments.

Planning that helps create productive learning environments focuses on two processes. First, consider the developmental levels of your students, and adjust your rules and procedures accordingly. Second, create a system of procedures and rules that can guide your students' behavior throughout the year.

2.3. What makes classroom management in urban classrooms unique?

First, because urban classrooms tend to be diverse, teachers need to make sure that all students understand classroom rules and procedures and how they contribute to learning. Second, urban classrooms tend to be large, making classroom management more challenging. Third, negative stereotypes often exist about urban students, resulting in teachers' teaching defensively rather than positively.

3.1. Explain how involving parents contributes to productive learning environments.

Productive learning environments focus on learning. Research indicates that when parents are involved, students are more willing to do homework, their long-term achievement is higher, their attitudes are more positive, and they behave more responsibly. Parental involvement supports the teacher's efforts and contributes to a safe, orderly, learning-focused environment.

3.2. What strategies are available to communicate with parents?

You can use a variety of strategies to communicate with parents. In addition to open houses, interim progress reports, and report cards, effective teachers send letters home, periodically send home packets of student work, and use newsletters, e-mails, and individual notes. Phone calls and home visits are also very effective.

4.1. Describe how effective teachers intervene when misbehavior occurs.

Effective teachers' interventions have two important characteristics. First, they take students' emotions into account, by avoiding loud, public, or sarcastic reprimands that embarrass or belittle students.

Second, the interventions are designed to teach, in addition to stopping unwanted behaviors. Demonstrating withitness and overlapping, ensuring that interventions are consistent, keeping verbal and nonverbal behavior congruent, and applying logical consequences all help to make your management understandable and reasonable, and students are more likely to comply when interventions for misbehavior make sense to them.

4.2. What actions, both short-term and long-term, should teachers take when encountering incidents of violence and aggression?

Short-term, teachers should intervene immediately to address the problem; this might consist of a personal intervention, or, if this isn't possible, they should immediately send for help. Long-term, teachers should involve parents and other school personnel in addressing the problems. Teachers should notify parents of the problem and seek the expertise and guidance of experienced school personnel.

11 Becoming an Effective Teacher

1.1. Define *motivation*, and describe the difference between *intrinsic* and *extrinsic motivation*.

Motivation is the energizing force behind student learning. *Extrinsic motivation* is motivation to engage in a behavior to receive some incentive, whereas *intrinsic motivation* is motivation to be involved in an activity for its own sake.

1.2. Describe the relationship between motivation and student achievement.

Learner motivation is a primary factor influencing students' achievement and satisfaction with school. In most cases, motivation is a more important factor than native ability.

1.3. Describe three factors within teachers' control that can increase students' motivation to learn.

Teachers can increase students' motivation to learn by beginning lessons with activities that attract students' attention, promoting high levels of student involvement in learning activities, and helping students apply topics to the real world.

2.1. What are the five essential steps in planning for instruction?

The steps in planning include the following:

1. Select topics. Standards, curriculum guides, textbooks, and the teacher's professional knowledge are sources that help make this decision.

2. Prepare learning objectives. Though the format for preparing learning objectives varies, the important aspect of preparing learning objectives is being clear about what you want students to know, understand, or be able to do.
3. Prepare and organize learning activities. Preparing and organizing learning activities often begin with finding or creating examples, as Shirley Barton did with her "pizzas" and "cakes."
4. Prepare assessments. Assessments that are created during planning instead of after learning activities have been completed help teachers focus their teaching on student learning outcomes.
5. Ensure instructional alignment. Instructional alignment means that teachers check that their learning activities and assessments are consistent with their objectives.

2.2. Planning in a standards-based environment involves an additional step beyond the planning steps described in this section of the chapter. What is this additional step?

When teachers' planning involves standards, the first step is to interpret the standard. Descriptions of standards vary; some are very specific, whereas others are quite general. When working with a standard described in general terms, teachers need to first decide what the standard means in terms of student learning, then they follow the rest of the planning steps: they plan learning activities and assessments.

2.3. Classify the following objectives into one of the cells of the taxonomy table in Figure 11.2, and explain your classification. (1) Students will identify examples of figures of speech such as similes, metaphors, and personifications in written paragraphs. (2) They will write original paragraphs that include those figures of speech.

Because figures of speech are concepts, and because being able to identify examples of them indicates understanding, the first objective would be classified in the cell where conceptual knowledge intersects with understand.

Writing paragraphs involves a procedure, and the fact that they must be original involves the cognitive process of creating, so the second objective would be classified in the cell where procedural knowledge intersects with create.

3.1. What are the essential teaching skills that all teachers should possess?

Essential teaching skills are the skills that all teachers, including those in their first year of teaching, should demonstrate regardless of topic or grade level. They include beliefs and behaviors such as caring, high efficacy, positive expectations, and enthusiasm. Effective teachers are also well organized, and they begin their lessons with reviews, attract and maintain attention, develop their lessons with questioning, provide their students with feedback, and help students apply what they've learned in new contexts.

3.2. As U.S. history students walk into their classroom, they see a large matrix comparing the climate, geography, and economies of the northern and southern states before the Civil War. As soon as the bell stops ringing, the teacher says, "Write a minimum of two differences each in the geography, climate, and economy columns of the chart." Students begin, and as they're writing the teacher takes roll. Which of the essential teaching skills does this example best illustrate? Explain.

Organization is the essential teaching skill best illustrated in this example. The teacher began the class right on time, and the chart was prepared and waiting when students walked into the room.

3.3. Shirley used her cardboard "pizzas" in her review and used her "cakes" to introduce the topic of equivalent fractions. Which essential teaching skill did the use of these materials best illustrate? Explain.

Focus is the essential teaching skill best illustrated by Shirley's use of the "pizzas" and "cakes." Each was an example that Shirley used to attract and maintain students' attention.

4.1. How are direct instruction, lecture–discussion, guided discovery, and cooperative learning similar and different?

All of these are instructional strategies, prescriptive approaches to teaching designed to help students acquire a deep understanding of specific forms of knowledge. They differ in the types of goals they're designed to help students reach. For example, direct instruction is designed to help students develop skills, such as adding fractions; lecture–discussion is designed to help students understand how ideas in a large body of information are related; and guided discovery is designed to help students understand concepts and other abstractions. Cooperative learning is designed to support each of the other strategies and helps students acquire social-interaction skills.

4.2. Which phase of direct instruction is most important for ensuring successful practice? Why?

The developing understanding phase is most important for ensuring student success during practice, and it is in this phase that we see the greatest difference between effective and ineffective teachers. If the developing understanding phase is ineffective, practice can be difficult and confusing. Remember, practice strengthens earlier understanding; it doesn't teach the skill. If teachers have to provide a great deal of explanation during practice, error rates increase and student achievement decreases.

4.3. A teacher places her third graders in groups of four and gives each group magnets and a packet containing a dime, a spoon, aluminum foil, a rubber band, a wooden pencil, a paper clip, and nails. She directs the groups to experiment with the magnets and items for 10 minutes, look for patterns, and record these on paper. After the groups have finished, she leads a discussion in which they identify characteristics of materials that are and are not attracted to magnets. The teacher is using which strategy, or strategies, in her learning activity?

The teacher in this case is using both guided discovery and cooperative learning. She had students work cooperatively to search for patterns in materials that are attracted to magnets, and the teacher then conducted a whole-group discussion and guided students to conclusions about the characteristics of magnetic materials.

12 Educational Reform and You

1.1. How has the current reform movement in our country been shaped by previous efforts at reform?

The current reform movement began in 1983 with the publication of *A Nation at Risk.* This report concluded that the United States was at risk of losing its international economic edge because of substandard education. A number of attempts at reform followed, such as establishing the National Council on Education Standards and Testing in 1993, passing the Goals 2000: Educate America Act in 1994, and holding the National Education Summit in 1996. Each attempt focused on standards and assessments designed to determine the extent to which the standards were met.

These efforts culminated in the No Child Left Behind Act of 2001, which required each state to create standards in reading and math and to design tests to assess students' attainment of these standards. The requirement that achievement gains for subgroups of American students, such as members of specific cultural minorities, also be reported was unique to this bill. Because of the political climate in our country, the future of the law and the form in which it exists is uncertain.

1.2. What are two common themes in the current reform movement?

Change and a focus on student achievement are two themes in the current reform movement. All reform efforts involve change in our current practices, and each of these efforts is focused on attempts to increase student achievement.

2.1. How will reform efforts that focus on the teacher affect your life in the classroom?

The way teachers are evaluated and merit pay systems are two reform efforts that will influence your life in your classroom. For example, it is likely that you will be evaluated in part by the way your students perform on standardized tests. And this evaluation might have an influence on your salary. This means that testing and the way your students perform on tests will be a significant part of your teaching life.

Second, you are likely to be involved in some form of merit pay system. This may have a significant impact on your school culture, which will also impact your classroom life.

2.2. What are the most common forms of teacher evaluation that you will encounter as a beginning teacher? How do these relate to value-added models?

The most common forms of teacher evaluation that you will encounter as a beginning teacher are principal observations and your students' scores on standardized achievement tests. Beginning teachers are typically observed several times during their first years of teaching, and the structured observation instrument can provide helpful feedback about your teaching.

One problem with using students' achievement test scores for evaluation purposes is that student aptitude and past achievement vary widely from school to school and even classroom to classroom. Value-added models of teacher evaluation attempt to statistically factor out these initial differences to provide a measure of the value you added to your students' learning.

2.3. What is merit pay? Why is it so controversial?

Merit pay is extra pay awarded for exemplary teacher performance. Typically, it results from a combination of principal ratings along with data from student achievement tests. The idea is to reward good teachers and hopefully identify other teachers needing help and remediation. A major reason it is controversial is that research is not clear about whether it actually motivates teachers to work harder or more effectively. Second, logistical problems in implementing these plans are considerable; unless these can be worked out, these systems will collapse. A third problem is teacher morale; for merit pay to be effective, it has to be accepted by teachers as a legitimate indicator of teacher expertise and productivity. Currently, existing systems are struggling to do this.

2.4. What are the two major professional associations? Why are they important to you as a beginning teacher?

The two major teacher professional organizations are the National Education Association (NEA) and the American Federation of Teachers (AFT). Both of these organizations provide valuable assistance to teachers, both through collective bargaining with districts as well as help with work conditions and liability issues. Currently, a number of states are considering limits on the abilities of these organizations to negotiate teacher employment issues.

3.1. Explain how reform efforts focusing on standards, testing, and accountability are influencing the curriculum and classroom instruction.

Standards are statements that specify what students should know or be able to do after a period of study. Because students are expected to meet the standards, and high-stakes tests are being used to ensure that they do, the standards are influencing the curriculum by dictating what is being taught. And direct methods of instruction that focus explicitly on the standards are becoming predominant.

3.2. Describe the relationship between assessment, standards, accountability, and high-stakes tests.

Assessment is the process that states use for holding students and teachers responsible for meeting standards. These assessments often exist in the form of high-stakes tests. The tests are high-stakes because test results are often used to determine if students will be promoted from one grade level to the next or if students will be allowed to graduate from high school.

3.3. What are national standards? How will they influence your life as a beginning teacher?

The national standards movement is a recent development in the standards movement, which received a major boost from No Child Left Behind legislation requiring each individual state to construct standards in basic skills areas such as reading and math. The national standards movement proposes to unify these diverse state standards into common ones for all states. It is very likely that you will encounter these new standards when you teach. You'll need to familiarize yourself with them and prepare yourself to use them in your teaching.

4.1. Explain how schools and schooling are being changed as a result of reform efforts.

Reform efforts are changing schools and schooling in several ways. For example, there are now alternatives to the regular public schools that we've all experienced. Some of these alternatives include charter schools, school vouchers, and home schooling. Schooling is being influenced by the emphasis on standards and performance-based programs that emphasize student-achievement data as a basis for rewarding teachers.

4.2. What do recent federal reform efforts have in common? What do they suggest about the future of reform in U.S. schools?

Recent federal reform efforts (e.g., Race to the Top) are focused on several important aspects of national reform: standards and assessment, improving low-performing schools, making teachers and principals more effective, and developing more-effective student data collection systems. In addition, federal efforts at reform have also emphasized teacher evaluation and parental choice in the form of charter schools. Recent federal reform efforts have also included monetary inducements, and these have proven effective in influencing state and district efforts. Tying reform efforts to competitive monetary rewards seems to be working, and we'll probably see additional initiatives in these areas.

4.3. In addition to reform efforts focusing on teacher tenure, teacher evaluation, merit pay, and limiting collective bargaining by professional organizations, how have states used charters to stimulate educational reform?

The charter movement is based on the idea that the educational bureaucracy is responsible for discouraging significant reform in our schools. The solution, charter advocates claim, is to create semiautonomous schools that have the freedom to innovate. These schools, if successful, would then serve as prototypes or models for reform efforts in regular schools. In addition, charter schools would offer educational alternatives to parents faced with substandard schools.

Unfortunately, the research on charter schools is mixed; the best are excellent, but others are either mediocre or subpar. Nevertheless, the charter movement is robust, aided by federal efforts and the support of political conservatives who wish to break what they see as a monopoly in education.

4.4. What are the two major forms of school choice? How are they similar and different?

The two major forms of school choice are charter schools and vouchers. They are similar in their philosophical underpinnings: Both are attempts to break up the perceived monopoly that exists in education, by providing more alternatives or choices to parents. They differ in how they propose to do this. Vouchers are, in one sense, less radical in that they maintain existing educational options and provide parents with tickets or vouchers to shop around and choose an alternative to their neighborhood schools. Charter schools, by contrast, create alternative schools, with self-contained governance and instructional systems.

13 Developing as a Professional

1.1. Describe the beliefs of beginning teachers.

Beginning teachers are idealistic and believe they will be very effective when they teach. They further believe that they'll be more effective than teachers who are now in the field, and they believe that their confidence in their ability to promote student learning will increase as they gain experience.

Beginning teachers believe that the most effective teachers are those best able to clearly explain the content they teach, and that if they thoroughly understand their content, they will figure out a way to help students learn it.

1.2. What are the most essential factors involved in finding a desirable job?

The most essential factors involved in finding a desirable job are developing a positive professional reputation and interviewing effectively. If you have developed a positive professional reputation, you'll earn supportive letters of recommendation, which make you more marketable.

Interviewers assess a variety of factors during an interview, such as your professional knowledge, personality, dress, use of language, and enthusiasm for teaching. How you come across in each of these areas will be significant in whether you're offered a job.

1.3. In which areas are teaching jobs most plentiful?

There are two categories of plentiful jobs. The first is related to content area. For example, jobs are plentiful in areas such as math, science (particularly chemistry and physics), special education, and foreign languages (particularly Spanish).

Many jobs also exist in challenging teaching situations, such as underperforming urban schools with high percentages of minority students and students whose native language isn't English.

2.1. What are the three stages of teacher development?

In the first stage, survival is uppermost on beginning teachers' minds. First-year teachers are preoccupied with management concerns and appearing competent in front of others. Anxiety and fatigue are common. After several years, consolidation occurs, and teachers become more confident about their ability to teach. Classroom management becomes routinized, which allows teachers to allocate more of their energies to teaching. In the third stage of teacher development, expertise/mastery, patterns emerge, and teachers begin to understand who they are and what it takes to be successful. The big picture starts to develop, and the focus shifts from survival to student learning and development.

2.2. Identify four factors that contribute to a successful first year of teaching.
Organization, classroom management, effective instruction, and knowing your students are four factors that will influence the success of your first year. For this reason, we describe them as "survival skills" for your first year of teaching. Each is important, but classroom management is one of the most essential: More beginning teachers leave the profession because of their inability to manage students than for any other reason.

2.3. What steps can you take to ensure that your first day of teaching is successful?
The most important factor for success on your first day of teaching is to overprepare. Get organized, and have lesson materials ready to go. Think through your management system, and be ready to share and even teach it to students. Introduce students to your content by actively involving them in a lesson. And finally, take the time to get to know each of your students. They will appreciate the effort and respond more readily during lessons.

2.4. What else can first-year teachers do to survive and thrive in their new schools?
Remember that you are part of a team, and get to know and enlist the aid of other members of your school team. Take the time to develop relationships with school secretaries and custodians; their help throughout the school year will be essential. Don't hide in your room during lunch breaks; visit the teachers' lounge, and find out which teachers are knowledgeable and willing to share their expertise. Informal mentors can be as helpful as formally assigned ones. Use these resources to figure out what the principal expects from his or her teachers. Be prepared for supervisory visits, and know what the principal will be looking for.

2.5. How are teacher evaluation systems created and used?
Educators base the design of teacher evaluation systems on research and theory that describe connections between teaching and learning. Educators gather and compile findings from a variety of sources and create observation instruments based on research. Administrators or supervising teachers then observe and evaluate teachers using the observation instruments as a guide.

2.6. What are the characteristics of successful induction programs?
Effective induction programs include systematic efforts to assist beginning teachers and to help them link their instruction to state and district standards. They also offer support with everyday problems, encourage teachers to develop a reflective professional attitude, and include professional development activities designed to increase mentors' effectiveness and provide compensation for mentors. In addition, new teachers in effective induction programs are observed and are given detailed feedback and support with planning and instruction.

3.1. What is InTASC? How has it influenced teacher preparation?
The Interstate Teacher Assessment and Support Consortium (InTASC) was created in 1987 to help states develop better teachers through coordinated interstate cooperation. It identified core standards for teacher preparation organized around 10 principles; these include knowledge of subject, knowledge of learners and human development, planning and instructional

strategies, as well as ways to work with parents and colleagues. These standards have improved the quality of teacher education and brought about greater uniformity in programs across states.

3.2. Describe two career-long professional-development opportunities available to you as a teacher.

Involving yourself in professional organizations, and attaining National Board certification are two long-term professional-development opportunities that can contribute to your professional growth and development.

3.3. What are five activities professional organizations support that are designed to improve teaching and schools?

Professional organizations aim to improve teaching and schools by (1) producing and disseminating professional publications that provide up-to-date research and information on trends in the profession; (2) providing professional-development activities for teachers; (3) holding yearly conferences that present theory and research about recent professional advances; (4) providing resources where teachers can find answers to questions about professional issues and problems; and (5) providing information to politicians and policy makers about important issues facing education.

REFERENCES

Aarons, D. I. (2010). Marketing scramble ahead amid a shifting landscape. *Education Week, 29*(17), 17.

Abington School District v. Schempp, 374 U.S. 203 (1963).

Abma, J. C., Martinez, G. M., & Copen, C. E. (2010). *Teenagers in the United States, sexual activity, contraceptive use, and childbearing. National survey of family growth 2006–2008.* Vital and Health Statistics, Series 23, No. 30.

Adams, C. (2011, Spring). Recess makes kids smarter. *Instructor,* 55–59. Retrieved from http://vnweb.hwwilsonweb.com.dax.lib.unf.edu/hww/results/external_link_maincontentframe.jhtml?_DARGS=/hww/results/results_common.jhtml.44

Adams, C. (2012). Eligible students missing out on advanced placement courses. *Education Week, 31*(21), 18.

Adler, M. (1982). *The Paideia proposal: An educational manifesto.* New York: Macmillan.

Adler, M. (1998). *The Paideia proposal: An educational manifesto.* (Reprint.) New York: Simon & Schuster.

Aikens, N., & Barbarin, O. (2008). Socioeconomic differences in reading trajectories: The contribution of family, neighborhood, and school contexts. *Journal of Educational Psychology, 100,* 235–251.

Alberto, P. A., & Troutman, A. C. (2013). *Applied behavior analysis for teachers* (9th ed.). Upper Saddle River, NJ: Pearson.

Alder, N. (2002). Interpretations of the meaning of care: Creating caring relationship in urban middle school classrooms. *Urban Education, 37*(2), 241–266.

Alexander, L. (2012). NCLB lessons: It is time for Washington to get out of the way. *Education Week, 31*(15), 40.

Allen, J. (2007). *Creating a welcoming school: A practical guide to home–school partnerships with diverse families.* New York: Teachers College Press.

Allen, R. (2002). Big schools: The way we are. *Educational Leadership, 59*(5), 36–41.

Alonso, G., Anderson, N., Su, C., & Theoharis, J. (2009). *Our schools suck: Students talk back to a segregated nation on the failures or urban education.* New York: New York University Press.

Alperstein, J. F. (2005). Commentary on girls, boys, test scores and more. *Teachers College Record.* Retrieved from http://tcrecord.org ID Number: 11874

Altman, L. (2008). *Sex infections found in quarter of teenage girls.* Retrieved from http://www.nytimes.com/2008/03/12/science/12std.html?_r=1

American Association of University Women. (1992). *How schools shortchange girls.* Annapolis Junction, MD: Author.

American Association of University Women. (1998). *Gender gaps: Where schools still fail our children.* Annapolis Junction, MD: Author.

American Association of University Women. (2006). *Drawing the line: Sexual harassment on campus.* New York: Harris Interactive.

American Bar Association. (2010). *Zero tolerance policy report.* Retrieved from http://www.maine.gov/education/speced/tools/b4se/reports/discipline/policyaba.pdf

American Educational Research Association, American Psychological Association, & National Council of Measurement in Education. (1999). *Standards for educational and psychological testing.* Washington, DC: AERA.

American Federation of Teachers. (2010). *2010 compensation survey.* Retrieved from http://www.aft.org/pdfs/pubemps/pecompsurvey0910.pdf

American Federation of Teachers. (2011). *About AFT teachers.* Retrieved from http://www.aft.org/yourwork/teachers/about.cfm

Amrein, A., & Berliner, D. (2003). The effects of high-stakes testing on student motivation and learning. *Educational Leadership, 60*(5), 32–38.

Anderson, J. (2011, June 2). At elite school, longer classes to go deeper. *New York Times,* pp. A18, A19.

Anderson, J. (2012, January 6). Students of online schools are lagging. *New York Times.* Retrieved from http://www.nytimes.com/2012/01/06/education/students-of-virtual-schools-are-lagging-in-proficiency.html?_r=1&ref=todayspaper

Anderson, L., & Krathwohl, D. (Eds.). (2001). *A taxonomy for learning, teaching, and assessing: A revision of Bloom's taxonomy of educational objectives.* New York: Addison Wesley Longman.

Anderson, M. (2011). Budget compromise puts vouchers back on track for students in D.C. *Education Week, 30*(29), 25.

Anderson, N. (2009, September 25). Unions criticize Obama school reform's reliance on tests, charters as "Bush III." *Washington Post.* Retrieved from http://www.washingtonpost.com/wp-dyn/content/article/2009/09/24/AR2009092403197.html

Anderson, N. (2011, March 3). Midwest union battles highlight debate over improving schools. *Washington Post.* Retrieved from http://www.washingtonpost.com/wp-dyn/content/article/2011/03/02/AR2011030203014.html

Anfara, V., & Mertens, S. (2008). Do single-sex classes and schools make a difference? *Middle School Journal, 40*(2), 52–57.

Applebome, P. (2011, March 10). The promise and costs of charters. *New York Times,* p. A23.

Aronson, E., Wilson, T. D., & Akert, R. D. (2010). *Social psychology* (7th ed.). Upper Saddle River, NJ: Pearson.

Ash, K. (2009). Policies target teacher–student cyber talk. *Education Week, 29*(10), 1, 14.

Ash, K. (2011). Prepping for common core. *Education Week, 31*(9), S7, S8.

Associated Press. (2010). Stiffer Title IX policies rolled out by Ed. Dept. *Education Week, 29*(30), 17.

Associated Press. (2011a). Ala. answers teacher exodus as 1,000-plus prepare to retire. *Education Week, 31*(11), 5.

Associated Press. (2011b). "Attack a Teacher Day" Facebook invitation prompts arrests. *Education Week, 30*(17), 8.

Associated Press. (2011c). Mo. repeals law limiting teacher–student messaging. *Education Week, 31*(10), 10–11.

Attiel, A., Sober, S., Numbers, R., Amasino, R., Cox, B., Berceau, B., Powell, T., & Cox, M. (2006). Defending science education against intelligent design: A call to action. *Journal of Clinical Investigation, 116,* 1134–1138.

Baker, B. (2012). *Revisiting that age-old question: Does money matter in education?* Albert Shanker Institute. Retrieved from http://www.shankerinstitute.org/images/doesmoneymatter_final.pdf

Baker, D. (2006, July 3). For Navajo, science and tradition intertwine. *Salt Lake Tribune,* D1, D5.

Bandura, A. (2001). *Social cognitive theory. In Annual Review of Psychology*. Palo Alto, CA: Annual Review.

Bandura, A. (2004, May). *Toward a psychology of human agency.* Paper presented at the meeting of the American Psychological Society, Chicago.

Banks, J. A. (2008). *An introduction to multicultural education* (4th ed.). Boston: Allyn & Bacon.

Banks, J. A., & Banks, C. A. (2010). *Multicultural education: Issues and perspectives* (7th ed.) Hoboken, NJ: John Wiley & Sons.

Banning Books in Miami. (2009). *Editorial.* Retrieved from www.nytimes.com/2009/02/11/opinion/11wed3.html

Barbour, M. K., & Reeves, T. C. (2009). The reality of virtual schools: A review of the literature. *Computers & Education, 52,* 402–416.

Barnoski, L. (2005). My purpose. *Education Week, 25*(13), 37.

Barton, P. (2006). The dropout problem: Losing ground. *Educational Leadership, 63*(5), 14–18.

Bauerlein, M. (2008). *The dumbest generation: How the digital age stupefies young Americans and jeopardizes our future.* New York: Penguin.

Bauman, S., & Del Rio, A. (2006). Preservice teachers' responses to bullying scenarios: Comparing physical, verbal, and relational bullying. *Journal of Educational Psychology, 98*(1), 219–231.

Bazelon, E. (2008, July 20). The next kind of integration. *New York Times.* Retrieved from http://www.nytimes.com/2008/07/20/magazine/20integration-t.html

Beets, M. W., Flay, B. R., Vuchinich, S., Snyder, F. J., Acock, A., Li, K-K., Burns, K., Washburn, I., & Durlak, J. (2009). Use of a social and character development program to prevent substance abuse, violent behaviors, and sexual activity among elementary school students in Hawaii. *American Journal of Public Health, 99*(8), 1438–1445.

Benner, A., & Mistry, R. (2007). Congruence of mother and teacher educational expectations and low-income youth's academic competence. *Journal of Educational Psychology, 99*(1), 140–153.

Bennett, C., McWhorter, L., & Kuykendall, J. (2006). Will I ever teach? Latino and African American students' perspectives on PRAXIS I. *American Educational Research Journal, 43*(3), 531–575.

Berger, K. (2007). Update on bullying at school: Science forgotten? *Developmental Review,* 90–126.

Berk, L. (2012). *Infants, children, & adolescents* (7th ed.). Boston: Allyn & Bacon.

Berk, L. (2013). *Child development* (9th ed.). Boston: Allyn & Bacon.

Berlin, L. (2009). Public school law: What does it mean in the trenches? *Phi Delta Kappan, 90*(8), 733–737,

Berliner, D. (2005, April). *Our impoverished view of educational reform.* Paper presented at the annual meeting of the American Educational Research Association, Montreal.

Berliner, D. (2009). *Poverty and potential: Out-of-school factors and school success.* Boulder, CO: Education and the Public Interest Center and Tempe, AZ: Education Policy research Unit. Retrieved from http://epicpolicy.org/publication/poverty-and-potential

Bethel School District No. 403 v. Fraser, 106 S. Ct. 3159 (1986).

Betts, J., & Tang, Y. E. (2011). *The effects of charter schools on achievement: A meta-analysis of the literature.* Seattle: National Charter School Research Project. Retrieved from http://www.crpe.org/cs/crpe/download/csr_files/pub_NCSRP_BettsTang_Oct11.pdf

Biddle, B. (2001). Poverty, ethnicity, and achievement in American schools. In B. J. Biddle (Ed.), *Social class, poverty, and education* (pp. 1–30). New York: Routledge Falmer.

Biggs, A., & Richwine, J. (2011, November 16). Are public school teachers really underpaid? Nope. *USA Today,* 11A.

Biskupic, J. (2010, September 30). In Louisville, a new turn in school integration: Court loss leads to income-based plan. *USA Today,* 1A–2A.

Bitter, G., & Legacy, J. (2008). *Using technology in the classroom* (7th ed.). Boston: Allyn & Bacon.

Black, S. (2008). Switching classes. *American School Board Journal, 195*(10), 47–49.

Blatchford, P., Bassett, P., & Brown, P. (2005). Teachers' and pupils' behavior in large and small classes: A systematic observation study of pupils aged 10 and 11 years. Journal of *Educational Psychology, 97*(3), 454–467.

Bloom, A. (1987). *The closing of the American mind.* New York: Simon & Schuster.

Bloom, B. (1981). *All our children learning.* New York: McGraw-Hill.

Bloom, B., Englehart, M., Furst, E., Hill, W., & Krathwohl, O. (1956). *Taxonomy of educational objectives: The classification of educational goals: Handbook 1. The cognitive domain.* White Plains, NY: Longman.

Bloom, H., & Unterman, R. (2012, January). Sustained positive effects on graduation rates. *MDRC Policy Brief.* Retrieved from http://www.mdrc.org/publications/614/policybrief.pdf

Board of Education of Independent School District No. 92 of Pottawatomie County v. Earls 536 U.S. 822, 1225. Ct. 2559 (2002).

Board of Education of the Westside Community School v. Mergens, 496 U.S. 226 (1990).

Bonner, J. (2011, October 31). Idaho is laboratory of teacher pay plans. *Deseret News,* A1, A9.

Bottoms, G., Presson, A., & Han, L. (2004). *Research brief: Linking career/technical studies to broader high school reform.* Southern Regional Education Board. Retrieved from http://www.sreb.org/programs/hstw/publications/briefs/LinkingCTStudies.asp

Boyd, A., & Bichao, S. (2012, February 14). Home-schooling demographics change, expand. *USA Today.* Retrieved from http://www.usatoday.com/news/education/story/2012-02-14/home-schools-secular/53095020/1

Boyd, D. Grossman, P., Ing, M., Lankford, H., Loeb, S., & Wyckoff, J. (2011). The influence of school administrators on teacher retention decisions. *American Educational Research Journal, 48*(2), 303–33.

Bracey, G. (2002). The 12th Bracey report on the condition of public education. *Phi Delta Kappan, 84,* 135–150.

Bracey, G. (2003). Not all alike. *Phi Delta Kappan, 84,* 717–718.

Bracey, G. (2005). And now, the Indian spelling gene. *Phi Delta Kappan, 87*(1), 91–93.

Bracey, G. (2008). Public versus private . . . again. *Phi Delta Kappan, 89*(5), 396–397.

Bradley v. Pittsburgh Board of Education, 913 F.2d 1064 (3d Cir. 1990).

Bransford, J., Brown, A., & Cocking, R. (Eds.). (2000). *How people learn: Brain, mind, experience, and school.* Washington, DC: National Academy Press.

Brenneman, R. (2011). Survey examines public's appetite for education news. *Education Week, 30*(27), 17.

Brill, S. (2009, August 31). The rubber room: The battle over New York's worst teachers. *New Yorker.* Retrieved from http://www.newyorker.com/reporting/2009/08/31/090831fa_fact_brill

Brimley, V., Verstegen, D., & Garfield, R. (2012). *Financing education in a climate of change* (11th ed.). Boston: Allyn & Bacon.

Brophy, J. (2006). Observational research on generic aspects of classroom teaching. In P. A. Alexander & P. H. Winne (Eds.), *Handbook of educational psychology* (2nd ed., pp. 755–780). Mahwah, NJ: Erlbaum.

Brophy, J. (2010). *Motivating students to learn* (3rd ed.). New York: Routledge.

Brown v. Bathhe, 416 F. Supp. 1194 (D. Neb. 1976).

Brown v. Board of Education of Topeka, 347 U.S. 483 (1954).

Brown, D. (2011). Should I take AP or dual enrollment courses? *Admission Center.* Retrieved from http://www.theadmissioncentre.com/2011/should-i-take-ap-or-dual-enrollment-courses/#axzz1nW2N7YQU

Brown, J. (2011). Middle school model re-thought. *Cincinnati Inquirer.* Retrieved from http://news.cincinnati.com/article/20111225/NEWS0102/312250017/Middle-school-model-re-thought

Bruning, R. H., Schraw, G. J., & Norby, M. M. (2011). *Cognitive psychology and instruction* (5th ed.). Upper Saddle River, NJ: Prentice Hall.

Bryk, A., Sebring, P., Allensworth, E., Luppescu, S., & Easton, J. (2010). *Organizing schools for improvement: Lessons from Chicago.* Chicago: University of Chicago Press.

Buck, S., Ritter, G., Jensen, N., & Rose, C. (2010). Teachers say the most interesting things—An alternative view of testing. *Phi Delta Kappan, 91*(6), 50–53.

Bullough, R., Jr. (1989). *First-year teacher: A case study.* New York: Teachers College Press.

Bullough, R., Jr. (2001). *Uncertain lives: Children of promise, teachers of hope.* New York: Teachers College Press.

Bureau of Labor Statistics. (2009). *Occupational outlook handbook, 2008–2009 edition.* Washington, DC: U.S. Government Printing Office.

Bureau of Labor Statistics. (2011). *Occupational outlook handbook, 2010–2011 Edition.* Washington, DC: Department of Labor.

Burkam, D., Michaels, D., & Lee, V. (2007). School grade span and kindergarten learning. *Elementary School Journal, 107*(3), 287–304.

Bushaw, W., & Gallup, A. (2008). The 40th annual Phi Delta Kappa/Gallup poll of the public's attitudes toward the public schools. *Phi Delta Kappan, 90,* 9–20.

Bushaw, W. J., & Lopez, S. J. (2010). A time for change: The 42nd annual Phi Delta Kappa/Gallup Poll of the Public's attitude toward the public schools. *Phi Delta Kappan, 92,* 9–26.

Bushaw, W., & Lopez, S. (2011). Betting on teachers: The 43rd annual Phi Delta Kappan/Gallup Poll of the public's attitudes toward the public schools. *Phi Delta Kappan, 93,* 9–26.

Business Wire. (2009, June 10). *Majorities of Americans continue to believe teacher pay too low.* Retrieved from http://findarticles.com/p/articles/mi_m0EIN/is_20090610/ai_n31971623/

Button, H., & Provenzo, E. (1989). *History of education in American culture.* New York: Holt, Rinehart & Winston.

California Department of Education. (2011). *Statewide enrollment by ethnicity.* Retrieved from http://dq.cde.ca.gov/dataquest/EnrollEthState.asp?Level=State&TheYear=2010-11&cChoice=EnrollEth1&p=2

California State Board of Education. (2008a). *Content standards.* Retrieved from http://www.cde.ca.gov/be/st/ss/

California State Board of Education. (2008b). *2003–2007 CST Released Test Questions*, p. 7. Retrieved from: http://www.cde.ca.gov/ta/tg/sr/documents/rtqgr11ela.pdf

Callister, T., & Burbules, N. (2004). Just give it to me straight: A case against filtering the Internet. *Phi Delta Kappan, 85*(9), 649–655.

Cambron-McCabe, N. (2009). Balancing students' constitutional rights. *Phi Delta Kappan, 90*(8), 709–713.

Campbell, F., Pungello, E., Burchinal, M., Kainz, K., Pan, Y., Wasik, B., Barbarin, O., Sparling, J., & Ramey, C. (2012, January 16). Adult outcomes as a function of an early childhood educational program: An Abecedarian Project follow-up. *Developmental Psychology*. Retrieved from http://psycnet.apa.org/psycinfo/2012-00549-001/

Campbell, P. (2007a). Edison is the symptom, NCLB is the disease. *Phi Delta Kappan, 99*(6), 438–443

Campbell, P. (2007b). High stakes for Edison: A rejoinder to John Chubb. *Phi Delta Kappan, 88*(6), 451–454.

Carey, B. (2010, December 12). Tracing the spark of creative problem-solving. *New York Times*. Retrieved from http://www.nytimes.com/2010/12/07/science/07brain.html?_r=1&ref=science

Carjuzaa, J., & Kellough, R. (2013). *Teaching in the middle and secondary schools* (10th ed.). Boston: Allyn & Bacon.

Carnegie Forum on Education and the Economy. (1986*). A nation prepared: Teachers for the 21st century*. Washington, DC: Author. (ERIC Document Reproduction Service No. ED268120)

Cascio, E. (2010). What happened when kindergarten went universal? *Education Next, 10*, 2. Retrieved April 2011 from http://educationnext.org/what-happened-when-kindergarten-went-universal/

Cavanagh, S. (2006a). Perkins bill is approved by Congress. *Education Week, 25*(44), 1, 27.

Cavanagh, S. (2006b). Possible road map seen in Dover case. *Education Week, 25*(10), 1, 10, 11.

Cavanagh, S. (2008). American culture seen to thwart girls' math development. *Education Week, 28*(9), 10.

Cavanagh, S. (2009). Parents schooled in learning how to help with math. *Education Week, 28*(22), 10–11.

Cavanaugh, S. (2010). Resurgent debate, familiar themes. *Education Week, 29*(17), 5–11.

Cavanagh, S. (2011a). Ambitious program signed into law in Indiana. *Education Week, 30*(30), 21.

Cavanagh, S. (2011b). California deficit clouds picture for K–12 funding. *Education Week, 30*(30), 1, 26.

Cavanagh, S. (2011c). Labor-curb plan eyed warily. *Education Week, 30*(23), 1, 20–21.

Cavanagh, S. (2011d). New laws curbing public worker bargaining besieged. *Education Week, 30*(28), 26, 28.

Cavanagh, S. (2011e). Online learning mandate on the move in Idaho. *Education Week, 31*(4), 10.

Cavanagh, S. (2011f). Pushed to improve—Race to Top, or not. *Education Week, 30*(26), 1, 22–23.

Cavanagh, S. (2011g). Race to Top now faces acid test. *Education Week, 30*(2), 1, 16.

Cavanagh, S. (2012a). Complex policy options abound amid international comparison. *Education Week, 31*(16), 6–10.

Cavanagh, S. (2012b). States dogged by lawsuits on K–12 funding. *Education Week, 31*(17), 1, 23.

Center for Public Education. (2011). *Starting out right: pre-k and kindergarten: full report*. Retrieved from http://www.centerforpubliceducation.org/Main-Menu/Organizing-a-school/Starting-Out-Right-Pre-K-and-Kindergarten/Starting-Out-Right-Pre-K-and-Kindergarten-full-report.html

Centers for Disease Control and Prevention. (2008). *Youth risk behavior surveillance—United States, 2007*. Retrieved from http://www.cdc.gov/HealthyYouth/yrbs/

Centers for Disease Control and Prevention. (2010). *Youth risk behavior surveillance system*. Retrieved from http://www.cdc.gov/HealthyYouth/yrbs/index.htm

Chalk v. U.S. District Court Cent. Dist. of California, 840 F.2d. 701 (9th Cir. 1988).

Chance, P. (1997). Speaking of differences. *Phi Delta Kappan, 78*(7), 506–507.

Chandler, M. (2012, January 3). Traditional schools blurring district lines. *Washington Post*. Retrieved from http://www.washingtonpost.com/local/education/2011/12/29/gIQAUIV-HZP_story_1.html

Chapman, C., Laird, J., Ifill, N., & KewalRamani, A. (2011*). Trends in high school dropout and completion rates in the United States: 1972–2009*. National Center for Education Statistics. Retrieved from http://nces.ed.gov/pubs2012/2012006.pdf

Charles, C. M., & Senter, G. W. (2012). *Elementary classroom management* (6th ed.). New York: Addison Wesley.

Chen, J. (2004). Theory of multiple intelligences: Is it a scientific theory? *Teachers College Record, 106*, 17–23.

Chesley, G. (2011). Now is the time to redefine teacher tenure. *Education Week, 30*(29), 44.

Chetty, R., Friedman, J., & Rockoff, J. (2011). *The long-term impacts of teachers: Teacher value-added and student outcomes in adulthood*. Retrieved from http://obs.rc.fas.harvard.edu/chetty/value_added.pdf

Chinni, D. (2011). Income inequality gap widens among U. S. communities over 30 years. *PBS NewsHour*. Retrieved from http://www.pbs.org/newshour/rundown/2011/03/income-inequality-gap-widens-among-us-communities-over-30-years.html

Chubb, J. (2007). Confluence is a cure: A reply to "Edison is the symptom, NCLB is the disease." *Phi Delta Kappan, 88*(6), 444–450.

Clark, R. C. (2010). *Evidence-based training methods: A guide for training professionals*. Alexandria, VA: ASTD Press.

Clement, M. (2008). Improving teacher selection with behavior-based interviewing. *Principal, 87*(3), 44–47.

Cochran-Smith, M., Feiman-Nemser, S. McIntyre, D. J. & Demers, K. (Eds.). (2008). *Handbook of research on teacher education* (3rd ed.). New York: Routledge.

Coleman, J., Campbell, E., Hobson, D., McPortland, J., Mood. A., Weinfield, F., & York, R. (1966). *Equality of educational opportunity*. Washington, DC: U.S. Department of Health, Education and Welfare.

Collins, G. (2011, December 3). Virtually educated. *New York Times*. Retrieved from http://www.nytimes.com/2011/12/03/opinion/virtually-educated.html?nl=todaysheadlines&emc=tha212&pagewanted

Common Core. (2011). *Learning less: Public school teachers describe a narrowing curriculum*. Retrieved from http://commoncore.org/ourreports.php

Common Core State Standards Initiative. (2010a). *Fifty-one states and territories join Common Core State Standards Initiative*. Retrieved from http://www.corestandards.org/

Common Core State Standards Initiative. (2010b). *Common Core State Standards for Mathematics*. Retrieved from http://www.corestandards.org/Files/K12MathStandards.pdf

Common Core State Standards Initiative. (2010c). *Common core state standards for English Language Arts and Literacy in History/Social Studies & Science*. Retrieved from http://www.corestandards.org/Files/K12ELAStandards.pdf

Commonwealth of Pennsylvania v. Douglass, 588 A.2d 53 (Pa. Super. Ct. 1991).

Compayre, G. (1888). *History of pedagogy* (W. Payne, Trans.). Boston: Heath.

Conant, J. (1959). *The American high school*. New York: McGraw-Hill.

Conroy, J. C., Davis, R. A., & Enslin, P. (2008). Philosophy as a basis for policy and practice: What confidence can we have in philosophical analysis and argument? *Journal of Philosophy of Education, 42,* 165–182.

Constantine, N., Jerman, P., Huang, A. (2007). California parents preferences and beliefs on school-based sexuality education policy. *Perspectives on Sexual & Reproductive Health, 39,* 169–175.

Cooper, H., Robinson, J. C., & Patall, E. A. (2006). Does homework improve academic achievement? A synthesis of research, 1987–2003. *Review of Educational Research, 76,* 1–62.

Cooperman, S. (2003). A new order of things. *Education Week, 22*(38), 30, 32.

Council for American Private Education. (2011). *Facts and studies*. Retrieved from http://www.capenet.org/facts.html

Council of Chief State School Officers. (2011). *2011 National teacher of the year*. Retrieved from http://www.pearsonfoundation.org/ccsso-toy/2011

Council of the Great City Schools. (2009). *Urban school superintendents: Characteristics, tenure, and salary. Sixth survey report*. Retrieved from http://www.cgcs.org/Pubs/Urban_Indicator_08-09.pdf

Council of the Great City Schools. (2011). *Urban school statistics*. Washington, DC. Retrieved from http://www.cgcs.org/site/default.aspx?pageid=75

Covay, E., & Carbonaro, W. (2010). After the bell: Participation in extracurricular activities, classroom behavior and academic achievement. *Sociology of Education, 83*(1), 20–45.

Cowan, R., & Sheridan, S. (2003). Investigating the acceptability of behavioral interventions in applied conjoint behavioral consultation: Moving from analog conditions to naturalistic settings. *School Psychology Quarterly, 18,* 1–21.

Coyne, M., Carnine, D., & Kame'enui, E. (2011). *Effective teaching strategies that accommodate diverse learners* (4th ed.). Boston: Pearson.

Coyne, R. (2011, August 29). Indiana vouchers nudge thousands into private schools. *Salt Lake Tribune*, A10.

Cuban, L. (1986). *Teachers and machines: The classroom use of technology since 1920*. New York: Teachers College Press.

Cuban, L. (1993). *How teachers taught: Constancy and change in American classrooms: 1890–1990* (2nd ed). New York: Teachers College Press, Teachers College, Columbia University.

Cuban, L. (2001). *Oversold and underused: Computers in the classroom*. Boston: Harvard University Press.

Cuban, L. (2003). *Why is it so hard to get good schools?* New York: Teachers College Press.

Cuban, L. (2004a). *The blackboard and the bottom line: Why schools can't be businesses*. Cambridge, MA: Harvard University Press.

Cuban, L. (2004b). The open classroom. *Education Next*. Retrieved from http://educationnext.org/theopenclassroom/

Cuban, L. (2005). *Growing instructional technology in U. S. classrooms*. 2005 J. George Jones & Velma Rife Jones Lecture: University of Utah, Salt Lake City.

Cuban, L. (2008). The turnstile superintendency? *Education Week, 28*(1), 26–27.

Cuban, L. (2010). *Larry Cuban on school reform and classroom practice: Part 2—high school reform again and again and again*. Retrieved from http://larrycuban.wordpress.com/2010/03/26/part-2-high-school-reform-again-again-and-again/

Cuban, L. (2012). Standards versus customization: Finding the balance. *Educational Leadership, 69*(5), 10–15.

Cullotto, K. (2011, March 25). As student absenteeism rises, a charter school fights back. *New York Times*. Retrieved from http://www.nytimes.com/2011/03/25/us/25cncabsent.html?r=1

Cushman, K. (2003). *Fires in the bathroom: Advice for teachers from high school students*. New York: The New Press.

Cushman, K. (2006). Help us care enough to learn. *Educational Leadership, 63*(5), 34–37.

Darden, E. (2008a). Policy, the law, and you. *American School Board Journal, 195*(4), 54–55.

Darden, E. (2008b). What not to wear. *American School Board Journal, 195*(1), 36–37.

Darling-Hammond, L. (2008). Knowledge for teaching: What do we know? In M. Cochran-Smith, S. Feiman-Nemser, D. J. McIntyre, & K. Demers (Eds.), *Handbook of research on teacher education* (3rd ed., pp. 1316–1323). New York: Routledge.

Darling-Hammond, L. (2012). Value-added teacher evaluation: The harm behind the hype. *Education Week, 31*(24), 32.

Darling-Hammond, L., & Bransford, J. (Eds.). (2005). *Preparing teachers for a changing world: What teachers should learn and be able to do*. San Francisco: Jossey-Bass.

Davis, M. (2010a). Schools factoring e-courses into the daily learning mix. *Education Week, April 28,* S4, S5.

Davis, M. (2010b). Social networking goes to school. *Education Week Digital Directions, Spring/Summer,* 16–23.

Davis, M. (2011). Training takes a hybrid turn. *Education Week: Virtual PD Creates Connections, 31*(9), S4, S6–S7.

DeBose, G., Jellinek, C., Mullenholtz, G., Walker, S., & Woods-Murphy, M. (2012). Teachers want to lead their profession's transformation. *Education Week, 31*(20), 23–24.

Delisle, J. (1984). *Gifted children speak out.* New York: Walker.

DeMitchele, T. (2007). School uniforms: There is no free lunch. *Teachers College Record.* Retrieved from http://www.tcrecord.org

Devlin-Scherer, R., Burroughs, G., Daly, J., & McCarten, W. (2007). The value of the teacher work sample for improving instruction and program. *Action in Teacher Education, 29*(1), 51–60.

Dewey, J. (1902). *The child and the curriculum.* Chicago: University of Chicago Press.

Dewey, J. (1906). *Democracy and education.* New York: Macmillan.

Dewey, J. (1923). *The school and society.* Chicago: University of Chicago Press.

Dewey, J. (1938). *Experience and education.* New York: Macmillan.

Dill, V. (2010). Students without homes. *Educational Leadership, 68*(3), 43–47.

Dillon, N. (2007). The trail to progress. *American School Board Journal, 194*(12), 21–24.

Dillon, S. (2008a, September 1). Hard times hitting students and schools. *New York Times.* Retrieved from http://www.nytimes.com/2008/09/01/education/01school.html?th&emc=th

Dillon, S. (2008b, November 13). School chief takes on tenure, and stirs a fight. *New York Times,* pp. A1, A19.

Dillon, S. (2008c, March 20). States' data obscure how few finish high school. *New York Times.* Retrieved from http://www.nytimes.com/2008/03/20/education/20graduation.html

Dillon, S. (2009, April 7). Report envisions shortage of teachers as retirements escalate. *New York Times.* Retrieved from http://www.nytimes.com/2009/04/07/education/07teacher.html?em

Dillon, S. (2010, September 1). Formula to grade teachers' skill gains acceptance, and critics. *New York Times*, pp. A1, A3.

Dillon, S. (2011a, March 31). Study says charter network has financial advantages over public schools. *New York Times,* p. A15.

Dillon, S. (2011b, June 15). U. S. students remain poor at history, tests show. *New York Times.* Retrieved from http://www.nytimes.com/2011/06/15/education/15history.html

Dilworth, M. (2011). *Mixed results reflect complexity of measuring the impact of National Board Certification.* American Institute for Research. Retrieved from http://www.caldercenter.org/research/Dilworth.cfm

Dimick, A., & Apple, M. (2005). Texas and the politics of abstinence-only textbooks. *Teachers College Record.* Retrieved from http://www.tcrecord.org ID Number 11855

Doe v. Renfrow, 635 F.2d 582 (7th Cir. 1980).

Donaldson, M., & Johnson, S. (2011, October 4). TFA teachers: How long do they teach? Why do they leave? *Phi Delta Kappan.* Retrieved from http://www.edweek.org/ew/articles/2011/10/04/kappan_donaldson.html?tkn=ROUF3k9ZdvpmgDUx9obttSJjFvDiipamx8Tl&cmp=ENL-EU-NEWS2

Doyle, C. (2010). All of my favorite students cheat: When dishonesty is a norm at school. *Education Week, 30*(2), 18–19.

Doyle, C. (2011). Back to the future. *Education Week, 31*(3), 25.

Doyle, W. (2006). Ecological approaches to classroom management. In C. M. Evertson & C. S. Weinstein (Eds.), *Handbook of classroom management: Research, practice, and contemporary issues* (pp. 97–125). Mahwah, NJ: Erlbaum.

Eagle, T., Gurm, R., Goldberg, C., DuRussel-Weston, J., Kline-Rogers, E., Palma-Dave, L., Aaronson, S., Fitzgerald, C., Mitchell, L., & Rogers, B. (2010). Health status and behavior among middle-school children in a midwest community: What are the underpinnings of childhood obesity? *American Heart Journal, 160*(6), 1185–1190.

Echevarria, J., & Graves, A. (2011). *Sheltered content instruction* (4th ed.). Boston: Allyn & Bacon.

Eckholm, E. (2009, March 11). As jobs vanish, motel rooms become home. *New York Times,* pp. A1, A16.

Editorial. (2012, February 15). In today's economy, age 16 is too soon to drop out of school. [Editorial]. *USA Today*, 6A.

Educational Testing Service. (2012). *The Praxis Series™: Principles of Learning and Teaching: Grades 7–12 (0524).* Retrieved from http://www.ets.org/Media/Tests/PRAXIS/pdf/0524.pdf

Edwards, J., Chronister, G., & Bomster, M. (2012). Executive summary: Equipping U.S. schools for the global fast lane. *Education Week, 31*(16), 4–5.

Eggen, P., & Kauchak, D. (2012*). Strategies and models for teachers: Teaching content and thinking skills* (6th ed.). Upper Saddle River, NJ: Pearson.

Eggen, P., & Kauchak, D. (2013). *Educational psychology: Windows on classrooms* (9th ed.). Upper Saddle River, NJ: Merrill/Pearson.

Eisenberg, M., Bernat, D., Bearinger, L., & Resnick, M. (2008). Support for comprehensive sexuality education: Perspectives from parents of school-age youth. *Journal of Adolescent Health, 42*(4), 352–359.

Eisner, E. (1993). *The educational imagination: On the design and evaluation of school programs* (3rd ed.). New York: Macmillan.

Eisner, E. (2003). Questionable assumptions about schooling. *Phi Delta Kappan, 84,* 648–657.

Eliot, L. (2010). The myth of pink & blue brains. *Educational Leadership, 68*(3), 32–36.

Emmer, E. T., & Evertson, C. M. (2013). *Classroom management for middle and high school teachers* (9th ed.). Upper Saddle River, NJ: Pearson.

Emmons, C., & Comer, J. (2009). Capturing complexity: Evaluation of the Yale Child Study Center School Development

Program. In R. Deslandes (Ed.), *International perspectives on contexts, communities, and evaluated innovative practices: Family–school community partnerships* (pp. 204–219). New York: Routledge.

Engel, S., & Sandstrom, M. (2010, July 23). There's only one way to stop a bully. *New York Times.* Retrieved from http://www.nytimes.com/2010/07/23/opinion/23engel.html

Engle v. Vitale, 370 U.S. 421 (1962).

EPE Research Center. (2011a). Graduation in the United States. *Education Week,* Diplomas Count, *30*(34), 26.

EPE Research Center. (2011b). Most of nation's largest school systems meeting expectations. *Education Week, Diplomas Count, 30*(34), 27.

Equity Project. (2012). *The Equity Project Charter School.* Retrieved from http://www.tepcharter.org/

ETR Associates. (2011). *National service-learning clearinghouse.* Retrieved from http://www.servicelearning.org

Evans, C., Kirby, U., & Fabrigar, L. (2003). Approaches to learning, need for cognition, and strategic flexibility among university students. *British Journal of Educational Psychology, 73,* 507–528.

Evertson, C. M., & Emmer, E. T. (2013). *Classroom management for elementary teachers* (9th ed.). Upper Saddle River, NJ: Pearson.

Fagen v. Summers, 498 P.2d 1227 (Wyo. 1972).

Faject, W., Bello, M., & Leftwich, S. A. (2005). Pre-service teachers' perceptions in beginning education classes. *Teaching and Teacher Education, 21*(6), 717–727.

Fallace, T. (2011). Tracing John Dewey's influence on progressive education. *Teachers College Record, 113*(3), 463–492.

Fast, J. (2008).*Ceremonial violence: A psychological explanation of school shootings.* New York: Overlook Press.

Federal Interagency Forum on Child and Family Statistics. (2010). *America's children in brief: Key national indicators of well-being, 2010.* Retrieved from http://www.childstats.gov/pdf/ac2010/ac_10.pdf

Feeding America. (2010). *Hunger study 2010.* Retrieved from http://feedingamerica.org/hunger-in-america/hunger-studies/hunger-study-2010.aspx

Feiman-Nemser, S. (2008). Teacher learning: How do teachers learn to teach? In M. Cochran-Smith, S. Feiman-Nemser, D. J. McIntyre, & K. Demers (Eds.), *Handbook of research on teacher education* (3rd ed., pp. 697–705). New York: Routledge.

Feinberg, W., & Soltis, J. (2004). *School and society* (4th ed.). New York: Teachers College Press.

Feistritzer, E. (2011). *Profile of teachers in U.S., 2011.* Washington, DC: National Center for Education Information.

Feldman, J., López, L., & Simon, K. (2006). *Choosing small: The essential guide to successful high school conversion.* San Francisco: Jossey-Bass.

Feller, B., & Hefling, C. (2012, February 9). Georgia among first states to get No Child Left Behind waiver. *Online Athens.* Retrieved from http://onlineathens.com/local-news/2012-02-09/georgia-among-first-states-get-no-child-left-behind-waiver

Fernandez, M. (2012, April 9). At Texas schools, making do on a shoestring. *New York Times,* p. A10.

Fertig, B. (2009). Choosing the direction of New York City Schools. *New Yorker.* Retrieved from http://www.wnyc.org/news/articles/123303

Finn, C., & Petrilli, M. (2009). Stimulating a race to the top. *Education Week, 28*(24), 31.

Finn, J., Gerber, S., & Boyd-Zaharias, J. (2005). Small classes in the early grades, academic achievement, and graduating from high school. *Journal of Educational Psychology, 97*(2), 214–223.

First Amendment Center. (1999). *The Bible and public schools: A First Amendment guide.* Nashville, TN: Author. Retrieved from http://www.freedomforum.org/publications/first/BibleAndPublicSchools/bibleguide_reprint.pdf

Fisher, D. (2006). Keeping adolescents "alive and kickin' it": Addressing suicide in schools. *Phi Delta Kappan, 87*(10), 784–786.

Fiske, E., & Ladd, H. (2010). The Dutch experience with weighted student funding. *Phi Delta Kappan, 92*(1), 49–53.

Fitzgerald, E. (2011). *Pay-to-play policy grows nationally as school budgets shrink.* Retrieved from http://www.newstimes.com/default/article/Pay-to-play-policy-grows-nationally-as-school-1383200.php

Flanigan, R. (2011). Networking professionals. *Education Week: Virtual PD Creates Connections, 31*(9), S10–S12.

Flanigan, R. (2012). U.S. schools forge foreign connections. *Education Week, 31*(19), S2–S4.

Fleischfresser v. Directors of School District No. 200, 15 F.3d 680 (7th Cir. 1994).

Fleming, N. (2011). Some efforts on merit pay scaled back. *Education Week, 31*(4), 1, 18.

Fleming, W. (2006). Myths and stereotypes about Native Americans. *Phi Delta Kappan, 88*(3), 213–216.

Florida Department of Education. (2007). *Sunshine state standards, Mathematics PreK–2.* Retrieved from http://etc.usf.edu/flstandards/sss/index.html

Florida Department of Education. (2008). *Florida Comprehensive Assessment Test.* Retrieved from: http://fcat.fldoe.org/fcatsmpl.asp

Florida Department of Education. (2010). *Next generation Sunshine State Standards.* Retrieved from http://www.floridastandards.org/Standards/FLStandardSearch.aspx

Foley, J. (2009). Time to update schools' reading lists. *Seattle Post Intelligencer.* Retrieved from http://www.seattlepi.com/local/opinion/article/Guest-Columnist-Time-to-update-schools-reading-1296681.php

Fong, T. P. (2007). *The contemporary Asian American experience: Beyond the model minority* (3rd ed.). Upper Saddle River, NJ: Prentice Hall.

Fossey, R., & Russo, C. (2008). Teachers' First Amendment rights are shrinking in the wake of a 2006 Supreme Court decision: That can't be good. *Teachers College Record.* ID Number: 14914. Retrieved from http://www.tcrecord.org

Franco, M. S., & Patel, N. H. (2011). An interim report on a pilot recovery program in a large, suburban midwestern high school. *Education, 132,* 15–27.

Frede, E., & Barnett, W. S. (2011). Why pre-K is critical to closing the achievement gap. *Principal, 90,* 8–11.

Freiberg, J. (1999). Sustaining the paradigm. In J. Freiberg (Ed.), *Beyond behaviorism: Changing the classroom management paradigm* (pp. 164–173). Boston: Allyn & Bacon.

Freire, P. (1989). *Pedagogy of the oppressed.* New York: Continuum Press.

Frey, W. H. (2011). *A demographic tipping point among America's three-year-olds.* Brookings Institute. Retrieved from http://www.brookings.edu/opinions/2011/0207_population_frey.aspx

Friedman, T. (2009, April 21). Swimming without a suit. *New York Times,* p. A20.

Friedman, T. (2010, August 25). Steal this movie, too. *New York Times,* p. A19.

Friesen, N. (2011). The lecture as a transmedial pedagogical form: A historical analysis. *Educational Researcher, 40,* 95–102.

Friess, S. (2009, April 13). A small Nevada town fears a damaging silence from its school bell soon. *New York Times,* p. A13.

Frosch, D. (2011, March 30). A trip to these principals may mean a paddling: Corporal punishment, dwindling over all, retains a hold in many public schools. *New York Times,* p. A15.

Gabriel, T., & Richtel, M. (2011, October 9). Inflating the software report card. *New York Times.* Retrieved from http://www.nytimes.com/2011/10/09/technology/a-classroom-software-boom-but-mixed-results-despite-the-hype.html?_r=1&nl=todaysheadlines&emc=tha23&pagewanted

Gaither, M. (2009). Homeschooling goes mainstream. *Education Next, 9*(1). Retrieved from http://educationnext.org/home-schooling-goes-mainstream/

Galley, M. (2004). Court blocks school ban on weapons images. *Education Week, 23*(16), 6.

Gallup. (2011). *Evolution, creationism, intelligent design.* Retrieved from http://www.gallup.com/poll/21814/evolution-creationism-intelligent-design.aspx

Gándara, P. (2010). The Latino education crisis. *Educational Leadership, 67*(5), 24–30.

Gao, H., Losh, S. C., Shen, E., Turner, J. E., & Yuan, R. (2007, April). *The effect of collaborative concept mapping on learning, problem solving, and learner attitude.* Paper presented at the annual meeting of the American Educational Research Association, Chicago.

Garcia, R. (2006). Language, culture, and education. In J. Banks, *Cultural diversity and education* (5th ed., pp. 266–291). Boston: Allyn & Bacon.

Gardner, H. (1983). *Frames of mind: The theory of multiple intelligences.* New York: Basic Books.

Gardner, H. (2008). E pluribus . . . a tale of three systems. *Education Week, 27*(34), 40.

Gardner, H. (2011, July 18). To improve U.S. education, it's time to treat teachers as professionals. *Washington Post.* Retrieved from http://www.washingtonpost.com/national/on-leadership/to-improve-us-education-its-time-to-treat-teachers-as-professionals/2011/07/18/gIQA8oh2LI_story.html

Gardner, H., & Moran, S. (2006). The science of multiple intelligences theory: A response to Lynn Waterhouse. *Educational Psychology, 41*(4), 227–232.

Garlick, D. (2010). *Intelligence and the brain: Solving the mystery of why people differ in IQ and how a child can be a genius.* Burbank, CA: Aesop Press

Gauld, J. (2012). Rebalancing learning with character education. *Education Week, 31*(18), 25.

Gay, G. (2005). Politics of multicultural teacher education. *Journal of Teacher Education, 56*(3), 221–228.

Gehring, J. (2002). Benefit of Illinois credit misses needy, study says. *Education Week, 22*(8), 11.

Gewertz, C. (2002). Edison buffeted by probe, loss of contracts. *Education Week, 22*(1), 3.

Gewertz, C. (2003). Vallas calls for cuts to private companies. *Education Week, 22*(29), 3.

Gewertz, C. (2006). H.S. dropouts say lack of motivation top reason to quit. *Education Week, 25*(26), 1, 14.

Gewertz, C. (2008). Consensus on learning time builds. *Education Week, 28*(5), 14–17.

Gewertz, C. (2010). Proposed standards go public: Math and English draft elicits kudos and doubts. *Education Week, 29*(25), 1, 14–15.

Gewertz, C. (2011a). Common-assessment consortia add resources to plans. *Education Week, 30*(21), 8.

Gewertz, C. (2011b). Higher ed.: Common core college-ready: But academics maintain some skills are missing. *Education Week, 31*(2), 1, 12–13.

Gewertz, C. (2011c). Progress is slow on common-standards implementation. *Education Week, 31*(4), 13.

Gewertz, C. (2012a). N. H. schools focus on competency. *Education Week, 31*(20), 1, 16.

Gewertz. C. (2012b). New details surface about common state assessments. *Education Week, 31*(15), 10.

Gladding, M. (2007). *A guide to ethical conduct for the helping professions* (2nd ed.). Upper Saddle River, NJ: Merrill/Pearson.

Glanzer, P. (2005). Moving beyond censorship: What will educators do if a controversy over "His Dark Materials" erupts? *Phi Delta Kappan, 87*(2), 166–168.

Gläscher, J., Rudrauf, D., Colom, R., Paul, L., Tranel, D., Damasio, H., & Adolphs, R. (2010). Distributed neural system for general intelligence revealed by lesion mapping. *Proceedings of the National Academy of Sciences of the United States of America, 107,* 4705–4709.

Glass, G. V., & Welner, K. C. (2011). *Online K–12 schooling in the U.S.: Uncertain private ventures in need of public regulation.* National Education Policy Center. http://nepc.colorado.edu/publication/online-k-12-schooling

Glasson, T. (2007). The imperial origins of the king's church in early America, 1607–1783. *William and Mary Quarterly, 64,* 859–61.

Goddard, R., Hoy, W., & Hoy, A. (2004). Collective efficacy beliefs: Theoretical developments, empirical evidence, and future directions. *Educational Researcher, 33*(3), 3–13.

Goldhaber, D., DeArmond, M., & DeBurgomaster, S. (2011). Teacher attitudes about compensation reform: Implications for reform implementation. *LexisNexis.* Retrieved from https://litigation-essentials.lexisnexis.com/webcd/app?action=DocumentDisplay&crawlid=1&doctype=cite&docid=64+Ind.+%26+Lab.+Rel.+Rev.+441&srctype=smi&srcid=3B15&key=1dc6a7a877115536b6e211b1a2bd0068

Goldin, C., & Katz, L. (2008). *The race between education and technology.* Cambridge, MA: Harvard University Press.

Goldsmith, P. (2011). Coleman revisited: School segregation, peers, and frog ponds. *American Educational Research Journal, 48*(3), 508–535.

Goldstein, D. (2006, May 6). Upset over anthem translation? Change your tune; it's old news. *Salt Lake Tribune,* A1, A4.

Goldstein, R. (2004). Who are our urban students and what makes them so different? In S. R. Steinberg & J. L. Kincheloe (Eds.), *19 Urban questions: Teaching in the city* (pp. 41–51). New York: Peter Lang.

Gollnick, D. (2008). Teacher capacity for diversity. In M. Cochran-Smith, S. Feiman-Nemser, D. J. McIntyre, & K. Demers (Eds.), *Handbook of research on teacher education* (3rd ed., pp. 249–258). New York: Routledge.

Gollnick, D., & Chinn, P. (2013). *Multicultural education in a pluralistic society* (9th ed.). Upper Saddle River, NJ: Merrill/Prentice Hall.

Good, T., & Brophy, J. (2008). *Looking in classrooms* (10th ed.). Boston: Allyn & Bacon.

Goodlad, J. (1984). *A place called school.* New York: McGraw-Hill.

Goodlad, J. I., Soder, R., & Sirotnik, K. A. (Eds.). (1990). *The moral dimensions of teaching.* San Francisco: Jossey-Bass.

Goodwin, B. (2010, December). Good teachers may not fit the mold. *Educational Leadership.* Retrieved from http://www.ascd.org/publications/educational-leadership/dec10/vol68/num04/Good-Teachers-May-Not-Fit-the-Mold.aspx

Gootman, E. (2009, June 5). Next test: Value of $125,000-a-year teachers. *New York Times.* Retrieved from http://www.nytimes.com/2009/06/05/education/05charter.html

Gootman, E., & Gebelof, R. (2008, June 19). Poor students lose ground in city's gifted programs. *New York Times,* p. A25.

Gordon, E. (2007). A context for the birth of "The Journal of Negro Education." *Journal of Negro Education, 76,* 198–203.

Gorski, P. (2008). Peddling poverty for profit: Elements of oppression in Ruby Payne's framework. *Equity & Excellence in Education, 41*(1), 130–148.

Gourley, C. (2009). What children write to authors: And what it may mean for schools. *Education Week, 29*(1), 26–27.

Goyette, K. (2008). Race, social background, and school choice options. *Equity & Excellence in Education, 4*(1), 114–129.

Graham, S. (2010). What educators need to know about bullying behaviors. *Phi Delta Kappan, 92,* 66–69.

Grant, C., & Agosto, V. (2008). Teacher capacity and social justice in teacher education. In M. Cochran-Smith, S. Feiman-Nemser, D. J. McIntyre, & K. Demers (Eds.), *Handbook of research on teacher education* (3rd ed., pp.175–200). New York: Routledge.

Gratz, D. (2009). Purpose and performance in teacher performance pay. *Education Week, 28*(24), 40.

Gratz, D. (2010). Looming questions in performance pay. *Phi Delta Kappan, 91*(8), 16–20.

Gray, L., Thomas, N., & Lewis, L. (2010). *Teachers' use of educational technology in U.S. public schools: 2009* (NCES 2010-040). Washington, DC: National Center for Education Statistics.

Green, C., Walker, J., Hoover-Dempsey, K., & Sandler, H. (2007). Parents' motivations for involvement in children's education: An empirical test of a theoretical model of parental involvement. *Journal of Educational Psychology, 99,* 532–544.

Green, E. (2010, March 7). Building a better teacher. *New York Times Magazine.* Retrieved from http://www.nytimes.com/2010/03/07/magazine/07Teachers-t.html?_r=1

Green, E. (2011, March 7). Study: $75M teacher pay initiative did not improve achievement. *Gotham Schools.* Retrieved from http://gothamschools.org/2011/03/07/study-75m-teacher-pay-initiative-did-not-improve-achievement/

Greene, J. P., & Winters, M. A. (2006). Getting ahead by staying behind: An evaluation of Florida's program to end social promotion. *Education Next, 6*(2), 65–69.

Greenhouse, L. (2007, June 26). Vote against banner shows divide in speech in schools. *New York Times.* Retrieved from http://www.nytimes.com/2007/06/26/washington/26speech.html

Gronke, A. (2009). Plugged-in parents. *Edutopia, 5*(1), 16.

Gross, J. (2008, January 12). Lack of supervision noted in deaths of home-schooled. *New York Times.* Retrieved from www.nytimes.com/2008/01/12/us/12bodies.html

Gruman, D., Harachi, T., Abbott, R., Catalano, R., & Fleming, C. (2008). Longitudinal effects of student mobility on three dimensions of elementary school engagement. *Child Development, 79,* 1833–1852.

Guggenheim, D. (Director). (2011). *Waiting for Superman* [Motion picture]. United States: Paramount Vantage.

Gugliemi, R. (2008). Native language proficiency, English literacy, academic achievement, and occupational attainment in limited-English-proficient students: A latent growth modeling perspective. *Journal of Educational Psychology, 100*(2), 322–342.

Gupta, Y. (2011). We must help students reach college. *Education Week, 30*(35), 26–27.

Gurian, M., & Stevens, K. (2007). *The minds of boys: Saving our sons from falling behind in school and life.* San Francisco: Jossey-Bass.

Gutierrez, M. (2012). Schools tackle teacher–student online conversations. *Education Week, 31*(17), 9.

Guttmacher Institute. (2011a). *Facts on American teens' sexual and reproductive health*. Retrieved from http://www.guttmacher.org/pubs/FB-ATSRH.html

Guttmacher Institute. (2011b). *Facts on teens' sources of information about sex*. Retrieved from http://www.guttmacher.org/pubs/FB-Teen-Sex-Ed.html

Guttmacher Institute. (2011c). Sex and STD/HIV education. *State Policies in Brief*. Retrieved from http://www.guttmacher.org/statecenter/spibs/spib_SE.pdf

Hafner, K. (2012, April 3). Giving women the access code. *New York Times,* D1, D4.

Hakel, M., Koenig, J., & Elliott, S. (Eds.). (2008). *Committee on evaluation of teacher certification*. Washington, DC: National Research Council.

Hakuta, K. (2011). Educating language minority students and affirming their equal rights: Research and practical perspectives. *Educational Researcher, 40*(4), 163–174.

Hallahan, D., Kauffman, J., & Pullen, P. (2012). *Exceptional learners: An introduction to special education* (12th ed.). Upper Saddle River, NJ: Allyn & Bacon/Pearson.

Hallinan, M. (2008). Teacher influences on students' attachment to school. *Sociology of Education, 81,* 271–283.

Halpern, D., Benbow, C., Geary, D., Gur, R., Hyde, J., & Gemsbacher, M. (2007). The science of sex differences in science and mathematics. *Psychological Science in the Public Interest, 8,* 1–51.

Halpern, D., Eliot, L., Bigler, R., Fabes, R., Hanish, L., Hyde, J., Liben, L., & Martin C. (2011). The pseudoscience of single-sex schooling. *Science, 333*(6050), 1706–1707.

Hampson, R., Leinwand, D., & Marcus, M. (2010, October 1). Has social networking gone too far? *USA Today,* A1–A2.

Hansen, D., Anderson, R., Frank, J., & Nieuwejaar, K. (2008). Reenvision the progressive tradition in curriculum. In F. M. Connelly, M. He, & J. Phillion (Eds.), *Sage handbook of curriculum and instruction* (pp. 440–459). Los Angeles: Sage Publications.

Hanushek, E. (1996). A more complete picture of school resource policies. *Review of Educational Research, 66,* 397–410.

Hanushek, E. (2011). Recognizing the value of good teachers. *Education Week, 30*(27), 34–35.

Hanushek, E., Rivkin, S., & Kain, J. (2005). Teachers, schools, and academic achievement. *Econometrica, 73,* 417–458.

Hardman, M., Drew, C., & Egan, W. (2011). *Human exceptionality* (10th ed.). Belmont, CA.: Wadsworth.

Harper, V. (2011). Denigrating the degree in Florida. *Education Week, 30*(16), 24–25.

Hart, D., Donnelly, T., Youniss, J., & Atkins, R. (2007). High school community service as a predictor of adult voting and volunteering. *American Educational Research Journal, 44*(1), 197–217.

Hartman, C. (2006). Students on the move. *Educational Leadership, 63*(5), 20–24.

Hattie, J. (2009). *Visible learning: A synthesis of over 800 meta-analyses relating to achievement*. New York: Routledge.

Hattie, J., & Timperley, H. (2007). The power of feedback. *Review of Educational Research, 77*(1), 81–112.

Haughney, C. (2010, July 13). Parents' real estate strategy: Schools come first. *New York Times*. Retrieved from http://www.nytimes.com/2010/07/13/nyregion/13appraisal.html

Hauser, D. (2008). Five years of abstinence-only-until-marriage education: Assessing the impact. *Advocates for Youth*. Retrieved from http://www.advocatesforyouth.org/publications/623?task=view

Haynes, C. (2008). *A teacher's guide to religion in public schools*. Nashville, TN. Retrieved from http://www.freedomforum.org/publications/first/teachersguide/teachersguide.pdf

Hazelwood School District v. Kuhlmeier, 484 U.S. 260 (1988).

Healy, M., & Bravo, V. (2011, November 20). Which is more rewarding? *USA Today*. Retrieved from http://www.scoop.it/t/snapshots/p/700215382/which-is-more-rewarding

Heilig, J., & Darling-Hammond, L. (2008). Students in a high-stakes testing context. *Educational Evaluation & Policy Analysis, 30,* 75–110.

Heitin, L. (2011). Evaluation system weighing down Tennessee teachers: Glitches in implementation could hurt other efforts. *Education Week, 31*(8), 1, 14–15.

Helgeson, V. (2012). *Psychology of gender* (4th ed.). Boston: Pearson.

Hellmech, N. (2007, March 29). No sugarcoating this: Kids besieged by food ads. *USA Today*, 9D.

Hendrie, C. (1999). Harvard study finds increase in segregation. *Education Week, 18*(41), 6.

Hendrie, C. (2005a). Court: Class strip searches unconstitutional. *Education Week, 24*(3), 3, 22.

Hendrie, C. (2005b). Legislation tightens fiscal oversight of California charters. *Education Week, 25*(7), 18.

Hess, F. (2010a). $pend money like it matters. *Educational Leadership, 68*(4), 51–54.

Hess, F. (2010b). Weighing the case for schools boards. *Phi Delta Kappan, 91*(6), 15–19.

Heward, W. (2009). *Exceptional children* (9th ed.). Upper Saddle River, NJ: Merrill/Pearson.

Heward, W. (2013). *Exceptional children* (10th ed.). Upper Saddle River, NJ: Pearson.

Hicks, M. (2010). *The digital pandemic: Reestablishing face-to-face contact in the electronic age*. Far Hills, NJ: New Horizon Press.

Hightower, A. (2012). On policy, student achievement, states pressing to measure up. *Education Week, 31*(16), 43–64.

Hill, C., Corbett, C., & Rose, A. (2010). *Why So Few? Women in science, technology, engineering, and mathematics*. Washington, DC: AAUW.

Hill, C., & Kearl, A. (2011). *Crossing the line: Sexual harassment at school*. Annapolis Junction, MD: American Association of University Women. Retrieved from http://www.aauw.org/learn/research/upload/CrossingTheLine_ExecSummary.pdf

Hirsch, E. (1987). *Cultural literacy: What every American needs to know*. Boston: Houghton Mifflin.

Hirsch, E. (2001). Seeking breadth and depth in the curriculum. *Educational Leadership, 59*(2), 22–25.

Hirsch, E. (2011, September 19). How to stop the drop in verbal scores. *New York Times*. Retrieved from http://www.nytimes.com/2011/09/19/opinion/how-to-stop-the-drop-in-verbal-scores.html?_r=1&nl=todaysheadlines&emc=tha212

Hoff, D. (2009a). Local educators prepare to use one-time funds. *Education Week, 28*(22), 1, 14–15.

Hoff, D. (2009b). National standards gain steam. *Education Week, 28*(23), 1, 20–21.

Hoffman, J. (2010, December 4). As bullies go digital, parents play catch up. *New York Times*. Retrieved from http://www.nytimes.com/2010/12/05/us/05bully.html

Hoffman, J. (2011, March 26). A girl's nude photo and altered lives. *New York Times*. Retrieved from http://www.nytimes.com/2011/03/27/us/27sexting.html

Hollins, E. (2012). *Learning to teach in urban schools: The transition from preparation to practice*. New York: Routledge.

Holmes, M., & Weiss, B. (1995). *Lives of women public schoolteachers: Scenes from American educational history*. New York: Garland Publishing.

Honawar, V. (2006). Md. Lawmakers fight school takeover plan. *Education Week, 25*(31), 25, 28.

Honawar, V. (2008). Performance-pay studies show few achievement gains. *Education Week, 27*(27), 7.

Honawar, V. (2009). Teacher gap: Training gets a boost. *Education Week, 28*(17), 28–29.

Honawar, V., & Olson, L. (2008). Advancing pay for performance. *Education Week, 27*(18), 26–31.

Hout, M., & Elliot, S. W. (2011). *Incentives and test-based accountability in education*. Washington, DC: The National Academies Press.

Howard, T., & Aleman, G. (2008). Teacher capacity for diverse learners: What do teachers need to know? In M. Cochran-Smith, S. Feiman-Nemser, D. J. McIntyre, & K. Demers (Eds.), *Handbook of research on teacher education* (3rd ed., pp. 157–174). New York: Routledge.

Howley, C., & Howley, A. (2004). School size and the influence of socioeconomic status on student achievement: Confronting the threat of size bias in national data sets. *Education Policy Analysis Archives, 12*(52). Retrieved from http://epaa.asu.edu/epaa/v12n52/

Hoye, J., & Stern, D. (2008). The career academy story. *Education Week, 28*(3), 24–25.

Hu, W. (2008, November 12). A school district asks: Where are the parents? *New York Times*, p. A25.

Hu, W. (2011, August 31). Bullying law puts New Jersey schools on spot. *New York Times*, pp. A1, A21.

Hu, W., & Gebeloff, R. (2011, May 26). Growth in education spending slowed in 2009. *New York Times*. Retrieved from http://www.nytimes.com/2011/05/26/education/26spending.html?_r=1&ref=education

Hubbard, B., & Mitchell, N. (2011, October 5). Test scores raise questions about Colorado Virtual Schools. *Education Week*. Retrieved from http://www.edweek.org/ew/articles/2011/10/05/07enc_virtualachieve.h31.html

Hughes, J. N., Chen, Q., Thoemmes, F., & Kwok, O. (2010). An investigation of the relationship between retention in first grade and performance on high stakes tests in third grade. *Educational Evaluation & Policy Analysis, 32,* 166–182.

Hulleman, C., & Barron K. (2010). Separating myth from reality. *Phi Delta Kappan, 91*(8), 27–31.

Hulse, C. (2006, May 16). Senate passes a bill that favors English. *New York Times*, p. A19.

Hurst, B., & Reding, G. (2009). *Professionalism in teaching* (3rd ed.). Upper Saddle River, NJ: Pearson.

Hussar, W., & Bailey, T. (2011). *Projections of education statistics to 2020* (39th ed.). Washington, DC: National Center for Education Statistics. Retrieved from http://nces.ed.gov/pubs2011/2011026.pdf

Hutton, T. (2005). The charter option: 5 big questions your board should ask before authorizing a charter school. *American School Board Journal, 192*(5), 16–20.

Hutton, T. (2008). Teaching and the Bible. *American School Board Journal, 195*(6), 38–41.

Hyman, I., Kay, B., Tabori, A., Weber, M., Mahon, M., & Cohen, I. (2006). Bullying: Theory, research, and interventions. In C. M. Evertson & C. S. Weinstein (Eds.), *Handbook of classroom management: Research, practice, and contemporary issues* (pp. 855–884). Mahwah, NJ: Erlbaum.

Ilg, T., & Massucci, J. (2003). Comprehensive urban high schools: Are there better options for poor and minority children? *Education and Urban Society, 36*(1), 63–78.

Illinois State Board of Education. (2008a). *Illinois Science Assessment Framework: Standard 12F—Astronomy (Grade 7)*. Retrieved from http://www.champaignschools.org/index2.php?header=./science/&file=MSCurriculum/astronomy

Illinois State Board of Education. (2008b). *2008 Science ISAT: Grades 4 and 7,* p. 45. Retrieved from http://www.isbe.state.il.us/assessment/pdfs/2008/Science_ISAT.pdf

Illinois State Board of Education. (2008c). *2008 Science ISAT: Grades 4 and 7,* p. 45. Retrieved from http://www.isbe.state.il.us/assessment/pdfs/2008/Science_ISAT.pdf

Imig, D., & Imig, S. (2008). From traditional certification to competitive certification: A twenty-five year retrospective. In M. Cochran-Smith, S. Feiman-Nemser, D. J. McIntyre, & K. Demers (Eds.), *Handbook of research on teacher education* (3rd ed., pp. 886–907). New York: Routledge.

Inan, F. A., Lowther, D. L., Ross, S. M., & Strahl, D. (2010). Pattern of classroom activities during students' use of computers: Relations between instructional strategies and computer applications. *Teaching and Teacher Education, 26,* 540–546.

Ingersoll, R. (2010). Who's teaching our children? *Educational Leadership, 67*(8), 14–20.

Ingersoll, R., & May, R. (2011). *Recruitment, retention, and the minority teacher shortage*. Philadelphia, PA: Consortium for Policy Research in Education, University of Pennsylvania Center.

Ingersoll, R., & Merrill, L. (2010). The teaching force: six trends. *Educational Leadership, 67*(8), 14–20.

Ingersoll, R., & Strong, M. (2011). The impact of induction and mentor programs for beginning teachers: A critical review of the research. *Review of Educational Research, 81*(2), 201–233.

Ingraham v. Wright, 430 U.S. 651 (1977).

Institute of Education Sciences. (2011). *Do low-income students have equal access to the highest-performing teachers?* National Center for Education Evaluation and Regional Assistance.

International Reading Association & National Council of Teachers of English. (2008). *Standards for the English language arts.* Retrieved from http://www.ncte.org/library/files/Store/Books/Sample/StandardsDoc.pdf

Interstate New Teacher Assessment and Support Consortium. (2011). *InTASC model core teaching standards: A resource for state dialogue.* Washington, DC: Council of Chief State School Officers.

Isaac, D. (2011, April). *C. E. Ayers challenge to Dewey: Is our faith in science and technology misplaced?* Paper presented at the annual meeting of the American Educational Research Association, New Orleans.

Isaacson, W. (2009). How to raise the standards in America's schools. *Time, 173*(16), 32–37.

Isseks, M. (2011). How PowerPoint is killing education. *Educational Leadership, 68,* 74–76.

Jackson, M. (2009). *Distracted: The erosion of attention and the coming dark age.* Amherst, NY: Prometheus Books.

Jackson, P. (1968). *Life in classrooms.* New York: Holt, Rinehart & Winston.

Jacobsen, D. (2003). *Philosophy in classroom teaching: Bridging the gap* (2nd ed.). Upper Saddle River, NJ: Prentice Hall.

Jadallah, M., Anderson, R., Nguyen-Jahiel, K., Miller, B., Kim, I., Kuo, L., Dong, T., & Wu, X. (2011). Influence of a teacher's scaffolding moves during child-led small group discussion. *American Educational Research Journal, 48*(1), 194–230.

Jaschik, S. (2010, September 14). Women lead in doctorates. *Inside Higher Ed.* Retrieved from http://www.insidehighered.com/news/2010/09/14/doctorates

Jason, G. (2011). Merit pay for teachers works, and the evidence now proves it. *American Thinker.* Retrieved from http://www.americanthinker.com/2011/04/merit_pay_for_teachers_works_a.html

Jemmott, J. B., Jemmott, L. S., & Fong, G. T. (2010). Efficacy of a theory-based abstinence-only intervention over 24 months. *Archives of Pediatrics & Adolescent Medicine, 164,* 152–159.

Jennings, R. (2011, March 16). The ads on the bus go round and round. *USA Today,* p. A3.

Jimerson, S., Pletcher, S., & Graydon, K. (2006). Beyond grade retention and social promotion: Promoting the social and academic competence of students. *Psychology in the Schools, 43*(1), 85–97.

Johnson, A. (2012). *Short guide to action research* (4th ed.). Upper Saddle River, NJ: Pearson.

Johnson, C. (2010). *Schools under fire from ACLU for 'pay for play athletic fees. Center for Investigative Reporting.* Retrieved from http://californiawatch.org/dailyreport/schools-under-fire-aclu-pay-play-athletic-fees-3740

Johnson, D., & Johnson, R. (2009). An educational psychology success story: Social interdependence theory and cooperative learning. *Educational Researcher, 38*(5), 365–379.

Johnson, D., & Johnson, R. (2013). *Joining together: Group theory and group skills* (11th ed.). Boston: Pearson.

Johnson, K. (2008, April 25). On the reservation and off, schools see a changing tide. *New York Times.* Retrieved from www.nytimes.com/2008/05/25/education/25hardin.html?th&emc=th

Johnson, T. W., & Reed, R. F. (2012). *Philosophical documents in education.* Upper Saddle River, NJ: Pearson.

Johnston, R. (1994). Policy details who paddles students and with what. *Education Week, 14*(11), 17–18.

Jones, J., & Saad, L. (2010). *Nurses top honesty and ethics list for 11th year.* Retrieved from http://www.gallup.com/poll/145043/nurses-top-honesty-ethics-list-11-year.aspx

Josephson Institute Center for Youth Ethics. (2010). *The ethics of American youth: 2010.* Retrieved from: http://charactercounts.org/programs/reportcard/2010/index.html

Kahlenberg, R. (2006). Integration by income. *American School Board Journal, 193*(4), 51–52.

Kahlenberg, R. (2011). The potential of interdistrict school choice. *Education Week, 30*(33), 24–25.

Kahlenberg, R. (2012). *The future of school integration: Socioeconomic diversity as an education reform strategy.* New York: Century Press.

Kaiser Family Foundation. (2004). *Survey snapshot: The digital divide.* Retrieved from www.kff.org

Kaiser, A. (2011). *Beginning teacher attrition and mobility: Results from the first through third waves of the 2007–2008 Beginning Teacher Longitudinal Study, U.S. Department of Education.* Washington, DC: National Center for Education Statistics. Retrieved from http://nces.ed.gov/pubs2011/2011318.pdf

Karrer, P. (2011). A letter to my president—the one I voted for . . . *Education Week, 30*(19), 23.

Kartal, G. (2010). Does language matter in multimedia learning? Personalization principle revisited. *Journal of Educational Psychology, 102,* 615–624.

Kauchak, D., & Eggen, P. (2012). *Learning and teaching: Research-based methods* (6th ed.). Boston: Pearson.

Kaufman, D., & Moss, D. (2010). A new look at preservice teachers' conceptions of classroom management and organization: Uncovering complexity and dissonance. *Teacher Educator, 45,* 118–136.

Kaufman, F. (2005). Diabesity. In P. Menzel, *Hungry planet: What the world eats* (pp. 242–243). Napa, CA: Material World Press.

Kedar-Voivodas, G. (1983). The impact of elementary children's school roles and sex roles on teacher attitudes: An interactional analysis. *Review of Educational Research, 20,* 417–462.

Keller, B. (2007). Gone again after five years? Think again. *Education Week, 26*(41), 26–30.

Kellough, R., & Carjuzaa, J. (2009). *Teaching in the middle and secondary schools* (9th ed.). Boston: Allyn & Bacon.

Kelly, M. (2011). *School violence: How prevalent is it?* Retrieved from http://712educators.about.com/cs/schoolviolence/a/schoolviolence.htm

Kelly, S., & Price, H. (2011). The correlates of tracking policy: Opportunity hoarding, status competition, or a technical-functional explanation? *American Educational Research Journal, 48*(3), 560–585.

Kennedy, M. (2006). Knowledge and vision in teaching. *Journal of Teacher Education, 57*(3), 205–211.

Kerman, S. (1979). Teacher expectations and student achievement. *Phi Delta Kappan, 60,* 70–72.

Kerr, D. (2012). Teens prefer texting over phone calls, e-mail. *CNET News.* Retrieved from http://news.cnet.com/8301-1023_3-57400439-93/teens-prefer-texting-over-phone-calls-e-mail/

Kimmel, M. (2008). *Guyland: The perilous world where boys become men.* New York: Harper Collins.

Kirylo, J. D., Thirumurthy, V., & Spezzini, S. (2010). Children were punished: Not for what they said, but for what their teachers heard. *Childhood Education, 86,* 130–131.

Kitzmiller et al. v. Dover Area School District, 04cv2688 (U.S. District Court for the Middle District of Pennsylvania, 2005).

Klein, A. (2011). Programs suffer cuts in funding. *Education Week, 30*(23), 1, 18.

Kliebard, H. (2002). *Changing course: American curriculum reform in the 20th century.* New York: Teachers College Press.

Koebler, J. (2012, January 9). Governors' association examines teacher merit pay. *U.S. News.* Retrieved from http://www.usnews.com/education/blogs/high-school-notes/2012/01/09/governors-association-examines-teacher-merit-pay

Kohn, A. (1996). By all available means: Cameron and Pierce's defense of extrinsic motivators. *Review of Educational Research, 66,* 1–4.

Konheim-Kalkstein, Y. (2006). A uniform look. *American School Board Journal, 193*(8), 25–27.

Konstantopoulos, S. (2008). Do small classes reduce the achievement gap between low and high achievers? Evidence from Project STAR. *Elementary School Journal, 108*(4), 275–291.

Koppich, J. (2010). Teacher unions and new forms of teacher compensation. *Phi Delta Kappan, 91*(8), 22–26.

Kosciw, J., & Diaz, E. (2006). *The 2005 National School Climate Survey: The experience of lesbian, gay, bisexual, and transgender youth in our nation's schools.* New York: Gay, Lesbian, & Straight Education Network.

Kostelnik, M., Onaga, E., Rohde, B., & Whiren, A. (2002). *Children with special needs.* New York: Teachers College Press.

Koth, C., Bradshaw, C., & Leaf, P. (2008). A multilevel study of predictors of student perceptions of school climate: The effect of classroom-level factors. *Journal of Educational Psychology, 100*(1), 96–104.

Kounin, J. (1970). *Discipline and group management in classrooms.* New York: Holt, Rinehart & Winston.

Kowalski, T., McCord, R., Peterson, G., Young, P., & Ellersen, N. (2011). *The American school superintendent: 2010 decennial study.* Washington, DC: American Association of School Administrators.

Kozol, J. (1991). *Savage inequalities.* New York: Crown.

Kozol, J. (2005). *The shame of the nation: The restoration of apartheid schooling in America.* New York: Crown.

Kraft, M. A. (2010). From ringmaster to conductor: 10 simple techniques that can turn an unruly class into a productive one. *Phi Delta Kappan, 91,* 44–47.

Krauss, S., Brunner, M., Kunter, M., Baumert, J., Blum, W., Neubrand, M., & Jordan, A. (2008). Pedagogical content knowledge and content knowledge of secondary mathematics teachers. *Journal of Educational Psychology, 100*(3), 716–725.

Kridel, C. (2010). *Encyclopedia of curriculum studies.* Los Angeles: Sage.

Kristoff, N. (2006, May 14). The model students. *New York Times,* Sect. 4, 13.

Kristoff, N. (2012, January 12). The value of teachers. *New York Times,* p. A21.

Krull, E., Oras, K., & Sisask, S. (2007). Differences in teachers' comments on classroom events as indicators of their professional development. *Teaching and Teacher Education, 23,* 1038–1050.

Kuhn, D. (2007). Is direct instruction the right answer to the right question? *Educational Psychologist, 42,* 109–113.

Kunzman, R. (2009). Understanding homeschooling: A better approach to regulation. *Theory and Research in Education,* 7(3), 311–330.

Labaree, D. (2008). An uneasy relationship: The history of teacher education in the university. In M. Cochran-Smith, S. Feiman-Nemser, D. J. McIntyre, & K. Demers (Eds.), *Handbook of research on teacher education* (3rd ed., pp. 290–306). New York: Routledge.

Lacey, M. (2011). January 7. Rift in Arizona as Latino class is found illegal. *New York Times.* Retrieved from http://www.nytimes.com/2011/01/08/us/08ethnic.html?pagewanted=all

Ladd, H. (2011). Teachers' perceptions of their working conditions: How predictive of planned and actual teacher movement? *Education Evaluation & Policy Analysis.* Retrieved from http://epa.sagepub.com/content/33/2/235.abstract

Laird, R. D., Pettit, G. S., Dodge, K. A., & Bates, J. E. (2005). Peer relationship antecedents of delinquent behavior in late adolescence: Is there evidence of demographic group differences in developmental processes? *Development and psychopathology, 17,* 127–144.

Lake, R., & Gross, B. (2012). Hopes, fears, and reality: A balanced look at charter schools in 2011. *National Charter*

School Resource Center. Retrieved from http://www.crpe.org/cs/crpe/download/csr_files/pub_crpe_HFR11_Jan12.pdf

LaMarche, G. (2011). The time is right to end "zero tolerance." *Education Week, 30*(27), 35, 37.

LaMorte, M. (2012). *School law: Cases and concepts* (10th ed.). Boston: Allyn & Bacon.

Langenegger, J. (2011, April). *Changes that stick: The role of sustaining forces*. Paper presented at the annual meeting of the American Educational Research Association, New Orleans.

Lareau, A. (2011). *Unequal childhoods: Class, race, and family life* (2nd ed.). Berkeley: University of California Press.

Lasser, J., & Fite, K. (2011). Universal preschool's promise: Success in early childhood and beyond. *Early Childhood Education Journal, 39*, 169–173.

Lau v. Nichols, 414 U.S. 563 (1974).

Lee v. Weismann, 112 S. Ct. 29649 (1992).

Lee, C. D., & Spratley, A. (2010). *Reading in the disciplines: The challenges of adolescent literacy*. New York: Carnegie Corporation of New York.

Lee, V. R. (2010). Adaptations and continuities in the use and design of visual representations in US middle school science textbooks. *International Journal of Science Education, 32*, 1099–1126.

Lemon v. Kurtzman, 403 U.S. 602 (1971).

Lemov, D. (2010*). Teach like a champion: 49 techniques that put students on the path to college*. San Francisco: Jossey-Bass.

Lenz, S. (2011, June 30). Males make up only 25% of Utah's teachers. *Deseret News*, pp. A1, A8, A10.

Leonard, J. (2008). *Culturally specific pedagogy in the mathematics classroom: Strategies for teachers of diverse students*. New York: Routledge.

LePage, P., Darling-Hammond, L., & Akar, H., with Gutierrez, C., Jenkins-Gunn, E., & Rosebrock, K. (2005). Classroom management. In L. Darling-Hammond & J. Bransford (Eds.), *Preparing teachers for a changing world: What teachers should learn and be able to do* (pp. 327–357). San Francisco: Jossey-Bass/Wiley.

Lewis, A. (2008). Learn from education's experience. *Phi Delta Kappan, 90*(4), 235–236.

Lewis, J., DeCamp-Fritson, S., Ramage, J., McFarland, M., & Archwamety, T. (2007). Selecting for ethnically diverse children who may be gifted using Raven's Standard Progressive matrices and Naglieri Nonverbal Abilities test. *Multicultural Education, 15*(1), 38–43.

Lezotte, L. W., & Snyder, K. M. (2011). *What effective schools do: Re-envisioning the correlates*. Bloomington, IN: Solution Tree Press.

Lichter, D., & Johnson, K. (2006). Emerging rural settlement patterns and the geographic distribution of America's new immigrants. *Rural Sociology, 71*(1), 109–131.

Lloyd, J. (2009, January 5) Number of home-schooled children in the rise. *USA Today*, p. A1.

Lomawaima, K., & McCarty, T. (2006). *To remain an Indian: Lessons in democracy from a century of Native American education*. New York: Teachers College Press.

Longfellow, C. (2008). Proven tools that work. *American School Board Journal, 195*(12), 25–27.

Lose, M. (2008). Using response to intervention to support struggling learners. *Principal, 87*(3), 20–23.

Lovelace, M. (2005). Meta-analysis of experimental research based on the Dunn and Dunn Model. *Journal of Educational Research, 98*(3), 176–183.

Lowe, J. I. (2011). Want to boost learning? Start with emotional health. *Education Week, 31*(13), 40, 32.

Lowery, A. (2012, January 6). Big study links good teachers to lasting gain. *New York Times*. Retrieved from http://www.nytimes.com/2012/01/06/education/big-study-links-good-teachers-to-lasting-gain.html?nl=todaysheadlines&emc=tha23

Macionis, J. (2011). *Society: The basics* (10th ed.). Upper Saddle River, NJ: Prentice Hall.

Macionis, J., & Parrillo, V. (2010). *Cities and urban life* (5th ed.). Upper Saddle River, NJ: Merrill/Prentice Hall.

Mailloux v. Kiley, 323 F. Supp. 1387 (D. Mass 1971), 448 F.2d 1242 (lst Cir. 1971).

Manchir, M. (2012). Twitter evolves as tool for little ones to tweet about school activities. *Education Week, 31*(24), 9.

Manning, A. (2010). Educators advised to be cautious on Facebook profiles. *Education Week, 30*(5), 8.

Manning, D. (1990). *Hill country teacher: Oral histories from the one-room school and beyond*. Boston: Twayne Publishers.

Manno, B. (2010). The new marketplace of school choice. *Education Week, 30*(13), 24–26.

Manzo, K. (2008). Election renews controversy over social-justice teaching. *Education Week, 28*(22), 1, 12–13.

Manzo, K. (2009a). Administration confront student "sexting." *Education Week, 28*(35), 8.

Manzo, K. (2009b, Spring/Summer). Global tech competition: Are U.S. students' tech skills keeping up with their international peers? *Digital Directions*, 16–19.

Margolis, E., & Romero, M. (2009). "The department is very male, very white, very old, and very conservative": The functioning of the hidden curriculum in graduate sociology departments. *Harvard Educational Review, 68*, 1–33. Retrieved from http://her.hepg.org/content/1q3828348783j851/?p=b05cc8ec246a433cb829d419ca2f49f7&pi=0

Margolis, J. (2010). What teacher quality is a local issue (and why Race to the Top is a misguided flop). *Teachers College Record*. Retrieved from http://www.tcrecord.org/Content.asp?ContentID=16023

Marsh, C., & Willis, G. (2007). *Curriculum: Alternative approaches, ongoing issues*. Upper Saddle River, NJ: Merrill/Pearson.

Marsh, H., & Kleitman, S. (2005). Consequences of employment during high school: Character building, subversion of academic goals, or a threshold? *American Educational Research Journal, 42*(2), 331–369.

Marsh, J., & McCaffrey, D. (2011/2012). What are achievement gains worth to teachers? *Phi Delta Kappan, 93*(4), 52–56.

Martineau, J. (2010). The validity of value-added models: An allegory. *Phi Delta Kappan, 91*(7), 64–67.

Martino, W., Kehler M., & Weaver-Hightower, M. (Eds.). (2009). *The problem with boys' education: beyond the backlash*. New York: Routledge

Maslow, A. (1968). *Toward a psychology of being* (2nd ed.). New York: Van Nostrand.

Mason, L. (2007). Introduction: Bridging the cognitive and sociocultural approaches in research on conceptual change: Is it feasible? *Educational Psychologist, 42*(1), 1–8.

Mastroprieri, M., & Scruggs, R. (2010). *The inclusive classroom* (4th ed.). Upper Saddle River, NJ: Merrill/Pearson.

Math.com. (2010). *Estimating and rounding decimals*. Retrieved from http://www.math.com/school/subject1/practice/S1U1L3/S1U1L3Pract.html

Mathematica Policy Research. (2007). *Impact of four abstinence education programs*. Retrieved from www.mathematica-mpr.com/abstinencereport.asp

Mathews, J. (2009, January 5). The latest doomed pedagogical fad: 21st century skills. *Washington Post,* p. B02.

Mattingly, M., & Stransky, M. (2010). *Young child poverty in 2009: Rural poverty rate jumps to nearly 29 percent in second year of recession*. Retrieved from http://www.carseyinstitute.unh.edu/publications/IB-Mattingly-childpoverty10.pdf

Maxwell, L. (2006). Web systems help schools screen visitors. *Education Week, 25*(32), 5, 16.

Maxwell, L. (2008). Sexual orientation. *Education Week, 28*(8), 5.

Maxwell, L. (2010). Vouchers draw bipartisan look. *Education Week, 29*(23), 1, 21.

Maxwell, L. (2012a). Achievement gaps tied to income found widening. *Education Week, 31*(23), 1, 22–23.

Maxwell, L. (2012b). Providers fear new Head Start rules could mean a shake out for the field. *Education Week, 31*(21), 22–23.

Maxwell, L. (2012c). States mull Obama's call to raise compulsory-attendance age. *Education Week, 31*(20), 1, 18.

Mayer, R. E. (2002). *The promise of educational psychology: Volume II. Teaching for meaningful learning*. Upper Saddle River, NJ: Merrill/Pearson.

Mayer, R., & Massa, L. (2003). Three facts of visual and verbal learners: Cognitive ability, cognitive style, and learning preference. *Journal of Educational Psychology, 95,* 833–846.

McAllister, G., & Irvine, J. (2002). The role of empathy in teaching culturally diverse students: A qualitative study of teachers' beliefs. *Journal of Teacher Education, 53,* 433–443.

McCarthy, M. (2009). Beyond the wall of separation: Church-state concerns in public schools. *Phi Delta Kappan, 90*(8), 714–719.

McCaslin, M., & Good, T. (1996). The informal curriculum. In D. Berliner & R. Calfee (Eds.), *Handbook of educational psychology* (pp. 622–670). New York: Macmillan.

McClatchy-Tribune (2011). Detroit deep in debt as manager leaves. *Education Week, 30*(31), 4, 5.

McCloskey, L., Pellegrin, N., Thompson, K., & Hakuta, K. (2008). Proposition 227 in California: A long-term appraisal of its impact on language minority achievement. *The Civil Rights Project*. Retrieved from http://civilrightsproject.ucla.edu/research/k-12-education/language-minority-students/proposition-227-in-california-a-long-term-appraisal-of-its-impact-on-language-minority-student-achievement

McCurdy, B., Kunsch, C., & Reibstein, S. (2007). Secondary prevention in the urban school: Implementing the behavior education program. *Preventing School Failure, 51,* 12–19.

McDevitt, T. M., & Ormrod, J. E. (2010). *Child development and education* (4th ed.). Upper Saddle River, NJ: Merrill/Pearson.

McDevitt, T. M., & Ormrod, J. E. (2013). *Child development and education* (5th ed.). Upper Saddle River, NJ: Pearson.

McDiarmid, G. W., & Clevenger-Bright, M. (2008). Rethinking teacher capacity. In M. Cochran-Smith, S. Feiman-Nemser, D. J. McIntyre, & K. Demers (Eds.), *Handbook of research on teacher education* (3rd ed., pp. 134–156). New York: Routledge.

McDonough, P. (2009). *TV viewing among kids at an eight-year high. Nielsen Wire*. Retrieved from http://blog.nielsen.com/nielsenwire/media_entertainment/tv-viewing-among-kids-at-an-eight-year-high/

McIntosh, S. (2011). *State high school tests: Changes in state policies and the impact of the college and career readiness movement*. Washington, DC: Center for Education Policy. Retrieved from http://www.cep-dc.org/displayDocument.cfm?DocumentID=385

McKinley, J. (2009, January 22). In Texas, a line in the curriculum revives evolution debate. *New York Times*. Retrieved from http://www.nytimes.com/2009/01/22/education/22texas.html

McMahon, S., Rose, D., & Parks, M. (2004). Multiple intelligences and reading achievement; An examination of the Teele Inventory of Multiple Intelligences. *Journal of Experimental Education, 73*(1), 41–52.

McNeil, M. (2008a). Governors face political hurdles in seeking power to appoint chiefs. *Education Week, 27*(20), 1, 20.

McNeil, M. (2008b). Overhaul school finance systems, researchers urge. *Education Week, 28*(11), 10–11.

McNeil, M. (2009). Rush to pump out stimulus cash highlights disparities in funding. *Education Week, 28*(22), 1, 26–27.

McNeil, M. (2011a). Delaware pushes to meet Race to Top promises. *Education Week, 30*(32). 1, 17–18.

McNeil, M. (2011b). Ohio vote to scrap bargaining law a labor victory—for now. *Education Week, 31*(12), 1, 26–27.

Medina, J. (2009a, January 29). Backers of mayoral school control face resistance. *New York Times*. Retrieved from http://www.nytimes.com/2009/01/29/education/29learn.html?partner=rss&emc=rss

Medina, J. (2009b, March 11). Boys and girls together taught separately in public school. *New York Times*, p. A24.

Medina, J. (2010, June 11). Scoring low, more pupils face school this summer. *New York Times*. Retrieved from http://www.nytimes.com/2010/06/11/nyregion/11summer.html?ref=education

Medina, J., & Gootman, E. (2008, September 2). New campaign under way to keep schools under Bloomberg's thumb. *New York Times,* p. C20.

MenTeach. (2010). Data about men teachers. *MenTeach*. Retrieved from http://www.menteach.org/resources/data_about_men_teachers

Mercurio, M., & Morse, C. (2007). "Tinkering" close to the edge. *Educational Leadership, 64*(6), 52–55.

Metiri Group. (2009). Focus on technology integration in America's schools. *National Trends Report: Enhancing Education Through Technology (EETT) Round 6, Fiscal Year 2007.* Washington, DC: The State Educational Technology Directors Association (SETDA). Retrieved from http://www.setda.org/c/document_library/get_file?folderId=6&name=DLFE-329.pdf

MetLife. (2009). *MetLife survey of the American teacher, Part 3: Teaching as a career.* Retrieved from http://www.metlife.com/assets/cao/contributions/foundation/american-teacher/MetLife_Teacher_Survey_2009_Part_3.pdf

MetLife. (2011). *MetLife Survey of the American teacher: Preparing students for college and careers part I: Clearing the path*. New York: Harris Interactive, Inc.

MetLife. (2012). *MetLife Survey of the American teacher: Teachers, parents and the economy.* MetLife, Inc. Retrieved from http://www.metlife.com/assets/cao/contributions/foundation/american-teacher/MetLife-Teacher-Survey-2011.pdf

Michener, J. (2006). Sex education: A success in our social-studies class. *Clearing House, 79*(5), 210–214.

Migration Policy Institute. (2010). *Top language spoken by English language learners nationally and by state.* National Center on Immigrant Integration Policy. Retrieved from http://www.migrationinformation.org/ellinfo/FactSheet_ELL3.pdf

Miller, G. (2012). Equal opportunity: A landmark law for children and education. *Education Week, 31*(15), 40.

Miller, M., Linn, R., & Gronlund, N. (2009). *Measurement and assessment in teaching* (10th ed.). Upper Saddle River, NJ: Merrill/Pearson.

Miller, P. (2011). A critical analysis of the research on student homelessness. *Review of Educational Research, 81*(3), 308–337.

Mills, G. (2011). *Action research: A guide for the teacher researcher* (4th ed.). Boston: Pearson.

Milner, H. R., & Tenore, F. B. (2010). Classroom management in diverse classrooms. *Urban Education, 45*, 560–603

Mithers, C. (2011). Are school nurses disappearing? *CNN Health*. Retrieved from http://www.cnn.com/2011/HEALTH/04/04/school.nurse.shortage.parenting/index.html.

Moir, E. (2008/2009). Knowing the drill. *Edutopia, 4*(6), 14.

Molnar, A., Boniger, F., Wilkinson, G., & Fogarty, J. (2009). *Click: The twelfth annual report on schoolhouse commercialism trends: 2008–2009.* Retrieved from http://nepc.colorado.edu/publication/schoolhouse-commercialism-2009

Molnar, A., Boniger, F., Wilkinson, G., Fogarty, J., & Geary, S. (2010*). Effectively embedded: The thirteenth annual report on schoolhouse commercializing trends: 2009–2010.* Retrieved from http://nepc.colorado.edu/publication/Schoolhouse-commercialism-2010

Molnar, A., Percy, S., Smith, P., & Zahorik, J. (1998). *1997–98 results of the Student Achievement Guarantee in Education (SAGE) program.* Milwaukee: University of Wisconsin–Milwaukee.

Monke, L. (2005/2006). The overdominance of computers. *Educational Leadership, 63*(4), 20–23.

Monte-Sano, C. (2008). Qualities of historical writing instruction: A comparative case study of two teachers' practices. *American Educational Research Journal, 45*(4), 1045–1079.

Moore, J. (2007, October). Suicide trends among youths and young adults 10–24 years—United States, 1990–2004. *Youth Today, 29.*

Moriarity, A. (2009). Managing confrontations safely and effectively. *Kappa Delta Pi Record, 45,* 78–83.

Morris v. Douglas County School District No. 9, 403 P.2d 775 (Or. 1965).

Morrison v. State Board of Education, 461 P.2d 375 (Cal. 1969).

Mozert v. Hawkins County Public Schools, 827 F.2d 1058 (6th Cir. 1987), cert. denied, 108 S. Ct. 1029 (1988).

Murray, F. (1986). *Necessity: The developmental component in reasoning*. Paper presented at the 16th annual meeting, Jean Piaget Society, Philadelphia.

Murray, F. (2008). The role of teacher education courses in teaching by second nature. In M. Cochran-Smith, S. Feiman-Nemser, D. J. McIntyre, & K. Demers (Eds.), *Handbook of research on teacher education* (3rd ed., pp. 1228–1246). New York: Routledge.

Murrell, Jr., P. C., Diez, M. C., Feiman-Nemser, S., & Schussler, D. L. (2011). *Teaching as a moral practice: Defining, developing, and assessing professional dispositions in teacher education*. Cambridge, MA: Harvard Education Press.

Nagel, D. (2009, April 2). Study ties student achievement to technology integration. *The Journal*. Retrieved from http://thejournal.com/Articles/2009/04/02/Study-Ties-Student-Achievement-to-Technology-Integration.aspx?p=1

National Association of State Boards of Education. (2007). *State education governance at-a-glance.* Retrieved from http://nasbe.org/index.php/file-repository?func=finishdown&id=212

National Board for Professional Teaching Standards. (2011a). *Certification stats for the NBCT class of 2011.* Retrieved from http://www.nbpts.org/about_us/nbct_class_of_2011/national_board_certifica

National Board for Professional Teaching Standards. (2011b). *What teachers should know and be able to do.* Retrieved from http://www.nbpts.org/UserFiles/File/what_teachers.pdf

National Campaign to Prevent Teen and Unplanned Pregnancy. (2010). *National data.* Retrieved from http://www.thenationalcampaign.org/national-data/default.aspx

National Campaign to Prevent Teen Pregnancy. (2010). *Teen sexual behavior and contraceptive use. Data from the Youth Risk Behavior Survey, 2009.* Retrieved from http://www.thenationalcampaign.org/resources/pdf/FastFacts_YRBS2009.pdf

National Center for Education Statistics. (2007). *The condition of education 2007.* Washington, DC: Author. Retrieved from http://nces.ed.gov/pubs2007/2007064.pdf

National Center for Education Statistics. (2009). *America's high school graduates: Results of the 2009 NAEP high school transcript study.* Retrieved from http://nces.ed.gov/nationsreportcard/pdf/studies/2011462.pdf

National Center for Education Statistics. (2010a). *Digest of education statistics: Table 7. Percentage of the population 3 to 34 years old enrolled in school, by age group; Selected years, 1940 through 2009.* Washington, DC: Author.

National Center for Education Statistics. (2010b). *Projections of education statistics to 2019.* Retrieved from http://nces.ed.gov/programs/projections/projections2019/tables/table_02.asp?referrer=list

National Center for Education Statistics. (2010c). *Public school graduates and dropouts from the common core of data: School year 2007–2008.* Washington, DC: Author.

National Center for Education Statistics. (2010d). *Status and trends in the education of racial and ethnic minorities.* Retrieved from http://nces.ed.gov/pubs2010/2010015/indicator2_7.asp#5

National Center for Education Statistics. (2010e). *Student effort and educational progress: Completions.* Washington, DC: Author.

National Center for Education Statistics. (2010f). *The condition of education 2010.* Washington, DC: U.S. Department of Education. Retrieved from http://nces.ed.gov/pubs2010/2010028.pdf

National Center for Education Statistics. (2010g). *The nation's report card: U.S. history, 2010.* Retrieved from http://nces.ed.gov/nationsreportcard/pubs/main2010/2011468.asp

National Center for Education Statistics. (2011a). *Characteristics of the 100 largest public elementary and secondary school districts in the United States: 2008–2009.* Retrieved from http://nces.ed.gov/pubs2011/2011301.pdf

National Center for Education Statistics. (2011b). *Condition of education, 2010.* Retrieved from http://nces.ed.gov/pubs2010/2010028.pdf

National Center for Education Statistics. (2011c). *Crime, violence, discipline, and safety in U.S. public schools, 2009–2010.* Retrieved from http://nces.ed.gov/pubs2011/2011320.pdf

National Center for Education Statistics. (2011d). *Digest of education statistics (NCES 2011-15). Chapter 2.* Washington, DC: U.S. Department of Education.

National Center for Education Statistics. (2011e). *Federal expenditures for education.* Washington, DC: Author. Retrieved from http://nces.ed.gov/ubs2005/2005074.pdf

National Center for Education Statistics. (2011f). *Projections of Education Statistics to 2020* (39th ed.). Retrieved from http://nces.ed.gov/pubs2011/2011026.pdf

National Center for Education Statistics. (2011g). *The condition of education 2011.* Washington, DC: Author.

National Center for Education Statistics. (2012). *Trends in high school dropout and completion rates in the United States: 1972–2009* (Compendium Report). Retrieved from http://nces.ed.gov/pubs2012/2012006.pdf

National Center for Women and Information Technology. (2010). *Fact sheet.* Retrieved from http://www.ncwit.org/about.factsheet.html

National Clearinghouse for English Language Acquisition. (2011). *The growing number of English learner students, 1998/1999–2008/2009.* Retrieved from http://www.ncela.gwu.edu/files/uploads/9/growingLEP_0708.pdf

National Commission on Excellence in Education. (1983). *A nation at risk: The imperative for educational reform.* Washington, DC: Government Printing Office. Retrieved from http://datacenter.spps.org/sites/2259653e-ffb3-45ba-8fd6-04a024ecf7a4/uploads/SOTW_A_Nation_at_Risk_1983.pdf

National Council of Teachers of Mathematics. (2008). *Math standards.* Retrieved from http://www.nctm.org/standards/

National Education Association. (2008). *Code of Ethics of the Education Profession, NEA Representative Assembly.*

National Education Association. (2009). *State affiliates.* Retrieved from http://www.nea.org/home/49809.htm

National Education Association. (2010a). *Rankings and estimates: Rankings of the states 2009 and estimates of school statistics 2010.* Retrieved from http://www.nea.org/assets/docs/010rankings.pdf

National Education Association. (2010b). *Status of the American school teacher 2005–2006.* Washington, DC: NEA.

National Education Association. (2011). *Rankings and estimates (2010–2011).* Retrieved from http://www.nea.org/assets/docs/HE/NEA_Rankings_and_Estimates010711.pdf

National Federation of State High School Associations. (2008). *2007–2008 high school athletics participation survey.* Retrieved September 2008 from http://www.nfhs.org/core/contentmanager/uploads/2007-08%20Participation%20Survey.pdf

National Middle School Association. (2010). *This we believe: Keys to educating young adolescents.* Westerville, OH: Author.

National School Boards Association. (2011). *School Boards Circa 2010: Governance in the Accountability Era.* Retrieved from http://www.nsba.org/Board-Leadership/Surveys/School-Boards-Circa-2010

Nelson, J. A. P., Young, B. J., Young, E. L., & Cox, G. (2010). Using teacher-written praise notes to promote a positive environment in a middle school. *Preventing School Failure, 54,* 119–125.

Neugebauer, R. (2011). Making the case for early childhood investments: Three arguments. *Exchange, 33,* 8–10.

New Jersey v. T.L.O., 105 S. Ct. 733 (1985).

Newby, T., Stepich, D., Lehman, J., Russell, J., & Leftwich, A. (2011). *Instructional technology for teaching and learning* (4th ed.). Upper Saddle River, NJ: Merrill/Pearson.

Newman, J. (2006). *America's teachers* (5th ed.). Boston: Allyn & Bacon.

Newman, R. (2008). Adaptive and nonadaptive help seeking with peer harassment: An integrative perspective of coping and self-regulation. *Educational Psychologist, 43*(1), 1–15.

Ngo, B., & Lee, S. (2007). Complicating the image of model minority success: A review of southeast Asian American education. *Review of Educational Research, 77*(4), 415–453.

Nichols, S., & Berliner, D. (2008) Why has high-stakes testing so easily slipped into contemporary American life? *Phi Delta Kappan, 89,* 672–676.

Nieto, S., & Bode, P. (2012). *Affirming diversity: The socio-political context of multicultural education* (6th ed.) Upper Saddle River, NJ: Allyn & Bacon/Pearson.

Noblit, G., Rogers, D., & McCadden, B. (1995). In the meantime: The possibilities of caring. *Phi Delta Kappan, 76,* 680–685.

Noddings, N. (2005*). The challenge to care in schools.* New York: Teachers College Press.

Noddings, N. (2010a). Moral education in an age of globalization. *Educational Philosophy and Theory, 42*(4), 390–396.

Noddings, N. (2010b). Teacher Tess in testing land. *Education Week, 30*(2), 19.

Noguera, P. (2003). The trouble with black boys: The role and influence of environmental and cultural factors on the academic performance of African American males. *Urban Education, 38*(4), 431–459.

Noguera, P. (2012). Saving black and Latino boys. *Phi Delta Kappan, 93*(5), 9–12.

Norenzayan, A., Choi, I., & Peng, K. (2007). Perception and cognition. In S. Kitayama & D. Cohen (Eds.), *Handbook of cultural psychology* (pp. 569–594). New York: Guilford Press.

Norris, N. (2004). *The promise and failure of progressive education.* Lanham, MD: Scarecrow Press.

Nucci, L. (2006). Classroom management for moral and social development. In C. Evertson & C. Weinstein (Eds.), *Handbook of classroom management: Research, practice, and contemporary issues* (pp. 711–731). Mahwah, NJ: Erlbaum.

Nucci, L. (2009). *Nice is not enough: Facilitating moral development.* Boston: Pearson.

Null, J. (2007). William C. Bagley and the founding of essentialism: An untold story in American educational history. *Teachers College Record, 109,* 1013–1055.

Oakes, J. (2008). Keeping track: Structuring equality and inequality in an era of accountability. *Teachers College Record, 110*(3), 700–712.

O'Connor, E. E., Dearing, E., & Collins, B. A. (2011). Teacher–child relationship and behavior problem trajectories in elementary school. *American Educational Research Journal, 48,* 120–162.

Oder, N. (2005). Oklahoma legislators urge limits on kid's books with gay themes. *Library Journal, 130*(11), 16–17.

Ogbu, J. (1999). Beyond language: Ebonics, proper English, and identity in a Black-American speech community. *American Educational Research Journal, 36,* 147–184.

Ogbu, J. (2003). *Black American students in an affluent suburb: A study of academic disengagement.* Mahwah, NJ: Erlbaum.

Ogbu, J., & Simons, H. (1998). Voluntary and involuntary minorities: A cultural-ecological theory of school performance with some implications for education. *Anthropology & Education Quarterly, 29*(2), 155–188.

Ogden, C., & Carroll, M. (2010). *Prevalence of obesity among children and adolescents: United States, trends 1963–1965 through 2007–2008.* Center for Disease Control and Prevention. Retrieved from http://www.cdc.gov/nchs/data/hestat/obesity_child_07_08/obesity_child_07_08.htm

Oliva, P., & Gordon, W. (2013). *Developing the curriculum* (8th ed.). Upper Saddle River, NJ: Allyn & Bacon/Pearson.

O'Meara, J. (2011). *Beyond differentiated instruction.* Thousand Oaks, CA: Corwin Press.

Oner, D., & Adadan, E. (2011). Use of web-based portfolios as tools for reflection in preservice teacher education. *Journal of Teacher Education, 62*(5), 477–492.

Orfield, G. (2009). *Reviving the goal of an integrated society: A 21 century challenge.* Los Angeles: The Civil Rights Project/Poyecto Dereschos Civiles at UCLA.

Orfield, G., Frankenberg, E., & Siegel-Hawley, G. (2010). Integrated schools: Finding a new path. *Educational Leadership, 68*(3), 22–27.

Orfield, G., & Siegel-Hawley, G. (2008). *The forgotten choice? Rethinking magnet schools in a changing landscape.* Retrieved from http://maec.ceee.gwu.edu/files/Civil_Rights_Project.pdf

Ornstein, A., Pajak, E., & Ornstein, S. (2011). *Contemporary issues in curriculum* (5th ed.). Boston: Allyn & Bacon.

Orr, A. (2009). Homework and diapers: How adults can help students juggle pregnancy, parenthood, and school. *Edutopia, 5*(1), 18–20.

O'Shea, M., Heilbronner, N., & Reis, S. (2010). Characteristics of academically talented women who achieve at high levels on the Scholastic Achievement Test—Mathematics. *Journal of Advanced Academics, 21,* 234–271.

Otterman, S. (2011, July 18). New York City abandons teacher bonus program. *New York Times.* Retrieved from http://www.nytimes.com/2011/07/18/education/18rand.html

Ou, S-R., & Reynolds, A. J. (2010). Grade retention, postsecondary education, and public aid receipt. *Educational Evaluation & Policy Analysis, 32,* 118–139.

Ozmon, H. A. (2012). *Philosophical foundations of education* (9th ed.). Boston: Pearson.

Palikoff, M., Porter, A., Smithson, J. (2011). How well aligned are state assessments of student achievement with state content standards? *American Educational Research Journal, 48*(4), 965–995.

Palka, M., & Sanders, T. (2011, June 30). New Jacksonville KIPP charter school scores at bottom on FCAT. *Florida Times-Union.*

Retrieved from http://jacksonville.com/news/metro/2011-06-30/story/new-jacksonville-kipp-charter-scores-bottom-fcat

Pallas, A. (2010/2011). Measuring what matters. *Phi Delta Kappan, 92*(4), 68–71.

Pang, V., Han, P., & Pang, J. (2011). Asian American and Pacific Islander students: Equity and achievement gap. *Educational Researcher, 40*(8), 378–389.

Papay, J. (2011). Different tests different answers: The stability of teacher value-added estimates across outcome measures. *American Educational Research Journal, 48*(1), 163–193.

Parham, J., & Gordon, S. (2011). Moonlighting: A harsh reality for many teachers. *Phi Delta Kappan, 92*(5), 45–51.

Park, S., Oliver, J. S., Johnson, T., Graham, P., & Oppong, N. (2007). Colleagues' roles in the professional development of teachers: Results from a research study of National Board certification. *Teaching and Teacher Education, 23,* 368–389.

Parker-Pope, T. (2008). *Hint of hope as child obesity rate hits plateau.* Retrieved from http://www.nytimes.com/2008/05/28/health/research/28obesity.html

Parker-Pope, T. (2009, February, 24). The 3 R's? A fourth is crucial, too: Recess. *New York Times.* Retrieved from http://www.nytimes.com/2009/02/24/health/24well.html?th&emc=th

Parker-Pope, T. (2010, July 20). Attention disorders can take a toll on marriage. *New York Times,* p. D5.

Partnership for 21st Century Skills. (2011). *Framework for 21st century learning.* Retrieved from http://www.p21.org/index.php?option=com_content&task=view&id=254&Itemid=119

Pashler, H., McDaniel, M., Rohrer, D., & Bjork, R. (2008). Learning styles: Concepts and evidence. *Psychological Science in the Public Interest, 9,* 105–119.

Patterson, G. (2012). Separating the boys from the girls. *Phi Delta Kappan, 93*(5), 37–41.

Patton, C., & Roschelle, J. (2008). Why the best math curriculum won't be a textbook. *Education Week, 27*(36), 32, 24–25.

Paulson, K. (2010, July 20). Sophomoric speech is free speech, too. *USA Today*, p. 9A.

Payne, C. (2008). *So much reform, so little change.* Boston: Harvard Education Press.

Payne, R. (2005). *A framework for understanding poverty.* Highland, TX: Aha! Process Press.

PBS LearningMedia. (2012). *National survey finds teachers want more access to classroom tech.* Retrieved from http://www.pbs.org/about/news/archive/2012/teacher-survey-fetc/

Peery, D. (2011). The colorblind ideal in a race-conscious reality: The case for a new legal ideal for race relations. *Northwestern Journal of Law & Social Policy, 6*(2), 473–495.

Pellegrino, A. M. (2010). Pre-service teachers and classroom authority. *American Secondary Education, 38,* 62–78.

Peregoy, S., & Boyle, O. (2009). *Reading, writing, and learning in ESL* (5th ed.). New York: Longman.

Perry, N. E., Turner, J. C., & Meyer, D. K. (2006). Classrooms as contexts for motivating learning. In P. A. Alexander & P. H. Winne (Eds.*), Handbook of educational psychology* (2nd ed., pp. 327–348). Mahwah, NJ: Erlbaum.

Pew Charitable Trust. (2010). *Pew Internet project: Teens and mobile phones.* Retrieved from http://www.pewtrusts.org/news_room_detail.aspx?id=58543

Pew Research Center. (2011). *Hispanic poverty rate highest in supplemental census measure.* Retrieved from http://pewresearch.org/pubs/2127/hispanics-poverty-rate-census-bureau-supplemental-poverty-measure

Piaget, J. (1952). *Origins of intelligence in children.* New York: International Universities Press.

Piaget, J. (1970). *The science of education and the psychology of the child.* New York: Orion Press.

Pitts, L. (2008). *Which books would Palin want to ban?* Retrieved from http://freep.com/apps/pbcs.dll/article?AID=/20080923/OPINION01/809230333/0/NEWS15

Plank, D. (2010). Assessing English-language learners: One size does not fit all. *Education Week, 31*(2), 20–21.

Pope, N. S., & Stenhagen, K. (2011, April). *Democracy, capitalism, and education: Reconsidering Dewey's failure to address economic life in his educational writings.* Paper presented at the annual meeting of the American Educational Research Association, New Orleans.

Popham, W. (2004). *American's failing schools: How parents and teachers can cope with No Child Left Behind.* New York: Routledge Falmer.

Popham, W. (2011). *Classroom assessment: What teachers need to know* (6th ed.). Boston: Pearson.

Poplin, M., Rivera, J., Durish, D., Hoff, L., Kawell, S., Pawlak, P., Hinman, I., Straus, L., & Veney, C. (2011). She's strict for a good reason: Highly effective teachers in low-performing urban schools. *Phi Delta Kappan, 92*(5), 39–43.

Porter, A. C. (2011). In common core, little to cheer about. *Education Week, 30*(37), 24–25.

Powell, P. J. (2010/2011). Repeating views on grade retention. *Childhood Education, 87,* 90–93.

Powers, T. G., Bindler, R. C., Goetz, S., & Daratha, K. B. (2010). Obesity prevention in early adolescence: Student, parent, and teacher views. *Journal of School Health, 80,* 13–19.

Prud'homme, A. (2011). *The ripple effect: The fate of fresh water in the twenty-first century.* New York: Simon & Schuster.

Public Agenda. (2002). *Sizing things up: What parents, teachers and students think about large and small high schools.* Retrieved from http://www.publicagenda.org/research/research_reports_details.cfm?list=21

Public Agenda. (2003*). Stand by me: What teachers really think about unions, merit pay, and other professional matters.* Retrieved from http://www.publicagenda.org/specials/standbyme

Public Agenda. (2004). *Teaching interrupted.* Retrieved from http://www.publicagenda.org

Pulliam, J., & Van Patten, J. (2007). *History of education in America* (9th ed.). Upper Saddle River, NJ: Merrill/Pearson.

Pulliam, J., & Van Patten, J. (2013). *History and social foundations of American education* (10th ed.). Upper Saddle River, NJ: Pearson.

Purdom, G. (2008, July 10). Schools cutting bus service because of fuel prices. *USA Today,* p. 3A.

Quaid, L. (2008, August 20). Study: Minority students more likely to be paddled. *Salt Lake Tribune,* p. A8.

Quillen, I. (2011a). Online options requires right fit. *Education Week, 31*(1), S18, S19.

Quillen, I. (2011b). Opportunity ripe for online ELL ed. *Education Week, 31*(1), S18, S19.

Quillen, I. (2011c). Virtual education advocates respond to a wave of criticism. *Education Week.* Retrieved from http://www.edweek.org/ew/articles/2011/11/23/13virtual.h31.html?tkn=URZFwJ9vRMyutipgkBEnZK1Mgtt1sbXTpud1&cmp=ENL-EU-NEWS1

Quillen, I. (2012). Ed-tech credential effort to start with online teachers. *Education Week, 31*(18), 11.

Radcliffe, J. (2010). Student tracking devices save money, raise concerns. *Education Week, 30*(8), 9.

Rainie, L. (2010). Internet, broadband and cell phone statistics. *Pew Internet and American Life Project.* Retrieved from http://www.pewinternet.org/Reports/2010/Internet-broadband-and-cell-phone-statistics.aspx

Raskauskas, J., & Stoltz, A. (2007). Involvement in traditional and electronic bullying among adolescents. *Developmental Psychology, 43*(3), 564–575.

Ravitch, D. (2000). *Left back: A century of failed school reforms.* New York: Simon & Schuster.

Ravitch, D. (2010a). Obama's Race to the Top will not improve education. *Huffington Post.* Retrieved from http://www.huffingtonpost.com/diane-ravitch/obamas-race-to-the-top-wi_b_666598.html

Ravitch, D. (2010b). *The death and life of the great American school system.* New York: Basic Books.

Ravitch, D. (2011). Obama's race to the top will not improve education. *Huff Post Politics.* Retrieved from http://www.huffingtonpost.com/diane-ravitch/obamas-race-to-the-top-wi_b_666598.html

Ray v. School District of DeSoto County, 666 F. Supp. 1524, (M.D. Fla. 1987).

Raymond, M. (2009). *Multiple choice: Charter school performance in 16 states.* Stanford University: Center for Research on Education. Retrieved from http://credo.stanford.edu/reports/MULTIPLE_CHOICE_CREDO.pdf

Ready, D., & Lee, V. (2008). Choice, equity, and the schools-within-schools reform. *Teachers College Record, 110*(9). Retrieved from http://www.tcrecord.org ID Number: 15178

Ready, D., & Wright, D. (2011). Accuracy and inaccuracy in teachers' perceptions of young children's cognitive abilities: The role of child background and classroom context. *American Educational Research Journal, 48*(2), 335–360.

Rebell, M., & Wolff, J. (2012). We can overcome poverty's impact on school success. *Education Week, 31*(17), 24–25.

Reese, W. (2005). *America's public schools: From the common school to No Child Left Behind.* Baltimore: Johns Hopkins University Press.

Reid, K. (2005). Sharing the load. *Education Week, 25*(12), 27–30.

Reis, S., Colbert, R., & Hébert, T. (2005). Understanding resilience in diverse, talented students in an urban high school. *Roeper Review, 27*(2), 110–120.

Resnick, M., & Bryant, A. (2010). School boards: Why American education needs them. *Phi Delta Kappan, 91*(6), 11–14.

Reupert, A., & Woodcock, S. (2010). Success and near misses: Pre-service teachers' use, confidence and success in various classroom management strategies. *Teaching and Teacher Education, 26,* 1261–1268.

Rhee, M., & Oakley, K. (2008). Rigor and relevance in teacher preparation. In M. Cochran-Smith, S. Feiman-Nemser, D. J. McIntyre, & K. Demers (Eds.), *Handbook of research on teacher education* (3rd ed., pp. 373–378). New York: Routledge.

Richardson, P., & Watt, H. (2005). "I've decided to become a teacher": Influences on career change. *Teaching and Teacher Education, 21,* 475–489.

Richtel, M. (2011, September 9). In classroom of future, stagnant scores. *New York Times.* Retrieved from http://www.nytimes.com/2011/09/04/technology/technology-in-schools-faces-questions-on-value.html?_r=1&pagewanted

Rideout, V., Foehr, J., & Roberts, D. (2010). *Generation M²: Media in the lives of 8- to 18-year-olds.* Menlo Park, CA: Kaiser Family Foundation.

Ridgers, N. D., Carter, L. M., Stratton, G., & McKenzie, T. L. (2011). Examining children's physical activity and play behaviors during school playtime over time. *Health Education Research, 26,* 586–595.

Riegle-Crumb, C., & King, B. (2010). Questioning a white male advantage in STEM: Examining disparities in college major by gender and race/ethnicity. *Educational Research, 39*(9), 656–664.

Rivkin, S. G., Hanushek, E. E., & Kain, J. J. (2001). *Teachers, schools, and academic achievement.* Amherst, MA: Amherst College.

Robelen, E. (2009). Growth of 'neovouchers' sparks debate over policies. *Education Week, 28*(16), 18–19.

Robelen, E., Adams, C., & Shah, N. (2012). Data show retention disparities. *Education Week, 31*(23), 1.

Roberts, S. (2007, November 17). In name count, Garcias are catching up to Joneses. *New York Times.* Retrieved from http://www.nytimes.com/2007/11/17/us/17surnames.html#

Roberts, W. (2006). *Bullying from both sides.* Thousand Oaks, CA: Corwin Press.

Roblyer, M., & Doering, A. (2013). *Integrating educational technology into teaching* (6th ed.). Upper Saddle River, NJ: Merrill/Prentice Hall.

Rochkind, J., Ott, A., Immerwahr, J., Doble, J., & Johnson, J. (2008). *Lessons learned, issue No. 3: New teachers talk about their jobs, challenges, and long-range plans.* Retrieved from http://www.tqsource.org/publications/LessonsLearned3.pdf

Rohrer, D., & Pashler, H. (2010). Recent research on human learning challenges conventional instructional strategies. *Educational Researcher, 39,* 406–412.

Romano, A. (2011, March 28). How dumb are we? *Newsweek,* pp. 56–60.

Romano, L. (2006, January 6). Fla. voucher system struck down: Court's ruling could affect programs in other states. *Washington Post,* p. A05. Retrieved from http://www.washingtonpost.com/wp-dyn/content/article/2006/01/05/AR2006010501983.html

Romboy, D., & Kinkead, L. (2005, April 14). Surviving in America. *Deseret Morning News, 155*(303), pp. 1, 11, 12.

Rosaen, C., & Florio-Ruane, S. (2008). The metaphors by which we teach: Experience, metaphor, and culture in teacher education. In M. Cochran-Smith, S. Feiman-Nemser, D. J. McIntyre, & K. Demers (Eds.), *Handbook of research on teacher education* (3rd ed., pp. 706–731). New York: Routledge.

Rose, L., & Gallup, A. (1998). The 30th annual Phi Delta Kappa/Gallup Poll of the public's attitudes toward the public schools. *Phi Delta Kappan, 80,* 41–56.

Rose, L., & Gallup, A. (2006). The 38th annual Phi Delta Kappa/Gallup poll of the public's attitudes toward the public schools. *Phi Delta Kappan, 88*(1), 51–53.

Rosenshine, B. (2008). *Five meanings of direct instruction.* Lincoln, IL: Center on Innovation and Improvement.

Rotherham, A. J. (2011). Fixing teacher tenure without a pass–fail grade. *Time U.S.* Retrieved from http://www.time.com/time/nation/article/0,8599,2044529,00.html

Rowe, M. (1986). Wait-time: Slowing down may be a way of speeding up. *Journal of Teacher Education, 37*(1), 43–50.

Russell, J. (2011). From child's garden to academic press: The role of shifting institutional logic in redefining kindergarten education. *American Educational Research Journal, 48*(2), 236–267.

Ryder, R., Burton, J., & Silberg, A. (2006). Longitudinal study of direct instruction effects from first through third grade. *Journal of Educational Research, 99,* 3, 179–191.

Sack-Min, J. (2007). The issues of IDEA. *American School Board Journal, 194*(3), 20–25.

Sackler, M. (Director). (2010). *The lottery* [Motion picture]. USA: Great Curve Films.

Saleh, M., Lazonder, A. W., & de Jong, T. (2007). Structuring collaboration in mixed-ability groups to promote verbal interaction, learning, and motivation of average-ability students. *Contemporary Educational Psychology, 32,* 314–331.

Saltman, D. (2011). Turning digital natives into digital citizens. *Harvard Education Letter, 27*(5). Retrieved from http://www.hepg.org/hel/article/511

Saltman, M. (2005). *The Edison schools: Corporate schooling and the assault on public education.* New York: Routledge/Falmer.

Salvia, J., Ysseldyke, J., & Bolt, S. (2010). *Assessment in special and inclusive education* (11th ed.). Boston: Cengage.

Samuels, C. (2006). Stricter school soda limits offered. *Education Week, 25*(36), 1, 18.

Samuels, C. (2009a). Abstinence education. *Education Week, 28*(16), 5.

Samuels, C. (2009b). Recess and behavior. *Education Week, 28*(20), 4.

Samuels, C. (2010). Proposal on Head Start aims to turn up heat on lagging programs. *Education Week, 30*(6), 7.

Samuels, C. (2011). Los Angeles names new superintendent. *Education Week, 30*(17), 4.

Samuels, C. (2012a). Budget pressures reshape work lives of superintendents. *Education Week, 31*(19), 8.

Samuels, C. (2012b). Indianapolis plan suggests blueprint for other districts. *Education Week, 31*(18), 1, 15.

Sanchez, J. (2009). Constitutional cases involving teachers. *Phi Delta Kappan, 90*(8), 724–728.

Sanders, T. (2011, December 10). Student grade recovery increases: Duval teachers question its message. *Florida Times Union.* Retrieved from http://m.jacksonville.com/news/metro/2011-12-10/story/student-grade-recovery-increases-duval-teachers-question-its-message

Sanders, W. L., & Rivers, J. C. (1996). *Cumulative and residual effects of teachers on student academic achievement.* Knoxville, TN: University of Tennessee Value-Added Research and Assessment Center.

Sandham, J. (2000). Home sweet school. *Education Week, 19*(20), 24–29.

Santa Cruz, N. (2010, June 10). Minority population growing in the United States, census estimates show. *Los Angeles Times.* Retrieved from http://articles.latimes.com/2010/jun/10/nation/la-na-census-20100611

Santos, F. (2012, March 8). Depth of teacher morale is shown in new survey. *New York Times,* p. A15.

Sawchuk, S. (2009a). "21st Century Skills" focus shifts W. Va. teachers' role. *Education Week, 28*(16), 1, 12.

Sawchuk, S. (2009b). Backers of "21st Century Skills" take flak. *Education Week, 28*(23), 1, 14.

Sawchuk, S. (2009c). Teacher training goes in virtual directions. *Education Week, 28*(26), 22–25.

Sawchuk, S. (2010a). New tacks target balancing teacher talent. *Education Week, 29*(35), 1, 16–17.

Sawchuk, S. (2010b, November 10). Professional development at a crossroads. *Education Week: Professional Development,* pp. S2–S4.

Sawchuk, S. (2010c). Study casts cold water on bonus pay. *Education Week, 30*(5), 1, 12–13.

Sawchuk, S. (2011a). Relaxed NEA evaluation policy incorporates many caveats. *Education Week, 30*(36), 6–7.

Sawchuk, S. (2011b). Teachers paid less in higher-minority schools. *Education Week, 31*(6), 5.

Sawchuk, S. (2011c). Unions striking back at bills to curb labor. *Education Week, 30*(26), 1, 14.

Sawchuk, S. (2012a) Access to teacher evaluations divides advocates. *Education Week, 31*(26), 1, 18.

Sawchuk, S. (2012b). Among top-performing nations, teacher quality, status entwined. *Education Week, 31*(16), 12–16.

Sawchuk, S. (2012c). Teacher education in data spotlight. *Education Week, 31*(15), 17.

Schimmel, D., Militello, M., & Eckes, S. (2011). Principals: An antidote to educational malpractice. *Education Week, 30*(33), 24–25.

Schimmel, D., Stellman, L., & Fischer, L. (2011). *Teachers and the law* (8th ed.). New York: Longman.

Schneider, J. (2011). Tech for all? Understanding our mania for education technology. *Education Week, 31*(6), 24.

Schoenberg, N. (2010). Kindergarten: It's the new first grade. *Chicago Tribune*. Retrieved from http://articles.chicagotribune.com/2010-09-04/features/sc-fam-0905-kindergarten-20100904_1_kindergarten-full-day-programs-early-grades

School Board of Nassau County, Florida v. Arline, 480 U.S. 273 (1987).

Schrimpf, C. (2006). This is me. In E. Keefe, V. Moore, & F. Duff (Eds.), *Listening to the experts* (pp. 87–90). Baltimore, MD: Brookes.

Schubert, W. (2008). Curriculum inquiry. In F. M. Connelly (Ed.), *Sage handbook of curriculum & instruction* (pp. 399–419). Los Angeles: Sage.

Schultz, F. (2012). New technologies engage students with disabilities.*Education Week, 31*(23), 14.

Schulz, L., & Bonawitz, E. (2007). Serious fun: Preschoolers engage in more exploratory play when evidence is confounded. *Developmental Psychology, 43*(4), 1034–1050.

Schunk, D. H., Pintrich, P. R., & Meece, J. L. (2008). *Motivation in education: Theory, research, and applications* (3rd ed.). Upper Saddle River, NJ: Merrill/Pearson.

Schussler, D., Stooksberry, L., & Bercaw, L. (2010). Understanding teacher candidate dispositions: Reflecting to build self-awareness.*Journal of Teacher Education, 61*(4), 350–363.

Schwarz, A. (2011, July 19). School discipline study raises fresh questions. *New York Times,* p. A14.

Schwerdt, G., & West, M. R. (2011). The impact of alternative grade configurations on student outcomes through middle and high school. *Harvard University Program on Education Policy and Governance Working Papers Series.* Retrieved from http://www.hks.harvard.edu/pepg/PDF/Papers/PEPG11-02_Schwerdt_West.pdf

Seider, S. (2009). An MI odyssey. *Edutopia, 5*(2), 26–29.

Sedlak, M. (2008). Competing visions of purpose, practice, and policy: The history of teacher certification in the United States. In M. Cochran-Smith, S. Feiman-Nemser, D. J. McIntyre, & K. Demers (Eds.), *Handbook of research on teacher education* (3rd ed., pp. 855–885). New York: Routledge.

Sergiovanni, T. (2009a). *Educational governance and administration* (6th ed.). Boston: Allyn & Bacon.

Sergiovanni, T. (2009b). *Principalship: The reflective practitioner perspective* (6th ed.). Boston: Allyn & Bacon.

Serrano v. Priest (1), 96 Cal. Rptr. 601, 487 P.2d 1241, Calif. (1971).

Sessions-Stepp, L. (2007, April 13). Study casts doubt on abstinence-only programs. *Washington Post.* Retrieved from http://www.washingtonpost.com/wp-dyn/content/article/2007/04/13/AR2007041301003.html

Shah, N. (2011a). Bullies operate anonymously on popular social network. *Education Week, 30*(27), 12–13.

Shah, N. (2011b). Charter schools. *Education Week, 30*(25), 5.

Shah, N. (2011c). Childhood hunger. *Education Week, 30*(22), 5.

Shah, N. (2011d). Federal data lay bare "opportunity gaps" across schools. *Education Week, 30*(36), 29.

Shah, N. (2011e). Policy fight brews over discipline. *Education Week, 31*(7), 1, 12

Shah, N. (2011f). School-meals makeover stirs the pot. *Education Week, 30*(27), 1, 22–23.

Shah, N. (2012). Rules aim to make school meals healthier. *Education Week, 31*(19), 16–19.

Shankar, S. (2011). Asian American youth language use: Perspectives across schools and communities. *Review of Educational Research, 35*(1), 1–28.

Sheldon, S. (2007). Improving student attendance with school, family, and community partnerships. *Journal of Educational Research, 199*(5), 267–275.

Shepard, L., & Smith, M. (1990). Synthesis of research on grade retention. *Educational Leadership, 47*(8), 84–88.

Sherer, Y. C., & Nickerson, A. B. (2010). Anti-bullying practices in American schools: Perspectives of school psychologists. *Psychology in the Schools, 47,* 217–229.

Simon, S. (2011, May 25). Public schools charge kids for basics, frills. *Wall Street Journal*, pp. A2, A14.

Simonson, M., Smaldino, S., Albright, M., & Zvacek, S. (2012). *Teaching and learning at a distance* (5th ed.). Upper Saddle River, NJ: Pearson.

Skiba, R. J., Michael, R. S., Nardo, A. C., & Peterson, R. L. (2002). The color of discipline: Sources of racial and gender disproportionality in school punishment. *Urban Review, 34,* 317–342.

Slavin, R. (2011). Job one for Title I: Use what works. *Education Week, 30*(26), 24.

Sleeter, C. (2005). *Un-standardizing curriculum: Multicultural teaching in the standards-based classroom.* New York: Teachers College Press.

Sleeter, C. (2008). Preparing White teachers for diverse students. In M. Cochran-Smith, S. Feiman-Nemser, D. J. McIntyre, & K. Demers (Eds.), *Handbook of research on teacher education* (3rd ed., pp. 559–582). New York: Routledge.

Small, G., & Vorgan, G. (2008). *iBrain: Surviving the technological alteration of the modern mind.* New York: William Morrow.

Smart, C. (2008, November 20). Wasatch school district may realign schools. *Salt Lake Tribune,* p. B3.

Smith v. Board of School Commissioners of Mobile County, 827 F.2d 684 (llth Cir., 1987).

Smith, C., Christoffersen, K., Davidson, H., & Herzog, P. S. (2011). *Lost in transition: The dark side of emerging adulthood.* New York: Oxford University Press.

Smith, F. (2005). Intensive care. *Edutopia, 1*(9), 47–49.

Smith, F. (2006). Learning by giving. *Edutopia, 2*(1), 54–57.

Smith, M. (2011, February 5). Marathon's tiny school district grabs at a lifeline. *New York Times*. Retrieved from http://

www.nytimes.com/2011/02/06/us/06ttschools.html?_r=2&pagewanted=2&ref=todayspaper

Smith, P., Molnar, A., & Zahorik, J. (2003). Class-size reduction: A fresh look at the data. *Educational Leadership, 61*(1), 72–74.

Solórzano, R. (2008). High stakes testing: Issues, implications, and remedies for English language learners. *Educational Researcher, 78,* 260–329.

Sommers, C. (2000). *The war against boys: How misguided feminism is harming our young men.* New York: Simon & Schuster.

Sommers, C. (2008). The case against Title-Nining the sciences. *Teachers College Record.* Retrieved from http://www.tcrecord.org

Song, J., & Felch, J. (2011). Times updates and expands value-added ratings for Los Angeles elementary school teachers. *Los Angeles Times.* Retrieved from http://www.latimes.com/news/local/la-me-value-added-20110508,0,930050.story

Sorenson, R. (2007). Bible board. *American School Board Journal, 194*(5), 32–34.

Sparks, S. (2010). Study finds fewer "dropout factory" schools. *Education Week, 30*(14), 12–13.

Sparks, S. (2011a). Learning declines linked to moving to middle school. *Education Week, 31*(13), 1, 23.

Sparks, S. (2011b). Panel finds few learning benefits in high-stakes exams. *Education Week, 30*(33), 1, 14.

Sparks, S. (2011c). Study finds safe schools are high-achieving, closely knit. *Education Week, 30*(31), 13.

Sparks, S. (2012, January 25). Small schools spur academic growth, says MDRC report. *Education Week.* Retrieved from http://blogs.edweek.org/edweek/inside-school-research/2012/01/small_schools_spur_academic_gr.html

Speer, N. (2008). Connecting beliefs and practice: A fine-grained analysis of a college mathematics teacher's collections of beliefs and their relationship to his instructional practices. *Cognition and Instruction, 26,* 218–267.

Sporkin, A. (2011). New publishing industry survey details strong three-year growth in net revenue, units. *Association of American Publishers.* Retrieved from http://www.publishers.org/press/44/

Spring, J. (2010). *Deculturalization and the struggle for equity: A brief history of the education of dominated cultures in the United States* (6th ed.). Boston: McGraw-Hill.

Spring, J. (2011). *American education* (15th ed.). Boston: McGraw-Hill.

Springer, M., & Gardner, C. (2010). Teacher pay for performance: Context, status, and direction. *Phi Delta Kappan, 91*(8), 8–14.

Standen, A. (2007) Gender matters: Educators battle over single-sex schools. *Edutopia, 3*(1), 46–49.

Starnes, B. (2006). What we don't know can hurt them: White teachers, Indian children. *Phi Delta Kappan, 87*(5), 384–392.

Steering Committee on Science and Creationism. (1999). *Science and creationism: A view from the National Academy of Sciences* (2nd ed.). Washington, DC: National Academies Press.

Steinhauer, J. (2011, March 10). Cuts to Head Start show challenge of fiscal restraint. *New York Times.* Retrieved from www.nytimes.com/2011/03/11/us/politics/11headstart.html

Sternberg, R. (2007). Who are bright children? The cultural context of being and acting intelligent. *Educational Researcher, 36*(3), 148–155.

Stewart, D., Blocker, G., & Petrik, J. (2013). *Fundamental philosophy* (8th ed.). Upper Saddle River, NJ: Pearson.

Stiggins, R. J., Arter, J. A., Chappius, J., & Chappius, S. (2010). *Classroom assessment for student learning: Doing it right-using it well.* Upper Saddle River, NJ: Allyn & Bacon/Pearson.

Stiggins, R. J., & Chappuis, J. (2012). *Introduction to student-involved assessment FOR learning* (6th ed.). Upper Saddle River, NJ: Allyn & Bacon/Pearson.

Stipek, D. (2002). *Motivation to learn* (4th ed.). Boston: Allyn & Bacon.

Stodgill, R., & Nixon, R. (2007). For schools, lottery payoffs fall short of promises. *New York Times.* Retrieved from www.nytimes.com/2007/10/07/business/07lotto.html

Stone v. Graham, 449 U.S. 39 (1981).

Stover, D. (2008). Take it to the limit. *American School Board Journal, 194*(11), 33–34.

Stover, D., & Hardy, L. (2008). As tutoring becomes a billion-dollar industry, are you doing what it takes to make a difference for your students? *American School Board Journal, 195*(2), 15–19.

Strange, M., Johnson, J., Showalter, P., & Klein, R. (2012). *Why rural matters 2011–2012.* Washington, DC: Rural School and Community Trust.

Strauss, V. (2011). Why merit pay for teachers sounds good—but isn't. *Washington Post.* Retrieved from http://www.washingtonpost.com/blogs/answer-sheet/post/why-merit-pay-for-teachers-sounds-good--but-isnt/2011/10/09/gIQAVb72YL_blog.html

Strong, M. (2009). *Effective teacher induction and mentoring: Assessing the evidence.* New York: Teachers College Press.

Stross, R. (2010, July 21). Computers at home: Educational hope vs. teenage reality. *New York Times.* Retrieved from http://www.nytimes.com/2010/07/11/business/11digi.html

Sturge-Apple, M., Davies, P., & Cummings, E. (2010). Typologies of family function: Implications for children's adjustment during the early school year. *Child Development, 81,* 1320–1335.

Stutz, T. (2007, May 12). 16% fail TAKS graduation test. *Dallas Morning News.* Retrieved from http://www.dallasnews.com/sharedcontent/dws/news/texassouthwest/stories/051207dntextaksfails.5c9ba6b1.html

Su, A. Y-L. (2007). The impact of individual ability, favorable team member scores, and student perception of course importance on student preference of team-based learning and grading methods. *Adolescence, 42,* 805–826.

Sullivan, A., Joshi, H., & Leonard, D. (2010). Single-sex schooling and academic attainment at school and through the lifecourse. *American Educational Research Journal, 47*(1), 6–36.

Swanson, C. (2008). Grading the states. *Education Week, 27*(18), 36–38.

Swanson, C. (2010). Progress postponed: Graduation rate continues decline. *Education Week, 29*(34), 22–23, 30.

Swanson, C. (2011). Nation turns a corner. *Education Week, 39*(34), 23–25.

Taines, C. (2012). Intervening in alienation: The outcomes for urban youth of participating in school activities. *American Educational Research Journal, 49*(1), 53–86.

Tamim, R. M., Bernard, R. M., Borokhovski, E., Abrami, P. C., & Schmid, R. F. (2011). What forty years of research says about the impact of technology on learning: A second-order meta-analysis and validation study. *Review of Educational Research, 81,* 4–28.

Tanner, L. (2009, April 7). Among 4-year-olds, 1 in 5 obese. *Salt Lake Tribune*, p. A7.

Tavernise, S. (2011, February 5). In census, young Americans increasingly diverse. *New York Times.* Retrieved from http://www.nytimes.com/2011/02/05/us/05census.html

Tavernise, S. (2012a, February 10). Rich and poor further apart in education. *New York Times*, pp. A1, A3.

Tavernise, S. (2012b, May 17). Whites account for under half of births in U.S. *New York Times,* Retrieved from http://www.nytimes.com/2012/05/17/us/whites-account-for-under-half-of-births-in-us.html?pagewanted=all

Terwiller, H., & Toppo, G. (2008, March 10). Home schooling takes a hit. *USA Today*, p. 5D.

Texas Education Agency. (2008a). *Texas essential knowledge and skills.* Retrieved from http://www.tea.state.tx.us/teks/

Texas Education Agency. (2008b). *Chapter 111. Texas essential knowledge and skills for mathematics: Subchapter A. Elementary.* Retrieved from http://www.tea.state.tx.us/rules/tac/chapter111/ch111a.html

Texas Education Agency. (2008c). *Texas Assessment of Knowledge and Skills (TAKS)—Spring 2006.* Retrieved from http://scotthochberg.com/files/taas/math4.pdf.

Texas Education Agency. (2011). *Chapter 112. Texas Essential Knowledge and Skills for Science Subchapter C. High School.* Retrieved from http://ritter.tea.state.tx.us/rules/tac/chapter112/ch112c.html

Thacher, N. (2010). No recess. *Education Week, 30*(12), 26–27.

Thomas, E., & Wingert, P. (2010, March 15). The key to saving American education. *Newsweek.*

Thomas, E., & Wingert, P. (2010, March 15). Why we can't get rid of failing teachers. *Newsweek,* pp. 24–27.

Thomas, N., & Lewis, L. (2010). *Teachers' use of educational technology in U.S. public schools: 2009* (NCES 2010-141). Washington, DC: National Center for Education Statistics.

Time Magazine U.S. (1969). Public schools: Sex in the classroom. *Time.* Retrieved from http://www.time.com/time/magazine/article/0,9171,901130-1,00.html

Tinker v. Des Moines Community School District, 393 U.S. 503 (1969).

Toch, T. (2009/2010). Seeding success in charter schools. *Phi Delta Kappan, 91*(4), 66–67.

Toch, T. (2010). Reflections on the charter school movement. *Phi Delta Kappan, 91*(8), 70–71.

Toch, T. (2011/2012). Vouchers redux. *Phi Delta Kappan, 93*(4). Retrieved from http://www.kappanmagazine.org/content/93/4/68.abstract

Tomlinson, C. (2005). *How to differentiate instruction in mixed-ability classrooms* (2nd ed.). Alexandria, VA: Association for Supervision and Curriculum Development.

Tompkins, G. (2013). *Language arts: Patterns of practice* (8th ed). Boston: Allyn & Bacon.

Tong, F., Lara-Alecio, R., Irby, B., Mathes, P., & Kwok, O. (2008). Accelerating early academic oral English development in transitional bilingual and structured English immersion programs. *American Educational Research Journal, 45*(4), 1011–1044.

Toppo, G. (2009, February 12). KIPP proves powerful point. *USA Today*, p. 6D.

Torff, B. (2011). Teacher beliefs shape learning for all students. *Phi Delta Kappan, 93*(3), 21–23.

Trinko, K. (2010, September 21). Political cowards love the sin tax. *USA Today,* p. 11A.

Trinko, K. (2011, April 19). Why school vouchers are worth a shot. *USA Today*, p. 9A.

Trotter, A. (2006). U.S. court backs school's decision to bar student's anti-gay T-shirt. *Education Week, 25*(34), 9.

Turnbull, A., Turnbull, R., & Wehmeyer, M. (2013). *Exceptional lives: Special education in today's schools* (7th ed.). Upper Saddle River, NJ: Pearson.

Turner, D. (2010, June 4). No class: 4-day school weeks gain popularity nationwide. *USA Today.* Retrieved from http://www.usatoday.com/news/education/2010-06-04-shorter-school-week_N.htm

Turner, S. (2010). The benefit of extracurricular activities in high school? Involvement enhances academic achievement and the way forward. *Academic Leadership Live, 8*(3). Retrieved from http://www.academicleadership.org/article/The_Benefit_of_Extracurricular_Activities_in_High_School

Tyack, D. (2003). *Seeking common ground: Public schools in a diverse society.* Cambridge, MA: Harvard University Press.

Tyack, D., & Hansot, E. (1986). *Managers of virtue: Public school leadership in American, 1820–1980.* New York: Basic Books.

Ubben, G., Hughes, L., & Norris, C. (2011). *The principal: Creative leadership for excellences in schools* (7th ed.). Boston: Allyn & Bacon.

Ubinas, L., & Gabrieli, C. (2011, August 23). Shortchanged by the bell. *New York Times.* Retrieved from: http://www.nytimes.com/2011/08/23/opinion/shortchanged-by-the-school-bell.html?_r=1&nl=todaysheadlines&emc=tha212

Underwood, J., & Webb, L. (2006). *School law for teachers.* Upper Saddle River, NJ: Pearson.

Urban, W., & Wagoner, J., (2009). *American education: A history* (4th ed.). New York: Routledge.

U.S. Bureau of Census. (2007a). American community survey (online). Retrieved from http://www.census.gov/acs/www/Products/index.html

U.S. Bureau of Census. (2007b). *Income, earnings, and poverty estimates released in American Fact Finder, 8/28/07.* Retrieved from http://factfinder.census.gov/home/saff/main.html?lang=en

U.S. Bureau of Census. (2008). *The Hispanic population in the United States.* Washington, DC: U.S. Government Printing Office.

U.S. Bureau of Census. (2009). *The foreign-born population in the United States: 2009.* Washington, DC: U.S. Government Printing Office.

U.S. Bureau of Census. (2010a). *Statistical abstract of the United States, 2010* (129th ed.). Washington, DC: U.S. Government Printing Office. Retrieved from http://www.census.gov/compendia/statab/

U.S. Bureau of Census. (2010b). *Table 232. Children who speak a language other than English at home by region: 2008.* Washington, DC: U.S. Government Printing Office.

U.S. Bureau of Census. (2011). *Income, poverty, and health insurance coverage in the United States: 2010.* Report P66N.238 Table B-2, pp. 68–73. Retrieved from http://www.census.gov/prod/2011pubs/p60-239.pdf

U.S. Bureau of Census. (2012). *Elementary and secondary education: Schools and enrollment. Table 241: Public elementary and secondary schools by type and size of school.* Retrieved from http://www.census.gov/compendia/statab/2012/tables/12s0241.pdf

U.S. Bureau of Indian Affairs. (1974). Government schools for Indians (1881). In S. Cohen (Ed.), *Education in the United States: A documentary history* (Vol. 3, pp. 1734–1756). New York: Random House.

U.S. Department of Education. (1995). *Digest of education statistics, 1994.* Washington, DC: U.S. Government Printing Office.

U.S. Department of Education. (2008). *Common core of data.* Washington, DC: Author.

U.S. Department of Education. (2009a). *Race to the top program: Executive summary.* Retrieved from http://www2.ed.gov/programs/racetothetop/executive-summary.pdf

U.S. Department of Education. (2009b*). School size.* Washington DC: Office of Vocational and Adult Education.

U.S. Department of Education. (2010). *The condition of education.* National Center for Education Statistics. Retrieved from http://nces.ed.gov/programs/coe/2010/section4/table-pal-1.asp

U.S. Department of Health and Human Services. (2009). *Child health USA, 2008–2009: Working mother and child care.* Retrieved from http://mchb.hrsa.gov/chusa08/pdfs/c08.pdf

U.S. Department of Health and Human Services. (2010). *Child maltreatment, 2009: National and state child abuse and neglect statistics.* Washington, DC: Author.

U.S. Department of Health and Human Services. (2011). Poverty guidelines. *Federal Register, 76*(12), 3637–3638.

U.S. English. (2011). *Official English: Why is official English necessary?* Retrieved from http://www.usenglish.org/view/10

U.S. Government Accounting Office. (2006). *No Child Left Behind Act: Additional assistance and research on effective strategies would help small rural districts.* Washington, DC: Government Printing Office.

Usdan, M. (2010). School boards: A neglected institution in an era of school reform. *Phi Delta Kappan, 91*(6), 8–10.

Van Horn, R. (2008). *Bridging the chasm between research and practice: A guide to major educational research.* Lanham, MD: Rowman & Littlefield Education.

Van Houtte, M., & Van Maele, D. (2011). The black box revelation: In search of conceptual clarity regarding climate and culture in school effectiveness research. *Oxford Review of Education, 37,* 505–524.

Vaughn, S., & Bos, C. (2012). *Strategies for teaching students with learning and behavior problems* (8th ed.). Upper Saddle River, NJ: Pearson.

Vedantam, S. (2010). *The hidden brain: How our unconscious minds elect presidents, control markets, wage wars, and save our lives.* New York: Spiegel & Grau.

Ventura, S. J., & Hamilton, B. E. (2011). U. S. teenage birth rate resumes decline. *NCHS Data Brief,* No. 58.

Viadero, D. (2005). Smoking-prevention programs in schools found ineffective for teens. *Education Week, 24*(26), 6.

Viadero, D. (2006). Rose reports influence felt 40 years later. *Education Week, 25*(41), 1, 21–24.

Viadero, D. (2008a). Career academies found to pay off in higher earnings. *Education Week, 27*(43), 10.

Viadero, D. (2008b). Research yields clues on the effects of extra time for learning. *Education Week, 28*(5), 16, 17.

Viadero, D. (2009a). Book probes scoring gaps tied to race. *Education Week, 28*(20), 1, 10, 11.

Viadero, D. (2009b). Delving deep: Research hones focus on ELLs. *Education Week, 28*(17), 22–25.

Vigeland, T. (2012, March 22). More men trading overalls for nursing scrubs. *New York Times,* p. F2.

Villegas, A., & Davis, D. (2008). Preparing teachers of color to confront racial/ethnic disparities in educational outcomes. In M. Cochran-Smith, S. Feiman-Nemser, D. J. McIntyre, & K. Demers (Eds.), *Handbook of research on teacher education* (3rd ed., pp. 583–605). New York: Routledge.

Virtual High School. (2009). Retrieved from http://www.govhs.org/website.nsf

Viteretti, J. (2009a). Should mayors run schools? *Education Week, 28*(28), 32, 26.

Viteretti, J. (2009b). *When mayors take charge.* Washington, DC: Brookings Institute Press.

Wald, J., & Thurau, L. (2010). Taking safety too far? *Education Week, 29*(22), 24, 25.

Walker, D. (2009). Effectiveness of state anti-bullying laws questioned. *Education Week, 29*(4), 7.

Wallace, J., Goodkind, S., Wallace, C., & Bachman, J. (2008). Racial, ethnic, & gender differences in school discipline among U.S. high school students: 1991–2005. *Negro Education Review, 59*(1–2), 47–62.

Walsh, M. (2000). Church–state rulings cut both ways. *Education Week, 19*(42), 1, 40–41.

Walsh, M. (2002). High court high noon. *Education Week*. Retrieved from http://www.policymattersohio.org/media/ew_voucher.pdf

Walsh, M. (2012). Speech cases turned aside by high court: Online activity by students remains contentious issue. *Education Week, 31*(18), 1, 22.

Warner, J. (2009, April 16). Dude, you've got problems. *New York Times*. Retrieved from http://warner.blogs.nytimes.com/2009/04/16/who-are-you-calling-gay/?em

Warnick, B. (2007). Surveillance cameras in schools: An ethical analysis. *Harvard Educational Review, 77*(3), 317–343.

Warnick, B., & Silverman, S. (2011). A framework for professional ethics courses in teacher education. *Journal of Teacher Education, 62*(3), 273–285.

Waterhouse, L. (2006). Multiple intelligences, the Mozart effect, and emotional intelligence: A critical review. *Educational Psychologist, 41*(4), 217–225.

Watt, H., & Richardson, P. (2007). Motivational factors influencing teaching as a career choice: Development and validation of the FIT-choice scale. *Journal of Experimental Education, 75*(3), 167–202.

Watzke, J. (2007). Longitudinal research on beginning teacher development: Complexity as a challenge to concerns-based stage theory. *Teaching and Teacher Education,* 23(1), 106–122.

Waxman, H., Huang, S., Anderson, L., & Weinstein, T. (1997). Classroom process differences in inner-city elementary schools. *Journal of Educational Research, 91*(1), 49–59.

Weinstein, C. S. (2007). *Middle and secondary classroom management* (3rd ed.). Boston: McGraw-Hill.

Weinstein, C. S., Romano, M. E., & Mignano, A. J., Jr. (2011). *Elementary classroom management: Lessons from research and practice* (5th ed.). New York: McGraw-Hill.

Weisberg, D., Sexton, S., Mulhern, J., & Keeling, D. (2009). The widget effect: Our national failure to acknowledge and act on difference in teacher effectiveness (Executive summary). *New Teacher Project*. Retrieved from http://widgeteffect.org/downloads/TheWidgetEffect_execsummary.pdf

Weiss, L. (2005). Book battle in Fayetteville, AR, rages on. *School Library Journal, 51*(11), 20.

Wells, A., & Frankenberg, E. (2007). The public schools and the challenge of the Supreme Court's integration decision. *Phi Delta Kappan, 89*(3), 178–188.

Whitcomb, J., Borko, H., & Liston, D. (2006). Living in the tension—living with the heat. *Journal of Teacher Education, 57*(5), 447–453.

Whitcomb, J., Borko, H., & Liston, D. (2007). Stranger than fiction: Arthur Levine's Educating School Teachers—The basis for a proposal. *Journal of Teacher Education, 58*(3), 195–201.

Wiggins, G. (2010). Why we should stop bashing state tests. *Educational Leadership, 67*(6), 48–52.

Wiggins, G., & McTighe, J. (2005). *Understanding by design* (2nd ed.). Upper Saddle River, NJ: Pearson.

Wight, V., Chau, M., & Aratani, Y. (2011). *Who are America's poor children?* Columbia University: National Center for Children in Poverty. Retrieved from http://www.nccp.org/publications/pdf/text_912.pdf

Wiles, J. W., & Bondi, J. C. (2011). *Curriculum development: A guide to practice* (8th ed.). Upper Saddle River, NJ: Merrill/Pearson.

Williams, J. (2003). Why great teachers stay. *Educational Leadership, 60*(8), 71–75.

Wilson, B., & Corbett, H. (2001). *Listening to urban kids: School reform and the teachers they want*. Albany, NY: State University of New York Press.

Wilson, S., & Tamir, E. (2008). The evolving field of teacher education: How understanding challenge(r)s might improve the preparation of teachers. In M. Cochran-Smith, S. Feiman-Nemser, D. J. McIntyre, & K. Demers (Eds.), *Handbook of research on teacher education* (3rd ed., pp. 908–936). New York: Routledge.

Wilson, S., & Youngs, S. (2005). Research on accountability processes in teacher education. In M. Cochran-Smith & K. Zeichner, *Studying teacher education: The report of the AREA panel on research and teacher education* (pp. 591–644). Mahwah, NJ: Erlbaum.

Winerip, M. (2011a, January 3). Teacher, my dad lost his job. Do we have to move? *New York Times*. Retrieved from http://www.nytimes.com/2011/01/31/education/31winerip.html?pagewanted=all

Winerip, M. (2011b, February 28). Seeking integration, whatever the path. *New York Times*, pp. A11, A13.

Winerip, M. (2011c, March 14). For Detroit schools, hope for the hopeless. *New York Times*, p. A13.

Winerip, M. (2011d, May 2). Homeless, but finding sanctuary at school. *New York Times*, p. A14.

Winerip, M. (2011e, November 7). In Tennessee, following the rules for evaluations off a cliff. *New York Times,* p. A16.

Winerip, M. (2011f, November 28). Principals protest role of testing. *New York Times,* p. A18.

Winitzky, N. (1994). Multicultural and mainstreamed classrooms. In R. Arends (Ed.), *Learning to teach* (3rd ed., pp. 132–170). New York: McGraw-Hill.

Winograd, K. (1998). Rethinking theory after practice: Education professor as elementary teacher. *Journal of Teacher Education, 49,* 296–303.

Winseman, A. (2005). *Religion in America: Who has none?* Retrieved from http://www.galluppoll.com/content/?ci=20329&pg=1

Winterfeld, A. (2008). *Nutrition rules. National Conference of State Legislatures*. Retrieved from http://www.ncsl.org/issues-research/health/state-legislatures-magazine-nutrition-rules-may.aspx

Winters, R. (2010, September 19). Is superintendent pay too super? *Salt Lake Tribune,* pp. A1, A6.

Wittwer, J., & Renkl, A. (2008). Why instructional explanations often do not work: A framework for understanding the effectiveness of instructional explanations. *Educational Psychologist, 43*(1), 49–64.

Wood, M. (2005). *High school counselors say they lack skills to assist gay, lesbian students.* Retrieved from www.bsu.edu/news

Woodward, T. (2002, June 20). Edison's failing grade. *Corporate Watch.* Retrieved from http://www.corpwatch.org/issues/PID.jsp?articleid=2688

Woolfolk Hoy, A., & Burke-Spero, R. (2005). Changes in teacher efficacy during the early years of teaching: A comparison of four measures. *Teaching and Teacher Evaluation, 21,* 343–356.

Woolfolk Hoy, A., Davis, H., & Pape, S. J. (2006). Teacher knowledge and beliefs. In P. A. Alexander & P. H. Winne (Eds.), *Handbook of educational psychology* (2nd ed., pp. 715–737). Mahwah, NJ: Erlbaum.

Woolfolk Hoy, A., Hoy, W., & Davis, H. (2009). Teachers' self-efficacy beliefs. In K. Wentzel, & A. Wigfield (Eds.), *Handbook of motivation in schools* (pp. 627–654). Mahwah, NJ: Erlbaum.

World of Sports Science. (2008). *Title IX and United States female sports participation.* Retrieved from http://www.faqs.org/sports-science/Sp-Tw/Title-IX-and-United-States-Female-Sports-Participation.html

Wubbels, T., Brekeimans, M., den Brok, P., & van Tartwijk, J. (2006). An interpersonal perspective on classroom management in secondary classrooms in the Netherlands. In C. M. Evertson & C. S. Weinstein (Eds.), *Handbook of classroom management: Research, practice, and contemporary issues* (pp. 1161–1191). Mahwah, NJ: Erlbaum.

Yarrow, A. (2009). State of mind. *Education Week, 29*(8), 21–23.

You Tube. (2011). *Miss USA—should math be taught in schools?* Retrieved from http://www.youtube.com/user/mackenziefegan

Young, M., & Scribner, J. (1997, March).*The synergy of parental involvement and student engagement at the secondary level: Relationships of consequence in Mexican-American communities.* Paper presented at the annual meeting of the American Educational Research Association, Chicago.

Younger, M., & Warrington, M. (2006). Would Harry and Hermione have done better in single-sex classes? A review of single-sex teaching in coeducational secondary schools in the United Kingdom. *American Educational Research Journal, 43*(4), 579–620.

Zahorik, J. (1991). Teaching style and textbooks. *Teaching and Teacher Education, 7,* 185–196.

Zehr, M. (2004). Va. plan would ease standards for home school parents. *Education Week, 23*(34), 26.

Zehr, M. (2008). Native American history, culture gaining traction in state curricula. *Education Week, 28*(11), 1, 12.

Zehr, M. (2009). NYC test sizes up ELLs with little formal schooling. *Education Week, 28*(23), 13.

Zehr, M. (2010a). Districts scramble to address increase in homeless pupils. *Education Week, 29*(20), 6–7.

Zehr, M. (2010b). KIPP middle schools boost learning gains, study says. *Education Week, 29*(36), 14.

Zehr, M. (2010c). More districts factoring poverty into student-assignment plans. *Education Week, 29*(31), 1, 20–21.

Zehr, M. (2010d). Public schools taking lesson from charters. *Education Week, 30*(11), 1, 12.

Zehr, M. (2011a). "It takes a village" to educate children in Indian district. *Education Week, 30*(28), 8–9.

Zehr, M. (2011b). KIPP and teachers' unions go toe to toe in Baltimore. *Education Week, 30*(24), 1, 14.

Zehr, M. (2011c). Study stings KIPP in attrition rate. *Education Week, 30*(27), 1, 24–25.

Zehr, M. (2011d). Transfer rates similar for KIPP, local schools. *Education Week, 30*(28), 10.

Zeldin, A., & Pajares, F. (2000). Against the odds: Self efficacy beliefs of women in mathematical, scientific, and technological careers. *American Educational Research Journal, 37,* 215–246.

Zernike, K. (2012, May 31). Judge defends penalty in Rutgers spying case, saying it fits crime. *New York Times,* p. A20.

Zigler, E. (2009). A new Title I. *Education Week, 28*(20), 34, 26.

Zirkel, P. (2007). Weird science? *Phi Delta Kappan, 88*(5), 414–416.

Zirkel, P. (2008a). Much ado about a C? *Phi Delta Kappan, 89*(4), 318–310.

Zirkel, P. (2008b). Unfunded mandate? *Phi Delta Kappan, 90*(2), 701–703.

Zirkel, P. (2009). School law all stars: Two successive constellations. *Phi Delta Kappan, 90*(8), 704–708.

Zirkel, P. (2010a). A tale of two cases. *Phi Delta Kappan, 92*(3), 76–77.

Zirkel, P. (2010b). In Rob we trust. *Phi Delta Kappan, 91*(8), 76–77.

Zirkel, P. (2010c). Teacher tenure is not the real problem. *Phi Delta Kappan, 92*(1), 76–77.

Zubrzycki, J. (2011a). Common core poses challenges for preschools. *Education Week, 31*(13), 1, 20–21.

Zubrzycki, J. (2011b). New laws take aim at bullying. *Education Week.* Retrieved from http://www.edweek.org/ew/articles/2011/10/19/08bully_ep.h31.html?tkn=TOZFASjzKIH7BUSNovjqB2C9hyLxck%2BcEdMI&cmp=ENL-EU-NEWS2

Zubrzycki, J. (2012). Single-gender schools scrutinized. *Education Week, 31*(17), 1, 12–13.

Zuger, S. (2008). Build better e portfolios. *Tech and Learning, 29*(1), 46–47.

Zumwalt, K., & Craig, E. (2008). Who is teaching? Does it matter? In M. Cochran-Smith, S. Feiman-Nemser, D. J. McIntyre, & K. Demers (Eds.), *Handbook of research on teacher education* (3rd ed., pp. 404–423). New York: Routledge.

GLOSSARY

A

Academic freedom. The right of teachers to choose both content and teaching methods based on their professional judgment.

Academic learning time. The amount of time students are both engaged and successful.

Academy. An early secondary school that focused on the practical needs of colonial America, offering math, navigation, astronomy, bookkeeping, logic, and rhetoric to both boys and girls.

Acceleration. A gifted and talented program that keeps the regular curriculum but allows students to move through it more quickly.

Accountability. The process of requiring students to demonstrate mastery of the topics they study as measured by standardized tests, as well as holding educators at all levels responsible for students' performance.

Action research. A form of applied teacher research designed to answer a specific school- or classroom-related question.

Adequate Yearly Progress (AYP). A provision of No Child Left Behind that requires students to demonstrate progress in statewide tests toward meeting state standards.

Administrators. People responsible for the day-to-day operation of a school.

Advanced Placement (AP) classes. Courses taken in high school that allow students to earn college credit, making college less time-consuming and expensive.

Allocated time. The amount of time a teacher designates for a particular content area or topic.

Alternative licensure. A shorter route to licensure for those who already possess a bachelor's degree.

American Federation of Teachers (AFT). The nation's second-largest teacher professional organization, founded in 1916 and affiliated with the AFL-CIO, a major national labor union.

American Recovery and Reinvestment Act. Legislation providing new federal aid to education designed to provide economic stimulus to the U.S. economy.

Assessment. The process teachers use to gather information and make decisions about students' learning and development.

Assimilation. A process of socializing people so that they adopt dominant social norms and patterns of behavior.

Assistive technology. A set of adaptive tools that support students with disabilities in learning activities and daily life tasks.

Autonomy. The capacity to control one's own professional life.

Axiology. The branch of philosophy that considers values and ethics.

B

Behavior disorders. The display of serious and persistent age-inappropriate behaviors that result in social conflict, personal unhappiness, or school failure.

Bilingual maintenance language programs. Language programs that place the greatest emphasis on using and sustaining the first language while teaching English.

Block grants. Federal monies provided to states and school districts with few restrictions for use.

Block scheduling. A high school scheduling option in which classes are longer but meet less frequently.

Buckley Amendment. A federal law, also called the Family Educational Rights and Privacy Act, that describes who may have access to a student's educational records.

Bullying. A systematic or repetitious abuse of power between students.

C

Career academy. An alternative to large, comprehensive high schools that places students in small, career-oriented learning communities.

Career technical schools. Schools designed to provide students with education and job skills that will enable them to get a job immediately after high school.

Caring. A teacher's investment in the protection and development of the young people in his or her classes.

Categorical grants. Federal funds targeted for specific groups and designated purposes like Head Start.

Censorship. The practice of prohibiting objectionable materials from being used in academic classes or, in some cases, from being placed in libraries.

Certification. Special recognition by a professional organization indicating that a person has met certain rigorous requirements specified by the organization.

Character education. A curriculum approach to developing student morality that emphasizes teaching and rewarding moral values and positive character traits, such as honesty, tolerance, and fairness.

Charter schools. Alternative schools that are independently operated but publicly funded.

Classroom management. Comprehensive actions teachers take to create an environment that supports and facilitates both academic and social-emotional learning.

Classroom organization. A professional management skill that includes preparing materials in advance, starting classes and activities on time, making timely and smooth transitions, and creating well-established routines.

Closure. A form of review occurring at the end of a lesson designed to help students organize what they've learned into a meaningful idea.

Collaboration. Joint communication and decision making among educational professionals to create an optimal learning environment for students with exceptionalities.

Collective bargaining. The process that occurs when a local chapter of a professional organization negotiates with a school district over the rights of the teachers and the conditions of employment.

Commercialization. Corporations using schools as avenues or arenas for advertising and other business ventures.

Common Core State Standards Initiative (CCSSI). A reform effort designed to establish a single set of clear educational standards for all states in English-language arts and mathematics.

Common school movement. A historical attempt in the 1800s to make education available to all children in the United States.

Communication disorders. Disorders that interfere with students' ability to receive and understand information from others or to express their own ideas or questions.

Compensatory education programs. Government attempts to create more equal educational opportunities for disadvantaged youth.

Comprehensive high school. A secondary school that attempts to meet the needs of all students by housing them together and providing curricular options (e.g., vocational or college-preparatory programs) geared toward a variety of student ability levels and interests.

Cooperative learning. A set of instructional strategies used to help learners meet specific learning and social-interaction objectives in structured groups.

Copyright laws. Federal laws designed to protect the intellectual property of authors, including printed matter, videos, computer software, and various other types of original work.

Corporal punishment. The use of physical, punitive disciplinary actions to correct student misbehavior.

Creationism. A religious view suggesting that the universe was created by God as described in the Bible, framed in terms designed to make it appear scientific.

Credentials file. A collection of important personal documents teachers submit when they apply for teaching positions.

Cultural diversity. The different cultures encountered in classrooms and how these cultural differences influence learning.

Culturally responsive classroom management. Classroom management that combines teachers' awareness of possible personal biases with knowledge of students' cultures.

Culturally responsive teaching. Instruction that acknowledges and capitalizes on cultural diversity.

Culture. The knowledge, attitudes, values, customs, and behavior patterns that characterize a social group.

Curriculum. Everything that teachers teach and students learn in schools. Also may include unintended outcomes from school experiences.

Cyberbullying. The use of electronic media to harass or intimidate other students.

D

Dame schools. One of the few examples of women teaching in colonial times; women taught small groups of children in their homes, funded by parents.

***De facto* segregation.** Segregation resulting from individuals' private decisions, primarily from housing or where people choose to live.

***De jure* segregation.** Segregation resulting from laws, such as those existing in many states that created schools that were supposedly "separate but equal."

Departmentalization. The organization of teachers and classes into separate academic areas.

Desists. Verbal or nonverbal communications teachers use to stop a behavior.

Detention. Similar to time-out, the taking away of students' free time by keeping them in school after regular dismissal times.

Development. The physical, intellectual, moral, emotional, and social changes that occur in students as a result of their maturation and experience.

Developmental programs. Programs that accommodate differences in children's development by allowing them to acquire skills and abilities at their own pace through direct experiences.

Differentiating instruction. The process of adapting instruction to meet the needs of students who vary in background knowledge, skills, needs, and motivations.

Digital portfolio. A collection of materials contained in an electronic file that makes personal information easy to edit and share with prospective employers.

Direct instruction. An instructional strategy designed to teach essential knowledge and skills through teacher explanation and modeling followed by student practice and feedback.

Disabilities. Functional limitations or an inability to perform a certain act, such as hear or walk.

Discipline. Teachers' responses to student misbehavior.

Discrepancy model of identification. One method of identifying students with exceptionalities that focuses on differences between classroom performance and tests, achievement and intelligence tests, or subtests within tests.

Distance education. Organized instructional programs in which teachers and learners, though physically separated, are connected through technology.

Dual enrollment. High school courses in which students are enrolled in college classes while still in high school.

Due process. A set of legal guidelines, based on the Fourteenth Amendment to the Constitution, that must be followed to protect individuals from arbitrary or capricious actions by those in authority.

E

Early childhood education. A general term encompassing a range of educational programs for young children, including infant intervention and enrichment programs, nursery schools, public and private pre-kindergartens and kindergartens, and federally funded Head Start programs.

Effective school. A school in which learning for all students is maximized.

Effective teaching. Instruction that maximizes learning by actively involving students in meaningful learning activities.

Emotional intelligence. The ability to manage emotions, control impulses, and behave in socially acceptable ways so an individual can cope with the world and accomplish goals.

Engaged time. The time students are paying attention and are actively involved in learning activities. Also called *time on task.*

English as a second language (ESL) programs. A wide variety of language programs emphasizing rapid transition to English through content-area instruction with no efforts to maintain students' native language.

English classical school. A free secondary school designed to meet the needs of boys not planning to attend college.

English learners (ELs). Students whose first language isn't English and who need help in learning to speak, read, and write in English (also called English language learners—ELLs).

Enrichment. A gifted and talented program that provides richer and more varied content through strategies that supplement usual grade-level work.

Epistemology. The branch of philosophy that deals with knowledge and questions of how we come to know what we know.

Equitable distribution. The practice of calling on all students—both volunteers and nonvolunteers—as equally as possible.

Essential teaching skills. Abilities that all teachers, including those in their first year, should have in order to help students learn.

Essentialism. An educational philosophy suggesting that specific knowledge and skills exist that all people should possess, such as basic skills in reading, writing, math, science, and social studies.

Establishment clause. The clause of the First Amendment that prohibits the establishment of a national religion.

Ethics. Sets of moral standards for acceptable professional behavior.

Ethnicity. A person's ancestry; the way individuals identify themselves with the nation they or their ancestors came from.

Exceptionalities. Learning or emotional needs that result in students' requiring special help to succeed and reach their full potential.

Explicit curriculum. The stated curriculum found in textbooks, curriculum guides, and standards, as well as other planned formal educational experiences.

Extracurriculum. The part of the curriculum consisting of learning experiences that go beyond the core of students' formal studies.

Extrinsic motivation. Motivation to engage in a behavior to receive some incentive.

Extrinsic rewards. Rewards that come from outside, such as job security and vacations.

F

Fair-use guidelines. Policies that specify limitations in the use of copyrighted materials for educational purposes.

Feedback. Information about existing student understanding used to enhance future learning.

Focus. Concrete objects, pictures, models, materials displayed on a document camera, and information written on the board that attract and maintain attention during learning activities.

Formative evaluation. The process of gathering information and providing feedback that teachers can use to improve their practice.

Free exercise clause. The section of the First Amendment that prohibits the government from interfering with individuals' rights to hold religious beliefs and freely practice religion.

Frequency. The number of questions teachers ask during a given period of instructional time.

Full-service schools. Schools that serve as family resource centers to provide a range of social and health services.

G

Gender bias. Discrimination based on gender that limits the growth possibilities of either boys or girls.

Gender-role identity. Societal differences in expectations and beliefs about appropriate roles and behaviors of the two sexes.

General pedagogical content knowledge. General principles of teaching and learning, such as the ability to maintain an orderly and learning-focused classroom and guide student learning using skilled questioning.

Gifted and talented. Students at the upper end of the ability continuum who need special services to reach their full potential.

Grade recovery. A controversial district policy where failing students are allowed to improve their grades by using online programs designed to improve their understanding and skills.

Grade retention. The practice of requiring students to repeat a grade if they don't meet certain criteria.

Grievance. A formal complaint against an employer alleging unsatisfactory working conditions.

Guided discovery. An instructional strategy designed to teach concepts and other abstractions by presenting students with data and assisting them in finding patterns through teacher questioning.

H

Head Start. A federal compensatory education program designed to help 3- to 5-year-old disadvantaged children enter school ready to learn.

High collective efficacy. The belief by teachers in their schools' ability to promote student learning regardless of external conditions; a pervasive factor in effective schools.

High-quality examples. Representations of content that ideally have all the information students need in order to learn a topic.

High-stakes tests. Standardized assessments that states and districts use to determine whether students will advance from one grade to another, graduate from high school, or have access to specific fields of study.

Homeschooling. An educational option in which parents educate their children at home.

I

Immersion programs. Language programs that emphasize rapid transition to English by exclusive use of the English language.

Implicit curriculum. The unstated and sometimes unintended aspects of the curriculum.

In loco parentis. A principle meaning "in place of the parents" that requires teachers to use the same judgment and care as parents in protecting the children under their supervision.

Inclusion. A comprehensive approach to educating students with exceptionalities that includes a total, systematic, and coordinated web of services.

Individualized education program (IEP). An individually prescribed instructional plan collaboratively devised by special education and general education teachers, resource professionals, and parents (and sometimes the student).

Individualized family service plan (IFSP). A comprehensive service plan, similar to an IEP, that targets the families of young children (birth to 2 years) who are developmentally delayed.

Induction programs. Professional experiences designed to help beginning teachers successfully transition into teaching.

Instruction. The strategies teachers use to help students reach learning goals in the curriculum.

Instructional alignment. The match between learning objectives, learning activities, and assessments.

Instructional strategies. Prescriptive approaches to teaching designed to help students acquire a deep understanding of specific forms of knowledge.

Instructional time. The amount of time left for teaching after routine management and administrative tasks are completed.

Integrated curriculum. A form of curriculum in which concepts and skills from various disciplines are combined and related.

Intellectual disabilities. Disabilities that include limitations in intellectual functioning indicated by difficulties in learning and problems with adaptive skills, such as communication, self-care, and social interaction (used to be called *mental retardation).*

Intelligence. The ability to acquire and use knowledge, solve problems, reason in the abstract, and adapt to new situations.

Intelligent design. A theory suggesting that certain features of the universe and of living things are so complex that their existence is best explained by an intelligent cause, rather than by an undirected process such as natural selection.

Interstate Teacher Assessment and Support Consortium (InTASC). An organization designed to help states develop better teachers through coordinated efforts to increase support for new teachers and to create improved teacher-evaluation systems.

Intervention. A teacher action designed to increase desired behaviors or to eliminate student misbehavior and inattention.

Intrinsic motivation. Motivation to be involved in an activity for its own sake.

Intrinsic rewards. Rewards that come from within oneself and are personally satisfying for emotional or intellectual reasons.

Involvement. The extent to which students are actively participating in a learning activity.

J

Junior high schools. Schools designed for early adolescents that are similar in form and focus to high schools.

K

KIPP (Knowledge Is Power Program). A national network of charter schools that targets at-risk students, stresses academics, and features extended school hours and mandatory homework.

L

Latchkey children. Children who go home to empty houses after school and who are left alone until parents arrive home from work.

Latin grammar school. An early college-preparatory school designed to help boys prepare for the ministry or a career in law.

Learning community. A classroom environment in which the teacher and students work together to help everyone learn.

Learning disabilities. The most frequently occurring exceptionality, involving difficulties in acquiring and using listening, speaking, reading, writing, reasoning, or mathematical abilities.

Learning objectives. Statements that specify what students should know or be able to do with respect to a topic or course of study.

Learning style. Students' personal approaches to learning, problem solving, and processing information.

Lecture–discussion. An instructional strategy designed to teach organized bodies of knowledge through teacher presentations and frequent questioning to monitor learning progress.

Licensure. The process by which a state evaluates the credentials of prospective teachers to ensure that they have achieved satisfactory levels of teaching competence and are morally fit to work with youth.

Local school board. A group of elected lay citizens responsible for setting policies that determine how a school district operates.

Logic. The branch of philosophy that examines the processes of deriving valid conclusions from basic principles.

Logical consequences. Outcomes that are conceptually related to misbehavior, linking students' actions and their consequences.

Looping. The practice of keeping a teacher with one group of students for more than a year.

Lower class. The socioeconomic level composed of people who typically make less than $25,000 per year, have a high school education or less, and work in low-paying, entry-level jobs.

M

Magnet schools. Public schools that provide innovative or specialized programs to attract students from all parts of a district.

Mainstreaming. The practice of moving students with exceptionalities away from segregated services and into general education classrooms, sometimes for selected activities only.

Mentors. Experienced teachers who provide guidance and support for beginning teachers.

Merit pay. A supplement to a teacher's base salary used to reward exemplary performance.

Metaphysics. The branch of philosophy that considers what we know.

Middle class. Socioeconomic level composed of managers, administrators, and white-collar workers who perform nonmanual work.

Middle schools. Special schools targeting grades 6–8 and designed to meet the unique social, emotional, and intellectual needs of early adolescents.

Modeling. The tendency of people to imitate others' behaviors and attitudes.

Montessori method. An approach to early childhood education that emphasizes individual exploration and initiative through learning centers.

Moral education. A curricular approach to teaching morality that emphasizes the development of students' moral reasoning.

Motivation. The energizing force behind student learning.

Multi-ability tasks. Learning activities that allow all students to succeed and develop their own learning strengths.

Multicultural education. A general term that describes a variety of strategies schools use to accommodate cultural differences in teaching and learning.

Multiple intelligences. A theory that suggests that overall intelligence is composed of eight relatively independent dimensions.

N

National Board for Professional Teaching Standards (NBPTS). A professional organization that sets voluntary standards for experienced teachers to recognize those who possess extensive professional knowledge.

National Education Association (NEA). The nation's oldest and largest teacher professional organization, founded in 1857.

Negligence. A teacher's or other school employee's failure to exercise sufficient care in protecting students from injury.

No Child Left Behind. A 2001 reauthorization of the Elementary and Secondary Education Act that mandates state-level testing in reading and math for grades 3–8 and holds individual schools accountable for student achievement in these areas.

Normal schools. Two-year postsecondary institutions developed in the early 1800s to prepare prospective elementary teachers, especially targeting women.

Normative philosophy. A description of the way professionals ought to practice.

Notoriety. The extent to which a teacher's behavior becomes known and is controversial.

Null curriculum. Topics left out of the course of study.

O

Old Deluder Satan Act. A landmark piece of legislation designed to create scripture-literate citizens who could thwart Satan's trickery.

Organization. The set of teacher actions that maximizes the amount of time available for instruction.

Overlapping. A teacher's ability to attend to two issues simultaneously.

P

Pay-for-performance plans. Plans that offer teachers higher salaries and bonuses for taking on extra responsibilities, working in high-need areas, or performing in exemplary ways.

Pedagogical content knowledge. A part of teachers' professional knowledge that includes the ability to represent abstract concepts in ways that students understand.

Perennialism. An educational philosophy suggesting that nature—including human nature—is constant and that schools should teach classic knowledge.

Personal teaching efficacy. Teachers' beliefs in their own ability to help all students learn, regardless of the conditions of the school or students' home lives and backgrounds.

Philosophy. The study of theories of knowledge, truth, existence, and morality.

Philosophy of education. A framework for thinking about educational issues, and a guide for professional practice.

Positive classroom climate. An environment in which learners feel physically and emotionally safe, personally connected to both their teacher and their peers, and worthy of love and respect.

Poverty thresholds. Household income levels that represent the lowest earnings needed to meet basic living needs.

Principal. The person who has the ultimate administrative responsibility for a school's operation.

Privatization. The move to outsource educational services to corporations.

Procedures. Management routines students follow in their daily learning activities.

Productive learning environment. A safe and inviting classroom that is orderly and that focuses on learning, providing opportunities for both social and personal growth.

Professional development. Programs designed to give teachers the tools they need to improve their teaching.

Professional ethics. A set of moral standards for acceptable professional behavior.

Professional learning communities. Groups of teachers who periodically meet online to discuss and improve their teaching.

Professional organization. An organization, usually nonprofit, seeking to advance a particular profession, the interests of individuals engaged in that profession, and the public interest.

Professional portfolio. A collection of materials representative of one's work that provides a concrete and effective way to document competence and qualifications.

Professionalism. Characteristic of an occupation having a specialized body of knowledge with emphasis on autonomy, decision making, reflection, and ethical standards for conduct.

Progressivism. An educational philosophy emphasizing curricula that focus on real-world problem solving and individual development.

Prompting. Providing additional questions and cues when students fail to answer correctly.

Property taxes. Taxes determined by the value of property in a school district primarily used to support education.

Punishment. The process of decreasing or eliminating undesired student behavior through some aversive consequence.

R

Race to the Top. A competitive reform effort by the U.S. Department of Education designed to spur innovation and reforms in state and local district K–12 education. Competing states were awarded points for satisfying certain educational policies.

Reduction in force. The elimination of teaching positions because of declining student enrollment or school funds. Also known as "riffing."

Reflection. The act of thinking about and analyzing one's actions.

Reforms. Suggested changes in education intended to increase student learning.

Resilient students. Students who are at risk who have been able to rise above adverse conditions to succeed in school and in other aspects of life.

Response to intervention (RTI) model of identification. A method of identifying a learning disability that focuses on the specific classroom instructional adaptations teachers use and their success.

Résumé. A document that provides a clear and concise overview of a person's job qualifications and work experience.

Rules. Guidelines that provide standards for acceptable classroom behavior.

S

School choice. A term describing a variety of programs designed to give families the opportunity to choose the school their children will attend.

School district. An administrative unit within a state, defined by geographical boundaries, and legally responsible for the public education of children within those boundaries.

Schools within schools. Smaller learning communities within larger schools where both teachers and students feel more comfortable.

Separate but equal. A policy of segregating minorities in education, transportation, housing, and other areas of public life if opportunities and facilities were considered equal to those of nonminorities. In education, the policy was implemented by creating separate schools with different curricula, teaching methods, teachers, and resources.

Service learning. An approach to character education that combines service to the community with content-learning objectives.

Sexting. The use of a cell phone to transmit sexual photos, videos, or texts; an increasing problem with students.

Sexual harassment. Unwanted and/or unwelcome sexually oriented behavior that interferes with a student's life.

Single-sex classes and schools. Classes and schools where boys and girls are segregated for part or all of the day.

Social justice. A movement in education that emphasizes human rights, fairness, and equity in the opportunities available to all members of society.

Social promotion. The process of promoting low-achieving students to the next grade so they can be with their peers, even if they're failing.

Social reconstructionism. An educational philosophy asserting that schools, teachers, and students should lead in alleviating social inequities in our society.

Social systems. Organizations with established structures and rules designed to promote certain goals.

Socioeconomic status (SES). The combination of family income, parents' occupations, and level of parental education.

Special education. Instruction designed to meet the unique needs of students with exceptionalities.

Standards. Statements specifying what students should know or be able to do after completing an area of study.

State board of education. The legal governing body that exercises general control and supervision of the schools in a state.

State office of education. Office responsible for implementing education policy within a state on a day-to-day basis.

State tuition tax-credit plans. A variation on school voucher programs in which parents are given tax credits for money they spend on private-school tuition.

Stereotype. A rigid, simplistic caricature of a particular group of people.

Students at risk. Students in danger of failing to complete their education with the skills necessary to function effectively in modern society.

Students with exceptionalities. Learners who need special help and resources to reach their full potential.

Summative evaluation. The process of gathering information about a teacher's competence, usually for the purpose of making decisions about retention and promotion. Can also apply to students' academic progress.

Superintendent. The school district's head administrative officer who, along with the district's administrative staff, is responsible for implementing policy in the district's schools.

T

Teach for America. An alternative licensure program that enables recent college graduates without state licensure to teach in hard-to-staff schools following a short period of training and supervision.

Teacher efficacy. Teachers' beliefs in their ability to promote learning and make a difference in students' lives, regardless of background or home conditions.

Teacher evaluation. The process of assessing teachers' classroom performance and providing feedback they can use to increase their expertise.

Teacher–student ratio. A measure of class size found by dividing the average number of students in classes by the number of classroom teachers.

Teacher tenure. A legal safeguard that provides job security by preventing teacher dismissal without cause, usually granted after a probationary period (typically 3 years).

Teaching contract. A legal employment agreement between a teacher and a local school board.

Theory. A set of related principles that are based on observation and used to explain the world around us.

Time-out. The process of removing a student from the class and physically isolating him or her in an area away from classmates.

Title I. A federal compensatory education program that funds supplemental education services for low-income students in elementary and secondary schools.

Transition programs. Language programs that maintain the first language until students acquire sufficient English to succeed in English-only classrooms.

21st-Century Skills. A curriculum reform movement focusing on the development of students' technological, analytical, and communication skills, which are needed to function effectively in the 21st century.

U

Underclass. People with low incomes who continually struggle with economic problems.

Upper class. The socioeconomic class composed of highly educated (usually a college degree), highly paid (usually above $170,000) professionals who make up about 5% of the population.

V

Value-added models. A form of teacher evaluation that recognizes and rewards teachers based on the amount students learn, as measured by students' performance on the difference between standardized pre- and post-tests.

Virtual schools. Schools offering comprehensive K–12 courses that connect teachers and students over the Internet.

Voucher. A check or written document that parents can use to purchase educational services.

W

Wait-time. The period of silence after a question is asked and after a student is called on to answer.

War on Poverty. A general term for federal programs designed to eradicate poverty during the 1960s.

Weighted student formula. Funding that allocates resources within a district to schools on a per-school basis according to student needs.

Withitness. A teacher's awareness of what is going on in all parts of the classroom at all times and the communication of this awareness to students, both verbally and nonverbally.

Working class (also called *lower middle class*). The socioeconomic level composed of blue-collar workers who perform manual labor.

Z

Zero-tolerance policies. Policies that call for students to receive automatic suspensions or expulsions as punishment for certain offenses, primarily those involving weapons, threats, or drugs.

NAME INDEX

SUBJECT INDEX

PHOTO CREDITS

© Paul Matthews Photography/Shutterstock, p. i; © Monkey Business/Fotolia, pp. 2, 36; © iofoto/Fotolia, p. 5; © Blend Images/SuperStock, p. 10; © Lisa F. Young/Fotolia, p. 20; © Corbis RF/Glow Images, p. 24; © David Grossman/Alamy, p. 27; Juanmonino/iStockphoto, p. 32; © micromonkey/Fotolia, p. 40; Rhoda Sidney/PH College, p. 42; © laurent hamels/Fotolia, p. 47; © Cleve Bryant/PhotoEdit, p. 50; © soupstock/Fotolia, p. 51; Tony Freeman/PhotoEdit Inc., p. 54; Rob Marmion/Shutterstock, pp. 62, 398; © Bob Ebbesen/Alamy, pp. 70, 87; KidStock/Blend RF, p. 76; © Stock Connection Blue/Alamy, p. 88; © Angela Hampton Picture Library/Alamy, p. 95; © Jim West/Alamy, pp. 100, 181, 212, 388; Hope Madden/Merrill, p. 82; Patrick White/Merrill, pp. 89, 280; © Vintage Images/Alamy, p. 106; © 1893 Gebbie & Co., p. 109; Courtesy of the Library of Congress, pp. 115, 128; Image Source, p. 120; Scott Cunningham/Merrill, p. 123; © H. Mark Weidman Photography/Alamy, p. 137; © Art Directors & TRIP/Alamy, p. 146; © Jim Cummins/CORBIS, p. 149; Gladskikh Tatiana/Shutterstock, p. 157; © Myrleen Pearson/Alamy, pp. 159, 325; © Radius Images/Alamy, p. 164; Graham Bell/Corbis, p. 168; Monkey Business Images/Shutterstock, pp. 176, 370; Katelyn Metzger/Merrill, p. 188; © Bob Daemmrich/Alamy, pp. 193, 387; © Marmaduke St. John/Alamy, p. 201; Pearson Learning Photo Studio, p. 205; Jacksonville-Courier/CLayton Statler/The Image Works, p. 218; Michael Newman/PhotoEdit Inc., pp. 221, 297; David Martin/Associated Press, p. 225; Nancy Louis/iStockphoto, p. 227; Anthony Magnacca/Merrill, pp. 231, 314, 341, 362, 432; Pearson Education Corporate Digital Archive, p. 231; Creatas/Thinkstock, p. 242; © Corbis Flirt /Alamy, p. 245; Don Ryan/Associated Press, p. 250; Will Hart/PhotoEdit, p. 252; Simon Podgorsek /iStockphoto, p. 255; michaeljung/Shutterstock, p. 257; © SCPhotos/Alamy, p. 259; AP photo/Daily Herald, Bill Zars, p. 269; © Blend Images/Alamy, pp. 276, 436; Ray Irvin/Merrill, p. 287; Supri Suharjoto/Shutterstock, p. 292; © BSIP SA/Alamy, p. 295; © Juice Images/Alamy, p. 299; Goodluz/Shutterstock, p. 306; © Image Source/Alamy, p. 310; © Michael Dwyer/Alamy, p. 323; © mauritius images GmbH/Alamy, p. 329; © WoodyStock/Alamy, p. 330; Dmitriy Shironosov/Shutterstock, pp. 338, 354, 380; © Ingor Normann/Fotolia, p. 343; Alexander Raths/Shutterstock, p. 361; Woodapple/Fotolia, p. 393; Buccina Studios/Getty Images, p. 408; ARENA Creative/Shutterstock, p. 414; Matt Antonino/Shutterstock, p. 421; © Sally and Richard Greenhill/Alamy, p. 431.